FOURTH EDITION

Teaching Language and Literacy

Preschool Through the Elementary Grades

James F. Christie
Arizona State University

Billie Jean Enz
Arizona State University

Carol Vukelich
University of Delaware

Boston Columbus Indianapolis New York San Francisco Upper Saddle River
Amsterdam Cape Town Dubai London Madrid Milan Munich Paris Montreal Toronto
Delhi Mexico City Sao Paulo Sydney Hong Kong Seoul Singapore Taipei Tokyo

Vice President, Editor-in-Chief: *Aurora Martínez Ramos*
Editorial Assistant: *Amy Foley*
Associate Sponsoring Editor: *Barbara Strickland*
Vice President, Director of Marketing: *Quinn Perkson*
Executive Marketing Manager: *Krista Clark*
Production Editor: *Gregory Erb*
Editorial Production Service: *TexTech International*
Manufacturing Buyer: *Megan Cochran*
Electronic Composition: *TexTech International*
Photo Researcher: *Annie Pickert*
Cover Designer: *Elena Sidorova*

Credits and acknowledgments borrowed from other sources and reproduced, with permission, in this textbook appear on appropriate page within text.

Library of Congress Cataloging-in-Publication Data

Christie, James F.
  Teaching language and literacy : preschool through the elementary grades / James Christie, Billie Jean Enz, Carol Vukelich. — 4th ed.
    p. cm.
  ISBN-13: 978-0-13-705762-7
  ISBN-10: 0-13-705762-8
  1. Language arts (Elementary)—Case studies. 2. Language arts (Preschool)—Case studies.
I. Enz, Billie. II. Vukelich, Carol. III. Title.
  LB1576.C5564 2010
  372.6—dc22

                                                                            2010004613

Printed in the United States of America

10 9 8 7 6 5 4 3 2 1   RRD-VA   14 13 12 11 10

www.pearsonhighered.com

ISBN-10: 0-13-705762-8
ISBN-13: 978-0-13-705762-7

ABOUT THE AUTHORS

James F. Christie is a professor of Advanced Studies in Education Policy, Leadership, and Curriculum at Arizona State University, where he teaches courses in early childhood education. His research interests include early literacy development and children's play. Dr. Christie has co-authored *Helping Young Children Learn Language and Literacy*, 3rd ed. (2008) and *Play, Development, and Early Education* (2005). He has been co-director of Early Reading First projects in San Luis and Somerton, AZ; Bullhead City, AZ; and Gallup, NM.

Billie Jean Enz is a professor of early childhood education in the College of Teacher Education and Leadership at Arizona State University, where she teaches courses in early childhood education. Her research interests include language and literacy development and family literacy. Dr. Enz has co-authored *Helping Young Children Learn Language and Literacy*, 3rd ed. (2008) and *Assessing Preschool Literacy Development* (International Reading Association, 2009). She is a co-principle investigator for First Things First External Evaluation for Arizona, which is a state-wide early childhood initiative.

Carol Vukelich is the L. Sandra and Bruce L. Hammonds Professor in Teacher Education and Director of the Delaware Center for Teacher Education at the University of Delaware. Her research and teaching interests include children's early literacy development and teachers' professional development, specifically coaching and reflection strategies. Dr. Vukelich has served as President of the Association for Childhood Education International and the International Reading Association's Literacy Development in Young Children Special Interest Group. She was a founder of the Delaware Writing Project, and serves as one of its co-directors. In addition to this book, other books by Dr. Vukelich include *Helping Young Children Learn Language and Literacy*, 2nd ed. (Allyn & Bacon, 2008); *Building a Foundation for Preschool Literacy: Effective Instruction for Children's Reading and Writing Development*, 2nd ed., (2009); and *Achieving EXCELLENCE in Preschool Literacy Instruction* (edited with Laura M. Justice, 2008). She works closely with colleagues Martha J. Buell and Myae Han on two Early Reading First projects.

CONTENTS

9   A Comprehensive Elementary Reading Program: Teaching Meaning and Skills   258

10   Creating Writers: Teaching Children to Write Well   290

11   Teaching the Mechanical Skills of Writing   321

PREFACE

Teaching Language and Literacy: Preschool through the Elementary Grades is about teaching the language arts, about facilitating children's reading, writing, speaking, and listening development in pre-kindergarten through the upper elementary grades. The language arts are essential to everyday life and central to all learning; through reading, listening, writing, and talking, children come to understand the world. To be a successful teacher of language and literacy, you need to understand how children's language and literacy develop and how to help children become fluent, flexible, effective users of oral and written language.

Children are at the center of all good language and literacy teaching. This principle underlies the three themes that run throughout this book: a perspective on teaching and learning that blends constructivism and science-based instruction, respect for diversity, and instruction-based assessment.

This book describes how children acquire language and literacy knowledge in many different contexts and how teachers can effectively promote the development of oral and written language. It also describes numerous science-based instructional practices teachers can use to enhance children's language and literacy knowledge. We believe that children construct their own knowledge about oral and written language by engaging in integrated, meaningful, and functional activities with other people. Children do not first "study" speaking, then listening, then reading, then writing. They learn by engaging in activities in which language and literacy are embedded. We also believe, however, that literacy skills can be increased via direct, systematic instruction. This instruction can often take the form of games and other engaging activities, but it also contains the elements of direct instruction: explanations, teacher modeling, guided practice, and independent practice.

New to This Edition

There are numerous new features to this edition that reflect recent developments in the field of language arts education.

- We continue to believe that it is important to frame the ideas presented in this book within the broader national context of what is happening in language and literacy in America. We have updated Chapter 1 to include new information about changes that have happened on the national scene—in part resulting from a new president and secretary of education—both with many new ideas. We begin with this description of the national landscape because of the significant effect recent policies and initiatives have had on the literacy field. Then, we describe the beliefs and the research base of the diverging views on the teaching of reading. We end with a set of principles that guide our view of the effective teaching of literacy in preschool and elementary classrooms.
- Since the publication in 2007 of the third edition of this book, much has been written about how to best support children's language and literacy development. Of course,

we have revised the ideas presented in this book so the information shared is reflective of what is known about language and literacy development today. Many references were eliminated because they provided outdated information, and many new references were added. A total of 24 percent of the references have been changed in this new edition.

■ The reviewers of the third edition of our book suggested that we clearly separate the early literacy information from the elementary literacy information. Therefore, after the chapter that lays the foundation for the ideas presented in the book (Chapter 1), Chapters 2–7 focus on the pre-K and kindergarten years, and Chapters 8–12 focus on the elementary years.

■ We have always maintained that children build knowledge by combining new information with what they already know. Thus, children's personal experiences, both at home and at school, are important factors in learning. In previous editions, the last chapter offered suggestions on how teachers could partner with parents in their children's literacy education. Our readers and reviewers told us that this inadvertently communicated an "Oh, by the way, teachers should work with their students' parents" message. We fully realize that parents are critically important partners in children's literacy development. We revised! In this edition, Chapters 2, 4, 5, 6, 7, 8, 9, 10, 11, and 12 include a *Family Focus* section with many new ideas. In addition, this edition includes an entire chapter on family literacy, and this chapter is situated early in the book.

■ In our diverse society, children come to school with vastly different backgrounds, both in terms of life experiences and language. This diversity needs to be taken into account when designing instructional activities for children and in evaluating children's responses to these activities. New illustrations of how teachers can work effectively with diverse learners can be found throughout this book. In many special features throughout this book, colleagues have described how to use science-based instructional strategies to meet all children's needs. Special emphasis is given to linguistic diversity. In a series of new special features, Luisa Araújo describes how teachers can help English language learners become bilingual and biliterate. In addition, Julia Park, Myae Han, and Sarah Hudelson and Irene Serna contribute one special feature. *Much* new information is available on how to support English language learners' language and literacy development. Nine of ten of these special features are new to this edition. We are grateful to our colleagues for sharing their knowledge with us.

■ Special emphasis in this edition also is given to working with children with special needs. Most teachers will have children with varying needs in their classrooms. Some will be identified as children with special needs; others will be waiting to be assessed so that teachers will better understand their special needs. Therefore, we include sections on working with special needs children in Chapters 5, 6, 8, 9, 10, and 11. Teachers need to know how to support all children's language and reading learning needs. Our colleagues Karen Burstein and Tanis Bryan, experts in special needs children's language and reading development, provide many of these special features. Thanks, colleagues!!

- We also are grateful to the many veteran teachers who describe how they provide their students with effective language arts instruction. This has been a feature of each of our previous editions. This edition includes seventeen *Trade Secrets*, each illustrating how the teaching strategies we describe can be applied to specific situations and how real teachers deal with practical problems that arise in the course of daily life in the classroom. Of the seventeen *Trade Secrets*, eight are new. In addition, two veteran teachers, Deanne McCredie and Sara McCraw, provide rich descriptions of their own or others' high-quality reading instruction. Thank you, thank you, colleagues!!
- Every child comes to school with a wealth of information about how written and spoken language works in the real world. To build on that student's knowledge through appropriate classroom activities, teachers must discover what each student already knows. Because we recognize that assessment—understanding what children know and have learned—cannot be separated from good teaching; instructionally linked assessment remains a strong theme in this edition. To elevate assessment to a more visible level, rather than weaving assessment strategies into select chapters, we have significantly reorganized and added new assessment information into two chapters, the first focusing on assessing young children's literacy development and the second focusing on older children's literacy development. Lest readers fail to see the link between assessment, planning, and instructing, we end each of these two chapters with reminders to use the gathered data to meet children's literacy needs and to use an Assess-Plan-Teach-Assess model.

Organization

We begin with the foundation of language and literacy learning. Chapter 1 describes the constructivist/emergent literacy and scientifically based reading research perspectives on children's language and literacy learning. Because we believe that both approaches to language and literacy learning have much to offer, we advocate for instruction that blends the two perspectives. By combining the two perspectives, we have created a set of basic principles of effective literacy instruction. We believe that these principles should guide how children are taught spoken and written language in preschool through elementary classrooms. These principles run throughout the book and underlie all the teaching strategies that we recommend in subsequent chapters.

Chapter 2 focuses on children's oral language development. It describes the phenomenal development of oral language that occurs in the first five years of life. We also cover the major theories of language development and discuss factors that contribute to variation in children's rate of language acquisition. Chapter 3 discusses family literacy and describes what children learn about reading and writing during the early years. This chapter sets the stage for the *Family Focus* features that are at the end of each of the remaining chapters.

Chapter 4 builds on Chapter 2's information by focusing on what families can do to facilitate children's oral language learning by providing opportunities for reciprocal conversation and discussion, contexts for language uses (e.g., dramatic play), and language-centered activities (e.g., sharing, movie and book reviews). We have added a new section on vocabulary instruction for young children.

Chapters 5 and 6 focus on strategies for teaching language and literacy at the preschool and kindergarten levels. Chapter 5 describes four strategies that form the foundation of developmentally appropriate preschool and kindergarten language arts programs: functional literacy activities, sharing literature, literacy play, and shared writing. In Chapter 6, we describe three other key components of a comprehensive early literacy program: writing instruction, reading instruction, and assessment. That chapter begins with a description of developmentally appropriate strategies for teaching "core" early reading skills (phonological awareness, alphabet knowledge, print awareness, word recognition, and phonics).

Chapter 7 begins with a discussion of the goals literacy professionals have identified as those that teachers should help their young learners meet. Then we consider the two general assessment approaches that teachers might use to gather information: ongoing or classroom assessment and on-demand or standardized assessment. We end this chapter, and section of the book, with a discussion of using the gathered assessment information to plan and deliver instruction.

Chapters 8 through 12 focus on elementary-grade reading and writing instruction and assessing older children's literacy performance. Chapter 8 discusses the components of the reading process that are the key objectives of elementary-grade reading instruction. Although this chapter's author, Mary Roe, discusses each component separately for clarity, she stresses that four of these skills (fluency, phonemic awareness, phonics, and vocabulary) coalesce and that the result is reading comprehension. Following this discussion, our colleague begins the description of how primary-grade teachers use their knowledge about the reading process to develop a reading program for the students in their classroom. Chapter 9 continues what Roe began with rich descriptions of how elementary-grade teachers help their students learn to construct a personal understanding of text and how they teach specific decoding and comprehension skills within a comprehensive approach to teaching reading. One of our colleagues, Sara McCraw, takes us into two first-grade classrooms to learn how three teachers use their knowledge of high-quality reading programs with their young students. Our colleague Deanne McCredie describes how, through the study of immigration, her third-graders used their language and literacy knowledge and at the same time learned content. Then we provide a description of a sixth-grade teacher's reading program. Chapter 10 describes the writing workshop and explains why it is an ideal strategy for helping elementary-grade students become proficient writers. In Chapter 11, we explain how instruction in mechanical skills—handwriting, spelling, capitalization and punctuation, and grammar—can be embedded within the writing workshop. Chapter 12 focuses on assessment of older children's literacy skills. We focus both on high-stakes, on-demand assessments that are used for accountability purposes and on ongoing assessment that is used to plan effective literacy lessons.

We have continued the use of a number of pedagogical features from earlier editions that are designed to make this book easier for students to read and comprehend. Most chapters begin with an introductory vignette that illustrates a major concept being presented in that chapter. The vignette is then "debriefed" in a manner that helps the reader begin to develop an interest in the topic. In addition, as part of the introduction, each chapter asks a series of *Think About* questions that enable readers to connect new material in the book with past personal experiences and prior knowledge. The beginning of each chapter also includes *Definitions* of key terms and a series of *Focus Questions* to alert the reader to the key concepts of that chapter. The *Summary* at the end of each chapter answers each focus question, providing a review of the key concepts in each chapter and giving readers an opportunity to self-check their comprehension. In addition, *Linking Knowledge to Practice* activities at the end of each chapter allow students to connect the theories and practices discussed in the book to practices they are observing or experiencing in real preschool, kindergarten, and elementary classrooms.

Supplements for Instructors and Students

The following supplements comprise an outstanding array of resources that facilitate learning about literacy instruction. For more information, ask your local Allyn & Bacon Merrill Education representative or contact the Allyn & Bacon Merrill Faculty Field Support Department at 1-800-526-0485. For technology support, please contact technical support directly at 1-800-677-6337 or http://247.pearsoned.com. Many of the supplements can be downloaded from the Instructor Resource Center at www.pearsonhighered.com/irc.

Help your students get better grades and become better teachers.

Instructor's Manual and Test Bank

For each chapter, the instructor's manual features a summary of main ideas and guiding focus questions; lesson plans for in-class discussion/processing activities, with extensions for out-of-class activities/assignments; information of which PowerPoint™ slides may be used in conjunction with the lecture and with processing activities; and handouts that may be used for in-class processing activities. The test bank includes multiple choice and essay questions that may be used to facilitate further class discussions, as journal topics, or as an assessment tool. (Available for download from the Instructor Resource Center at www.pearsonhighered.com/irc.)

PowerPoint™ Presentation

Designed for teachers using the text, the PowerPoint™ Presentation consists of a series of slides (ten to twenty per chapter) that can be shown as is or used to make overhead transparencies. The presentation highlights key concepts and major topics for each chapter. (Available for download from the Instructor Resource Center at www.pearsonhighered.com/irc.)

PEARSON
myeducationkit

Dynamic Resources Meeting Your Needs

MyEducationKit is a dynamic website that connects the concepts addressed in the text with effective teaching practice. Plus, it's easy to use and integrate into assignments and courses. Whenever the MyEducationKit logo appears in the text, follow the simple instructions to access a variety of multimedia resources geared to meet the diverse teaching and learning needs of instructors and students. Here are just a few of the features that are available:

- **Online study plans, including self-assessment quizzes, resource material, and flashcards.**
- **Gradetracker, an online grade book.**
- **A wealth of multimedia resources, including classroom video, expert video commentary, student and teacher artifacts, case studies, and strategies.**
- **Web links to important national organizations and sites in your field.**

Study Plan.   A MyEducationKit Study Plan is a multiple choice assessment with feedback tied to chapter objectives. A well-designed Study Plan offers multiple opportunities to fully master required course content as identified by the objectives in each chapter:

- *Chapter Objectives* identify the learning outcomes for the chapter and give students targets to shoot for as they read and study.
- *Multiple Choice Assessments* assess mastery of the content. These assessments are mapped to chapter objectives, and students can take the quiz as many times as they want. Not only do these quizzes provide overall scores for each objective, but they also explain why responses to particular items are correct or incorrect.
- *Essay Questions* encourage consideration of chapter topics. Hints and feedback are provided.

Assignments and Activities.   Designed to save instructors preparation time and enhance student understanding, these assignable exercises show concepts in action (through video, cases, and/or student and teacher artifacts). They help students synthesize and apply concepts and strategies they read about in the book.

Multimedia Resources.   The rich, media resources you will encounter throughout MyEducationKit include:

- *Videos:* The authentic classroom videos in MyEducationKit show how real teachers handle actual classroom situations. Discussing and analyzing these videos not only deepens understanding of concepts presented in the text, but also builds skills in observing children and classrooms.
- *Student & Teacher Artifacts:* Real K-12 student and teacher classroom artifacts are tied to the chapter topics in your text and offer practice in working with the different materials teachers encounter daily in their classrooms.
- *Case Studies:* A diverse set of robust cases illustrates the realities of teaching and offers valuable perspectives on common issues and challenges in education.
- *Web Links:* On MyEducationKit you don't need to search for the sites that connect to the topics covered in your chapter. Here, you can explore web sites that are important in the field and that give you perspective on the concepts covered in your text.

General Resources on MyEducationKit.   The Resources section on MyEducationKit is designed to help students pass their licensure exams, put together effective portfolios and lesson plans, prepare for and navigate the first year of their teaching careers, and understand key educational standards, policies, and laws. This section includes:

- *Licensure Exams:* Contains guidelines for passing the Praxis exam. The *Practice Test Exam* includes practice multiple-choice questions, case study questions, and video case studies with sample questions.
- *Lesson Plan Builder:* Helps students create and share lesson plans.
- *Licensure and Standards:* Provides links to state licensure standards and national standards.
- *Beginning Your Career:* Offers tips, advice, and valuable information on:
  - Resume Writing and Interviewing: Expert advice on how to write impressive resumes and prepare for job interviews.
  - Your First Year of Teaching: Practical tips on setting up a classroom, managing student behavior, and planning for instruction and assessment.
  - Law and Public Policies: Includes specific directives and requirements educators need to understand under the No Child Left Behind Act and the Individuals with Disabilities Education Improvement Act of 2004.

Visit *www.myeducationkit.com* for a demonstration of this exciting new online teaching resource.

Acknowledgments

Many outstanding educators helped us write this book. Our very special thanks go to Mary Roe for her significant contribution to this book on the new theory and research on elementary-grade reading instruction and to Luisa Araújo for her many special features on English language learners. Like us, these colleagues sat before their computers for many days. From Luisa, we learned how our ideas about teaching the language arts are appropriate for use with children whose primary language is a language other than English. From Mary, we learned how to use the new research on the reading process to develop high-quality reading programs for elementary students. We also extend a special thanks to Sara McCraw and Deanne McCredie for helping us hear teachers' and children's voices during rich language and literacy times in real classrooms. From them, we learned how the ideas on the reading process Mary presented come alive in elementary classrooms. Several of our colleagues added their special insights to this book, and we thank them. Karen Burstein and Tanis Bryan helped us better understand the special needs of exceptional children. Bonnie Albertson shared a rich description of a state's creation of its standardized assessment instrument. Barbara Gaal Lutz helped us better understand the writing of English language learners. Patricia Scott and Noreen Moore taught us about new technology to enhance classroom writing programs. We thank each of them for their important contributions to this book.

Many classroom teachers shared their secrets, showing how theory and research link with quality classroom practice. We are grateful to Karen Eustace from Arizona; and Deirdra Aikens, Lisa Albert, Gaysha Beard, Katrin Blamey, Dawn Downes, Christine Evans, Debby Helman, Noreen Moore, Jackie Shockley, and Bernadette Watson from Delaware for their description of exemplary teaching practices. From these teachers, and others like them, we have seen how exciting language and literacy learning can be when teachers and children are engaged in purposeful language arts activities. From them, and their students, we have learned much.

Several of our colleagues played roles in the construction of this book through their willingness to engage us in many conversations about children's language and literacy learning. Never unwilling to hear our ideas and to share their own, colleagues Kathy Roskos, John Carroll University; Laura Justice, Ohio State University; Lisa Albert, Bonnie Albertson, Katie Blamey, Martha Buell, Peggy Dillner, Brenda Dorrell, Dawn Downes, Christine Evans, Martha Ford, and Myae Han, University of Delaware; and Rebecca Marek and Pilla Parker, U.S. Department of Education, have greatly helped us frame our arguments.

Doctoral student Sohyun Han of the University of Delaware has been helpful in contributing features, locating references, cross-checking the reference list, constructing the index, and so forth.

The students and Early Reading First teachers we have nurtured and taught—young children, college students, and inservice teachers—have also influenced the development of our ideas. Their questions, their talk, their play, their responses, their enthusiasm—each one of them has taught us about the importance of the language arts in our lives. Their positive response to our ideas fueled our eagerness to share those ideas more broadly. What better honor than to learn that a "black market" of photocopies of the early drafts of the chapters of this book had developed on our campuses.

Additionally, we would like to thank the reviewers for this edition: W. Leah Calvert, Appalachian State University; Diane S. Maletta, Purdue University North Central; and Susan Harris-Sharples, Wheelock College.

Finally, our families have helped us write this book. Our grandchildren and grand-nieces and -nephews have provided wonderful examples of their use and enjoyment of oral and written language. The story of their journey to being competent language users brings life to the research and theory discussed in our book. Mary Christie, Don (Skip) Enz, and Ron Vukelich gave us time to write but also pulled us from our computers to experience antique shows, museums, trips, home repairs—life. And then, of course, there is our extended family—our parents, David and Dorothy Palm, Art and Emma Larson, Bill and Jeannine Fullerton, John and Florence Christie—who provided our early reading, writing, speaking, and listening experiences and helped us know firsthand the joys of learning and teaching the language arts.

Jim Christie
Billie Enz
Carol Vukelich

PART ONE

Foundations

1 Foundations of Language and Literacy

In recent years, the field of literacy has been thrust into the spotlight. A flurry of new studies, consensus reports, and national literacy policies have had a significant effect on literacy instruction in the United States. Being in the spotlight is, as Margery Cuyler (1991) reported in her delightful children's book *That's Good! That's Bad!*, good and bad. What's good is that additional financial resources have been funneled into the literacy field. The resulting research has enriched our knowledge about literacy and the teaching of reading. This research, detailed throughout this book, has identified (1) the key language and early literacy skills preschool children need to know and be able to do if they are to become successful readers, (2) effective instructional strategies that teachers of young children need to use to support their young learners' language and literacy development, (3) five key elements crucial to elementary children's reading success, (4) methods and approaches for teaching the key elements to elementary children, and (5) effective ways to engage parents in their children's literacy development. Funded initiatives, in the form of national policies and programs described later in this chapter, provided incentives for educators to begin to use the new research-based strategies to teach children the key skills.

The bad news is that while the new resources, research findings, and initiatives provide rich resources to improve literacy instruction, they also present educators with some daunting challenges. Teachers are experiencing mounting pressure to increase children's literacy development, raising concerns that drill and practice, workbooks, basal readers, and other types of "developmentally inappropriate" instruction will find their way into the school system. Many educators are concerned that elementary school practices will be pushed down to the preschool level. Preschool teachers also worry that academic instruction (i.e., a teacher standing before a group of young children and delivering content) will replace the preschool staples of children learning through play and adults reading stories to children purely for the enjoyment of the literature. Elementary school teachers worry that reading instruction will become one-dimensional with an exclusive focus on skills, as opposed to a comprehensive literacy program that focuses on all aspects of reading and writing. For example, phonics, an identified key element to helping children become good readers, might become the instructional approach to teaching reading, with all children experiencing a systematic phonics program (even those who have already mastered phonics). Elementary teachers worry that they no longer will be free to make decisions about the when, why, how, and to whom they provide instruction in the key elements of reading and writing; all children will receive the same instruction in the same dosage.

This book draws on current research and best practices, blending the previously held theory- and research-based instructional practices that have proved successful in supporting children's reading, writing, and speaking development with the new scientifically based reading research. Our goal is to provide teachers with the foundations—the core content and the best-practice teaching strategies—needed to provide high-quality reading, writing, and speaking programs for children from preschool through elementary school. While some in the field want to divide reading instruction into "camps"—at the preschool level, emergent literacy versus scientifically based reading research instruction, and at the elementary level, reading workshop instruction versus basal reading instruction—we believe that the two views need to be merged to provide an effective reading, writing, and speaking program for all children.

We begin this book with a brief overview of the recent key U.S. policies and initiatives that have affected the teaching of reading at the preschool and elementary levels. Because of the significant effect these policies and initiatives have had on the literacy field, we start with this description of the national landscape. Then, we describe the beliefs and the research base of the diverging views on the teaching of reading. We end with a set of principles that guide our view of the effective teaching of literacy in preschool and elementary classrooms.

Before Reading This Chapter, Think About . . .

- Your beliefs about how young children first learn to read and write. At what age do children begin to learn about literacy? Is knowledge about reading and writing transmitted from adults to young children, or do children construct this knowledge on their own?
- Your beliefs about effective language and literacy instruction. How can teachers best help young children become skilled speakers, listeners, readers, and writers?
- Your memories about how you learned to talk, read, and write. Do you recall, for example, reading cereal labels at an early age? Do you recall writing messages to loved ones?
- Your memories about how you were taught to read and write in elementary school. Do you recall being explicitly taught how to sound out words? Do you recall reading aloud? Do you remember engaging in silent reading? Do you remember being taught how to be aware of your understanding of the passages you were reading?

Focus Questions

- How have U.S. literacy polices and initiatives affected preschool and elementary reading instruction?
- How did the standards movement change literacy instructional practices and the assessment of children?
- How is the emergent literacy perspective different from the scientifically based reading research perspective on young children's early literacy learning?

BOX **1.1**

Definition of Terms

annual yearly progress (AYP): Using 2001–2 achievement data, U.S. states were required to set expectations for growth in student achievement that is continuous and substantial (shows increases each year) such that all students (100 percent) will be judged proficient in reading and math no later than the 2013–14 academic year. (See www.ed.gov/policy/elsec/guid/secletter/020724.html.)

benchmarks: Expected or anticipated skills or understandings at various developmental levels (e.g., by third grade, students will know and be able to . . .).

comprehension: A complex cognitive process; an active process that requires an intentional and thoughtful interaction between the reader and the text.

content standards: Define the knowledge and skills that students must attain in each content area (e.g., English language arts, mathematics, science).

fluency: Reading out loud with speed, accuracy, and proper expression.

grade level expectations: What students are expected to demonstrate that they know and can do at each grade level.

phonemic awareness: Phonemes are the smallest units of sound in a language. English consists of approximately forty-one phonemes. Phonemic awareness refers to the ability to focus on and manipulate these phonemes in spoken words. (Official definition is from www.nationalreadingpanel.org/faq/faq.htm#7.)

phonics instruction: A way of teaching reading that stresses learning how letters correspond to sounds and how to use this knowledge in reading and spelling. (Official definition is from www.nationalreadingpanel.org/faq/faq.htm#9.)

■ What principles should guide teachers when teaching language and literacy? How can teachers effectively communicate and involve parents in their child's literacy learning?

National Literacy Policies and Initiatives

National literacy policy changed dramatically at the beginning of the twenty-first century. At the pre-kindergarten (pre-K) and primary-grade levels, these policies placed early literacy directly on center stage. At the pre-K level, a growing body of research indicated that early exposure to oral language and literacy skills (skills such as phonological awareness and alphabet knowledge) put children at an advantage for later reading achievement. This research pressed policy makers to institute new initiatives that changed instructional practices in early childhood programs. These new pre-K policies grew out of movements begun in the 1980s. The publication of the scientifically based findings of the National Reading Panel suggested that all students need explicit instruction in phonics, *fluency, comprehension, phonemic awareness*, and vocabulary development. The resulting national legislation mandating instruction in these key areas in federally funded programs dramatically changed reading instruction. In this section, we provide a brief history of the genesis of several significant national literacy policies.

The Standards Movement

In 1983, the National Commission on Excellence in Education prepared a report titled *A Nation at Risk*. The commissioners warned that a "rising tide of mediocrity" in our schools threatened our future as a nation. Action was needed. The solution recommended by the commissioners was the creation of standards. High and rigorous standards, the commissioners believed, would restore the nation's place in the world.

Standards? What are they? Standards define the knowledge and skills that students— all students—must attain. They clarify and raise expectations. Because they identify what all students must know and be able to do, they define what is to be taught and what level of student performance is expected.

Following the publication of *A Nation at Risk,* a few states and some national professional organizations (such as the National Council of Teachers of Mathematics) began to develop standards in the core content areas (English language arts, mathematics, science, and social studies). Two subsequent events pushed states into high gear. The first was the 1989 meeting in Charlottesville, Virginia, of the nation's governors. A significant outcome of this education summit was a list of eight goals aimed at improving education. Goals 3 and 8 are particularly relevant to our interests. Goal 3 reads, "By the year 2000, American students will leave grades 4, 8, and 12 having demonstrated competency in challenging subject matter including English, mathematics, science, history, and geography." Goal 8 reads, "By the year 2000, all children will start school ready to learn." Collectively, these eight goals (known as Goals 2000 because of the date by which they were to be achieved) provided a set of directions for improving public education.

The second event that nudged states' standards-writing efforts forward was the passage of the Educate America Act (Goals 2000, Title III, Educate America Act, 1994). This legislation provided federal funding to states to support their writing of standards. To receive these federal funds states had to (1) develop reliable state assessments at three grade spans; (2) align local curricula to state standards and assessments; and (3) educate teachers and the general public about the standards. These funds allowed many states to support the work of committees of teachers, administrators, parents, and other key stakeholders (business leaders, school board members, legislators, and other community leaders) to draft academic *content standards* with grade-level *benchmarks* (what students must demonstrate they know and can do by a particular grade), commonly called GLEs, or *grade level expectations*.

By the mid- to late 1990s, the standards were developed, and states' attention turned toward the three conditions noted above. State departments of education held meetings to introduce the public and educators to the standards and the grade level expectations. Groups of educators began the work of aligning their curricula to their state's standards. Did the chosen reading series provide the district's students with the opportunity to learn the content by the designated time? If not, new series would need to be ordered or adjustments made to when the content would be delivered. Finally, state departments of education began to select or design standardized assessments (tests) linked to their standards. Were students achieving the standards? The massive effort of implementing K–12 standards-based education reform was under way. By 2004, all but one state (Iowa) had adopted K–12 standards. (See Figure 1.1 for an example of one state's English language arts standards.) By 2006, states were making revisions to their earlier K–12 standards, revisions aimed at ensuring consistency with the new knowledge about each of the content areas.

FIGURE 1.1   Delaware's English Language Arts Content Standards and the Performance Indicators for the End of K–5

English Language Arts Content Standards

Standard One: Students will use written and oral English appropriate for various purposes and audiences.

Standard Two: Students will construct, examine, and extend the meaning of literary, informative, and technical texts through listening, reading, and viewing.

Standard Three: Students will access, organize, and evaluate information gained through listening, reading, and viewing.

Standard Four: Students will use literary knowledge gained through print and visual media to connect self to society and culture.

(Indicators of required performance for each standard at four grade clusters—K–3, 4–5, 6–8, and 9–10—are provided. One such set of indicators for K–5 students for one standard, Standard One, is detailed below.)

Performance Indicator for the End of K–Grade 5

Writers will produce texts that exhibit the following textual features, all of which are consistent with the genre and purpose of the writing:

Development: The topic, theme, stand/perspective, argument, or character is fully developed.

Organization: The text exhibits a discernible progression of ideas.

Style: The writer demonstrates a quality of imagination, individuality, and a distinctive voice.

Word Choice: The words are precise, vivid, and economical.

Sentence Formation: Sentences are completed and varied in length and structure.

Conventions: Appropriate grammar, mechanics, spelling, and usage enhance the meaning and readability of the text.

Writers will produce examples that illustrate the following discourse classifications:

1. **Expressive** (author-oriented) texts, both personal and literary, that
   a. reveal self-discovery and reflection;
   b. demonstrate experimentation with techniques, which could include dialogue;
   c. demonstrate experimentation with appropriate modes, which include narration and description;
   d. demonstrate experimentation with rhetorical form.
2. **Informative** (subject-oriented) texts that
   a. begin to address audience;
   b. exhibit appropriate modes, which could include description, narration, classification, simple process analysis, simple definitions;
   c. conform to the appropriate formats, which include letters, summaries, messages, and reports;
   d. contain information from primary and secondary sources, avoiding plagiarism.

(continued)

FIGURE 1.1   Continued

3. **Argumentative and persuasive** (audience-oriented) texts that
   a. address the needs of the audience;
   b. communicate a clear-cut position on an issue;
   c. support the position with relevant information, which could include personal and expert opinions and examples;
   d. exhibit evidence of reasoning.

Speakers demonstrate oral-language proficiency in formal and informal speech situations, such as conversations, interviews, collaborative group work, oral presentations, public speaking, and debate. Speakers are able to

1. **Formulate** a message, including all essential information.
2. Organize a message appropriately for the speech situation.
3. **Deliver** a message,
   a. beginning to control volume, tone, speed, and enunciation appropriately for the situational context;
   b. using facial expression to reinforce the message;
   c. maintaining focus;
   d. creating the impression of being secure and comfortable, and in command of the situation;
   e. incorporating audiovisual aids when appropriate.
4. **Respond** to feedback, adjusting volume and speed, and answering questions.

Source: Delaware Department of Education.

As this book goes to press, President Obama's secretary of education, Arne Duncan, has set aside $350 million dollars of the Department of Education's budget for the creation of national standards in the four core content areas. He invited states to join the department in this initiative and to nominate content area specialists for service on the standards-writing committees. To date, forty-five states have responded positively to his invitation. Once national standards are created, the U.S. Department of Education will consider the development of an assessment that all states could use to assess their young citizens' attainment of the expected skills or understandings. The standards movement continues to be viewed as an important means to improve the quality of education in America.

Elementary and Secondary Education Act (Formerly Known as the No Child Left Behind Act)

The passage of the Elementary and Secondary Education Act, Public Law 107-110, originally passed as the No Child Left Behind (NCLB) Act in 2001, dramatically increased the importance of the standards-based reform efforts. Before, to obtain some federal education funds (like Title I funds to improve the quality of education in high-poverty schools and/or give extra help to struggling students), the federal government required states to have standards. With the passage of the act, the federal government began requiring states to hold schools and students, *all* students, accountable for meeting the state's content standards. The act requires states to assess annually the success of students in grades 3–8 in meeting state standards in reading, mathematics, and science. It also requires states to design and then implement an accountability system that holds students and the education system (schools and districts) responsible for all students' achievement in the specified content areas. Further, every state's accountability system must ensure that all groups of students reach proficiency. Assessment results must be broken out by poverty (family socioeconomic status), race, ethnicity, disability, and limited English proficiency. Student performance within each group must show improvement; no group can be left behind. The law requires that not later than twelve years after the end of the 2001–2 school year, all students in each group must meet or exceed the state's proficiency level of academic achievement on the state assessments. School districts and schools that fail to make *annual yearly progress* (AYP) toward the statewide proficiency goals are required to design plans to improve their students' performance. Should these plans fail to produce the desired results, the school districts and schools are subject to corrective action and restructuring measures aimed at getting them back on course so that all their students meet the state standards in reading and mathematics (and eventually science). (For the details of the act, see www.ed.gov/policy/elsec/guid/ states/index.html.) While Congress continues to support the ideas of NCLB, the act is now referred to by its official name, the Elementary and Secondary Education Act.

Reading First. Reading First was a component of the Elementary and Secondary Education Act. This program called for high-quality, evidence-based reading programs in the nation's poorest schools in kindergarten through grade 3. Reading First provided funding to help states and local school districts serving low-income children eliminate reading deficits by establishing high-quality, comprehensive reading instruction, instruction built on the scientific research described in the National Reading Panel (2000) report (see below). States received Reading First funds and then awarded subgrants to eligible school districts through a competitive process. School districts receiving Reading First funds were required to provide their teachers with professional development on scientifically based reading programs and instructional strategies; to implement the selected reading program with fidelity; and to assess the children's reading achievement through ongoing, valid, and reliable screening, diagnostics, and classroom-based assessments. Specifically, teachers were to be provided with professional development in the essential reading skills (phonemic awareness, phonics, fluency, vocabulary, and comprehension), and children were to be offered explicit instruction in each of the skills identified by the National Reading Panel as key to children's reading achievement. (These key skills are discussed later in this book.)

By requiring schools to use "what works," the federal government hoped to improve student achievement and ensure that all children learn to read well by the end of third grade. In 2008, the Institute of Education Sciences (IES) at the U.S. Department of Education published its research findings on Reading First. These findings were interpreted by many as indicating that Reading First was not successful in meeting its goals. Reading First did result in grade one and two teachers providing their students with much more instructional time focused on the five essential components of reading instruction promoted by the program (phonemic awareness, phonics, vocabulary, fluency, and comprehension), and teachers received much more professional development in scientifically based reading instruction practices and support from full-time reading coaches. And it did have a positive effect on first-graders' ability to decode. However, Reading First did not result in a significant impact on students' reading comprehension test scores in grades 1, 2, or 3 (Gamse, Jacob, Horst,

Boulay, & Unlu, 2008). As a result of these disappointing findings, President Obama's fiscal year (FY) 2010 budget included no funding for the Reading First program.

Good Start, Grow Smart.   The Elementary and Secondary Education Act also drew attention to the need to prepare young children before they started school. Supported by the burgeoning body of research on the importance of the early years in children's later achievement, some of which is discussed in this book, and the findings that some children enter school with deficits that put them at risk for long-term academic achievement, the George W. Bush administration developed a plan to strengthen early learning to equip young children with the skills they need to start school ready to learn. This initiative, known as Good Start, Grow Smart (2002), addressed two major areas:

PEARSON
myeducationkit™

Go to the Assignments and Activities section of Chapter 1 in the MyEducationKit and complete the activity entitled "Head Start." As you watch the video and answer the accompanying questions, note in what ways Head Start has changed in recent years, changes aimed at strengthening this program for low income children.

1. *Strengthening Head Start:* Congress's 1999 reauthorization of Head Start mandated a set of learning goals for children enrolled in Head Start, goals such as "develop phonemic, print, and numeracy awareness, recognize a word as a unit of print, and identify at least 10 letters of the alphabet" (*Good Start, Grow Smart,* 2002, p. 8). From the administration's perspective, the goals had not been fully or effectively implemented by 2002. Hence, the administration directed the Department of Health and Human Services (HHS) to develop an accountability system for Head Start to ensure that every Head Start center assesses each child's early literacy, language, and numeracy skills at the beginning, middle, and end of each year and that every center analyzes the data to judge the progress of the children toward the stated learning goals.

2. *Partnering with states to improve early childhood education:* The Bush administration asked states to engage in three activities aimed at defining quality criteria for early childhood education. The first activity was to develop voluntary guidelines (standards) in prereading and language that aligned with their K–12 standards for children ages three through five. (See Figure 1.2 for one state's language and early reading standards.) The second was to develop a plan for offering education and training activities to child care and preschool teachers and administrators. The third activity was to design a plan for coordinating at least four early childhood programs funded with federal and/or state dollars. Ultimately, the administration's goal was for states to take steps that would help prepare children to be ready to learn before they entered kindergarten.

In addition, HHS was directed to implement a national training program, called Project STEP, to show Head Start teachers early literacy teaching techniques. If Head Start children were to be able to demonstrate the identified early literacy and language skills, then their Head Start teachers would need training in research-based strategies so that they could provide Head Start children with high-quality instruction.

Further, the administration provided funding to identify effective prereading and language curricula and teaching strategies. Preschool Curriculum Evaluation Research (PCER) researchers evaluated the impact of fourteen preschool curricula on children's prereading and language learning. During Year 1, the children participated in a preschool program that

---

ORAL EXPRESSION

The child will develop listening and speaking skills by communicating
experiences and ideas through oral expression.

- Listen with increasing attention to spoken language, conversations, and stories read aloud.
- Correctly identify characters, objects, and actions in a picture book as well as stories read aloud, and begin to comment about each.
- Make predictions about what might happen in a story.
- Use two words to ask and answer questions to include actions.
- Use appropriate language for a variety of purposes (e.g., ask questions, express needs, get information).
- Engage in turn-taking exchanges and rules of polite conversation with adults and peers.
- Listen attentively to stories in a whole-class setting.

VOCABULARY

The child will develop an understanding of words and word meanings
through the use of appropriate vocabulary.

- Use single words to label objects.
- Listen with increasing understanding to conversations and directions.
- Follow simple, one-step oral directions.
- Engage in turn-taking exchanges with adults and peers.
- Use new vocabulary with increasing frequency to express and describe feelings and ideas.

PHONOLOGICAL AWARENESS

The child will manipulate the various units of sounds in words.

- Successfully detect beginning sounds in words.
- Listen to two one-syllable words and blend together to form the compound word (e.g., *Rain, bow* is *rainbow*).
- Identify words that rhyme; generate simple rhymes.
- Listen to a sequence of separate sounds in words with three phonemes and correctly blend the sounds to form the whole word (e.g., cat = /k/ /a/ /t/).

FIGURE 1.2   Virginia's Literacy Foundation

(continued)

LETTER KNOWLEDGE AND EARLY WORD RECOGNITION

The child will demonstrate basic knowledge of the alphabetic principle.

- Correctly identify ten to eighteen alphabet (uppercase) letters by name in random order.
- Select a letter to represent a sound (eight to ten letters).
- Correctly provide the most common sound for five to eight letters.
- Read simple or familiar high-frequency words, including his or her name.
- Notice letters around him or her in familiar, everyday life, and ask how to spell words, names, or titles.

PRINT AND BOOK AWARENESS

The child will demonstrate knowledge of print concepts.

- Identify the front of a book.
- Identify the location of the title of a book.
- Identify where reading begins on a page (first word or group of words).
- Demonstrate directionality of reading left to right on page.
- Identify part of the book that "tells the story" (print as opposed to pictures).
- Turn pages one at a time from the front to the back of a book.

WRITTEN EXPRESSION

The child will write using a variety of materials.

- Copy letters using various materials.
- Print first name independently.
- Print five to eight letters with a pencil using appropriate grip.
- Copy simple words (three to five letters).
- Use inventive spellings to convey messages or tell stories.

FIGURE 1.2   Continued

used a particular language and early reading curriculum, and their progress in achieving important language and early reading skills was measured against children's progress in a control center where the teachers continued teaching as they had in the past. All children were followed into kindergarten and first grade in an effort to understand the long-term effects of the preschool curriculum on the children's reading achievement. The results indicated that the majority of the curricula had no statistically significant impact on any of the student-level measures. (Readers can find the full executive summary of the PCER research at http://ies.ed.gov/ncer/pubs/20082009/ and obtain a copy of the full report from the Institute of Education Sciences, National Center for Education Research.)

Early Reading First. Funded in the Elementary and Secondary Education Act and as a part of the George W. Bush administration's Good Start, Grow Smart initiative, Early Reading First was a competitive grant program. It provided funding to local educational agencies and to public and private organizations serving low-income preschool children. The program was created to address the growing concern that many of the nation's children begin kindergarten without the necessary foundation to benefit fully from formal school instruction. Therefore, the intent of the program was to transform existing preschool programs into centers of excellence that prepared young children to enter kindergarten ready to learn and that served as models for other preschool programs to emulate. The program's goals included the following: (1) to enhance preschool, particularly low-income, children's language, cognitive, and early reading development by using scientifically based teaching strategies; (2) to demonstrate language and literacy activities based on scientifically based reading research that support young children's oral language, phonological awareness, print awareness, and alphabet knowledge; (3) to use screening assessments to identify preschool-age children who may be at risk for reading failure; and (4) to create high-quality language and print-rich environments. To achieve these goals, funded programs had to provide teachers with high-quality professional development experiences that build their knowledge of scientifically based language and early reading research and instructional teaching practices.

Using Scientifically Based Reading Research to Make Curricular and Instructional Decisions

Intertwined with the standards-based educational reform agenda described above is the requirement that federally funded programs, such as Early Reading First and Reading First, use curricula, programs, and instructional methods that have been "proven" to be effective. The official definition of what is acceptable as proof of effectiveness first appeared in federal legislation in 1999 in the Reading Excellence Act (see www.ed.gov/inits/FY99/REAguidance/sectionB.html). This statute defined acceptable research as "scientifically based reading research." As defined, this research applies "rigorous, systematic, and objective procedures to obtain valid knowledge relevant to reading development, reading instruction, and reading difficulties." The term *scientifically based research* was specifically defined in the Elementary and Secondary Act. This legislation identified several features that must be present to meet the criteria of scientifically based research (see Box 1.2).

Why has the use of scientifically based reading research been judged to be so important to the literacy field? In *Teaching Reading Is Rocket Science,* Louisa Moats (1999, p. 5) provides one explanation:

> Low reading achievement, more than any other factor, is the root cause of chronically under-performing schools, which harm students and contribute to a loss of public confidence in our school system. . . . Thanks to new scientific research—plus a long-awaited scientific and political consensus around this research—the knowledge exists to teach all but a handful of severely disabled children to read well. . . . In medicine, if research found new ways to save lives, health care professionals would adopt these methods as quickly as possible, and would change practices, procedures, and systems. Educational research has found new ways to save young minds by helping them to become proficient readers; it is up to us to promote these new methods throughout the education system.

BOX 1.2

Scientifically Based Research

The Elementary and Secondary Education Act defines "scientifically based research" as detailed below.

Scientifically based research includes research that

(i) employs systematic, empirical methods that draw on observations or experiment;

(ii) involves rigorous data analyses that are adequate to test the stated hypotheses and justify the general conclusions drawn;

(iii) relies on measurements or observational methods that provide reliable and valid data across evaluators and observers, across multiple measurements and observations, and actual studies by the same or different investigators;

(iv) is evaluated using experimental or quasi-experimental designs in which individuals, entities, programs, or activities are assigned to different conditions with appropriate controls to evaluate the effects of the condition of interest, with a preference for random-assignment experiments, or other designs to the extent that those designs contain within-condition or across-condition controls;

(v) ensures that experimental studies are presented in sufficient detail and clarity to allow for replication, or, at a minimum, offer the opportunity to build systematically on their findings; and

(vi) has been accepted by a peer-reviewed journal or approved by a panel of independent experts through a comparably rigorous, objective, and scientific review.

Source: Public Law 107-110, the Elementary and Secondary Education Act (formerly known as the No Child Left Behind Act of 2001), pp. 126–127.

While the jury is still out on the strength of scientifically based reading research as *the* tool to change underperforming schools into performing schools and nonreaders into readers, without doubt, it has had a significant impact on educators' thinking about how children become successful readers, writers, and speakers.

The National Reading Panel

To understand which approaches to teaching children to read are supported by scientifically based reading research, Congress directed that the National Reading Panel (NRP) be formed to assess the status of research-based knowledge about reading. Using the definition of scientifically based reading research presented in Box 1.2, the panel reviewed articles published in peer-reviewed journals on the following topics: alphabetics (phonemic awareness instruction and phonics instruction), fluency, comprehension (vocabulary instruction, text comprehension instruction, teacher preparation and comprehension strategies instruction), teacher education and reading instruction, and computer technology and reading instruction. The panel suggests that it missed reporting on some areas that likely are important to children's reading achievement (e.g., writing development, self-regulation, motivation) because of the lack of an adequate number of investigations that met the criteria of scientifically based reading research. The panel reported the following conclusions relative to the five key elements it identified as crucial to children's reading success (NRP, 2000).

1. *Phonemic awareness:* Teaching children to manipulate the sounds in language (phonemes) helps them learn to read. In fact, phonemic awareness training improves students' phonemic awareness, spelling, and reading, with the effects on reading lasting well beyond the end of the training.

2. *Phonics:* Systematic *phonics instruction* leads to significant positive benefits for students in kindergarten through sixth grade and for children who are having difficulty learning to read. It enhances children's success in learning to decode, spell, and comprehend text.

3. *Vocabulary:* Vocabulary development has long been considered important for reading comprehension. The panel concluded that vocabulary should be taught both directly and indirectly. Repetition and seeing vocabulary words several times are important.

4. *Comprehension:* Text comprehension is improved when teachers use a combination of reading comprehension techniques such as question answering, question generation, and summarization. When students are able to use these techniques successfully, they perform better in recalling, answering questions, generating questions, and summarizing texts.

5. *Fluency:* Guided repeated oral reading has a significant and positive impact on word recognition, reading fluency, and comprehension for students of all ages.

The National Early Literacy Panel

A few years after the publication of the National Reading Panel's findings, the National Institute for Literacy, a unit within the U.S. Department of Education, created the National Early Literacy Panel (NELP) and directed the panel to conduct a synthesis of the scientific research on the development of early literacy skills in children ages zero to five. The goal was to understand how teachers could help young children develop the early literacy skills linked to the successful development of readers and writers during the school year, what instructional programs and interventions supported the development of early literacy skills and/or conventional literacy skills, and with whom the interventions worked best. After several years of studying the literature, using procedures similar to those used by the National Reading Panel, the National Institute for Literacy published the NELP results of the meta-analysis of the scientifically based reading research literature (National Center for Family Literacy, National Early Literacy Panel, & National Institute for Literacy, 2008).

This analysis revealed that (1) the strong to moderate predictors of success in reading and writing are alphabet knowledge, phonological awareness (PA) (specifically phonemic awareness), concepts about print and print knowledge, oral language, rapid automatic naming, writing or name writing, and visual processing; (2) interventions to teach code-related skills (especially PA) are highly successful; (3) shared reading interventions that used interactive reading styles help promote children's print knowledge and oral language skills; (4) age, socioeconomic level and race did not seem to alter the effectiveness of the various interventions; and (5) interventions that produced the largest effects usually were conducted one-on-one or in small group instructional activities and were teacher directed and focused on helping children use these skills. The NELP report is important because it identified what preschool teachers must focus on in early literacy, and it helped to inform educators and the public about why these skills are important. (Readers can obtain a full copy of the NELP report at www.nifl.gov/nifl/publications/pdf/NELPReport09.pdf.)

A Continuum of Instructional Approaches or "The Reading Wars"

The field of elementary-grade reading instruction has witnessed a century-old debate between the proponents of two very different views of how to teach reading. On one side are the supporters of meaning-based approaches that stress comprehension, connected reading, good literature, and the integration of reading and writing. These approaches assume that if children engage in lots of meaningful reading and writing activities with support from teachers and peers, they will acquire literacy. The terms *literature based* and *whole language* are sometimes used to describe this perspective. On the other side are proponents of a skills-based view who emphasize direct instruction on skills such as phonics, alphabet recognition, and fluency that enable children to decode written texts. The assumption is that once children are taught to recognize written words fluently, they will comprehend the texts that they read. The end point for both approaches is the same: fluent reading with good comprehension. This debate, however, has often been harsh, politicized, and polarized, leading some to use the term *reading wars* to characterize the discourse between the two groups (Joyce, 1999).

Emergent Literacy Approach

Until the late 1990s, the field of pre-K reading had largely escaped the bitter debate that was raging at the elementary level. Emergent literacy was the predominant view of early reading and writing, and most conceptions of best practice stemmed from this meaning-centered perspective. According to this view, children begin learning about reading and writing at a very early age by observing and interacting with adults and other children as they use literacy in everyday life activities (Sulzby & Teale, 1991). For example, young children observe the print on cereal boxes to select their favorite brands, watch as their parents write notes and read the newspaper, and participate in special literacy-focused routines such as storybook reading with a parent or older sibling. On the basis of these observations and activities, children construct their own concepts about the functions and structure of print and then try them out by engaging in emergent forms of reading and writing, which often are far removed from the conventional forms used by adults. Based on how others respond to their early attempts, children make modifications and construct more sophisticated systems of reading and writing. For example, early attempts at writing often shift from scribbles, to random streams of letters (e.g., SKPVSSPK), and to increasingly elaborate systems of invented spelling such as *JLE* for *jelly* (Sulzby, 1990). Eventually, with many opportunities to engage in meaningful literacy activities, much interaction with adults and peers, and some incidental instruction, children become conventional readers and writers.

Proponents of emergent literacy believed that, if provided with the right kinds of environments, experiences, and social interactions, most children require very little formal instruction to learn to read and write. Early childhood language arts programs based on the emergent literacy perspective feature the following components:

- Print-rich classroom settings that contain large numbers of high-quality children's books, displays of conventional print (e.g., alphabet friezes, charts written by teachers), functional print (helper charts, daily schedules, labels), student writing, and play-related print (empty cereal boxes in the home center)
- Frequent storybook reading by the teacher with lots of student interaction
- Shared reading of big books coupled with embedded instruction on concepts about print (e.g., book concepts such as *author* and *title* and the left-to-right sequence of written language)
- Shared writing experiences in which the teacher writes down oral stories dictated by children
- Projects and/or thematic units that link language, reading, and writing activities
- Opportunities for children to engage in meaningful reading and writing during "center time" activities, and a family literacy component

Emergent literacy proponents contend that these types of emergent literacy experiences build on what children have already learned about written language, provide a smooth transition between home and school, and help ensure initial success with learning to read and write. The teacher's role is to provide the materials, experiences, and interactions that enable children to learn to read and write. Direct instruction on skills such as alphabet recognition and letter–sound relationships is only used with children who fail to learn these skills through meaningful interactions with print. This approach is described in detail in Chapter 5.

Scientifically Based Reading Research Approach

By the late 1990s, the standards movement and other national literacy policies and initiatives described at the beginning of this chapter began to have an impact on the field of early literacy. As James Christie (2008, p. 26) noted,

> Many policymakers became disenchanted with the education establishment's rather relaxed emergent literacy approach to early reading instruction. There was an increased call for effective "science-based" methods of instruction to turn back the tide of rising reading disabilities.

By 2002, initiatives such as Good Start, Grow Smart and the Early Reading First grant program, products of this disenchantment, pushed a skills-based approach to early literacy instruction, often referred to as scientifically based reading research (SBRR), into prominence. Perhaps the most valuable contribution of the SBRR movement has been the identification of the "core" knowledge and skills that young children must have to become successful readers (Snow, Burns, & Griffin, 1998). Longitudinal studies have shown that preschool-age children's *oral language* (expressive and receptive language, including vocabulary development), *phonological awareness,* and *alphabet knowledge* are predictive of reading achievement in the elementary grades. *Print awareness,* which includes concepts of print (e.g., left-to-right, top-to-bottom sequence), book concepts (author, title), and sight word recognition, has also been found to be positively correlated with reading ability in the primary grades. The NELP report, as noted above, added *rapid automatic naming, writing or name writing,* and *visual processing* to this earlier list.

SBRR investigators have also focused on identifying effective strategies for teaching this core literacy content to young children. One of the most consistent research findings is that core early literacy skills can be increased via *explicit, systematic instruction.* This instruction can often take the form of games and other engaging activities, but it also contains the elements of direct instruction: explanations, teacher modeling, guided practice, and independent practice.

Scientifically based reading research instruction occurs in both large and small group settings. Large group instruction occurs during "circle time" when the entire class sits on the floor near the teacher; it may include the following:

- Songs, such as "Down by the Bay," coupled with instruction on rhyme production ("Did you ever see a whale with a polka-dot . . . (tail), Down by the bay.") [SBRR skill: phonological awareness.]
- Storybook reading, coupled with instruction on vocabulary (after reading "Did you see llamas eating their pajamas, Down by the bay," the teacher asks, "Does anyone know what a llama is?"). [SBRR skill: oral language.]
- Alphabet charts with a poem for each letter that contains many examples of the "target" letter. For example, after reading a poem for the letter P ("Patty Panda likes to draw, holds a pencil in her paw . . ."), the teacher asks children to come up and point to the words that contain P and say the letter name. [SBRR skill: alphabet knowledge.]
- Every pupil response activity in which all children have a chance to respond at the same time. For example, the teacher might say a series of words, some of which begin with the /p/ sound and some that do not. Children hold their thumbs up if a word starts with the sound of p. [SBRR skill: phonological awareness.]

Instruction can also be conducted in small groups. The advantage is that if an activity requires that one child respond at a time, all children get multiple opportunities to participate. For example, using a pocket chart, a teacher could give a small group of children each a high-frequency word flash card (my, the, is, big, fast) or a rebus picture card (truck, cat, girl, house). After reviewing the words on the cards, the teacher would help the children build sentences by saying words and having the children bring up their cards and place them in the chart ("My cat is big"; "The truck is fast"; "My house is big"). [SBRR skill: print awareness.]

PEARSON myeducationkit

Go to the Assignments and Activities section of Chapter 1 in the MyEducationKit and complete the activity entitled "Building Phonological Awareness." As you watch the video and answer the accompanying questions, note the rhyming words the children experience as they sing the songs and hear the poem.

PEARSON myeducationkit

Go to the Assignments and Activities section of Chapter 1 in the MyEducationKit and complete the activity entitled "Building Phonemic Awareness." As you watch the video and answer the accompanying questions, note the teacher's focus on the p sound, the first sound in several words in the nursery rhyme. Note how she did not draw the children's attention to the letter p but rather focused on the sound. Had she asked the children to point to the letter in the nursery rhyme that made the p sound, she would have been teaching phonics, not phonemic awareness.

Children also need opportunities to practice and consolidate what has been taught in large and small group settings. This chance usually occurs during an "activity" time during which children work individually or in small groups in learning centers. It requires that the teacher link the center activities to the skills being taught in the curriculum.

Blended Instruction: A Comprehensive Literacy Program

Both the emergent literacy and SBRR approaches to early literacy instruction have their advantages. Emergent literacy programs provide opportunities for children to learn about literacy on their own and with help from the teacher and peers. Learning can occur at the appropriate pace for each child and can build on what he or she already knows. This approach provides children with rich opportunities to acquire oral language and move through the developmental progressions in emergent reading and writing. The downside is that not all children are ready or able to take full advantage of these learning opportunities. Some children have a tendency to "fall through the cracks" in emergent literacy programs and make very little progress. Such children need to be directly taught vocabulary, phonological awareness, alphabet, and concepts of print before they can fully profit from the learning experiences in an emergent literacy program.

We advocate instruction that blends together the key components of both approaches (Figure 1.3). This instructional approach features the print-rich classrooms, storybook reading, shared writing, projects/units, and meaningful center-based literacy activities advocated by proponents of emergent literacy, coupled with explicit instruction and practice on core language and literacy skills featured in the SBRR approach. Blended instruction is therefore a comprehensive approach to early literacy instruction that combines the best aspects of the emergent literacy and SBRR perspectives.

Fortunately, we are not alone in this view. Most, if not all, of the comprehensive pre-K early literacy curricula developed since 2002 are blended programs. All have been strongly influenced by the SBRR perspective and use the term *science-based instruction* in

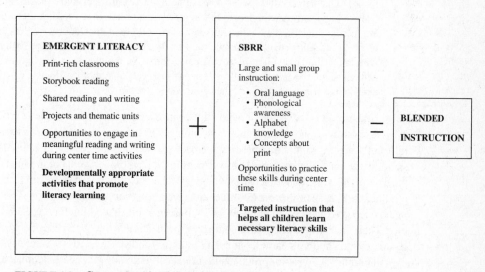

FIGURE 1.3   Comprehensive Literacy Instruction

their promotional literature. These new programs place heavy emphasis on the "big four" science-based skills: oral language, phonological awareness, alphabet knowledge, and print awareness. Direct instruction on these skills in large and small group settings is also now a standard feature, although the nature and intensity of this instruction varies from program to program. These programs also include the main components recommended by emergent literacy: frequent storybook reading, print-rich classroom environments, and center activities that involve reading and writing. Box 1.3 describes the comprehensive literacy program that was used in an Early Reading First grant project in Arizona and continues to be used in these classrooms, years after the Early Reading First funding ended.

Of course, how teachers implement a curriculum has a big influence on how appropriate and effective the curriculum will be for specific groups of children. Susan Neuman and Kathy Roskos (2005) give an example of an observation they made in a preschool that used a commercially published early literacy curriculum fitting our definition of a comprehensive literacy program. The classroom did have a print-rich environment, but the instruction that Neuman and Roskos observed was not developmentally appropriate for the three-and-a-half and four-year-old children participating in the lesson. Here is a vignette that describes the lesson:

> The local school administrator recommends an exemplary school for us to visit. We watch a day unfold in a room filled with print. The walls are adorned with words; pocket charts, alphabet letters, numbers, signs, and environmental print claim every available space. A big book stands ready in the circle area, accompanied by a pointer for tracking print. The children sit "station style," with "quiet hands and feet," in their designated space in the circle and sing "Stop, Look, and Listen" along with their teacher. The day is about to begin.
>
> Taking flash cards in hand, the teacher begins, "Good morning, Charley. Do you know the first two letters of your name?" Charley moves tentatively to the board and slowly writes *C* and *H*. Moving to the next child, then the next, the teacher follows a similar routine. Some fourteen children later, she reviews many of the letters, asking children to spell the names of the helpers of the week. The days of the week are next, and children repeat them in chorus. They compare the letters in Monday with the letters in Tuesday, then Tuesday with Wednesday, and Tuesday with Thursday. What follows is the Counting Calendar and "My, oh my, it's the thirtieth of the month," and so the children count each day up to thirty. Finally, with an "I like how you're listening" some forty-five minutes later, circle time is about to end. Even so, the transition allows for one last teachable moment focusing on the *t-t-t* in *teacher,* the *m-m-m* in *Ms.,* and the *j-j-j* in *jingle.* (p. 22)

This vignette shows that it is possible to take a comprehensive literacy curriculum and skew it one way or the other, resulting in too little or too much instruction. There is nothing inherently wrong with the activities themselves: writing the letters in children's names, spelling the names of classroom helpers, reciting the days of the week, comparing the letters in the days of the week, counting, and sounding out the initial sounds in words. In fact, with a few modifications, each of these activities could have been a very effective lesson. The problem is that the lesson contained all these activities, making it much too long for three- and four-year-olds. These instructional activities could have been shortened (e.g., writing the beginning letters in several children's names, but not all fourteen) and spread across several days.

For guidance in appropriate instructional early literacy practices, Neuman and Roskos send preschool teachers to *Learning to Read and Write: Developmentally Appropriate*

BOX 1.3
The Arizona Centers for Excellence in Early Education Project

The Arizona Centers for Excellence in Early Education (ACE[3]) was an Early Reading First project that served children in twenty-four Head Start and state-funded preschools in San Luis and Somerton, Arizona. A vast majority of these children were learning English as a second language. Like all Early Reading First projects, the primary goal of ACE[3] was to promote preschoolers' readiness for kindergarten by teaching them "science-based" early reading skills: oral language, phonological awareness, alphabet knowledge, and concepts of print.

The program used a commercially published curriculum, *Doors to Discovery* (Wright Group/McGraw-Hill, 2002), which is a good example of a comprehensive early literacy program. The *Doors* program is organized into one-month "explorations" or units that focus on topics that appeal to young children, such as transportation, nature, food, and school. The *Doors* curriculum consists of three interrelated components:

1. **Large group time:** Song and Rhyme posters were used as a warm-up and to teach phonological awareness (e.g., rhyme recognition). They were followed by shared reading of big books in which the teacher encouraged children to read along and engage in book-related talk. Three shared reading books were used in each unit: a narrative storybook, an informational book, and a concept book. When stories were initially introduced, the teacher did a "picture walk" to introduce key concepts and vocabulary. Instruction on concepts of print, phonological awareness, and alphabet knowledge are incorporated into the shared reading sessions.
2. **Discovery centers:** During a sixty-minute period, children engaged in self-selected activities in a variety of learning centers, including dramatic play, art, blocks, writing, mathematics, and science. Many of these activities were

linked to the theme and to the stories that were read during shared reading. The teacher manual contains lists of theme-related Wonderful Words that the teachers used with the children while they were engaging in center activities. Discovery centers were stocked with theme-related literacy props and materials, providing children with a print-rich environment. For example, during the unit on transportation, the dramatic play center was turned into a gasoline station. Props included a gas station sign (e.g., "Chevron") and a cardboard gas pump with a label ("gas") and numerals to represent the gallons and cost of gas that was pumped.

3. **Small group time:** During the second ten-minute segment of discovery center time, the teacher met with small groups of students and conducted a vocabulary lesson using an Interactive Book, a wordless big book that contains illustrations related to the unit theme. For example, *Our Big Book of Driving,* which was used in the unit on transportation, contains pictures of different types of vehicles (bus, ambulance, motorcycle), parts of a car (door, tire, speedometer), and a scene of a busy intersection. Children were encouraged to discuss the pictures.

Once a week, during the third ten-minute segment of discovery center time, the teacher also taught a small group lesson using *Our Big Scrapbook,* a blank big book. In a variation of the language experience approach or shared writing, the teacher recorded the children's oral language while the children watched. The subject of the children's dictation was usually photographs of children's play activities or their artwork. For example, children drew pictures of the type of vehicle their parents drove. Each child then dictated a sentence ("My mom drives a blue van"), which the teacher wrote below the picture. The children's contributions were

(continued)

BOX **1.3** Continued

then pasted or taped to the blank pages of the scrapbook. Completed scrapbooks were placed in the classroom library center for children to read during the center time.

A positive feature of this program was the way in which the different components and activities were linked together around the current theme. The following vignette occurred during a unit on building and construction:

> During large group circle time, the teacher and children sang a song that had to do with building a tree house. The teacher paused to point out the words that rhymed in the story and then encouraged the children to come up with other words that ended with the same rhyming sound. She also focused on several tool-related vocabulary terms: hammer and nail. Next, the teacher did a shared reading lesson with a big book about building a doghouse. Before reading the book with the children, she did a "picture walk," engaging the children in a discussion about objects in the photos in this informational book. The teacher focused children's attention on several tool vocabulary terms:

hammer, nail, saw, measuring tape, and safety goggles. Then the teacher read the book and encouraged the children to read along. Some were able to do so because of the simple text and picture clues. During center time, several children chose to play in a dramatic play center that was set up as a house construction site. There was a "house" made out of large cardboard boxes as well as toy tools (hammers, saw, measuring tape, level), safety goggles, hard hats, some golf tees that were used as make-believe nails, and several signs ("Hard Hat Area," "Danger," "Construction Site"). Two girls and a boy spent thirty minutes in the center, using the toy tools to measure, plan, and build the house. During this play, they used the target vocabulary repeatedly and also explored the uses of the tools. For example, when the boy attempted to use the toy saw without first putting on his safety goggles, one of the girls reminded him to put on the goggles. The dramatic play center was used as a means to provide children with an opportunity to practice and consolidate the vocabulary and concepts that were being taught in the instructional part of the curriculum.

Practices, the 1998 joint position statement published by the International Reading Association (IRA) and the National Association for the Education of Young Children (NAEYC), and the International Reading Association's more recent position statement, *Literacy Development in the Preschool Years* (2005a). These two position statements define a set of principles or recommendations to guide preschool teachers' teaching practices, parents, and policy makers and community leaders. Neuman and Roskos (2005b) summarize the principles related to preschool teachers' teaching practices:

> The research-based statement stresses that for children to become skilled readers, they need to develop a rich language and conceptual knowledge base, a broad and deep vocabulary and verbal reasoning abilities to understand messages conveyed through print. . . . It recognizes that children also must develop code-related skills: an understanding that spoken words are composed of small elements of speech (phonological awareness), the idea that letters represent these sounds (the alphabetic principle), and the knowledge that there are systematic correspondences between sounds and spellings. But . . . *meaning,* not sounds or letters, drives children's earliest experiences with print. . . . Although specific skills like alphabet knowledge are important to literacy development, children must acquire these skills . . . [through] meaningful experiences. (p. 23)

Note a level of consistency between these skills and at least some of those identified as key language and early literacy skills in the position statement with those identified by SBRR research. The difference, then, is not in the key skills as much as in instructional strategies some preschool educators elect to use to teach these skills. Neuman and Roskos's view is that pre-kindergarten teachers should use "content- and language-rich instruction" that includes "time, materials, and resources that . . . build language and conceptual knowledge; a supportive learning environment . . . different group sizes (large, small, individual) . . . to meet the needs of individual children; and opportunities for sustained and in-depth learning, including play" (2005b, p. 26). To this list of suggestions could be added the position statement's perspective: "But the ability to read and write does not develop naturally, without careful planning and instruction" (IRA/NAEYC, 1998, p. 3).

The challenge, then, for early childhood educators is to carefully plan and teach the key elements through meaningful experiences. Our goal is to provide teachers with research-based information on how to combine the emergent literacy and the scientifically based reading research perspectives to create an effective blended early literacy program, one with meaningful experiences and with direct, developmentally appropriate instruction in the key early literacy areas.

PEARSON
myeducationkit

Go to the Assignments and Activities section of Chapter 1 in the MyEducationKit and complete the activity entitled "Creating a Print-Rich Environment." As you watch the video and answer the accompanying questions, note the many different ways that print is incorporated into this classroom.

PEARSON
myeducationkit

Go to the Assignments and Activities section of Chapter 1 in the MyEducationKit and complete the activity entitled "Creating Purposeful Environments for Emergent Readers and Writers." As you watch the video and answer the accompanying questions, note the variety of opportunities to experience print in this kindergarten classroom and the teacher's purposes for providing these many experiences.

A Comprehensive Literacy Instructional Program

We believe that to provide preschool through elementary school children with a high-quality, effective reading, writing, and speaking program, the two perspectives need to be interwoven, and that both views make significant contributions to such a program. Children need meaningful interactions with print in print-rich environments and in books. They need social interactions with their peers and their teachers in literacy events. They need many opportunities to engage in meaningful reading, writing, and speaking events. In addition, they need explicit instruction in reading, writing, and speaking skills.

By combining the two perspectives, we have created a set of basic principles of effective literacy instruction. These principles should guide how children are taught spoken and written language in preschool through elementary classrooms.

Effective Teachers Provide Children with a Print-Rich Classroom Environment

High-quality literacy programs require a literacy-rich environment with many materials to support children's learning. As Neuman and Roskos with colleagues Wright and Lenhart (2007, p. 38) explain, a print-rich classroom environment matters in students' language and literacy development:

No doubt about it, the environment is a powerful teacher! What it contains—the objects, materials, settings, and language—jump start all kinds of social, emotional, and cognitive learning. When you consciously design appealing physical space and structures, you invite . . . children into a wide variety of language and literacy experiences, not to mention endless opportunities for interaction. Using basic design elements, . . . [teachers can] create a lively place that teaches, that promotes choices and activity, and that is full of talking, reading, and writing, and the real joy of learning.

Rich physical environments do not just happen; the creation of a classroom environment that supports children's learning, teachers' teaching, and the curriculum requires forethought. Some characteristics of this type of classroom environment include a well-stocked library corner and writing center; lots of functional print; theme-related literacy props in play areas; and displays of children's writing. This type of environment offers children opportunities to talk, listen, read, and write to one another for real-life purposes.

Effective Teachers Demonstrate, Model, and Scaffold Instruction

Because children will try to do what others do, demonstrating and modeling literacy events will lead to children imitating these events. When a teacher reads books to young children, children independently pick up the books and say words in ways that would lead a listener to think they are reading. The children sound as though they are reading words, yet their eyes are focused on the illustrations. When children see parents and teachers using print for various purposes—writing shopping lists, looking up information in a book, and writing notes—they begin to learn about the practical uses of language and to understand why reading and writing are activities worth doing.

Deborah Rowe (1994) provides an example of a preschool teacher's demonstration of the use of exclamation points. The teacher is sitting in the writing center with a small group of children. She writes a get-well card to a sick colleague. She writes: "Dear Carol, We hope you get well SOON!!!" She explains, "exclamation mark, exclamation mark, exclamation mark. Because I want her to get well *soon*." Moments later, Kira and Hana talk about exclamation marks.

KIRA: And this is [pause] extamotion [*sic*] point. How come?

HANA: Put three cause it's big letters.

Still later, Hana and Kira include exclamation marks in their writing. Kira writes the letters *COI* over and over inside one band of a rainbow and exclamation marks inside another band, and Hana writes her name and fills the bottom of the page with upside-down exclamation marks (Rowe, 1994, pp. 168–169). This preschool teacher probably did not set out to teach her young students about exclamation points. In the act of writing and talking about her writing, she demonstrated to curious, observant preschool apprentices the purpose of using an exclamation mark. Notice how she showed her student "observers" what is done during reading and writing. She acted as a writer, not as a teacher of reading and writing. In this way, she shared with the children how a reader or a writer thinks as well as acts.

Effective Teachers Explicitly Teach Children Skills That Research Supports as Key Elements of Reading, Writing, and Speaking

Scientifically based reading research has identified key skills of early and later reading. This literature tells us that early language and literacy instruction should focus on the core content: the knowledge, skills, and dispositions that are predictive of later reading success (i.e., alphabet knowledge, phonological awareness, concepts about print and print knowledge, oral language). Writing research and theory has identified the elements of quality expressive, informative, and persuasive texts (e.g., organization, development). There is a rich body of language development research to help teachers understand the key features of oral language (e.g., phonology, syntax, semantics, pragmatics). In each area, research has identified effective instructional strategies for teaching children these skills, elements, and features. Many of these instructional strategies call for teachers to explicitly teach children: large groups of children, small groups of children, and individuals. In all instances, the strategies used should be appropriate for the age of the children.

Effective Teachers Read to Children Daily and Encourage Them to Read Books on Their Own

Living in a print-rich world provides children with many opportunities to read *contextualized* print. That is, children form hypotheses about what words say because of the context in which the words are embedded. As described in other sections of this chapter, children learn to read cereal boxes, stop signs, and the McDonald's sign early in life. While making such connections with print is important, young children also need multiple experiences with decontextualized print. Neuman and Roskos (1993) explain the meaning of decontextualized print:

> Essentially, . . . unlike contextualized print experiences, written language has meaning apart from the particular situation or context of its use. The meaning of decontextualized print is derived from the language itself and from the conventions of the literary genre. Over time, [children] develop a frame, or sense of story, a mental model of basic elements of a story. (p. 36)

Reading stories to children is one of the best ways to familiarize them with decontextualized print. Effective teachers plan numerous opportunities for storybook reading experiences. These teachers read aloud daily to individual children, small groups of children, and the whole class. Hearing stories read aloud, however, is not enough for children of any age. Studies have shown the importance of talking about the books read (Heath, 1983; Whitehurst & Lonigan, 1998). Many teachers begin their read-alouds by engaging children in a discussion related to the story they are about to read. While reading, the teacher might invite the children to make comments, to share reactions, or to ask questions. After reading, the teacher will likely engage the children in a discussion aimed at extending their understanding of the story. This framework for read-alouds has been called a "grand conversation" (Clay, 1991) and more recently has been referred to as holding "extratextual conversations" (Cabell, Justice, Vukelich, Buell, & Han, 2008). Such conversations help children understand how to process the decontextualized text found in books.

Is there ever a time when children are too old to be read to? Absolutely not! Teachers whose students are reading independently should select texts (novels, magazine articles, newspaper articles) that are above the students' independent reading level but at their listening and interest level. Reading aloud to elementary-aged students allows teachers to engage in such behaviors as modeling fluent and expressive reading, stopping to model thinking about the text, and making connections between and among other texts.

It is also important to provide opportunities for children to read books to themselves and to one another. Through such occasions, children have the opportunity to practice what they have learned during the interactive storybook readings and to refine the strategies needed to construct meaning from texts. To learn to enjoy making meaning from written texts, each person must do the work, the thinking, independently. Children learn to read by reading.

Effective Teachers Provide Opportunities for Children to Collaborate and Help Each Other Learn about Language and Literacy

Of course, teachers are not the only people in the classroom environment who offer demonstrations of literacy. "Knowledgeable teachers understand that the social, collaborative nature of learning to read and respond to books goes beyond the relationship between adult and child, teacher and student, and includes peers" (Galda, Cullinan, & Strickland, 1993). This statement about learning to read is equally applicable to learning to write. Creating a "community of literacy learners" is often suggested in the professional literature. Children select books to "read" because their peers have selected the book. Children talk to each other about books they are reading or have had read to them. Children turn to each other for information and help in decoding or spelling words. "How do you spell *morning*?" "What's this word say?"

When teachers know that learning is a social act and that readers, writers, and speakers develop new understandings as a result of the rich exchange of ideas in collaborative learning contexts, they intentionally create new kinds of classroom participation opportunities for their students. For example, these teachers provide their students with opportunities to engage in discussion groups about books, to form literacy clubs, or to work in small groups to investigate specific topics within a content area.

Such collaborative learning opportunities will not "just happen." Teachers must create an environment in which children can demonstrate for, or coach, each other. Several researchers have documented what happens when teachers create such opportunities. For example, researchers (e.g., Christie & Stone, 1999; Vukelich, 1993) have studied how play in literacy-enriched play settings provides children with opportunities to teach each other. Carol Vukelich (1993), for example, studied how children teach each other about the functions, features, and meaning of print in play. The following peer-to-peer interaction illustrates how one child coaches another child about how to spell his name.

Jessie is the forest ranger. She is seated at the entrance to the campsite, directing potential campers to get a sticker from her before entering the campground, and *then* she'll tell them which tent they can use.

JESSIE: Ronald, how do you spell your name?

RONALD: *R.* [Jessie writes *r.*] No, it's the big kind.

[Ronald forms the letter with his finger on the table. Jessie writes *R.*] Good!

JESSIE: What else?

[Jessie writes as Ronald dictates each letter of his name, looking up at him after each one. When finished, she gives Ronald the sticker with his name on it.] (p. 390)

This example was from a kindergarten classroom. Similar rich examples of teachers and children learning together in literacy-enriched environments are reported in the literature about elementary children's literacy development, particularly relative to the teaching of writing. As children write and share their texts with their peers and teachers, they come to understand the needs of their audience in addition to gathering specific feedback on the quality of their writing (e.g., "Does my beginning make you want to read more?"). As the following example illustrates, seven-year-old Kristi had learned much by sharing her writing with her peers.

Kristi is about to begin a new story. She sits, staring at her paper and twiddling her pencil. Suddenly she grabs a piece of scrap paper, leaps up, and approaches her friend Shannon.

KRISTI: What do you want to know about my burned hand?

SHANNON: How did you do it?

[Kristi moves on, approaching Charlie.]

KRISTI: What do you want to know about my burned hand? Shannon wants to know how I did it.

CHARLIE: What did you do after you burned it?

And so Kristi proceeded, one by one, asking several of her peers what they would like to know about her burned hand. When her teacher questioned her use of this strategy, Kristi responded, "I might as well find out what they want to know before I begin my piece, rather than after!" Clearly, Kristi had developed a sense of writing for others, not just herself.

Should opportunities to learn from each other stop at the end of the primary grades? Of course not! In their recent meta-analysis of writing instruction research, Steve Graham and Dolores Perin (2007, p. 463) showed that "collaborative arrangements where students [in grades 4–12] help each other with one or more aspects of their writing [planning, drafting, and/or revising] had a strong and positive impact on writing quality." As a result of their finding, they encourage teachers to "develop instructional arrangements in which adolescents [can] work together" (p. 466).

When teachers value children's contributions and celebrate what they know, children see the strengths in each other. Within such a supportive climate, children practice what they know and take the risks necessary for learning to occur. This kind of environment encourages children to learn from themselves, from each other, and from the teacher.

Effective Teachers Provide Opportunities for Children to Use Language and Literacy for Real Purposes and Audiences

Most research on learning supports the proposition that knowing the reason for a learning situation and seeing a purpose in a task help children learn. Through their lives outside the classroom, children have experienced a wide variety of purposes for writing to various audiences. If children are allowed to experiment with paper and pencils and to write on topics of their choice, these purposes will begin to show up in their early attempts at writing. They will jot down lists of things they need to do, make signs for their doors warning intruders to stay out, and write letters to the editor to complain about injustices.

Similarly, children have experienced many opportunities to read for real purposes. They have shopped in grocery and toy stores, and sometimes they have screamed when their parent refused to purchase the cereal or toy whose label they read and wanted. They have told the car driver who slowed but didn't come to a full stop at the stop sign to STOP! They have read the address on an envelope collected at the mailbox and said, "You won't like this one. It's a bill!"

Notice how many of these reading and writing opportunities are literacy events woven into daily life. The event defines the purpose of the literacy activity. When children read and write for real people, for real purposes, and in ways that are linked with their lives outside of school, they are more likely to be motivated, and motivation is believed to result in learning that is deep and internalized (Gambrell & Mazzoni, 1999). Furthermore, through such meaningful literacy events, school and community are bridged. Just outside the walls of every school are a number of real problems awaiting study. Reading and writing for real purposes abound.

Effective Teachers Support Children's Experimentations with Print

As we blend the two perspectives, it is important that teachers allow children a "risk-free" environment in which they practice and integrate new skills they are learning with what they already know. Years ago, young children were not considered to be writing until they were writing conventionally, that is, correctly forming the letters and spelling the words. They were not considered to be reading until they could correctly recognize numerous printed words. In the 1970s, Marie Clay (1975) and Charles Read (1971) helped us understand emergent forms of writing and reading. We learned that children construct, test, and perfect hypotheses about written language. Their research led Elizabeth Sulzby and her colleagues (Sulzby, 1985a, 1985b; Sulzby, Barnhart, & Hieshima, 1989) to create developmental sequences that children pass through on their way to becoming conventional readers and writers.

While excellent teachers continue to model correct forms of writing during guided writing and to support and scaffold children's reading and writing efforts, excellent teachers realize that children continue to develop and evolve to more conventional forms of reading and writing through practice and time. Teachers' support for the construction of knowledge through experimentation and risk taking does not end when children's print understandings more closely resemble that of adults. When children reach this stage in their literacy development, teachers support their efforts to search for and construct new meanings in reading and through writing. They encourage them to test the word: Does it make sense in this sentence? They work to make children strategic readers, readers who dare to employ different strategies with different texts read for different purposes. These teachers and their children view reading and writing as meaning making or producing events.

Effective Teachers Use Multiple Forms of Assessment to Find Out What Children Know and Can Do and They Use That Data to Make Instructional Decisions

Is the child's development following the expected stages? Is the child acquiring the core-content early literacy skills or the crucial-element early elementary skills? Today, teachers use standardized and curriculum-based measures and other ongoing measures to assess children's progress in acquiring the crucial elements or core content skills.

Not so long ago, the literacy field recommended against the use of standardized tests, particularly with young children and particularly paper-and-pencil group-administered tests. For example, the 1998 joint statement by the International Reading Association and the National Association for the Education of Young Children had the following to say about testing young children:

> **Accurate assessment** of children's knowledge, skills, and dispositions in reading and writing will help teachers better match instruction with how and what children are learning. However, early reading and writing cannot simply be measured as a set of narrowly defined skills on standardized tests. These measures often are not reliable or valid indicators of what children can do in typical practice, nor are they sensitive to language variations, culture, or experiences of young children. Rather, a sound assessment should be anchored in real-life writing and reading tasks and continuously chronicle a wide range of children's literacy activities in different situations. Good assessment is essential to help teachers tailor appropriate instruction to young children and to know when and how much intensive instruction on any particular skill or strategy might be needed. (IRA/NCTE, 1998, p. 38)

This joint statement advised teachers of young children to use multiple indicators to assess and monitor children's development and learning. We concur.

Now, however, the field also acknowledges that standardized assessments—such as the *Peabody Picture Vocabulary Test* (Dunn & Dunn, 1997), the *Individual Growth and Developmental Indicator* (IGDI; Early Childhood Research Institute on Measuring Growth and Development, 2000), and the *Phonological Awareness Literacy Screening* (Invernizzi, Meier, Swank, & Juel, 1999)—can provide teachers with valuable information. Repeated use of the same instruments allows teachers to chronicle children's development over time. Neither standardized nor informal ongoing assessment should be used alone, however. When multiple sources of data are used, the likelihood of an accurate understanding of children's literacy knowledge and learning is increased (IRA/NCTE, 1994).

Teachers must use both kinds of assessment to improve their instruction. Teachers must gather information, analyze the information, and use what they learn to inform their instruction. In fact, that is a key purpose of assessment. The Assess-Plan-Teach-Assess model must be central to teachers' classroom assessment procedures.

Effective Teachers Recognize That Some Children Need Explicit Instruction in Order to Become Proficient Readers and Writers—and They Provide the Needed Intensive Intervention

This principle is closely related to the previous principle. It has gained increased prominence because of Response to Intervention (RTI), a relatively new federal initiative. RTI is the result of the recent reauthorization of the Individuals with Disabilities Education Act (IDEA; Public Law 108-446), the law that defines the federal rules for special education. The ultimate goal of RTI is to ensure that all struggling children have the opportunity to participate in intensive interventions *prior to* their being identified as having a learning disability. The interventions used must be intensive (maybe as much as an extra hour of instruction each day) and supported by research that proves their effectiveness. Each child's progress must be monitored carefully so that adjustments in the intervention can be made as needed in order to produce accelerated growth to meet the annual yearly progress criteria.

Though RTI's origin is special education legislation, it is not simply a special education initiative. Because the law requires schools to demonstrate that a child's reading difficulty is not the result of a lack of "appropriate instruction in reading, including the essential components of reading instruction, as defined in section 1208(3) of the Elementary and Secondary Act" before the process of the child's consideration for special education begins (Department of Education, 2006, p. 46786), the child's classroom teachers play a central role in the implementation of this law. This provision has resulted in schools nationwide beginning to use a three-tiered model of classroom reading instruction. In Tier 1, classroom teachers provide their students with high-quality classroom reading instruction in the essential components of reading (e.g., reading comprehension strategies, phonics, fluency, phonemic awareness, and vocabulary). Tier 1 instruction should result in most children (estimates are 75–80 percent) reading proficiently with this level of support. Progress monitoring assessments are used to identify children whose learning rate is insufficient. Identified children receive supplemental support in small groups of two to three students. Instruction in Tier 2 is focused on each small group's specific skill needs and is designed to increase the children's learning rate. Estimates are that an additional 10–15 percent of the children will be proficient readers with Tier 2 instruction. The remaining 5–10 percent of the children who continue to struggle receive Tier 3 instruction. Tier 3 is intensive, individualized tutorial interventions. Assessing to monitor children's growth, planning, and teaching are integral to each tier. Children who continue to struggle after Tier 3 interventions are then formally assessed for special education services.

RTI is the model for school-aged children. A similar instructional model is developing for use in preschool, called Recognition and Response (R&R; Coleman, Buysse, & Neitzel, 2006). Like RTI, R&R includes four essential components: tiered interventions with the intensity of the instruction corresponding to the children's support needs; screening and assessing using multiple sources of information (e.g., checklists, observations, work sampling) to monitor the children's progress toward key benchmarks; teachers' use of research-based curriculum and instruction in all tiered-intervention levels; and the use of a collaborative (e.g., parents, teachers, specialists) problem-solving process for making decisions about what is the best intervention to meet each child's learning needs.

Effective Teachers Respect and Make Accommodations for Children's Developmental, Cultural, and Linguistic Diversity

Children arrive in the classroom with different individual language and literacy needs. Our challenge is to offer good fits between each child's strengths and needs and what we try to give the child. The instruction we provide needs to dovetail with where children are developmentally and with their language and culture.

Some children will come to school having learned how to talk in ways that are consistent with their teachers' expectations; other children will not. "We come to every situation with stories: patterns and sequences of events which are built into us. Our learning happens within the experience of what important others did" (Bateson, 1979, p. 13). In other words, the ways in which we make meaning and use words are dependent on the practices shared by the members of our community: the words chosen; the sentence structures used; the decision to talk after, or over, another's comment; and so on. As Allan Luke and Joan Kale (1997, p. 13) point out, "Different cultures make meaning in different ways, with different patterns of exchange and interaction, text conventions and beliefs about reading and writing." Given our increasingly diverse communities composed of many different cultures, teachers are more challenged than ever before to understand what this diversity means for their teaching and for their children's learning.

Only since the 1980s have researchers investigated early literacy learning in non-mainstream homes and communities. In one pioneering study, Shirley Brice Heath (1983) described how children growing up in one working-class community learn that reading is sitting still and sounding out words, following the rules, whereas children in another working-class community learn that being able to tell a story well orally is more important than being able to read written texts. These conceptions of literacy were quite different from those found in children from middle-class families. The important question is, should these types of cultural differences be viewed as deficits that must be "fixed" for children to succeed in school, or should these differences be viewed as positive characteristics that teachers can take advantage of when helping children learn language and literacy? Curt Dudley-Marling and Krista Lucas (2009) worry that too many teachers respond negatively to their poor and non-English-speaking students' language and cultural experiences, viewing these children's experiences as deficits rather than as assets. They argue that the claims of language deficiencies in these children and their families are unwarranted and that teachers must view the language differences as "just that —differences" and that teachers must build on their "students' linguistic, cultural, and cognitive 'funds of knowledge' to teach them what they need to achieve success" (p. 369). Teachers must exhibit "respect for students' knowledge, who they are, and where they come from" (p. 369).

Will children with different experiences meet teachers who have engaged in the study of the children's communities' ways with words and texts? Will their teachers provide scaffolded language activities and instruction that will enable these children to be successful in their efforts to learn mainstream English? Will they meet teachers who have redesigned reading lessons so the lessons better fit the speech events the children are accustomed to at home and in their community? Will their teachers understand and value the patterns of teaching and learning evidenced in their homes and build on these patterns so that these children are drawn into the school world? Will their teachers understand that these children might be quiet in school because their parents have taught them to show respect by being quiet and deferential? Throughout this book we give pointers on providing culturally sensitive language and literacy instruction. If these guidelines are followed, the answers to the above questions will be a resounding yes.

A significant and rapidly growing group of diverse learners are second-language learners, and the vast majority are from homes where Spanish is the primary language (Tabors, Paez, & Lopez, 2003). The population of children who speak English as a second language was estimated at 3.5 million in the year 2000 and is projected to grow to 6 million by 2020 (Faltis, 2001). Of this group, those children who speak little or no English are referred to as limited English proficient. Other children are bilingual and can speak both

English and their native language with varying degrees of proficiency. These children's native language might be Spanish, Portuguese, Japanese, or some other world language. When they come to school, second-language learners are typically competent users of their native language, and this competence is a strength to be exploited by sensitive teachers.

We have included Special Feature sections in select chapters of this book that focus on second-language and bilingual learners' literacy development. From these features, readers will learn which strategies presented in this book are appropriate for use with children whose primary language is a language other than mainstream English and which strategies need to be adapted to meet the needs of these children.

Effective Teachers Build Partnerships with Families

Collin (1992, p. 2) refers to the parents' nurturing role in their child's literacy development as "planting the seeds of literacy." Almost all parents want to plant these seeds, but many are unsure of the best way to begin. Similarly, most parents and other primary caregivers vastly underestimate the importance of their role in helping children become competent language users. Throughout this text we will discuss strategies teachers can use to enhance language and reading and writing opportunities in the home.

Research over the past few decades has consistently demonstrated that families provide the rich social context necessary for children's language development (Black, Puckett, & Bell, 1992; Field, Woodson, Greenberg, & Cohen, 1982; Weiss, Lilly-White, & Gordon, 1980; White, 1985). The thousands of hours of parent–child interactions from the moment of birth through the preschool years provide the foundation for language. Research has long documented that children differ in their ability to learn and use new words (Smith & Dickinson, 2002). In an effort to understand what accounts for these differences, researchers Betty Hart and Todd Risley (1995) documented parent and child interactions during the first three years of children's lives. The research team observed forty-two families from different socioeconomic and ethnic backgrounds one hour each month for two and a half years. Their data revealed vast differences in the amount of language spoken to children. Children from welfare homes heard an average of 616 words an hour; children from working-class families heard 1,251 words an hour; whereas children from professional homes heard 2,153 words per hour! If one thinks of words as dollars, the children from these different socioeconomic homes would have significantly disparate bank accounts. Further, this long-term study revealed that early language differences had a lasting effect on children's subsequent language accomplishments both at age three and at age nine. In other words, talk between adults and children early in life makes a significant difference.

Likewise, parents play a critical role in helping children learn about print. Many children learn about literacy very early. This task is accomplished quite naturally as children sit on the laps of parents, other family members, or caregivers sharing a storybook. Being read to at home facilitates the onset of reading, reading fluency, and reading enjoyment. Unfortunately, many parents do not have the resources or literacy legacy to offer their children (Enz & Foley, 2009) and research suggests that this is especially true for low-income homes (Christian, Morrison, & Bryant, 1998; Griffin & Morrison, 1997). This lack of parental involvement may have a significant effect on the children's learning throughout their schooling. For example, Billie Enz's (1992) study of 400 high school sophomores revealed that

70 percent of the remedial readers could not recall being read to by their parents as children, while 96 percent of the students in advanced placement courses reported that their parents had read to them regularly. In essence, it appears that a child's future literacy and subsequent success in school depend on parents' ability and willingness to provide the child with thousands of planned and spontaneous encounters with print (Enz & Searfoss, 1995).

Helping parents understand their role as their child's first and most impactful literacy model is one of a teacher's most important tasks. To fulfill this responsibility, teachers at all grade levels must interact with parents constantly! However, this role may be more challenging than many teachers initially anticipate. This text will provide practical suggestions for providing resources for families and developing two-way communications with families.

Effective Teachers Recognize the Importance of Reflecting on Their Instructional Decisions

The importance of "learning by doing," standing back from each teaching/learning event to learn from one's teaching, is not new. John Dewey (1938) is usually credited with proposing the importance of this activity and Donald Schon (1983) with reintroducing the idea into the educational literature. To reflect is to take an active role in studying one's own instructional decisions to enhance one's knowledge and make informed decisions. Not all such reflections will be on past actions (retrospective); some might be on the potential outcomes of future actions (anticipatory), and others will be "in action" while teaching (contemporaneous) (van Manen, 1995). To reflect is to put a new lens on one's teaching: to consider and reconsider the procedures for technical accuracy (e.g., the procedural steps to follow while conducting a guided reading lesson), the reasons for instructional actions and outcomes, and the underlying assumptions of actions that impact social justice (e.g., curriculum mandates that affect teacher decision making or inequities that inhibit student learning).

Being a reflective practitioner is important for literacy teachers who seek to provide learning experiences that meet each child's instructional needs. As the decision makers, these teachers determine which literacy skills or components to teach and when to move their community of learners toward the desired instructional goals, adjusting the when and how to meet each learner's needs. Reflection is central to making these critical decisions.

Summary

In this chapter, we briefly explained the significant impact of recent national policies on the literacy field and compared the constructivist approaches to literacy learning (emergent literacy and reading workshop) with the new scientifically based reading research approach to literacy learning. We believe that the best literacy practices use strategies from both approaches. We firmly believe that teachers must use evidence (from research and from their students' performance) to guide their teaching.

In subsequent chapters, we provide many explanations of how to implement teaching strategies aimed at promoting different aspects of language and literacy development. In addition, the themes of respect for student diversity and instruction linked to assessment appear throughout the book. When appropriate, Special Features about the special needs of

PEARSON
myeducationkit

To check your comprehension on the content covered in this chapter, go to the MyEducationKit for your book and complete the Study Plan for Chapter 1. Here you will be able to take a chapter quiz and receive feedback on your answers.

second-language learners are included. Further, a section titled Assessment: Discovering What Children Know and Can Do is included in several chapters.

To summarize the key points from this chapter, we return to the focus questions at the beginning:

■ *How have U.S. literacy policies and initiatives affected preschool and elementary reading instruction?*

Beginning with the 1983 (*A Nation at Risk*) suggestion that students be held to high and rigorous standards, to the passage of the No Child Left Behind Act in 2001 requiring schools and school districts to hold all students responsible for demonstrating that they know the content of the standards, national policies have had a significant impact on literacy instruction in the United States. Two literacy programs were funded by the NCLB Act: (1) Reading First, a program that provides funding to help states and local school districts serving low-income children eliminate reading deficits by establishing high-quality, comprehensive reading instruction built on the scientific research; and (2) Early Reading First, a program that aims to transform existing preschool programs into centers of excellence that prepare young children to enter kindergarten ready to learn to read and write. To obtain these funds, agencies must demonstrate that they will use reading programs and instructional strategies that are consistent with scientifically based reading research and that they will provide teachers with extensive professional development on these programs and strategies. The required use of "scientifically based reading research"— research that meets a set of specific criteria—has received a mixed response from the literacy field.

Recent national initiatives and legislation have drawn attention to the need to prepare children before they start school. From the reauthorization of Head Start, to the writing of pre-kindergarten literacy standards, to funded research and preschool-teacher professional development programs, to President George W. Bush's Good Start, Grow Smart initiative, the nation now recognizes the importance of children's early years to their later academic success, particularly their reading achievement.

■ *How did the standards movement change literacy instructional practices and the assessment of children?*

The Elementary and Secondary Education Act requires states and school districts to hold all students, grades 3 through 8, responsible for demonstrating that they know the content of their state's English language arts standards. Specifically, this act requires states to assess students' success annually in meeting state standards in reading, mathematics, and, soon, science. To ensure that all students demonstrate progress toward proficiency in "meeting the standards," each state was required to design an accountability system. All students must meet or exceed the state's standards no later than twelve years after the end of the 2001–2 school year. Clearly, if students are to "know" the standards, then the curriculum must be aligned with the standards. Teachers must ensure that their students have the opportunity to learn the content specified by the standards.

- *How is the emergent literacy perspective different from the scientifically based reading research perspective on young children's early literacy learning?*

The emergent literacy perspective suggests that children learn about language and literacy by observing, exploring, and interacting with others. Children assume the role of apprentice: mimicking, absorbing, and adapting the words and literacy activities used by more knowledgeable others. As they engage in social interactions, children integrate new experiences with prior knowledge, constructing and testing hypotheses to make meaning.

The scientifically based reading research perspective argues that children need to be explicitly taught those skills that the research literature has identified as predictive of later reading success. To date, twelve variables have been identified as predictive of later reading success (italics indicate those skills evidencing the highest correlation with school-age decoding): *alphabet knowledge,* print knowledge, *oral language/vocabulary,* environmental print, invented spelling, listening comprehension, *phonological memory,* rapid letter naming, *phonemic awareness,* visual memory, and *visual perceptual* skills.

A key difference between the two perspectives, then, is the early literacy practices recommended as appropriate: explicit instruction versus allowing the children to acquire the skills of literacy through multiple interactions with print and more knowledgeable others. Unfortunately, to date there are few research-based suggestions on early literacy instructional strategies and programs. What do appropriate instructional strategies look and sound like? Teachers of young children must ensure that inappropriate strategies do not creep into their teaching practices as they shift to teaching the skills identified as central to children's success as readers.

- *What principles should guide teachers when teaching language and literacy?*

Effective teachers

- Provide children with a print-rich classroom environment
- Demonstrate, model, and scaffold instruction
- Explicitly teach children skills that research supports as key elements of reading, writing, and speaking
- Read to children daily and encourage them to read books on their own
- Provide opportunities for children to collaborate and help one another learn about language and literacy
- Provide opportunities for children to use language and literacy for real purposes and audience
- Support children's experimentations with print
- Use multiple forms of assessment to find out what children know and can do and then use that data to make instructional decisions
- Recognize that some children need additional instruction in order to become proficient readers and writers—and provide the needed intensive intervention
- Respect and make accommodations for children's developmental, cultural, and linguistic diversity
- Recognize the importance of reflecting on their instructional decisions

LINKING KNOWLEDGE TO PRACTICE

1. Access your state's Department of Education Web site and bookmark your state's English language arts standards and grade-level benchmarks. Don't forget to look for the pre-K standards as well. Compare what your state expects third-graders to know with what a neighboring state expects third-graders to know.

2. Observe a teacher in a nearby classroom. How does this teacher's language and literacy instruction match up with the teaching principles described in this chapter?

2 Oral Language Development

Perched in the shopping cart, nine-month-old Dawn babbles away to her mother. As they approach the checkout register, the clerk greets her mother. Dawn smiles, loudly says "Hi!" and waves her hand. The startled clerk smiles at Dawn and begins to talk to her. Dawn, obviously pleased with this attention, now babbles back to the clerk.

As this scenario reveals, the power of language is evident to even its youngest users. Dawn demonstrates that she knows how to use language to express—and realize—her desire to become a significant, communicating member in her world. By age eighteen months, Dawn will have a vocabulary of dozens of words, and she will begin speaking in rule-governed, two-word sentences. By thirty-six months, her vocabulary will number in the hundreds of words, and she will be using fully formed, five- and six-word sentences.

Children's oral language development is remarkable. Lindfors (1987, p. 90) outlines the typical accomplishments of young language learners:

> Virtually every child, without special training, exposed to surface structures of language in many interaction contexts, builds for himself—in a short period of time and at an early stage in his cognitive development—a deep-level, abstract, and highly complex system of linguistic structure.

How does Dawn—and every other human child, for that matter—learn to communicate? How does this development occur so rapidly and without any seeming effort on the part of children or their parents? This question has fascinated scholars and parents for hundreds of years and is the subject of this chapter.

Before Reading This Chapter, Think About . . .

- What were your first words? Although you probably do not recall uttering those words, maybe your parents or older siblings recollect your having spoken to them.
- How do you think children acquire language? Is language development primarily a matter of genetics (an inborn ability to learn languages), the types of experiences and support children receive from their parents and other people, or a combination of these factors?
- When do children begin to express their thoughts orally? Why do some children develop language early while others experience language delays?

■ Have you ever been in a situation in which everyone around you used a language you don't know? How did you feel? How did you communicate with these speakers?

Focus Questions

■ What are the major views on how children's language develops? Which aspects of language development does each view adequately explain?
■ What are the major components of language?
■ How do the structures of an infant's brain develop? How does this structural development affect language acquisition?
■ What factors affect children's rate of language acquisition?
■ How does children's acquisition of a second language compare with their first language acquisition? What should adults do to make it easier for children to learn English as a second language?

Language Acquisition Theories

There are four views on how children learn language: behaviorism, linguistic nativism, social interactionism, and the neurobiological perspective. We present a brief description of

---

BOX 2.1

Definition of Terms

behaviorist perspective: the view that language acquisition is a result of imitation and reinforcement.

cerebral cortex: the largest part of the brain, composed of two hemispheres that are responsible for higher brain functions, including thought and language.

myelineation: a process in which the neurons of the brain become coated with a white substance known as myelin, which facilitates the transmission of sensory information and promotes learning.

morphemes: the smallest units of meaning in oral language. The word *cats* contains two morphemes: *cat* (name of a type of animal) and *s* (plural).

nativist perspective: the view that language development is a result of an inborn capacity to learn language.

neurobiological perspective: the view that language acquisition can be explained by studying the structural development of the brain.

neurons: the impulse-conducting cells that make up the brain.

otitis media: an inflammation of the inner part of the ear that can impede language acquisition.

phoneme: the smallest unit of sound in a language. There are approximately forty-four phonemes in English.

pragmatics: rules that affect how language is used in different social contexts.

semantics: the part of language that assigns meaning to words and sentences.

synapses: connections between the neurons of the brain.

syntax: rules for arranging words into sentences.

social-interactionist perspective: the view that language development is a result of both genetics and adult support.

each perspective in this chapter. Our experiences as parents, teachers, and researchers lead us to believe that the *social-interactionist perspective* most realistically accounts for similarities and differences in young children's language development. Therefore, we present a more detailed description of what is presently known about children's language acquisition from this perspective. However, we also acknowledge the importance of the new neurobiological information provided by neuroscientists to help us understand the biology of language acquisition. Together, the social-interactionist perspective and the *neurobiological perspective* provide important insights for teachers and future teachers on how children acquire language(s). In Figure 2.1, we summarize these four views of language acquisition.

Behaviorist Perspective

The *behaviorist perspective* suggests that nurture—the way a child is taught or molded by parents and the environment—plays a dominant role in children's language development. Through the first half of the twentieth century, this was the prevalent view. Researchers and teachers believed that all learning (language included) is the result of two basic processes— classical and operant conditioning (Skinner, 1957). Behaviorists attribute receptive language to associations that result from classical conditioning. For example, every time the baby is

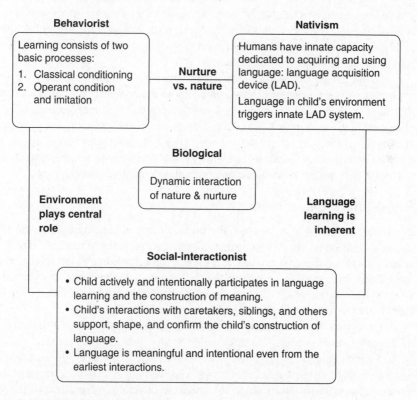

FIGURE 2.1   Theoretical Perspectives on Language Acquisition

offered a bottle, the mother names the object, "Here's the bottle." After numerous repetitions with the adult presenting the action/object and phrase, the baby learns that the clear cylinder filled with food is called a bottle.

Behaviorists suggest that through operant conditioning, infants gradually learn expressive language by being rewarded for imitating the sounds and speech they hear. For instance, a baby spontaneously babbles and accidentally says or repeats the sound "mama." The mother responds joyfully, hugging and kissing the baby, saying "Yes, Mama!" The baby, given this reward, is reinforced and attempts to repeat the behavior. Once the behavior is repeated and rewarded often enough, the child connects the word to the object or event.

Nativist Perspective

The *nativist perspective* of learning and development, with its emphasis on nature, is at the opposite end of the continuum from the behaviorist perspective. According to the nativist view, a person's behavior and capabilities are largely predetermined. Nativists believe every child has an inborn capacity to learn language. If these theorists were using computer terminology, they would say that humans are hardwired for language. Noam Chomsky (1965) called this innate capacity a language acquisition device (LAD). Nativists posit that the LAD allows children to interpret phoneme patterns, word meanings, and the rules that govern language. For example, when children first begin to use past tenses, they often overgeneralize certain words, such as *goed* for *went,* or *thinked* for *thought.* Since *goed* and *thinked* are not words that children would hear adults say, these examples illustrate that children are using some type of internal rule system, not simple imitation, to govern their acquisition of language.

Nativists also believe that this innate language structure facilitates the child's own attempts to communicate, much the same way as the computer's wiring facilitates the use of a number of software programs. Nativists believe that language learning differs from all other human learning in that a child learns to communicate even without support from parents or caregivers. They view the environment's role in language acquisition as largely a function of activating the innate, physiologically based system. Environment, these theorists believe, is not the major force shaping a child's language development.

Social-Interactionist Perspective

Social interactionists do not come down on either side of the nature versus nurture debate; rather, they acknowledge the influence of genetics and parental teaching. They share with behaviorists the belief that environment plays a central role in children's language development. Likewise, along with nativists, they believe that children possess an innate predisposition to learn language. In addition, social interactionists stress the child's own intentional participation in language learning and the construction of meaning.

Lev Vygotsky's theory (1978) forms the foundation of the social-interactionist view of language development. Vygotsky believed that language develops in the context of social interaction and language use. As children experience the wide variety of functions and forms of language, they internalize the way that their society uses language to represent meaning. Social experiences shape the language the child internalizes. At the same time, the child is making an internal effort to assign meanings to experience and to communicate

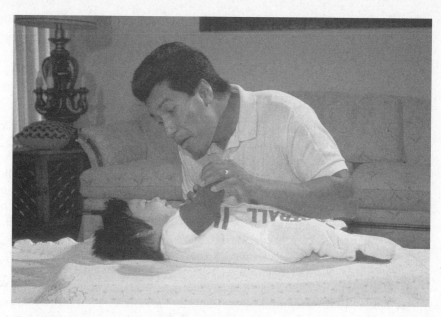

The social-interactionist perspective highlights the importance of infants' "verbal bouts" with caregivers.

with the outside world. These efforts are simultaneous. Two forces, within and without the child, work together to propel language learning.

The social interactionist's point of view emphasizes the importance of the infant's verbal negotiations or "verbal bouts" (Golinkoff, 1983) with caregivers. These negotiations occur partly because mothers or other caretakers treat children's attempts at speech as meaningful and intentional (Piper, 1993). An example is shown by eleven-month-old Dawn, standing by the garage door. Dawn is patting the door.

DAWN: "Bice!"

MOM: "Do you want ice?"

DAWN: (shaking her head) "Biiisse."

MOM: (opening the garage door) "Bise?"

DAWN: (pointing at the bike) "Bise."

MOM: "You want to go for a bike ride?"

DAWN: (raising her arms, nodding her head vigorously) "Bice!"

As Dawn's mother (and most mothers) begins to make sense of her child's speech, she also begins to understand her child's meaning and/or intent. Lev Vygotsky (1962) described this type of adult support, or scaffolding, as facilitating the child's language growth within the zone of proximal development, the distance between a child's current level of development and the level at which the child can function with adult assistance. In the preceding example, the mother's questions enable Dawn to successfully communicate using a one-word sentence, something she could not have done on her own. Parents also support children's efforts to learn language by focusing the child's attention on objects in the immediate environment and labeling each object and its action.

A Biological Perspective

The psychologists, linguists, and anthropologists who developed the three preceding perspectives of language acquisition had to infer the origins of language and brain activity from careful, long-term observations of external behavior. Over the past two decades, technological innovations have enabled neuroscientists to study the brain at a cellular level. Brain-imaging techniques are noninvasive procedures that allow researchers to graphically record and simultaneously display three-dimensional, color-enhanced images of a living brain as it processes information (Sochurek, 1987). These data provide researchers with a better way to understand the organization and functional operations of the brain.

According to this perspective, the capacity to learn language begins with brain cells called neurons. *Neurons* emerge during the early phases of fetal development, growing at the fantastic rate of 250,000 per minute (Edelman, 1995). As neurons multiply, they follow a complex genetic blueprint that causes the brain to develop distinct but interdependent systems—brain stem and limbic system, cerebellum and cerebral cortex (MacLean, 1978). New brain-imaging technology has allowed scientists to locate specific areas in the brain that are dedicated to hearing, speaking, and interpreting language. Thus, the nativist linguistic theory of language acquisition is, in part, correct—the human brain has dedicated structures for language, and infant brains are born capable of speaking any of the 6,000-plus human languages (Kuhl, 1993). However, infants are not disposed to speak any particular language, nor are they born language proficient. The language that a child learns is dependent on the language that the child hears spoken in the home (Kuhl, 2008).

In fact, the recent discoveries in neurobiology support elements of the nativist, behaviorist, and social-interactionist views of language development. These biological findings reveal that language learning is a reciprocal dialogue between genetics (nature) and environment (nurture). Clearly, infants are born with key brain areas genetically dedicated to language functions. Yet, for children to learn the language of their culture, it is necessary that they have consistent, frequent opportunities to interact with a persistent caregiver who models the language with the child. Likewise, neuroscientists agree that a child's language capacity is dependent on the quality of language input. Parents and caregivers who consistently engage in conversation with their infants actually help their children develop neural networks that lead to language fluency and proficiency (Healy, 1994, 1997; Kotulak, 1997; Sprenger, 1999).

Linguistic Vocabulary Lesson

Linguistics is the study of language. To better understand the complexities of linguistic acquisition, we provide a brief discussion of the components of linguistic structure: phonology, morphology, syntax, semantics, and pragmatics.

Phonology

The sound system of a particular language is its phonology, and the distinctive units of sound in a language are its *phonemes*. Individual phonemes are described according to how speakers modify the airstream they exhale to produce the particular sounds.

Phonological development begins when sounds of speech activate neural networks in the infant's brain. This process begins during the last three months of prenatal development as babies are able to hear intonation patterns from their mother's voice (Shore, 1997).

Although the mechanical aspects of the auditory system are in place at birth, the neural network that supports language acquisition is just beginning to develop. Verbal interactions with caregivers allow babies to clearly hear sounds of their native language(s) and observe how the mouth and tongue work to create these unique sounds. Simultaneously, as babies babble, they gain motor control of their vocal and breathing apparatus. Interactions with caregivers allow babies an opportunity to listen, observe, and attempt to mimic sounds they hear and the mouth and tongue movements they see. Through this process, babies begin to specialize in the sounds of their native language(s). The developmental window of opportunity (sometimes called the critical period) for mastering sound discrimination occurs within the first six months of an infant's life. By this time, babies' brains are already pruning out sensitivity to sounds that are not heard in their environment (Kuhl, 1993). This pruning is so efficient that children actually lose the ability to hear phonemes that are not used in their mother tongue. Children who consistently hear more than one language during this time may become native bi- or trilinguals, as they retain the ability to hear the subtle and discrete sounds.

Another important aspect of the English phonology is its prosody, or the stress and intonation patterns of the language. Stress refers to the force with which phonemes are articulated. Where the stress is placed may distinguish otherwise identical words (RECord [noun] versus reCORD [verb]). Intonation, on the other hand, refers to the pattern of stress and of rising and falling pitch that occurs within a sentence. These changes in intonation may shift the meaning of otherwise identical sentences:

IS she coming? (Is she or is she not coming?)
Is SHE coming? (Her, not anyone else)
Is she COMING? (Hurry up; it's about time)

Babies as young as four and five months begin to experiment with the pitch, tone, and volume of the sounds they make and often produce sounds that mimic the tonal and stress qualities of their parents' speech.

Morphology

As babies' phonological development progresses, they begin to make *morphemes*. Morphemes are the smallest units of meaning in oral language. While babies may begin to make wordlike sounds (echolalia) around six to eight months, morphemes will not emerge until around a baby's first birthday. These real words are made up of one or more phonemes and fall into several categories:

Lexical—individual meaning carrying words, such as *cat, baby*.

Bound—units of sound that hold meaning (like *re, un*) but must be attached to other morphemes (*reorder, unbend*).

Derivational and inflectional—usually suffixes that change the class of the word; for example: noun to adjective—*dust* to *dusty;* verb to noun—*teaches* to *teacher.*

Compound—two lexical morphemes that together may form a unique meaning, such as *football* or *cowboy.*

Idiom—an expression whose meaning cannot be derived from its individual parts; for example, *Put your foot in your mouth* carries a very different meaning from the visual image it conjures up.

Syntax

Syntax refers to how morphemes, or words, are combined to form sentences or units of thought. In English, there are basically two different types of order: linear and hierarchical structures. Linear structure refers to the object–verb arrangement. For example, *Building falls on man* means something very different than *Man falls on building.* Hierarchical structure refers to how words are grouped together within a sentence to reveal the speaker's intent. However, different languages have unique and inherent rules that govern syntax. A speaker of English might say: *The long, sleek, black cat chased the frightened tiny, gray mouse.* A language with syntactical rules that differ from English could state it this way: *Chasing the gray mouse, tiny and frightened, was the cat, long, sleek, and black.*

Shortly after their first birthdays, most children are able to convey their intentions with single words. Have you ever heard a young child use the powerful words *no* and *mine*? More complex, rule-driven communication usually emerges between the ages of two and three, when children are able to construct sentences of two or more words.

Though children have prewired capacity for language rules (such as past tense), adult scaffolding or support plays a significant role in extending and expanding a child's language development. For instance, when Joe says *deenk,* his day care teacher can extend and clarify Joe's intentions: *Joe, do you want to drink milk or juice*? If Joe says, *I drinked all the milk,* his teacher might tactfully expand his statement. *Yes, Joe, you drank all of your milk.* This type of subtle modeling is usually the most appropriate way to support children as they learn the conventional forms and complexities of their language. However, even when adults expand a child's speech, the child's own internal rule-governing system may resist modification until the child is developmentally ready to make the change. The following interaction between a four-year-old and an interested adult illustrates this phenomenon (Gleason, 1967):

CHILD: My teacher holded the baby rabbits and we patted them.

ADULT: Did you say your teacher held the baby rabbit?

CHILD: Yes.

ADULT: What did you say that she did?

CHILD: She holded the baby rabbits and we patted them.

ADULT: Did you say she held them tightly?

CHILD: No. She holded them loose.

Semantics

"How would you differentiate among the following words that a blender manufacturer has printed under the row of buttons: stir, beat, puree, cream, chop, whip, crumb, mix, mince, grate, crush, blend, shred, grind, frappe, liquify?" (Lindfors, 1987, p. 47). *Semantics* deals with the subtle shades of meaning that language can convey. Variations in language meanings generally reflect the values and concerns of the culture. For instance, dozens of Arabic words may be dedicated to describing the camel's range of moods and behaviors. The Polynesian language has many words that define variations in the wind; likewise, Eskimo languages include many words for snow.

Knowledge of word meaning is stored throughout the brain in a vast biological forest of interconnected neurons, dendrites, and *synapses*. Beyond culture, children's ongoing personal experience allows them to connect words and meaning. Since words are symbolic labels for objects, events, actions, and feelings, a child may initially call all four-legged animals *kitty*. However, after several firsthand encounters with kitties (with the support of adults who can help label and describe the event) a child will likely develop the concepts and vocabulary to discriminate kitties from doggies, kittens from cats, and eventually Persians from Siamese.

Pragmatics

Sitting in his bouncer, two-month-old Marcus studies his mother's face as she talks to him. In a high-pitched voice, she exaggerates her words in a singsong manner: *Lookeee at Mommeeee. I see baabee Marceee looking at Mommeee.* Baby Marcus appears to mimic her mouth movements and responds to her conversations with smiles, wiggles, and very loud coos. After Marcus quiets, his mother knowingly responds to her baby's comments, *Yes, you're right, Mommeee does love her Marceee-Boy.*

When parent and child engage in singsong conversation of "parentese" and baby vocalizations, the basic conventions of turn taking are learned, but rarely does the teacher or student realize that a lesson was being taught. *Pragmatics* deals with the conventions of becoming a competent language user. These include rules on how to engage successfully in conversation with others, such as how to initiate and sustain conversation, how to take turns, when and how to interrupt, how to use cues for indicating subject interest, and how to tactfully change subjects.

Pragmatics also refers to the uses of language (spoken and body) to communicate one's intent in real life. The message of a speaker's actual words may be heightened or may even convey the opposite meaning depending on the manner in which the words are delivered. This delivery may include inflection, facial expressions, or body gestures. Take, for example, this statement: *I'm having such a great time.* Imagine that the person who is saying this phrase is smiling easily and widely, with eyes making direct contact with the person with whom she is sharing her time. Now, picture the person saying *I'm having such a great time* while sneering and rolling her eyes (see Figure 2.2). Though the words are identical, the intent of the two speakers is obviously completely different. Further, pragmatics deals with an increasing conscious awareness of being able to accomplish goals through the use of language.

Children who are learning two languages simultaneously may also begin to exhibit the body languages that often accompany particular cultures. For example, four-year-old

FIGURE 2.2   Language Is More Than Words

Hasina Elizabeth speaks both Arabic (dad's language) and British-English (her mother's tongue). At her young age Hasina is fluent and responds back in the language with which she is prompted, using both gestures and dialect. When her mother asks, "Do you want bis- cuits?" (English cookie), Hasina responds by straightening her back, lifting her chin, and saying, "Why, yes. Thank you!" All mannerisms would suggest a very proper British lady. The following morning when her dad asks the same question in Arabic, she responds by leaning in close to him and holding her hands out with with a bold hand gesture, ("Thank you very much"), she replies. Though the words were nearly the same her physical posture and facial expressions reflect the cultural mannerism that her parents model when they speak to her. Hence, we see that language is more than the words alone—it also includes nonverbal interactions and mannerism (Mayberry & Nicoladis, 2000).

As children mature, they are able to use social registers—or the ability to adapt their speech and mannerisms to accommodate different social situations. This level of commu- nicative competence can be observed in children as young as five as they engage in pretend play. During dramatic play children may easily switch roles—baby to parent, student to teacher, customer to waiter—by using the vocabulary, mannerisms, and attitudes that con- vey the role they wish to play.

In reviewing these linguistic structures—phonology, morphology, syntax, semantics, and pragmatics—it seems amazing that children acquire these components naturally.

Parents rarely teach these intricate conventions directly. Instead, children acquire these communication skills by listening, imitating, practicing, observing, and interacting with supportive caregivers and peers.

Observing the Development of Children's Language

"One of the most remarkable cognitive achievements of early childhood is the acquisition of language" (Black, Puckett, & Bell, 1992, p. 179). By the time they enter school, most children have mastered the basic structures of language and are fairly accomplished communicators. Though individual variations do occur, this rapid acquisition of language tends to follow a predictable sequence.

This progression will be illustrated by following Dawn from infancy through second grade. Dawn is the child of educational researchers. Her development is like that of almost every other normal child throughout the world, except that it was documented by her researcher-parents. Dawn's parents used a simple calendar-notation procedure to collect information about their children's language development. When Dawn's parents reviewed the date book/calendar each morning, new words were recorded. Thus, it became quite easy to document Dawn's growth over time. When these busy parents had a reflective moment, they recorded their recollections (vignettes) of an event and dated it. Often, at family celebrations, a video camera was used to record the events of Dawn's use of language in great detail. Occasionally, videotapes also documented story times. By using the calendar vignettes and the videotapes, Dawn's parents were able to marvel at her growth and development.

In Dawn's seven-year case study, we observe her language acquisition from a social-interactionist perspective and a neurobiological view. By intertwining the two views we can easily see how Dawn's language development is a dynamic interaction of her intentions, the physical coordination of her mouth and tongue, her neural development, and the support of her family members. This complex dance of nurture and nature reveals that Dawn's skills do not automatically develop at a certain point in brain maturation but, by the same token, without a particular level of neural growth, Dawn would not be able to accomplish her goals.

Birth to One Month

During the first month of Dawn's life, most of her oral communication consisted of crying, crying, crying. The greatest challenge her parents faced was interpreting the subtle variations in her cries. It took about three weeks for them to understand that Dawn's intense, high-pitched cry meant she was hungry. Dawn's short, throaty, almost shouting cries indicated a change of diaper was necessary, while the whining, fussy cry, which occurred daily at about dinner time, meant she was tired.

At birth, the human brain is remarkably unfinished. Most of the 100 billion neurons, or brain cells, are not yet connected. In fact, there are only four regions of the brain that are fully functional at birth including the brain stem, which controls respiration, reflexes, and heartbeat, and the cerebellum, which controls the newborn's balance and muscle tone. Likewise, infants' sensory skills are rudimentary; for instance, newborns can only see objects within twelve to eighteen inches of their faces. Still, newborns are able to distinguish between faces and other objects and they recognize the sound of their parents' voices.

Two to Three Months

During the second to third months after Dawn's birth, she began to respond to her parents' voices. When spoken to, Dawn turned her head, focused her eyes on her mother or father, and appeared to listen and watch intensely. Her parents and grandparents also instinctively began using an exaggerated speech pattern called *parentese* (often called *baby talk*). Until recently, parents were cautioned against using parentese with their infants because it was believed to foster immature forms of speech. However, recent studies have demonstrated that this slowed-down, high-pitched, exaggerated, repetitive speech actually seems to facilitate a child's language development because:

- The rate and pitch of parentese perfectly matches the infants' auditory processing speed. As babies mature their brain eventually reaches normal speech rates.
- Parentese also allows babies many opportunities to see and hear how sounds are made and, thus, to learn how to control their own vocal apparatus. As babies carefully observe parents, siblings, and other caregivers, they often mimic the tongue and mouth movements they see (Cowley, 1997; Field, Woodson, Greenberg, & Cohen, 1982; Healy, 1994; Shore, 1997).

During the first three months of life, the number of neural synapses, or connections, increases twenty times to more than 1,000 trillion. These neural connections are developed through daily verbal and physical interactions that the infant shares with parents, siblings, and other caregivers. Daily routines such as feeding and bathing reinforce and strengthen particular synapses, while neural networks that are not stimulated will eventually wither away in a process called *neural pruning*.

Four to Six Months

During conversations with her parents, Dawn would often move her mouth, lips, and eyes, mimicking the facial movements of her parents. At the beginning of the fourth month, Dawn discovered her own voice. She delighted in the range of sounds she could make and sometimes chuckled at herself. At this point, Dawn (and most normally developing infants) could make almost all of the vowel and consonant sounds. She cooed and gurgled end-lessly, joyfully experimenting with phonemic variations, pitch, and volume. When spoken to, she often began her own stream of conversation, called "sound play," which would par-allel the adult speaker. At six months, Dawn was becoming an expert at imitating tone and inflection. For example, when her mother yelled at the cat for scratching the furniture Dawn used her own vocal skills to yell at the poor animal, too.

The *cerebral cortex*, the part of the brain that is responsible for thinking and problem solving, represents 70 percent of the brain and is divided into two hemispheres. Each hemi-sphere has four lobes—the parietal, occipital, temporal, and frontal. Each of these lobes has numerous folds, which mature at different rates as the chemicals that foster brain develop-ment are released in waves. This sequential development explains, in part, why there are optimum times for physical and cognitive development. For instance, when a baby is three or four months old, neural connections within the parietal lobe (object recognition and eye–hand coordination), the temporal lobe (hearing and language), and the visual cortex have begun to strengthen and fine-tune. This development allows babies' eyes to focus on objects that are more than two feet away from their faces. This new ability allows babies to recognize themselves in a mirror and begin to visually discern who's who. At this same time, babies begin to mimic the tongue and mouth movements they see. Babies also experiment with the range of new sounds they can make. These trills and coos are also bids for attention, as most babies have begun to make simple cause-and-effect associations, such as crying equals Momma's attention.

Six to Nine Months

During her sixth month, Dawn's muscle strength, balance, and coordination allowed her to have greater independent control over her environment as she mastered the fine art of crawling and stumble-walking around furniture. These physical accomplishments stimulated further cognitive development, as she now had the ability to explore the world under her own power.

At seven months, Dawn's babbling increased dramatically. However, the sounds she produced now began to sound like words, which she would repeat over and over. This type of vocalizing is called *echolalia*. Though "MmmaaaMmmaaa" and "DddaaaDdaaa" sounded like "Mama" and "Dada," they were still not words with a cognitive connection or meaning.

In her eighth month, Dawn's babbling began to exhibit conversation-like tones and behaviors. This pattern of speech is called *vocables*. While there were still no real words in her babble, Dawn's vocalizations were beginning to take on some of the conventions of adult conversation, such as turn taking, eye contact, and recognizable gestures. These forms of prelanguage are playlike in nature, being done for their own sake rather than a deliberate use of language to communicate a need or accomplish a goal.

At approximately nine months, Dawn first used real, goal-oriented language. As her father came home from work, she crawled to him shouting in an excited voice, "Dada, Dada," and held her arms up to him. Dawn's accurate labeling of her father and her use of body language that expressed desire to be picked up were deliberate actions that revealed that Dawn was using language to accomplish her objectives.

As a child matures, the actual number of neurons remains relatively stable. However, the human brain triples its birth weight within the first three years of a child's life. This change is caused as neurons are stimulated and synapse connections increase, as the message-receiving dendrite branches grow larger and heavier. In addition, the long axons over which sensory messages travel gradually develop a protective coating of a white, fatty substance called *myelin*. Myelin insulates the axons and makes the transmission of sensory information more efficient. *Myelineation* occurs at different times in different parts of the brain and this process seems to coincide with the emergence of various physical skills and cognitive abilities. For instance, the neuromuscular development during the first months of life is dramatic. Within the first six months, helpless infants develop the muscle tone and coordination that allows them to turn over at will. Babies develop a sense of balance and better eye–hand coordination as neural connections in the cerebellum and parietal lobe strengthen. This allows most six-month-old babies to sit upright, with adult support, and successfully grasp objects within their reach. The ability to hold and inspect interesting items gives babies a lot to "talk" about.

Between six and seven months, the brain has already created permanent neural networks that recognize the sounds of a child's native language(s) or dialect. Next, babies begin to distinguish syllables, which soon enables them to detect word boundaries. Prior to this, "doyouwantyourbottle?" was a pleasant tune, but was not explicit communication. After auditory boundaries become apparent, babies will hear distinct words, "Do / you / want / your / BOTTLE?" As sounds become words that are frequently used in context to label a specific object, the acquisition of word meaning begins. At this stage of development, babies usually recognize and have cognitive meaning for words such as *bottle, momma,* and *daddy.* Their receptive or listening vocabulary grows rapidly, though it will take a few more months before their expressive or oral language catches up.

From about the eighth to the ninth month, the hippocampus becomes fully functional. Located in the center of the brain, the hippocampus is part of the limbic system. The hippocampus helps to index and file memories and, as it matures, babies are able to form memories. For instance, babies can now remember that when they push the button on the busy box it will squeak. At this point, babies' ability to determine cause-and-effect and remember words greatly increases.

Nine to Twelve Months

Between age nine months and her first birthday, Dawn's expressive (speaking) and receptive (listening and comprehending) vocabulary grew rapidly. She could understand and comply with dozens of simple requests, such as "Bring Mommy your shoes" or the favorite label-the-body game, "Where is Daddy's nose?" In addition, Dawn's command of nonverbal gestures and facial expressions were expanding from waving "bye-bye" to scowling and saying "no-no" when taking her medicine. In addition, holophrastic words began to emerge, in which one word carried the semantic burden for a whole sentence or phrase. For example, "keeths," while holding her plastic keys, purse, and sunglasses meant "I want to go for a ride," or "iith" meant "I want some ice." Dawn also used overgeneralized speech in which each word embraced many meanings. For instance, *doll* referred not only to her favorite baby doll but to everything in her toy box, and *jooth* stood for any type of liquid she drank.

At the end of the first year, the prefrontal cortex, the seat of forethought and logic, forms synapses at a rapid rate. In fact, by age one, the full cortex consumes twice as much energy as an adult brain. This incredible pace continues during the child's first decade of life. The increased cognitive capacity and physical dexterity stimulates curiosity and exploration and a deep desire to understand how things work. Neural readiness, in combination with countless hours of sound play and verbal exchanges with loving caregivers, allows most children to begin speaking their first words.

PEARSON
myeducationkit

Go to the Assignments and Activities section of Chapter 2 in the MyEducationKit and complete the activity entitled "Language Sample: 18-month-old boy." As you watch the video and answer the accompanying questions, note how he imitates his parents' phone behaviors.

Twelve to Eighteen Months

At this time Dawn's vocabulary expanded quickly. Most of her words identified or labeled the people, pets, and objects that were familiar and meaningful to her. Clark's research (1983) suggests that young children between one and six will learn and remember approximately nine new words a day. This ability to relate new words to preexisting internalized concepts, then remember and use them after only one exposure, is called *fast mapping* (Carey, 1979).

Because chronological age is not a reliable indicator of language progression, linguists typically describe language development by noting the number of words used in a sentence, which is called "mean length of utterance" (MLU). At this point, Dawn was beginning to use two-word sentences such as "Kitty juuth." Linguists call these two- and three-word sentences "telegraphic speech" as they contain only the most necessary of words to convey meaning. However, these first sentences may have many interpretations; for instance, Dawn's sentence "Kitty juuth" might mean "The kitty wants some milk," or "The kitty drank the milk," or even "The kitty stuck her head in my cup and drank my milk." Obviously the context in which the sentence was spoken helped her parents to better understand the intent or meaning of her communication.

By 18 months neural synapses have increased and strengthened, and are beginning to transmit information quite efficiently; hence, most toddlers begin to experience a language "explosion." Brain-imaging technology clearly reveals that the full cortex is involved in processing language. During this time children are able to learn as many as twelve words a day.

Eighteen to Twenty-four Months

Around age eighteen months to two years, as Dawn began using sentences more frequently, the use of syntax became apparent. "No shoes" with a shoulder shrug meant she couldn't find her shoes, but "Shoes, no!" said with a shaking head, meant Dawn did not want to put on her shoes.

At two years of age, most children have fully wired brains and nimble fingers, and are sturdy on their feet. Though they are generally aware of cause and effect, they are still unable to foresee potential problems. In other words, children's physical abilities may exceed their common sense. By this time, most children are able to use language to communicate their needs and accomplish their goals. Increased neural activity, plus verbal expression and physical skill, also give rise to greater independence. At this time parents may hear "No!" quite often.

Biologically, the brain is fully functional by this time. The remainder of a child's language development relies on the experiences and opportunities the child has to hear and use language with more experienced language users.

Twenty-four to Thirty-six Months

Though Dawn's vocabulary grew, her phonemic competence did not always reflect adult standards. Many of her words were clearly pronounced (*kitty, baby*), while others were interesting phonemic attempts or approximations (*bise* for *bike*, *Papa* for *Grandpa, bawble* for *bottle*); others were her own construction (*NaNe* for *Grandma*). At this age, most children are unable to articulate perfectly the sounds of adult speech. Rather, they simplify the adult sounds to ones they can produce. Sometimes this means they pronounce the initial sound or syllable of a word (*whee* for *wheel*), and at other times they pronounce only the final sound or syllable (*ees* for *cheese*). Another common feature is temporary regression, meaning that they may pronounce a word or phrase quite clearly, then later produce a

PEARSON
myeducationkit

Go to the Assignments and
Activities section of Chapter 2
in the MyEducationKit and
complete the activity entitled
"Language Sample: 3-year-
old boy." As you watch the
video and answer the accompanying questions, note how
much development has
occurred in just three
years—most children go
from saying a few words
to telling entire stories.

shortened, less mature version. This, too, is a normal language developmental phase for all children. Thus, it is important that parents accept
their child's language and not become overly concerned with correcting
their pronunciation.

Likewise, children's early attempts to use sentences need thoughtful support, not critical correction. Parents can best support their child's
attempts to communicate through extensions and expansions. Extensions
include responses that incorporate the essence of a child's sentence but
transform it into a well-formed sentence. For example, when Dawn said,
"ree stor-ee," her father responded, "Do you want me to read the storybook to you?" When parents and caregivers use extensions they model
appropriate grammar and fluent speech and actually help to extend a
child's vocabulary.

When parents use expansions, they gently reshape the child's
efforts to reflect grammatically appropriate content. For example, when
Dawn said, "We goed to Diseelan," instead of correcting her ("We don't
say *goed,* we say *went*") her mother expanded Dawn's language by initially confirming the intent of Dawn's statement while modeling the correct form, "Yes, we
went to Disneyland."

The adaptations parents make when talking to young children, such as slowing the
rate of speech, using age-appropriate vocabulary, questioning and clarifying the child's
statements, and extensions and expansions, occur in all cultures. These early interactions
with children and the gradual and building support is called parentese or, more gender-
specifically, *motherese* and *fatherese.* When parents use this form of support they are actually helping their children gain communicative competence and confidence (White, 1985).

Between the ages of two and three years, Dawn's language had developed to the point
where she could express her needs and describe her world to others quite well. In addition
to using pronouns, she also began to produce grammatical inflections: *-ing,* plurals, the past
tense, and the possessive.

Statements	Age
"I lub you, Mama."	2.0*
"Boot's crywing."	2.1
"Dawn's baby dawl."	2.2
"My books."	2.4
"Grover droppted the radio."	2.6
"Cookie monster shutted the door."	2.8
"She's not nice to me."	2.9
"Daddy's face got stickers, they scratch."	3.0

*Indicates age by years and months.

Dawn also loved finger plays such as "Itsy, Bitsy Spider" and "Grandma's Glasses,"
poems such as "This Little Pig," and songs such as "Jingle Bells," "Yankee Doodle," and the
"Alphabet Song." She was also beginning to count and echo-read with her parents when
they read her favorite stories, like the "Three Little Pigs." Dawn would "huff and puff and
blow your house down" as many times as her parents would read the story.

Three to Five Years

Dawn had become a proficient language user. She could make requests, "Please, may I have some more cake?" and demands, "I need this, now!" depending on her mood and motivation. She could seek assistance, "Can you tell me where the toys are?" and demonstrate concern, "What's the matter, Mama?" She sought information about her world, "Why is the moon round one time and just a grin sometimes?" She could carry on detailed conversations just as she did in the grocery store at 4.0 (four years and zero months):

MOM: Dawn, what juice did you want?

DAWN: Orange juice. But not the kind that has the little chewy stuff in it.

MOM: That is called pulp.

DAWN: Pulp—ick! I don't like it because it tasted badly.

MOM: Well, do you remember what kind has the pulp?

DAWN: You know, it comes in the orange can and has the picture of the bunny on it.

MOM: Well, there are several kinds in orange cans.

DAWN: Mom, I know that, cause orange juice is orange. But this one I don't like, at all, has a bunny on it.

MOM: Can you remember the name?

DAWN: Yeah, the writing words have A-B-C-O.

MOM: Oh, I know, the store's brand, ABCO.

DAWN: Yes, here it is. Now DON'T BUY IT!!

Four to Five Years

Dawn began to engage in dramatic play, using her knowledge of common events in familiar settings such as the grocery store and the doctor's office to act out life scripts with other children. These dramas allowed Dawn and her peers the opportunity to use their language in many functional and imaginative ways. Her favorite script was the restaurant, as she always enjoyed being the waitress, describing the daily special to her customers, then pretending to write their orders.

Jim Johnson, Jim Christie, and Thomas Yawkey (1999) suggest that during dramatic play, two types of communication can occur. First, *pretend communication* takes place when a child assumes a role and talks, in character, to other characters in the drama. The second type, *metacommunication,* occurs when the children stop the ongoing dramatic-play script and discuss the plot or character actions. The following is an example of metacommunication between Dawn and her friend Jennifer at age 5.6 years:

DAWN: Pretend you ordered pizza and I have to make it, okay?

JENNIFER: Okay, but it should be cheese pizza, 'cause I like it best.

DAWN: Okay, I can use yellow strings (yarn) for the cheese.

JENNIFER: Waitress, I want yellow cheese pizza, in a hurry. I'm hungry.

What Is Normal Language Development?

While the process of learning to talk follows a predictable sequence, the age at which children say their first word may vary widely from one child to another. Developmental guidelines provide descriptions of specific behaviors and delineate the age at which most children demonstrate this physical or cognitive skill. This type of information helps parents and physicians anticipate normal physical and cognitive growth. While physical maturation is easy to observe, cognitive development is less obvious. Fortunately, children's language development provides one indication that their cognitive abilities are developing normally. In Table 2.1, we present the average ages for language acquisition. While most children demonstrate language skills well within the normal age range, some do not. If a child's language is delayed more than two months past the upper age limits, caregivers should seek medical guidance, as delays may indicate problems (Copeland & Gleason, 1993; Weiss, Lilly-White, & Gordon, 1980). Early identification of problems leads to appropriate intervention.

While helpful, developmental guidelines are not perfect. To determine norms, data must be collected on specific populations. In most cases these data were collected on middle-income Caucasian children born in modern industrial-technological societies. Since this sample does not represent the world's population, the upper and lower age limits of these "universal" norms must be interpreted carefully.

Factors Contributing to Variation in Rate of Language Acquisition

Because the critical period for language development occurs within the first thirty-six months of a child's life, significant language delay may indicate specific medical or cognitive problems. Beyond medical problems, there are several factors that could modify the rate of normal language production. We review these factors in the following discussion.

Gender Differences

Are there differences in the rate and ways that boys and girls develop language fluency and proficiency? This question reflects another facet of the ongoing nature versus nurture debate. Observational research consistently reveals that a majority of girls talk earlier and talk more than the majority of boys. It is also true that the majority of late talkers are young boys (Healy, 1997; Kalb & Namuth, 1997). However, it is difficult to determine whether differences in the rate of language acquisition are biological or if biological differences are exaggerated by social influences. There is evidence for both views. For example, neurobiological research offers graphic images that illustrate how men's and women's brains process language somewhat differently (Corballis, 1991; Moir & Jessel, 1991). Though this research appears to support nature as the dominant factor in language differences, it is also important to consider how powerful a role nurture plays. Experimental research consistently documents differential treatment of infants based on gender. In other words, men and women tend to cuddle, coo at, and engage in lengthy face-to-face conversations with baby girls. Yet, with baby boys, adults are likely to exhibit "jiggling and bouncing" behaviors but

TABLE 2.1 Language Development Chart

Age in Months	Typical Language Development
0–3	Majority of communication consists of crying because larynx has not yet descended. Turns head to the direction of the family's voices. Is startled by loud or surprising sounds.
3–6	Begins to make cooing sounds to solicit attention from caregivers. Makes "raspberry" sounds. Begins to play with voice. Carefully observes caregiver's face when being spoken to, often tries to shape mouth in a similar manner.
6	Vocalization with intonation. Responds to his or her name. Responds to human voices without visual cues by turning his or her head and eyes. Responds appropriately to friendly and angry tones.
12	Uses one or more words with meaning (may be a fragment of a word). Understands simple instructions, especially if vocal or physical cues are given. Practices inflection. Is aware of the social value of speech.
18	Has a vocabulary of approximately five to twenty words. Vocabulary is made up chiefly of nouns. Some echolalia (repeating a word or phrase over and over). Much jargon with emotional content. Is able to follow simple commands.
24	Can name a number of objects common to his or her surroundings. Is able to use at least two prepositions such as *in, on, under.* Combines words into a short sentence, largely noun–verb combinations. Approximately two thirds of what child says should be understandable. Vocabulary of approximately 150 to 300 words. Rhythm and fluency often poor; volume and pitch of voice not yet controlled well. Can use pronouns such as *I, me, you.* *My* and *mine* are beginning to emerge. Responds to such commands as "Show me your eyes (nose, mouth, hair)."
36	Is using some plurals and past tenses: "We played a lot." Handles three-word sentences easily: "I want candy." Has approximately 900 to 1000 words in vocabulary. About 90 percent of what child says should be understandable. Verbs, such as "let's go, let's run, let's climb, and let's play," begin to predominate. Understands most simple questions dealing with his or her environment and activities. Relates his or her experiences so that they can be followed with reason. Is able to reason out such questions as "What do you do when you are hungry?" Should be able to give his or her sex, name, and age.

(continued)

TABLE 2.1 Continued

Age In Months	Typical Language Development
48	Knows names of familiar animals.
	Names common objects in picture books or magazines.
	Knows one or more colors and common shapes.
	Can repeat four digits when they are given slowly.
	Can usually repeat words of four syllables.
	Demonstrates understanding of *over* and *under*.
	Often engages in make-believe.
	Extensive verbalization as he or she carries out activities.
	Understands such concepts as *longer* and *larger* when a contrast is presented.
	Much repetition of words, phrases, syllables, and even sounds.
60	Can use many descriptive words, both adjectives and adverbs, spontaneously.
	Knows common opposites: *big–little, hard–soft, heavy–light.*
	Speech should be completely intelligible, despite articulation problems.
	Should be able to define common objects in terms of use (hat, shoe, chair).
	Should be able to follow three commands given without interruptions.
	Can use simple time concepts: morning, night, tomorrow, yesterday, today.
	Speech on the whole should be grammatically correct.
72	Speech should be completely intelligible and socially useful.
	Should be able to tell a rather connected story about a picture, seeing relationships between objects and happenings.
	Can recall a story or a favorite video.
	Should be able to repeat sentences as long as nine words.
	Can describe favorite pastimes, meals, books, and friends.
	Should be using fairly long sentences and should use some compound and some complex sentences.

are not as likely to engage in sustained face-to-face verbal interactions. Perhaps girls talk earlier and talk more because they receive more language stimulation (Huttenlocher, 1991).

Socioeconomic Level

Numerous studies have long documented the differences in the rate of language acquisition and the level of language proficiency between low and middle socioeconomic families (Hart & Risley, 1995; Morisset, 1995; Walker, Greenwood, Hart, & Carta, 1994). These studies found that children, especially males, from low-income homes were usually somewhat slower to use expressive language than children from middle-income homes. These findings likely reflect social-class differences both in language use in general and in parent–child interaction patterns. For example, Betty Hart and Todd Risley (1995) estimate that, by age four, children from professional families have had a cumulative total of 50 million words addressed to them, whereas children from welfare families have been exposed to

57

only 13 million words. The children from professional families have had more than three times the linguistic input as welfare families' children; this gives them a tremendous advantage in language acquisition.

Results of long-term observations of middle-income and lower-income families concluded that all mothers spent a great deal of time nurturing their infants (e.g., touching, hugging, kissing, and holding), but that there were differences in the way mothers verbally interacted with their children. Middle-income mothers spent a great deal more time initiating verbal interactions and usually responded to and praised their infants' vocal efforts. Middle-income mothers were also more likely to imitate their infants' vocalizations. These verbal interactions stimulate neural-synapse networks that foster expressive and receptive language. It is still unclear why lower-income mothers do not engage their children in verbal interactions at the same level as middle-income mothers. The authors of these studies speculate that this may be a reflection of social-class differences in language use in general.

Cultural Influences

The rate of language acquisition may be somewhat different for children of different cultures. Since spoken language is a reflection of the culture from which it emerges, it is necessary to consider the needs verbal language serves in the culture. Communication may be accomplished in other meaningful ways (Bhavnagri & Gonzalez-Mena, 1997). Janet Gonzalez-Mena (1997, p. 70) offers this example:

> The emphasizing or de-emphasizing of the verbal starts from the beginning with the way babies are treated. Babies carried around much of the time get good at sending messages nonverbally—through changing body positions or tensing up or relaxing muscles. They are encouraged to communicate this way when their caregivers pick up the messages they send. They don't need to depend on words at an early age. Babies who are physically apart from their caregivers learn the benefits of verbal communication. If the babies are on the floor in the infant playpen or in the other room at home, they need to learn to use their voices to get attention. Changing position or tensing muscles goes unperceived by the distant adult.

Likewise, some cultures do not view babies' vocal attempts as meaningful communication. Shirley Brice Heath (1983) describes a community in which infants' early vocalizations are virtually ignored and adults do not generally address much of their talk directly to infants. Many cultures emphasize receptive language, and children listen as adults speak.

Medical Concerns

Beyond gender, socioeconomic, and culture differences, other reasons that children's language may be delayed include temporary medical problems and congenital complications. In Special Feature 2.1, "She Just Stopped Talking," we provide an example of one the most common childhood problems—otitis media—that, left unattended, could cause significant language delays and speech distortion and ultimately difficulty in learning to read and write.

PEARSON myeducationkit™

Go to the Assignments and Activities section of Chapter 2 in the MyEducationKit and complete the activity entitled "Hearing and Vision Screening." As you watch the video and answer the accompanying questions, note the way young children's vision and hearing are tested in school settings.

She Just Stopped Talking

On her first birthday, Tiffany mimic-sang "Hap Birffaay meee" over and over. She said "Sank oo" when she received her birthday gifts and "Bye, seeoo" when her guests left. Later that summer, after a bad bout with an ear infection, Tiffany's mother noticed she was turning up the volume on the television when she watched *Sesame Street*. A few days later, after several restless nights, Tiffany became very fussy and irritable and began tugging on her ear. Her parents again took her to the doctor, who diagnosed another ear infection. After a ten-day treatment of antibiotics, Tiffany appeared to be fine, except that she seemed to talk less and less.

About a month later, the situation worsened. Tiffany would not respond to her mother's speech unless she was looking directly at her mother. At that point Tiffany had, for the most part, stopped talking.

Tiffany's story is all too common. She was suffering from *otitis media*, an inflammation of the middle part of the ear. The symptoms of otitis media usually appear during or after a cold or respiratory infection. Because fluid can collect in the middle ear (behind the eardrum) without causing pain, children with otitis media may not complain. The following is a list of possible symptoms; any one of these symptoms could indicate that a child has otitis media:

- earaches or draining of the ears
- fever
- changes in sleeping or eating habits
- irritability
- rubbing or pulling at the ears
- cessation of babbling and singing
- turning up the television or radio volume much louder than usual
- frequently needing to have directions and information repeated
- unclear speech
- use of gestures rather than speech
- delayed speech and language development.

From twelve months through four years of age, language development is at its peak. Even a temporary hearing loss during this time interferes with speech articulation and language learning. Otitis media causes temporary loss of hearing when the fluid pushes against the eardrum. The pressure prevents the eardrum from vibrating, so sound waves cannot move to the inner ear and the child's hearing is greatly distorted or muffled. Consequently, final consonant sounds and word endings are often unheard, and words blend into one another. Because one of the main reasons people talk is to communicate, a child who cannot understand what is said becomes frustrated and easily distracted. This type of hearing loss may continue for up to six weeks after the ear infection has healed.

Though hearing loss caused by otitis media is described as "mild and fluctuating," it is a major cause of speech distortion and language delay in the preschool years. If left untreated, young children with recurrent and persistent otitis media may develop permanent hearing loss, speech distortions, language delays, and problems with focusing attention.

When Tiffany's parents realized that she had stopped speaking, their pediatrician referred them to an otolaryngologist (ear, nose, and throat specialist). The doctor was pleased that Tiffany's parents had written down new words she used on the family calendar. As the doctor reviewed the calendar, it became apparent that Tiffany's normal language development had virtually stopped. He did not seem surprised when her parents mentioned that she had also stopped babbling and singing and that she no longer danced when music was played. Because Tiffany's pediatrician had already tried three months of antibiotics to control the infection with no success, the specialist suggested surgically placing bilateral vent tubes in the eardrum to drain the fluid from the middle ear. When the fluid is drained, the eardrum can then vibrate freely once again and normal hearing may be restored.

After a brief operation (approximately thirty minutes), eighteen-month-old Tiffany began to speak once again. Though her hearing was restored, the doctor suggested that Tiffany and her parents visit a speech therapist to help her fully regain her language.

Within a year, Tiffany's development was progressing normally, and by age three, the surgically implanted tubes naturally fell out of her eardrums. Since that time, Tiffany has not had a recurrence of otitis media.

Congenital Language Disorders

For most children, learning to communicate is a natural, predictable developmental progression. Unfortunately, some children have congenital language disorders that impair their ability to learn language or use it effectively. The origin of these disorders may be physical or neurological. Examples of physical problems include malformation of the structures in the inner ear or a poorly formed palate. Neurological problems include dysfunction in the brain's ability to perceive or interpret the sounds of language.

Though the symptoms of various language disorders may appear similar, effective treatment may differ significantly, depending on the cause of the problem. For example, articulation problems caused by a physical malformation of the palate might require reconstructive surgery, whereas articulation problems caused by hearing impairment might require a combination of auditory amplification and speech therapy. Two of the most common symptoms of congenital language disorders are disfluency and pronunciation.

Disfluency. Children with fluency disorders have difficulty speaking rapidly and continuously. They may speak with an abnormal rate—too fast or too slow; in either case, their speech is often incomprehensible and unclearly articulated. The rhythm of their speech may also be severely affected. Stuttering is the most common form of this disorder. Many children may have temporary fluency disruptions or stuttering problems as they are learning to express themselves in sentences. Children who are making a transition to a second language may also experience brief stuttering episodes. It is important for parents and teachers to be patient and supportive, as it may take time to distinguish normal developmental or temporary lapses in fluency from a true pathology. Stuttering may have multiple origins and may vary from child to child. Regardless of cause, recently developed treatment protocols have been effective in helping stutterers.

Pronunciation. Articulation disorders comprise a wide range of problems and may have an equally broad array of causes. Minor misarticulations in the preschool years are usually developmental and will generally improve as the child matures. Occasionally, as children lose their baby teeth, they may experience temporary challenges in articulation. However, articulation problems that seriously impede a child's ability to communicate needs and intentions must be diagnosed. Causes of such problems may include malformation of the mouth, tongue, or palate; partial loss of hearing due to a disorder in the inner ear; serious brain trauma; or a temporary hearing loss due to an ear infection (Copeland & Gleason, 1993).

English Language Learning

BY LUISA ARAÚJO

Do you know any families who are raising children who speak a home language other than English or who speak both English and the caregivers' native language? In this chapter you have learned that the *input,* or the kind of linguistic information children are exposed to from an early age, influences their language development. You have learned that children have a natural instinct to learn language, that there are predictable stages of language development and that parents support children's efforts to learn language in specific ways. In situations in which children are learning English as a second language (ESL), caregivers' responses to children's vocalizations and verbal bouts are as important as in first language (L1) situations. Valuing communicative interactions and expanding on children's language initiatives optimizes language learning (Fennell, Byers-Heinlein, & Werker, 2007; Kuhl, 2004).

Young children who learn two languages from birth to the age of five experience what experts call *simultaneous bilingualism* (Bialystok, 1991). When they learn a second language (L2) after the age of five they experience sequential bilingualism. Decades of research have shown that bilingual children do not experience any cognitive or language impairments as a result of learning two languages (August & Hakuta, 1997). They are quite capable of maintaining the two language systems separately and of communicating effectively in both. Interestingly, neurolinguistic findings indicate that when five-year-old bilingual children retell a story in their two languages they activate the same brain area, regardless of the language in which they do the retelling (Kim, Relkin, Lee, & Hirsch, 1997). Bilingual adults who have learned a second language after the age of seven, on the other hand, activate different brain areas depending on whether they do the retelling in their first or second language. This tells us that children who acquire a second language before the age of five behave like native speakers because indeed they are (Sakai, 2005). They process the two languages in the same brain area at the same time that they are able to keep them separate.

At times, however, children may engage in *code-switching,* the alternate use of two languages from sentence to sentence, or even within the same sentence. Code-switching is a rule-governed language behavior also used by adult bilinguals (Grosjean, 1982; Lessow-Hurley, 2000). It can be used to emphasize a point, to express ethnic solidarity, and to fill a lexical need. For example, a Spanish–English speaker may reiterate the same message in the two languages to emphasize an order: "Get up now. Levántate!"

A bilingual child who has been exposed to two languages from birth may show this linguistic sophistication in school in addition to the ability to converse with ease in two languages. Parents and teachers may even witness with awe how easily children are able to translate adequately from one language to another depending on the need to address speakers who speak only one language.

Recent estimates tell us that in 2010, more than 30 percent of all school-age children will come from homes in which the primary language is not English (U.S. Citizenship and Immigration Services, 2001). These children will acquire the second language—English—in the school setting (sequential bilingualism) and the majority of these English language learners (ELLs) are Spanish speakers (Goldenberg, 2008). English language learners are individuals who are learning English. The term is usually used in education to refer to students who are acquiring English as a second language (ESL). The term *ELL* is now preferred over "limited English proficiency (LEP)" as it highlights accomplishments rather than deficits. Most ELL children attend English-only language classrooms. Some attend first-language classrooms where only their L1 is used or bilingual programs where both English and the home language are used (Tabors, 1998).

English language learners progress through a series of levels of English proficiency. In English-only early childhood settings a specific sequence explains second-language development: home language use, preproduction, early production, and speech emergence (Goldenberg, 2008; Tabors, 1998). First, young children may speak their home language because they have not yet discovered that a different language is used in the new setting. During the preproduction phase, children are taking in the new language and go through what is called the "silent period," which may take from one to three months (Krashen, 1981; Saville-Troike, 1988). Children may understand most of the discourse addressed to them in the second language, but are unable to speak it. In the third phase, students are capable of saying one- or two-word utterances. In the fourth phase, speech emerges and children are able to produce longer phrases and sentences. In considering these levels we must bear in mind that they reflect general trends and that there is variation from child to child. Also, these levels explain only the English oral development of ELLs. In looking at literacy proficiency, including progression in reading and writing, additional developmental levels need to be considered.

Lindfords (1987) and Tabors and Snow (1994) have documented how social interactions assist young children in negotiating meaning while their oral English proficiency increases. Following the silent period, children begin to use formulaic expressions they memorize and that assist them in communicating with others. They may say, "Don't do that" or "Wanna play?" to maintain and initiate interactions with other children. When they begin using one- or two-word utterances and longer sentences, their telegraphic discourse may be marked by the ungrammatical speech that characterizes younger monolingual children. For example, in creatively constructing new sentences they may overgeneralize plural formation (*foot – foots*) and past tense rules for regular verbs (*eat – eated*). This indicates that children are actively constructing language, using words according to morphological and syntactic rules to form sentences. First and foremost, young children try to figure out how to use the language they know to meet their social needs (Wong-Fillmore, 1991a). Their desire to interact with other children, to play and make friends is what drives language learning.

Preschool ELL children have been observed to employ a variety of strategies to learn the second language (Tabors, 1998). Some will repeat to themselves, in a very low voice, the new language they hear. Others will attempt to communicate on early

exposure by using gestures, mimes, and cries. In fact, it seems that personality traits and the characteristics of the social setting interact to create learning opportunities. A willingness to communicate and take risks in a nonthreatening social context invites communicative interactions that foster language development. For example, a second-language learner may communicate by saying, "Dog run" to mean that the dog is running. A teacher who promotes the kind of interactions that facilitate language development will provide a scaffold by saying, "Yes, the dog is running." As Goldenberg (2008) states, "Students who are beginning English speakers will need a great deal of support, sometimes known as 'scaffolding,' for learning tasks that require knowledge of English. For example, at the very beginning levels, teachers will have to speak slowly, with clear vocabulary and diction, and use pictures, objects, and movements to illustrate the content being taught. They should expect students to respond either nonverbally (e.g., pointing or signalling) or in one or two-word utterances" (p. 23).

Early childhood educators can help young ELL children by having a set of daily routines and by providing access to activities that are not highly demanding in terms of communication (Tabors, 1998). Daily routines help children predict events and thus learn expected language behaviors. Activities built around a housekeeping area, a sandbox with toys, or a block area engage children in play without the added pressure of having to communicate in specific ways. In addition, teachers should use lots of nonverbal communication or combine gestures with talk, keep messages simple, talk about the here and now, emphasize the important words in sentences, and repeat key words in a sentence. This will help children learn new vocabulary as will the regular reading of picture books because the pictures carry the message.

Indeed, storybook reading provides an authentic linguistic *input* that is easy to understand because it is contextually embedded (pictures). Moreover, it seems that language learning can be optimized when teachers explain the vocabulary using gestures, synonyms, and examples. A recent preschool study shows how explaining new vocabulary helped Portuguese-speaking children learn vocabulary from storybook reading (Collins, 2005). Vocabulary learning is a

(continued)

English Language Learning   Continued

crucial component of literacy instruction, because vocabulary building in the early years is associated with good reading performance in third grade (Sénéchal, Ouellette, & Rodney, 2006).

Young ELL children need to feel increasingly able to communicate and to feel socially accepted. Teachers may use a buddy system, whereby an outgoing English-speaking child is paired with an ELL child, to help second-language children feel more affectively connected and socially accepted. Similarly, teachers should show children that their home language is socially accepted and valued. As their

English proficiency increases, it is easy for children to lose their native language (Wong-Fillmore, 1991b). Asking parents to come to the classroom and share their language and culture will affirm that bilingualism is an asset and not a limitation.

Source: Araújo, Luisa (2002). The literacy development of kindergarten English-language learners. *Journal of Research in Childhood Education, 16*(2), 232–247. Reprinted by permission of Luisa Araújo and the Association for Childhood Education International, 17904 Georgia Avenue, Suite 215, Olney, MD. Copyright © 2002 by the Association.

It is important to remember that some children may simply show delayed language development; this may mean that a child is gaining control over speaking mechanisms at a slower rate than same-age peers or has had limited opportunity to hear speech or interact with others. Children who are learning a second language may also appear to have articulation difficulties when they attempt to use their second language. As we explain in the next section, anyone learning a new phonemic system will experience some difficulty in expressing new sound combinations. "Bilingual children should be assessed in their native language and referred for therapy only if an articulation disorder is present in that language" (Piper, 1993, p. 193). Caregivers and teachers need to be careful not to confuse the normal course of second-language acquisition with speech disorders.

Family Focus: Developing Language Over Time

How do parents engage young children in language? Table 2.2 provides simple suggestions that will help enrich parent–child verbal interactions.

TABLE 2.2   How Parents Can Scaffold Young Children's Language

Birth to Six Months	Six to Eighteen Months	Eighteen Months to Three Years
Use "parentese" intentionally to stimulate and extend infant's attention span.		
Talk frequently at close proximity to the infant's face. At about three to four months the child will begin to babble back. Engage in these two-way conversations!		

TABLE 2.2   How Parents Can Scaffold Young Children's Language

Describe actions and objects that are encountered in the daily routine (while dressing, changing, feeding, shopping, cleaning, preparing meals, etc.).	Continue to talk frequently all day long, describing actions and objects that are encountered in daily routines.	Talk frequently all day long, but now ask the child questions and wait for the child to respond. Engage in two-way conversations as often as possible.
Modulate voice and vary intonation to match levels of enthusiasm, emotion, meaning.	Use words to describe your feeling(s). *Mom is so happy!*	Use words to describe your feelings and ask child to use words to describe his or her feelings.
Talk face-to-face at a distance where infant can clearly see the adult's mouth and facial expressions as he or she speaks.	Talk face-to-face at a distance where child can clearly see the adult's mouth and facial expressions as he or she speaks.	Talk face-to-face at a distance where the child can clearly see the adult's mouth and facial expressions as he or she speaks.
Use a second language naturalistically if parent is bilingual.	Use a second language naturalistically if parent is bilingual.	Use a second language naturalistically if parent is bilingual.
Introduce songs and music at different times throughout the day and sing simple songs.	Continue to sing songs and engage in finger plays.	Encourage children to sing songs and sing along with them. Children love to sing with their families.
	Hold child and read plastic, board, or cloth books on a daily basis to share new words and/or to repeat reading familiar books that the child enjoys.	Parent and child may co-hold the books several times a daily (five to ten minutes only). Child may begin to "read" along. Use your finger to point to the words as you read in order to share new words and/or to repeat reading familiar books that the child enjoys.
	Deliberately point out and label simple attributes of objects (smooth, rough, hot, big, square, round, blue, red, striped, wet, etc.).	Ask the child to describe the attributes of objects. Reinforce his or her descriptions and add to the descriptions.
	Deliberately point out objects that are the same, or different (e.g., smooth/round, hot/cold, big/little, up/down, over/under, open/shut, wet/dry).	Ask the child to tell you how objects are the same or different.
	Read rhyming stories, songs, or finger plays with rhyming words with the child frequently.	Read rhyming stories or plays with rhyming words with the child frequently, pointing out how/where words sound alike and sound different.
		Play simple word games (e.g., the opposites game, complete the rhyme/ complete the song phrase, etc.).

Summary

Children's acquisition of oral language is truly remarkable. By the time they enter kindergarten, most children have mastered the basic structures and components of their native language, all without much stress or effort. How did the information contained in this chapter compare with what you were able to discover about your own first words and early language learning? Which of the four perspectives described above comes closest to your view about children's language development?

PEARSON myeducationkit™

To check your comprehension on the content covered in this chapter, go to the MyEducationKit for your book and complete the Study Plan for Chapter 2. Here you will be able to take a chapter quiz and receive feedback on your answers.

To summarize the key points about oral language development, we return to the guiding questions at the beginning of this chapter:

■ *What are the major views on how children's language develops? Which aspects of language development does each view adequately explain?*

Four competing perspectives have been used to explain how children acquire language. The behaviorist perspective emphasizes the important role of reinforcement in helping children learn the sounds, words, and rules of language. This view handily explains the imitative aspects of initial language learning. Nativists stress the importance of children's inborn capacity to learn language and suggest that a portion of the brain is dedicated to language learning. Nativist theory explains how children "invent" their own two- and three-word grammars and overgeneralize rules for past tense ("He goed to the store") and plural ("I saw two mouses today!"). The social-interactionist perspective emphasizes the importance of both environmental factors and children's innate predisposition to make sense of language and use it for practical purposes. According to this view, children learn about language by using it in social situations. The social-interactionist view highlights the role of parental support in language acquisition. Finally, new technology has allowed scientists to observe how the brain perceives, interprets, and expresses language. These developments have led to a new perspective of children's language learning, the neurobiological view, which complements the three earlier views on language development. This perspective explains how the structural development of the brain is related to language acquisition. It helps explain why children's experiences during infancy have such a crucial effect on later language learning.

■ *What are the major components of language?*

The major components of language are (1) phonology—the sounds that make up a language; (2) morphology—the meaning-bearing units of language, including words and affixes; (3) syntax—the rules for ordering words into sentences; (4) semantics—the shades of meaning that words convey; and (5) pragmatics—the social rules that enable language to accomplish real-life purposes.

■ *How does the structure of an infant's brain develop? How does this structural development affect language acquisition?*

At birth, the human brain is remarkably unfinished. Most of the 100 billion neurons or brain cells are not yet connected. During the first month of life, the number of neural synapses or connections increases 20 times to more than 1,000 trillion. As a child matures, the actual number of neurons remains stable; however, the number of synapse connections increases, and the message-receiving dendrite branches grow larger and heavier. At age one, the full cortex consumes twice as much energy as an adult brain. This neural readiness, in combination with countless hours of sound play and verbal exchanges with loving caregivers, allows most children to begin speaking their first words at this age.

By eighteen months, neural synapses have increased and strengthened and are beginning to transmit information efficiently. Hence most toddlers begin to experience a language explosion, particularly in the areas of vocabulary and syntax. During this time, children are able to learn as many as twelve words a day. Thus, the neurobiological perspective reveals how the rapid development of the brain during the first few years of life makes it possible for children to acquire language so quickly and efficiently. This perspective also explains why the first thirty-six months are a critical period for language development.

■ *What factors affect children's rate of language acquisition?*

While language development follows a predictable sequence, the rate at which children acquire language varies tremendously. Gender, socioeconomic level, and cultural influences all can affect the rate of language acquisition. A child's language learning can also be impeded by illnesses, such as otitis media, and by a variety of congenital problems of a physical and/or neurological nature. Parents and caregivers are cautioned to seek a medical diagnosis if language development is significantly delayed, as early identification and treatment can often avoid irreparable disruption of the language acquisition process.

■ *How does children's acquisition of a second language compare with their first language acquisition? What should adults do to make it easier for children to learn English as a second language?*

In many ways, second-language acquisition in young children is similar to their acquisition of their first language. In learning a new language, children engage in the creative construction of the rules of the new language, and this creative construction occurs within the context of multiple social interactions as children use the new language with others.

Adults working with second-language learners need to focus both on making themselves understood by children and on encouraging these children to use their new language. Adults need to focus on the learners' communicative intentions, not on the conventionality of their utterances. Children should be encouraged but not forced to use the new language, and children should not be belittled for hesitancy in trying it. Adults need to recognize that children are learning English even if they are not responding verbally. Adults need to encourage other children who are native speakers of English to have patience with ESL learners and to assist them in their learning. Finally, adults should value the native languages that children bring to school with them and encourage them to continue to use their native languages.

LINKING KNOWLEDGE TO PRACTICE

1. Interview two parents and two early childhood teachers regarding how they believe children learn language. Consider which theory of language acquisition best matches each interviewee's beliefs.

2. Interview a school nurse or health care aide about the numbers of children she or he sees who are affected by illnesses and congenital problems. From the health care worker's perspective, what effect do these medical problems have on children? How often should children be screened for auditory acuity? If a family has limited financial recourses, what agencies can provide medical services?

3. Observe a second-language learner in a preschool or day care setting. Does the second-language learner comprehend some of the talk that is going on in the classroom? How does the child communicate with other children? How does the teacher support the child's second-language acquisition? Are other children helping? Does the second-language learner have any opportunities to use his or her native language?

CHAPTER

3   Family Literacy

Four-year-old Evan, from Arizona, was visiting his grandparents in Vermont during the Christmas holiday. Opening the drapes one morning, he viewed snow-covered trees and fields. Evan gasped, "Grammie, who spilled all the sugar?" His grandmother responded, "Evan, that's very clever. It sure looks like sugar. Actually, it's snow."

Clearly, Evan's unfamiliarity with snow didn't prevent him from drawing a clever comparison. His grandmother responded by first showing appreciation for Evan's deduction and then providing the correct word, *snow.* Evan had a great opportunity to learn about the qualities of snow through conversations with his parents, grandparents, and older sister as they played together in the snow. During these adventures, they offered appropriate words for and information about all the new sights, sounds, tastes, smells, and feelings. By the end of the week, Evan knew the difference between wet and powder snow. He made snow angels, helped build a snowman and snow fort, engaged in a snowball war, and had an exhilarating ride on a sled. The new experiences he shared with older and more snow-experienced language users allowed Evan to build new vocabulary and cognitive understandings.

Chapter 2 discussed how infants and toddlers learn their native language through complex social interactions with parents, siblings, and other caregivers. These individuals are essentially a child's first and most important teachers. Throughout the preschool years, the family plays a significant role in helping children become accomplished language users. In this chapter, we examine the talk that goes on in homes and describe ways parents can support and enrich language development.

Likewise, for children living in a culture that values literacy, the process of learning to read and write begins very early, often before their first birthdays. In recent years, researchers have made great progress in expanding our understanding of early literacy development. We now know that children acquire written language in much the same way that they learn oral language. Both are social, constructive processes. With oral language, children listen to the language that surrounds them, detect patterns and regularities, and make up their own rules for speech. Children then try out and refine these rules as they engage in everyday activities with others. Similarly, with written language, children observe the print that surrounds them and watch their parents and others use reading and writing to get things done in daily life. They then construct their own concepts and rules about literacy, and they try out those ideas in social situations. With experience, these child-constructed versions of reading and writing become increasingly similar to conventional adult forms. Yet, as noted in Chapter 1, children need more instruction from adults to become readers and writers than they do to become speakers.

Before Reading This Chapter, Think About . . .

Your home language environment when you were a child.

- Did you engage in lengthy conversations with your parents and siblings?
- Did you have an appreciative audience when you told stories about your own experiences?
- Did your family discuss the TV shows that you watched?

Your early experiences with storybooks.

- What were your favorite books as a young child?
- Do you recall snuggling into an adult's lap and sharing a storybook? Did this happen regularly, at bedtime? On the bus?

Focus Questions

- How can parents best facilitate their children's oral language development?
- What home factors affect young children's literacy development?
- What does early literacy look like in a language other than English?

Home Talk: A Natural Context for Learning and Using Language

Evan's family helped him understand and label his new experience with snow. Their language support was natural and was guided by Evan's constant questions: Why doesn't this snow make a snowball? Why can't I make an angel on this snow? Evan's learning while he played was nothing new or extraordinary; he has received language support from his parents and sibling from the moment he was born. His parents and older sister intuitively supported his attempts to communicate. When Evan was an infant his parents, like most parents, naturally used parentese. That is, they talked to him in higher-pitched tones, at a slower rate of speech, and with exaggerated pronunciation and lots of repetition of phrases. Parentese helped Evan hear the sounds and words of his native language. Between the age of eighteen months and three years, as Evan's communicative competence grew, his family

---

BOX **3.1**

Definition of Terms

personal narrative: a story told in the first person about a personal experience.

scaffolding: temporary assistance that parents and teachers give to children to enable them to do things that they cannot do on their own.

intuitively adjusted their verbal responses so that he could easily learn new vocabulary and grammatical structures.

In Special Feature 3.1, we describe the types of verbal *scaffolding* Evan's family and most adults automatically use to support children's language development. This type of scaffolding is a prime example of Vygotsky's (1978) zone of proximal development, in which adults help children engage in activities that they could not do on their own. Through ongoing interactions with his parents, sister, and other caregivers, Evan (and most children) quickly learn basic conversation skills (Danst, Lowe, & Bartholomew, 1990; Manning-Kratcoski & Bobkoff-Katz, 1998; Norris & Hoffman, 1990). By age three, Evan, like most children, had learned to take turns, back-channel (use fillers like "uh-huh" to keep conversations going), be polite, and make appropriate responses (Menyuk, 1988). He knew how to engage in conversations with adults and his peers.

SPECIAL FEATURE 3.1

Caregivers' Strategies for Supporting Children's Language Development

In almost all cases, caregivers intuitively scaffold children's language development. These communication strategies have been observed across all cultures.

- *Expansions.* Adult recasts the child's efforts to reflect appropriate grammar. When adults use expansions they help introduce and build new vocabulary.
  Child: Kitty eat.
  Adult: Yes, the kitty is eating.
- *Extensions.* Adult restates the child's telegraphic speech into a complete thought and may add new information in response to the child's comments.
  Child: Kitty eat.
  Adult: Kitty is eating his food.
  Child: Kitty eat.
  Adult: The kitty is hungry.
- *Repetitions.* Adult facilitates the development of new sentence structure by repeating all or part of the child's comment.
  Child: Kitty eat.
  Adult: Time for kitty to eat. Time for kitty to eat.

- *Parallel talk.* Adult describes the child's actions. Parallel talk is an effective way to model new vocabulary and grammatical structure.
  Child: Kitty eat.
  Adult: Jimmy is watching the kitty eat.
- *Self-talk.* Adult describes their actions. Like parallel talk, self-talk effectively models new vocabulary and grammatical structures.
  Adult: I'm feeding the kitty.
- *Vertical structuring.* Adult uses questions to encourage the child to produce longer or more complex sentences.
  Child: Kitty eat.
  Adult: What is the kitty eating?
  Child: Kitty eat cat food.
- *Fill-ins.* Adult structures the conversation so that the child must provide a word or phrase to complete the statement.
  Adult: The kitty is eating because she is—
  Child: Hungry!

Source: Adapted from Manning-Kratcoski, A., & Bobkoff-Katz, M. (1998). Conversing with young language learners in the classroom. *Young Children,* 53(3): 30–33.

Go to the Assignments and
Activities section of Chapter 3
in the MyEducationKit and
complete the activity entitled
"Emergent Literacy Devel-
opment." As you watch the
video and answer the accompanying questions, note how
the moms in this video
actively engage their little
ones in the reading and
writing process.

In fact, the most important component of learning language is actually engaging children, even infants, in verbal bouts. In Chapter 2 we discussed how families provide the rich social context necessary for children's language development. The thousands of hours of parent–child interactions from the moment of birth through the preschool years provide the foundations for language. As children acquire language, they are able to share with others what they feel, think, believe, and want. Although most children begin to use their expressive vocabuary in the second year of life, research has long documented that children differ in their ability to learn and use new words (Smith & Dickinson, 1994). In an effort to understand what accounts for these differences, researchers Betty Hart and Todd Risley (1995) documented parent and child interactions during the first three years of children's lives.

Their research team observed forty-four families from different socioeconomic and ethnic backgrounds one hour each month for two and a half years. Their data revealed vast differences in the amount of language spoken to children. Children from homes that received welfare assistance heard, on average, 616 words an hour; children from working-class families heard 1,251 words an hour; and children from professional homes heard 2,153 words per hour. If one thinks of words as dollars, the children from these different socioeconomic homes would have significantly disparate bank accounts. Further, this long-term study revealed that early language differences had a lasting effect on children's subsequent language accomplishments both at age three and at age nine. In other words, talk between adults and children early in life makes a significant difference. To look at an example of how this languge difference begins to multiply, observe the following language of three parents when interacting with their babies when preparing to eat a meal.

MOM 1:   Okay, Crystal, let's eat.

MOM 2:   Okay, Paulie, it's time to eat our lunch. Let's see what we are having? Yes, let's have carrots.

MOM 3:   Okay, Teryl, it's lunchtime. Are you hungry? Mommy is so hungry! Let's see what we have in the refrigerator today. What is this? It's orange. Could it be peaches? Could it be apricots? Let's see! See the picture on the jar? That right, it carrots.

The number of words spoken during these simple interactions clearly illustrates how children can have vastly different experiences in hearing language.

Encouraging Personal Narratives

Evan's family played a vital role in helping him interpret, label, and recall his new experiences with snow. Back in Arizona, Evan had many stories to tell his teacher and playmates at preschool. For the next several months, each time he spoke with his grandparents, he relived his snow-day tales. The stories, or personal narratives, that Evan told helped him make sense of this new experience, broadened his vocabuary, and reinforced his expressive language skills. Likewise, each time Evan told the story about how the snowball he threw at his sister knocked off the snowman's nose and made his dad laugh, he deepened his memory of the event.

Children's personal narratives are a window into their thinking. Their language also reveals how they use current knowledge to interpret new experiences. Evan's first interpretation of a snowy field was to relate it to a recent incident with a broken sugar bowl. These verbal expressions of new mental constructions can be both fascinating and humorous. Likewise children's personal narratives offer insight into their language development and overall intellectual, social, and emotional growth.

Though children instinctively know how to put experiences, feelings, and ideas into story form, parents and caregivers can encourage their children's language development by offering many storytelling opportunities and attentively listening while children share their accounts of events (Canizares, 1997). Though nothing can replace quiet and private time to listen to children, many working parents report that they use the time in the car, bus, or subway going to and from day care and/or errands to listen carefully to their children.

Children often share what they know or have learned in story form. This is because the human brain functions narratively—for most of us it is much easier to understand and remember concepts when we are given information in story form rather than as a collection of facts. Since the human brain retains information more efficiently in story form, parents can explain new information using stories (Sprenger,1999). For example, when five-year-old Tiffany wanted to know how to tie her shoelaces, her daddy told her the following story:

> Once upon a time, there were two silly snakes [the shoelaces] who decided to wrestle. They twisted around each other and tied themselves together very tightly [first tie]. The snakes became scared and tried to curl away from each other [the loops]. But the snakes tripped and fell over each other and tied.

As discussed in Chapter 2, most children develop language within normal developmental guidelines. However, that is not the case for all children. Some children experience language delays or significant articulation difficulties. While most children develop language well within the normal developmental guidelines (see Chapter 2), such is not the case for all. Special Feature 3.2 offers suggestions for parents and teachers for how to support children who experience language delays.

SPECIAL FEATURE 3.2
Supporting Children Who Experience Language Delays or Speech Challenges

KATHY EUSTACE

I teach in an inclusion preschool of four-year-olds. Each year nearly half my students exhibit some type of speech production challenge. As their teacher I see one of my roles as being a language facilitator for *all* my students. Whether the child is classified as typically developing or exhibits a speech production disorder, or presents evidence of language delay, each is merely at a specific stage of development. My job is the same for all students: to assess their current level of ability, support mastery at this stage, and then help them learn the skills necessary to move on to

(continued)

the next stage. The most common challenges I see when I work with children include articulation disorders, fluency disorders, and language delay.

Articulation disorders account for the majority of all speech production difficulties in young children. These generally involve the mispronunciations of the *s, r, l, th,* and *sh* sounds. The child either:

- omits the sound completely (e.g., *alt* for *salt*),
- substitutes one sound for another consistently (e.g., *wabbit* for *rabbit*), or
- distorts or does not produce the sounds precisely (e.g., *Eidabeth* for *Elizabeth*).

Nearly all children experience some level of misarticulation while they are learning to speak and most children correct through normal development. Speech therapy is usually only necessary if the misarticulations prohibit others from understanding the child's verbal communication or if the problem persists and becomes embarrassing for the child.

Fluency disorders occur when the normal rate of speech "flow" is atypical. Stuttering is one form of fluency disorder. Stuttering occurs when repetitions of sounds interrupt the child's flow of speech, for example, *ppppp please.* Cluttering is another form of disfluency. Cluttering involves excessively fast speech in which word boundaries are often obscured or garbled, for example, *Idonwnnagotoleep* for *I don't want to go to sleep.* Once again, nearly all children occasionally stutter and/or clutter when they are excited or tired. Disfluency disorders are not considered problematic unless they are constant and prevent a child from communicating his or her intentions.

Language delay is diagnosed when children have difficulty understanding a communicated message or expressing their thoughts verbally as contrasted to a developmental standard. For example, a two-year-old who responds in one- or two-word sentences is developmentally normal, but a four-year-old who only responds in one- or two-word sentences would be classified as language delayed.

Language delays may be exhibited as a primary condition caused by temporary health concerns such as colds or ear infections. Other more serious causes of language delay also include language-impoverished home environments or damage to the areas of the brain that process language. Language delays also occur as secondary symptoms to other physical conditions such as mental retardation, autism, cleft palate, or cerebral palsy.

While there are many reasons children may not acquire the typical language skills expected for their age, the cause is less important than the treatment. For example, a child may exhibit language delays due to mental retardation or a child with normal intelligence may not have acquired normal language due to temporary hearing loss or an environment that was not verbally interactive. Regardless of the circumstance, the instructional goal is to increase the production of verbal communication, and therefore the treatment is nearly identical.

When I plan activities for my inclusive class, I plan language opportunities that would be appropriate for a range of abilities, from the typically developing child to the children who exhibit speech production challenges to language delays. I also facilitate student participation based on the ability level of each child, always keeping the child's individual goals in mind. The activities are open-ended and designed to elicit responses at all four levels. The following examples are based on a discussion I had with my class after we had read *Little Cloud* by Eric Carle (Scholastic, 1996).

- *Level 1*—involves an indication that the child has a receptive understanding of a new concept, in this case, clouds. At this level I merely ask the child to demonstrate his or her understanding of the new concept by pointing to a visual representation of the concept. *Where are the clouds in this picture, Jamie?*

SPECIAL FEATURE 3.2 Continued

- *Level 2*—asks a child to use a one-word response to communicate. This one word may help me gauge a child's receptive understanding or a linguistic concept, or it may include a targeted speech sound that is typically mispronounced by this child. For example, *On this page what did Little Cloud turn into? Gustavo? Yes, that is right RRRRabbit.*
- *Level 3*—involves a multiword response from a child whose goal it is to increase his

or her mean length of utterance or who is working on syntax. *Can you tell me three or four things that Little Cloud changes into? Sarafina?*

- *Level 4*—involves helping children make inferences or comparisons. This level of response gives children an opportunity to elaborate their thoughts and to work on the aspect of their language that is in question. *How are sheep and clouds alike? Who helped Little Cloud make the rain?*

PEARSON
myeducationkit

Go to the Assignments and Activities section of Chapter 3 in the MyEducationKit and complete the activity entitled "Reading to Children." As you read the article and conduct the reading activity, think about how you prepared this reading in order for both you and the children to be successful.

PEARSON
myeducationkit

Go to the Assignments and Activities section of Chapter 3 in the MyEducationKit and complete the activity entitled "Story Time: Large Group." As you watch the video and answer the accompanying questions, note how this teacher keeps all young children physically engaged in this storybook reading.

Reading Storybooks

Research reveals a connection between the amount of time adults spend reading storybooks to children and the level of children's oral language development. The stories, pictures, and accompanying adult-to-child interactions facilitate language use and increase expressive and receptive vocabulary. Further, children who have been read to frequently are better able to retell stories than children who have had few opportunities to engage in story time (Barrentine, 1996; Durkin, 1966). Caregivers may also encourage discussion and comprehension by asking open-ended questions about the stories they read. Children often relate to the characters and story lines, and, when encouraged, they reveal interesting views. The following conversation occurred when Dominique was four years old, after a reading of *Goldilocks and the Three Bears*.

MOM: What part of the story did you like the best?

DOMINIQUE: When Goldilocks kept messing up baby bear's stuff.

MOM: Who did you like best in the story?

DOMINIQUE: Baby bear.

MOM: Why?

DOMINIQUE: 'Cause baby bear is like me. All of his stuff is wrecked up by Goldilocks, like Sheritta [her eighteen-month-old sister] messes up mine.

Notice that Dominique's mother asked open-ended opinion questions and accepted her child's responses. This type of question encourages oral responses and children's personal interpretation of the story. Adults should refrain from asking interrogation or detail questions, such as "What did

Goldilocks say when she tasted the second bowl of porridge?" Detail questions tend to make story time something to be avoided, not enjoyed.

As children snuggle in a parent's lap or beside their parent in a chair or bed, story time creates a comforting, private time to talk together and learn new vocabulary. However, in today's culturally, linguistically, and socioeconomically diverse society, teachers may find that some of their students' parents are unsure how to successfully engage their children in story time. Special Feature 3.3 offers a model teachers may wish to share with parents.

SPECIAL FEATURE 3.3
Language Development via Storybook Reading

In recent years, studies have revealed that home literacy experiences, or the lack of them, profoundly influence children's later literacy development and language development. However, storybook reading is not an instinct. Knowing how to interact with children and storybooks takes time and practice. One simple approach that significantly increases a child's involvement in the story time experience is called "dialogic reading." It involves parents asking questions (see Figure 3.1, Closed- and Open-Ended Questions) about the stories as they read, such as asking children to describe what they are seeing on the page. In addition, parents are also encouraged to add information.

The following scene illustrates the dialogic reading approach. Dad is reading Jane Manning's *Who Stole the Cookies from the Cookie Jar?* (HarperFestival, 2001) to three-year-old Jasper. Before Dad even begins the story, he asks Jasper about the cover illustration.

DAD: Jasper, who is on the cover?

JASPER: Doggie, kitty, piggy, rabbit, and mouse.

DAD: Look, Jasper. Do you see that the book is shaped like our cookie jar?

JASPER: Daddy, see the cookies, they are chocolate chip!

DAD: Your favorite, Jasper. The title of this book is *Who Stole the Cookies from*

the Cookie Jar? Who do you think stole the cookies?

JASPER: I think Piggy or Cookie Monster.

The reading and conversation about this twelve-page storybook lasted more than a half hour with Jasper deeply engaged with describing the richly detailed illustrations and guessing who had stolen the cookies.

In addition to dialogic reading, there are other simple and enjoyable strategies parents can use to help their children get the most from story time:

- Read the same books again and again. Children learn new things each time they hear a story and look at the pictures.
- Ask children to find and label objects. This helps to keep them involved in the story.
- Ask open-ended questions. Asking questions like "What do you think will happen next?" or "What was your favorite part of the story?" encourages children to share their feelings and opinions. Figure 3.1 provides several examples of open-ended questions.
- Expand your child's answers. Adding to your child's responses encourages him or her to interact with you and keeps him or her involved.
- Read with enthusiasm. Taking on the voices of the three little pigs and the wolf is fun and exciting and brings the story to life.

FIGURE 3.1   Closed- and Open-Ended Questions

Closed-ended questions usually only require a single-word answer—"yes" or "no"— or require the "right answer." Open-ended questions, on the other hand, have no right or wrong answers and encourage students to talk more and to use richer language.

This set of example questions for early primary-grade children refers to Maurice Sendak's *Where the Wild Things Are*.

Closed-Ended Questions	Open-Ended Questions
Did you like Max?	What did you think about Max?
Why did Max get in trouble?	How did you feel when Max's mother sent him to bed?
Were the wild things monsters?	Tell me about the wild things. What did they look like?
What did Max do to the wild things?	Why did Max stare at the wild things?
Did you like the story?	What part of the story did you like best?

Remember to ask questions before, during, and after the story as this helps to maintain child involvement.

Television as a Language Tool

Television has been a major influence on family life in almost all U.S. households since the 1950s. In the 1980s the availability of video rentals and inexpensive video players, video movies, and video storybooks, cartoons, and games added yet another dimension to television watching. During the 1990s, it was estimated that 99 percent of U.S. homes had at least one television set. By the 2000s most U.S. homes reported multiple TVs and children learning to use remote tuners before they mastered dining utensils (Schnabel, 2009). In addition, the TV is usually in the part of the home where most family interactions occur (Miller, 1997). Sadly, the average child between two and five years of age will spend twenty-seven hours a week viewing television programming. Anything that occupies children for so many hours a week deserves careful consideration.

Time.   Research regarding the amount of time young children watch TV and the effect of viewing on later academic success is inconclusive, though the data clearly suggest that watching for many hours per day or week has a negative effect on children's academic performance. Susan Neuman (1988) suggests that more than four hours of TV viewing a day has a negative effect on children's reading achievement. Likewise, Angela Clarke and Beth Kurtz-Costes's (1997) study of low-socioeconomic African American preschool children shows that children who watched the most television (between thirty and fifty-five hours per week) exhibited poorer academic skills than their peers who watched fewer than twenty-five hours per week. On the other hand, moderate amounts of TV viewing may be beneficial. The Center for the Study of Reading's landmark report "Becoming a Nation of Readers" suggests that there is actually a positive link between watching up to ten hours of television a week and reading achievement (Rice, Huston, Truglio, & Wright, 1990). Clarke and Kurtz-Costes (1997) suggest that the variation in researchers' findings may be due in part to the home climate. They suggest that *who* watches TV with young children and *how* TV is watched may have a greater effect on children's learning than simply the *amount* of TV viewing.

Choosing Programming for Children.   Selecting appropriate children's programming has become more challenging in recent years. In addition to regular public access, cable service may offer as many as 100 options to choose from each hour of the day. And though there are a number of proven classics—such as *Sesame Street*—children's programs change from year to year. One way parents can determine the quality of children's programming is through considering children's needs. Diane Levin and Nancy Carlsson-Paige (1994) created a list of children's developmental needs and suggested program criteria to accommodate these concerns.

Active Viewing.   Children are extremely impressionable, and television's visual imagery is a powerful force in their lives. Therefore, it is important for parents to help guide and mediate the viewing process. Susan Miller (1997) suggests a number of ways parents and caregivers may interact with children as they view television.

- *Watch television together.* Help children interpret what they see on the screen.
- *Talk about the programs.* Conversations initiated by television programming offer opportunities to discuss a wide variety of issues.
- *Observe children's reactions.* Ask children to label or describe their feelings.
- *Foster critical thinking.* Ask children what they think about a program. Would they have handled the problem differently? Did they agree with the character's actions?
- *Extend viewing activities.* Children are often motivated to learn more about a topic or activity once television has sparked their interests.

In short, though the television can be a powerful tool in children's learning, careful consideration of how much and what programming and how children view that programming is needed.

Home Literacy Experiences

As explained in Chapter 1, interest in emergent literacy began with studies of early readers, children who learned to read before they entered kindergarten. This research led to investigations of what preschool-age children typically learn about print. At the same time, researchers began to investigate children's home literacy experiences, seeking to discover the factors that promote early literacy acquisition.

Early studies on home literacy learning focused on umbrella characteristics such as family income and parents' levels of education (Sulzby & Teale, 1991). Results revealed positive relationships between these variables and reading achievement in the early grades. For example, children from middle-income families tend to be better readers than those from low-income families. Unfortunately, such findings do little to explain how these variables directly affect children's literacy growth.

More recent studies have narrowed their research focus and have attempted to describe the actual literacy-related experiences that children have at home. These home literacy studies have identified several factors that appear to have important roles in early literacy acquisition. These factors are described in the sections that follow.

■ *Access to print and books.* In order to learn about literacy, young children must have opportunities to see lots of print and must have easy access to books. Plentiful home supplies of children's books have been found to be associated with early reading (Durkin, 1966), interest in literature (Morrow, 1983), and positive orientation toward schooling (Feitelson & Goldstein, 1986).

Because of the literate nature of our society, all children are surrounded by large amounts of environmental print. For example, they see print on product containers (Cheerios, Pepsi), street signs (Stop), and store signs (McDonald's, Pizza Hut). Differences do occur, however, in children's exposure to books and other forms of reading materials. Bill Teale's (1986) descriptive study of the home environments of twenty-four low-income preschoolers revealed that, while some of the homes had ample supplies of children's books, other homes contained none. This is not to suggest that all children from low-income families lack exposure to reading materials at home. However, those children who do not have access to books at home are at a great disadvantage in acquiring literacy.

■ *Adult demonstrations of literacy behavior.* Children also need to observe their parents, other adults, or older siblings using literacy in everyday situations (Smith, 1988). When children see their family members use print for various purposes—writing shopping lists, paying bills, looking up programs in the television listings, and writing notes to each other—they begin to learn about the practical uses of written language and to understand why reading and writing are activities worth doing. If their parents happen to model reading for pleasure, so much the better. These children see literature as a source of entertainment. Children's exposure to these types of functional and recreational literacy demonstrations has been found to vary greatly.

■ *Supportive adults.* Early readers tend to have parents who are very supportive of their early attempts at literacy (Morrow, 1983). While these parents rarely attempt to directly teach their children how to read and write, they do support literacy growth by doing such things as (1) answering their children's questions about print; (2) pointing out letters and words in the environment; (3) reading storybooks frequently; (4) making regular visits to the local library; (5) providing children with a wide variety of experiences such as trips to stores, parks, and museums; and (6) initiating functional literacy activities (such as suggesting that a child write a letter to grandmother or help make a shopping list).

The amount of such support that children receive during the preschool years varies greatly from family to family, and these differences have been found to have a considerable effect on children's literacy learning during kindergarten and the elementary grades (Christian, Morrison, & Bryant, 1998).

■ *Independent engagements with literacy.* Young children need to get their hands on literacy materials and to have opportunities to engage in early forms of reading and writing. This exploration and experimentation allows children to try out and perfect their growing concepts about the functions, forms, and conventions of written language.

Independent engagements with literacy often take place in connection with play. Don Holdaway (1979) has described how, as soon as young children become familiar with a storybook through repetitive read-aloud experiences, they will begin to play with the books and pretend to read them. He believes that this type of reading-like play is one of the most important factors promoting early literacy acquisition.

Young children also incorporate writing into their play. Sometimes this play writing is exploratory in nature, with children experimenting with different letter forms and shapes. At other times, emergent writing occurs in the context of make-believe play. Figure 3.2 is an example of this type of play-related writing. Four-year-old Ben was engaging in dramatic play in the housekeeping center. He wrote a Post-it Note message to another child, who was acting out the role of his mother, informing her that he was at soccer practice.

Young children also use literacy in functional, nonplay situations. An excellent example is Glenda Bissex's (1980) account of how her four-year-old son Paul, after failing to get her attention by verbal means, used a stamp set to write "RUDF" (Are you deaf?). He also attempted to secure his privacy by putting the sign "DO NOT DSTRB GNYS AT WRK" (Do not disturb. Genius at work) on his door.

FIGURE 3.2   Ben's Post-it Note: "Gone to soccer practice. Be back at 4."

Opportunities to engage in these types of independent engagements with literacy depend on access to books and writing materials. As mentioned previously, research on children's home environments indicates that there are wide discrepancies in the availability of children's books and other reading materials. Similar differences also exist in the availability of writing materials. Teale's (1986) descriptive study of the home environments of low-income preschoolers revealed that only four of twenty-four children had easy access to paper and writing instruments. He noted that these particular children engaged in far more emergent writing than did the other subjects in the study.

■ *Storybook reading.* Storybook reading is undoubtedly the most studied aspect of home literacy. Quantitative studies have attempted to establish the importance and value of parents' reading to their children. A meta-analysis of twenty-nine studies spanning more than three decades indicated that parent–preschooler storybook reading was positively related to outcomes such as language growth, early literacy, and reading achievement (Bus, van Ijzendoorn, & Pellegrini, 1995).

Other studies have attempted to describe and analyze what actually takes place during storybook-reading episodes and to identify the mechanisms through which storybook reading facilitates literacy growth (e.g., Altwerger, Diehl-Faxon, & Dockstader-Anderson, 1985; Heath, 1982; Holdaway, 1979; Snow & Ninio, 1986; Taylor, 1986; Yaden, Smolkin, & Conlon, 1989). These studies have shown that parent–child storybook reading is an ideal context for children to receive all of the previously mentioned factors that promote literacy acquisition:

1. Storybook reading provides children with access to enjoyable children's books, building positive attitudes about books and reading.

Family Focus: Parent Workshops

One highly effective strategy for involving and directly informing parents of preschool and kindergarten students about how to support their children's language and literacy learning is through parent workshops. The purpose of the workshops is to share explicit information about the children's development and the class curriculum, and to provide practical suggestions that parents may use at home to support their child's learning (Brown, 1994).

To begin, the teacher should design a "Needs Assessment Survey" to determine parents' special interests and needs. In Figure 3.3, we provide an example of a survey that covers possible workshop topics, meeting times, and child care needs.

After the survey has been returned and the results tallied, the early childhood teacher should publish and "advertise" the schedule of workshops. We recommend the teacher select the top two or three topics and identify the time(s) and day(s) listed as convenient for most of the parents. Generally, the most convenient meeting place is the classroom or the school's or center's multipurpose room. Scout troops, parent volunteers, or older students may provide child care. Teachers should be sure to have parents confirm their participation in the workshop (see Figure 3.4). This will allow the teacher to prepare sufficient materials and secure appropriate child care arrangements. Send reminders the day before the workshop. Don't

(continued)

Family Focus: Parent Workshops   Continued

be surprised if only a few parents attend initially. Parent workshops may be a new concept and it might take a little time for parents to become comfortable with this approach to parent/teacher interactions.

Teachers must *prepare* for a parent workshop. They need adequate supplies. They may need to organize the room. They need to set up refreshments. (Parent–teacher organizations or center budgets can

Dear Parents,

Did you know you are your child's first and most important teacher? One of my responsibilities as a teacher is to work and share all my teaching colleagues for the benefit of the special student we share–your child. I would like to conduct several workshops this year, and I need to know what topics you are most interested in learning about. Please complete the survey and have your child return it by _____. Place "X" by topics you would like to attend.

____Storytelling techniques   ____Linking Play and Literacy

____Writers Workshop   ____Kitchen Math and Science

____Rainy Day Fun   ____Learning Motivation

____Other_____

_____

What is the most convenient day? What time is the most convenient for you to attend a workshop?

____Monday   ____Tuesday   ____9:00am ____4:00pm ____7:00pm____

____Wednesday   ____Thursday

____Friday   ____Saturday

Would I use a child-care service if one was provided?

____Yes—list number of children needing care ____.

____No.

FIGURE 3.3   Needs Assessment Survey

Dear Parents:

The topics that most most of you wanted to learn more about were

Writing Workshop, Kitchen Math and Science, and Rainy Day Fun!

The times that were convenient for most of you were:

    Wednesdays at 7:00 p.m. and Saturdays at 9:00 a.m.

I have used this information to create a schedule of workshops for the Fall semester. Please fill out the personal information and put an X by the workshops you plan to attend. All workshops will be in my classroom. Refreshments will be served. Dress comfortably as we might be getting messy. Children will be cared for in the cafeteria by the Girl Scouts and their leaders.

_____

Name_____ Phone_____

Number of children needing child care_____.

____Writers Workshop—Wednesday, October 2, 7:00–8:30 p.m.

____Kitchen Math and Science—Saturday, November 4, 9:00–10:30 a.m.

____Rainy Day Fun—Wednesday, November 9, 7:00–8:30 p.m.

FIGURE 3.4   Workshop Confirmation Letter

often reimburse teachers for refreshments.) Teachers need to prepare name tags, double-check child care arrangements, develop an evaluation form for the workshop, and create a detailed lesson plan!

There are several points for teachers to remember when running a parent workshop. First, the workshop should begin promptly. Second, start with a "get acquainted" activity to put people at ease and begin the workshop on a relaxed, positive note. Third, remember that parents should not be lectured to; instead, they should experience hands-on, highly engaging activities. After the parents have engaged in the activity

(continued)

Family Focus: Parent Workshops   Continued

provide brief, specific information about the theory underlying the process. Most important, remember to *smile*. When the teacher has a good time, the parents will also! Finally, have parents complete the workshop evaluation form; this will help to continually refine the quality of the workshops (see Figure 3.5).

Workshop Name_____ Date_____

List two activities you enjoyed or learned the most about.

1.

2.

List any information that was not useful to you.

The workshop was (mark all that apply):

____clear   ____confusing   ____enjoyable   ____boring

____too short   ____too long ____informative

Any other comments?

Thanks for attending!

FIGURE 3.5   Workshop Evaluation Form

2. During storybook reading, parents present children with a model of skilled reading. Children see how books are handled, and they hear the distinctive intonation patterns that are used in oral reading.
3. Parents provide support that enables young children to take an active part in storybook reading. Early storybook-reading sessions tend to be routinized, with the parent first focusing the child's attention on a picture and then asking the child to label the picture. If the child does so, the parent gives positive or negative feedback about the accuracy of the label. If the child does not volunteer a label, the parent provides the correct label (Snow & Ninio, 1986). As children's abilities grow, parents up the ante, shifting more of the responsibility to the children and expecting them to participate in more advanced ways.
4. Storybook reading encourages independent engagements with literacy by familiarizing children with stories and encouraging them to attempt to read the stories on their own (Holdaway, 1979; Sulzby, 1985a).

Other researchers have studied how cultural factors affect the manner in which parents mediate storybook reading for their children. Shirley Brice Heath (1982) found that middle-class parents tended to help their children link book information with other experiences. For example, John Langstaff's popular predictable book *Oh, A-Hunting We Will Go* (Macmillan, 1974) contains the following lines:

Oh, a-hunting we will go.
A-hunting we will go.
We'll catch a lamb
And put him in a pram
And then we'll let him go.

To help the child understand the term *pram,* a middle-class parent might say, "The pram looks just like your sister's baby carriage." Working-class parents, on the other hand, had a tendency to not extend book information beyond its original context and would simply define the word *pram* for the child. Sulzby and Teale (1991) speculate that these differences in story-reading style may have a considerable effect on children's early literacy acquisition.

Case Studies

The following section presents two case studies of early literacy development. Tiffany, a native English speaker, is the subject of the first case study. The second study describes Alicia's literacy acquisition. Alicia is a native speaker of Spanish, and English is her second language. There are many interesting similarities and differences in the early literacy acquisition of these two girls.

Tiffany

Tiffany's parents began reading to her soon after birth, and by one year, she was actively participating in storybook-reading sessions. Now, more than two years later, thirty-month-old

Tiffany has begun to attempt to read on her own. The story begins in her bedroom, where she was looking at Richard Scarry's *Best Word Book Ever* (Western Publishing Company, 1980) with her sister Dawn. Though her house has many children's books, this book was one of her favorites. Tiffany delighted in labeling the pictures and describing the actions of the Bunny family as they engage in familiar, everyday situations. As Tiffany pointed to the pictures of Nicki Bunny going to the doctor for a checkup, both she and Dawn laughed at the animals who are all dressed up in clothing: "Nicki Bunny wears shoes!" While attempting to read this text, Tiffany displayed many aspects of her concepts about print, including book handling and turning pages (starting at the front of the book and progressing to the back), as well as an appreciation of storybook reading.

On the way to the grocery story several months later, Tiffany's family passed a McDonald's sign. Thirty-three-month-old Tiffany shouted with gleeful recognition, "Donald's—ummm, eat burgers." Tiffany, like most children brought up in a literate culture, had already begun to recognize that her world is full of environmental print. Though Tiffany's reading of the McDonald's sign came more from interpreting the color and shape of the logo than from differentiating letters, it demonstrated her understanding that print carries meaning—another important developmental milestone.

Tiffany was also beginning to demonstrate an understanding that writing, as well as oral language, communicates meaning. Waiting with her mother in the bank, thirty-six-month-old Tiffany took a handful of bank forms. While her mother talked to the bank manager, Tiffany occupied herself by using a pen to fill out the many forms. Her writing contained many squiggly lines and some picture like forms. When Tiffany's mother asked her what she had written, Tiffany replied, "I write, 'Tiffy can buy money'" (see Figure 3.6). At this stage, it is typical for children's writing to include both pictographs (pictures that represent writing) and scribble writing. Notice that her scribbling has the appearance of an adult's English cursive writing.

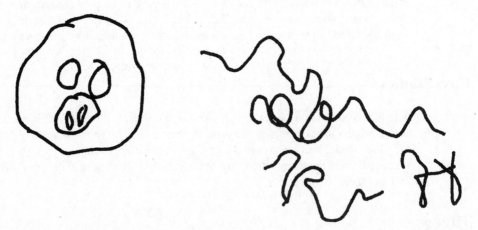

FIGURE 3.6   Tiffany (Age Thirty-six Months) Writes a Note Using Drawing and Scribbles: "Tiffy Can Buy Money."

Sitting on her Daddy's lap, forty-two-month-old Tiffany was reading him the story of Maurice Sendak's *Where the Wild Things Are* (Scholastic, 1963):

> *This bad boy in the wolf pajamas is mean to his mommy.*
> *He runs away 'cause he is mad.*
> *He gets in a boat, like "rubba a dub"* [Tiffany's bathtub toy boat]
> *Then he meets some big bad chicken monsters and yells at them.*
> *They make him the King, 'cause he yelled so loud!!!*
> *Then he goed home 'cause he wanted to eat.*

The story she told consisted of her interpretations of the text's illustrations, and she used a storytelling tone as she held the book and turned the pages. As explained earlier, this behavior is indicative of Elizabeth Sulzby's category of emergent reading, "attending to pictures, forming oral stories" (Sulzby & Barnhart, 1990). Though Tiffany's oral retelling of the story was fairly accurate, her father noted that she did not include the monster refrain—"and they rolled their terrible eyes, gnashed their terrible teeth, and showed their terrible claws!" Her omission of this salient part of the story was probably caused by the fact that, during this stage of emergent reading, story retelling is guided by the illustrations rather than by the words in the text. As the pictures did not explicitly detail this refrain, Tiffany lacked the visual cues that would have triggered the recitation of this phrase.

At age four years, Tiffany continued to refine her understanding of the many functions of print. Sitting at her child-sized table in her pretend playhouse, with her best friend, Becca, Tiffany pondered over a piece of paper with her pencil in her mouth:

TIFFANY: What do you think the babies will eat?

BECCA: Baby food, Tiff.

TIFFANY: I know that! What kind of baby food?

BECCA: Oh, I think the orange stuff, but not the green.

TIFFANY: [Now writing this information down.] Okay. What else?

BECCA: You need to write down cat food and take the coupons.

TIFFANY: [Pulling out a bunch of coupons from her drawer, she sorts through them until she finds the Purina Cat Chow coupon.] Yeah, that coupon says "free cat food."

Tiffany had now begun to produce letterlike forms (see Figure 3.7). Though she continued to use pictographs, Tiffany could distinguish print from pictures. Pointing to the drawing she said, "This is a picture of baby food." She went on to describe her letterlike forms with the comment, "This says buy peaches and diapers."

This episode also reveals that Tiffany was continuing to expand her environmental print vocabulary. In fact, she was becoming quite adept at recognizing dozens of product names. This ability was fostered by parental praise and encouragement each time Tiffany joined her parents as a member of the grocery-shopping expedition.

At age four, Tiffany started preschool. One of the first academic activities her preschool teachers undertook was helping the children to recognize and print their own name. As is often the case, Tiffany's first attempts to print her name were somewhat frustrating.

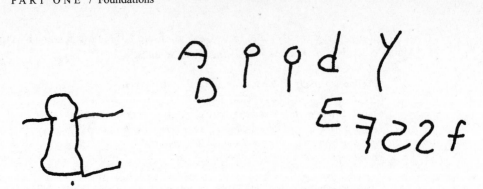

FIGURE 3.7   Tiffany (Age Forty-eight Months) Writes a Shopping List.

Though she was quite accomplished at making letterlike forms, trying to reproduce specific letters in a specified sequence was definitely a challenge. At that time, Tiffany received a chalkboard from her grandparents. The new writing implement seemed to inspire her to practice more frequently, and soon Tiffany had mastered the fine art of printing her name.

Along with printing her name, Tiffany, as well as most of her preschool classmates, was becoming interested in naming and printing the alphabet. This interest was sparked by her teachers through direct, developmentally appropriate instruction. Prior to her preschool experience, Tiffany only casually watched the *Sesame Street* letter segments, paying attention instead to the social drama of the *Sesame Street* characters. However, between the ages of four and five years, Tiffany became an astute alphabet hunter—shouting with great authority the names of the letters as they flashed across the television screen. Tiffany sang the alphabet song, read alphabet books, did alphabet puzzles and alphabet dot-to-dot worksheets, and molded clay letters. She diligently wrote alphabet symbols with every type of writing tool imaginable—markers, pens, pencils, and water paints and paint brushes. She wrote her letters on every surface conceivable, including her bedroom walls! Her all-time favorite alphabet activity was writing her letters with soap crayons on the bathtub/shower wall.

Tiffany's new proficiency with letter formation resulted in the production of many strings of random capital and lowercase letters, or using Sulzby's (1990) terminology, strings of nonphonetic letter strings. Notice that though Tiffany knew many upper- and lowercase letters, she was not yet forming words or clustering her letters in wordlike units (see Figure 3.8).

Soon after Tiffany entered preschool, she became interested in joining her sister Dawn (age seven) in playing school. During these dramatic play sessions, Tiffany would listen to Dawn as she read basal texts and their favorite literature. In the role of teacher, Dawn would ask factual questions during and after reading storybooks to Tiffany. For example, after reading Maurice Sendak's *Where the Wild Things Are* (Harper & Row, 1984), Dawn asked, "What did the monsters say to Max? What did Max say to the monsters?" Dawn would model writing letters on the chalkboard and then ask Tiffany to copy what she had written. Tiffany did her best to reproduce the words that Dawn wrote. Every so often, Tiffany would run out to her mom and proclaim, "Look it! What it say?"

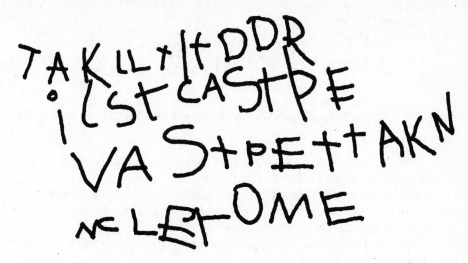

FIGURE 3.8   Tiffany (Age Fifty-four Months) Writes a Stream of Random Letters.

Later in the year, when Dawn was at school, Tiffany would play school by herself, only this time she was the teacher. Dressed in a long white pleated skirt, heels, and jacket, she looked like Ms. O'Bannon, her sister's second-grade teacher. She would "read" stories to her teddy bear and to rows of doll students, and she would use her ruler to point to alphabet cards posted on the wall. She would ask Teddy to pay attention and ask Annie (a doll) to tell her what the letters said. It is interesting to note that, when Tiffany pretended to be the teacher, her writing became more conventional. She carefully wrote her letters as she practiced saying the phrases that Dawn had used earlier: "Start at the top, draw a flat-hat top, then find the middle and draw a straight line. Now you see, you have a *T*."

Sitting in her miniature rocker holding her beloved baby doll Ramalda, four-and-a-half-year-old Tiffany began reading another favorite story, *Old Hat, New Hat* by Stan and Jan Berenstain (Random House, 1970). Pointing to the pictures, Tiffany recited the story line, "new hat, new hat, new hat" and "too feathery, too scratchy," then the rousing finale, "just right, just right, just right!" Tiffany's recitation involved following the pictures and recalling the phrases she had heard and repeated with her parents virtually dozens of times. At this point in her development, her storybook reading was beginning to sound like reading as she imitated the expression and phrasing her parents used when they read this story to her.

When Tiffany began kindergarten at age five, she could recognize most alphabet letters. During her kindergarten year, Tiffany learned that each alphabet letter made a specific sound, but some alphabet letters made two or three sounds. For Tiffany, this phonics knowledge was an exciting step toward literacy. She reveled in baking Big Bird's brown banana bread with butter and studying the scientific qualities of bubbles and bouncing balls billions of times.

Her teacher, Ms. C., also modeled the writing process at the end of each day. She began by asking the children to summarize what they had learned that day, and as the

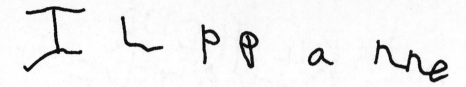

FIGURE 3.9   Tiffany (Age Sixty Months) Uses Invented Spelling in Her Journal.

children volunteered ideas, she would write their statements. While Ms. C. wrote, she would ask, "Who knows what letter Baby Bear starts with? What other sounds do you hear?" This type of informal modeling provided the spark that ignited Tiffany's reading-writing connection. This very sensitive teacher also had the kindergarten children write in their journals at their own developmental level. The writing sample in Figure 3.9 illustrates one of Tiffany's first invented-spelling journal entries. At this point, she was beginning to separate her words.

Alicia

Irene Serna and Sarah Hudelson present a second case study of early literacy. This one features Alicia, who came from a home in which Spanish was the primary language. When she entered kindergarten, Alicia was speaking perfect Spanish but was only partially proficient in oral English. She was fortunate to attend a bilingual kindergarten in which she was allowed to learn to read and write in Spanish and then transfer what she had learned to English literacy. It is interesting to compare Alicia's acquisition of reading and writing in Spanish with Tiffany's literacy development in English. As you will see, there are many interesting parallels.

Alicia's Early Literacy Development in Spanish

IRENE SERNA AND SARAH HUDELSON

As Tiffany's case study illustrates, young children begin to read and write English by engaging in daily literacy activities with family members and teachers. These adults support early literacy by creating opportunities for reading and writing and by responding to children's requests for assistance. What does early literacy look like in a language other than English? Alicia, a Spanish-speaking kindergartner we came to know through our research, provides a good example of how children construct their literacy in Spanish (Serna & Hudelson, 1993).

Alicia's Home Language and Literacy.   Spanish was the dominant language in Alicia's home. Her mother reported that Alicia had requested that books be read to her since she was four years old. In addition, Alicia had been eager to engage in writing within family activities. At home, Alicia helped produce shopping lists, notes, and cards sent to family members. Of course, these were written in Spanish. Clearly, Alicia came from a very literate home environment that featured frequent storybook reading, many opportunities to write in connection with daily activities, and adults who supported her early attempts at reading and writing. In this regard, Alicia's early literacy development was quite similar to Tiffany's and that of other English-speaking children who come from supportive home environments. There was one significant difference—Alicia reported that her mother and grandmother frequently told her *cuentos* (folktales) and family stories. Thus, storytelling (oral literacy) was also a strong part of Alicia's home literacy experiences.

Alicia's Literacy Development in Kindergarten. Though Alicia participated in a bilingual Head Start program as a four-year-old, when she entered kindergarten, her score on an oral language proficiency test identified her as limited English proficient. Two thirds of the children in her bilingual kindergarten program spoke English, and one third spoke Spanish. Alicia used both languages to socialize with her peers. However, she primarily used Spanish to explain her thinking, to narrate stories, and to express herself personally. At the beginning of kindergarten, Alicia only discussed books that were read aloud in Spanish. By the latter half of the year, she was discussing books read in both languages. This was particularly helpful to the monolingual children because Alicia could interpret books and communications in English or Spanish. Alicia's role in the classroom became that of translator. Thus, while her one year of Head Start was not sufficient time for Alicia to develop oral proficiency in English, the second year of bilingual programming in kindergarten did allow her to develop bilingual abilities.

Writing. Beginning in October of her kindergarten year, Alicia was asked to write in a journal for forty-five minutes daily. Throughout the year, she also drew and wrote in learning logs to record information from study in thematic units. She contributed to group language experience charts, which summarized findings from the children's thematic studies. In her earliest journal entries, Alicia wrote a patterned and familiar phrase in English, "I love my mom." A November entry demonstrated that Alicia had moved from producing a patterned phrase to creating a label for her picture: *"Mi papalote"* (my kite). In November, Alicia also wrote her first sentence describing a picture, *"Yo ciro mi babe Martinsito"* (I love my baby Martincito), using both invented (*ciro* for *quiero*) and conventional spelling. She also wrote additional patterned sentences, *"Mi Nana bonita come sopa Mi mami bonita come sopa"* (My pretty grandmother eats soup. My pretty mother eats soup). In December, Alicia repeated phrases to write two lines of text describing her picture, *"Los colores del arco iris son bonitos Colores del arco ids"* (The colors of the rainbow are pretty. The colors of the rainbow). Her writing did not become more expressive until February when she wrote about playing in the pile of snow that had been trucked to the school (see Figure 3.10).

This February sample demonstrates that Alicia's invented spellings included most sounds in each syllable, that the vowels were standardized, and that she confused some of the consonants. Though she put spaces between most words, conventional word separation was not used consistently.

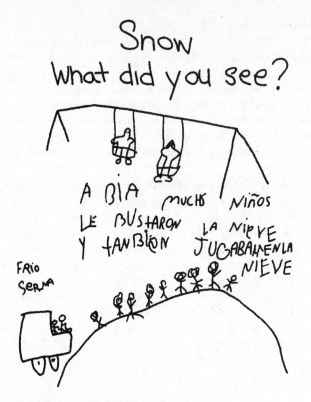

Snow
What did you see?

A BIA MUCHIS NIÑOS
LE BUSTARON LA NIPYE
Y +ANBION JUGABAHENLA
NIEVE

FRIO
SERMA

FIGURE 3.10   Alicia's February Writing Sample

In April, Alicia wrote a personal narrative about her little cousin Martincito, primarily describing how she cared for and played with him. Figure 3.11 contains two of the ten sentences she wrote in this personal narrative. Written over a three-week period, Alicia's personal narrative illustrates that her invented spellings were very close approximations of standard Spanish spellings. Alicia also separated words more consistently. Syntactically, all of her sentences were complete, and all grammatical inflections were correct. By the end of kindergarten, Alicia was the classroom's most fluent writer in Spanish. As a result, other children often asked her to write their personal narratives.

Reading.   From September through February, Alicia retold stories from familiar, predictable picture books using some of the story language in Spanish and some in English. In March, her first story was typed for publication (in Spanish). Alicia read this text for the first time using letter–sound cues and a phonetic decoding strategy (i.e., she tried to sound out the words). While this initial reading was not very smooth, Alicia practiced reading the words until she could reread her own story fluently. From March to the end of the year, Alicia used this same strategy with familiar, predictable books in Spanish. Initially, each book was read utilizing the phonetic decoding strategy, focusing on sounding out unfamiliar words. Subsequently, she reread the text until she could read it fluently. Alicia chose to read books that had plain print, with only one or two lines of text per page. She rejected books

Yo LueGo
coN mi
PRimíto
A LAS   ESooNdiDAS
CUANDo
Yo   AGO
UNa Ma RoMa
e me
coPeA

Alicia's Spelling	Conventional Spanish Spelling	English Translation
Yo juego	Yo juego	I play
con mi	con mi	with my
primito	primita	little cousin
alas escondidas	a las escondidas	hide-and-seek
Cuando	Cuando	When
Yo ago	yo hago	I make
una ma roma	una moroma	a somersault
e me copea	el me copea	he copies me

FIGURE 3.11   Alicia's April Writing Sample

with too many words or italic print. By the end of May, Alicia read the Spanish versions of Maurice Sendak's *Where the Wild Things Are* (Harper & Row, 1963) and Robert Kraus's *Herman the Helper* (Windmill, 1974), familiar and unfamiliar texts, respectively. She made a few mistakes, primarily grammatical. She did not correct these mistakes, but they were rather minor and did not change the meaning of the story. Alicia read more effectively, using multiple cues (letter–sound, meaning, and grammatical) as well as illustrations to decode unfamiliar words. Alicia also demonstrated that she was reading to construct the meaning of each text because she was able to retell each story accurately. By the end of kindergarten, Alicia had become a fluent writer and reader in Spanish. She was able to use sophisticated invented spellings that were very close approximations of standard Spanish spellings, and she could compose coherent narrative stories. Alicia learned to read in Spanish through reading both her own writing and familiar, predictable books. By April, Alicia was reading picture books fluently and independently. She was able to use multiple cueing systems and reading strategies in Spanish.

Summary

This chapter began with a review of the many ways parents can support their child's language development within the home. To summarize the key points about facilitating oral language learning, we return to the guiding question at the beginning of this chapter:

PEARSON
myeducationkit™

To check your comprehension on the content covered in this chapter, go to the MyEducationKit for your book and complete the Study Plan for Chapter 3. Here you will be able to take a chapter quiz and receive feedback on your answers.

- *How can parents best facilitate their children's oral language development?*

Parents can promote their children's oral language by scaffolding their language, encouraging them to tell personal narratives about their experiences, reading stories to them on a regular basis, and monitoring their children's TV viewing and encouraging active viewing.

- *What home factors affect young children's literacy development?*

Several factors have been identified as having important roles in early literacy acquisition:

1. Opportunities to see lots of print and have easy access to books
2. Opportunities to observe adults using literacy in everyday situations
3. Supportive adults who support children's literacy development by answering children's questions, pointing to letters, taking the children to the library, providing children with a wide variety of experiences, and initiating functional literacy activities
4. Literacy materials that support children's engagement in early forms of reading and writing
5. Experiences with adults who share books with children

- *What does early literacy look like in a language other than English?*

Children learn the dominant language of their home. When these homes—be they English-speaking, Spanish-speaking, or Arabic-speaking—provide a literate model, typically the young children who live in them are eager to engage in talking, writing, and reading in the home's dominant language. So early literacy across languages looks quite similar. Some cultures and families emphasize oral storytelling in addition to reading and writing. Adults in these homes share stories with their young literacy learners and with each other. Of course, children from families whose dominant language is a language other than English will enter school using the language that works for them in their home environment. A quality program that supports these children's emergence as readers and writers is important.

LINKING KNOWLEDGE TO PRACTICE

1. Read a storybook with a child three years or older. Ask the child to point to where you should begin reading. Does the child know that you will read the print, not the pictures? After you have read the story to the child, ask the child to read the story to you. What form does the child use to read the story (e.g., attending to pictures, forming oral stories; attending to pictures, forming written stories; attending to print)? When you have finished reading the book, select an important word from the story. Can the child tell you the name of the letters in this word? Say a word that rhymes with this word. Now, it's the child's turn. Can the child say another word that rhymes with this word? Say a word that begins with the same sound. Can the child say a word that begins with the same sound? Point to each letter. Can the child say the sound of each letter? Can the child blend the letter sounds to form the word? Compare your findings with those gathered by your colleagues.

2. Plan a parent workshop that will help parents become effective storybook readers. Present your workshop plan to the class.

PART TWO

Early Language and Literacy Instruction

4 Facilitating Early Language Learning

San Luis Preschool teacher Mrs. Lemos uses a commercially published curriculum to teach early language and literacy skills to the English language learners in her classroom. The curriculum is organized into thematic units focusing on broad themes that are of interest to young children. This month, Mrs. Lemos's class is studying building and construction. The curriculum has identified approximately twenty target words that are to be directly taught to children, including the names of tools (hammer, saw, safety goggles, tape measure, nails) and construction equipment (dump truck, backhoe, crane). On this particular day, Mrs. Lemos is teaching the target tool words. She begins circle time with the shared reading of a rhyme poster. While the primary function of the poster is to teach rhyme identification (a phonological awareness skill), Mrs. Lemos also highlights two tool words in the rhyme. She has children make a hand motion when hammer is mentioned and use their fingers to show how small the tiny little nails are. Next, Mrs. Lemos does a shared reading of a big book about a father and daughter building a doghouse. This informational book has very few text words but contains several photographs that contain pictures of tools. Even though the tools are not mentioned in the text, Mrs. Lemos pauses to discuss them. She first asks, "What kind of tools will they need to build the doghouse?" As she reads each page, she points to each of the tools in the illustrations and asks, "Does anyone know the name of this tool?" She chuckles when, after pointing to several nails in one picture, a child responds, "Tiny little nails," repeating the phrase used earlier in the rhyme poster. After the story is read, children go to center time. Mrs. Lemos has arranged the environment to provide additional opportunity to encounter and use tool words. Several regular-size copies of the doghouse book have been placed in the classroom library for independent or partner reading. There are black-line masters of tools for the children to color and label in the art center. Finally, the dramatic play center has a cardboard frame that resembles a doghouse, and it contains toy replicas of all of the tools mentioned in the doghouse book: plastic hammers, nails (actually wood golf tees), measuring tape, safety goggles, and toy circular saw. Two girls and a boy spend a half hour playing together, pretending to build a doghouse. In this play, the names of tools are used numerous times, and the children help each other learn how to properly use each tool. For example, one of the girls reminds the boy to put on his safety goggles when using the saw!

Research has shown that oral vocabulary is a strong predictor of elementary-grade reading comprehension (Dickinson & Tabors, 2001) and that strength of this relationship increases progressively from grade 1 to grade 7 (Snow, 2002). Other aspects of young children's oral language, including listening comprehension and grammar, also have important roles in later literacy achievement (National Early Literacy Panel, 2008).

Chapter 2 discussed how infants and toddlers learn their native language through complex social interactions with parents, siblings, and other caregivers. These individuals are essentially a child's first and most important teachers. Chapter 3 explained how, throughout the preschool years, the family plays a significant role in helping children become accomplished language users. We examined the talk that goes on in homes and described ways parents can support and enrich language development.

However, a child's family is not the only source of language stimulation. Preschool teachers can also play a crucial role in promoting language development, particularly in the case of children who are not exposed to rich language at home. In their extensive home–school study of young children's oral language environments, Patton Tabors, Catherine Snow, and David Dickinson (2001, p. 326) found that "excellent preschools can compensate for homes that offer well below average access to language and literacy support." Note that this applies to *excellent* preschools—schools where teachers expose children to rich language models and opportunities, like Mrs. Lemos in the example above.

In a recent chapter entitled "Characteristics of Classroom Environments Associated with Accelerated Literacy Development," Renée Casbergue, Lea McGee, and April Bedford (2008, p. 170) summarize research-based teacher practices in a language- and literacy-rich classroom:

- Teacher provides opportunities for extended talk.
- Teacher frequently uses rare words.
- Teacher frequently employs language extension activities.
- Teacher provides opportunities for children to use analytic and predictive talk.
- Teacher plans for conversations with children throughout the day.
- Teacher plays with and talks to children in centers.
- Teacher extends children's dramatic play by modeling new "scripts."

In this chapter, we examine the ways teachers can provide children with these types of excellent language learning activities. Strategies include rich teacher discourse, reciprocal conversations, classroom activities that encourage language use, activities that focus children's attention on language, and direct instruction on vocabulary.

Before Reading This Chapter, Think About . . .

- The conversations that took place in your classroom when you were in school. Were they mainly teacher-centered exchanges in which you and your classmates responded to questions asked by the teacher, or did you have the opportunity to engage in two-way conversations with the teacher and other students?
- Sharing or show-and-tell. What did you like about this activity? What, if anything, did you not like about it?
- The make-believe play you engaged in when you were a child. What were some of the favorite roles and themes that you acted out during this play?
- How was vocabulary taught by your teachers? Did they use picture cards, real objects, workbooks, dictionaries, or other methods to teach you the meaning of new words?

Focus Questions

- What is the initiation, response, evaluation (IRE) pattern of class talk? What problems are associated with this type of discourse? How can teachers provide students with more stimulating conversations in the classroom?
- How do group activities, learning centers, and dramatic play promote oral language acquisition?
- What can teachers do to promote language-rich dramatic play?
- How can sharing or show-and-tell be turned into a valuable oral language activity?
- How should teachers teach new vocabulary words?
- What can teachers do to optimize oral language experiences for bilingual and second-language learners?
- How can teachers encourage parents to extend language development at home?

Teacher Discourse

Every school day offers dozens of possibilities for verbal interactions (Smith & Dickinson, 1994). Unfortunately, research indicates that these opportunities are often overlooked in traditional transmission-oriented classrooms. Studies have shown that in many classrooms the teacher dominates the language environment, which does little to promote the children's oral language growth (Cazden, 1988; Howard, Shaughnessy, Sanger, & Hux, 1998; Wells, 1986). For example, in some classrooms:

- Teachers spend most of the time talking *to* rather than talking *with* children.
- Teachers dominate discussions by controlling how a topic is developed and who gets to talk.

BOX **2.1**

Definition of Terms

active listening: the listener combines the information provided by the speaker with his or her own prior knowledge to construct personal meaning.

dramatic play: an advanced form of play in which children take on roles and act out make-believe stories and situations.

initiation, response, evaluation (IRE): a pattern of classroom talk in which the teacher asks a question, a student answers, and the teacher either accepts or rejects that answer and then goes on to ask another question.

metalinguistic awareness: the ability to attend to language forms in and of themselves. For example, a child may notice that two words rhyme with each other.

metaplay language: comments about play itself ("I'll be the mommy, and you be the baby").

pretend language: comments that are appropriate for the roles that children have taken in dramatic play. For example, a child pretending to be a baby might say, "Waah! Waah!"

vocabulary: children's knowledge of word meanings.

- Children spend most of their time listening to teachers.
- When children do talk, it is usually to give a response to a question posed by the teacher.
- Teachers tend to ask testlike, closed-ended questions that have one correct answer (that the teacher already knows).

The typical pattern of classroom discourse is characterized by teacher initiation, student response, and teacher evaluation. In this *initiation, response, evaluation (IRE)* pattern, the teacher asks a question, a student answers, and the teacher either accepts or rejects that answer and goes on to ask another question (Galda, Cullinan, & Strickland, 1993). For example, before the following discussion, the kindergarten children had listened to *The Three Little Pigs.*

> **TEACHER:** What material did the pigs use to build their first house?
>
> **BOBBIE:** They used sticks.
>
> **TEACHER:** Yes. That is correct, the pigs used sticks for the first house. What did the pigs use to build the third house?
>
> **MANUEL:** They used cement.
>
> **TEACHER:** No. Who remembers what the book says? Jon?
>
> **JON:** Bricks.
>
> **TEACHER:** Yes. The pigs used bricks.

Notice how the teacher's questions are not real questions; rather, they test whether these young students recalled specific details of the story. Notice also that these children have no opportunity to construct their own meaning of the story by combining text information with their prior knowledge. For example, Manuel's answer, *cement,* suggests that Manuel was making inferences based on prior experience. The teacher's negative response to Manuel's comment probably communicates to him that it is incorrect to make inferences when reading. This response sends a message to students that one should recall exactly what is said in the text. Finally, notice that there is absolutely no interaction from student to student. The turn-taking pattern is teacher–student–teacher–student.

These types of IRE interactions are sometimes appropriate because teachers do need to get specific points across to students (Dyson & Genishi, 1984). Problems ensue, however, if this is the only type of talk that is taking place in the classroom. IRE discussions do not provide the type of language input and feedback that "advance children's knowledge of language structure and use" (Menyuk, 1988, p. 105). In addition, these teacher-dominated exchanges do not allow students to negotiate and build meaning through dialogue (Hansen, 1998).

What can early childhood teachers do to provide children with more stimulating experiences with language? We offer four recommendations:

1. Engage students in reciprocal discussions and conversations.
2. Provide ample opportunities for activity-centered language that invite (and, at times, require) students to use language to get things done.

3. Provide language-centered activities that focus students' attention on specific aspects of language.
4. Provide direct, systematic vocabulary instruction.

In the sections that follow, we present guidelines for implementing each of these recommendations.

Reciprocal Discussions and Conversations

Teachers' verbal interaction styles set the general tone for classroom language environments. The worst-case scenario occurs when a teacher insists on absolute silence except during teacher-led initiation, response, evaluation discussions. Such environments definitely limit continued oral language development. Other teachers provide ideal language environments by engaging students in genuine conversations, conducting stimulating reciprocal discussions, and allowing children to converse with each other at a moderate volume during classroom learning activities, using "inside voices" (soft voices that do not disrupt classroom learning).

Teachers have many opportunities to talk with students throughout the school day, ranging from one-to-one conversations to whole-group discussions. Following is an example of an effective conversation between Ms. E., a preschool teacher, and Roberto, age four:

ROBERTO: See my new backpack, Teacher?

MS. E.: What a neat backpack, Roberto. Show it to me.

ROBERTO: It has six zippers. See? The pouches hold different stuff. Isn't it neat?

MS. E.: I like the different-size pouches. Look, this one is just right for a water bottle.

ROBERTO: Yeah. The arm straps are great too. See, I can make 'em longer.

MS. E.: Yes [nods and smiles]. It fits your arms perfectly. Where did you get this nifty backpack?

ROBERTO: We got it at the mall.

MS. E.: What store in the mall?

ROBERTO: The one that has all the camping stuff.

MS. E.: The Camping Plus store?

ROBERTO: Yeah. That's the one.

Notice how Ms. E. allowed Roberto to take the lead by listening carefully to what he said and by responding to his previous statements. She let him do most of talking, using back channeling (nodding and smiling) to keep the conversation going. Ms. E. asked only three questions, and they were genuine: she wanted to know where Roberto purchased the backpack.

Reciprocal conversations are not restricted to one-to-one situations. Teachers can also engage children in genuine discussions pertaining to ongoing instructional activities. Cory Hansen (1998) gives an example of group discussion of George MacDonald's 1872 classic, *The Princess and the Goblin* (Puffin Books). The chapter book is being discussed by a group of kindergarten students in Chris Boyd's classroom.

Previously in the story, the grandmother had given the princess a gift of a glowing ring from which a thread would lead her to comfort if she were frightened. The princess assumed it would lead her to her grandmother, but one night it led her deep into a cave and stopped at a heap of stones. The chapter ("Irene's Clue") ends with the princess bursting into tears at the foot of the rocks. Curdie, the fearless miner's son, was missing.

PEARSON
myeducationkit™

Go to the Assignments and Activities section of Chapter 4 in the MyEducationKit and complete the activity entitled "Conducting an Investigation: Small Group Taste Test Activity." As you watch the video and answer the accompanying questions, note how the small group setting and the teacher's informal, responsive style promotes reciprocal conversations with the children about the "taste test."

JOSEPH: I think that Curdie's on the other side of the rocks.

MRS. B.:   Where'd you get the clue for that?

ANNA: Because the strings led her to the mountain. That means it was close to Curdie because Curdie lived by the mountain.

KIM: Maybe Curdie's on the other side of the stones!

JAMAL: I think her grandmother was a goblin since she could have went through the rocks.

JORDAN: I know. Maybe—when she was falling asleep on the other side—but how could the goblins be that fast?

ANNA: Because they're magic.

RICHARD: I know how Curdie got to the other side.

JOSEPH: Maybe Curdie's in the heap of stones.

MRS. B.:   What makes you say that?

JOSEPH: Because in the last chapter—"Curdie's Clue"—it said they piled the rock—a big stone in the mouth of the cave.

KIM: The grandmother said the ring always led to the grandmother's bedroom so she . . .

ANNA: No it didn't. It said, "This will take me to you—wherever it takes you, you go." And the grandmother said, "Wherever it takes you, you will go."

MRS. B.:   Can you think of any reason why the princess should go to the cave?

JOSEPH: Because it said, "You must not doubt the string."

ADAM: The grandmother said the thread would lead to her but it ended up leading her to Curdie.

ALONDRA: I think the grandmother knows about Curdie.

KIM: It's because her grandmother wanted her to save Curdie!

ANNA: That was the clue.

JAMAL: To get Curdie out cuz she know about him.

JOSEPH: Yeah. (Hansen, 1998, pp. 172–173)

Here, Mrs. B. let the students take the lead by listening closely to what they said and responding to their comments. Her questions were genuine (she did not know what the children's responses would be) and were open-ended in nature ("What makes you say that?"). By welcoming the children's viewpoints, she encouraged them to bring their personal interpretations to the story. Also notice that the children talked to each other; they engaged in real conversations. The teacher facilitated this child–child turn-taking pattern by encouraging the students to respond to others' ideas.

Ms. E.'s and Mrs. B.'s effective use of reciprocal questions allowed students to engage in authentic discussion with the teacher and each other. Obviously, the way a teacher interacts with children influences the way children communicate. Therefore, it is important for teachers to reflect on the quality of their conversations and discussions with students of all ages.

As teachers work with the students in their classrooms it is important to remember that many children do not speak academic or "standard" English. Teachers must be sensitive and respectful to the wide range of dialects they hear, always remembering that the language of the child's home must be valued even as teachers help children learn a more academic vocabulary. Special Feature 4.1 offers some guidance for teachers in understanding and supporting language variation.

SPECIAL FEATURE 4.1
Understanding and Supporting Language Variation

Welcome to my home. Please, do come in.
Hey yaw'l. Jes come rite-on in ta mah plaaace.
Dude, catch the pad. Wanna crash?

As you read the sentences above, did you begin to form mental images about the speakers? Did you make predictions about their ages, places of origins, and social status? If you did, then you are not alone; the study of dialects offers a fascinating look at how the language we use is linked to our social identity. Likewise, the study of dialects often provides the most vivid illustration of how language changes over time (Hazen, 2001).

Many people believe that there is only one correct form of English, what is often called Standard English. According to this view, the phrase "My sister is not home" will always be preferred to the phrase "My sister ain't home." Linguists, however, suggest that what is appropriate language depends on the situation. In many contexts, "My sister ain't home" is more acceptable. This wording, called Rhetorically Correct English, suggests

that what is "correct" varies and is governed by the speaker's intention, the audience, and the context (Crystal, 1995; Demo, 2000).

Unfortunately, dialect discrimination is widely tolerated in the United States. Many people believe that there is only one kind of appropriate English that all children should learn and that all teachers should be required to teach. Today, however, even this long-held view is being challenged. In the mid-1990s, the Oakland, California, school board proposed that Ebonics be accepted as a school language. The outcry against this idea was national: the frequent response was that only Standard English should be taught in schools. When educator-linguist Lisa Delpit (1997, p. 6) was asked if she was for or against Ebonics her answer was complex:

> My answer must be neither. I can be neither for Ebonics nor against Ebonics any more than I can be for or against air. It exists. It is the language spoken by many of our African-American children. It is the language they heard as their

(continued)

mothers nursed them and changed their diapers and played peek-a-boo with them. It is the language through which they first encountered love, nurturance, and joy. On the other hand, most teachers of those African-American children who have been least well-served by the educational system believe that their students' chances will be further hampered if they do not learn Standard English. In the stratified society in which we live, they are absolutely correct.

As Delpit suggests, no matter how accepting teachers may be of a child's home language in the classroom, a child's dialect may serve as a source of discrimination as he or she matures. So what is the role of the teacher? According to Lily Wong-Fillmore and Catherine Snow (2000, p. 20), "Teachers must provide children the support needed to master the English required for academic development and for jobs when they have completed school. However, this process does not work when the language spoken by the children—the language of their families and primary communities—is disrespected in school."

In summary, teachers need to teach children the dialect of school and work. To accomplish this goal, teachers need to provide the same type of scaffolding parents used when children were first learning to talk (Manning-Kratcoski & Bobkoff-Katz, 1998). Teachers must extend and expand children's language in a respectful manner, for example, as a simple expansion:

CHILD: That ain't right

TEACHER: I agree, this isn't right.

Notice how the teacher recasts the child's effort in Standard English. Notice also that the teacher does not emphasize the correct form, but uses it naturally. When adults use expansions, they introduce and help children build new vocabulary.

Contexts That Encourage Language Use

What students say and do is greatly influenced by where they are and what is around them. For example, as Evan played in the snow, he learned snow-related vocabulary with his family. Teachers must create dynamic learning environments that are contexts for language development. In other words, the curriculum must give children something to talk about. In the following section, we describe how teachers can use group activities, learning centers, and dramatic play to expand students' learning and opportunities to use language.

Group Activities

Teachers can support language by involving children in group activities that encourage, and at times necessitate, verbal interaction. What sort of activities would require children to talk? As Celia Genishi (1987) points out, "Almost every object or activity presents an opportunity for talk when teachers allow it to" (p. 99). Likewise, researchers Susan Burns, Peg Griffin, and Catherine Snow (1999) suggest that "sociodramatic play activities give children a chance to develop language and literacy skills, a deeper understanding of narrative, and their own personal responses to stories" (p. 72). In the following vignette, we provide an illustration of a whole-group activity that required a rather large group of multilingual, four-year-old children to reveal and assert needs and wants and connect with themselves and others.

The young students have been learning about manners and balanced meals. As part of a culminating activity, the entire room has been transformed into a restaurant. Twelve little tables are draped with tablecloths, and on each table sits a vase of flowers. Today, the teachers are waitresses, and a few parents have volunteered to cook real food. The children must choose between the Panda Café (spaghetti, meatballs, garlic toast, juice or milk) or the Café Mexico (burrito, chips, salsa, juice or milk). Each café has a menu with words and pictures. The children must select the specific items they wish to eat and give their orders to the waitress. The waitress takes the children's orders on an order form and gives the order form to the cooks. The cooks fill the orders exactly as the children request. Then, the waitress returns with the food and the order form and asks the children to review the order.

TEACHER: What café would you like, sir?

ROBERTO: [Points to menu.]

TEACHER: Which café? You must tell me.

ROBERTO: The Café Mexico.

TEACHER: Right this way, sir. Here is your menu. Take a moment to decide what you want to eat. I'll be right back to take your order.

ROBERTO: [Looks over the menu and shares his choices with his friend by pointing to the items he wants.]

TEACHER: OK, sir. What would you like?

ROBERTO: [Points to the items on the menu.]

TEACHER: Please, sir. You will have to tell me.

ROBERTO: [Hesitates for a few seconds.] I want the burrito and chips and juice.

TEACHER: Do you want salsa? [She leans over so he can see her mark the items on the order form.]

ROBERTO: No. [Firmly.]

Notice how the teachers organized this activity so that the children had to verbally express their needs multiple times throughout the restaurant adventure. In addition, the children had many opportunities to see how print is used in real life. Teachers, however, are not the only valuable source of language input. Children can also gain valuable oral language practice from talking with peers who are not as skilled as adults in initiating and maintaining conversations. To encourage peer-to-peer interactions, these teachers also created a miniature version of the restaurant in a dramatic play learning center. In this center, Roberto and his classmates will be able to play restaurant together for a few weeks.

As teachers of children observe their students in a variety of learning situations that require the children to use their language skills, they will often notice some who are having difficulty with the production of speech. Good teachers know that children with speech challenges and language delays should receive specialized support, as explained in the section on helping children with special needs at the end of this chapter.

Learning Centers

Because children's learning and language is greatly influenced by their environment, good teachers guide children's language development through the deliberate structuring of the

Go to the Assignments and
Activities section of Chapter 4
in the MyEducationKit and
complete the activity entitled
"Learning Centers." As you
watch the video and answer
the accompanying questions,
note how the learning centers
are clearly defined and articulated so that children know
what to do in each area.

classroom environment. For example, the teachers in the previous vignette
created a restaurant to encourage talk about food, ordering meals, taking
orders, cooking meals, and the like. Later, as the children interacted
together in the restaurant play center, they continued to help each other
build and reinforce their knowledge of restaurants. In learning center classrooms, the teacher's role is to set up the environment, observe as children
interact with the materials, supply help and guidance when needed, and
engage in conversations with the children around the materials and the children's use in their learning. A good deal of the teacher's effort is expended
on the setting-up or preparation phase. Centers are created when the teacher
carves the classroom space into defined areas. Readers seeking more information on establishing centers will find *The Creative Curriculum for Early
Childhood Education* (Dodge & Colker, 1992) a useful resource. This book
presents detailed, easy-to-follow instructions for setting up popular interest
areas (centers). It also contains practical tips on schedules, routines, and
other aspects of classroom management, plus good suggestions for encouraging parental
involvement.

Dramatic Play

Another context for activity-centered language is *dramatic play*, which occurs when children take on roles and use make-believe transformations to act out situations and stories
episodes. For example, several children might adopt the roles of family members and pretend to prepare dinner, or they may become superheroes who are engaged in fantastic
adventures. This type of play—also called sociodramatic, make-believe, pretend, or imaginative play—reaches its peak between the ages of four and seven.

Go to the Assignments and
Activities section of Chapter 4
in the MyEducationKit and
complete the activity entitled
"The Restaurant." As you
watch the video and answer
the accompanying questions,
note how the teacher encourages rich language by taking
on the role of customer and
joining in the restaurant play.
Also, observe how, once the
teacher leaves the play, the
children continue to engage
in complex play-related
conversations.

Although to some dramatic play appears simple and frivolous at
first glance, close inspection reveals that it is quite complex and places
heavy linguistic demands on children (Burns et al., 1999; Fessler, 1998).
In fact, Jerome Bruner (1983, p. 65) reported that "the most complicated
grammatical and pragmatic forms of language appear first in play activity." When children work together to act out stories, they face formidable
language challenges. They not only need to use language to act out their
dramas, but they must also use language to organize the play and keep it
going. Before starting, they must recruit other players, assign roles,
decide on the make-believe identities of objects (e.g., that a block of
wood will be used as if it were a telephone), and plan the story line. Once
started, language must be used to act out the story, keep the dramatization heading in the right direction (e.g., be sure that everyone is doing
things appropriate to their role), and reenergize the play if it is becoming
repetitious and boring.

To accomplish these tasks, children must use two different types
of language: (1) *pretend language* that is appropriate for their roles and
(2) *metaplay language* about the play itself. Children switch between
their pretend roles and their real identities when making these two types

of comments. This linguistic complexity is illustrated in the following example (Johnson, et al. 1999, p. 1):

> Three preschoolers are enacting a domestic scene in their classroom's housekeeping corner. John has taken the role of the father; Wendy is the mother; and George, the youngest of the three, has reluctantly agreed to be the baby.

WENDY: Baby looks hungry. Let's cook him some food. [Pretend.]

JOHN: Okay. [Pretend.]

WENDY: [Addressing George.] Cry and say that you're hungry. [Metaplay]

GEORGE: But I'm not hungry. [Metaplay]

WENDY: Pretend that you are! [Metaplay]

GEORGE: [Using a babyish voice.] I'm hungry. [Pretend.]

WENDY: [Addressing John.] Father, what should we have for dinner? [Pretend.]

JOHN: How about eggs? [Pretend.]

WENDY: I'll go get some eggs from the 'frigerator. [She goes to a wall shelf and takes several cube-shaped blocks.] [Pretend.]

GEORGE: Aah! I'm hungry! [Pretend.]

WENDY: [Pretending to scold George.] Be quiet! [She puts the blocks in a toy pan and places the pan on the toy stove.] The eggs are cooking. Father, you'd better set the table.

JOHN: Okay. [Pretend.]

GEORGE: Let me help, Daddy. [Pretend.]

JOHN: No! Babies don't set tables! You're just supposed to sit there and cry. [Metaplay]

In this example, Wendy is in her role as mother when she makes her initial comment about the baby. She reverts to real-life identity when she tells George what to say next and to pretend to be hungry. Then she shifts back to the role of mother when she asks father what he wants for dinner.

To take full advantage of dramatic play's potential as a medium for language development, attention needs to be given to three factors: (1) the settings in which play occurs, (2) the amount of time allocated for play activities, and (3) the type of teacher involvement in play episodes.

It is important to remember that children play best at what they already know. Therefore, dramatic play settings need to be familiar to children and consistent with their culture (Neuman, 1995). For example, the domestic play themes, such as parents caring for a baby or a family eating a meal, are very popular with young children because these are the roles and activities with which they are most familiar. For this reason, we recommend that preschool and kindergarten classrooms contain a housekeeping play center equipped with props that remind children of their own homes. Not only do such centers encourage dramatic play, but they also provide a context in which children can display the types of literacy activities they have observed at home.

The range of children's play themes and related literacy activities can be greatly expanded by the addition of a theme center to the classroom. These centers have props and furniture that suggest specific settings that are familiar to children, such as a veterinarian's

Dramatic play is an ideal medium for promoting oral language development.

office, restaurant, bank, post office, ice cream parlor, fast-food restaurant, and grocery store. (Table 4.1 contains lists of literacy materials that can be used in a variety of theme centers.) For example, a veterinarian's office might be divided into two areas: a waiting room with a table for a receptionist and chairs for patients, and an examination room with another table, chairs, and a variety of medical props (doctor's kit, scales, etc.). Stuffed animals can be provided as patients. Theme-related literacy materials—appointment book, patient folders, prescription forms, wall signs, and so on—should also be included to encourage children to reenact the literacy activities they have observed in these settings. Children will use their knowledge of visits to the doctor to engage in play with their peers. The following scenario illustrates how three preschoolers verbalize their knowledge of what occurs at the animal hospital.

SERGIO: [The vet is looking at the clipboard.] It says here that Ruffy is sick with worms.

MARIE: [Owner of a toy kitty named Ruffy.] Yep, uh huh. I think she ate bad worms.

SERGIO: That means we gotta operate and give Ruffy big horse pills for those worms.

JOY: [The nurse.] Okay, sign here. [Hands Marie a big stack of papers.] Sign 'em all. Then we'll operate. But you gotta stay out in the people room. You could faint if you stay in here.

TABLE 4.1 Literacy Materials Added to Play Settings in the Christie and Enz Study

Home Center	Business Office
Pencils, pens, markers	Pencils, pens, markers
Note pads	Note pads
Post-it notes	Telephone message forms
Baby-sitter instruction forms	Calendar
Telephone book	Typewriter
Telephone message pads	Order forms
Message board	Stationery, envelopes, stamps
Children's books	File folders
Magazines, newspapers	Wall signs
Cookbooks, recipe box	
Product containers from children's homes	
Junk mail	

Restaurant	Post Office
Pencils	Pencils, pens, markers
Note pads	Stationery and envelopes
Menus	Stamps
Wall signs ("Pay Here")	Mailboxes
Bank checks	Address labels
Cookbooks	Wall signs ("Line Starts Here")
Product containers	

Grocery Store	Veterinarian's Office
Pencils, pens, markers	Pencils, pens, markers
Note pads	Appointment book
Bank checks	Wall signs ("Receptionist")
Wall signs ("Supermarket")	Labels with pets' names
Shelf labels for store areas ("Meat")	Patient charts
Product containers	Prescription forms
	Magazines (in waiting room)

Airport/Airplane	Library
Pencils, pens, markers	Pencils
Tickets	Books
Bank checks	Shelf labels for books
Luggage tags	("ABCs," "Animals")
Magazines (on-board plane)	Wall signs ("Quiet!")
Air sickness bags with printed instructions	Library cards
Maps	Checkout cards for books
Signs ("Baggage Claim Area")	

Carol Woodard (1984), a teacher who has had considerable success with theme centers in her university's laboratory preschool, recommends that one theme center be introduced at a time and left for several weeks. Then the center can be transformed into another theme. She also advises locating these centers near the permanent housekeeping center so that children can integrate the theme center activities with their domestic play. Children acting as parents for dolls, pets, or peers in the housekeeping area might, for example, take a sick baby to the doctor theme center for an examination. Or, children might weld or examine cars in the classroom garage (Hall & Robinson, 1995). Woodard found that children, particularly boys, began engaging in more dramatic play when the theme centers were introduced.

Dramatic play requires providing a considerable amount of time for children to plan and initiate. If play periods are short, then children have to stop their dramatizations right after they have started. When that happens frequently, children tend to switch to less advanced forms of play, such as functional (motor) play or simple construction activity, which can be completed in brief sessions.

Research has shown that preschoolers are much more likely to engage in rich, sustained dramatic play during thirty-minute play periods than during shorter fifteen-minute sessions (Christie, Johnsen, & Peckover, 1988). Our experience indicates that even longer periods are needed. For example, Billie Enz and Jim Christie (1997) spent a semester observing a preschool classroom that had forty-minute play periods. Very often, the four-year-olds had just finished preparing for a dramatization when it was time to clean up. Fortunately, the teachers were flexible and often let the children have an extra ten to fifteen minutes to act out their dramas. We recommend that center time last for at least sixty minutes whenever possible.

For many years, it was believed that teachers should just set the stage and not get directly involved in children's play activities. This hands-off stance toward play has been seriously challenged by a growing body of research that suggests that classroom play can be enriched through teacher participation. Teacher involvement has been found to assist non-players to begin to engage in dramatic play, to help more proficient players enrich and extend their dramatizations, and to encourage children to incorporate literacy into their play episodes (Enz & Christie, 1997; Roskos & Neuman, 1993). Teachers, however, need to use caution because overzealous or inappropriate forms of involvement can interfere with ongoing play and can sometimes cause children to quit playing altogether (Enz & Christie, 1997).

The simplest and least intrusive type of teacher involvement in play is observation. By watching children as they play, teachers demonstrate that they are interested in the children's play and that play is a valuable, worthwhile activity. Observation alone can lead to more sustained play. Jerome Bruner (1980) reported that preschoolers' play episodes lasted roughly twice as long when a teacher was nearby and observing than when children played completely on their own. In addition, the children were more likely to move toward more elaborate forms of play when an adult was looking on.

Observation can also provide clues about when more direct forms of teacher involvement in play are appropriate. A teacher may find that, despite conducive play settings, some children rarely engage in dramatic play. Or, the teacher may notice that there is an opportunity to extend or enrich an ongoing play episode, perhaps by introducing some new element or problem for children to solve (Hall, 1999). Both situations call for active teacher involvement.

Chapter 5 describes three roles that are ideal for initiating and extending dramatic play: the stage manager role, in which the teacher supplies props and offers ideas to enrich play; the coplayer role, in which the teacher actually takes on a role and joins in the children's play; and the play leader, who stimulates play by introducing, in a role, some type of problem to be resolved. (For more information about these roles and other roles that teachers can adopt during play, see Jones and Reynolds, 1992.)

In addition to promoting language acquisition, dramatic play encourages children to help one another learn academic skills and content (Hansen, 1998; Christie & Stone, 1999), make friends, and develop important social skills (Garvey, 1977). Peer-to-peer interaction is particularly important for the growing numbers of students who are learning English as a second language and need help with more basic aspects of oral language (Fessler, 1998). For these reasons, dramatic play centers need to be a prominent feature in early childhood classrooms.

Language-Centered Activities for Children

Beyond creating contexts that encourage language and facilitate verbal interactions, teachers can also provide activities that focus specifically on language. Read-alouds, sharing, storytelling, and language play all fall into this category. Storybook reading can be an ideal context for promoting attentive listening and oral discussion skills, as will be discussed in Chapter 5. We discuss the remaining four language-centered activities below.

PEARSON
myeducationkit™

Go to the Assignments and Activities section of Chapter 4 in the MyEducationKit and complete the activity entitled "Active Listening." As you read the artifact and answer the accompanying questions, note how these activities focus on a specific language skill: active listening. This is why the activity is "language-centered."

Sharing

Sharing, or show-and-tell, is a strategy designed to promote students' speaking and listening abilities. Traditionally, sharing has been a whole-class activity in which one child after another gets up, takes center stage, and talks about something of her or his own choosing, often some object brought from home (Gallas, 1992). Children in the audience are expected to listen quietly and not participate.

In this traditional format, sharing is not a very productive language experience for the child who is speaking or for those who are listening. The large group size can intimidate the speaker and reduce participation because only a small percentage of students get to share on a given day. If many students share, it becomes a very drawn-out, boring affair. The lack of participation on the part of the audience leads to poor listening behavior. Listening is an active, constructive process in which listeners combine information provided by a speaker with their own prior knowledge to build personal meaning. Mary Jalongo (1995) relates a teacher's definition of listening that captures the essences of *active listening*: "It is hearing and making and shaping what you heard—along with your own ideas—into usable pieces of knowledge" (p. 14). The passive role of the audience in traditional sharing works against this process.

With two modifications, sharing can be transformed into an exceptionally worthwhile language activity. First, group size should be "small enough to reduce shyness, encourage interaction, permit listeners to examine the object, and afford everyone a long enough turn without tiring the group" (Moffett & Wagner, 1983, p. 84). Groups of three to six students are ideal for this purpose. Second, listeners should be encouraged to participate by asking questions of the child who is sharing. "Let the sharer/teller begin as she will. When she has said all that initially occurs to her, encourage the audience by solicitation and example to ask natural questions" (Moffett & Wagner, 1983, p. 84). The teacher's role is to model questioning that encourages elaboration and clarification (When did you get? What happened next? What's that for?). After asking one or two questions, teachers should pause and encourage the audience to participate. Prompts (Does anyone have questions for Suzy?) may sometimes be needed to get the process started. Once children realize that it is acceptable for them to participate, prompting will no longer be necessary.

This peer questioning stimulates active listening by giving the audience a reason to listen to the child who is sharing. Children know that to ask relevant questions they are going to have to listen very carefully to what the sharer has to say. The child who is sharing benefits as well. Children can be encouraged to elaborate their brief utterances or organize their content more effectively and to state it more clearly (Moffett & Wagner, 1983).

Teachers can add variety to sharing by occasionally giving it a special focus. For instance, they can ask students to bring in an item that:

- Has a good story behind it, which encourages narrative discourse
- They made or grew, which facilitates explanation or description
- Works in a funny or interesting way, which fosters expositive communication

Storytelling

Telling stories to children is also very worthwhile. The direct connection between the teller and audience promotes enjoyment and active listening. Marie Clay (1989) describes some of the values of storytelling:

> Storytelling is more direct than story reading. Facial expressions, gestures, intonations, the length of pauses, and the interactions with the children's responses create a more direct contact with the audience, dramatic in effect. The meaning can be closer to the children's own experiences because the teller can change the words, add a little explanation, or translate loosely into a local experience. (p. 24)

The first stories that children tell usually involve real-life experiences: they relate something that has happened to them. Sharing can be an ideal context to allow children to tell these types of stories in the classroom. Small-group, interactive sharing provides feedback that enables children to tell clearer, better-organized stories about personal experiences (Canizares, 1997).

Some children need assistance in broadening the range of their storytelling to imaginative, fictional stories. The following suggestions can help with this task.

- Open up the sharing period to include fantasy stories. Once teachers begin permitting their children to tell "fictional" stories, the children may begin sharing imaginative, creative stories that feature language that is much richer than that used in their show-and-tell sharing (Gallas, 1992).
- Encourage children to retell the stories contained in their favorite storybooks. Books remove the burden of creating an original story to tell. Story retelling has other benefits

for children, including enhanced oral fluency and expression and improved story comprehension (Morrow, 1985).

■ Have children make up words for the stories in wordless picture books, such as *Pancakes for Breakfast* by Tomie dePaola (Harcourt, Brace, Jovanovich, 1978). Here again, the book is providing the content for the child's story.

■ Link storytelling with play and writing. Vivian Paley (1990) has developed a strategy in which children come to a story table and dictate a story that the teacher writes down. During this dictation, the teacher asks the children to clarify any parts of the story that are unclear or difficult to understand. The teacher reads the story plays to the class. Finally, children serve as directors and invite classmates to join in acting out their stories. Children enjoy watching their stories dramatized, motivating them to create additional imaginative stories.

Language Play

In addition to using language in their dramatic play, children also play with language. This intentional "messing around" with language begins as soon as children have passed through the babbling stage and have begun to make words (Garvey, 1977). This play involves the phonological, syntactic, and semantic aspects of language. By age two, language play becomes quite sophisticated. Ruth Weir (1962) placed a tape recorder in her two-and-a-half-year-old son Anthony's crib and turned it on after he had been placed in his crib for the evening. During this presleep time, Anthony engaged in an extensive amount of systematic language play. He experimented with speech sounds ("Babette Back here Wet"), substituted words of the same grammatical category ("What color. What color blanket. What color mop. What color glass."), and replaced nouns with appropriate pronouns ("Take the monkey. Take it." and "Stop it. Stop the ball. Stop it."). These monologues constituted play because language was being manipulated for its own sake rather than being used to communicate.

Young children also make attempts at humor, playing with semantic aspects of language. Kornei Chukovsky (1976) explains that "hardly has the child comprehended with certainty which objects go together and which do not, when he begins to listen happily to verses of absurdity" (p. 601). This play, in turn, leads children to make up their own nonsense. Chukovsky uses his two-year-old daughter as an example. Shortly after she had learned that dogs say "bow wow" and cats say "miaow," she approached him and said, "Daddy, 'oggie— miaow!" and laughed. It was his daughter's first joke!

Children gain valuable practice while engaging in these types of language play. They also begin to acquire *metalinguistic awareness*, the ability to attend to language forms as objects in and of themselves. Courtney Cazden (1976) explains that when language is used for its normal function—to communicate meaning—language forms become transparent. We "hear through them" to get the intended message (p. 603). When children play with language, the situation is reversed. The focus is on the language, on the grammatical rules and semantic relationships they are manipulating.

The type of language play children engage in is also age related (Geller, 1982). At age three, children like to repeat traditional rhymes ("Mary had a little lamb"). They eventually begin to make up their own nonsense rhymes, playing with sound patterns ("Shama sheema / Mash day n' pash day"). By ages five and six, children delight in verbal nonsense

("I saw Superman flying out there!") and chanting games ("Cinderella, dressed in yellow / Went upstairs to kiss her fellow / How many kisses did she get? / 1, 2, 3, 4, 5"), which are forms themselves rather than meaning. Children become aware of the sounds ("Teddy bear, Teddy bear, turn around, Teddy bear, Teddy bear, touch the ground").

The obvious educational implication is that language play should be encouraged and supported at school (Cazden, 1976). Judith Schwartz (1983) recommends that teachers try three things to stimulate their students to play with language:

1. Teachers should create a climate that allows play to flourish, a classroom atmosphere in which "children and teacher laugh easily and often."
2. Teachers should serve as a model by sharing humorous anecdotes, word play, folk literature, jokes, and stories with children and by using gentle humor in interpersonal relationships with children.
3. Teachers should value each child's contributions by allowing many opportunities for sharing oral and written language play.

Songs and Finger Plays

Sitting on the floor with a small group of preschoolers, Ms. K. begins:

> *Where is Thumbkin?*
> *Where is Thumbkin?*
> *Here I am! Here I am!*
> *How are you today, sir?*
> *Very well, I thank you.*
> *Run away, Run away.*

The three- and four-year-old children quickly join in and immediately start the finger movements that accompany this familiar song. Very young children love to sing. The human fondness for a catchy tune and a snappy, clever rhyme begins early. Beginning in infancy and continuing on throughout their childhood, children experiment with their voices and the sounds that they can make. Singing encourages risk-free language play, especially for children who are learning a second language (Freeman & Freeman, 1994; Jackman, 1997). Singing songs in a new language allows children to make safe mistakes as they experiment with the new phonemic system, in a similar way as toddlers may begin to sing jingles they hear on the television long before they can actually speak in full sentences. As noted in a report by Catherine Snow and her colleagues (1998), singing songs is an important literacy activity.

Therefore, teachers of young children would be wise to build in singing as part of their language arts curriculum (Collins, 1997). In particular, children enjoy songs that offer repetition and chorus, such as "Polly Put the Kettle On," "Mary Had a Little Lamb," and "Here We Go Round the Mulberry Bush"; provide repeated words or phrases that can be treated like an echo, such as "Miss Mary Mack" and "She'll Be Comin' Round the Mountain"; require sound effects or animal noises, such as "If You're Happy and You Know It" and "Old MacDonald Had a Farm"; tell a story, such as "Hush, Little Baby," "Humpty Dumpty," and "Little Bo Peep"; and ask questions, such as "Where Is Thumbkin?" and "Do

You Know the Muffin Man?" In addition to singing, many songs or poems include finger plays. Do you recall the "Itsy-Bitsy Spider" and how your fingers became the spider that climbed up the waterspout? Children's minds are fully engaged when they act out the words of a song or poem with their fingers (Collins, 1997).

Many preschool and kindergarten teachers write the songs the children love to sing on chart paper or purchase the big book format of these beloved songs. As the children sing, the teacher uses a pointer to underline each word. The follow-the-bouncing-ball approach to teaching reading is quite effective with some children (Segal & Adcock, 1986). Singing is a wonderful way for children to play with and enjoy language.

Vocabulary Instruction

Vocabulary refers to children's knowledge of word meanings. While vocabulary acquisition is one of the key components of oral language development, it also plays an important role in early literacy. Research has shown that the size of children's vocabulary at age three is strongly associated with reading comprehension at the end of third grade (Hart & Risley, 2003). Research has also shown that vocabulary growth is promoted through direct instruction of targeted words and by arranging experiences so that children encounter these targeted words frequently in different contexts (McCardle & Chhabra, 2004). Because vocabulary size and rate of growth are central to the acquisition of early literacy skills, vocabulary development is one of the key instructional objectives in scientifically based reading research (SBRR) curriculums.

Vocabulary learning can be promoted through direct instruction of word meanings (Biemiller, 2004) and through incidental learning from contexts that provide rich verbal opportunities (Biemiller, 2004; Roskos, Tabors, & Lenhart, 2009; Weizman & Snow, 2001). Early childhood teachers have traditionally used incidental approaches to provide vocabulary instruction, looking for "teachable moments" during storybook reading and classroom conversations to build children's knowledge of word meanings. What is new in SBRR programs is that vocabulary instruction is intentional and preplanned, as well as incidental. Specifically, teachers decide in advance to teach selected words to children, and both high-utility root words (Biemiller & Slonim, 2001) and "rare words" (Hirsch, 2003) are targeted for instruction. High-utility root words refer to uninflected words that occur with high frequency in oral language. These words are useful to know because they can be used to create many related words (*move > moved, moveable, remove,* etc.). Rare words refer to specialized vocabulary needed for development of domain knowledge in content areas (e.g., *excavate, backhoe, scoop, blueprint, plaster,* etc.). Often, these targeted words are connected to other parts of the academic curriculum—an ongoing thematic unit, books that are being read, field trips, and so on. These vocabulary–curriculum connections provide opportunities for children to encounter the targeted words repeatedly in a short period of time—a crucial factor in word learning (Stahl, 2003). The vignette of Mrs. Lemos's vocabulary instruction at the beginning of this chapter is an excellent example of this type of integrated teaching.

Given the important role of vocabulary in early and later literacy development and that many children from low-income families tend to lag far behind their middle-class peers in learning new words (Hart & Risley, 1995), one would expect vocabulary to be a high instructional priority in preschool, kindergarten, and the middle grades. Unfortunately, this is not the case. Susan Neuman and Julie Dwyer (2009) report that vocabulary instruction is "missing in action" in early education. They cite research by Beck and McKeown (2007) and the research synthesis by the National Reading Panel (2000) as showing that little explicit, intentional teaching of vocabulary occurs in pre-K, kindergarten, and the primary grades. In addition, Neuman and Dwyer found that the major commercially published early literacy curriculums do a mediocre job of systematically teaching vocabulary.

Day care, preschool, and kindergarten teachers must consistently work to enhance children's language development. Fortunately, the school day offers numerous opportunities for both direct instruction and incidental oral interactions. However, teachers of young children must be diligent and mindful to create vocabulary learning moments. Kathy Roskos, Patton Tabors, and Lisa Lenhart (2009) suggest that teachers who are also playful, planful, and purposeful are successful in helping children to develop oral language competence and simultaneously expand their vocabulary.

Trade Secret 4.1 demonstrates how Ms. V., a kindergarten teacher, playfully, planfully, and purposefully employs classroom routines to intentionally offer explicit vocabulary instruction.

TRADE SECRET 4.1
Explicit Vocabulary Instruction

Ms. V. is working with predominantly English-speaking kindergarten children from lower-socioeconomic homes. Most of these children are able to share their wants and needs and express their feelings, but Ms. V. has noticed that most of the children have limited vocabularies. Her *purpose* is to help them build expressive vocabulary. The scenario below describes Ms. V.'s explicit vocabulary activities beginning with a game she *plays* with the children once or twice a week. She usually *plans* her target words to extend a storybook or a social studies or science lesson. Ms. V. begins by explicitly introducing new vocabulary words to the children the minute they enter the classroom.

- *Morning greeting.* "Martine, you are clever," whispers Ms. V. into Martine's ear. Moving to Jorge, she again whispers, "Jorge, you are so smart." Kevin is next; Ms. V. whispers, "Kevin, you are so bright." And she repeats the procedure with several more

children, as the class assembles for group time.
- *Group time.* Ms. V. continues to extend the new words *clever, smart,* and *bright* during group time. She tells the class, "I whispered a word to many of you this morning as you came in the door. But I didn't use exactly the same word. So listen closely! If I told you that you were clever, please stand up!" Four children stand. "Great. This is the word *clever* [holding a word card that will later go on the vocabulary word wall]. If I told you that you were smart, stand up! If I told you that you were bright, stand up!" She asks the children to repeat the words on the card as she points to them on the chalkboard. Then she asks the children, "What do you think is the meaning of these words? Turn to your neighbor and tell them what *smart* means. Can some of you share your ideas? Do you agree? Smart means knowing a lot of things? Okay, what does

---

TRADE SECRET 4.1 Continued

clever mean? Tell another partner." Children begin to offer their ideas; Ms. V. listens and nods. She says, "Jason and Gabby think *clever* also means someone knows a lot of stuff but they might be sort of tricky. What do the rest of you think?" Now the children discuss *bright*. Two young ladies, Hannah and Emma, suggest *bright* may have something to do with knowing a lot of stuff, but it also means really colorful, like Rainbow Brite dolls. Ms V. takes a large piece of construction paper and asks the children if they can agree that *bright, clever,* and *smart* all mean knowing a lot. The children agree, and she writes this common definition on the paper and then puts the three words below. She asks the children if there are any other words they can think of that also mean knowing a lot of stuff. Connor suggests *brilliant.* "Ron said that Hermione [*Harry Potter*] is brilliant when she had a really good idea." Ms. V. congratulates Connor on being very clever! Ms. V. adds *brilliant* to the list. She reminds the students that today they are going to try to use their new words and listen to see if Ms. V. uses them.

- *Activity time.* During centers, Ms. V. roams the room and catches the children being clever, smart, brilliant, bright. Each time she uses the words the children repeat it loudly. Each time a child uses the word (correctly) in a sentence the other children in the center clap. Using these new words is exciting and immediately reinforced.

- *Snack time.* During snack time today the children's comments are full of the target words. *This snack will make us brilliant! Milk is a drink for smart kids. Clever kids eat carrots.* The children are pleased when Ms. V. claps for their efforts.

- *Story time.* Today the children hear *The Gingerbread Boy* by P. Galdon. After Ms. V. reads the story, she asks the children to describe the different characters. Elija suggests, "The Gingerbread Boy thought he was smart, but really he wasn't because he kept teasing everyone else." Ariel comments, "The fox was clever—smart and tricky— since he caught the Gingerbread Boy." Gabby exclaims, "Wow, brilliant!"

- *Outdoor play.* On the playground Tony is heard shouting, "I'm the smartest"; under her breath Kara responds by saying to her teacher, "No, he's just fast; that doesn't mean he knows a lot."

Ms. V.'s clever use of words was brilliant, don't you think? A few moments of preparation and a great deal of determination are helping her bright young students become even smarter.

Family Focus: Sharing the Curriculum

Communicating with parents about the curriculum and how children learn is essential. These communications help build a classroom community and offer parents effective ways to continue learning opportunities at home.

Teacher-written instructional publications are designed to describe the children's learning activities or directly inform parents about specific literacy and language concepts. They may include informal news flashes, weekly notes, and a more formal monthly newsletter that features regular columns, such as Dear Teacher, Family Focus, and Center Highlights. With the growing number of homes with computers and Internet access, some teachers now publish their classroom instructional publications on a classroom Web site or share through a listserv. Of course,

(continued)

Family Focus: Sharing the Curriculum   Continued

teachers must check with their children's parents to learn which homes have access to these services.

Informal Weekly Notes

Because consistent communication helps create a sense of community, the authors strongly recommend weekly, or at minimum bimonthly, notes. Frequent communications give teachers the opportunity to

- Provide a bond between school and home experiences
- Extend parents' understanding of developmentally appropriate curricula
- Involve parents in assessing the child's growth and development
- Encourage parents to reinforce and enrich children's learning
- Strengthen the working partnership between parents and teacher

Weekly notes are typically one page in length and generally include (1) information about upcoming events; (2) items about children's achievements; (3) explanations about the curriculum that help parents understand how children learn to read and write; (4) practical and developmentally appropriate suggestions for working with children; and (5) recognition of parents who have helped support classroom learning—for example, parents who accompanied the class on a field trip (Gelfer, 1991).

It is important that informal weekly notes be reader-friendly and brief and suggest successful activities for parents and children to do together. These suggestions typically are well received if they are stated in a positive, proactive manner—for example, "Reading to your child just ten minutes a day helps your child become a better reader," not, "Your child will not learn to read unless you read to her or him."

Figure 4.1 is a sample of an informal weekly note. Observe how Ms. Jones reviews the previous week's activities, taking the opportunity to thank parents who have provided supplies or support. Next, she describes the focus of this week's curriculum and provides suggestions that will help parents reinforce this information at home. Notice how Ms. Jones uses friendly, everyday language to introduce

and explain new concepts, and suggests realistic, content-appropriate literacy activities that encourage parents to become involved in classroom learning.

News Flashes

There are times when events occur that require immediate publication or an upcoming activity warrants attention, such as reminding parents that their children will attend school for only a half day because of parent–teacher conferences or alerting parents that their children will be on the TV news tonight. Teachers may use news flashes to inform parents about TV programming that is relevant to curriculum the class is currently studying. News flashes might also be used to tell a parent about a noteworthy event in the child's life that day (e.g., Zack wrote his first letter today!)

Monthly Newsletters

Like weekly notes, monthly newsletters create a sense of community. The goal of monthly newsletters should be to provide parents with specific information about children's literacy development. In addition, monthly newsletters offer parents an opportunity to preview the curriculum and classroom projects for the upcoming month. As most parents have extremely busy schedules, monthly newsletters help them plan ahead and thus increase the likelihood that they will be able to participate in school activities. Monthly newsletters are generally two or three pages in length and typically use a two- or three-column format. Regular features, such as Dear Teacher, Family Focus, Curriculum Overview, Center Highlights, and Monthly Calendar inform parents in a direct, but fun and interesting manner. In Figure 4.2, we provide a sample kindergarten newsletter written for the month of October. Notice the regularly featured columns.

Dear Teacher Letters

As the sample newsletter demonstrates, parents frequently have questions about reading to their children. An effective way to address these inquires is through Dear Abby–type letters. The teacher frames the questions based on common concerns she hears from the parents. The following are examples of typical parent questions, similar to those in Jim Trelease's *Read Aloud Handbook* (2006).

Dear Parents:

Last week our field trip to the hospital was exciting and we learned even more about how doctors and nurses serve our community. Have your child read you the story they wrote and illustrated about what we learned on our hospital journey. One of the most exciting stops in the hospital was the baby nursery. All of the children were interested in their own first stay at the hospital. Perhaps you will be able to share your memories about that event. A great big thank you to Mrs. Delgato and Cecille Ortiz for helping to chaperon. They also helped our students write their stories.

This week we will discuss fire safety at home and school. Our first lesson is called "Stop, Drop, and Roll," which teaches us what to do if our clothes catch on fire. Next, we will discuss the proper use and storage of matches and lighters. We will also map a safe exit from our room in case of fire and review appropriate behavior during an emergency (no talking, listen to teacher's directions, leave all possessions, walk the planned escape route). We will actually have a schoolwide fire drill to practice these skills. Because you and your child's safety is so important, I am asking that you work with your child to draw and label a map of your house and design the best fire escape route. Drawing the map and labeling the rooms of your house teach your child vocabulary words and reinforce the fire safety concepts I am teaching in school. On Friday we will go to our local Fire Station. Attached to this note is a permission slip. Since this is a walking field trip, I will need at least four parent volunteers. I hope you can join us. To help all of us learn more about fire safety, the Fire Marshall will provide the children and their families with a booklet called "Learn Not To Burn." The book is available in Spanish also. If you would like additional copies, let me know. Please review this informative and entertaining booklet with your child.

To learn even more about fire safety and fire fighters, you might wish to read the following books to your child. These books are available in the classroom, school, and local public library.

EL Fuego, by Maria Ruis and Josep McParramon, Harron's.
Pumpers, Boilers, Hooks and Ladders: A Book of Fire Engines,
by Leonard Everett Fisher, Dail Press.
Fire Fighters, by Ray Brockel, Children's Press.
Curious George at the Fire Station, by Margret and H.A. Rey, Houghton Mifflin.
Puedo Ser Bombero, by Rebecca Hankin, Children's Press.
The Whole Works: Careers in a Fire Department, by Margaret Reuter, Children's Press.

If you have any personal experiences in the area of fire safety, please let me know and you can be an Expert Speaker for our classroom.

Sincerely, Mrs. Jones

FIGURE 4.1   Informal Weekly Note

DEAR TEACHER: My three-year-old often becomes restless when I read stories to him. What can I do to keep his interest? *Signed, Wiggle-Worm's Mom*

DEAR WIGGLE-WORM'S MOM: While most children enjoy having stories read to them, most young children also have a short attention span. Hence, younger children need to be actively involved in the reading.

Asking your son to predict what he thinks will happen next or asking him to point to a character or discuss some aspect of the illustration is an excellent way to keep his attention. This approach also increases children's vocabulary!

DEAR TEACHER: I have three children, and our evenings are hectic to say the least! I also work, so the time I have is limited. When is

(continued)

Family Focus: Sharing the Curriculum   Continued

Ms. Jones' October Newsletter

Kindergarten Curriculum

 It's October and the Kinder-gartners in Ms. Jones' class are learning about our 5 senses—Halloween style! During this month we will learn about sight: how our eyes work, and eye health and safety. We will also have our vision tested. We will study the super sense of smell: How the nose and olfactory nerves work, and how smell and memory are related. We will learn how the ear hears and discover how hearing aids work. We will test our tongues to determine how the sense of taste works to detect sweet, salty, sour, and bitter. Finally, we will learn about the largest organ on our bodies—our skin! The sense of touch can teach us many things about our world.

Dear Teacher: Questions about Reading.

Dear Teacher,
Hola! Both my husband and I speak and read Spanish. Though our son speaks both languages, would it confuse him if we read him story books in Spanish?
Signed, Bilingual/Biliterate

Dear Bi-double L,
How wonderful it is that your son is already speaking two languages! It is perfectly fine to read books written in Spanish to him in Spanish—just as you would read books written in English to him in English. While he is learning to read in both languages, he will also begin to write in English and Spanish.

**Parent Partnership:
Your Child Learns to Write.**

DR TUTH FRE ILS MI TUTH
PLS HEL ME FD et

Can you read this? This is a note to the tooth fairy. It was written by a child who lost her first baby tooth. Let's decode this note together.

DR TUTH FRE ILS MI TUTH

Dear Tooth Fairy, I lost my tooth.

PLS HEL ME FD et

Please help me find it.

As adults, we have been conditioned to read only conventional spelling. On first glance, this note may resemble only a string of letters. On closer inspection, we detect that its writer is trying to convey an important message. When young children begin to use print, their parents and teachers should encourage all attempts. Treating a child's scribbles or letter streams as important and meaningful encourages the child to continue her efforts. As she experiments with reading and writing, her understanding of the rules of our language increases. Eventually, develop-mental or invented spelling matures into more conventional spelling. To read more about this process you might want to read *Spell. . . is a four letter word* by J. Richard Gentry, (1987) from Heinemann Publishing Company in Portsmouth, New Hampshire.

(cont.)

FIGURE 4.2   Monthly Newsletter

the best time and for how long should I read to my kids? *Signed, Watching the Clock*

DEAR WATCHING: Excellent question! Many parents have multiple responsibilities, and

time is always an issue. The best time is whenever you can consistently schedule about fifteen to twenty minutes alone. For most parents, that time appears to be just

**Preparing for
Parent/Student/Teacher Conferences**

Conferences are wonderful opportunities for parents, student, and teacher to sit beside one another to share the students' work and review their progress. In our class each student will share the contents of his/her portfolio with both parents and teacher.

In the first half of the 20-minute conference, students will display and discuss their writing and perhaps read some of their stories. They will explain why certain products were included in the portfolio and why they believe these particular pieces best demonstrate their learning efforts. The students will also show the parents and teacher some of the work they completed at the beginning of the school year and compare it to how they are performing today. During this part of the conference, it is important for parents to listen to the student's self-evaluation. Parents are encouraged to ask open-ended questions, such as:

- What did you learn the most about?
- What did you work the hardest to learn?
- What do you want to learn more about?

These questions encourage students to analyze their own learning and also help them set new learning goals for themselves. Parents should not criticize the child's work or focus on any negative aspect of any material that is presented from the portfolio. Negative comments will only inhibit learning and dampen excitement about school. During the last ten minutes of the conference, the student will be excused so that parents and teacher have an opportunity to talk about any concerns the parents may have. Be sure to complete the Preconference Questionnaire and return it prior to the conference so that the teacher may be better prepared to discuss your concerns.

October Calendar

3rd	– Visit with the eye doctor: vision testing
7th	– Visit the audiologist: hearing tests
15th	– My Favorite Smells Day: bring in your favorite smell
18th	– Taste-testing day
19th	– School pictures day–dress bright
23rd	– Touch and tell day
28th–29th	– Parent/Student/Teacher Conference
31st	– Halloween/5 senses party

Remember: Weekly notes will provide details for each event.

Story Books for October

Georgie's Halloween, by Robert Bright (Doubleday)
The Teeny-Tiny Woman, by Paul Galdone (Clarion)
The Berenstain Bears: Trick or Treat, by Stan and Jan Berenstain (Random House)
Clifford's Halloween, by Norman Bridwill (Scholastic)
ABC Halloween Witch, by Ida Dedage (Garrard)
Who Goes Out on Halloween, by Sue Alexander (Bank Street)
It's Halloween, by Jack Prelutsky (Greenwillow)

FIGURE 4.2 Continued

before bed. However, some parents report that they find time right after the evening meal. Whenever you feel rested and can give your children fifteen to twenty minutes of undivided time is the best time to read to them.

DEAR TEACHER: My four-year-old son wants to hear the same story over, and over, and over. Is this normal? Shouldn't I read a new book each night? *Signed, Repeating Myself*

DEAR REPEATING: As adults we tend to like variety, but most young children between

(continued)

Family Focus: Sharing the Curriculum   Continued

the ages of two and seven have a favorite story, and this storybook may be as comforting to them as their best-loved stuffed toy. So the question becomes how to have both variety and comfort. At this age, favorite books tend to be short, so one suggestion is to read two or three books at story time. Try reading the new books first and the favorite book last. When your child begins to read along with you, this is the perfect time to have him read this favorite book to you or to another child in your household. Frequently a child's favorite book becomes the first one he will read independently.

DEAR TEACHER: When I read my five-year-old daughter a book at story time, I worry about her comprehension skills. Should I ask questions? *Signed, Just the Facts*

DEAR FACTS: I'm so glad you asked that question. The stories you read will frequently inspire your child to share many of her thoughts, hopes, and fears. These discussions are obviously more important than reciting any particular detail. In fact, quizzing chil-

dren about story details will only make story time an unpleasant activity for both of you. Instead, ask open-ended, opinion questions, such as "Which was your favorite part?" or "Why do you think Max stared at the Wild Things?" Story time will also motivate your children to ask you questions! Take your time, share your views, and allow your child to hear your thought process. This activity will do more to teach them about story interpretation than 1,000 fact questions! P.S. Did you know that Sendak's relatives served as the model for the Wild Things?

DEAR TEACHER: What is the best way to help my child develop new vocabulary? *Signed, Wondering about Words*

DEAR WORDS: Children are word sponges and the best way to help them learn new words is through experiences such as going on family field trips to the zoo or museum. To prepare for these adventures you can use storybooks or factual texts to help establish your child's background. Likewise, watching kids, science shows are also an exceptional way to build vocabulary words and concepts.

Strategies for Teaching English Language Learners

LUISA ARAÚJO

Second-language acquisition research shows that several variables affect language learning (Lessow-Hurley, 2000). As we discussed in Chapter 2, the effect of age is well documented and there is general agreement that younger is better. Neurolinguistic findings indicate that children who acquire a second language before the age of five behave like native speakers, whereas children who learn a second language after puberty tend to speak a second language with an accent (Pinker, 1995; Sakai, 2005). However, second-language proficiency entails the mastery of

other language aspects related to semantics, syntax, and pragmatics. Indeed, children between the ages of five and twelve may have a cognitive advantage over younger children because they are more mature and they already know a first language. This may make them especially apt at figuring out how to learn the language needed for school. Similarly, many adults are proficient in a second language, even though they may have an accent when they speak.

Jim Cummins (1994) proposes two complementary notions that describe second-language development in a school setting. Children need to develop *basic interpersonal communicative skills (BICS)* and *cognitive academic language proficiency (CALP)* in order to communicate effectively and to perform academic tasks. BICS is the ability to communicate fluently in a second language; for example, the ability to talk about personal experiences, likes, and dislikes. CALP entails effective performance of cognitively demanding academic tasks that involve processing decontextualized language; for example, the ability to solve a math story problem requires the understanding of CALP. Conversational fluency in BICS is often acquired to a functional level within about two years of initial exposure to the second language. However, children may take five to seven years to catch up to native speakers in academic aspects of the second language (Collier, 1987; Cummins, 1994; Thomas & Collier, 1997). Students who arrive in the United States with a few years of schooling in their primary language reach grade-level performance after five years (Lessow-Hurley, 2000).

As Claude Goldenberg (2008) states, "Academic English—the type of language that is essential for school success—is particularly difficult to master because it is generally not used outside of the classroom and it draws on new vocabulary, more complex sentence structures, and rhetorical forms not typically encountered in non-academic settings. Knowing conversational English undoubtedly helps in learning academic English, but the latter is clearly a more challenging task that requires more time" (p. 13). Several states, such as California, use ELL developmental levels in their state Language Arts Standards to place students in a language proficiency continuum. These levels range from beginning to advanced, with two or three intermediate levels, and may have separate language behavior descriptors according to oral language comprehension and production, reading, and writing. It is quite common for ELL children to take longer to move from intermediate to advanced levels than to move from a beginning level to an intermediate one (Goldenberg, 2008). Again, this is because it takes time to achieve full command of the language to perform academic tasks.

Failure to take into account the BICS/CALP (conversational/academic) distinction may result in discriminatory psychological assessment of bilingual students and premature exit from language support programs (Cummins, 1994). These programs are designed to assist learners in developing the conversational and academic skills necessary for their success in mainstream classrooms. English as a second language (ESL) support programs are usually pullout programs where children work on developing conversational skills and knowledge of academic content. The pullouts are done on a daily basis or a few times a week for about an hour each day and the students work with a teacher specialised in ESL methodologies.

ESL instruction optimizes language learning through the use of comprehensible input and contextualization. According to Krashen (1981), *comprehensible input* is modified language that is provided by the teacher. ESL teachers make sure that they present language that is only a little beyond a child's capabilities. In addition, they work on increasing children's academic proficiency by providing contextual cues for the understanding of cognitively demanding tasks. When teaching the Civil War, an ESL teacher might use a map of the United States and show cause-and-effect relationships using a diagram with arrows. These strategies will ensure that students who do not know the second language very well do not fall behind academically and can also be used by regular classroom teachers. In fact, ESL teachers and regular classroom teachers should plan together and devise instructional strategies that maximize language learning. As Lessow-Hurley (2000) indicates, English acquisition is facilitated by the use of:

- Slow but natural levels of speech
- Clear enunciation
- Short, simple sentences
- Repetition and paraphrasing
- Controlled vocabulary and idioms
- Visual reinforcement through the use of gestures, props, pictures, films, demonstrations, and hands-on activities
- Frequent comprehension checks

Although there is no doubt that these modifications optimize language learning, it is also true that "good instruction for students in general tends to be good instruction for English Language Learners in particular" (Goldenberg, 2008, p. 17).

(continued)

Strategies for Teaching English Language Learners   Continued

Supporting English language learning in English-only settings entails providing good instruction in general, making modifications where necessary and teaching ESL as a separate subject at a distinct time during the day. ESL teachers, because they work with small groups of ELL children, can spend more time on oral English and can be more focused on their use of instructional time. Effective strategies in these complementary teaching–learning situations should comprise the following:

- Graphic organizers that make content and the relationships among concepts and different lesson elements visually explicit
- Additional time and opportunities for practice, either during the school day, after school, or for homework
- Redundant key information, for example, visual cues, pictures, and physical gestures about the lesson content and classroom procedures
- Identifying, highlighting, and clarifying difficult words and passages within texts to facilitate comprehension, and more generally greatly emphasizing vocabulary development
- Helping students consolidate text knowledge by having the teacher, other students, and ELLs themselves summarize and paraphrase

- Giving students extra practice in reading words, sentences, and stories in order to build automaticity and fluency
- Providing opportunities for extended interactions with teacher and peers
- Adjusting instruction (teacher vocabulary, rate of speech, sentence complexity, and expectations for student language production) according to students' oral English proficiency
- Targeting both content and English language objectives in every lesson (Goldenberg, 2008, p. 20)

It is also ideal to help ELL learners become aware of what they already know in their first language so that they can apply this knowledge in their second language. For example, students should be able to identify cognate words like *elefante* and elephant because this can assist them in spelling and in developing comprehension skills (Goldenberg, 2008).

Source: Araújo, Luisa (2002). The literacy development of kindergarten English-language learners. *Journal of Research in Childhood Education, 16*(2), 232–247. Reprinted by permission of Luisa Araújo and the Association for Childhood Education International, 17904 Georgia Avenue, Suite 215, Olney, MD. Copyright © 2002 by the Association.

Strategies for Children with Special Needs: Speech Delays

KAREN BURSTEIN AND TANIS BRYAN

When children come to school, they are expected to be able to communicate. Language is the ability to communicate using symbols; it includes comprehension of both oral and written expression. Speech is one component of oral expression. Many young children come to school with delays in speech and language (comprehension and expression). Speech problems such as misarticulations and dysfluencies are frequently seen in young children with and without special needs. Less obvious are problems understanding others' speech.

Fortunately, the majority of children with language problems are able to successfully participate in all aspects of general education with a few modifications to the environment or curriculum.

Frequently, children with language problems receive special education services from a speech and language pathologist. However, the classroom teacher also has important roles to fulfill: (1) monitoring children's comprehension of instructions and classroom activities, and (2) providing opportunities for oral language practice and interaction with peers and adults.

The following are strategies that classroom teachers can use to help promote speech development in children with oral language delays:

- Collaborate with the speech and language pathologist in selecting activities, materials, and games that promote language development.
- Model appropriate grammar, rhythm, tone, and syntax.
- Keep directions simple, brief, and to the point.
- For students who have difficulty expressing themselves, do not rely solely on open-ended questions.
- Use yes or no questions that are easier to answer.
- When students with speech problems speak, give them your full attention and ensure that other students do the same.
- Errors should not be criticized. Pay attention to the content of the child's message. Do not call attention to misarticulations, especially dysfluencies, as the problem may become more serious if attention is called to it (Lewis & Doorlag, 1999).
- Children who stutter may improve their speech quality if alternate styles of communication are used, such as whispering, singing in a higher or lower pitch, or choral reading.
- Give children with special needs multiple opportunities across the day to converse with you.
- Encourage parents to routinely engage in conversations using children's new words, experiences, and relationships.

Special strategies are also needed to help language-delayed children learn the meanings of new words (receptive vocabulary) and be able to use them. These strategies include:

- Teach vocabulary in all subjects: math, science, social studies, health, and so on.
- Assess each child's prior knowledge before introducing a new topic.
- Have students develop a word book of new words for practice. Pair these words with pictures.
- Encourage children to ask about words they do not understand. Pair these new words with concepts already known.
- Have students paraphrase new words they are acquiring.
- Use physical demonstrations of words, such as verbs and prepositions, that are difficult to explain. Show children the meanings of these words.
- Have students physically demonstrate the meanings of words.
- Use manipulatives that children can handle to teach new words.
- Give multiple examples of word meanings.
- Teach students to use picture dictionaries to locate unfamiliar words.
- Keep parents informed of these special strategies and urge them to continue their use outside of school.

For children with more severe special needs, secure the services of a specialist in augmentative communication. These individuals have specific skills in communication boards, electronic communication devices, and computer voice synthesis. For more information about this special area, visit www.dati.org, a Web site sponsored by the DuPont Hospital for Children and the University of Delaware.

Summary

This chapter began with a review of the many ways parents can support their child's language development within the home. The remainder of the chapter described ways that teachers can provide young children with stimulating oral language experiences that promote active listening and more precise, sophisticated speech. How did your own experiences at home and at school compare with those described in this chapter? Did you recall other types of beneficial oral language activities that were not covered?

To summarize the key points about facilitating oral language learning, we return to the guiding questions at the beginning of this chapter:

■ *What is the initiation, response, evaluation (IRE) pattern of class talk? What problems are associated with this type of discourse? How can teachers provide students with more stimulating conversations in the classroom?*

The IRE pattern of discourse occurs when a teacher asks a question, a student answers, and the teacher either accepts or rejects that answer and goes on to ask another question. These types of question-and-answer exchanges do not provide the type of language input and feedback needed to advance children's language skills. Teachers can provide richer oral language experiences for children by engaging them in reciprocal conversations and discussions: listening closely and responding to their comments; asking genuine, open-ended questions; welcoming the interjection of personal experiences; and encouraging child–child turn-taking interactions.

■ *How do group activities, learning centers, and dramatic play promote oral language acquisition?*

These types of activities create language content (i.e., give children something to talk about). In addition, children must use language to participate successfully in these types of activities.

■ *What can teachers do to promote language-rich dramatic play?*

Teachers can promote language-rich play by (1) providing settings equipped with theme-related, culturally relevant props; (2) scheduling lengthy play periods; and (3) being actively involved in children's play activities.

■ *How can sharing or show-and-tell be turned into a valuable oral language activity?*

Traditional sharing involves having one child speak to the entire class. This activity can be transformed into a valuable oral language activity by limiting group size and encouraging children in the audience to participate actively by asking questions and making comments.

■ *How should teachers teach new vocabulary words?*

Vocabulary learning can be promoted through direct instruction of word meanings and through incidental learning from contexts that provide rich opportunities to hear and use new vocabulary words. Teachers should attempt to connect words that are being taught to other parts of the academic curriculum: ongoing thematic units, books that are being read, field trips, and so on. These vocabulary–curriculum connections provide opportunities for children to encounter the targeted words repeatedly in a short period of time—a crucial factor in word learning

■ *What can teachers do to optimize oral language experiences for bilingual and second-language learners?*

Supporting English language learning in English-only settings entails providing good instruction in general, making modifications where necessary (e.g., the use of comprehensible input and contextualization), and teaching ESL as a separate subject at a distinct time during the day.

LINKING KNOWLEDGE TO PRACTICE

1. Visit an early childhood classroom and observe children interacting in a dramatic play center. Notice the theme that the children are acting out and the roles that they are playing. Record examples of both metaplay language and pretend language.

2. Observe students engaging in a sharing (show-and-tell) activity. Describe the teacher's role and the students' behavior (both the speaker and the audience). Did this sharing time involve most of the students in active listening?

3. Based on a classroom experience, write a one-page weekly note for parents.

4. Work with a group of colleagues to write a monthly newsletter for your class (the one for which you are reading this book).

5. Write a Dear Teacher question-and-answer column for inclusion in a preschool classroom's newsletter. Make a photocopy for everyone in your college class.

CHAPTER

5   Emergent Literacy Strategies

As Isaac enters his kindergarten classroom, he and his classmates collect laminated helper necklaces from their name pockets on the attendance chart. Each necklace has a tag listing a classroom task. Isaac "reads" his tag: Errand Runner. He checks the nearby Helper Board, where all the duties for each task have been described in both words and pictures. Today he will run errands for his teacher, such as taking the attendance count to the center's office. Yesterday, Isaac was Pencil Sharpener, which involved gathering and sharpening pencils. He hopes to be Pet Feeder tomorrow.

In Chapter 1, we overviewed the emergent literacy perspective. According to this view, the literacy learning process shares much in common with oral language development. Literacy acquisition, like oral language development, begins early. For many children, literacy development begins in infancy when caregivers read storybooks to them and when children begin to notice print in the environment. Literacy learning is an active, constructive process. By observing print and having stories read to them, young children discover patterns and create their own early versions of reading and writing that initially have little resemblance to conventional forms: the story they "read" may be quite different from the one in the book, and their writing may look like drawing or scribbles. As children have opportunities to use these early forms of literacy in meaningful social situations and as they interact with adults who draw their attention to the features and functions of print, their constructions become increasingly similar to conventional reading and writing.

Home literacy experiences help children develop an awareness of the forms and functions of print. Therefore, developmentally appropriate early childhood programs feature literacy activities that mirror the types of literacy experiences found in enriched home environments, such as print-rich settings, storybook reading, demonstrations of various forms of literacy, and many opportunities for children to engage in meaningful reading and writing activities. Such experiences build on what children have already learned about written language, provide a smooth transition between home and school, and help ensure initial success with language arts instruction.

As stated in Chapter 1, we believe that effective early literacy programs should blend the best emergent literacy strategies with the best strategies from the scientifically based reading research (SBRR) approach. This chapter describes four strategies that form the foundation of developmentally appropriate preschool and kindergarten language arts programs: functional literacy activities, sharing literature, literacy play, and shared writing. These strategies are particularly valuable because they provide a broad spectrum of learning opportunities appropriate for children at different ages and with different prior experience with print. When used with groups of children, opportunities exist for *all* children to gain valuable knowledge about literacy. We firmly believe that these emergent literacy strategies should be major components in every early literacy curriculum.

Before Reading This Chapter, Think About . . .

- How you used print as a child. Did you write notes to your family? Did you pretend to write checks? Send a letter to Santa? Write a thank-you card to Grandma?
- Advertising logos you remember from your childhood. Could you spot a McDonald's a mile away? Did your favorite toy or snack food have a special logo or trademark?
- The favorite books from your childhood. Did you have one or two favorite books that you liked to have your parents, siblings, or other adults read to you? Did you have a favorite book that you liked to read on your own?
- How you played house as a child. Did you have real cereal boxes and egg cartons for your pretend kitchen? Did an interested adult join in your pretend play?

Focus Questions

- What are functional literacy activities, and how can teachers use these activities in a preschool or kindergarten classroom?
- How can teachers set up a well-designed library center?
- What are the characteristics of effective adult storybook reading?
- How can dramatic play centers be used to encourage young children's literacy development?
- How do shared writing and interactive writing increase a child's understanding of print and facilitate reading development?
- How can teachers share information about emergency literacy with parents?

Functional Literacy Activities

A child's home reading experiences are usually functional in nature. Children watch their parents and older siblings use reading and writing to accomplish real-life purposes. They often join in these activities (e.g., reading food labels and signs in the environment). It is important that teachers provide opportunities for children to continue to learn about functional qualities of reading and writing.

In the vignette at the opening of this chapter, note how the helper necklaces in Isaac's classroom provide the same type of functional literacy experiences that children have at home. The print on the helper necklaces serves a real purpose and assists with everyday

B O X **5.1**

Definition of Terms

environmental print (EP): includes the real-life print children see in the home or community, including print on food containers and other kinds of product boxes, store signs, road signs, and advertisements. Because the situation gives clues to the print's meaning, EP is often the first type of print young children recognize and understand.

functional literacy activities: reading and writing activities that accomplish real-life purposes, such as writing lists and reading directions.

functional print: print that guides everyday classroom activity (e.g., labels, lists, directions, sign-up sheets).

interactive writing: an extension of shared writing in which children share the pen with the teacher to write a text.

literacy-enriched dramatic play centers: socio-dramatic play centers that are enhanced with appropriate theme-related literacy materials, such as recipe cards, cookbooks, and food containers for the kitchen area of the house-keeping center.

shared book experience: the teacher reads a big book with enlarged print and encourages children to read along on parts that they can remember or predict.

shared writing: the teacher works with whole groups, small groups, or individual students to write down the children's oral language stories. These highly contextualized stories are easy for children to read.

activities (classroom chores). The surrounding context—the chores that are done on a daily basis in the classroom—makes the print on the necklaces easy to recognize and understand.

Functional literacy activities provide opportunities for children who are at different stages in their literacy development to learn new skills and concepts. For example, if Isaac is just beginning to learn about the meaning and functions of print, then the helper necklaces provide an opportunity to learn that print can inform him about his assigned chores and help him remember these chores. If he has already acquired this basic concept, then the necklaces provide opportunities to learn about the structure of print. For example, he may eventually learn to recognize some of the printed words on the necklaces (*runner, pencil, pet*) or to figure out some related letter–sound relationships (the letter *p* represents the sound that *pencil* and *pet* begin with).

In the sections that follow, we describe two types of print that can provide children with functional literacy activities. Environmental print exists in everyday life outside of school, and functional print is connected with classroom activities.

Bringing Environmental Print into the Classroom

At home and in their neighborhoods, young children are surrounded by print that serves real-life functions: labels on cereal boxes and soft drink cans, road signs, billboards, and restaurant menus. This type of print is referred to as *environmental print* (EP). Because the situation gives clues to the print's meaning, EP is often the first type of print that young children can recognize and understand.

The educational benefits of EP are very controversial. On the one hand, proponents of emergent literacy believe that EP is a valuable instructional resource. For example, Prior and Gerard (2004) state:

> We believe . . . that with the assistance of an adult, a child is easily able to recognize the letters in environmental print. Furthermore, we believe that using these highly motivating and visually appealing materials creates a meaningful foundation for learning about the alphabetic principle. In addition, we have found that when teachers use environmental print as an instructional tool to teach letters and sounds, the print in the actual environment serves as a constant reinforcement of the reading skills children are learning in school. (p. 9)

Other researchers with a bent toward the SBRR point of view have argued that EP is of little instructional importance. For example, Ehri and Roberts (2006) found evidence that children did not focus on the alphabet letters in EP. Rather, children tended to focus on more visually salient cues such as color and logo designs. This led Ehri and Roberts to conclude that "even though children may be able to read environmental print, this capability does not appear to promote letter learning" (p. 121).

Our position is that, because EP is so meaningful and easy to read, it should be available in all preschool and kindergarten classrooms. In order for this print to promote alphabet knowledge and phonics, teachers need to draw children's attention to letters that occur in EP. We recommend the following EP strategies:

- *EP alphabet chart.* The teacher places pieces of chart paper around the room for every letter of the alphabet. Each day, children bring to class product labels that they can "read." During circle time, these labels are read and attached to the correct chart. For example, the Kix (cereal) label would go on the *K k* page. Then the group reads the labels on all the charts, starting with the *A a* page. After several months, when most of the chart pages are full, the teacher can use the product labels from the charts to make books such as "I Can Read Cereals" (Enz, Prior, Gerard, & Han, 2008).
- *EP folders.* Selected pieces of EP can be attached to file folders to make EP books (Anderson & Markle, 1985). For example, a pizza book could be made by pasting or laminating the product logos from pizza advertisements, coupons, and delivery containers onto the inside surfaces of a file folder. Children can decorate the front cover with pizza-related illustrations. Other book possibilities include toothpaste, cookies, milk, cereal, and soft drinks. These EP folders should be placed in the classroom library so that children can show off to their friends how well they can read this type of contextualized print.
- *EP walks.* The strategy of EP walks involves taking a class for a walk in the neighborhood surrounding the school (Orellana & Hernández, 1999). Before leaving, the children are told to be on the lookout for EP. As examples of EP are encountered during the walk, they are pointed out by the teacher or by the children. After the children return to the classroom, they draw pictures of the print they could read on the walk. The pictures are put into a group book, which the teacher reads aloud to the class. The children can then take turns reading EP items in the book.
- *Literacy-enriched dramatic play.* As will be explained later in this chapter, EP can be used as props in children's dramatic play. For example, empty product boxes such

as cereal containers and milk cartons can be used in the kitchen area of housekeeping or home centers. As children act out home-related themes such as making dinner, they will have opportunities to attempt to read the print on the containers.

Functional Print Connected with Classroom Activities

Unlike environmental print that is found in the world outside of school, *functional print* is connected with everyday classroom activities. This print is practical as well as educational. The helper necklaces in the opening vignette help children remember their assigned chores, making the classroom run more smoothly. Simultaneously, the necklaces offer children opportunities to learn about the functions and structure of print. As with all functional print, the context helps children discover the meaning of the print (Strickland & Schickedanz, 2004).

In the sections that follow, we describe the major types of functional print that are commonly found in preschool and kindergarten classrooms: labels, lists, directions, schedules, calendars, messages, sign-in and sign-up lists, and inventory lists.

Labels.   As illustrated by the helper necklaces in the vignette at the beginning of this chapter, labels may be used to delineate tasks that students are assigned to complete, such as line leader, pencil sharpener, pet feeder, and paper passer. Labels can also be used to help organize the classroom. For example, cubbies can be labeled with children's names so that students know where their belongings are stored. Containers can be labeled to designate their contents, and labels can be used on shelves to indicate where materials are to be stored. Labels can also be used to designate different areas of the classroom (library, home center, blocks, games, art), informing children about the types of activities that are supposed to take place in each location. Finally, labels can be used to convey information. For example, teachers often use labels to identify objects in displays (e.g., types of seashells) and pictures ("This is a . . ."). In classrooms with children whose primary language is not English, teachers write the labels in English and, when possible, in the children's home language (e.g., Spanish). Need help with the translating? Go to www.google.com/webmasters/igoogle/wordmonkey.html.

Lists.   Lists have a variety of practical classroom uses. Attendance charts can be constructed by placing each child's picture and name above a pocket. The children sign in by finding their name card in a box and by matching it with their name on the chart. After the children become familiar with their printed names, the pictures can be removed. In Trade Secret 5.1, a preschool teacher offers another way of using this approach to take attendance and document ongoing literacy development.

Teachers can use a second set of name tags to post jobs on a helper chart (see Figure 5.1). This chart, which is an alternative to the helper necklaces described at the beginning of this chapter, contains a description of jobs needing to be done and display pockets that hold the children's name cards. When attendance and helper charts are used on a daily basis, children quickly learn to recognize their own names and the names of their classmates.

Directions.   Instructions can be posted for using equipment such as tape recorders and computers. Classroom rules (e.g., "We walk in our classroom") can be displayed to remind children of appropriate behavior. In addition, children can create their own personal directives.

FIGURE 5.1   Helper Chart

For example, a child may place a "Look, don't touch!" sign on a newly completed art project or block structure. At first, children will need help from the teacher or from peers in reading these types of directions. Soon, however, they will learn to use the surrounding context to help them remember what the directions say. Teachers can facilitate this process by constantly referring children to these posted directions. For example, if a child is running in the classroom, then the teacher could direct the child's attention to the "We walk in our classroom" sign and ask, "What does that sign say?"

Directions can also include recipes for cooking or instructions for art activities. The information can be put on wall charts. Even very young children can follow simple directions that use both words and pictures.

TRADE SECRET 5.1

Connecting Names and Faces

Ms. Martinez uses a visual approach to help her three- and four-year-old preschool students recognize their names and document their literacy growth over time. During the first day of school, Ms. Martinez takes an individual picture of each student using a digital camera. After the child's image has been printed, she asks each child to write his or her name on a piece of construction paper. (If the child's writing is completely illegible, then she writes the child's name conventionally next to the child's personal script and explains, "This is how I write your name."). She places the child's picture above the name and places the page in a clear plastic protector. She places the pictures on a child's eye-level bulletin board. She uses the bulletin board to help the children take attendance (as the children enter the room in the morning they attach a brightly painted clothespin to their pictures).

In five or six weeks, Ms. Martinez repeats this process. She takes new pictures of the children and again asks them to print their names on a new piece of construction paper. In addition, she asks them to write anything else they would like to share. She is always amazed at how much the children's ability to print their names and their understanding about print has developed during the first few weeks. Instead of sending the first set of pictures home, she organizes the pages in a "book" titled "Our Class" and places the book in the library. It is one of the children's favorite library books.

Schedules.   A daily schedule can be presented at the beginning of class to prepare children for upcoming activities. Pictures can be used to help children remember the different segments of the day (see Figure 5.2). When children ask what is going to happen next, the teacher can help them use the chart to figure it out.

Calendars.   A calendar can be set up at the beginning of each month and used for marking children's birthdays, parties, and other special events (field trips, classroom visitors, when a student's dog had puppies, etc.). The teacher can encourage the children to use the calendar to determine how many more days until a special event takes place and to record events of importance to them.

Messages.   Often, unforeseen events change the day's plans. It's raining, so there can be no outdoor playtime. Instead of simply telling children, some teachers write a message. For example:

> Circle time will be first thing this morning.
> We have a special visitor!
> She will share her cookies with us.

Because these messages inform children about activities that directly affect their day, even the youngest children quickly learn to pay close attention to these notices.

Sign-In and Sign-Up Lists.   Children can write their names on lists for a variety of functional purposes. For example, kindergarten teacher Bobbi Fisher (1995) writes the date and

SCHEDULE

9:00	Opening
9:10	Free-Choice Time
10:00	Circle Time
10:30	Snack
10:45	Outdoor Play
11:30	Go Home

FIGURE 5.2   Daily Schedule

day at the top of large nine-by-eighteen-inch piece of drawing paper and has her students write their names on the paper each morning when they first arrive in the classroom. Fisher and her assistant teacher also sign the list. During circle time, the list is read to the class as a means of taking attendance and to build a sense of community. As the students become familiar with each other's printed names, they take over the activity. Fisher periodically uses this sign-in procedure to assess the students' emerging writing abilities.

Lists can also be used to sign up for popular classroom centers and playground equipment. Teachers can have children sign up on lists to use popular centers such as the block and dramatic play areas. If children do not get a chance to use the area on a given day, then they could be first in line to use it the next day. Sign-up sheets are also used to get turns using tricycles on the playground.

Children should be encouraged to use emergent forms of writing. If a child's writing is completely illegible, then the teacher may need to write the child's name conventionally next to the child's personal script. The teacher can explain, "This is how I write your name." Once the child's name is recognizable, this scaffold can be discontinued.

Inventory Lists.   Lists can also be used to create inventories of the supplies in different classroom areas. Susan Neuman and Kathy Roskos (2007) give an example of a chart that contains an inventory of the supplies in the art area. The list contains a picture and the name of each item as well as the quantity of each item available. The sign informs children that there are eight paintbrushes, twelve pairs of scissors, lots of paper, and so on. During cleanup, children can use this information to make sure the center is ready for future use.

Sharing Literature with Children

As early as 1908, Edmond Huey wrote about children's acquisition of reading and noted that "the key to it all lies in the parents reading aloud to and with the child" (p. 332). Today, after decades of research on the teaching of reading, we continue to agree with Huey. More recently, Marilyn Adams (1990) summarized what many educators believe and what research supports: "The single most important activity for building the knowledge and skills eventually required for reading appears to be reading aloud to children" (p. 46). This single act—parents and teachers reading aloud to children—has received more research attention than any other aspect of children's literacy development. The findings of this vast body of research support the claims of Huey and Adams.

Why is storybook reading so important for young children's language and literacy development? The following points summarize key research findings in this area:

- To succeed in school, children need experiences with decontextualized language. Decontextualized language is language for which there is no support available in the immediate environment to help children make meaning. Storybook reading provides children with models for decontextualized language (Dickinson, Temple, Hirschler, & Smith, 1992).
- Storybook reading exposes children to more complex grammar and to vocabulary that is not used in everyday conversations (Beck, McKeown, & Kucan, 2002; Brabham & Lynch-Brown, 2002).
- Read-alouds contribute to children's understanding of literary elements (Sipe, 1998).
- Storybook reading builds children's content knowledge (Leal, 1994).

According to the National Early Literacy Panel's (2008) report, the greatest impact of shared reading is on children's oral language and print knowledge outcomes. Following the panel's analysis of the studies that met their high quality standard, the panel concluded that "shared reading . . . can have a significant, substantial, and positive impact on young children's oral language skills and on young children's print knowledge" (p. 155).

What the National Education Goals Panel (1997) said more than a decade ago still holds:

> Early, regular reading to children is one of the most important activities parents can do with their children to improve their readiness for school, serve as their child's first teacher, and instill a love of books and reading. Reading to children familiarizes them with story comprehension such as characters, plot, action, and sequence ("Once upon a time," "and they lived happily ever after"), and helps them associate oral language with printed text. Most important, reading to children builds their vocabularies and background knowledge about the world. (p. 20)

Unfortunately, not all children have equal access to this wonderful literacy-building experience. Data suggest that only about 45 percent of children younger than three and 56 percent of three- to five-year-olds are read to daily by their parents (National Education Goals Panel, 1997). More recent research (Yarosz & Barnett, 2001) suggests that households in which reading experiences are the most infrequent exhibit three characteristics: (1) English is not spoken as a primary language, (2) the mother is Hispanic, and (3) the mother's educational level is below the twelfth grade.

This section is about how to share books with young children. We begin by explaining how teachers can set up inviting library centers in their classrooms and how they can effectively read stories to young children. Finally, we discuss how preschool teachers can encourage parents to read to their children on a regular basis.

Selecting Good Books for Children

Selecting the right book is the first step toward a successful story-reading session. Helen Ezell and Laura Justice (2005) suggest that there are three criteria teachers should use when selecting books: (1) narrative content (themes and topics need to be appropriate to young children and presented using vocabulary that children can understand); (2) print (the size needs to be large enough for the children to see and positioned to make the print prominent on the page in order to provide opportunities for adult and children to talk about the print); and (3) physical characteristics (the composition and shape, illustrations, and packaging need to be appealing and appropriate for the age of the child). The careful selection of quality picture storybooks can play an important role in young children's development.

To help teachers with the task of making appropriate selections of quality books, we suggest readers consider obtaining a copy of Barbara Zulandt Kiefer, Janet Hickman, and Susan Hepler's (2007) book, *Charlotte Huck's Children's Literature*. This book is a rich resource for teachers of children of all ages. It alerts readers to title after title of outstanding literature, noting the likely age of children who would enjoy each book most. At the end of each chapter, readers will find pages and pages of recommended titles. The latest (ninth) edition of this book reproduces many pages from quality picture books and picture storybooks for teachers' examination. This book is a *must* for every teacher's professional library.

In addition to selecting high-quality books for sharing with children, teachers should ensure that they expose their young students to a variety of genres: counting books, alphabet books, predictable books, folktales, fantasy, narrative, poetry, and more, including informational books. Today, a growing number of informational (or expository) texts for young children are published annually. Nell Duke and V. Susan Bennett-Armistead (2003, pp. 20–23) summarize several reasons teachers must include informational books in their story-reading sessions.

- The reading of informational texts will dominate the children's reading in their later schooling.
- This kind of text is ubiquitous to society; it is what people outside school read.
- Informational text is the preferred reading material of some children.
- Informational text builds children's knowledge of the natural and social world.
- Informational text may help build children's vocabulary and other kinds of literacy knowledge (e.g., graphical devices such as diagrams and tables).

In addition, a recent study by Lisa Price, Anne van Kleek, and Carl Huberty (2009) revealed that children and their parents had longer, more complex discussions during informational book sharing than when narrative storybooks were read and discussed. This implies that reading informational books to young children may also help promote oral language development.

Not only must teachers include informational books in the classroom libraries, but they also must read informational books aloud. Sadly, survey data suggest that teachers read very few informational texts (less than 15 percent of all books read) in their read-aloud sessions (Yopp & Yopp, 2000). Through reading informational books, teachers can not only build children's background knowledge about a range of topics but also introduce children to a range of text structures that are different from the narrative text structures (Vukelich, Evans, & Albertson, 2003).

Finally, teachers should be sure to share tales representative of various cultures. Many resources locate high-quality multicultural literature. The most up-to-date information on multicultural books can be found on the World Wide Web. A variety of sites can be found using the descriptor "multicultural children's literature" with any of the major search engines.

Once appropriate selections have been made, the teacher's challenge is to organize the books to make them accessible to their students. Students should be encouraged to read, read, read voluntarily.

Classroom Library Centers

A key feature of a classroom for young children is a well-stocked, well-designed, well-organized library center that is distinct from other areas in the classroom. Classroom libraries promote independent reading by providing children with easy access to books and a comfortable place for browsing and reading. Children have been found to read more books in classrooms with libraries than in ones without libraries (Morrow & Weinstein, 1982). As Stephen Krashen (1987, p. 2) has pointed out, this finding supports "the commonsense view that children read more when there are more books around."

The mere presence of a classroom library is not enough to ensure heavy use by young children, however. The library must contain an ample supply of appropriate and interesting books for children to read. Design features are also important. Lesley Morrow and Carol Weinstein (1982) found that children did not choose to use "barren and uninviting" library corners during free-play time. When the design features of centers were improved, however, children's library usage increased dramatically.

Unfortunately, classroom libraries are not a universal feature of early childhood classrooms, and many of the libraries that do exist were not designed well. Jann Fractor, Marjorie Woodruff, Miriam Martinez, and Bill Teale (1993) collected data on the libraries in eighty-nine kindergartens through second-grade classrooms and found that only 58 percent of classes had a library center. Only 8 percent of these classroom libraries were rated as being good or excellent (having large numbers of books, partitions, ample space, comfortable furnishings, book covers rather than book spines facing out on book shelves, and book-related displays and props). The vast majority of libraries were rated as basic, containing small numbers of books and few desirable design characteristics.

Books. To attract and hold children's interest, a classroom library must be stocked with lots of good books to read that are in excellent condition and in ample supply. Experts recommend that classroom libraries contain five to eight books per child (Fractor et al., 1993). According to these guidelines, a class of twenty children would require 100 to 160 books. According to the newly revised *Early Language and Literacy Classroom Observation: Pre-K Tool* (Smith, Brady, & Anastasopoulos, 2008), an instrument often used to evaluate the quality of preschool classroom's language and literacy environments, a pre-K classroom should include books on a range of topics that are important to young children, of varying difficulty of text (e.g., wordless to first readers), of multiple genres (e.g., fictional narratives, poetry, concept books), and inclusive of diversity in characters and family structures. These books should be divided into a core collection and one or more revolving collections. The core collection should be made up of high-quality literature that remains constant and

A well-designed library center invites children to read books.

available all year. Included here should be books that appeal to most of the children in class and that most children will enjoy reading on more than one occasion. Lesley Morrow (2005) also recommends that the books be color-coded according to type. For example, all animal books could be identified with blue dots on their spines so they can be clustered together on a shelf marked *Animals*. Each category would be distinguished by a different color. Morrow also suggests a simpler alternative of storing books in plastic tubs or cardboard boxes, with labels on the front describing the type of book in the container.

Revolving collections change every few weeks to match children's current interests and topics being studied in class. For example, if several children become hooked on one author such as Tomie dePaola or Maurice Sendak, collections of that author's books could be brought into the library to capitalize on this interest. If the class is studying seeds and plants, then picture storybooks and informational books relating to these topics could be added. When student interest shifts to a new author or when a new topic is under investigation, the old sets of revolving books are replaced with new ones.

Quality and variety are also of utmost importance in selecting books for the classroom library (Fractor et al., 1993). To motivate voluntary reading and instill positive attitudes toward written texts, books must catch children's attention, hold their interest, and captivate their imaginations. Only high-quality literature will achieve these goals.

Physical Characteristics. A number of physical features have been identified that make libraries attractive to children and that promote book reading (Morrow, 1983, 2001):

- *Partitions.* Bookshelves, screens, large plants, or other barriers set the library center apart from the rest of the classroom, giving children a sense of privacy and providing a cozy, quiet setting for reading.
- *Ample space.* There should be room enough for at least five or six children to use the library at one time.
- *Comfortable furnishings.* The more comfortable the library area, the more likely it is that children will use it. Soft carpeting, chairs, old sofas, beanbags, and a rocking chair all help create a comfortable atmosphere for reading.
- *Open-faced and traditional shelves.* Traditional shelves display books with their spines out, whereas open-faced shelves display the covers of books. Open-faced shelves are very effective in attracting children's attention to specific books. Researchers have found that when both types of shelves are used, kindergartners chose more than 90 percent of their books from the open-faced displays (Fractor et al., 1993). Traditional shelves are also useful because they can hold many more books than open-faced shelves. Many teachers rotate books between traditional and open-faced shelves, advertising different books each week.
- *Book-related displays and props.* Posters, puppets, flannel boards with cutout figures of story characters, and stuffed animals encourage children to engage in emergent reading and to act out favorite stories. Stuffed animals also are useful as listeners or babies for children to read to. (Posters are available from such sources as the Children's Book Council, 67 Irving Place, New York, NY 10003; the American Library Association, 50 East Huron Street, Chicago, IL 60611; and the International Reading Association, 800 Barksdale Road, Newark, DE 19711.)

PEARSON
myeducationkit™

Go to the Assignments and Activities section of Chapter 5 in the MyEducationKit and complete the activity entitled "Creating a Puppet." As you watch the video and answer the accompanying questions, note the rich language that the two girls use while making their book-related puppets.

- *Labeling the center.* Like cordoning off the area from the classroom space, symbolic cues help define the space and identify appropriate activities for young children. Using print, "Library Corner," and symbols associated with a library—book jackets, a photograph of a child looking at a book—helps even the youngest child read the label for the corner.
- *Writing center.* Some teachers like to place a writing center near the library corner. This accessibility seems to prompt young children to make illustrations and write in their personal script or dictate a sentence to an adult about the stories they are reading.

To this list, Miriam Smith and David Dickinson (2002) add:

- *Listening center.* Typically this is a table large enough for four to eight children to gather around a cassette or CD player, put on headphones, and listen to taped stories. The teacher provides multiple copies of the book on tape or CD so that children can turn the pages of the book as the story unfolds.

Remember, the better designed the library corner, the more use children will make of it; that is, more children will choose to participate in book reading and literature-related activities during free-choice periods. Therefore, a classroom library corner that is voluntarily used by few children is suspected to be a poorly designed center. What might an enticing library corner look like? A drawing of a possible library corner for an early childhood classroom is shown in Figure 5.3.

Effective Story-Reading Strategies

Research suggests that the frequency with which children participate in shared reading during the preschool years has a positive influence on their language and early reading skills (Snow et al., 1998). Attention to quantity alone is insufficient, however. The quality of the story-reading sessions also is important.

The verbal interaction between adult and child that occurs during story readings has a major influence on children's literacy development (Cochran-Smith, 1984). Much of the early research on effective story-reading techniques reports on the interactions between a parent and child during story reading.

Some of this research discusses the affective benefits of story reading. For example, researchers such as David Yaden, Laura Smolkin, and Laurie MacGillivray (1993, p. 60) describe story reading as a pleasurable activity: "Children learn very quickly that bringing a book to a parent or caregiver will begin a certain predictable and, for the most part, pleasurable activity." Teale (1986) describes the exchange as a dance, a choreographed interaction between adult and child reader (sometimes the adult and sometimes the child) and listener (sometimes the adult and sometimes the child).

A growing number of researchers have studied preschool teachers' reading styles and the impact of their interaction style on their young learners' literacy development. Each of these researchers (e.g., Brabham & Lynch-Brown, 2002; Hargrave & Sénéchal, 2000; Justice, Kaderavek, Fan, Sofka, & Hunt, 2009; Reese & Cox, 1999) discovered that teachers who had children predict, analyze, generate word meanings, and draw conclusions *as they read* had a significantly positive impact on children's vocabulary development, memory

FIGURE 5.3   Library Center

abilities, and print skills. Key features of adult behaviors during reading include (1) encouraging children to participate while the adult is reading by using evocative techniques to assist the children in using language, techniques such as asking "wh" questions that require the children to engage in novel speech; (2) providing children with feedback in the form of instructive information by expanding what the children said, praising and correcting errors; (3) adapting the reading style to the children's growing linguistic abilities, moving beyond what the children already know to new information; and (4) drawing children's attention to the print in book (print referencing). As Sonia Cabell and her colleagues (2008) point out, it

Family Focus: Sharing Instructional Materials and Offering Guidance

Preschool teachers frequently recommend that parents read to their young children (Becker & Epstein, 1982). Unfortunately, many parents face great financial hardships and cannot provide a large number of quality reading materials in their homes. Nor do they have time or easy access to public libraries. Further, parents may not know how to encourage and engage their children's interest in reading (Richgels & Wold, 1998). To help parents to fulfill their role as partners in literacy programs, it is vital for teachers to work with these families to offer easy access to books of all kinds (Brock & Dodd, 1994) and guidance in how to use them (McGee & Richgels, 1996).

Classroom Lending Library

Susan Neuman's 1999 study examined the effect of flooding more than 330 child care centers with storybooks. The results of her study confirm that children who have access to high-quality storybooks and teachers who are trained to support children's storybook interactions score significantly higher on several early reading achievement measures than children who have not experienced high-quality storybooks and trained teachers. In other words, it is critically important for young children to have easy access to high-quality storybooks and expository texts. Further, it is essential that parents and child care providers know how to support a child's early interactions with print. Though most public schools possess libraries, children generally are restricted to borrowing only one or two books a week. Some child care centers use public libraries with similar restrictions. While this may be appropriate for older children who can read chapter books, this quantity is insufficient for young children who are learning how to read. Young children should have the opportunity to have at least one new book an evening. One way to ensure early literacy development at home and foster the home–school connection is through a classroom lending library. A classroom lending library allows children to check out a new book each day, thus ensuring that all parents have an opportunity to read to their child frequently.

The acquisition of quality books for daily checkout is the first step in establishing a classroom lending library. Since the children will exchange their book each day, all a teacher needs to begin a library is one book per child.

Managing the classroom lending library requires that all books contain a library pocket and identification card. The teacher needs to create a classroom library checkout chart. When a child borrows a book, she simply removes the book's identification card and replaces it in her or his name pocket on the classroom checkout chart. The teacher can see at a glance what book each child has checked out.

The rules that accompany the classroom lending library are simple. A child may borrow one book each day. When the book is returned, the child may check out another. Teaching the children to manage the checkout routine is easy. When the children enter the classroom in the morning, they return their books to the library by removing the book's identification card from their name pocket. They place the identification card back in the book's library pocket, and they place the book back on the shelf. The children may select new books anytime throughout the day.

Book Bags

Yet another way to encourage family participation and successfully engage and guide parents' literacy interactions with their children is through book bags (Barbour, 1998–1999). Like writing briefcases, book bags may be checked out of the classroom lending library for a week at a time. Book bags contain a collection of high-quality books and offer informal, interactive activities for extending children's language and literacy acquisition. When designing the bags, teachers need to consider their children's developmental stages, interests and experiences, and literacy levels. The book bags (nylon gym bags) typically contain three or four books and activities inspired by a specific theme (see Figure 5.4 for sample book bag themes). In addition, each bag contains two response journals (one for the child and one for the parent). Each bag also contains an inventory that

(continued)

Family Focus: Sharing Instructional Materials and Offering Guidance   Continued

helps parents and children keep track of and return materials assigned to each bag.

Teachers typically initiate the program by sending home a letter describing the program. In addition to the introductory letter, each family also receives a contract. The terms of the contract are simple: Parents promise to spend time regularly reading to their children; children promise to spend time with the books and activities and treat each bag with care; and teachers promise to instill a love of reading

in children and to manage the program. All three participants sign the contract.

The book bag project has been highly successful in many teachers' classrooms. The book bags supply parents with appropriate materials and explicit guidance, which in turn empower and motivate them to become teachers of their own children, encourage them to provide supportive home learning environments, and expand their knowledge of how to interact with their children.

FIGURE 5.4   Sample Book Bag Themes

Counting Theme
Hillanbrand, W. (1997). *Counting Crocodiles.* Orlando: FL: Harcourt Brace.
Kirk, D. (1994). *Miss Spider's Tea Party.* New York: Scholastic.
Barbieri-McGrath, B. (1998). *Hershey's Counting Board Book.* Wellesley, MA: Corporate Board Book.

Alphabet Theme
Wilbur, R. (1997). *The Disappearing Alphabet.* New York: Scholastic.
Alexander, M. (1994). *A You're Adorable.* New York: Scholastic.
Martin, B., & Archambault, J. (1989). *Chicka, Chicka, Boom Boom.* New York: Simon & Schuster Children's Publishing.

Rhyming Books
Goldston, B. (1998). *The Beastly Feast.* New York: Scholastic.
Slate, J. (1996). *Miss Bindergarten Gets Ready for Kindergarten.* New York: Scholastic.
Wood, A. (1992). *Silly Sally.* Orlando: FL: Harcourt Brace.
Degen, B. (1996). *Jesse Bear, What Will You Wear?* New York: Simon & Schuster Children's Publishing.
London, J. (1997). *Froggy Gets Dressed.* New York: Viking Children's Press.
Regan, D. (1998). *What Will I Do if I Can't Tie My Shoe?* New York: Scholastic.

is the "extratextual conversations" that teachers have with children during storybook reading that are so important to children's language and literacy development.

Classroom Read-Alouds

When a parent and a child read together, the child typically sits in the parent's lap or snuggles under the parent's arm. Many parents establish a bedtime reading ritual, cuddling with the child for a quiet reading time before the child goes to bed. Teachers of the youngest children, infants, and toddlers should follow parents' lead and apply what is known about how parents read to infants and toddlers to their reading to their young students. The low teacher–child ratio recommended by the National Association for the Education of Young Children for

PEARSON
myeducationkit

Go to the Assignments and
Activities section of Chapter 5
in the MyEducationKit and
complete the activity entitled
"Individual Story Time: Preschool." As you watch the
video and answer the accompanying questions, note how
the teacher asks questions
and give prompts to keep
the child actively engaged
in the storybook reading.

PEARSON
myeducationkit

Go to the Assignments and
Activities section of Chapter 5
in the MyEducationKit and
complete the activity entitled
"Reading to Toddlers." As
you watch the video and
answer the accompanying
questions, note how the
child gets increasingly
engaged in the story as
it progresses.

infant (one adult to one infant) and toddler (one adult to four toddlers) programs supports this kind of adult–child interaction, although with toddlers,
such one-on-one reading together requires some careful arranging (Bredekamp, 1989). We recommend that teachers create a daily reading ritual.
Some day care centers connect with church groups or nearby residential
facilities for elderly citizens for the explicit purpose of having adults come
to the center just before naptime to read to the children. Now, like at home,
every child can have a lap, a cuddle, and a "grandparent" all alone.

The older the children, the larger the number of children in the
group permitted by law. The typical kindergarten class, for example, is
often one teacher for twenty (unfortunately, sometimes even more) children. These teachers are challenged to keep read-alouds enjoyable, pleasurable experiences. Of course, selecting age- and interest-appropriate
books is important. Read-aloud experiences are one way to ensure that
high-quality literature is accessible to all students, something that is
especially important for children who have had few storybook experiences outside school.

The *how* of reading is also important. Even when there are too
many children for everyone to cuddle next to the adult reader, physical
comfort is important. Having a special carpeted area for reading to the
group is important. This area is often next to the library center. Nancy
asks her young learners to sit in a semicircle. Patty asks her young learners to sit on the X marks she has made with masking tape on the carpet.
Lolita asks her three-year-olds to sit or lie wherever they like in the small,
carpeted area, as long as they can see the pictures and the words. Each day
a different child gets to snuggle with her. In all these classrooms, the
teacher sits at the edge of the circle or the carpet on a low chair, holding
the picture book about at the children's eye level. The chair the teacher sits
in to read from is a special chair, used both for teacher read-alouds and for
the children to read their own writing to the class. Each teacher calls this chair *the author's
chair*. Nancy, Patty, and Lolita have mastered reading from the side. Thus, the children can
see the illustrations and the print while the teacher reads. These teachers know the story they
are about to read. They have carefully selected it and read it through in advance, practicing
how it will sound when read aloud. They know how to read it with excitement in their voices.
They are careful not to overdramatize, yet they use pitch and stress to make the printed dialogue sound like conversation. They show that they enjoy the story.

The following sequence describes the typically recommended read-aloud strategies:

1. *Select high-quality literature.* A key element to a successful read-aloud experience is
   the book that is being read. Try to find books that will appeal to the children's interest,
   evoke humor, stimulate critical thinking, stretch the imagination, and so on. Although
   a good story is always effective, also try to include informational books and poetry
   written for young audiences. A great source for locating good read-aloud books is
   Jim Trelease's (2006) *The Read-Aloud Handbook.* Trelease's book is also available at
   www.trelease-on-reading.com.

2. *Show the children the cover of the book.* Draw the children's attention to the illustration on the cover ("Look at the illustration on this book!"). Tell the children the title of the book, the author's name, and the illustrator's name. ("The title of this book is. . . . The author is. . . . The illustrator is. . . .") Point your finger to the title, the author's name, and the illustrator's name as you read each. Remind the children that the title, author's name, and illustrator's name are always on the front cover of the book. Remember that these are new concepts for young children.

3. *Ask the children for their predictions about the story* ("What do you think this story might be about?"). Take a few of the children's predictions about the story's content. ("Let's read to see what this story is about.")

4. *Or, provide a brief introduction to the story.* You might provide background information about the story, connect the topic or theme of the story to the children's own experience, draw the children's attention to the book's central characters, clarify vocabulary that might be outside the children's realm of experiences, and so on. Keep the introduction brief so that there is ample reading time.

5. *Identify where and what you will read.* Two important concepts about print for young children to learn are that readers read the print, not the pictures, on the pages and where readers begin reading. Begin read-alouds by identifying where you will start reading and what you will read. Repeating this important information often ("Now, I'll begin reading the words right here") weaves it into the read-aloud. Be sure to point to the first word on the page as you say where you will begin. Eventually, the children will be able to tell you where to begin reading. After many exposures to this important concept, you might playfully ask, "Am I going to read the words or the pictures in this book?" and "Where should I begin reading?"

6. *Read with expression and at a moderate rate.* When teachers read with enthusiasm and vary their voices to fit different characters and the ongoing dialogue, the story comes alive for children. It is also important to avoid reading too quickly, which Trelease (1989), a leading authority, claims is the most common mistake adults make when reading aloud. He recommends reading slowly enough that children can enjoy the pictures and can make mental images of the story.

7. *Read stories interactively.* Encourage children to interact verbally with the text, peers, and the teacher during the book reading. Pose questions throughout the book reading to enhance the children's meaning construction and to show how one makes sense of text (Fisher, Flood, Lapp, & Frey, 2004). Encourage children to offer spontaneous comments, to ask questions, to respond to others' questions, and to notice the forms and functions of print features (words, punctuation, letters) as the story unfolds. Use these during-reading book discussions to help children understand what to think about as a story unfolds. As indicated earlier, adults (teachers and parents) who use an interactive reading technique facilitate children's language, particularly vocabulary, and early reading development.

8. *Read favorite books repeatedly.* Not every book you read has to be a book the children have never heard before. In fact, repeated readings of books can lead to enhanced comprehension, better postreading discussions, and children's acquisition of expressive and receptive vocabulary (Martinez & Roser, 1985; Morrow, 1988; Sénéchal, 1995). In addition, reading a book three or more times increases the likelihood that

young children will attempt to select that book during free-choice time and will try to reenact or read it on their own (Martinez & Teale, 1988). Of course, the benefits of repeated reading should be balanced against the need to expose children to a wide variety of literature.

9. *Allow time for discussion after reading.* Good books arouse a variety of thoughts and emotions in children. Be sure to follow each read-aloud session with a good conversation and with questions and comments ("What part of the story did you like best?" "How did you feel when . . . ?" "Has anything like that ever happened to you?" "Who has something to say about the story?"). Such open-ended questions invite children to share their responses to the book that was read. After listening to a book read aloud, children want to talk about the events, characters, parts they liked best, and so forth. As children and teacher talk about the book together, they construct a richer, deeper understanding of the book.

When teachers follow the preceding guidelines, they can help ensure that their story reading has the maximum impact on children's literacy learning. Notice how these guidelines encourage educators to make both meaning and print an explicit focus of the storybook reading.

Shared Reading

Teachers usually read picture books to their classes by holding the books so that the children can see the illustrations and by pausing occasionally to elicit students' reactions to the stories or to ask story-related questions. This traditional whole-class read-aloud experience differs from parent–child storybook reading interactions in a very important way: Most children can see only the pictures, not the print. To remedy this situation, Holdaway (1979) devised the *shared book experience*, a strategy that uses enlarged print, repeated readings, and increased pupil participation to make whole-class storybook reading sessions similar to parent–child reading experiences. Today, the shared book experience has become an important component of a quality early literacy program.

PEARSON
myeducationkit

Go to the Assignments and Activities section of Chapter 5 in the MyEducationKit and complete the activity entitled "Shared Reading—The Second Reading in a K-3 Multilingual Classroom." As you watch the video and answer the accompanying questions, note the fluency and expression of the children's choral reading.

To use this strategy, the teacher first needs to select an appropriate book. Andrea Butler and Jan Turbill (1984) recommend stories that have (1) an absorbing, predictable story line; (2) a predictable structure, containing elements of rhyme, rhythm, and repetition; and (3) illustrations that enhance and support the text. These features make it easy for children to predict what is coming up in the story and to read along with the teacher.

Once a book has been selected, an enlarged copy needs to be obtained, which can be done in several ways. The teacher can (1) rewrite the story on chart paper, using one- or two-inch tall letters and hand-drawn illustrations; (2) make color transparencies of the pages from the original picture book and use an overhead projector; or (3) acquire a commercially published big book (about twenty-four by twenty-six inches) version of the story. Scholastic and Wright Group/McGraw-Hill, for example, publish enlarged versions of a number of high-quality picture books. Initially, only picture storybooks were available in the big book size. Today, informational books also can be located in big book size. These ready-made big books have the advantage of saving teachers time by eliminating the need to make enlarged texts. Understandably, they are expensive because they include large versions of the original illustrations.

Unlike when regular-size books are shared with children, big books permit all children to see the print. Teachers may take advantage of the enlarged print by drawing young children's attention to the print in the same ways that a parent draws a child's attention to the print in a regular-size book during a read-aloud. Typically, teachers use a pointer to point to the words as they read big books and invite the children to read along, particularly to the words in a familiar text or to the refrain in a book. As children "read" along with the teacher, they internalize the language of the story. They also learn about directionality (reading from left to right with return sweeps), one important convention of print.

Through the use of big books, teachers can introduce children to other aspects of print: to letter–sound relationships (phonics); to the sequence of letter sounds in words (phonemic awareness); to the difference between letters, words, and sentences; to the spaces between words; to where to start reading on the page; to reading left to right; to return sweeps; to punctuation. In addition, through the use of big books, teachers are able to further children's development of important concepts about books (e.g., the front and back of a book, the difference between print and pictures, that pictures on a page are related to what the print says, that readers read the print, where to begin reading, where the title is and what it is, what an author is, what an illustrator is). In essence, using big books teaches print knowledge, phonological awareness, alphabet knowledge, vocabulary and language, and comprehension skills in context. Read Trade Secret 5.2 to discover how a Head Start teacher Lynn Taylor uses big books with her four-year-olds.

TRADE SECRET 5.2
Ms. Taylor's Shared Reading of *Tabby Tiger, Taxi Driver*

LISA ALBERT AND KATRIN BLAMEY

Ms. Taylor's preschool children read together every day. The following describes how she engages in shared reading with her young children. She begins reading with the big book displayed on the big book easel. The book is closed with children looking at the front cover.

The First Reading

Ms. Taylor begins by reading the children the title, author, and illustrator of the book, pointing to each word as she reads with her pointer, a long stick with a mini hand on the end. "The title of our book is *Tabby Tiger, Taxi Driver*. How many words are in our title? Let's count." The children

count as Ms. Taylor points to the words. She does this to build the children's understanding of the concept of *word*.

"What do you see on the cover of this book?" She asks this question in an attempt to build their background knowledge and help the children to understand what happens in this story. The children respond in chorus, "Tabby Tiger!" as she is a familiar character they have grown to love. "What else do you see?" Ms. Taylor asks. The children respond with everything from "taxi" to "tall buildings" to "a hat." After talking about all of the pictures, she asks the children, "What do you think will happen in this story?" Several of the children say that Tabby will clean her car. "Why do you think that?" One child responds, "Because Tabby

TRADE SECRET 5.2 Continued

has a towel in her hand." Ms. Taylor records a few of the children's predictions on a large piece of chart paper. She then leads the class through a picture walk of the book, looking at each page and asking children to describe what is happening in the pictures. She stops a few pages short of the end of the book though, just as Tabby is driving down a hill. Ms. Taylor does this to help build suspense and leave the children excited about reading the story tomorrow to find out what happens.

The Second Reading
The children rush to the rug today, eager to find out what happens to Tabby. Ms. Taylor begins by reviewing the children's predictions from the day before. She asks if anyone would like to revise their prediction, making each child think about whether they still think their prediction is right. One child shouts out, "I think Tabby is going to crash!" Ms. Taylor explains that good readers make predictions when they read and then look to see if they were right. She reads the title, author, and illustrator again. "Can anyone remind me what the author did?" "She wrote the words," several children reply.

She starts reading the story asking questions on every page. "Where is Ms. Sheep going?" One child yells out, "The supermarket!" "How did you know that?" She leads the class to look at the picture, which shows a grocery cart full of food, and discusses how the pictures tell us what the words say. She repeatedly asks the children to describe what happened to Tabby Tiger on each page, as the children laugh at each accident Tabby has. Her questions are mostly open-ended, encouraging many different children to respond. When they get near the end of the story, the children get very excited to see that Tabby crashed into the pond. Ms. Taylor asks, "How do you think Tabby feels now?" One child responds, "Sad." "Why is she sad?" A child exclaims, "Because she is stuck in the pond!" At the end of the story, they discuss what Tabby needs to do when she drives. The children talk about how she needs to be careful so she doesn't hit things.

Ms. Taylor's goal during this reading was to engage the children in the story. She invites comments and questions on every page in order to build children's comprehension of what happened. She wants the children to understand that readers have to build meaning with a text. Readers think and analyze what they read, making decisions about what they would have done, or what the characters should do.

The Third Reading
Ms. Taylor begins, "Let's look at our cover again today. What things do you see around Tabby Tiger?" One child responds that she is on the road. Another child talks about the tall buildings." Ms. Taylor confirms each answer by saying yes and pointing to it on the cover. "Nice job noticing all of the different things on the cover. You can find all of these things in the city. Can you say, 'city'?" The children respond in chorus, "city." "A city is a place with tall buildings, many cars, and lots of people live there. Tabby drives her taxi in a city. Have you ever been in a city?" One child tells about his trip to New York, and how he even got to ride in a taxi. Ms. Taylor does this to build the children's vocabulary and to help them make connections to the story's content. She knows that one of the strongest predictors of children's reading success is their knowledge of words and their meanings.

As she rereads the story today, she encourages the children to read with her. She points to each word, and slows down at the end of each sentence so the children can fill in the last word. She reviews the vocabulary word, *city,* by asking children on different pages how they can tell that Tabby is still in the city. The children describe the tall buildings on each page and one child shares a story about how she saw a hotdog stand in the city that was just like the one Mr. Elephant had. Ms. Taylor concludes the reading by having the children help to write a shared letter to Tabby Tiger about how to be a careful driver. The children volunteer sentences as she records them on large chart paper. The children help her sound out the words and remember what to write. She models by thinking aloud about what letters to write, where to add punctuation, and the format of a letter.

Linking Literacy and Play

In Chapter 4, dramatic play is described as an ideal context for developing young children's oral language. Dramatic play can also offer a context in which children can have meaningful, authentic interactions with reading and writing in early childhood classrooms (Roskos & Christie, 2000, 2007). The following vignette, which involves four-year-old preschoolers, illustrates some of the advantages of integrating play and literacy:

> With some teacher assistance, Noah and several friends are getting ready to take a make-believe plane trip. The elevated loft in the classroom has been equipped with chairs and has become the plane, and a nearby theme center has been turned into a ticket office. Noah goes into the ticket office, picks up a marker, and begins making scribbles on several small pieces of paper. The teacher passes by with some luggage for the trip. Noah says, "Here Kurt! Here are some tickets." The teacher responds, "Oh great. Frequent flyer plan!" Noah then makes one more ticket for himself, using the same scribblelike script. The teacher distributes the tickets to several children, explaining that they will need these tickets to get on board the plane. As Noah leaves the center, he scribbles on a wall sign. When asked what he has written, Noah explains that he wanted to let people know that he would be gone for a while.

The most obvious benefit of linking literacy and play is that play is fun. When children incorporate literacy into their play, they begin to view reading and writing as enjoyable skills that are desirable to master. Yet there are benefits of linking play and literacy beyond fun. Following a critical review of the play and literacy research, Kathy Roskos and James Christie (2004) suggest three ways that play can serve literacy:

1. By providing settings that promote literacy activity, skills, and strategies
2. By serving as a language experience that can build connections between oral and written modes of expression
3. By providing opportunities to teach and learn literacy

Like functional literacy, linking literacy and play is a broad-spectrum instructional strategy that offers children many opportunities to learn a variety of skills and concepts. In addition, children can learn these skills in many ways, including observation, experimentation, collaboration, and instruction. As a result, there are meaningful opportunities for children at different levels of development to learn new skills and to consolidate newly acquired skills that are only partially mastered. Unlike narrowly focused skill-and-drill activities, opportunities exist for every child in the classroom to advance his or her literacy development.

Literacy-Enriched Dramatic Play Centers

Nigel Hall (1991) recommends that classroom play areas be subjected to a print flood, an abundance of reading and writing materials that go along with each area's play theme. The goal is to make these play centers resemble the literacy environments that children encounter at home and in their communities. For example, a pizza parlor center can be equipped the following props:

- Cardboard pizza crusts (large circles)
- Felt pizza ingredients (tomato sauce [large red circles the same size as the cardboard crusts], pepperoni, black olives, onions, etc.)

- Pencils, pens, markers
- Note pads for taking orders
- Menus
- Wall signs ("Place Your Order Here," "Pay Here," "Shirts and Shoes Required")
- Employee name tags
- Pizza boxes with company name and logo
- Cookbooks
- Bank checks, money, and credit cards
- Newspaper ads and discount coupons

These props invite children to incorporate familiar pizza-parlor-based literacy routines into their play. Research has shown that this print-prop strategy results in significant increases in the amount of literacy activity during play (Neuman & Roskos, 1992, 1997).

In addition, this literacy-enriched play setting provides children with opportunities to learn important concepts about print. At the most basic level, the literacy props illustrate that print has meaning. Children demonstrate this awareness when they point to a menu or wall sign and ask the teacher or peer, "What does that say?" These print props also provide opportunities for children to learn more advanced concepts such as the difference between a letter and a word. Literacy terms, such as *letter* and *word,* are often used by children and adults during play in print-enriched centers.

The pizza parlor setting contains many examples of the functional uses of print. Print is used to convey information on menus and pizza boxes. Signs such as "Place Your Order Here" and "The Line Starts Here" illustrate the regulatory function of print. Pizza parlors also are associated with literacy routines—sets of reading and writing actions that are ordinary practices of a culture (Neuman & Roskos, 1997). These routines demonstrate the instrumental functions of print and present opportunities for children to use emergent forms of writing and reading. Customers can read or pretend to read menus while placing orders. Waiters and counter clerks can use note pads to write down orders that will later be used by the chefs to determine which types of pizzas to bake. Chefs can consult cookbooks for information on how to prepare pizzas. Once the pizzas are baked, customers can use discount coupons from the newspaper to reduce the cost of their meals and pay their bill by writing checks. Not surprisingly, research has shown that adding print-related props to play areas results in significant increases in the amount of literacy activity during play (Roskos & Christie, 2004).

As young children have repeated exposure to print props, opportunities arise for developing alphabet and sight word recognition. Some children may learn to recognize the letter *p* because it is the first letter in *pizza.* Others may learn to recognize entire words such as *pepperoni, menu,* and *cheese.* Research has shown that children learn to recognize environmental print in play settings (Neuman & Roskos, 1993; Vukelich, 1994).

Opportunities also exist to learn comprehension skills. Neuman and Roskos (1997) have detailed how playing in print-enriched settings can lead children to develop several types of strategic knowledge that have a role in comprehending text. In a pizza parlor setting, children have opportunities to:

- *Seek information.* A child might ask a playmate about the identity of a word on the pizza menu.

- *Check to see if guesses and hypotheses are correct.* A child might ask the teacher, "Is this how you spell *pizza*?"
- *Self-correct errors.* While writing the word *pizza* on a sign, a child might exclaim, "Oops, *pizza* has two *z*'s!"

Checking and correcting are self-regulatory mechanisms that build a base for cognitive monitoring during reading.

Preparatory Experiences

Matching the play settings to children's experiences outside the classroom is important. Children can play only what they know. Nigel Hall and Anne Robinson (1995), for example, used a mechanic's garage as a setting for classroom play and as a stimulus for multiple kinds of reading and writing. Prior to initiating the garage play theme, the children were taken on a field trip to a neighborhood mechanic's garage. This firsthand, direct experience greatly increased the children's understanding of what goes on in a mechanic's garage, helped them plan and construct a realistic garage play center, and enhanced their subsequent play.

Teacher Involvement in Play

Lev Vygotsky (1978) has described how adult interaction can facilitate children's development within the children's zone of proximal development. That is, adults can help children engage in activities that go beyond their current level of mastery, which the children could not do on their own without adult mediation. Many opportunities for this type of adult scaffolding occur when children are engaged in dramatic play in literacy-enriched settings (Roskos & Neuman, 1993). Teachers can encourage children to incorporate literacy activities into ongoing play episodes and can help children with reading and writing activities that the children cannot do independently, both of which, in turn, can promote literacy growth. Carol Vukelich (1994) found that when adults assumed the role of a more knowledgeable play partner with kindergartners in print-rich play settings, the children's ability to read environmental print was enhanced.

The following vignette illustrates how one teacher used literacy scaffolding to enrich her four-year-olds' pizza parlor dramatization.

> Channing and several friends ask their teacher whether they may play pizza parlor. The teacher says yes and brings out a prop box containing felt pizza pieces, pizza boxes, menus, tablecloths, and so on. The children spend about ten minutes separating the pizza ingredients (olives, pepperoni slices, onions, and cheese shavings made out of felt) into bins. When they have finished, the teacher asks which pizza shop they would like to be today. They respond, "Pizza Hut." While the children watch, the teacher makes a sign with the Pizza Hut name and logo. Channing requests, "Make a 'Closed for business' sign on the back." The teacher turns over the paper and writes "CLOSED FOR BUSINESS." She then hangs the "CLOSED" sign on the front of the play center. The children spend another ten minutes rearranging furniture and setting up the eating and kitchen areas in their pretend restaurant. When the children have finished their preparations, the teacher asks, "Is it time to open?" Channing responds, "Yeah. Switch the sign now." The teacher turns the "CLOSED" sign

over so that the Pizza Hut logo is showing. The teacher then pretends to be a customer, reads a menu, and orders a pizza with pepperoni, green peppers, onions, and lots of cheese. Once the cooks have piled the appropriate ingredients onto the pizza, the teacher carries it over to a table and pretends to eat it. When she finishes eating, she writes a make-believe check to pay for her meal.

The teacher played several important roles in this episode. First, she served as *stage manager,* supplying the props that made the pizza play possible. She also provided scaffolding, making signs that the children could not make on their own. The "Pizza Hut" and "CLOSED" signs provided environmental print for the children to read and also created an opportunity for the children to demonstrate their growing awareness of the regulatory power of print. The pizza shop could not be open for business until the "CLOSED" sign was taken down.

The teacher also served as a *coplayer,* taking on a role and becoming a play partner with the children. Notice that she took the minor role of customer, leaving the more important roles (pizza cooks) to the children. While in the role of customer, the teacher modeled several literacy activities, such as menu reading and check writing. Several children noticed these behaviors and imitated them in future play episodes.

Research has revealed that teachers assume a variety of roles when interacting with children during play (Enz & Christie, 1997; Roskos & Neuman, 1993). The keys to successful play involvement are for teachers to observe carefully and to choose an interaction style that fits with children's ongoing play interests and activities. The teachers' ability to switch styles to fit the children's play agenda appeared to be as important as the specific interaction styles the teachers used.

When teachers set up literacy-enriched play settings and become involved in play in appropriate ways, they provide children with opportunities for meaningful engagements with emergent reading and writing. They help children see different uses for familiar props and create new props, expand the children's repertoire of play themes and roles by exposing them to new experiences (through field trips, guest speakers, and carefully chosen videos), and help children use appropriate strategies to plan and carry out their play (Bodrova & Leong, 2003).

Play-related literacy activities go hand in hand with such functional, real-world writing activities as signing up to use a popular center, making an invitation to class parties or performances, writing a message to the custodians ("Plz du nt tch"), and so on. Both types of literacy engagements give children opportunities to form, try out, and perfect their own hypotheses about the function and structure of print.

Shared Writing

The language experience approach (LEA), which became popular in the 1970s (Allen, 1976; Veatch, Sawicki, Elliot, Flake, & Blakey, 1979), has children read texts composed of their own oral language. Children first dictate a story about a personal experience, and the teacher writes it down. The teacher reads the story back to the children and then gives them the opportunity to read it themselves. Sometimes the children illustrate their dictated sentences. This strategy is now referred to as *shared writing*.

The shared writing strategy is an excellent means for teachers to demonstrate the relationship between speaking, writing, and reading. It can help children realize (1) that what is said can be written down in print, and (2) that print can be read back as oral language.

Like functional print and play-based literacy, the language experience or shared writing strategy presents children with many learning opportunities. At the most basic level, shared writing helps children learn that the purpose of written language is the same as that of oral language: to communicate meaning. For other children, the strategy enables teachers to demonstrate explicitly the structure and conventions of written language. The children watch as the teacher spells words conventionally, leaves spaces between words, uses left-to-right and top-to-bottom sequences, starts sentences and names with capital letters, ends sentences with periods or other terminal punctuation marks, and so on. This method is an ideal way to show children how the mechanical aspects of writing work.

Shared writing has the additional advantage of making conventional writing and reading easier for children. By acting as scribe, the teacher removes mechanical barriers to written composition. The children's compositions are limited only by their experiential backgrounds and oral language. Reading is also made easier because the stories are composed of the children's own oral language and are based on their personal experiences. This close personal connection with the story makes it easy for children to predict the identity of unknown words in the text.

A number of variations of shared writing have been developed. In the sections that follow, three that are particularly appropriate for use with young children are described: group stories, individual stories, and shared writing

Group Stories

This strategy begins with the class having some type of shared experience: The class takes a field trip to a farm, to a zoo, across the street to the supermarket, to see a play; the class guinea pig has babies; the class completes a special cooking activity or other project. As described in Trade Secret 5.3, shared reading of literature can also lead to a shared writing experience. Whatever the event, the experience should be shared by all members of the group so that everyone can contribute to the story.

The following is a description of how a kindergarten teacher might engage children in a group shared story-writing experience:

1. The teacher begins by gathering the children on the rug in the whole-group area to record their thoughts about the experiences—to preserve what they recall in print. Teachers often begin with a request to "tell me what you remember about . . . ?"
2. As children share their memories, the teacher records exactly what the children say. The teacher does not rephrase or correct what a child says. The teacher records the children's language, just as they use it. The sentence structure, or syntax, is the child's. The spellings, however, are correct. As the teacher writes the child's comments on a large sheet of chart paper with a felt-tip marker in print large enough for all the children to see, the teacher verbalizes the process used to construct the text. (The teacher might choose to write on the chalkboard, overhead transparency, or chart paper.)

When doing group experience stories, the teacher takes sentences from only a small number of students. Taking sentences from all the children would make the sitting

TRADE SECRET 5.3
Shared Writing

San Luis Preschool teacher Mrs. Lemos links shared reading with shared writing activities. Today she has just finished reading the big book *There Was an Old Lady Who Swallowed a Fly,* by Simms Taback (2000, Scholastic). It is one of the children's favorite books. Mrs. Lemos has decided to use the children's enthusiasm for the story as a stimulus for a group experience story, with a twist—it will be a group letter. Mrs. Lemos starts the lesson by saying, "Maybe today we can write a letter to the Old Lady Who Swallowed the Fly. Who would like to help me write the letter?" Almost all of the children raise their hand and shout out, "Me! Me!" Mrs. Lemos has already written the beginning of the letter at the top of a large piece of chart paper. She reads this to the children: "Dear Old Lady. . . ." Then she says, "Okay, what do we want to say next?" She picks Dileanna, who says, "Don't eat a fly and don't eat lots of candy." Mrs. Lemos writes down Dileanna's words, repeating them as they are written. Once she has written the words, Mrs. Lemos rereads Dileanna's sentence. Then she asks, "Why shouldn't she eat lots of candy?" and a child responds, "Because it's not good for us!" Mrs. Lemos then says, "What else can we say?" Keetsia volunteers, "Don't eat all of the animals," and Mrs. Lemos write this down and reads it back to class. As Mrs. Lemos writes *eat,* Nubia shouts out, "No, Mrs. Lemos, *eat* starts with a *t*!" Mrs. Lemos sounds out the word (/ê- t/) and says, "Yes, *eat* does have a *t,* but it comes at the end of the word. Eat starts with the /ê/ sound. What letter makes that sound?" Several children respond *E.* The children continue contributing things that the Old Lady shouldn't eat: a cow and a spider. Then Mrs. Lemos asks, "Should we put anything else?" and several children mention healthy food. So Mrs. Lemos concludes the story with, "You should eat healthy foods." Nubia again helps with the spelling, pointing out that *healthy* starts with an *h.* Mrs. Lemos then rereads the story:

> Dear Old Lady,
> Don't eat a fly and don't eat lots of candy.
> Don't eat all of the animals.
> Don't eat a cow.
> Don't eat a spider.
> You should eat healthy foods.

Then Mrs. Lemos writes, "From your friends," and reads it to the class. Dileanna says, "And our names so she knows." Mrs. Lemos responds, "That's a good idea. Each of you can come up and write your name so she knows who wrote this letter. Roberto, would you like to come first?" All of the children then take turns writing their names at the end of the letter. Finally, Mrs. Lemos says, "We're going to read our letter one more time" and reads it again with class. The children have figured out what the print says by this point and are able to read along fluently with Mrs. Lemos.

time too long for the young learners. If a student's contribution is vague or unclear, the teacher might have to ask the child to clarify the point or may have to do some *minor* editing to make the sentence comprehensible to the rest of the class. The teacher must exercise caution when a student's contribution is in a divergent dialect (e.g., "He ain't funny."). Changing this utterance to so-called standard English may be interpreted as a rejection of the child's language. This, in turn, might cause the child to cease to participate in future experience stories. In such cases it is usually better to accept the child's language and not change it.

3. When the whole story is created, the teacher rereads it from beginning to end, carefully pointing to each word and emphasizing the left-to-right and return-sweep progression. Then the class reads the story as a group (a practice called *choral reading*). Often a child points to the words with a pointer as the class reads.

4. The teacher hangs the story in the writing center, low enough so interested children can copy the story. Because the teacher wrote the story on chart paper (teachers' preferred medium for group stories), the story can be stored on the chart stand and reviewed periodically by the class. Sometimes the teacher rewrites each child's sentence on a piece of paper and asks the originator to illustrate his or her sentence. The pages are then collected into a book, complete with a title page listing a title and the authors' names, and placed in the library corner. These books are very popular with the children. Other times, the teacher makes individual copies of the story—via photocopying or word processing—for each child.

Individual Experience Stories

In an individual experience story, each student meets individually with the teacher and dictates her or his own story. As the child dictates, the teacher writes the story. Because the story is not intended for use with a group audience, editing can be kept to a minimum, and the child's language can be left largely intact. Once the dictation is completed, the teacher reads the story back to the child. This rereading provides a model of fluent oral reading and gives the child an opportunity to revise the story ("Is there anything you would like to change in your story?"). Finally, the child reads the story.

Shared writing is an excellent way to teach the structure and conventions of writing.

A variety of media can be used to record individual experience stories, each with its own advantages. Lined writing paper makes it easier for teachers to model neat handwriting and proper letter formation. Story paper and unlined drawing paper provide opportunities for children to draw illustrations to go with their stories. Teachers can also use the classroom computer to make individual experience stories. Children enjoy watching the text appear on the monitor as the teacher keys in their story. Word processing programs make it easy for the teacher to make any changes the children want in their stories. Stories can then be printed to produce a professional-looking text.

Individual experience stories can be used to make child-generated books. One approach is to write children's stories directly into blank books. Blank books are made of sheets of paper stapled between heavy construction paper or bound in hard covers. An alternative approach is to staple completed experience stories between pieces of heavy construction paper. For example, books can be made up of one student's stories ("Joey's Book") or of a compilation of different children's stories ("Our Favorite Stories" or "Our Trip to the Fire Station"). Child-authored texts can be placed in the classroom library for others to read. These books tend to be very popular because children like to read what their friends have written.

Individual experience stories have several important advantages over group stories. The direct personal involvement produces high interest and motivation to read the story. There is a perfect match between the child's experiences and the text, making the story very easy to read. Children also feel a sense of ownership of their stories and begin to think of themselves as authors.

The one drawback to this strategy is that the one-to-one dictation requires a considerable amount of teacher time. Many teachers make use of parent volunteers or older students (buddy writers) to overcome this obstacle. Another strategy is to have a tape recorder available for children to dictate their stories. Teachers can then transcribe the children's compositions when time allows. Of course, children miss out on valuable teacher modeling when tape recordings are used.

Interactive Writing

An extension of the group experience story approach is known as *interactive writing*. Like the creation of the group experience story described above, interactive writing follows a series of steps (Boroski, 1998). A significant difference is that the teacher shares the pen with the children, inviting them to write some of the letters and words on the chart paper. There are six recommended steps of interactive writing:

1. Negotiate a sentence. The teacher and the children collaborate to write a meaningful sentence that can be read.
2. Count the number of words on fingers. The teacher repeats the agreed-on sentence slowly, putting up one finger for each word spoken. Then, the teacher and the children say and count the number of words in the sentence.

PEARSON
myeducationkit

Go to the Assignments and Activities section of Chapter 5 in the MyEducationKit and complete the activity entitled "An Interactive Writing Activity." As you watch the video and answer the accompanying questions, note how the teacher helps the children write the sentence, "We made apple-tasting graphs."

PEARSON
myeducationkit

Go to the Assignments and Activities section of Chapter 5 in the MyEducationKit and complete the activity entitled "Interactive Writing." As you watch the video and answer the accompanying questions, note how first graders are able to do more of the writing on their own compared with the kindergartners in the previous video.

3. Recall each word to be written and stretch the word. The teacher articulates each word slowly, stretching the word to help the children hear each phoneme of each word.

4. Using a felt-tip pen, the teacher invites a child to volunteer to take the pen and write part of the word or the whole word on the chart paper.

5. Point and read. The teacher or a child points to each word written on the chart, and everyone reads the word aloud.

6. Recall the sentence and begin again at step 3. At step 5, there will now be two words to read.

In Trade Secret 5.4, Noreen Moore describes how Sue Reichle, a kindergarten teacher, uses an adapted version of the above six steps.

TRADE SECRET 5.4
Scaffolded Interactive Writing

NOREEN MOORE

Ms. Sue's kindergarten class is clustered attentively around her on the colorful alphabet carpet as she finishes her read aloud of Robert Munsch's *Moira's Birthday*. Ms. Sue asks the children if they can make a text-to-self connection. Immediately hands bolt up in the air, waving frantically; the children are anxious to share their connections between the text and their own birthdays. Lila describes her cake with pink flowers, Bryce talks about his cake shaped like Mickey Mouse, and Cameron recounts her birthday party at Build-a-Bear.

Ms. Sue takes this opportunity to engage in an interactive writing activity in which children write about their text-to-self connections. After several children have shared their connections, the class votes on which child's text-to-self connection they would like to write about as a group. In an almost unanimous vote, the children decide to write about Bryce's birthday cake.

Bryce shares his text-to-self connection with the class again. He proudly announces, "My cake was Mickey Mouse."

Ms. Sue asks the children to count the words in Bryce's sentence. All of the children count aloud using their fingers, "one . . . two . . . three . . . four . . . five," as Ms. Sue repeats the sentences and counts on her fingers, "My . . . cake . . . was . . . Mickey . . . Mouse." Next, Ms. Sue draws

five lines, representing each of the words in the sentence, on a piece of chart paper. As she draws the five lines, she repeats Bryce's sentence, "My . . . cake . . . was . . . Mickey . . . Mouse." With the lines clearly displayed, she invites individual children to go to the chart paper and write a word in Bryce's sentence. Jonathan approaches the chart paper first and writes "My" with a capital "M" because it is the first word in the sentence. As a child writes a word on the chart paper, the children sitting on the carpet write the word themselves using a pointer finger in one hand as the pen and the palm of their other hand as the paper. After each word, Ms. Sue praises the child who wrote the word on the chart paper and asks the children sitting on the carpet to show her the "writing" they did on the palm of their hands. The class continues in this way until Bryce's sentence is written.

Next, the children write their own text-to-self connections independently at their tables. Many children have mastered drawing lines to represent the words in their writing. They use clothespin space men to help them leave spaces between words. Other children request Ms. Sue's help in drawing the lines to match the words in their sentence after they dictate it to her. Ms. Sue continues to circulate the room checking in on children and talking to them about their writing. Soon, all children have written a successful sentence and they are enjoying illustrating what they have written.

Strategies for Teaching English Language Learners

MYAE HAN

Classroom Environment

Imagine yourself in a subway station trying to find a way to get to the other station. Add a little more imagination; you are in a foreign country, and everything is labeled in a language you cannot read. How would you find your way?

This may be how new immigrant children feel when they enter the classroom in the United States for the first time. Fortunately, most preschool classrooms are filled with hands-on materials and activities for the children's engagement. Teachers can modify their classroom environment to make easy access for ELLs. An environment that thoughtfully accommodates the cultural and linguistic needs of children helps smooth ELLs' adjustment and transition from home to school. Such environments also support ELL children's language and literacy development. Below are several strategies to make the classroom environment more welcoming for ELL children.

- Include pictures and words in each ELL child's first language when labeling classroom areas and objects.
- Display the daily schedule with pictures, such as story time, snack time, cleanup, hand washing, etc. This gives a general sense of daily structure.
- Display the children's names with pictures and verbalize them as often as possible. Have other English-speaking children say the names of ELL children. This supports positive peer relationships. Peer partners are very helpful in a classroom with a diverse population. Researchers have found that peer tutoring has a positive impact for both English-speaking and ELL children (Hirschler, 1994).
- Have ample play materials that children can play with without assistance. Teachers should ensure that they are providing places in the classroom where ELL children can feel comfortable, competent, and occupied.
- Early in the school year, it is desirable to stick with a strict routine to minimize the ELL children's confusion. This helps the ELL children to adjust in the classroom and feel more secure sooner.
- Include a picture dictionary in the classroom library.

Free-Play Time/Center Time/Choice Time

Most preschool classrooms provide a free-choice time during the day. Researchers found that lengthy play periods (at least forty-five to sixty minutes) can promote children's self-expression and self-direction (Isenberg & Jalongo, 1993). Children become self-directed learners when they know that they have enough time during the school day to complete the learning activities they have chosen. Free-play time is also less stressful than structured group time for ELL children. It also is a time when the classroom adults can provide individual support to the ELL children within the context of joyful activities.

What can teachers do to support ELLs during free-play time? Tabors (1997) recommends two strategies: running commentary and context-embedded language. Running commentary is a strategy called "talking while doing." When teachers use this strategy, they explain their actions or others' actions as an activity unfolds. For example, a teacher might say, *"I'm getting some writing paper from the shelf here and I'll need a Magic Marker from the writing tools box. I'm writing a note to myself to remember to get popcorn for the children tomorrow. I write 'p-o-p-c-o-r-n [saying each letter as she writes it]."* Context-embedded language is language related to the immediate situation, particularly in the course of sociodramatic play. In child-initiated activities, the child creates a context first, and then the teacher follows the child's action verbally so that the teacher's language is more meaningful to children. For example, Martinec and De'Zebbra are building in the block corner. The teacher says, *"De'Zebbra is putting one block down. Martinec is putting one block on top of De'Zebbra's block. De'Zebbra is putting one block on top of Martinec's block."* The teacher

(continued)

Strategies for Teaching English Language Learners   Continued

continues this description of the children's actions in this context until she says, *"Look! Martinec and De'Zebbra built a tall tower!"*

Storybook Time
Large-group story time is one of the most challenging times for teachers with ELL children. Teachers fear that these children may not understand the story but still need to listen to a book. The following are several suggestions for ways teachers might make storybook reading more successful:

- Start with patterned books or predictable books. These books are highly repetitive and have simplified texts that make it easy for ELL children to become engaged with them. Gradually expand beyond predictable books to books consistent with the children's interests. When choosing books, consider the vocabulary, length, and cultural sensitivity.
- When children are not following the book's words, talk the story rather than reading it. Also consider the use of puppets or storytelling props to assist children's understanding of story. For example, one of the popular children's books *There Was an Old Lady Who Swallowed a Fly* can be better understood with a prop of a big old lady. Before the story is read, say the names of the animals. As the story

is read, attach the animal figures to the old lady's stomach.
- Keep storybook reading time short. Don't make storybook reading time a patience contest. If the book is too long, it is fine to stop in the middle and finish at a later time.
- Consider small group book reading. Instead of having one large group story time, teachers can have small group story time with different groups of children during free-choice time or by splitting the group into two groups and having the teacher read to one group while the classroom assistant reads to the other group. When grouping children, flexible grouping (mixing ELL children with English-speaking children) is recommended. However, depending on the type of book, the content, and level of difficulty, the teachers may consider grouping only the ELL children together on some occasions.
- Repeated reading is important. Read the same book at least three or four times. Children get more information each time they listen to the story. It is also important to remember to focus on different aspects of the story each time the book is read. For example, during each reading, focus on different vocabulary words, predictions of what will happen next, comprehension questions, or alphabet letters.

Strategies for Children with Special Needs

KAREN BURSTEIN AND TANIS BRYAN

On Your Mark
Teachers in preschools, kindergartens, and the primary grades are increasingly likely to have students with special needs in their classrooms. Typically, the majority of these children have speech and/or language impairments, developmental delays, and learning disabilities. A smaller number of these children have mental and or emotional disturbances, sensory

disabilities (hearing or visual impairments), and physical and health impairments. The latter reflects increases in the number of children surviving serious chronic conditions (e.g., spina bifida, cystic fibrosis) and attending school as well as increases in the number of children with less life-threatening but nonetheless serious health (e.g., asthma) and cognitive (e.g., autism) problems.

Public policy and law, including the 1997 Individuals with Disabilities Education Act (IDEA), along with humane and ethical considerations dictate that children with disabilities receive optimal educational programs, given our knowledge bases and resources. Further, IDEA stipulates that children with special needs be provided their education in classes with their same-age peers to the greatest extent possible.

One of the primary goals of early education is to prepare all young children for general education classrooms. Making this a reality for children with special needs requires that teachers make accommodations and adaptations that take into account the individual student's special needs. Teachers' willingness to include students with disabilities and their skillfulness in making adaptations are critical determinants of effective instruction. This special feature outlines strategies and suggestions for teachers who have young students with special needs in their classrooms. Our purpose is to provide suggestions for making adaptations so that teachers feel comfortable, confident, and successful including these students in their classrooms.

Get Set

Cognitive, physical, sensory, developmental, physical, emotional—there are so many variations in development! It is not reasonable to expect general education teachers or special education teachers to be experts on every childhood malady. The primary lesson to remember is that children are far more alike than they are different from one another. Whatever their differences, children desire and need the company of other children. They are more likely to develop adaptive behaviors in the presence of peers. Children with special needs can succeed academically and socially in mainstreamed settings (Stainback & Stainback, 1992; Thousand & Villa, 1990).

Setting the stage for an inclusive classroom takes somewhat more planning. Effective planning includes input and support from the school administration, other teachers, parents of children with special needs, and possibly the school nurse. Early and frequent collaboration with your special education colleagues is particularly helpful. There are signifi-

cant differences between general and special education teachers' perspectives on curriculum and methods of instruction. Sometimes they differ in expectations for children.

Collaboration works when teachers constructively build on these different points of view. For collaboration to work, teachers have to respect different points of view, have good listening skills, and be willing to try something new. Here are some strategies for collaboration:

- Attend the student's multidisciplinary team meeting.
- Keep a copy of the individual family service plan (IFSP) or individualized education plan (IEP) and consult it periodically to ensure that short- and long-term goals are being achieved.
- Arrange to have some shared planning time each week with others who work with students with special needs.
- Brainstorm modifications/adaptations to regular instructional activities.
- Identify who will collect work samples of specific tasks.
- Assess the student's language, reading, and writing strengths, and give brief probes each week to check on progress and maintenance.
- Share copies of student work with your collaborators and add these artifacts to the student's portfolio.
- Collaborate with families. Parents are children's first and best teachers. Additionally, they possess personal knowledge of their children that far surpasses any assessment data we may collect.

Go

As previously mentioned, the majority of children with special needs have difficulties in language, reading, and written expression. Research indicates that these problems stem from deficits in short-term memory, lack of self-awareness and self-monitoring strategies, lack of mediational strategies, and inability to transfer and generalize learned material to new or novel situations. Hence, many students with special needs may have difficulty in classroom settings

(continued)

Strategies for Children with Special Needs   Continued

that utilize a high degree of implicit teaching of literacy. These students typically can benefit from explicit instruction. Here are some general teaching strategies that teachers can use to support students with special needs:

- Establish a daily routine on which the student with special needs can depend.
- Allocate more time for tasks to be completed by students with special needs.
- Structure transitions between activities, and provide supervision and guidance for quick changes in activities.
- Adapt the physical arrangement of the room to provide a quiet space free of visual and auditory distractions.
- Plan time for one-on-one instruction at some point in the day

- Use task analysis to break learning tasks into components.
- Recognize the different learning styles of all students, and prepare materials in different ways—for example, as manipulatives, audio recordings, visual displays, and the like.
- Try cross-ability or reciprocal peer tutoring for practice of learned material.
- Consistently implement behavior change programs.
- Encourage all students to respect and include students with special needs in their academic and play activities.
- Establish a routine means of communication with parents.
- Locate strategies that help parents select materials that are developmentally and educationally appropriate for their students.

Summary

When most children enter preschool or kindergarten, they already possess considerable knowledge about reading and writing. Teachers can capitalize on this prior learning by using a number of effective yet remarkably simple instructional strategies that link home and school literacy learning. In this chapter, we discussed four strategies that form a solid foundation for an effective, developmentally appropriate early childhood language arts program: functional literacy activities, storybook reading, play-based literacy, and the language experience approach/shared writing.

PEARSON
myeducationkit™

To check your comprehension on the content covered in this chapter, go to the MyEducationKit for your book and complete the Study Plan for Chapter 5. Here you will be able to take a chapter quiz and receive feedback on your answers.

- *What are functional literacy activities, and how can teachers use these activities in a preschool or kindergarten classroom?*

Functional print (labels, lists, directions, and schedules) is ideal for beginning readers because the surrounding context helps explain its meaning. This contextualized print is easy for young children to read and helps them view themselves as real readers. In addition, functional literacy activities help develop the concept that reading and writing have practical significance and can be used to get things done in everyday life. This realization makes print more salient to children and provides important motivation for learning to read and write. Functional print also presents opportunities for children to learn to recognize letters and words in a highly meaningful context.

■ *How can teachers set up a well-designed library center?*

A well-stocked and managed classroom library should be a key feature of every early childhood classroom. To encourage young children to engage in book reading in this area, the classroom library must be well designed, with partitions, ample space, comfortable furnishings, open-faced and traditional bookshelves, and book-related props and displays. Teachers will know quickly if their classroom library meets the criteria for being well designed; inviting classroom libraries are heavily used by the children.

■ *What are the characteristics of effective adult storybook reading?*

What adults say—the verbal interaction between adult (parent or teacher) and child—during story readings has a major influence on children's literacy development. During storybook readings, children learn about the turn taking inherent in all conversation. The adult helps the child negotiate the meaning of the text, assisting by relating the content to personal experiences, providing information, asking questions, and setting expectations. Who talks the most and the content of the talk varies with the child's age.

Specific read-aloud strategies have been recommended for use in early childhood classrooms. A general read-aloud structure includes the following: read aloud every day, select high-quality literature, show and discuss the cover of the book before reading, ask children to make predictions about the story, provide a brief introduction, identify where and what you will read, read with expression at a moderate rate, read some stories interactively, read favorite stories repeatedly, and allow time for discussion after reading.

Shared reading through the reading of big books is also recognized as a critically important practice in quality early childhood literacy programs. Big books permit all children to see the print, something not possible when teachers read aloud from a regular-size book. By using big books, teachers can introduce children to the conventions of print and the concepts about books.

■ *How can dramatic play centers be used to encourage young children's literacy development?*

Dramatic play provides an ideal context for children to have meaningful, authentic interactions with print. Dramatic play offers children of all ages and abilities multiple low-risk opportunities to explore and experiment with reading and writing.

■ *How does shared writing increase a child's understanding of print and facilitate reading development?*

The shared writing strategy involves having the teacher write stories that children dictate. In interactive writing, the teacher and child share the pen, both writing to create the text (with the child doing most of the writing). The resulting child-authored stories are a dynamic means to demonstrate the connections among talking, reading, and writing. As the teacher writes the children's speech, the children immediately see the one-to-one correspondence between spoken and written words. Because the children are the authors of these highly contextualized stories, they can easily read the stories. Experience stories can be composed either by a single child or by a group of children. Group stories are more time efficient, but individual stories are more personalized and ensure a perfect match between reader and text. In interactive writing, the teacher shares the pen with the children, inviting them to write some of the letters and words.

LINKING KNOWLEDGE TO PRACTICE

1. Visit a preschool or kindergarten classroom and record the different types of functional literacy activities and the ways they are used in the classroom. How did the children respond to or use functional print within classroom? Did the teacher refer to the functional print?

2. Observe a library center in an early childhood classroom and evaluate its book holdings and design features. Are there a large number and wide variety of books available for the children to read? Are any basic types of books missing? Does the library center contain partitions, ample space, comfortable furnishings, open-faced and traditional bookshelves, and book-related props and displays? Is there a writing center nearby?

3. Select a specific read-aloud strategy. Using this strategy, tape yourself during a read-aloud with a small group of children. Analyze your read-aloud style for the strategies suggested in this chapter. What goals would you set for yourself?

4. With a partner, design plans for a literacy-enriched play center. Select a setting appropriate for a group of children. Describe how this center might be created in a classroom. What literacy props could be placed in the play center? What functional uses of print might be used to convey information? What literacy routines might children use in this center? What roles might children and teacher play? How might you scaffold children's play and literacy knowledge in this play center?

5. Observe a shared writing activity. Describe how the teacher used this opportunity to teach children about the forms and functions of print.

CHAPTER

6

Teaching Early Reading and Writing

Martha Vasquez, teacher in a "reverse mainstream" preschool classroom in the Somerton school district in southwestern Arizona, is in the middle of a thematic unit on water and sea creatures. Today she has decided to center her instruction on syllable segmenting, a phonological awareness skill that is part of her state's Early Learning Standards. She begins by holding up cards with children's first names written on them. She asks the children first to recognize whose name is on the card and then clap and count the number of syllables in the name. The children have become quite good at this, quickly shouting out the names (e.g., "Christopher") and number of syllables ("three"). The children enjoy the activity and are very engaged. Next up is the poster part of the lesson. Mrs. Vasquez first asks children how many syllables are in the word poster, *and the children shout out "two!" Then she reads the rhyme poster, which is about a submarine. While the main purpose of the poster is to teach rhyme recognition, Mrs. Vasquez focuses on vocabulary and syllable segmenting. She reads the poster with the children, encouraging them to make motions that go with the rhyme (e.g., putting their fingers together to make pretend glasses for the word* periscope). *Then she asks individual children to count the syllables in several words from the poster (e.g.,* submarine). *Finally, she moves onto the vocabulary phase of the lesson. As before, she asks the children how many syllables are in the word* vocabulary. *She says the word in syllable segments and holds up a finger for each syllable. The children clap each syllable. Four children quickly shout out "five!" Being able to count the syllables in a five-syllable word is quite an accomplishment for four-year-olds! Next, Mrs. Vasquez holds up picture/word cards that contain words related to the unit theme. She asks the children to say the word and then asks them a question about it. For example, after the children identify the picture of a whale, she asks, "Where would you find a whale?" Several children respond, "In the ocean!" She also has them make motions for the words when appropriate (as with* wave). *When words contain more than one syllable (e.g.,* rainbow), *Mrs. Vasquez asks the children to clap and count syllables. The academic level of these activities is quite high for preschool, especially since two thirds of the children in this reverse mainstreamed classroom have identified special needs. But all students seem able to successfully participate (two assistant teachers are there to help), and they appear to enjoy showing off their rapidly growing literacy skills.*

Mrs. Vasquez's instruction exemplifies the scientifically based reading research (SBRR) approach to early literacy instruction. She is directly teaching her students skills that will prepare them to learn to read in kindergarten and the primary grades. When she has children recognize their classmates' written names, she is teaching them print awareness. When she has them count the number of syllables in words, she is teaching a phonological awareness skill. When she has children identify, use, and discuss the words on the picture/word cards, she is directly teaching them new vocabulary. Since many of her children are English language learners, this latter skill is particularly important.

It is important to note that this type of direct, focused instruction is only part of the literacy instruction that the children in Mrs. Vasquez's classroom receive. She also reads them several books every day. In addition, the children have an hour-long center time in which they choose what to do. On the day described above, Mrs. Vasquez read the book *Rainbow Fish* by Marcus Pfister (North-South Books, 1992) to the class, and children had the following choices: (a) engage in dramatic play in an ocean-theme center, complete with a cardboard boat; (b) play with miniature replicas of sea creatures; (c) play a game where they can "catch" letters with a fishing pole with a string and magnet on the end; and (d) make a cut-and-paste picture of the Rainbow Fish with multicolored scales, and read books in the library with the teacher.

Mrs. Vasquez's literacy program is an example of what we refer to as a comprehensive curriculum. It combines emergent literacy strategies (described in Chapter 5) with scientifically based instructional strategies. Mrs. Vasquez directly teaches skills contained in the Arizona Early Learning Standards. The syllable segmenting activities described above help her children master the following standard: *Strand 2 Prereading Processes, Concept 3—Sounds and Rhythms of Spoken Language: c. Identifies syllables in words by snapping, clapping, or other rhythmic movement.* We believe that such a combination is the most effective way to help young children learn to read and write.

This chapter begins with a description of developmentally appropriate strategies for teaching "core" early reading skills, including phonological awareness, alphabet knowledge, print awareness, word recognition, and phonics. Next, strategies for teaching early writing are discussed, including the writing center, the writing workshop, interactive writing, and publication.

Before Reading This Chapter, Think About . . .

- How you learned the names of the letters of the alphabet. Did you learn by singing the alphabet song?
- How you learned the sounds letters make. Do you remember phonics workbooks or learning phonics rules (e.g., when two vowels go walking, the first one does the talking)?
- How you learned to write (not handwriting, but actual writing). Do you remember writing messages to special people, maybe messages that were lines and lines of scribble? Do you remember writing on walls, much to someone's dismay?

Focus Questions

- Which reading skills should early childhood teachers provide in order to give their children an opportunity to learn?

- What is the difference between phonological awareness, phonemic awareness, and phonics? In what sequence do young children typically acquire these skills? What does this sequence suggest about classroom instructional strategies?
- How might early childhood teachers introduce young children to the letters of the alphabet?
- Why is a writing center an important area in the preschool classroom? How might an adult teach in the writing center?
- How does a teacher teach during a writing workshop?
- Why is it important to publish children's writing?

Early Reading Instruction

As discussed in Chapter 1, scientifically based reading research (SBRR) came into prominence in the late 1990s, along with the movement to establish early childhood academic standards and skill-oriented policy initiatives such as No Child Left Behind and Good Start, Grow Smart. Whereas emergent literacy has relied primarily on qualitative forms of research, the SBRR perspective uses well-designed correlational studies and tightly controlled experiments. Proponents of SBRR believe that these types of rigorous "scientific" research can reveal: (1) the skills and concepts that young children need to master to become proficient readers and writers and (2) the most effective strategies for teaching this content.

Perhaps the SBRR movement's most valuable contribution to early literacy education has been the identification of "core" knowledge and skills that young children must have to become successful readers. Longitudinal studies have shown that preschool-age children's oral language (expressive and receptive language, including vocabulary development), phonological awareness, and alphabet knowledge are predictive of reading achievement in the elementary grades (Snow et al., 1998). Print awareness, which includes concepts of print (e.g., understanding how print can be used) and conventions of print (e.g., left-to-right,

BOX **6.1**

Definition of Terms

alphabetic principle: the idea that that there is a relationship between alphabet letters, or groups of letters, and the sounds of oral language.

onsets: the beginning parts of words.

phonemes: the individual sounds that make up spoken words.

phonemic awareness: the awareness that spoken words are composed of individual sounds or phonemes.

phonics: the relationship between sounds and letters in written language.

phonological awareness: the awareness of the sound structure of oral language.

rimes: the endings parts of words.

writing center: an area in the classroom that is stocked with materials (different kinds of paper, different writing tools) to invite children to write.

top-to-bottom sequence), has also been found to be positively correlated with reading ability in the primary grades (Snow et al., 1998).

SBRR investigators have also focused on identifying effective strategies for teaching this core literacy content to young children. One of the most consistent research findings is that young children's phonological awareness and alphabet knowledge can be increased via direct, systematic instruction (National Early Literacy Panel, 2008). This instruction can often take the form of games and other engaging activities, but it also contains the elements of direct instruction: teacher modeling, guided practice, and independent practice.

In the sections that follow, we provide examples of how "core" early reading skills are taught in the SBRR approach: phonological awareness, alphabet knowledge, phonics, and print awareness. Examples of teaching the other core skill—oral language—are presented in Chapter 4.

Phonological and Phonemic Awareness

A "massive body of work has established that phonological awareness is a critical precursor, correlate, and predictor of reading achievement" (Dickinson, McCabe, Anastaspoulos, Peisner-Feinberg, & Poe, 2003, p. 467), and discriminating units of language (i.e., words, segments, phonemes) is linked to successful reading (Carnine, Silbert, & Kameenui, 2004; National Reading Panel, 2000). Clearly, phonological and phonemic awareness are two closely related skills that play an important role in early literacy development. *Phonological awareness* is a broader term, referring to awareness of the sound structure of speech. *Phonemic awareness* is an advanced subset of phonological awareness that involves awareness that spoken words are composed of individual sounds or *phonemes* (Yopp & Yopp, 2000). Both are important for all young children to possess if they are to become successful readers. These phonological processing skills lay the foundation for learning *phonics*, the relationships between letters and the sounds that they represent.

Marilyn Adams (1990) suggests that if children are to succeed at reading, especially if the reading program they meet in the primary grades relies heavily on phonics, phonemic awareness is the most crucial component of an early literacy program. Early childhood teachers must look for ways to help their young children attend to the sounds in the language. This is a new challenge for early childhood teachers. In the past, children have been denied phonological and phonemic awareness instruction because teachers did not realize the importance of this skill. Children were first taught to recognize letters and then taught the sounds associated with the letters (i.e., phonics). Now we know that before phonics instruction can be fully useful to young children, they need phonemic awareness. They must be aware of the individual sounds in words before they can begin to match these sounds up with letters. By not teaching phonological and phonemic awareness, teachers were making it difficult for many children to learn phonics!

Growth in phonological awareness begins in infancy, so even the teacher of the youngest child is a phonological awareness instructor. Initially, babies hear language as one big "blah, blah, blah." However, as

PEARSON
myeducationkit™

Go to the Assignments and Activities section of Chapter 6 in the MyEducationKit and complete the activity entitled "Phonemic and Phonics Instruction." As you watch the video and answer the accompanying questions, note how the teacher begins this lesson by focusing on letter sounds (phonemic awareness instruction) and ends the lesson by adding print (phonics instruction).

discussed in Chapter 2, babies quickly learn to distinguish the unique phonemes that make up their native language. These early speech lessons occur naturally as most adults use "parentese" to communicate with infants (parentese is an exaggerated, slowed, higher-pitched, and highly articulated form of speech that allows infants to see and hear their native language; see Chapter 2). Phonological awareness begins when young children are able to hear the boundaries of words; for example, *Seethekitty* becomes *See the kitty*. As sounds become words that are frequently used in context to label specific objects, the acquisition of word meaning begins.

The ability to hear distinct words and make meaningful associations usually emerges between nine and eighteen months (Cowley, 1997; Stern, 2000), and children quickly become specialists in their native tongue. However, as children begin to hear and consistently produce the discrete sounds that comprise their language, the ability to hear and accurately produce the phonemes of other languages rapidly diminishes. Robert Sylvester (1995) calls this process "neural selectivity." The networks for phonemes that aren't in the local language may atrophy over time due to lack of use. This creates a challenge for children who do not speak the language of instruction when they enter school, as they often experience difficulty with hearing the phonemes and word boundaries of a second language.

Research has revealed a developmental trajectory in children's acquisition of phonological processing skills (see Figure 6.1). In general the movement is from larger units to smaller units. Marilyn Adams (1990) suggests that before young children can become aware of phonemes—the individual sounds that make up spoken words—they first must become aware of larger units of oral language. Thus, children must first realize that spoken language is composed of words, syllables, and sounds. They need to learn to recognize when words rhyme by ending with the same sound and instances where several words begin with the same sound (i.e., alliteration). They also need to be able to segment sentences into words, and words into syllables. As mentioned earlier, this broader understanding is referred to as phonological awareness.

FIGURE 6.1   Phonological Processing Skills

PHONOLOGICAL AWARENESS

(1) Rhyme—words that end with same sound
(2) Alliteration—words that start with same sound
(3) Word and syllable segmenting—divide sentences into individual words and divide words into syllables

PHONEMIC AWARENESS

(4) Phoneme isolation (/kan/, /kar/, & /kap/ begin with /k/ sound)
(5) Blending phonemes (/k-a-t/ = /kat/)
(6) Segmenting phonemes /kat/ = /k-a-t/
(7) Manipulating phonemes

- deletion   /Snapple/ - /Sn/ = /apple/
- addition   /p/ + /art/ = /part/
- manipulation   /kat/ - /a/ + /o/ = /kot/

Once these skills are mastered, children can begin to focus on the individual sounds of language and develop phonemic awareness. When children have fully mastered phonemic awareness, they are able to take individual sounds and blend them into whole words, break down words into individual sounds, and even manipulate the sounds in words (e.g., replace the middle sound of a word with another sound, so that *cat* become *cut* and *fan* becomes *fun*).

Research is clear that phonological awareness and phonemic awareness are metalinguistic abilities (Adams, 1990). As such, children not only must be able to recite and play with sound units but also must understand that sound units map onto parts of language. While children's initial entry into phonological awareness might be through recitations and playing with sound units, such activities appear to be insufficient. Explicit instruction is required (Snow et al., 1998). In addition, teachers are cautioned against focusing too much attention on rhyming. Though rhyme is a good starting point for building awareness of the sounds of language, rhyming has not been found to be a significant predictor of children's reading skills (e.g., Mann & Foy, 2003; Muter & Diethelm, 2001).

In the sections that follow, we describe a number of strategies that teachers can use to increase children's phonological and phonemic awareness. We have ordered these to match the general development sequence of phonological processing.

Phonological Awareness.   Phonological awareness activities focus children's attention on the sounds of words. In rhyming activities, children learn to recognize when words end with the same sound. In alliteration activities, the focus shifts to the beginning sounds of words. Segmenting activities help children learn to break oral sentences up into individual words and take individual words and break them up into syllables. Onset and rime activities involve segmenting initial sounds from ending syllables in selected groups of words. These activities make children aware of the sounds of language and lay the foundation for phonemic awareness.

Rhyme.   Rhyme activities focus children's attention on the ending sounds of words (e.g., *bee, flea, we*). There are two levels of rhyme awareness: rhyme identification, in which children can indicate which words rhyme, and rhyme production, in which children can, when given examples of rhyming words (*fat, cat, mat*), come up with other words that fit the rhyme pattern (*rat, sat, Laundromat*). Identification is the easier of the two. Research by Fernandez-Fein and Baker (1997) showed that children's knowledge of nursery rhymes and the frequency that they engage in word play were both strong predictors of children's phonological awareness. It is not surprising, therefore, that many research-based strategies for promoting phonological awareness in preschool and kindergarten use playful activities such as singing songs, reciting nursery rhymes, reading books that play with the sounds of language, and gamelike activities (e.g., Adams, Foorman, Lundberg, & Beeler, 1998).

Rhyme identification instruction often begins by inviting children to recite or sing well-known nursery rhymes such as "Jack and Jill,"

PEARSON
myeducationkit™

Go to the Assignments and Activities section of Chapter 6 in the MyEducationKit and complete the activity entitled "Matching Sounds." As you watch the video and answer the accompanying questions, note how this playful center time activity helps children practice rhyming and the varying levels of support (scaffold) the children need.

PEARSON
myeducationkit™

Go to the Assignments and Activities section of Chapter 6 in the MyEducationKit and complete the activity entitled "Activities that Foster Phonemic Awareness." As you read the artifact and answer the accompanying questions, note the developmentally appropriate ways that children can be helped to develop their ability to rhyme.

TRADE SECRET 6.1

A Rhyme Production Activity

In a video published by Allyn and Bacon (2000), kindergarten teacher Grant Clark demonstrates how a song/book, *Down by the Bay* by Raffi (Crown, 1987), can be used to help children learn to produce rhyming words that fit a pattern. *Down by the Bay* is a predictable song that has the refrain "Did you ever see a goose kissing a moose, Down by the bay?" "Did you ever see a whale with a polka-dot tail, Down by the bay?" The two words that fit in the blanks always rhyme: fly–tie, bear–hair. When Mr. Clark reads the book to the class,

he pauses slightly before reading the second word. This enables the children to use their knowledge of rhyme and the clues given by the book illustrations to come up with the second part of the rhyme. After he has finished reading the book, he continues to sing the song with the children, letting the children come up with their own pairs of rhyming words, some of which are quite amusing. For example, one girl came up with "Did you ever see a book kissing a hook, Down by the bay?"

"Humpty Dumpty," or "Hickory Dickory Dock." After children become familiar with the rhyme, the teachers can go back and highlight the rhyming words, pointing out that these special words end with the same sound. Then teachers can help children identify the rhyming words. Once children are able to identify these words, teachers can repeat a rhyme, pausing before the words that rhyme, giving children time to predict the upcoming word ("Humpty Dumpty sat on a wall. Humpty Dumpty had a big _____.") (Ericson & Juliebö, 1998). This is the first step toward rhyme production. Ultimately, teachers can present the rhyming words from a story and ask children to supply more words that fit the rhyme pattern ("In this story, *wall* and *fall* rhyme—they end with the same sound. Can you think of other words that rhyme with *wall* and *fall*?").

Trade Secret 6.1 illustrates how kindergarten teacher Grant Clark uses the popular song *Down by the Bay* to help children learn to go a step beyond rhyme identification and produce their own rhymes.

A few words of caution: Beware of *only* providing children with rhyming activities. The research literature clearly shows that children's ability to rhyme is a consistently weak predictor of their later reading comprehension (National Early Literacy Panel, 2008).

Alliteration.   Alliteration occurs when two or more words begin with the same sound (e.g., *Bibbity bobbity bumble bee*). As with rhyme, there are two levels of alliteration awareness: (1) identification—recognizing that several words start with the same sound; and (2) production—after hearing several words that begin with the same sound (*sand, sailboat, seal, sun*), children can produce other words that start with same sound (*sing, snake*). As with rhyme, instruction begins by reading or singing songs and stories that contain examples of alliteration (e.g., "My baby brother Bobby bounced his favorite ball."). The teacher should first point out and explain the examples of alliteration ("*Baby, brother, Bobby,* and *ball* all start with the same sound, /b/."). Then children can be asked to identify the words that "start alike." Once children can recognize alliteration, they can be helped to come up with other words that start with the same sound.

San Luis Preschool teacher Lisa Lemos systematically introduces her children to a letter and its sound every two weeks using a published program, *Sound, Rhyme and Letter Time* (Wright Group/McGraw-Hill, 2002). For example, she introduced the sound of the letter *S* by showing children a chart that contains pictures of objects that start with this sound (*sun, seal, sailboat, sandwich, sand, sunglasses, seashell*). She began by having the children identify the objects on the poster. Most of Mrs. Lemos's children are English language learners, so this helped to build vocabulary as well as phonological awareness. Next, she pointed out the names of all the objects that begin with the same sound: /s/. She then had the children take turns identifying and saying the names of the objects. She then asked if the children knew any other words that start with this sound. At the beginning of the school year this was a challenge for the children. On this day, however, one child was able to come up with a Spanish word, *sol,* that starts with the /s/ sound. Mrs. Lemos praised the child for coming up with such an excellent example, commenting that both *sol* and its English counterpart *sun* start with the /s/ sound. Later that day, she sent a note home with the children, telling their families that the class is studying the letter *S* and requesting objects from home that begin with the /s/ sound. The next day, about half of the children brought objects to share. The children took turns sharing their objects with the class. For example, Alexis showed a small replica of a star and said its name. Mrs. Lemos said, "Yes, *star* begins with the /s/ sound." Then Mrs. Lemos wrote the word *star* on the whiteboard and drew a small picture of a star. Next, Izac shared his stuffed snake (which was a big hit with his classmates), and Mrs. Lemos added *snake* and a drawing of a snake to the whiteboard. After adding the names and drawings of all the objects that the children have brought to share, Mrs. Lemos put a big sun in the middle of the *S* web. This web remained up for the remainder of the two weeks that the /s/ sound was studied. Through these activities, Mrs. Lemos was helping her children master the Arizona Early Learning Standard *Strand 2 Prereading Processes—Concept 3 Sounds and Rhythms of Spoken Language: d. Recognizes when different words begin or end with the same sound.*

Word and Syllable Segmenting.   Activities that help children learn how to segment sentences into words and words into syllables help set the stage for full phonemic segmentation—the ability to divide words up into individual sounds.

■ *Word segmenting.* The goal is to develop children's awareness that oral language is made up of strings of individual words. Children initially have difficulty with word boundaries. For example, young children often think that *before* is actually two words (because of syllable segmentation) and that *once upon a time* is one word (because the words are often blended together with little pause in between). Teachers can help children divide speech up into separate words by reciting familiar nursery rhymes (e.g., "Jack and Jill") and inviting the children to join in. The teacher then explains that rhymes are made up of individual words. She recites the rhyme again, clapping as each word is spoken. Children then join in, clapping the words along with the teacher. This is continued until the children can clap the words accurately. Finally, the teacher reconstructs the rhyme by inviting each child to say one word of the rhyme in sequence (Wright Group, 1998). Activities in which children track print, such as the shared reading of big books described in Chapter 5, are also effective ways to help children discover the concept of word.

■ *Syllable segmenting.* Activities that develop the ability to analyze words into separate syllables take segmenting to the next stage. Syllables are a unit of spoken language larger than a phoneme but smaller than a word. Once children can divide words up into syllables (*begin* can be divided into *b••g•n*), full phonemic awareness is just a step away (*begin* can be segmented into *b-•-g-•-n*). The vignette at the beginning of this chapter describes how Martha Vasquez teaches this important skill. She begins by having children clap and count the syllables in their classmates' names. She then has children clap and count syllables in a rhyme poster and in vocabulary words on picture/word cards. What we like best about Mrs. Vasquez's approach is that she keeps returning to this skill throughout the day, giving children many brief but focused opportunities to practice and perfect it.

Onset and Rime Substitution. Onsets and *rimes* are often used as an instructional bridge between phonological and phonemic awareness. Onsets and rimes are "families" of words that end with the same vowel and consonant cluster (e.g., *-at*: *bat, cat, fat, hat, mat, rat, sat*). The beginning consonant is referred to as the onset and the medial vowel and ending consonant are called the rimes. Onset and rime substitution activities, in which the child substitutes different onsets with a set rime (*c-ake, b-ake, sh-ake, m-ake*) are the easier phonemic awareness activities because the word is only broken into a beginning and ending part (*f-ake*) rather than into individual phonemes (*f-•-k*). Onsets and rimes also build a foundation for learning the sounds represented by vowels. In the primary grades, onsets and rimes are often used as a way to teach long and short vowel sounds because rimes have consistent letter–sound relationships. The vowel *a* represents many different sounds but when it is paired with *ke,* forming the *ake* rime, it almost always represents the long *a* sound. In primary-grade phonics instruction, rimes are often referred to as phonograms or word families. Trade Secret 6.2 presents an example of a preschool onset and rime lesson.

TRADE SECRET 6.2
An Onset and Rime Activity

New Castle County, Delaware, Head Start teacher Debby Helman uses an onset and rime activity as a transition from circle time to getting-ready-for-lunch time. Ms. Helman begins by telling the children that to leave the circle today they are going to play a game with rhymes. She begins, "Listen to this word: *hop*. Now if I take the /h/ away from *hop* and I put a /p/ on /op/, what new word did I make? /p/-/op/." The children are quiet. Just as she is about to speak, Jemelda shouts, "Pop!" Ms. Helman compliments her and invites her to go wash her hands for lunch. She asks, "Who can put a different letter sound on /op/ and make a different rhyming word?

[pause] When you see a red light you _____." A child shouts, "Stop!" Ms. Helman says, "Right! /St/ on /op/ makes /st/-/op/." She invites the child who provided the word *stop* to go wash his hands. She says, "We wash up spills with a ___op." Kathryn says, "Mop!" Ms. Helman says, "Kathryn took the /p/ off /op/, put on an /m/, and made *mop*." Kathryn goes to wash her hands. These examples have helped the children understand how to play this game. Soon the children produce *shop, cop, top, bop, nop,* and more /-op/ words. [Notice that *nop* is a nonsense word. It is acceptable to play this game with nonsense words.]

Phonemic Awareness.   Through the phonological awareness exercises described above, children become aware that the words in speech are composed of sequences of individual sounds or phonemes. This conscious awareness of phonemes sets the stage for children to discover the alphabetic principle that there is a relationship between letters and sounds. Learning these letter–sound relationships, in turn, facilitates "sounding out" written words that are in children's oral vocabulary but are not familiar in print (Stanovich, 1986).

On entering school, children's level of phonemic awareness is one of the strongest predictors of success in learning to read (Adams, 1990). In fact, phonemic awareness has been shown to account for 50 percent of the variance in children's reading proficiency at the end of first grade (Adams et al., 1998).

Unfortunately, phonemic awareness is difficult for many young children to acquire. Marilyn Adams and her colleagues (1998, p. 19) report that phonemic awareness eludes roughly 25 percent of middle-class first-graders and substantially more of those who come from less literacy-rich backgrounds. Furthermore, these children evidence serious difficulty in learning to read and write.

One reason that phonemic awareness is difficult to learn is that there are few clues in speech to signal the separate phonemes that make up words (Ehri, 1997). Instead, phonemes overlap with each other and fuse together into syllabic units. Adams and her colleagues (1998) give the example of *bark*. They point out that this word is not pronounced /b/, /a/, /r/, /k/. Instead, the pronunciation of the medial vowel *a* is influenced by the consonants that precede and follow it. Because phonemes are not discrete units of sound, they are very abstract and are difficult for children to recognize and manipulate (Yopp, 1992). This is why most children need direct instruction on phonemic awareness. The challenge is to make this instruction appropriate for young children. We believe that strategies presented below meet this important criterion.

Phoneme Isolation.   Phoneme isolation activities focus children's attention on the individual phonemes, the smallest units of sound, that make up words. This is the beginning of true phonemic awareness.

- *Sound matching.* Children decide which of several words begins with a specific sound (Yopp & Yopp, 2000). For example, the teacher can show children pictures of familiar objects (*cat, bird, monkey*), and ask which begins with the /b/ sound.
- *Sound isolation.* Children are given words and asked to tell what sound occurs at the beginning, middle, or ending (Yopp, 1992). For example, the teacher can ask, "What's the sound that starts these words: *time, turtle, top*?" Or she can ask children to "Say the first little bit of *snap*" (Snow et al., 1998).

Phoneme Blending.   In blending activities, children combine individual sounds to form words. The game "What am I thinking of?" is a good way to introduce blending to preschoolers (Yopp, 1992). The teacher tells the class that he is thinking of an animal. Then he says the name of the animal in separate phonemes: "/c/-/a/-/t/." Children are then asked to blend the sounds together and come up with the name of the animal.

Phoneme Segmenting.   Segmenting is the flip side of blending. Here, teachers ask children to break words up into individual sounds (Stahl, Duffy-Hester, & Stahl, 1998). Lucy Calkins (1994) calls the ability to segment words "rubber-banding," stretching words out to hear the individual phonemes. For example, the teacher can provide each child with counters and

Elkonin boxes, a diagram of three blank squares representing the beginning, middle, and ending sounds in a word (e.g., ☐☐☐). Children are asked to place counters in the boxes to represent each sound in a word. For the word *cat,* a marker would be placed in the left-hand square for /c/, another in the center square for /a/, and a third in the right-hand square for /t/. The props are designed to make this abstract task more concrete for children.

Phoneme Manipulation.   Phoneme manipulation is the most advanced form of phonemic awareness. These activities require children to add or substitute phonemes in words:

- *Phoneme addition.* Say a word and then say it again with a phoneme added at the beginning (*an > fan*) or end (*an > ant*).
- *Phoneme deletion.* Say a word and then say it again without the initial (*farm > arm*) or ending (*farm > far*) sound.
- *Phoneme substitution.* Substitute initial sounds in lyrics of familiar songs (*Fe-Fi-Fiddly-i-o > De-Di-Diddly-i-o*) (Yopp, 1992).

In a video published by Allyn and Bacon (2000), kindergarten teacher Grant Clark demonstrates how the book *The Hungry Thing* by Jan Slepian and Ann Seidler (Scholastic, 1971) can be used to teach phoneme manipulation. In the book, a large creature comes into town with a sign saying "Feed me." When asked what it would like to eat, the creature mispronounces the name of a series of foods. For example, if it wants pancakes, it says "shmancakes." The adults try to come up with complicated interpretations (e.g., schmancakes are a strange kind of chicken), but a little boy figures out that one just needs to substitute a different beginning sound to make sense of what the creature is saying (*schmancakes > fancakes > pancakes*). Once the children in his class catch on to the pattern, Mr. Clark pauses and sees if the children can figure out what food the creature wants (*tickles > pickles*). The children soon are shouting out the correct names of the food as soon as the creature mispronounces the words. After reading the story, Mr. Clark follows up by playing a game. He reaches into a bag, which he says is his lunch bag, and describes a food item, mispronouncing the initial sound like the creature in the story. For example, when he grabs the replica of a clump of grapes, he says, "Oh, these must be napes!" Then he asks the children what they think *napes* are. They quickly catch on and say "grapes!" He then pulls out a simple cardboard replica of a cluster of grapes. Next is *phizza,* and so on.

Alphabet Knowledge

Alphabet identification in kindergarten is a strong predictor of later reading achievement (Chall, 1996), and the National Early Literacy Panel (2008) has identified alphabetic knowledge as a core component of early literacy instruction. In addition, research indicates that the phonemic awareness instruction is more effective when it is taught along with alphabet knowledge (Ehri, Nunes, Willows, Schuster, Yaghoub-Zadeh, & Shanahan, 2001). As discussed above, phonemes are not discrete units in speech (Adams et al., 1998). Instead, phonemes are influenced by adjacent sounds in words. Alphabet letters provide a concrete representation for the "elusive" phonemes that make up words.

What do children seem to be learning when they begin to name and write alphabet letters? By the time young children say the alphabet letter names, they have begun to make discoveries about the alphabet. Children who have had experiences with print come to understand that the squiggles on the paper are special; they can be named. Toddler Jed, for example, called all letters in his alphabet books or in environmental print signs either *B* or *D* (Lass, 1982). At this very young age, he had already learned that letters were a special form of graphics with names. Three-year-old Frank associated letters with things that were meaningful to him. He argued with his mother to buy him the *Fire truck* (not just the car) because "It's like me!" He pointed to the *F.* (Incidentally, his argument was successful.) Giti pointed to the *z* on her blocks and said, "Look, like in the zoo!" (Baghban, 1984, p. 30). These three young children have learned to associate letters with things important to them.

Alphabet knowledge can be divided into two subskills: identification and naming. Alphabet identification involves being able to point out a letter that someone else names. For example, a teacher might ask a child to point to the letter *C* on an alphabet frieze (a chart that lists all of the letters in alphabetical order). Alphabet naming requires naming a letter that someone else points to. For example, the teacher could point to the letter *C* on the alphabet chart and ask, "What's the name of this letter?" Of the two skills, naming is the more difficult.

PEARSON
myeducationkit

Go to the Assignments and Activities section of Chapter 6 in the MyEducationKit and complete the activity entitled "Transition Activity: Alphabet." As you watch the video and answer the accompanying questions, note how this teacher of young children uses a transition from group time to lining up to leave the classroom to reinforce a literacy skill, alphabet knowledge.

We have also included phonics—the study of letter–sound relationships—in this section. Once children have developed phonemic awareness and have begun to learn to identify the letters of the alphabet, they can begin to learn the sounds that are associated with those letters. So we have categorized phonics as the most advanced aspect of alphabet learning. Many pre-K and kindergarten teachers make phonics the capstone of their teaching of each letter. What often happens in large group phonics instruction with four-year-olds is that children with good phonemic awareness learn letter–sound relationships as a result of this teaching, whereas children who are slower in developing phonological processing skills will receive extra exposure to letters and their names. This is not necessarily bad, as long as the teacher understands what each child is expected to get out of the instruction. Of course, a preferable alternative is to use small group instructions tailored to needs of individual children.

Should early childhood teachers expect all children to identify and name all letters of the alphabet by the time the children are five? Certainly not! However, state early childhood academic standards always include alphabet knowledge as a key instructional objective. For example, the Arizona Early Learning Standards and the 1999 reauthorization of Head Start (*Good Start, Grow Smart,* 2002, p. 8) both specify that by the end of preschool, children should be able to name at least ten letters of the alphabet. Children in Early Reading First programs are expected to be able to name nineteen letters of the alphabet. So building alphabet knowledge does need to be a key component of early literacy programs.

While it is generally accepted that alphabet knowledge should be an instructional objective, there is some controversy over which specific letters to teach and the order in which to teach them. Some argue that different letters should be taught to each child. For example, Lea McGee and Don Richgels (1989) believe that it is preferable to teach letters that match children's current interests and activities. In order to deliver this type of individualized alphabet instruction, teachers need to observe closely to learn about the types of contexts in which children notice letters (e.g., environmental print, computer keyboards, books, friends' T-shirts). These contexts provide wonderful opportunities for informal talk and instruction about the alphabet. Examples of "informal" alphabet learning activities include:

- *Environmental print.* Bring environmental print items to class (empty cereal boxes, cookie bags, etc.) and encourage children to read the print's message and discuss prominent letters (e.g., the letter *C* on a box of corn flakes).
- *Reading and writing children's names.* As discussed in Chapter 5, printed versions of children's names can be used for a variety of functional purposes, including attendance charts, helper charts, sign-up lists, and so on. Names of classmates have inherent high interest. Take advantage of every opportunity to read these names and to call attention to letters in the names ("Look, Jenny's and Jerry's names both start with the same letter. What letter is it?").

PEARSON

myeducationkit™

Go to the Assignments and Activities section of Chapter 6 in the MyEducationKit and complete the activity entitled "Name Lotto: Upper and Lower Case Alphabet." As you watch the video and answer the accompanying questions, note the children's enjoyment and the level of support, the scaffolding, the teacher provides during this alphabet teaching activity.

- *Traditional manipulatives.* Many traditional early childhood manipulatives can be used to support children's alphabet letter name learning. These manipulatives include alphabet puzzles, magnetic uppercase and lowercase letters, felt letters, letter stencils, and chalk and chalkboards.
- *Writing.* Whenever children engage in writing, on their own or with a teacher (e.g., shared writing), their attention can be drawn to the letters of the alphabet. Remember that even if children are using scribbles or another personalized form of script, they are attempting to represent the letters of the alphabet and thus are learning about letters.
- *Alphabet books.* Many types of alphabet books are available. For young children who are just learning the alphabet, books with simple letter–object associations (e.g., illustrations that show a letter and objects that begin with the sound associated with the letter) are most appropriate (Raines & Isbell, 1994). Alphabet books offer an enjoyable way to introduce children to letters and the sounds they represent. Research has shown that repeated reading of ABC books can promote young children's letter recognition (Greenewald & Kulig, 1995).

It is also beneficial for children to make their own alphabet books. These child-made ABC books typically have a letter at the top of each page. Children then draw pictures and/or cut and paste illustrations of objects that begin with the sound of each letter. They can also write any words they know that contain the target letter. An adult can label the pictures.

Other researchers recommend that the alphabet be taught in a systematic order to all children, using more direct forms of instruction. Two basic assumptions underlie this position. First, it is assumed that it is difficult for teachers to individualize alphabet instruction for all the children in their classroom. If this individualization is not done effectively, some children will "fall through the cracks" and not learn much about the alphabet. Second, it is assumed that there is logical sequence for alphabet instruction. Some letters should be taught before others. For example, Treiman and Kessler (2003) discovered that young children learn letters in about the same order. For example, *O* is one of the easiest letters for children between the ages of three and seven to recognize. Letters such as *D, G, K, L, V,* and

Direct, systematic instruction on selected letters promotes alphabet knowledge.

Y are more difficult for children and typically are among the last children recognize. Hence, Bowman and Treiman (2004) suggest that teachers should expose children to the printed letters in the order of difficulty, introducing the easiest letters first to build the foundation, followed by the more difficult letters.

Further, looking at lower socioeconomic kindergarten classrooms, researcher Ray Reutzel (2009) found that teaching a letter a day, in any order, was a more successful approach than the traditional letter-a-week method. He hypothesizes that more frequent exposures to alphabet letters help young children to learn the letters significantly better than the duration of exposure.

We strongly recommend a blended approach, providing children with the individualized, informal forms of alphabet learning described above plus systematic instruction on selected letters. The order of the letters can be based on ease of learning or on other curriculum factors. For example, teachers may wish to focus on letters that fit with the stories and experiences highlighted in the curriculum. If the class is going to take a field trip to the fire station, for example, it might be an ideal time for them to learn the letter *F*. This letter will be encountered on the field trip, in shared reading of books about fires and firefighters, in play activities connected with the theme, and in shared writing.

The following are some of the strategies that we recommend for direct instruction on the alphabet.

Songs.   The "traditional" alphabet song is the way children are most often introduced to letters at home (Adams, 1990). While there are some advantages to learning the names of letters in this fashion (e.g., the names give children a peg on which to attach perceptual information about letters), the song can also lead to misconceptions (e.g., that *lmnop* is one letter). In addition, Schickedanz (1998) argues that learning to recite the alphabet from memory is a trivial accomplishment that contributes little to children's learning to read. Yet the report by the National Research Council (Burns et al., 1998) suggests singing the alphabet song as one of many activities early childhood teachers should use to support children's literacy learning.

Other songs can also be used to help children learn the alphabet. For example, Marla Chamberlain, who teaches at the San Luis Preschool in Arizona, uses a song with the lyrics

> Can you find the letter _?
> The letter _?
> The letter _?
> Can you find the letter _,
> Somewhere in this room?

She writes the lyrics on five large pieces of tagboard with slots to hold different letters. The class currently is studying the letter *M,* so she has written this letter on four cards that can be placed in these slots. The song now becomes:

> Can you find the letter M?
> The letter M?
> The letter M?
> Can you find the letter M,
> Somewhere in this room?

Mrs. Chamberlain sings the song with the children and then waits for them to answer the question posed by the song. Most of the children hold up their hands. One child says "monkey," pointing to a picture of a monkey on a poster that has an upper- and lowercase *M* on it. Another child points to the class calendar and says "Monday." Because of the slots, this song chart can be used for practice in identifying all of the letters that the class studies.

Letter Charts.   Letter charts contain a letter (usually its upper- and lowercase forms) and pictures of objects that start with the letter. Teachers can purchase or make these, using pictures from magazines, environmental print, and so on. As described above in the section on teaching alliteration, San Luis Preschool teacher Lisa Lemos systematically introduces her children to a letter and its sound every two weeks, using a published program, *Sound, Rhyme and Letter Time* (Wright Group/McGraw-Hill, 2002). This program provides a letter poster showing pictures of objects that begin with a "target" letter. For example, the letter *S* poster has pictures of a sun, seal, sailboat, sandwich, sand, sunglasses, and a seashell. During the first week, Mrs. Lemos focuses on the sound of the letter, helping children realize that all of the objects on the chart start with the same sound, /s/. She also helps children come up with other words that start with the /s/ sound. During the second week, Mrs. Lemos teaches children about the letter *S.* She begins by reviewing the words represented on the poster, reminding the children that all these words begin with the /s/ sound. Next she writes a label for each picture on a Post-it Note, with the first letter in a different color, and places the labels on the pictures. She points out that all of the words start with the same letter, *S.* Next Mrs. Lemos removes the labels from the poster and has the children put the labels back on the chart next to the corresponding object. When they do this, Mrs. Lemos asks them to say the letter name, letter sound, and whole word. This is repeated over several days so that all of the children get several turns. By using this two-week routine with each letter, Mrs. Lemos is helping her children development phonemic awareness, letter recognition, and phonics.

Alphabet Word Walls.   A word wall is a collection of words displayed on a classroom wall that is used for instructional purposes. In an alphabet word wall, large upper- and lowercase letters are arranged on the wall in alphabetical order, and words that begin with each letter are posted below. Each day, one or two special words are selected for placement on the word wall. These words can come from the stories, rhymes, songs, and poems that the class is reading. They can also include children's names, familiar environmental print, and words from thematic units, and they are placed under the letters that they start with. At the pre-K level, teachers often include a picture to go along with each printed word. Picture supports tends to get phased out in kindergarten. The teacher can use the words on the word wall to reinforce letter identification and letter naming. Lisa Lemos uses her word wall during transitions from large group to small group instruction. She asks each child to point to a letter that she says (letter identification), or she will say the name of a letter, hand the pointer to a child, and ask the child to point to the letter (letter naming). Each child gets a turn before going to the next activity, and Mrs. Lemos helps those who have difficulty. Usually children can quickly point to or name the letters because the pictures that go with the words and the familiar environmental print give helpful clues.

Games.   Games are frequently used in SBRR instruction to provide children with the practice needed to consolidate and retain the skills that are being taught through direct instruction. When practice activities are put into a game format, skill practice can become fun and enjoyable for children. They will persist at games much longer than activities such as worksheets and workbook exercises. On the day that author Jim Christie was observing Martha Vasquez's syllable segmenting instruction, described at the beginning of this chapter, Ms. Vasquez had also planned an alphabet game for her preschoolers to play during center time. The game involved fishing for letters that were on little replicas of fish. The children would catch the fish with magnets on strings suspended from small poles. One of Vasquez's assistant teachers, Christian Garibay, stationed himself in the dramatic play area so that he could scaffold the children's play with the letters. When children caught a letter, he would ask them to name it. What was remarkable is that a group of five boys spent more than thirty minutes engaging in this letter naming practice.

At the San Luis Preschool, teacher Lisa Lemos has her children play a game that combines alphabet practice with the traditional "A Tisket, a Tasket, a Red and Yellow Basket" song. A small group of children sits on the floor, and Mrs. Lemos gives one of them a letter carrier hat and a small basket that contains large pieces of poster paper, each with a letter written on it. While the children sing the "tisket, tasket" song, the "mail carrier" walks around the group and gives one child a letter from the bag. The child who receives the letter then must say the name of the letter. Then this child becomes the mail carrier. Again, the game format and make-believe role-playing ensure high levels of child engagement.

Researcher Judy Schickedanz (1998) recommends two alphabet games that are particularly useful in reinforcing young children's growing alphabet knowledge:

1. *Alphabet-matching puzzles,* in which the children match loose letter tiles with letters printed on a background board.

2. *Alphabet clue game,* in which the teacher draws part of a letter and then asks children to guess which letter he or she is thinking of. After children make their guesses, the teacher adds another piece to the letter and has the children guess again.

Phonics Instruction

Phonics involves using the *alphabetic principle* (letters have a relationship with the sounds of oral language) to decode printed words. Young children differ greatly in their need for instruction in this important decoding skill. Stahl (1992, p. 620) explains: "Some will learn to decode on their own, without any instruction. Others will need some degree of instruction, ranging from pointing out of common spelling patterns to intense and systematic instruction." Thus, as in all other aspects of literacy instruction, it is important for phonics teaching to match the needs of individual students.

The children who learn phonics more or less on their own simply need to be provided with the types of meaningful reading and writing activities described in Chapters 4 and 5—shared reading and writing, literacy-enriched play, and functional literacy activities. As these children engage in these purposeful literacy activities, they gradually discover the relationship between letters and sounds.

Those who need a moderate amount of assistance profit from what Morrow and Tracey (1997) term "contextual instruction." This type of instruction occurs in conjunction with the same types of activities described in the preceding paragraph—shared reading and writing, literacy-enriched play, and functional literacy activities. The only difference is that while children are engaging in these activities, the teacher draws children's attention to letter–sound relationships that are present.

Morrow and Tracey (1997) give an example of how one teacher, Mrs. M., drew her students' attention to the letter *M* and its sound during an activity that involved both shared writing and functional writing:

> Because her class had finished putting on a show for their grandparents, Mrs. M. thought it would be a good idea if they wrote a thank-you note to the music teacher who assisted them with the performance. The note was composed by the students with the teacher's help. She wrote the note on the board and sounded out each word to help the students with spelling. After they finished writing, Mrs. M. read the entire note and had the students read the note aloud:
>
> **MRS. M.:**   How should we start this letter?
>
> **Student:**   Dear Mr. Miller.
>
> **Mrs. M.:**   Very good. [as she writes] "Dear Mr. Miller" has three words. *Dear* is the first word, *Mr.* is the second word, and *Miller* is the third word. I just realized that my name and Mr. Miller's name both begin with the same letter, *M.* Let's say these words together, "Mr. Miller, Mrs. Martinez." (p. 647)

This type of spontaneous teaching can occur in connection with all the literacy learning activities described in Chapters 4 and 5. Of course, such teaching requires a teacher who is on the lookout for teachable moments involving letter–sound relationships. Because most, if not all, preschool and kindergarten classes contain some children who need moderate assistance, we recommend that teachers make an effort to take advantage of these types of teaching opportunities when they arise.

Another way to help children acquire knowledge about phonics is through writing (IRA/NAEYC, 1998; Stahl, 1992). Once children have reached the invented spelling stage in their writing development, they begin to use their knowledge of letter names and letter–sound relationships to spell words. During this stage, children spell words the way that they sound rather than how they are conventionally spelled. For example, a child may spell the word *leave* with the letters *lev* because this is how the word sounds. When children use invented spelling, their attention is naturally focused on letter–sound relationships.

Research indicates that temporary use of invented spelling can promote children's reading development (IRA/NAEYC, 1998). For example, a study by Clarke (1988) found that young children who were encouraged to write with invented spelling scored higher on decoding and reading comprehension tests than children who were encouraged to use conventional spelling. The National Early Literacy Panel's (2008) recent meta-analysis of the research supports the importance of writing as a predictor of children's later reading and writing skills.

Print Awareness

According to the National Research Council (1999, p. 27), "a child's sensitivity to print is a major first step toward reading." Print awareness is a broad term that refers to children's ability to recognize print, ranging from contextualized environmental print (e.g., the word *Cheerios* on a cereal box) to decontextualized written words (e.g., the print in a children's book). Print awareness also encompasses concepts about print, including book concepts (author, illustrator, title, front, back) and conventions of print (directionality, capitalization, punctuation). Research has shown that young children's knowledge of concepts of print is moderately correlated with reading ability in the primary grades (National Early Literacy Panel, 2008), and thus concepts of print are an instructional objective of SBRR instruction.

In Chapter 5 we described a number of emergent literacy strategies that can be used to promote print awareness, such as functional print, shared reading, shared writing, and literacy-enriched play. Trade Secret 6.3 describes another way that shared reading can contribute to children's print awareness. In this strategy, teachers use "print-salient" books and make reference to print during story reading.

In the sections that follow, we describe how print awareness can be taught through more direct forms of instruction: teaching concepts about print and the key word strategy.

Teaching Concepts about Print.   According to Laura Justice and Helen Ezell (2004), print knowledge includes the following dimensions:

- *Print concepts.* Understanding print and text features such as a book's cover page elements (title, author, illustrator), print organization (left to right, left to right with return sweeps to the next line), and book organization (left-to-right page turning)
- *Letters.* Understanding that letters are discrete units of written language that link up to make words and that each print shape is called an alphabet letter and it has a name and makes a sound (or sometimes more than one sound)
- *Words.* Understanding that words are discrete units of written language that are made up of letters
- *Print-to-speech connections.* Understanding of the relationship between words and letters in print and in speech

TRADE SECRET 6.3
Selecting Print-Salient Books

Sonia Cabell and her colleagues (2008) suggest that teachers need to include an explicit focus during storybook reading on print. Laura Justice and Helen Ezell (2002) suggest two approaches for teachers use: select print-salient books for reading and incorporate print references in reading interactions.

Print-salient books are books where print is a key component of the design of the book; these are books that make print worth talking about. Some examples include: *Chicka Chicka Boom Boom* by Bill Martin Jr. and John Archambault (Simon & Schuster, 1989), *Click, Clack, Moo: Cows That Type* by Doreen Cronin (Simon & Schuster, 2000), and *The Crunching Munching Caterpillar* by Sheridan Cain (Tiger Tales, 2000). While reading any book, teachers can do such things as track the print, point to the print within the illustration, and ask questions, like "What do you think I'm reading, the pictures or the word?" or "This words says 'Danger!'" or "This is the letter S,

just like in your name." or "What is this letter?" Print-salient books offer special opportunities to invite children to attend to the print in the book. For example, in *Click, Clack, Moo: Cows That Type,* the cows write Farmer Brown a letter demanding electric blankets. One whole page is the letter from the cows to Farmer Brown. Another page contains a letter from the cows telling him that the hens want electric blankets also; they, too are cold! On other pages, print is embedded into the illustration. For example, on one page, a hen holds a sign "Closed. No milk. No eggs." The hens are on strike. On other pages the word *moo* is enlarged and in bold print. The book provides many opportunities for teachers to draw children's attention to its print.

Including print-referencing strategies into adult–child or children storybook reading interactions is important to do because when teachers do not reference print during their storybook reading children do not attend to the print in the storybook (Justice, Bowles, & Skibbe, 2006).

Early Reading First projects are required to teach print awareness by providing print-rich classroom environments and teaching book concepts during shared reading and shared writing. Early Reading First teachers also use more direct forms of instruction to teach specific concepts about print. Head Start teacher Connie Felix uses direct instruction to help her children in San Luis, Arizona, learn the distinction between pictures, words, and alphabet letters. Mrs. Felix has prepared a large chart with three columns labeled Picture, Word, and Letter. An example of each is pasted next to the label (e.g., there is photograph next to the label Picture and a written word next to the label Word). She has put a number of cards into a bag. Each card contains an example of a picture, word, or letter. She begins by explaining each of these concepts. The children are very interested, and several quickly recognize the examples that Mrs. Felix has provided ("That's an *A*" and "It's *cat*"). Children take turns drawing a card out of the basket. When they have drawn a card, they tell the class what is on the card, say to which category it belongs, and tape it to the correct column on the chart. If a child struggles, classmates help out. For example, Angela picks a card with a classmate's name on it. She recognizes the name and says "Elian." Mrs. Felix prompts her with the question, "Which type is it? A picture, word, or letter?" When Angela does not respond, several classmates chime in, "It's a word." Angela then places the card in the correct column and feels proud that she has done this correctly.

Key Words.   The key word strategy, developed by Sylvia Ashton-Warner (1963), is an effective way to build young children's ability to recognize words. It is a very simple and elegant
strategy: children choose words that they want to learn to recognize—words that have personal
meaning for each child. Real-life experiences, favorite children's books, writing workshop, and
language experience stories are primary sources for these key words. Children learn to recognize these words quickly because of their high meaning and personal significance.

The key word strategy is often associated with emergent literacy because of its focus
on personal meaning, learning by doing, and social interaction. However, the key word strategy also meets the specifications for a SBRR strategy because it involves direct instruction.
It features teacher modeling, guided practice, and independent practice. We have included
key words in this section because we believe that it is one of the most effective ways to
directly teach pre-K and kindergarten children to recognize whole words.

Here is how the key word strategy works: The teacher asks each child in the class to
pick a favorite word that he or she would like to learn to read. This word is written on a
large card while the child watches. (This is sometimes done in circle time so that the whole
class learns about each child's key word.) The children then write their key words plus any
other words that they remember. Finally, they engage in various games and practice activities with their key words.

The following are some of the key word games and practice activities recommended
by Jeanette Veatch and her associates (1979, pp. 30–32):

- *Retrieving words from the floor.* The children's words (with young children this will
  be the words of a partner or a small group) are placed face down on the floor. On the
  signal, each child is to find one of her or his own words, hold it up, and read it aloud.
- *Claiming the cards.* The teacher selects many words from the class, holds them up,
  and the child who "owns" each word claims it.
- *Classifying words.* The teacher selects categories that encompass all of the words
  selected by the children. The categories are introduced, and labels are placed on the
  floor for each category. The children must then decide in which category their words
  belong. For example, the children who have animal words would stand next to the
  sheet of paper that says *animals.*
- *Making alphabet books.* Children record their words in the correct section of an
  alphabet book that is divided by initial letters. This is a good example of how children
  can learn about words and letters simultaneously.
- *Illustrating.* The child can draw a picture about the key word, dictate the word to a
  teacher to write on a card, and then copy the word into a picture dictionary word
  book.
- *Finding words.* Children might find their key words in books, magazines, and
  newspapers.

Veatch and her colleagues recommend that children collect key words and keep them
in a box or on a ring file known as a "word bank." Another possibility is to have children
keep their key words in a word book. In this variation, the teacher writes a word on a card
for the child, then the child copies the word into his or her word book. Periodically, the
teacher can have children review their words in their word banks or word books. Besides

TRADE SECRET 6.3
My Word Book

BERNADETTE WATSON

As the children entered the classroom, Ms. Watson greeted them, gave them a three-by-five-inch card, and asked them, "What is your word for today?" Children answered. Amanda said, "elephant." Ms. Watson positioned her hand to write *elephant* on the card. Before she wrote the word, she asked Amanda how she decided on this word as her word for the day. Amanda had seen a program on television about elephants the night before and had decided, right then and there, that *elephant* would be her word today.

> "So," asked Ms. Watson, "what letter do you think *elephant* begins with?"
> "I don't know," responded Amanda.
> "It's an *E*," said Ms. Watson. "What letter is next?" She stretched the sound, "L-l-l-l-l."

Amanda responded, "*L*!"
"You're right," exclaimed Ms. Watson, "and then it's another *e,* and a *p-h-a-n*. And what do you think the last letter is? T-t-t-t-t."
Amanda said, "*T*!"
"Absolutely," said Ms. Watson.

Amanda took her card with *elephant* written on it with her and set off to locate her word book. Having found it, she sat at a table to copy her word into her book. First she drew a picture of an elephant. Above it, she copied the word *elephant.* At the beginning of the year, that is all she would have done. Now, she also wrote a sentence under the picture: "isnt.v" (I saw on TV).

When she was done, Amanda took her book to the library center. Here she might read her words to herself or to a friend. The pictures she had drawn greatly help her remember her word for the day.

providing opportunities for children to practice recognizing key words, word banks and word books serve other valuable functions. They provide children with a concrete record of their reading vocabulary growth. It is very motivating for children to see their collections of words grow larger and larger. In addition, the words can be used to help children learn about letters and the sounds with which they are associated. For example, if children are learning the sound associated with *b,* the teacher can have children find all the words in their collections that begin with that letter.

Trade Secret 6.4 describes a variation of the word bank strategy in which children write their key words in a word book. Notice how the teacher, Bernadette Watson, prompts Amanda to use letter–sound relationships when she writes Amanda's key word, *elephant,* on the card.

Early Writing Instruction

Even the youngest of children like to write—not only on paper, but also on walls and floors. As Pam Oken-Wright (1998) notes, "The urge to make one's mark is such a strong one that it is manifest on many a bedroom wall, executed with whatever implement was handy or seemed exciting" (p. 76). Early childhood teachers, then, must take advantage of this natural urge by providing a variety of writing materials to their young writers, learning to ask the right question at the right time, and providing the right instruction at the right time to nudge their young writers' development (Schickedanz & Casbergue, 2004). In this section, we explore the "what" and "how" of writing instruction in an early childhood classroom.

The Context for Writing: The Writing Center

A *writing center* is a special area in the classroom that is stocked with materials that invite children to write. When setting up such a center, teachers need to remember that writing is a social act. Teachers typically provide a table and chairs in the writing center because they know of children's need for talk while writing. Children want to share their writing with peers, know what their peers are writing, and ask for assistance with the construction of their text.

Gather the Needed Materials.   In addition to a table and chairs, teachers stock the writing center with materials that invite children to write and to play with writing materials. Such materials include but are not limited to the following:

- Many different kinds of paper (e.g., lined theme paper, typical story paper, discarded computer or office letterhead paper with one side clean, lots of unlined paper, paper cut into different shapes to suggest writing about particular topics, paper folded and made into blank books, stationery and envelopes, cards)
- Various writing tools (e.g., pencils, markers—be certain to purchase the kind that can withstand the kind of pressure young children exert as they write—crayons, felt-tip pens, a computer or computers with a word processing program)
- Writing folders for storage of each child's writing efforts
- A box or file drawer in which to store the file folders
- Lists of children's names
- Children's names and photos laminated on card stock
- Magic or gel slates
- Dry erase board and markers
- Three-by-five-inch cards
- Letter stamps and stamp pads
- Homemade blank books
- Hole punch, stapler, scissors, tape

Notice that oversize (fat) pencils and special primary-lined paper were not recommended as the only paper and pencils to be provided. For young children, Miriam Martinez and Bill Teale (1987) recommend unlined paper because it does not signal how writing is supposed to be done. Children are freer to use the emergent forms of writing—pictures used as writing, scribble writing, letterlike units, and so on—that do not fit on the lines of traditional lined writing paper or story paper (e.g., top half blank, bottom half lined).

In addition to these required items, many teachers include the following items in their classroom writing center:

- A bulletin board for displaying such items as samples of the children's writing, examples of different forms of writing (e.g., thank-you notes, letters, postcards, stories), writing-related messages (e.g., "Here's our grocery list"), messages about writing (e.g., "Look at this! Shawn's sister published a story in the newspaper"), and the children's writing

- Posters showing people engaged in writing
- Clipboards for children who want to write somewhere other than at the table
- Mailboxes (one for each child, the teacher, the principal or center director, and other appropriate persons, as determined by the children) to encourage note and letter writing
- Alphabet strips on the writing table so that children have a model readily available when they begin to attempt to link their knowledge of letter sounds with their knowledge of letter formations

Most teachers introduce the materials to the children gradually, that is, they do not place all these materials in the writing center on the first day of school, which young children would find overwhelming. They make the writing center new and exciting over the year by regularly adding new materials and tools. Pam Oken-Wright (1998) suggests that when new materials are added to the writing center, it is important not to substitute the new for the old; young children like the familiar along with the new.

Arrange the Materials. With so many different materials in the writing center, keeping the supplies orderly and replenishing them can take up time. Some teachers label the places where the various tools and paper belong in the writing center, which helps all the children know where to return used materials and helps a child "clerk" know how to straighten the center at cleanup time. Further, labeling the places where the items belong permits a quick inventory of missing and needed items. Figure 6.2 provides an illustration of a well-equipped, well-arranged writing center.

Computers and Word Processing. A growing number of early childhood classrooms have computers in the writing center. Teachers in these classrooms are indeed fortunate! So are the children in these classrooms. Doug Clements and Julie Sarama (2003) summarized the research on young children and technology. In the language and reading area, they report that computers facilitate increased language use (children talk more to peers when they are at the computer than at other activities). Software programs can help children develop pre-reading skills as well. In writing, children "using word processors write more, have fewer fine motor control problems, [and] worry less about making mistakes. Young children cooperatively plan, revise, and discuss spelling, punctuation, spacing, and text meaning and style" (pp. 36–37). Notice the two chairs in front of each computer in Figure 6.2. This arrangement encourages increased talk between peers. Technology expert Patricia Scott highly recommends the following software packages for their user-friendly qualities; that is, young children can easily use them to write: *Orly's Draw-a-Story* (Broderbund, 1999), *Kid Works Deluxe* (Davidson, 1995), *Storybook Weaver Deluxe* (The Learning Company, 2004), and *Paint, Write, and Play* (The Learning Company, 1996).

Marilyn Cochran-Smith, Jessica Kahn, and Cynthia Paris (1986) point out that all writers, regardless of age, require time at the computer when their attention is focused on learning word processing skills. For example, Bev Winston, a kindergarten teacher, introduced her young students to word processing during the school's orientation days, those

FIGURE 6.2   A Well-Equipped Writing Center

days that precede the first full day of school. Then she watched her children as they played with word processing during their center time and provided instruction as each child needed it. Word processing is a tool to preserve children's important first writings. It is important for teachers to keep this in mind. Young children need time to experiment with this tool just as children need time to experiment with pencils, pens, markers, and so forth.

Teachers' Role.   Materials alone, however, even well-organized materials in beautifully arranged writing centers, are not enough. Children also need opportunities to interact with their teachers in the writing center. They need their teachers to sit beside them to support their writing efforts. Sometimes teachers will support by selecting a writing tool and paper and modeling a form of writing, such as writing a letter to a friend, writing a thank-you note, or making a sign for the coat cubbies asking the children to please put their snow boots in the bottom of their cubbies. While teachers engage in this modeling, they talk aloud, describing their thinking, stretching words to hear the letter sounds, asking for assistance, and so on. At other times, teachers will support a child's writing, particularly those students who have begun to associate sounds with letters, by helping the child stretch out the words to hear the letter sounds and select the correct letter to represent each sound. Just as in teachers' involvement with children during their play, such adult interactions can facilitate children's learning within their zone of proximal development. Through such support, teachers can stretch children beyond their current level of knowledge, and children can do what they could not do independently. In turn, children's literacy growth can be promoted, both in terms of their knowledge about the purposes of writing and in terms of their understanding of how sound is mapped onto print in the language.

Writing in Other Centers

We believe that every center in the classroom should be literacy enriched. Every center should have print materials (e.g., books, magazines, pamphlets) connected with the topic under investigation available for the children's use. In addition, every center should include props to support the children's writing explorations (e.g., paper and writing implements). Miriam Smith, Joanne Brady, and Louisa Anastasopoulos's (2008) *Early Language and Literacy Classroom Observation, Pre-K Tool* directs observers to look at the early writing environment provided for the children's explorations and to note the kind of support the teacher provides for the children's writing. When every center has writing tools, children can use writing to achieve a variety of purposes and practice using the form of writing (linear scribble, phonics-based spellings) that serves their need at the moment. In the science center, for example, teachers should provide forms to encourage children's recording of their scientific observations. Addie, a delightful four-year-old, was studying the life cycle of the butterfly when we met her. Because paper and writing tools were available, she recorded her discovery (see Figure 6.3). (After we requested a copy of her writing for publication in this book, she made poster copies of her discovery for every person in her neighborhood.) Writing tools in the library center encourage children to use books as models for their writing. For example, a child might write their own version of Eric Carle's *The Very Hungry Caterpillar*. When blue paper and writing tools were available in the block center, children made "blueprints" of the building they intended to construct, labeling the rooms. The blueprints that lined the walls of the block center during the construction unit provided a model for the children's drawing and writing. Using paper in the math center, children in Eileen Feldgus and Isabel Cardonick's (1999, p. 72) classrooms made bar graphs to illustrate their classmates' answer to a question (e.g., "Have you ever had a cast?"), wrote their observations of different objects' weight, and recorded their guesses of how many objects were in a jar. Clearly, putting writing tools at children's fingertips allows them to use those tools for multiple purposes.

The Writing Workshop

By the time children reach kindergarten, many teachers add a writing workshop, with some direct teaching of writing, to the daily schedule at least once a week.

The writing workshop was first described by Donald Graves (1983) in his book *Writing: Teachers and Children at Work*. All members of the writing workshop meet to

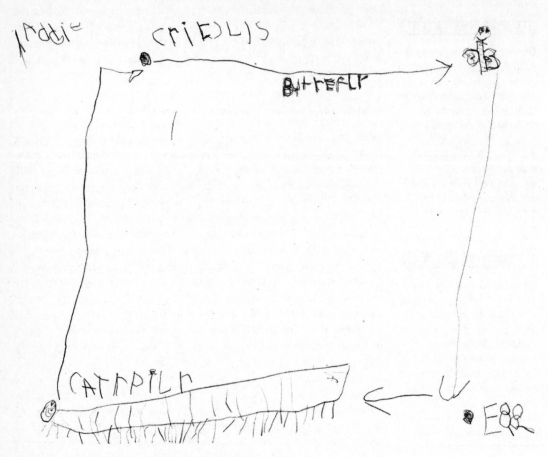

FIGURE 6.3   Life Cycle of a Butterfly by Addie

intensively study the art and craft of writing. The workshop typically has the following components:

- *Focus lesson.* A five-minute lesson to teach children about the writing process ("I want to make a change in my writing. I'm going to *revise.* Here's how I'll do it."); a procedural aspect of the writing program ("We help our friends while they write. We say things like, 'Tell me more about your dog. What color is he?'"); a quality of good writing ("I can tell more about my dog by adding his color, black. So I'll write 'I hv a blk dg.'"); a mechanical feature of writing ("Always make *I* a capital, a big letter."); or about why people write ("We need to make a list.").
- *Writing.* A ten- to fifteen-minute period during which children write and meet with peers and the teacher.
- *Group share.* A ten-minute period during which one or two children read their writing pieces to the group and receive positive feedback and content-related questions.

TRADE SECRET 6.5
Teaching about Sound–Symbol Relationships: An Invented-Spelling Focus Lesson

BERNADETTE WATSON

Teacher: I didn't tell you this before. I went on a trip to New York this weekend. The New York Marathon, a running race, was on this weekend, so there was a lot of traffic! It took us a long time to get to New York. That's what I'm going to write about today. I'm going to start by drawing a picture. I'll just draw a road. That will help me remember what I'm going to write about. [Teacher draws a road.] I'm going to write "I went to New York City." Will you help me write the words? "I." Oh, that's an easy one. [Writes "I" on the board.] W-e-n-t. [Stretches word.] "w"-"w"-"w."

CHILD: "Y."

TEACHER: It does sound like a "Y." We'll use "Y" for that sound. E-N-T.

CHILDREN: "N!" "N!" [Teacher writes "N."]

TEACHER: W-E-N-T-T-T

CHILDREN: "T!" [Teacher writes "T."]

TEACHER: to

CHILD: I know how to spell to—"t" "o."

TEACHER: How do you know that?

CHILD: I don't know. I just do. [Teacher writes *to*.]

Although the writing workshop was originally designed for use in the elementary grades (see Chapter 10), it can be easily adapted for use with younger children. One kindergarten teacher, for example, has used variations of the workshop approach—focus lessons and group share time—to help her students develop as writers.

Focus Lessons. Focus lessons are short lessons that focus on an aspect of writing. In Trade Secret 6.5, kindergarten teacher Bernadette Watson uses focus lessons to teach her students how to match letter sounds with the correct letter symbols. In one lesson, she helped the children sound out the spellings of the words in the sentence "I went to New York." She stretched the words out (e.g., w-e-n-t) and focused the children's attention on the sound of each letter ("What letter makes the /w/ sound?") or letter cluster ("How about /ent/?"). Because she knows that her students will not fully understand the relationship between sounds and symbols as a result of one lesson, she weaves the content of this lesson into many lessons and reinforces this understanding when she talks with her young writers about their writing.

Writing Time. The focus lesson is followed by a time for the children to write. Ms. Watson teaches in a public school and has an occasional parent as a teacher assistant. She presents a writing lesson on Monday. Five children begin their free-play time in the writing center, writing with Ms. Watson's support and reading their text to her before they leave the writing center. The other children proceed to centers of their choice. Tomorrow another five children will begin their free-play time in the writing center. Each child begins free-play in the writing center once each week. The children can choose to write on more than their writing day, but all children must write at least one day each week. Requiring the children to begin their play in the writing center one day each week allows Ms. Watson time to support and observe each child's writing development at least once each week.

While the children write, Ms. Watson and other adults who might be in the classroom meet with the young writers about their writing. The opportunity to talk while writing is a critically important component of writing workshop. The talk is about the content and the mechanics (usually the letter–sound relationships) of the piece. Through conferences, teachers can provide one-on-one instruction, providing the child with just the right help needed at that minute.

Group Share Time.   The workshop is culminated by group share time. During the group share session, two or three children sit, one at a time, in the author's chair and share their pieces with the other writers in the class. Typically, the other children are gathered at the sharing writer's feet, listening attentively while the writer reads the piece and preparing to make comments or ask questions. The following describes one group share in Bernadette Watson's kindergarten classroom.

> **DEMETRI:** I like your story.
>
> **MS. WATSON:**   Remember, Demetri, when we talked about how we tell the writer what we really liked about his or her story? Can you tell Aaron what you liked about his story?
>
> **DEMETRI:**   I really liked the part where you thought you would get a dog because I want a dog, too.
>
> **AARON:**   Thanks.

The classroom rule is that the writer calls on three children for a question or a comment. The first response is a comment. The other two must be questions. Ms. Watson uses this time to help her students begin to understand the difference between a comment (statement or sentence) and a question. Learning the difference takes a lot of practice.

Through group shares, young children learn that writing is meant to be shared with others. Writers write to communicate their thoughts and ideas with their readers. Young children also learn how to share their writing with others (reading in a loud voice so that others can hear, holding their writing so others can see) and about the difference between a question and a comment. Teachers use children's texts and questions and comments as a context to teach about writing.

We return to the writing workshop in Chapters 10 and 11. There, we describe how the workshop is used in the elementary grades.

Publishing Children's Writing

"Helping children make and publish their own books taps into [their] love of creating and owning written words" (Power, 1998, pp. 31–32). Brenda Power suggests several reasons teachers should help young children publish their writing in books. Making their own books helps children learn the following:

- To hold the book right side up and to turn the pages correctly
- That books have covers, titles, and authors

- Letters and sounds through writing a book and how to decode words by reading their own words
- About the importance of an author and an illustrator to a book

To publish with young children is to take their written texts and do something special with them. To publish is to make the writing public, to present it for others to read. There are many different ways to publish young children's writing. For example:

- Ask each child to bring an eight-and-a-half-by-eleven-inch clear plastic frame to school. (Of course, frames must be purchased for those children whose parents cannot provide them.) Have the children publish their work by mounting their selected pieces, one at a time, in their frames. Hang the frames on the back wall of the classroom on a Wall of Fame.
- String a clothesline across the classroom. Using clothespins, clip the children's writings to the clothesline.
- Punch a hole in the upper-left corner of several pages. Construction paper can be used for all pages. If not, include a piece of colored construction paper or poster board on the top and bottom of the pile of pages for the book's cover. Thread string, yarn, or a silver ring through the hole to hold the book together.
- Purchase a low-cost photo album with large, stick-on plastic sleeves. (They can be found at discount stores and occasionally at flea markets or rummage and garage sales.) Place one page of each child's writing in one of the plastic sleeves. The same photo album can be used again and again as one piece of writing can be substituted for another piece of writing.
- While engaging in a special experience, take photographs of the children. Glue the picture to a piece of construction paper. Ask each child to select a photo. Ask the child to write about the chosen picture on a piece of white paper. Cut the white paper into an interesting shape and mount it on the construction paper below the photo. Laminate each page and put the pages together with spiral binding.
- Cover a large bulletin board with bright paper or fabric. In large cutout letters, label the bulletin board something like "Young Authors" or "Room 101 Authors." Divide the bulletin board evenly into rectangular-shaped sections, one section for each child in the class, using yarn or a marker. Label each section with a child's name. Encourage each child to mount one piece of writing in his or her special section each week. A staple or pushpin might be used to mount the writing.

These suggestions are but a few of the many ways that children's writing might be published. We repeat: Publishing with young children means making their writing public and available for others to read. It is developmentally inappropriate to require young children to revise or recopy their writing, although sometimes they are willing to add to their text. Most young children do not have the attention span or interest to make revisions or to recopy the text.

If the child's writing is a personal script—that is, if it is a form of emergent writing that needs the child's reading for meaning to be constructed—then the teacher might elect to include a conventionally spelled version of the message with the child's personal script version. It is important to include the child's personal script version on the page with the conventionally spelled version to avoid taking ownership from the child.

Strategies for Teaching English Language Learners

Young English language learners (ELLs) face a major task: they are charged with the task of acquiring a second language while simultaneously developing their first. A recent extensive review of the research on ELL children sponsored by the Institute of Education Sciences and the U.S. Department of Education reported that, despite a paucity of rigorous experimental research, sufficient evidence exists to provide five proven and practical strategies to improve early literacy skills with ELL children (Gersten, Baker, Shanahan, Linan-Thompson, Collins, & Scarcella, 2007). These five strategies have been analyzed and reviewed by the *What Works Clearinghouse*:

1. Conduct formative assessments with English learners using English language measures of phonological processing, letter knowledge, and word and text reading. . . .
2. Provide focused, intense small group interventions for English learners determined to be at risk for reading problems. . . .
3. Provide high-quality vocabulary instruction throughout the day. . . .
4. Provide curricula and supplementary curricula to accompany core reading and mathematics series. . . . Accompany with relevant training and professional development for the teachers. . . .
5. Ensure that teachers of English learners devote approximately 90 minutes a week to instructional activities in which pairs of students at different ability levels or different English proficiency levels work together on academic tasks. (Gersten et al., p. 2)

Similarly, the Center on Instruction has published a set of recommendations for promoting reading development in ELL children (Francis, Rivera, Lesaux, Kieffer, & Rivera, 2006, pp. 30–31), including the following:

1. ELLs need early, explicit, and intensive instruction in phonological awareness and phonics in order to build decoding skills.

2. K–12 classrooms across the nation must increase opportunities for ELLs to develop sophisticated vocabulary knowledge.
3. Reading instruction in K–12 classrooms must equip ELLs with strategies and knowledge to comprehend and analyze challenging narrative and expository texts.
4. Instruction and intervention to promote ELLs' reading fluency must focus on vocabulary and increased exposure to print.

Note that both sets of recommendations are closely related to the SBRR strategies discussed in this chapter. Instruction and assessment for ELL children should focus on the same "core" early literacy skills that are at the foundation of the scientifically based approach: phonological awareness, alphabet knowledge, print awareness, and vocabulary. Beyond the ideas recommended in this chapter (several researchers comment on the value of using the activities described in this book with *all* children), are there any evidence-based suggestions specifically for helping young ELL children develop these key language and reading skills?

Vocabulary

Theresa Roberts (2008) discovered that sending books home in the child's primary language for a caregiver to read while the teacher read the same book in English in the classroom helped low-income preschoolers whose primary language was Hmong or Spanish to learn a substantial number of words in English.

Eurydice Bauer and Patrick Manyak (2008) suggest that to make language comprehensible to children learning a new language teachers need to accompany oral explanations and read-alouds with visuals, realia, gestures, and dramatization to illustrate key concepts and vocabulary. Such a strategy, of course, is appropriate for use with all children.

Researchers (Bear, Helman, Templeton, Invernizzi, & Johnston, 2007) point out the importance of connecting learning with the learners' personal experiences. A strategy recommended is the use of cognates. When the English word is similar to the first language word (e.g., *colores* and *colors*), the teacher should highlight the similarities.

Phonological Awareness

David Dickinson and his colleagues (Dickinson, McCabe, Clark-Chiarelli, & Wolf, 2004) recommend teaching ELL children whose primary language is Spanish phonological awareness in Spanish; there is a strong transfer of performance on phoneme deletion and rhyme recognition from Spanish to English. What kinds of activities? Hallie Kay Yopp and Lilia Stapleton (2008) suggest engaging in sound play in the Spanish language (for example, pointing out the rhymes in songs and poems or substituting sounds in each repetition of a verse of a song), teaching tongue

twisters, selecting Spanish books that "exploit the sounds of the language" (p. 379), including books like *Vamos a Cazar un Oso* (*We're Going on a Bear Hunt,* Kane/Miller, 1998), *Albertina anda Arriba: El Abecedario* (*Albertina Goes Up: An Alphabet Book,* AIMS International, 1993), and *Los Nanas de Abuelita: Canciones de Cuna, Trabelenguas y Adivinanzas de Suramerica* (*Grandmother's Nursery Rhymes,* Henry Holt, 1996). Whether or not someone in the preschool speaks the child's home language, the parents should be encouraged to engage in these activities to support their children's reading development. (And, of course, while reading parents can teach their children new words and concepts about print—all of the key language and literacy skills.)

Family Focus: Creating a Book Nook and Author's Corner

ALLISON MULLADY

Parents can help support children's emerging reading and writing skills at home by creating a book nook and/or author's corner. In the corner of a family room or child's bedroom, parents can gather all types of literacy materials. For instance, all the children's books and magazines can be collected and placed on a small bookshelf or placed in baskets for children to peruse. Parents can include a rocking chair or large pillows to encourage reading.

Parents can also create an author's corner by collecting paper of all types and writing implements

such as crayons, markers, and pencils. Some parents have even included safety scissors and tape to encourage more creative books. Parents then can include a writing place, using a small table and chairs. Children can write their own books that can be "published" and placed in the book nook.

Parents who create such special literacy places in their homes report significant increases of literacy activities and more opportunities to encourage young readers and writers.

Courtesy of the authors

Strategies for Children with Special Needs: Writing Instruction

KAREN BURSTEIN AND TANIS BRYAN

Most young children with special needs do not have physical impairments. However, many may experience delays in both fine and gross motor development. These delays may affect a child's ability to effectively grasp a pencil or shape letters and numbers. Large or ball-shaped crayons are often effective writing tools for children who have not developed a pencil grip. Many commercial built-up pencils or pencil grips are also available. When using these grips, be sure to instruct the child in the proper finger and hand placement on the pencil. For very young children with special needs, tracing letters in sand is a good place to start. Practicing letter structure in finger paints or liquid soap is also effective. Paper used by young children can be brightly colored to produce a contrast between the writing and the background. Initially, plain paper without lines is preferable to that with lines, as printing is similar to drawing. Using successive approximation of the appropriate size and shape of letters can be accomplished with wide-lined paper with different-colored lines. These lines serve as cues for the child to stop or go. Young children with more severe special needs may require the support and services of occupational therapists. These therapists can provide you with expertise and specialized equipment to promote fine motor development.

Written expression by young children with special needs may present several problems for the teacher and the child, as writing is both a process and a product that requires physical and cognitive skills. The written product should be assessed using observable and measurable goals that correspond with the strengths and weaknesses of the child. Teachers need patience and repeated observations of children's written work in order to effectively evaluate and plan for writing instruction. The following are strategies for promoting written expression by young children with special needs:

- Allocate time for writing each day.
- Have children create simple stories from tangible objects that they can touch and manipulate, rather than asking for a memory or a concept. For example, give a ball to the child and ask the child to tell you about this ball. Have an adult serve as a scribe for the child and take dictation, writing down the story as it is composed. When the child is able, ask the child to copy the dictated copy and draw a picture of the ball.
- Compliment children on the content of their stories. Ask for more information about the topic and help them expand their stories.
- Develop a template for writing—for example, putting name and date on a specific area of the paper.
- Exhibit examples of *all* children's writing.
- Celebrate the child's successes!

Summary

Whereas Chapter 5 described activities that can implicitly teach children how to write and read, this chapter dealt with explicit literacy instruction. It described a variety of developmentally appropriate strategies that teachers can use to teach children to write and read. Each skill has been found to be important to children's success as readers and writers. What have you learned?

- *Which early reading skills should early childhood teachers provide in order to give their children an opportunity to learn?*

PEARSON
myeducationkit

To check your comprehension on the content covered in this chapter, go to the MyEducationKit for your book and complete the Study Plan for Chapter 6. Here you will be able to take a chapter quiz and receive feedback on your answers.

The National Early Literacy Panel (2008) was formed to synthesize the early literacy research to this question. To date, this panel has identified eleven variables as important components of an early literacy program: alphabet knowledge, print knowledge, environmental print, invented spelling, listening comprehension, oral language/vocabulary, phonemic awareness, phonological short-term memory, rapid naming, visual memory, and visual perception skills. Of this list, the "broader" early reading skills include phonological and phonemic awareness, alphabet letter recognition, phonics, word recognition, and print awareness. Early childhood teachers must ensure that they provide their young learners with opportunities to learn each of these key skills by using a variety of explicit and implicit teaching procedures and activities.

■ *What is the difference between phonological awareness, phonemic awareness, and phonics? In what sequence do young children typically acquire these skills? What does this sequence suggest about classroom instructional strategies?*

Phonological awareness (realization that spoken language is composed of words, syllables, and sounds) is broader than phonemic awareness (realization that words are composed of phonemes). Both concepts are important for all young children to know if they are to become successful readers. Whereas phonological and phonemic awareness just involve sound, phonics involves learning the relationship between letters and the sounds they represent. The instructional sequence now recommended by research is to begin by helping children build the basic concepts of phonological awareness, then move toward helping children develop awareness that words are composed of phonemes, and finally help children develop awareness of letter–sound associations. Therefore, the instructional sequence is from broad concepts to smaller and smaller ones.

■ *How might early childhood teachers introduce young children to the letters of the alphabet?*

Some readers probably learned the names of the letters of the alphabet by singing the alphabet song. Today, the value of this activity gets mixed reviews. Some readers probably learned the names of the letters of the alphabet by studying a different letter each week. This approach receives some criticism today. Early childhood teachers should teach their young learners the names of the letters through explicit instruction. A teacher should remember that most children will not know the names of all the letters of the alphabet before they recognize and read whole words. A skillful teacher can link children's attention to highly meaningful words and key letters simultaneously.

■ *Why is a writing center an important area in the preschool classroom? How might an adult teach in the writing center?*

A writing center is that area of the classroom where the teacher has stocked materials (different kinds of papers, various writing tools, alphabet strips, computers) that invite children to write. The teacher is an important other in the writing center. As a cowriter, the teacher writes alongside the children and models the writing process, informally teaching children about the forms (letters, thank-you notes) and features (spelling, letter formation) of print. As a skilled writer, the teacher can teach children as he or she writes by casually talking about letter–sound relationships, how to begin a letter, or what might be said in a letter.

■ *How does a teacher teach during a writing workshop?*

Each writing workshop begins with a focus lesson. The goal of such lessons is to teach children about some aspect of writing (e.g., how to make revisions, how to add describing words, how to spell words). The focus lesson is followed by writing time. During writing time, the teacher talks with individual children about their writing. Here, the teacher might help a child stretch words to hear sounds, add details to the child's drawing, or talk with the child about the topic of the piece. Through conferences, the teacher provides one-on-one instruction. After the writing time, two or three children will share their work with their peers and the teacher. Now, the teacher and the other children can ask questions about the writing.

■ *Why is it important to publish children's writing?*

Publishing helps young children understand that they write so that others can read their thoughts. Making young children's writing efforts public is important. The publishing process need not be complicated.

LINKING KNOWLEDGE TO PRACTICE

1. Visit a classroom set up for three-year-olds and a classroom set up for five-year-olds in an early childhood center. Draw a diagram of each classroom's writing center, and make a list of the writing materials the teacher has provided. Describe the differences between the writing center set up for three-year-olds and the one for five-year-olds. Observe the classrooms' teachers as they interact with the children in the writing center. Describe what they talk about with the children.

2. Create descriptions of several developmentally appropriate phonological or phonemic awareness activities, from the most basic concepts to the more advanced, that might be used with young children. Make copies of your activities for others in your class.

3. Create a description of several developmentally appropriate alphabet recognition activities for use with young children. Make copies of your activities for others in your class.

4. Search the Internet for sites describing activities to help children develop each of the key early reading skills. Prepare a brief description of each site. Make copies of your discoveries for others in your class.

7 Assessing Early Literacy: Finding Out What Young Children Know and Can Do

Mrs. Saenz is observing four-year-old Martine and Monique playing together in the post office center. The children are pretending to be post office people and are busy sorting letters into a mail sorter (a plastic office sorter that is divided into twenty-four slots, each labeled with an alphabet letter sticker). As she watches the children put the letters in the slots, Mrs. Saenz notices that Martine is accomplishing this task by recognizing the first letter of each name, then matching it to the appropriately labeled slot. She also notices that Monique, who is learning English, is simply putting the letters into the slots without paying any attention to the names on the envelopes. After a few moments, Martine stops Monique.

> **MARTINE:** No, Monique. Look at the name. See the big letter? That letter tells you to put it in this mailbox.
>
> **MONIQUE:** What it say?
>
> **MARTINE:** It says B. I think it is for Bobby. See? [He puts the letter in the B mailbox.]
>
> **MONIQUE:** Gimme. [She reaches for another letter.] What it say?
>
> **MARTINE:** It says R.
>
> **MONIQUE:** [Thinking for a moment, she starts to sing the alphabet song. She puts her hand on each letter as she sings it.]
>
> **MARTINE:** That helps find 'em fast, uh?

Mrs. Saenz carefully observes this interaction and makes brief anecdotal notes describing what Monique and Martine know and can do. This information will also help her to adjust instruction to better meet both children's learning needs.

In several of the preceding chapters we have presented strategies for implicit and explicit instruction in early literacy. While these instructional activities form the core of an effective language arts program, they cannot stand alone. Two other elements are needed to ensure that the instructional strategies meet the needs of every child in the class: teachers need to know what to teach and whether these activities achieve their intended aims.

We begin this chapter by discussing the goals literacy professionals have identified as those that teachers should help their young learners meet. Then we consider the two general assessment approaches that teachers might use to gather information: ongoing or classroom assessment and on-demand or standardized assessment. In the past, teachers of young children mostly used ongoing or classroom assessments. However, today standardized assessments have become increasingly prevalent across the country. Therefore, we agree with Kathy Short, Jean Schroeder, Gloria Kauffman, and Sandy Kaser (2002, p. 1999): "Educators can no longer afford to ignore these tests since the results are often used to make life-altering decisions about students and curriculum and to evaluate teachers and programs."

Before Reading This Chapter, Think About . . .

- Your own experiences with standardized tests. Were you required to take a test, like the Scholastic Aptitude Test or the Graduate Record Examination, and score above a minimum level to gain admission to your undergraduate or graduate program?
- How your teachers assessed your literacy progress. Did you take spelling tests? Did you read stories and answer comprehension questions? Did you ever evaluate your own progress?
- How information about your literacy progress was shared with your parents. Did your parents read your report card? Did your parents attend conferences? Were you involved in sharing information about your progress with your peers or parents?

Focus Questions

- What is important for teachers to know about children's literacy development?
- What two general approaches might teachers use to assess their children's literacy learning?
- What types of ongoing assessment tools are used to collect information about children's progress?
- How do teachers use the information they collect?

Determining What Children Know and Can Do

Instruction and assessment are intertwined in excellent literacy instruction. In the opening vignette, Ms. Saenz observed two children with differing levels of alphabet recognition. Ms. Saenz's careful observations are supported by developmental guidelines created by early childhood experts. She knows that though Martine and Monique differ in their ability to recognize alphabet letters, both are making remarkable progress. She also knows that as a second-language learner, Monique has made tremendous strides. Further, Ms. Saenz's observations provide her with a better understanding of the different strategies (alphabet song and one-to-one letter matching) Monique is using to learn the name of each of these symbols. The lessons Ms. Saenz will teach tomorrow are guided by the observations she made of what and how the children learned today.

In 2004, the National Association for the Education of Young Children and the National Association of Early Childhood Specialists in State Departments of Education

BOX **7.1**

Definition of Terms

criterion-referenced test: a test used to compare a student's progress toward mastery of specified content, typically content the student had been taught. The performance criterion is referenced to some criterion level such as a cutoff score (e.g., a score of 60 is required for mastery).

norm-referenced test: a test designed to compare one child against a group of children.

on-demand assessment: a type of assessment that occurs during special time set aside for testing. In most cases, teaching and learning come to a complete stop while the teacher conducts the assessment.

ongoing assessment: a form of assessment that relies on the regular collection of children's work to illustrate children's knowledge and learning. The children's products are created as they engage in daily classroom activities. Thus, children are learning while they are being assessed.

standardized test: the teacher reads verbatim the scripted procedures to the students. The conditions and directions are the same whenever the test is administered. Standardized tests are one form of on-demand testing.

---

prepared a joint position statement on curriculum, assessment, and program evaluation. These two major early childhood associations agreed that "reliable assessment [should be] a central part of all early childhood programs"; the purpose of assessment, these educators believe, should be to assess children's "strengths, progress and needs" (NAEYC/NAECS-SDE, 2004, pp. 51, 52). What teachers learn from assessing their children today should determine what they teach tomorrow—the Assess-Plan-Teach-Assess model.

The primary purpose of early childhood assessment, then, is to improve instruction. As Lorrie Shepard, Sharon Kagan, and Emily Wurtz (1998) note:

> When children are assessed as part of the teaching–learning process, then assessment information tells caregivers and teachers what each child can do and what he or she is ready to learn next. Finding out, on an ongoing basis, what a child knows and can do helps parents and teachers decide how to pose new challenges and provide help with what the child has not yet mastered. This type of assessment guides teachers' instruction. Teachers also use their assessment of children's learning to reflect on their own teaching practices so that they can adjust and modify curricula, instructional activities, and classroom routines that are ineffective. (p. 52)

However, increasingly administrators need to collect evidence to document the effectiveness of the instructional program and to assess the children's progress toward a set of learning goals. This is assessment for accountability purposes.

What Is Important for Teachers to Know about Children's Literacy Development?

Teachers must begin assessment by determining what they value. To do so, they need to answer these questions: What is important for us to know about our children's development as readers, writers, speakers, and listeners? What do these young learners need to know and be able to do when they exit the preschool years? Today, they have a resource to help them answer these questions. Early childhood educators (sometimes along with parents, administrators, and higher education faculty) in nearly every state in the United States have worked together to create language and early literacy standards (or building blocks, or learning foundations; various terms are used interchangeably). See, for example, Figure 1.2 in Chapter 1 for a copy of one state's, Virginia's, language and early reading standards. In addition, some national groups have defined standards or outcomes. Head Start has developed an outcomes framework, defining six framework domains: listening and understanding; speaking and communicating; phonological awareness; print awareness and concepts about book knowledge; early writing; and alphabet knowledge.

Standards are important because they express shared expectations for children. That is, the educators in each state or national group have agreed upon what they value. Further, once stated, all educators have a common language for assessing children's progress toward those goals or outcomes. Standards not only guide teachers' assessment of children's progress but also what teachers teach. As Assistant to the Secretary of Education for Early Childhood Education Barbara Bowman (2006) said in her keynote address at NAEYC's National Institute for Early Childhood Professional Development, "Standards say clearly that teachers are responsible for organizing the learning environment so that children learn" (p. 46).

We begin this section by exploring the most appropriate ways teachers might gather information about their children's literacy development. We describe the tools for the ongoing gathering of information about children's language and literacy learning. Readers should know that it is generally believed to be more difficult to determine what young children know and can do than what older children know and can do. Both the nature of early learning and young children's developing language skills provide teachers and caregivers with assessment challenges.

Two Kinds of Assessment

Once teachers have decided what is important for them to know about their children's literacy development, they must then decide how to gather this information. Teachers use two kinds of assessment to measure children's progress toward the achievement of the state standards: ongoing and on-demand. Charlene Cobb (2003) uses an analogy to describe the difference between the two forms.

> A visit to the doctor's office is to [ongoing] assessment what an autopsy is to [on-demand assessment]. Let's say you see a doctor, for either a perceived need or a regular checkup. The doctor examines you, makes a diagnosis, and provides a treatment based on his or her discovery and your needs. This is a form of ongoing assessment. Suppose you come home from the doctor and find out that your neighbor has suddenly died. You're told that nobody knows what happened, but an autopsy is planned. An autopsy is [like an on-demand assessment.] [On-demand assessments] are done to determine what happened. (p. 386)

Why both kinds of assessments? Sandra Heidemann, Claire Chang, and Beth Menninga (2004, p. 87) describe the kinds of assessments the teachers use in their very successful early childhood project in Minnesota and why assessment is important to the success of their project: "In effective assessment systems, teachers use multiple measures, such as informal observations, work sampling, and documentation along with more formal assessment, to guide their instruction."

Teachers assess, then, *to guide their decisions about what to teach.* Effective teachers engage in an Assess-Plan-Teach-Assess model. These four elements are central to quality teaching.

We begin by considering ongoing assessment because this is the kind of assessment used most frequently by teachers of young children. Engaging in this kind of assessment demands that teachers be very careful observers of young children.

Ongoing Assessment

Ongoing assessment relies on regularly collecting artifacts to illustrate children's knowledge and learning. "It is the process of gathering information in the context of everyday class activities to obtain a representative picture of children's abilities and progress" (Dodge, Heroman, Charles, & Maiorca, 2004, p. 21). The artifacts (the children's products) are produced by the children while they engage in their daily classroom activities, such as those described in every chapter in this book. The products of these activities, then, serve the dual purposes of instruction and assessment. Because teachers are gathering *samples* of children's work to illustrate what the children know and can do, ongoing assessment sometimes is called *work sampling*. Ongoing assessment differs from on-demand assessment in several ways:

- Children work on their products for varying amounts of time, and the procedures or directions often vary across the classroom or across classes in the building.
- What each child and the teacher select as evidence of literacy learning may be different, not only across the children in the school or center but also across the children in a teacher's class.
- The classroom teacher analyzes each child's performance on the tasks and makes judgments about each child's learning.
- The classroom teacher's judgments are used immediately to define the child's next learning goal. The assessment, then, has an immediate effect on instruction for each child.
- The assessment of the work produced over time in many different contexts permits the teacher and the child to gather more than a quick snapshot of what the child knows and is able to do at a given moment.

Ongoing assessment, then, permits both the teacher and the student to examine the child's knowledge and learning. Young learner Phyllis shares what this means as she uses her journal to describe her growth as a reader and writer:

> I comed to this school a little bit nervous, you know. Nothin'. [She shakes her head for added emphasis.] I couldn't read or write nothin'. Look at this. [She turns to the first few pages of her writing journal.] Not a word! Not a word! [She taps the page and adds an aside.]

And the drawin's not too good. Now, look at this. [She turns to the end of the journal.] One, two, three, four. Four pages! And I can read 'em. Listen. [She reads.] Words! [Nodding her head.] Yup! Now I can read and write a lotta words!

Ongoing Assessment Tools

Phyllis's journal is one of several tools her teacher uses to gather information about Phyllis's literacy learning. Like Phyllis, her teacher can compare the writing at the beginning and at the end of the journal to learn about Phyllis's literacy development over time. Each tool permits teachers to gather information about their children's literacy learning while the children perform the kinds of activities described in this book. Readers were introduced to several of these tools in previous chapters.

PEARSON
myeducationkit™

Go to the Assignments and Activities section of Chapter 7 in the MyEducationKit and complete the activity entitled "Observing Children in Authentic Contexts." As you watch the video and answer the accompanying questions, note the teacher's system for recording anecdotal notes on the child's behavior and her plans for using them.

Anecdotal Notes. These are teacher notes describing a child's behavior. In addition to the child's name, the date, and the classroom area, the specific event or product should be described exactly as it was seen and heard. The following is an example of one of kindergarten teacher Karen Valentine's anecdotal notes:

> Martia
> 9/25
> M./ in the library center "reading" a page in a big book. As she reads, she points to the words. She runs out of words before she is done reading (each syllable = pointed to word). She tries again, and again, and again, and again. She leaves, shaking her head.

Teachers use many different kinds of paper (e.g., computer address labels, notepads, paper in a loose-leaf binder, index cards, Post-it Notes) to make anecdotal records of children's behavior.

In the Opening Doors to Literacy Early Reading First project, the Head Start teachers have developed an anecdotal note system that helps them gather information for the descriptions of their children's behaviors that are required three times per year. They use a sheet of sticky computer labels. A child's name is put on each label. They are very careful to ensure that there is a label for every child in the class. Through the week, they write short notes describing the children's behavior, much like the note above. At the end of the week, they remove the label and attach the note to each child's folder. The next week, they begin again with a blank computer label sheet. A benefit of computer label sheets is that at a glance teachers can see which children have been observed and which have been overlooked.

Teachers use anecdotal notes to describe the strategies children use to decode words, the processes children use while they write, the functions of writing children use while they play, and characteristics of children's talk during a presentation to the class. Note that anecdotal notes describe exactly what occurred and what was said verbatim, with no judgment or interpretation applied.

Vignettes or Teacher Reflections. Vignettes are recordings of recollections of significant events made after the fact, when the teacher is free of distractions. Vignettes are like

Teacher observations of children's work provide an important summary of what the teacher noticed over the year.

anecdotal notes except that they are prepared some time after a behavior has occurred and are based on a teacher's memory of the event. Though vignettes are used for many of the same purposes as those identified for anecdotal notes, these after-the-fact descriptions can be more detailed than anecdotal notes and are particularly useful when recording literacy behavior that is significant or unique for a specific child.

For example, Ms. Valentine observed a student attempting to control his peers' behavior by writing a sign and posting it in an appropriate place. She did not have time to record a description of the student's behavior immediately. As soon as the children left for the day, she recorded her recollection of the event:

For days Jamali had been complaining about the "mess" left by the children getting drinks at the classroom water fountain after recess. "Look at that mess! Water all over the floor!" At his insistence, the class discussed solutions to the problem. While the problem wasn't solved, I thought there was less water on the floor. Evidently, Jamali did not. Today he used the "power of the pen" to attempt to solve the problem. He wrote a sign:

BEWR!! WTR SHUS UP
ONLE TRN A LITL
(Beware! Water shoots up. Only turn a little.)

He posted his sign over the water fountain. This was the first time I had observed him using writing in an attempt to control other children's behavior.

Vignettes, then, are recollections of significant events. Because teachers can write vignettes when they are free of distractions, they can be more descriptive about the child's concern that drove the literacy-oriented behavior, and they can connect this event to what is known about the child's previous literacy-oriented behaviors.

Checklists.   Checklists are observational aids that specify which behaviors to look for and provide a convenient system for keeping records. They can make observations more systematic and easier to conduct. The number of checklists available to describe children's literacy development seems almost endless! In Figure 7.1, we provide an example of a checklist for assessing young children's book-related understandings.

FIGURE 7.1   Checklist for Assessing Young Children's Book-Related Understandings

_____ can
       (Child's name)

Concepts about Books	Date	Comments
look at the picture of an object in a book and realize it is a symbol for the real object	_____	_____
handle a book without attempting to eat or chew it	_____	_____
identify the front, back, top, and bottom of a book	_____	_____
turn the pages of a book correctly, holding the book upright	_____	_____
point to the print when asked, "What do people look at when they read?"	_____	_____
show how picture and print connect	_____	_____
point to where a reader begins reading on a page	_____	_____
point to a book's title on cover	_____	_____
point to a book's author on cover	_____	_____
point to a book's illustrator on cover	_____	_____
recognize specific books by their covers	_____	_____

Conventions of Print		
show that a reader reads left to right with return sweeps	_____	_____
find a requested letter or provide the letter's name	_____	_____

FIGURE 7.1   Continued

Concepts about Books	Date	Comments
ask questions or make comments about letters	_____	_____
ask questions or make comments about words	_____	_____
read words or phrases	_____	_____
read sentences	_____	_____
read along while adult reads familiar stories	_____	_____

Comprehension of Stories

	Date	Comments
answer and ask literal questions about story (provide example)	_____	_____
answer and ask interpretive questions about story (provide example)	_____	_____
answer and ask critical questions about story (provide example)	_____	_____
ask questions about story	_____	_____
say new words and dialogue from story	_____	_____
retell stories	_____	_____
by relying on pictures and with help to recall details	_____	_____
without book and with knowledge of the details	_____	_____
without book and with knowledge of key story elements	_____	_____
setting	_____	_____
characters	_____	_____
theme (what main character wanted or needed)	_____	_____
episodes or events (___/___)	_____	_____
ending	_____	_____
climax ending resolution	_____	_____
sequence	_____	_____
from beginning to middle	_____	_____
from middle to end	_____	_____
connect information in stories to events in his/her life	_____	_____
use own experiences to understand character's feelings and motivation	_____	_____

Attitude Toward Books

	Date	Comments
participate in book-sharing routine with caregiver	_____	_____
listen attentively to a variety of genres	_____	_____
voluntarily look at books	_____	_____
show excitement about books and reading	_____	_____
ask adults to read to him/her	_____	_____
use books as resource for answers to questions	_____	_____

Checklists are useful because they provide information that teachers can see at a glance, showing what children can do. Teachers have learned that (1) children sometimes engage in a behavior one day that does not reappear for several weeks, and (2) many different variables (e.g., a storybook being read, other children in the group) can affect the literacy behaviors children show. Hence, teachers are careful to record the date of each observation and to use the checklist many times over the year in an attempt to create an accurate picture of their children's literacy development.

Video and Audio Recordings.   Teachers often use audiotaping to document children's reading progress. For example, teachers might record children's reading of a favorite book to study reading attempts or children's retellings of stories read to them to study story comprehension.

Teachers use videotape to capture children's literacy behaviors in a variety of contexts. Some teachers focus the camera lens on an area of the classroom, such as the dramatic play area or the writing center, to gather information about children's literacy-related social interactions during their play and work. Viewing the tapes provides valuable information not only about the children's knowledge of context-appropriate oral language and their ability to engage in conversations with others but also about the children's knowledge of the functions of writing.

Products or Work Samples.   Some products, such as samples of children's writing, can be gathered together in a folder. If the children's original works cannot be saved (e.g., a letter that is sent to its recipient), a photocopy can be made of the product. Other products, such as three-dimensional structures the children have created with labels written by them, might not be conveniently saved. In these cases, a photograph—still or video—can be made. Because memories are short, the teacher should record a brief description of the product or the activity that resulted in the product.

Addressing Storage Problems

Mrs. Saenz has developed an assessment notebook that helps her organize information about children's literacy learning. Her notebook consists of several sections. One section contains a checklist she has developed to document children's emergent writing. Another section contains a checklist she created to document emergent reading behaviors, including information about concepts of print and alphabet recognition. Mrs. Saenz's notebook also has a section for writing vignettes. To prompt her memory of an event, Mrs. Saenz uses a digital camera that allows her to take pictures of the children engaging in specific literacy behaviors. Later in the day, she downloads and prints the photos, and writes her interpretation of the event on the bottom margin of each photo. In addition, the camera automatically dates the picture, making it easier for Mrs. Saenz to document this information quickly. Using these various tools results in the accumulation of many items that need to be stored someplace.

For teachers to maintain this kind of assessment system, they must be very well organized! Typically, teachers maintain a folder for each child. Many teachers find that folders with pockets and center clasps for three-hole-punched paper are better storage containers than file folders. Interview forms, running-record sheets, and other similar papers can be three-hole-punched, thus permitting easy insertion into each child's folder. When anecdotal notes and vignettes are written on computer address labels, the labels can be attached to the inside covers of each child's folder. When these notes are written on index cards, the cards can be stored in one of the folder's pockets. Also, a resealable plastic sandwich bag might be stapled inside each child's folder to hold an audiotape. The class's folders might be housed in a plastic container or in hanging files in a file cabinet.

On-Demand Assessment

Teachers use, or are required to use, another kind of assessment to understand their students' literacy learning. This kind of assessment is often referred to as the assessment of learning or *on-demand assessment* (Johnston & Costello, 2005). Think of on-demand assessments as an annual physical checkup. Periodically, we all need to stop what we are doing to take a formal measure of the state of our health. On-demand assessments occur at specific times, like once a year or every three months. For example, on Tuesday all kindergarten children in the school district may be asked to take a pencil-and-paper test. They might be asked to listen to several short stories composed of two or three sentences. Then the children would be asked to put an X on the picture that best matches each story. They may be asked to circle the letters said aloud by the teacher. They might be asked to listen to sounds said aloud by the teacher (e.g., *b*) and to circle the letter that makes that sound.

Standardized Tests

Most readers likely would label these kinds of on-demand assessments as *tests*. On-demand assessments are administered, scored, and interpreted in the same way for all test takers. Each student taking the test hears the same passages and answers the same questions. When all variables are held constant, the assessment is known as a *standardized test*.

The Elementary and Secondary Act specifies that "evidence-based research" relies on measures and observational methods that provide reliable and valid data. *Reliability* refers to the consistency of the data—if the same test is administered to the same child on consecutive days, the child's score should be similar. And if two different teachers administer an assessment to the same child, again the scores should be similar if the assessment is reliable. *Validity* refers to the extent to which an assessment really measures what it claims to measure.

Standardized assessments use carefully scripted procedures so that the conditions and directions are always the same whenever the test is administered. Each student taking the test hears the same directions, is given the same test items, and has the same amount of time. This "standardization" helps to increase the reliability of the assessment. It is not surprising, therefore, that the evidence-based approach makes heavy use of standardized types of assessment.

In Table 7.1, we provide a description of several of the standardized assessments in reading currently in use in early literacy programs.

TABLE 7.1 Standardized Reading Measures Used with Young Children

Title/Publisher	Purpose	Description	When to Use It
Dynamic Indicators of Basic Early Literacy Skills (DIBELS)— Letter Naming Fluency	To assess fluency with which children identify letter names. To identify children at risk of reading difficulty early, before a low reading trajectory is established	Individually administered, timed phonemic awareness task. Randomly ordered lower- and uppercase letters are presented to children for one minute: children are instructed to name as many letters as they can	Beginning kindergarten through fall of first grade or until children are proficient at accurately producing forty to sixty letter names per minute
Phonemic Segmentation Fluency Publisher: CBM Network, School Psychology Program, College of Education, University of Oregon http://dibels.uoregon.edu/	Assess children's ability to segment orally presented words into phonemes. To identify children who may be at risk of reading difficulty	Individually administered, timed phonological awareness task. Words are orally presented to children for one minute; children are instructed to segment each word into individual phonemes (i.e., sounds)	Winter of kindergarten through first grade or until children are proficient at accurately producing thirty-five to forty-five phonemes per minute
Early Reading Diagnostic Assessment Publisher: Harcourt	Diagnostic information specifying strengths and needs	Individually administered diagnostic test. Provides specific information about a child's reading skills	Grades K–3. Individually administered
Gates MacGinite Reading Tests, Third Edition Publisher: Riverside Publishing Company	Commercially published test designed to identify specific strengths and weaknesses in reading comprehension	Achievement test designed to assess a child's knowledge of important background concepts of reading, identify strengths and weaknesses in the area of beginning reading, and serve as a measure of reading skills for children who make less than average progress in reading by the end of first grade	Level "PRE" and "R" for use with beginning kindergartners to assess background concepts; Level "R" for measuring reading skills of students who are not making adequate progress; other seven levels used to provide a general assessment of reading achievement

TABLE 7.1 Continued

Title/Publisher	Purpose	Description	When to Use It
IDEA Proficiency Test (IPT) Publisher: Ballard & Tigh	To determine the English language skills of students who have a non-English language background	Children are assessed on oral language abilities, writing, and reading. Asked to write their own stories and respond to a story	Administered to children K–12
Individual Growth and Developmental Indicator (IGDI)	To identify children's phonological awareness strengths and weaknesses	Three components to the test: picture naming, rhyming, and alliteration. Takes approximately five minutes to administer	Used for ages three to five
PALS Pre-K http://pals. virginia. edu/PALS-Instruments/ PALS-PreK.asp	To provide information on children's strengths and weaknesses	Measures name-writing ability, upper- and lowercase alphabet recognition, letter sound and beginning sound production, print and word awareness, rhyme awareness, and nursery rhyme awareness	Used in fall of pre-K and can be used as a measurement of progress in the spring
Peabody Picture Vocabulary Test-III (PPVT-IV) Publisher: American Guidance Service	To measure receptive vocabulary acquisition and serve as a screening test of verbal ability	Student points to the picture that best represents the stimulus word	Beginning at age two-and-a-half years to ninety-plus years
The Phonological Awareness Test (PAT) Publisher: LinguiSystems	To assess students' phonological awareness skills	Five different measures of phonemic awareness (segmentation of phonemes, phoneme isolation, phoneme deletion, phoneme sub-stitution, and phoneme blending) and a measure of sensitivity to rhyme	Beginning the second semester of kindergarten through grade 2
Test of Preschool Early Literacy Publisher: Pro-Ed	To identify children at risk of having problems or developing problems in literacy	Individually administered. Provides information about print knowledge, single-word oral vocabulary and definitional vocabulary, and phonological awareness.	Used for ages three to six
Word-Attack Subtest of the Woodcock Reading Mastery Test-Revised Publisher: American Guidance Service	To assess children's ability to apply knowledge of letter-sound correspondences in decoding complex nonwords	Individually administered test consisting of a series of increasingly complex nonwords that children are asked to sound out as best as they can	Kindergarten through Grade 12 as a screening measure

There are two types of standardized tests: criterion-referenced and norm-referenced.

Criterion-Referenced Tests.   These tests are developed with a specific set of objectives that reflect district, state, or federal learning standards. The goal of *criterion-referenced tests* is for all students to demonstrate mastery of the information and skills they have been taught.

Some early childhood programs administer criterion-referenced tests. Teachers in these programs arrange to meet individually with each child three or four times a year to administer the assessment as one means of gathering specific information about each child's literacy development. For example, these teachers might ask children to show them the front of the book or how to turn the book's pages; to point to the title; to demonstrate their understandings of print by showing them where they should begin reading, where to go after reading a line of text, and what is read, the print or the pictures; to point to a letter, a word, a period, and a question mark; to listen to a story and read along, pointing while they read, when they can; or to retell the story. In Special Feature 7.1, we describe a criterion-referenced assessment procedure used by an Early Reading First project in Yuma, Arizona.

SPECIAL FEATURE 7.1
Curriculum-Based Measurement

TANIS BRYAN AND CEVRIYE ERGUL

An important part of teaching early literacy skills is continuous monitoring of children's learning. Although teachers "take in" thousands of bits of information about their students' learning every day, preschool teachers need reliable and valid measures to help them evaluate young children's development of the early literacy skills being taught in their classrooms. Over the past thirty years curriculum-based measurement (CBM) has been developed to help teachers monitor children's progress. The intent is for teachers to collect technically sound but simple data in a meaningful fashion to document students' growth and determine the necessity for modifying instructional programs.

Critical early literacy skills assessed with preschool CBMs on phonological awareness, alphabet letter naming, and oral language. CBM test stimuli are drawn from the curriculum. Teachers administer CBMs weekly across the school year and use the data for instructional planning. Teachers find CBM a feasible addition to their schedules because it is fast (two minutes per child weekly), inexpensive, and easy to administer. Because CBM is directly connected to daily instruction, the information is useful to teachers. Teachers use CBM to continuously measure their students' gains, determine if their students are learning at the expected rate, and evaluate their instructional strategies. Ideally, a team of teachers collaborate in each step of doing CBM.

Here is a step-by-step description of how teachers use CBM:

Step 1: Select children.   Teachers can select two to four children who are monitored weekly or rotate two to four children each week so that all children in the classroom are monitored monthly. It's important that each cohort include a child with learning delays or problems, such as a child who has developmental delays or disabilities, and/or a child at risk for disabilities. Include a child with typical achievement and/or a child with high achievement to help figure out if a particular child is having a problem or if all the children are making errors, and the instruction is missing its mark (e.g., the material is too difficult for everyone).

Step 2. Develop CBMs.   Teachers take a close look at the curriculum and weekly lesson plans and decide which vocabulary, sounds, and letters will be emphasized each week. Each CBM should assess: receptive vocabulary ("show me"), expressive vocabulary ("tell me"), letter identification, and alliteration (identification of initial sounds). The CBM should include six to eight words, two to four alphabet letters, and two sounds for alliteration from each week's lesson plan. It is important to use the same number of words, sounds, and letters each week because this allows teachers to evaluate the children's development across time.

A score sheet is prepared for each child (see Figure 7.2). The score sheet lists the sources for the items, such as the book/page or poster that shows the words in the item, and provides space for comments and descriptions of the types of errors (e.g., okay with initial sounds but unable to pronounce the rest of the word, mispronunciation of the whole word, certain types of mispronunciations of words or letters) or any other event that influenced the child's responses (e.g., off-task behavior, sick, weather too hot).

Step 3: Administer CBMs.   CBMs are administered at the same time each week, following the same procedures and wait time for each child. On receptive vocabulary, the child is shown a poster or page that has several pictures from the lesson and asked to "Show me _____". On expressive vocabulary and letter identification, the child is shown a poster or book page and asked to name the object or letter pointed to. On alliteration, the child is shown a card with the target word illustrated at the top of the card and three other illustrations in a row at the bottom of the card. One of the illustrations should have the same initial sound as the target word. Two sample items should be provided. The teacher displays each card and sounds out the words. The child is asked to point to one of the three pictures at the bottom with the same initial sound as the target picture.

Step 4: Analysis.   At the end of each week or month, each child's scores on each test are summed and a graph is prepared (see Figure 7.3). The horizontal axis indicates the week of the unit and the vertical axis presents the number of correct responses on each CBM subtest. Graphs give teachers an overview of each child's mastery of the curriculum. Teachers compare the performance of children with special needs, at risk, typical achieving, and high achieving.

Step 5: Using the results.   First, teachers establish expectations for students. Should every child get every item on every CBM? Should every child get three of the four items? Teachers reviewing the data should ask: (a) are one or two children not meeting expectations, (b) are all children not meeting expectations, or (c) are all the children exceeding expectations? We recommend that teachers use the performance of the typical or average achieving student to establish an expectation line. Then teachers can evaluate whether the child with disabilities or at risk for disabilities or an English language learner is learning at about the same rate as typical children or needs additional instruction.

Teachers are encouraged to include parents in the process by sending parents (or discussing)

(continued)

ACE3 CBM SCORE SHEET – UNIT [VROOM VROOM] / WEEK [One]

Child's Name _____   School _____

Date of Test _____   Examiner _____

Purpose: Track how well the child is learning the vocabulary words and letters you are teaching using DOORS.

Directions: Read the script in the box below. Enter the scores on the left side column.

Letter Identification
Letter Card (card with all letters):

D d _____   L l _____   M m _____   J j _____

correct _____

Show Me
Our Big Book of Driving: Pages 2-3.

Van _____

Bicycle _____

Motorcycle _____

Fire Truck _____

correct _____

Tell Me
Picture Word Cards: Pull the word cards for the following items:

Taxi _____   Bus _____

Tire _____   Stop sign _____

correct _____

Comments: _____

LETTER IDENTIFICATION:

Present the letter card to the child, and

*Say, "We are going to look at this card with all these letters. Tell me the name of letter I point to."

SCORE:
1 Point = correct answer or self-correction within approximately 3 seconds.
0 Point = incorrect answer.
NA (No Answer) = Asked twice and no answer at the end of three seconds.

SHOW ME (Identification):

Open the lap book version of "Our Big Book of Driving" to pages 2-3. Place the book in front of the child and

Say, "We are going to look at these pictures. Point to the picture that I tell you."

"Show me the _____ ."

SCORE:
1 Point = correct answer or self-correction within approximately 3 seconds.
0 Point = incorrect answer.
NA (No Answer) = Asked twice and no answer at the end of three seconds.

TELL ME (Production):

Place the word cards in front of the child and

*Say, "We are going to look at these pictures. Tell me the name of the picture I point to."

"Point to each picture and say, "Tell the name of this ."

SCORE:
1 Point = correct answer or self-correction within approximately 3 seconds.
0 Point = incorrect answer.
NA (No Answer) = Asked twice and no answer at the end of three seconds.

ACE3 CBM SCORE SHEET (ALLITERATION)
'VROOM VROOM' / WEEK 1

Alliteration (Picture cards)

Toy _____   Toilet _____

Toaster _____   Toes _____

correct _____

Comments: _____

ALLITERATION (Identification of initial sounds):

Use alliteration picture cards.

1. Sample item 1

"Say, "Here is a picture of bread. It starts with the 'b' sound." Repeat the word and say "Now look at these pictures. Which one starts with "b." Name each bottom picture. If child does not get correct answer, say the top picture's name and correct answer emphasizing initial sounds.

2. Sample item 2

Repeat the instructions of sample item 1 using the pictures' names in this sample.

3. Test items 1 and 2

"Say, "Here is a picture of a (picture name). Now which one of these pictures starts with the same sound." Name the top picture and then point to each picture in the bottom and say out loud.

SCORE:
1 Point for each correct answer or self-correction within approximately 3 seconds.
0 Point = incorrect answer.
NA (No Answer) = Asked twice and no answer at the end of three seconds.
Sample responses are not scored.

FIGURE 7.2   CBM Score Sheet

SPECIAL FEATURE 7.1 Continued

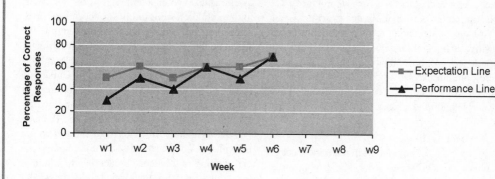

A Sample CBM Graph

FIGURE 7.3   Sample CBM Graph

an explanation of CBM, the words and letters being focused on in each exploration or week, and the child's graph. The teacher should explain the graph, noting positive changes in the child's progress. Parents also should be provided activities to do at home that support classroom learning.

Norm-Referenced Tests.   These tests are designed to measure the accomplishments of one student relative to the whole class, or to compare one classroom of pre-K students to another classroom within the same school or center, or to compare all the classrooms in a district, or to compare all children across the country. Norm-referenced standardized tests can be used to determine whether a school's curriculum reflects national expectations of what children should know at a specific grade level and to compare students to one another.

Special Feature 7.2 by Karen Burstein, an evaluation expert, provides useful information about both types of standardized assessments. In addition, Dr. Burstein describes the assessments used in the Arizona Centers of Excellence in Early Education Early Reading First project.

SPECIAL FEATURE 7.2

Standardized Assessment of Young Children

KAREN BURSTEIN

During the past twenty years, assessment of young children has assumed increased prominence, as seen in the Elementary and Secondary Act of 2001's emphasis on yearly testing. Today early childhood teachers are frequently expected to administer and interpret multiple standardized tests as well as conduct informal evaluations of children across the year. The notion of testing

(continued)

young children evokes passionate debate among teachers and scholars. To some it provides reliable measures for examining programs and attainment of standards; to others it conjures up negative images of subjecting children to trying experiences of questionable value. That said, there continues to be a push to test children in order to track their progress in preschool. What are early childhood educators to do?

Reasons for Testing

As assessments of young children are increasing, teachers and scholars ask why. The driving force behind assessment lies in the results: What information does the assessment yield? Who can use it? What is the benefit to the child? There are four primary reasons for assessment (Shepard, Kagan, & Wurtz, 1998):

1. *Accountability.* Districts/schools are compared across communities, and the question posed is whether they are achieving state standards or benchmarks. For this purpose, early childhood programs are likely to be using Dynamic Indicators of Basic Early Literacy Skills (DIBELS), its preschool counterpart *Get It, Got It, Go!* (Individual Growth and Development Indicators), and AIMS Web. These are standardized, individually teacher-administered measures of early reading skills that are responsive to the implementation of teaching methods consistent with scientifically based reading research. These tests provide districts and schools with benchmark information and teachers with child-specific skills attainment. The instruments are administered approximately three times annually and yield results on children's acquisition of skills in sound (phonemic awareness), alphabet, letter, vocabulary, and oral reading fluency.

2. *Identify children who are not benefiting from instruction and refer for special education or additional services.* Since the implementation of IDEA (formerly P.L. 94-142) in 1975, the most

common reason for administering standardized assessments to young children is to assist in determining children's eligibility for special services. These tests include standardized measures of IQ, such as the Wechsler Preschool and Primary Scale of Intelligence (WPPSI) or the Stanford-Binet Intelligence Scales for Early Childhood (Early SB5), and measures of different areas of child development such as the Vineland Social-Emotional Early Childhood Scales and Peabody Picture Vocabulary Test-IV. All of these tests are individually administered and some require special training or advanced credentials to administer and interpret. Students' raw scores are usually converted into standard scores that fall along a continuum that allows for comparisons of individuals to a "normal" distribution of same-age children. They typically do not indicate academic strengths or weaknesses and generally do not help teachers develop instructional plans. The advantage of standardized assessments is that they expedite the process of determining eligibility for special services. However, important educational decisions should be based on multiple sources of information including observations, work samples, and family interviews.

3. *Program evaluation and progress monitoring.* One of the most prevalent and high-profile models of program evaluation was the Head Start National Reporting System (NRS). Early in 2003, the Bush administration announced its intention to require all four- and five-year-olds in the federal Head Start program to be assessed at the beginning and end of each program year. The NRS assessments were standardized and measured a limited set of skills that include expressive and receptive English vocabulary, uppercase letter naming, and early math skills such as number identity and simple addition and subtraction. Teachers administered the NRS, but it was scored by an external organization that sent reports of overall program outcomes to Head Start and local administrations. The primary focus of the NRS was the

SPECIAL FEATURE 7.2 Continued

overall progress that groups of children made in each Head Start program. The NRS was not designed to assess the school readiness of individual children (*Head Start In Focus,* April 2003).

Programs can also be evaluated at the local level. For example, all Early Reading First projects are required to have an evaluation plan to measure their effectiveness in boosting pre-K children's school readiness. The Arizona Centers of Excellence in Early Education (ACE[3]), discussed earlier in this book, developed an evaluation model that included semiannual administration of a battery of standardized assessments, semimonthly systematic classroom observations, and weekly curriculum-based measurements. Many adequate "skills-specific" measures exist, so assessments were selected based on reliability and validity reported by test publishers and the test "fit" with the population of children being assessed (i.e., the populations were represented in the norming samples). A team of local substitute teachers were trained to be the examiners. The ACE[3] assessment battery provided an English language fluency level for each child and a baseline of each child's knowledge of initial sounds and rhymes, areas of competence in print awareness, a measure of receptive vocabulary, and the number and names of the letters recognized. Upon completion of the battery, teachers received the ACE Preschool Continuum of Progress (see Figure 7.4), an easy-to-understand summary of each child's assessment results, and a set of graphs of overall class results. Parents were provided with similar information and, at the end of the year, an exit summary of their child's skills in each area.

4. *Inform teachers of students' instructional needs.* From the teacher's perspective, the most important reason for assessment is to obtain accurate information about the instructional needs of students. The Assess-Plan-Teach-Assess model of instruction directs teachers to:

- know the content of the early childhood education standards in their community;
- align their classroom curriculum to these standards;
- assess each child's skill attainment on these standards;
- plan instruction that is responsive to children's assessed needs and skills;
- deliver instruction that explicitly targets needs; and
- reassess to ensure that children are learning the content that was delivered.

Within this model, assessment is a critical step in good instruction. As the call for assessment has increased, there are now a plethora of measures covering a myriad of skills. Even curriculum developers have begun to develop standardized measures aligned with their materials. However, the vast majority of standardized assessments are limited in their scope and number of items. Couple this limitation with the dramatic developmental variations in young children and one can begin to understand the consequences of trying to use standardized assessments to fully inform teachers of the needs of their students. Teachers need specific information from multiple models of assessment in order to develop effective plans and activities for their classes. Each teacher's skill repertoire should include not only standardized assessment but also knowledge about child development and strong skills in observation techniques, work sampling, parent interviewing and collaboration, curriculum alignment, and curriculum-based measurement (see Special Feature 7.1).

FIGURE 7.4   ACE Preschool Continuum of Progress

ACE Preschool Continuum of Progress: Niño at a glance!

Child Name _____   **Program Year** _____

Teacher: _____   **Center/Site:** _____

The purpose of this form is to assist parents and teachers to make appropriate educational goals for children enrolled in the ACE program and to track progress across the school year. It concludes with a summary and end of the year report to families.

Curriculum Based Assessment Results (initial, midyear, end of year)

Letter Identification   1) _____ 2) _____ 3) _____
Initial Sounds (alliteration) 1) _____ 2) _____ 3) _____
Rhyming   1) _____ 2) _____ 3) _____
Get Ready to Read   1) _____ 2) _____ 3) _____
CBM Quarterly   1-Letter name) _____ Show Me) _____ Tell Me) _____ Alliteration) _____
                     2-Letter name) _____ Show Me) _____ Tell Me) _____ Alliteration) _____
                     3-Letter name) _____ Show Me) _____ Tell Me) _____ Alliteration) _____
                     4-Letter name) _____ Show Me) _____ Tell Me) _____ Alliteration) _____

Developmental Assessment (name) _____ Brief Summary _____
_____
_____

Summary of teacher observations and anecdotal records _____
_____
_____
_____

Parent Goals (What the parent wants the child to work on during the program year): _____
_____
_____
_____

IEG Individual Education Goals: _____
  1) _____
  2) _____

Goals from IEP to be supported in the classroom: _____
_____

Monthly Explorations/Theme:

September _____
Circle each of the letter names that the child has learned. Letter names learned: F   M
Instructional Modifications: 0) no modification necessary   1) modify classroom   2) more instruction
          3) more practice   4) more structured play   5) more parent involvement   6) other _____
Social development activities:
Activities sent home:

[Note: Page 2 contains reports on the remaining monthly explorations and themes, and Page 3 contains reports of the parent conferences that are conducted in the fall and spring.]

Family Focus: Sharing Assessment Results With Parents

Children are complex, social individuals who must function appropriately in two very different cultures—school and home. Parents need to understand how a child uses his or her social skills to become a productive member of the school community. Likewise, experienced teachers appreciate the child's home life and recognize its significant influence on a child's behavior and ability to learn. Partnerships reach their full potential when parents and teachers share information about the child from their unique perspectives, value the child's individual needs and strengths, and work together for the benefit of the child.

The best opportunity teachers have for engaging parents in this type of discussion is during parent–teacher conferences. Conferences should feature a two-way exchange of information. There are generally two types of parent–teacher conferences—preestablished conferences that review the child's classroom progress, and spontaneous conferences that deal with a range of specific concerns that occur throughout the year.

Progress Review Conference

The progress review conference is an opportunity for parents and teachers to share information about children's social interactions, emotional maturity, and cognitive development. One way to help a parent and teacher prepare to share information during the conference is a preconference questionnaire. The teacher sends the questionnaire home to the parent to complete and return prior to the conference. In Figure 7.5, we present the notes made by Manuel's mother as she prepared for her conference with Ms. Jones, her son's kindergarten teacher. The information Mrs. Romero provides also tells Ms. Jones what concerns she has; therefore, Ms. Jones has a better idea about how to focus the conference. Remember, it may be necessary to have this letter and questionnaire translated into the language spoken in the home.

During a progress review conference, the teacher shares information about the child's academic progress. In addition to academic progress, most parents want to know about their children's social interactions and classroom behavior. The observational data that the teacher has recorded helps provide a more complete picture of the child in the classroom context.

When working with parents, teachers are encouraged to use a structured format during the progress review conference. The structure keeps the conference focused and increases the chance of both teachers' and parents' concerns being adequately discussed. Billie Enz and Susie Cook (1993) recommend that progress review conferences be structured as follows:

- *Positive statement and review conference format.* The teacher's first sentence helps establish a foundation for a proactive conference. Positive statements are sincere and usually personal—for example, "Your child is so eager to learn." Next, the teacher should briefly review the three steps of the conference: (1) parent input, (2) teacher input, and (3) closure. Reviewing the conference process relieves stress and actually helps keep the conference moving in a positive direction.
- *Ask for parental input.* "First, I am going to ask you to share with me what you have observed about your child this year that makes you feel good about his learning and then what concerns you have about his progress." It is important for parents to focus on their child's academic and social strengths when they meet with you. It is also important for you to know the parents' view of their child's major academic and social concerns.
- *Offer teacher input.* "Then I will share some of your child's work with you and my observations

PEARSON
myeducationkit™

Go to the Assignments and Activities section of Chapter 7 in the MyEducationKit and complete the activity entitled "A Conference with Kayla's Mom." As you watch the video and answer the accompanying questions, note how the teacher prepared for the conference with Kayla's mother and the similarities and differences between the format of this progress review conference and the format described by Billie Enz and Susie Cook.

(continued)

Family Focus: Sharing Assessment Results With Parents   Continued

Dear Parent,

To help us make the most of our time, I am sending this questionnaire to help facilitate our progress review conference. Please read and complete the questions. If you have any other concerns, simply write them down on the questionnaire and we will discuss any of your inquiries during our time together. I look forward to getting to know both you and your child better.

1. How is your child's overall health?
   Good, but Manuel gets colds alot.

2. Are there specific health concerns that the teacher should know about? (include allergies)
   Colds and sometimes ear infections.

3. How many hours of sleep does your child typically get?
   About 9

4. Does your child take any medication on a regular basis? If so, what type?
   He takes penicillin when he has ear infections.

5. What are the names and ages of other children who live in your home?
   Maria, 9; Rosalina, 7; Carlos, 3.

6. How would you describe your child's attitude toward school?
   He likes school.

7. What school activity does your child enjoy most?
   P.E. and art

8. What school activity does your child enjoy least?
   Math

9. What are your child's favorite TV shows?
   Power Rangers, Ninja Turtles

   How many hours of TV will your child generally watch each night?
   Three

10. What is the title of your child's favorite storybook?
    Where the Wild Things Are.

11. How often do you read to your child?
    His sisters read to him most nights.

12. What other activities does your child enjoy?
    Playing soccer.

Other concerns:
I can't read his writing. His sisters' was good in Kindergarten.

FIGURE 7.5   Preconference Questionnaire

about his progress. We'll discuss ideas that will continue to encourage his learning."

- *Closure.* "So, let's review the home and school [or center] activities that we think will best help your child continue to progress."

The success of the parent–teacher relationship depends on the teacher's ability to highlight the child's academic and social strengths and progress.

When areas of concern are discussed, it is important to provide examples of the child's work or review the observational data to illustrate the point. Often, the issues that parents reveal are directly related to concerns the teacher has. Whenever possible, connect these concerns, as this reinforces the feeling that the teacher and the parents have the same goals for helping the child learn. It is essential to solicit the parents' views and suggestions for helping the child

Student's name: *Manuel Romero*   Parent's name: *Mary Romero*

Conference date: *Nov. 1*   Time: *4:30 p.m.*

Positive Statement: *Manuel is so eager to learn*

Review Conference steps:
Our conference today will consist of three parts. First, I will ask you to review your child's progress, sharing with me both academic/social strengths and areas of concern. Next, I'll review Manuel's work with you and discuss his academic/social strengths and areas in which we will want to help him grow. Finally, we will discuss the main points we discussed today, and review the strategies we decided would help Manuel continue to make progress.

1. Ask for Parent Input: What have you observed about Manuel this year that makes you feel good about his learning? (Take notes as parent is sharing)
Manuel likes school, drawing, friends, stories.

What are your main concerns?
His writing looks like scribbles. He's not reading yet but he likes stories read to him.

2. Teacher Input: I would like to share some observations about Manuel's work and review both areas of strengths and skills that need to be refined. *Manuel interest in reading is wonderful. He is eager to write in class journal. Though his printing is still developing, he is beginning to use "invented" spelling. Look at this example in his portfolio.*

MT M*p*N PR RG2
Mighty Morphin Power Rangers

Notice how he is separating the words. Ask him to read his work for you if you are having difficulty decoding or deciphering it. His printing skills will improve naturally with time and encouragement. He is really progressing well. Sometimes young girls develop finger muscles sooner. We need to support his efforts. Manuel enjoys sharing his writing in class with his friends and his art work is full of detail. Manuel has many friends and gets along easily with others.

3. Closure: Let's review those things we talked about that will facilitate continued success. (Teacher needs to write down this information as the parent talks)

a. *Manuel's printing is "okay" for him.*

b. *Manuel is writing. I am surprised to see that he really is writing. I just need to have him read for me. Then it's easier for me to figure out what his*
c. *letters say.*

FIGURE 7.6   Progress Review Conference Form

and also to provide concrete examples about how they might help the child learn.

To make sure both teacher and parents reach a common understanding, briefly review the main ideas and suggestions for improvement that were discussed during the conference. Allow parents to orally discuss their views of the main ideas of the conference. Check the parents' perceptions. Finally, briefly

(continued)

Family Focus: Sharing Assessment Results With Parents   Continued

record the parents' oral summary on the conference form. Figure 7.6 is a progress review conference form from Manuel's conference.

Child–Parent–Teacher Conferences

A rather new innovation in progress review conferences is the inclusion of the student. The child participates equally—sharing work, discussing areas in which he or she has noticed improvement, and establishing academic and/or social goals. This type of conference requires that the children are active participants in selecting what work will be featured in their portfolios. In addition, the teacher must begin to help children develop the skill to evaluate their own performance. For example, an editing checklist, such as the one described in Chapter 11, may be created with the children, for use in the writing workshop. The checklist also serves as an instructional guide. Children consult the checklist to make sure they have used correct punctuation, have begun sentences with capital letters, or have asked another student to proofread their work. Child–parent–teacher conferences are a natural outgrowth of frequent child–teacher conferences.

Because a three-way conference may be a new experience for parents, it is important for the teacher to establish guidelines for parents and students. A letter sent home explaining the format of the conference and discussing each person's role is essential. Parents are encouraged to ask open-ended questions, such as:

"What did you learn the most about?"
"What did you work the hardest to learn?"
"What do you want to learn more about?"

Questions such as these encourage students to analyze their own learning and also help them to set new goals. Parents should not criticize the child's work or focus on any negative aspect of any material that is presented during the conference. Negative comments, particularly from parents, will only inhibit learning and dampen excitement about school.

PEARSON myeducationkit™

Go to the Assignments and Activities section of Chapter 7 in the MyEducationKit and complete the activity entitled "Communicating with Parents." As you watch the video and answer the accompanying questions, consider how establishing a positive relationship with parents through phone calls to share news about their child doing something great can have a positive impact on the parent-teacher relationship.

Assessing English Language Learners

In the discussion of this chapter's opening vignette, Ms. Saenz demonstrated her sensitivity to the challenges of accurately assessing Monique's language and literacy learning. She knows that the results from the assessment process can be used to make many vital decisions. She wants the conclusions she reaches about her English language learner (ELL) children's development to be valid. She is sensitive to the recommendations for assessing ELL children Julia Park provides in Special Feature 7.3.

SPECIAL FEATURE 7.3
Assessing English Language Learners

JULIA PARK

Research suggests that assessment problems often stem from a lack of training, awareness, and sensitivity (Santos, 2004). To do a good job of assessing young children whose home language is not English, skill, sensitivity, and knowledge of the child's culture and language are required (Biggar, 2005). Deepening one's understanding of the impact of culture and language on the assessment process is the first step. The best-practice recommendations for appropriate assessment of young children whose home language is not English are as follows:

1. *Learn about ELLs' literacy background.* Teachers should never assume that students who share the same language will observe the same cultural practices or understand the same types of texts. In understanding that ELLs differ in the literacy practices of their native language, teachers may be in a better position to determine whether those literacy practices are facilitating or interfering with the development of literacy in English.

2. *Use screening and assessment for appropriate purposes and determine the purpose of assessment beforehand.* Assessment strategies should help teachers find out what students know and can do, not what they do not know and cannot do. Also, when the purpose for assessment is determined beforehand, better decisions about what information should be gathered can be made.

3. *Decide how to assess children.* Multiple forms of evaluation through a variety of authentic assessment tools should be conducted to fairly assess the placement and progress of children and to plan instruction.

4. *Use culturally and linguistically appropriate assessment tools.* In assessing young ELLs, great emphasis should be given to the alignment of assessment tools and procedures with the specific cultural and linguistic characteristics of the children being assessed.

5. *Adopt a multidimensional approach including alternative assessments (observations, journals, conferring, questionnaires, and portfolios).* Alternative assessment tasks are more appropriate and fair ways to measure academic progress. They provide teachers the ability to identify what students need.

6. *Assess in nontraditional ways.* Because ELLs are in the process of acquiring language as they acquire content, teachers need to ensure that their assessment addresses the linguistic component of the learning continuum. Therefore teachers should provide ELLs with opportunities to demonstrate knowledge in nontraditional ways such as the opportunity to show and practice knowledge in nonlanguage-dependent ways (drawing pictures, building structures).

7. *Consider modifications for ELLs who are in the process of acquiring English.* Allow a qualified bilingual professional to assist with the assessment.

8. *Begin assessment with several examples and simplify directions.* Giving the directions in the student's native language could also be a consideration.

9. *Allow students to use their language abilities to complete literacy tasks and to express their knowledge in the language they know best.* Oftentimes, knowledge of the first language means that students possess linguistic skills that can assist them in mastering literacy tasks in the second language.

10. *Involve families in the assessment process.* When conducting assessments, professionals should seek assistance from a family member or cultural guide to confirm their interpretations of the child's behavior during the assessment process.

(continued)

SPECIAL FEATURE 7.3 Continued

11. *Include a qualified representative of the child's cultural and linguistic group to assist in the interpretation of the results when bilingual professionals are not available.*

12. *Always consider to what degree perceived developmental delays are related to cultural or child-rearing practices, difficulties in translation, or other cultural variables.*

Using Assessment Data to Plan Early Literacy Instruction

It is unacceptable if a teacher is still teaching the same way she/he was teaching twenty years ago. We, as a profession, have learned incredible amounts about how students learn best. . . . If [we] teach well, maintain best practices, make instructional decisions based on [our] students' needs, and make decisions that are reflective of [the principles of learning we hold], [our] students will learn. They will learn well, and they will pass the test. (Buckner, 2002, p. 215)

We strongly agree that no single test score should be used alone to judge a child's progress in language, reading, and writing development. However, *if* most of the students in a classroom do not perform as expected on a standardized test, then teachers must be prepared to reconsider their methods of teaching language, reading, and writing. Teachers need to ask themselves, What could I have done better or differently? Others certainly will raise this question. Did I not spend enough time explicitly teaching phonological awareness? Did I not support my children's language development by explicitly teaching vocabulary and expanding or elaborating on their talk? Teachers must be able to respond by defending their teaching practices and by learning what legitimately needs revising to support children's language, reading, and writing development. Teachers need to study the reported testing data to understand what their children could do well and what was challenging for their children. These data can guide teachers' examination of their teaching practices.

What do I teach tomorrow? Early childhood teachers do not teach a program; they teach children. One of the book's authors recently asked kindergarten teachers to submit a copy of a week's language and literacy lesson plans. Almost every teacher submitted a photocopy of pages from the reading program teacher's guide. There were no indications of adjustments made based on children's needs. Information must be gathered, using on-demand and ongoing assessment procedures, to help teachers know what their young students know and can do—and cannot do. This information, then, determines what the teacher teaches tomorrow.

PEARSON
myeducationkit™

To check your comprehension on the content covered in this chapter, go to the MyEducationKit for your book and complete the Study Plan for Chapter 7. Here you will be able to take a chapter quiz and receive feedback on your answers.

Summary

Chapters 3 through 6 presented the instructional strategies that create the framework for an effective early childhood language arts curriculum. However, these strategies by themselves are not sufficient to construct a program that ensures optimal language and literacy learning for all children. This chapter presented another key ingredient—assessment.

- *What is important for teachers to know about children's literacy development?*

Teachers need a thorough knowledge of language and literacy guidelines for young children. This information may be obtained from several sources, including state standards and nationally defined outcomes.

- *What two general approaches might teachers use to assess their children's literacy learning?*

Teachers use two kinds of assessment to measure their children's progress toward the achievement of the state standards: ongoing and on-demand.

- *What types of ongoing assessment tools are used to collect information about children's progress?*

Changes in what we know about language literacy learning have necessitated major changes in our ways of measuring young children's literacy accomplishments and progress. In addition to on-demand assessments that provide samples of student literacy behavior, teachers rely on ongoing assessment procedures that are connected with the daily literacy activities that take place in the classroom. This ongoing assessment makes heavy use of systematic observation and the collection of samples of children's work. The classroom library, writing center, and dramatic play areas are ideal settings for this type of assessment, and anecdotal notes, vignettes, and checklists provide effective ways to record data.

- *How do teachers use the information they collect?*

Teachers (and children) collect information and store it. Teachers analyze the products and information to assess each child's progress over time. These types of authentic assessments provide just the type of information that teachers need to know to provide effective literacy learning experiences for children.

LINKING KNOWLEDGE TO PRACTICE

1. One way teachers determine what they want and need to know about children's literacy development is by reviewing national, state, and local standards. Contact your state and a local school district to obtain a copy of the local standards for language arts at the pre-K and kindergarten levels. Given what you have learned about children's early literacy development in this textbook, do these standards appear to be reasonable goals for language arts instruction at these levels?

2. Interview a pre-K or kindergarten teacher about the information-gathering tools that he or she typically uses to collect information about children's literacy development. How does the teacher use this information to adjust instruction to meet each child's language and literacy needs?

PART THREE

Elementary Grade Literacy Instruction

8

Elementary Reading: Expanding the Foundation for Ongoing Literacy Learning

MARY F. ROE

Adam is in the sixth grade. He receives high grades in his language arts class, and his teacher considers him a capable reader, but he does not fare as well in his social studies class. Outside school, he has read every Harry Potter book and recently began reading Tolkien's trilogy.

Janet is just starting first grade. She enjoys listening to books read to her and can easily talk about them. She can identify her name and several words that frequently appear in her books, but is unable to read the simplest of texts independently.

Juan is bilingual. He speaks Spanish at home and learned to read in his native language. He started school in the United States in third grade. Now in fourth grade, he attends a class for second-language learners twice a week. In addition, he receives reading assistance from a Title I paraprofessional, a federal program established to help students like Juan. His classroom teacher remains concerned about his reading achievement, especially his ability to contribute to classroom discussions about assigned texts from his basal anthology.

Each of these three students has a teacher who is responsible for helping them read better. To accomplish that goal, the teachers must have a rich and deep understanding of reading. Armed with theoretical and practical understandings, the teacher can make the "just-right" instructional choices that allow not only students like Juan, Adam, and Janet to read better, but also myriad other readers the teacher will encounter in his or her professional journey. Today's classrooms do not hold readers who are cookie-cutter versions of each other. Therefore, helping all children read better demands responsive teachers who realize that as long as they teach, they will engage in lifelong learning. The goal remains constant: intentionally selecting from a wealth of scientifically based possibilities those strategies that will help each student be a better reader. Parents and guardians turn to teachers for reading expertise and expect that teachers, whether novice or experienced, will not fail their children. Meeting this challenge demands more than enjoying the company of children. It depends on knowledge, versatility, and gumption. In this chapter, we help teachers begin the task of becoming a reading teacher scholar.

Before Reading This Chapter, Think About . . .

■ A text you recently read for pleasure. What type of text was it: a magazine, a newspaper, a novel, a historical account? Why did you find it pleasurable? Were you aware of the processes you used to obtain meaning from it?

■ A text recently assigned for you to read. Did you find it easier or more difficult to read than the text you read by choice? Were you aware of the processes you used to obtain meaning from it? How did those processes compare with what you noticed when you read for pleasure?

■ How you learned to read. Do you remember being taught to read, or did reading just magically begin? While in grades 1 through 6, what do you remember most about reading in and out of school? How do those reading contexts compare?

Focus Questions

■ What are the components of the reading process?

■ Beyond a reader's proficiency in the specific features of this process, what else contributes to reading achievement?

■ What classroom events would you expect to see during the time assigned for reading?

■ What attributes define a successful reading teacher?

BOX **8.1**

Definition of Terms

comprehension: an ability to combine what you know (i.e., prior knowledge) with an author's words to understand a text.

comprehension strategies: approaches used by readers to assist their understanding of a text (e.g., visualizing, determining importance, monitoring and adjusting, predicting, making inferences, summarizing, analyzing, posing questions, using fix-up strategies).

flexible grouping: the formation of temporary groups to address specific student reading needs.

sight vocabulary: words that are immediately and correctly pronounced and understood by a reader (i.e., known at the level of automaticity).

text structure: the organization of a text (i.e., narrative or exposition).

vocabulary: words that hold conceptual meaning for readers and that they can appropriately understand when reading a text.

word identification strategies: cues used by readers to pronounce an unknown word (i.e., contextual cues, morphemic cues, and graphophonic cues).

word meaning strategies: cues used by readers to infer the meaning of an unknown word (i.e., definition, appositive, example, antonym, synonym, grouping, summary, and simile).

Understanding the Reading Process

PEARSON
myeducationkit™

Go to the Assignments and
Activities section of Chapter
8 in the MyEducationKit and
complete the activity entitled
"Defining Reading Compre-
hension." As you watch the
video and answer the accompanying questions, note the
balance children must maintain between word recognition and comprehension.

PEARSON
myeducationkit™

Go to the Assignments and
Activities section of Chapter
8 in the MyEducationKit and
complete the activity entitled
"Dimensions of Comprehen-
sion." As you watch the
video and answer the accompanying questions, note
the four dimensions of
comprehension.

Reading is comprehending. Perhaps you have heard that statement before. It has upheld the test of time. This statement makes reading sound like a simple process when it is actually a complex, challenging process. We begin this chapter by briefly describing the history of reading and shedding light on past trends and current misconceptions.

Explanations of the process that supports reading comprehension have undergone many changes. In earlier times, comprehension was believed to rest on a reader's ability to say words quickly and accurately (Mathews, 1966). Reading in this era was viewed as no more compli-cated than understanding oral language. Break the code, say the words, and comprehension followed. More recently, this perspective became labeled as a *bottom-up* approach. By privileging the text (the print on the page, i.e., starting from the bottom), reading experts believed that meaning resided in the words and a reader's ability to say them quickly and accurately. Classroom reading programs that reflected this stance placed a heavy emphasis on word identification strategies such as phonics.

Move forward a few years and an alternative explanation was put forth. This perspective viewed comprehension as residing in the head of a reader. Within this view, typically called a *top-down* approach, a reader acquired a text's meaning by using his or her prior knowledge to under-stand it. Although decoding the words was essential, decoding alone was insufficient to signal comprehension. As the famous quote by John Locke suggests, it was the *thinking* that made the reader know the mean-ing of the words.

Driven by the early research conducted by educational psycholo-gists and cognitive scientists (Anderson, Pichert, & Shirey, 1983; Brans-ford, Barclay, & Franks, 1972), a third perspective arose that views reading as an interaction between the text and the reader. Typically called an interactive or sociocultural view of reading (Au, 2006), this position holds that *comprehension* stems from an interplay between the words on the page and the understand-ings that a reader brings to them. A continuous and reciprocal action exists between what is in the reader's head and what is on the page. As Gretchen Owocki explains (2005, p. 5), "Socio-cultural theory of learning recognizes that children's life experiences provide a foundation from which all new learning occurs." This perspective allows a teacher to embrace the five key psychological components noted by the National Reading Panel (2000)—rate and fluency, phonemic awareness, phonics, comprehension, and vocabu-lary)—as well as what Marjorie Lipson and Karen Wixson (2003) call learner and context factors. Four of these components of reading (fluency, phonemic awareness, phonics, and vocabulary) coalesce, and the result is comprehension. We discuss each component sepa-rately to help readers grasp the complexity of this process and the information a teacher needs to help all students read better.

Psychological Contributors to Reading

As previously mentioned, several text-driven processes allow a reader to access a text's message. Sometimes, the word is one the reader recognizes immediately; the word is in the reader's sight word vocabulary. At other times, readers need to draw on one of numerous *word identification strategies* to help them say the word. Once a word is pronounced, a reader must attach meaning to it. Of course, readers with large speaking vocabulary are at an advantage over readers with limited speaking vocabularies. When the reader does not know a word, he or she is prompted to use any of a number of *word meaning strategies*. Reading, however, is more than saying individual words and knowing their meanings. Readers must handle connected text. This requires the use of comprehension strategies. Expert readers initially make a decision and then adjust their thinking as necessary to maintain meaning. They perform these mental gymnastics (saying words, attaching meaning, and understanding the whole connected text) simultaneously and without pause. More novice readers, and those older readers who struggle, must work harder. To assist all readers, a teacher needs a rich and deep grasp of each piece a reader uses: word identification, vocabulary, and comprehension strategies.

Word Identification

Some readers possess a large *sight vocabulary* and recognize a word immediately. They can quickly turn their attention to the big ideas and nuances of the words as presented in the text. Of course, that is not true of all readers. Some readers are still developing large reading vocabularies. They must rely on several word identification strategies to assist them. Approaching word identification *strategically* rather than as a skill requires a plan for directing the entire process of saying words. It demands problem solving, a road map of sorts to guide a reader's actions. A strategy holds ongoing value for readers. In addressing word identification, readers have several options.

PEARSON
myeducationkit

Go to the Assignments and Activities section of Chapter 8 in the MyEducationKit and complete the activity entitled "Context Clues." As you watch the video and answer the accompanying questions, note how the teacher helps the student identify and label the strategies he is using to make meaning.

■ First, students with large speaking vocabularies find using context helpful. A reader who uses context predicts an unknown word by using the sense of the text. Consider the following sentence from *Knuffle Bunny* (Willems, 2004): *Then they left*. Previously, a dad and his daughter had gone to a Laundromat. This three-word sentence appears once they finish their laundry. If *left* is unknown, then readers who hold this word in their oral (i.e., speaking) vocabulary can reasonably infer this word's pronunciation.

■ Readers can also use a second strategy, graphophonic cues, which is often called phonics. Those who use this strategy must understand that words are composed of subsounds (phonemes); must know the sound that each letter represents (in the above example, the consonant sounds for *l, f,* and *t* and the short sound for *e*); must synthesize them or blend them to say the word; and then must check to make sure that the word makes sense. Good readers often combine these strategies. With the word *left,* a host of words would make sense in the general sentence (e.g., Then they played, danced, or sang). These words, however, do not cohere with this story's events and do not coincide with this word's first letter.

. ■ When using morphemic analysis for saying unknown words, a reader must first identify the affixes, expose the root, and then pronounce and recombine these pieces. Such analysis occurs, for example, with words like *helped,* which is also found in *Knuffle Bunny*. Although some novice readers may know the word *help,* they can become perplexed when they see *helped.* Identifying the suffix (i.e., *ed*) and exposing the root (i.e., *help*) is an example of morphemic analysis. Of importance, only a word's spelling confirms its pronunciation, and a reader should never be led to think otherwise. Because word identification cues are often misunderstood and inappropriately presented, a fuller explanation of each is warranted.

Graphophonic Cues.   Using cues driven by a word's spelling requires students to understand the sounds that letters generally represent, the unique sounds of some letter combinations, and generalizations that control letter sounds. Because phonics applies to syllables, when readers encounter multisyllabic words, they must first apply syllabication generalizations. (Refer to Table 8.1 for a listing of letter sounds, sound combinations, generalizations that control letter sounds, and syllabication generalizations.) The use of the term *generalizations* is intentional and important.

Parents who designate a bedtime rule, a teacher and students who compose classroom rules, or a school principal who posts playground rules expect their children or students to follow them without exception. Such is not the case with phonics. Exceptions exist. Good readers understand flexibility and good teachers promote it. Table 8.2 uses additional words from *Knuffle Bunny* to further underscore the helpfulness and complexity of using phonics.

Morphemic Analysis Cues.   As described above, readers who use morphemic analysis must be well grounded in commonly occurring prefixes and suffixes (collectively called affixes). A teacher's goal is to make sure his or her students identify affixes as a unit and pronounce them correctly. (Refer to Table 8.3 for a listing of common prefixes and suffixes.) For more novice readers, attending to *-s, -ed,* and *-ing* makes sense because these suffixes often appear in the simplest of words. It is important for novice readers to know that *-ed* can assume three pronunciations: /d/ as in *tied,* /t/ as in *stopped,* and /ed/ as in *acted.* Although a student's oral language often corrects a mispronunciation of this word ending, a teacher must be prepared to understand this misstep and, if necessary, explicitly address it. An examination of the words in the texts that a student reads determines the affixes that matter at a particular point in time.

Context Cues.   Context cues come from two sources: syntactic cues (the grammatical use of a word) and semantic cues (the meaning of the text). For example, the following sentence appears in *Kira-Kira* (Kadohata, 2004, p. 9): *It was a sweltering day when Uncle Katsuhisa arrived in Iowa to help us move to Georgia.* Assuming that a reader was unable to pronounce *sweltering,* the reader might infer that the word must describe *day* and therefore serve as an adjective. Syntax provides that information. Then, if a reader also considers

TABLE 8.1   Using Phonics for Word Identification

Letter Sounds	Explanation	Sample Words
consonant sounds	Letters other than a, e, i, o, and u are called consonants.	bet, cat, dog, four, gum, hat, jog, kit, like, me, no, pig, run, sun, tip, van, won, yes, zoo Note: /q/ typically represents the sound /kw/ as in quit, /x/ the sound /ks/.
short and long vowel sounds	a, e, i, o, and u are called vowels. Vowels can represent two sounds: short and long. At times, y and w can function as a vowel.	short vowel examples: cat, beg, ill, on, up long vowel examples: ate, eel, ice, bone, use
ch, th, wh, ph, ng, sh	These consonant combinations, called consonant digraphs, represent a single sound.	chip, this, thin, when, phone, sang, ship
oi, oy, ou, ow	These vowel combinations, called diphthongs, represent a single sound.	boil, coy, out, owl

Generalizations For Letter Sounds	Explanation	Sample Words
c/g	c and g can represent two sounds: a hard sound as in *cat* and *go* and a soft sound as in *city* and *gym*. To guide a reader's initial decision, c and g usually represent their soft sound when followed by e, i, or y and their hard sound when followed by a, o, and u.	Soft sound: mice, cent, gem, page Hard sound: cut, come, gut, gave
r-controlled vowels	When an r appears after a vowel, one of three r-controlled sounds is possible.	car, fir, or
silent-e generalization	When a syllable or word ends in a single consonant and an e, the vowel usually represents its long sound and the e is silent (i.e., does not represent a sound).	tone, bake, cute, cite, muse
double vowel generalization	When two vowels appear next to each other, the first vowel usually represents its long sound and the second is silent.	boat, seem, team, aim
open syllables	When a syllable ends in a vowel sound, the vowel usually represents its long sound.	go, me, hi
closed syllables	When a syllable ends in a consonant sound, the vowel usually represents its short sound.	bug, mat, set, hit, pot, tug

TABLE 8.1   Continued

Generalizations For Syllabication	Explanation	Sample Words
VCCV	When two consonants appear next to each other, usually divide between the consonants.	matter (mat/ter) album (al/bum)
VCV	When two vowels are separated by a single consonant, the syllabication division usually occurs after the vowel.	cater (ca/ter) bison (bi/son)
Vcle	When a word ends in an le, the consonant before it usually stays with it and the -le is always pronounced /ul/.	sparkle (spar/kle) kindle (kin/dle)

Note: The following texts provide fuller accounts of decoding and phonics: P. M. Cunningham (2005), *Phonics they use* (Boston: Allyn and Bacon); B. J. Fox & M. A. Hull (2002), *Phonics for the teacher of reading* (Columbus, Ohio: Merrill); and D. D. Durkin (1981), *Strategies for identifying words* (Boston: Allyn and Bacon).

the time of year when this section of the story took place and the story's geographical setting, the reader could (and, one hopes, would) use semantic information to identify the word. Remember that the best readers combine strategies. In a closer consideration of *sweltering,* the reader could start with context and combine this word's spelling when making a final decision. If that proved unsuccessful, then the next step would require morphemic analysis: eliminating the suffix, *-ing,* to expose the root, *swelter.* From here, the reader would know to expect two syllables because this word has two letters that represent vowel sounds. Next, the reader would apply the vowel–consonant–vowel–consonant (VCCV) syllabication generalization, pronounce each syllable, and combine the pieces. Because *swelter* follows the applicable generalizations, a reader who took this path likely would succeed in pronouncing it.

Are you impressed with all that you are doing when you read to identify words, many of them new to you? Identifying words is a challenging task for novice and struggling readers. As the previous examples confirm, the use of word identification strategies is complex. Teachers must teach this area well, and students must strategically call upon the options available to them when they encounter an unknown word. Once readers under-stand their options, they can use a cue or combination of cues efficiently and successfully. If well taught, readers will develop what Marie Clay (1991) called a "self-extending" sys-tem. The options can be accessed without prompting or assistance and can be used success-fully. In addition, if teachers maintain the important links between an attention to word identification and real reading, then readers will not fall into the trap of believing that reading is saying words with accuracy and speed or accepting a mindless response to the printed page.

Selecting a text for or by a student at the just-right level of challenge will prevent word identification from overwhelming the reader. As a rule of thumb, a reader should encounter no more than four errors per 100 words of text. This maximum number of errors

TABLE 8.2   Applying Phonics to Real Texts

Words	Generalizations That Apply	Exceptions
so, she, be	Individual consonant sounds; open syllable generalization; consonant digraph, *sh*; long vowel sounds; blending demand: two phonemes	to
as, did, not, went, but	Individual consonant sounds; closed syllable generalization; short vowel sounds; blending demand: two to four elements	put, was
home, time, those	Individual consonant sounds; consonant digraph, *th*; silent-*e* generalization; long vowel sounds; blending demand: three elements	whole, were
please	Individual consonant sounds; double vowel generalization; long vowel sounds; blending demand: three or four phonemes (depending on whether the reader perceives *pl* as a consonant cluster)	Said
daddy, fussy, mommy	Syllabication generalization (VCCV) *dad/dy, fus/sy, mom/my*; individual consonant sounds; closed syllable generalization; short vowel sounds *y* as a long-*e* sound	

TABLE 8.3   Common Prefixes and Suffixes

Prefixes	Suffixes
ab-	-tion
ad-	-ment
de-	-ate
dis-	-ance
com-	-able
im-	-ity
pre-	-ous
pro-	-ence
per-	-ic
un-	-age
ex-	-tive
sub-	-ness
bi-	-ful
non-	-ism
retro-	-sion

provides opportunities for a reader to be strategic in using word identification strategies and does not present so many roadblocks that meaning (and a student's enjoyment of reading) is sacrificed. One study (Shannon, 1988) found that the most successful readers of school-assigned materials made two errors per 100 words read. The weakest readers, however, made at least eighteen errors per 100 words. A teacher must continually monitor the texts that students read to make sure that students do not experience the discouragement that results from their need to employ word identification strategies too often. As Althier Lazar (2004) reminds us, "Children, even those who struggle with reading, can develop as readers when they are given lots of texts they can read and when they have highly knowledgeable teachers to guide their progress" (p. 18). Teachers who remember that reading is compre-hending and who explain and model word identification strategies at just the right moment to students who make immediate use of the strategies make strides toward this important goal. (See Figure 8.1 for an example of a word identification lesson.)

Word Meaning

Although some students need to say words to read better (use appropriate word identifica-tion strategies), others need to increase the number of words that are meaningful to them. In other words, they must build their *vocabularies,* both reading and oral. Although acknowl-edging that readers must know word meanings may seem obvious, like word identification, careful examination of this obvious concept reveals its complexity.

For some students, especially those with large oral vocabularies, merely saying a word triggers its meaning. At other times, students' correct pronunciation of a word may lead a teacher to assume that the students know its meaning when in fact they do not. For these students, word meaning assistance is required. A student's needs can vary. For some words, readers need to know their multiple meanings and select the one that applies in the text being read. For example, a student reading the book *Sadako and the Thousand Paper Cranes* must understand that *crane* in this instance refers to a bird and not to a piece of construction equipment. The youngest of readers needs to understand homophones, words such as *to, too,* and *two* that sound the same but have different meanings. At some point, all readers will encounter a word for which they know the concept but not the label. An example is when a sixth-grade student reads a science text and encounters *platyhelminthes*. Students might understand flatworms, but they need to add this new scientific label for that concept. In addi-tion, all readers eventually must learn a word and its concept simultaneously. For instance, this process might have occurred for you while reading this chapter and adding the term *phonemic awareness* to your professional language.

In addressing these various vocabulary needs, teachers have several choices. Of course, they can directly teach the unknown word. Although potentially helpful and appropriate, however, limitations exist for the number of words a teacher can select for this instruction. If a teacher decides to offer a definition, then the teacher should move beyond a simple statement. Instead, students benefit from an initial and student-friendly explanation of a word's meaning followed by opportunities to engage in applying its meaning. Teachers can accomplish that by having students respond to questions or complete activities that use the target words. For example, after addressing the words *meander, scamper, sprint,* and *saunter,* a teacher might ask students if a turtle would meander or scamper? Or, students might work in groups to place words with comparable meanings together.

Beyond providing explanations and follow-up activities to learn new words, teachers can direct students to use a reference such as a dictionary or online source. The availability of an appropriate source limits the helpfulness of this option. As Bill Nagy and Judy Scott

FIGURE 8.1   A Word Identification Lesson

Declarative

"Today we're going to learn how to increase the accuracy of words that we say by using our understanding of what we're reading and a word's spelling."

Conditional

"Good readers say words quickly and correctly. Increasing your accuracy with pronouncing words can allow you to exhibit this attribute and, in some instances, improve your understanding of what you read."

Procedural

"Let's see how this works. The first thing I want to do is to confirm that the word I say matches the spelling of the word the author used. Let me use a sentence you recently encountered as an example."

[Show the student the sentence:]

> When Martin Luther King Jr. was a boy many laws would not allow black people to go to the same places as whites.

"I begin reading and say, When Martha—

"Then, I notice that the author's word ends in an /n/ and doesn't match the word I said, *Martha*. I look at the word more closely—*Mar–tin, Martin*.

"As I read further [return to the sentence], I have another reason to know that Martha would be incorrect since Martha is not a name typically given to a boy and this person is male.

"Let's do one together. Listen to these two words: presence, presentation. Do you expect them to be spelled the same?"

[Student response.]

"Okay, so if I read this sentence [show it to the student],

> Soccer had not been very popular in the United States up to this point, but Pele's presence had a dramatic effect.

"I would immediately know to look again at this word if I pronounced it *presentation*. Now I'm thinking, Do I know another word that matches this spelling and makes sense? Can you help me?"

[Student says *presence*.] "Let's try one more. You see this sentence." [show it to the student] He could not afford a soccer ball so he fashioned one.

"and read it this way:

> He could not afford a soccer ball so he finished one.

[I will say the sentence without showing it to the student.]

"Did you hear a word that did not match its spelling? Can you point to it?" [Student responds appropriately.]

"Now, read the sentence silently and see if you can think of a word that matches its spelling and makes sense."

[Student begins using phonics, /f/a/sh/, and says *fashioned*.]

FIGURE 8.1   Continued

"Let's review. What are two things you want to do before you settle on a word's pronunciation?"

[Student responds appropriately: Make sure it matches the spelling of the word and makes sense.]

"Correct, so anytime you read, remember this important strategy. I will be checking with you to see how this strategy helps."

This future reading provides independent practice. Listen to the student read aloud on regular occasions to monitor the success.

Notes: Success with this strategy depends on the unknown or incorrect word being part of a student's oral vocabulary. In this lesson, the student held this information. Nonetheless, the teacher must be prepared to provide additional instruction if the student encounters words that are unknown conceptually (oral language) as well as in print (reading vocabulary).

The text examples for this lesson come from the *Qualitative Reading Inventory* (Leslie & Caldwell, 2006).

(2000) note, too often students find dictionary definitions confusing or misleading. As they explain:

> Definitions, the traditional means of offering concentrated information about words to students, do not contain the quantity or quality of information that constitutes true word knowledge. Students can gain some word knowledge from definitions, but generally only if they are given other types of information about the word and opportunities to apply this information in meaningful tasks. (p. 280)

Simply stated, instead of assisting readers' comprehension, definitions can further cloud it. In addition, and on a practical note, ask yourself whether you read with a dictionary at your side. Most readers do not. Taking time away from reading to access dictionary definitions becomes time consuming and intrusive.

A final option involves teaching readers to use context strategies for inferring the meaning of an unknown word. Although readers should not be expected to infer a perfect definition, unless that is the teacher's goal, they often can make a decision that allows them to keep reading without a comprehension break.

Expecting readers to use context to infer the meaning of an unknown word depends on the types of assistance an author makes available. This assistance can take several forms: definition, appositive, example, summary, synonym, antonym, grouping, and simile.

■ *Definition.* The most helpful context provides a definition. Informational texts and textbooks often provide this level of help. Generally, definitions follow this pattern: X (the unknown word) is X (a definition). For example, in Chapter 1, you read that "Reading First was a component of the No Child Left Behind Act." As an expert reader, you easily and quickly linked the information on each side of the linking verb to obtain accurate information about Reading First. For some students, this mental act needs explicit instruction and modeling.

■ *Appositive.* In appositive assistance, a reader encounters an unknown word followed by an appositive, a descriptive phrase set off from the rest of the sentence by commas. We just used this type of clue in the preceding sentence to explain an appositive. A reader needs to understand this grammatical structure to grasp that the phrase means the same thing as the word, typically a noun that comes before it. A student reading narratives often finds out more about a character through an appositional phrase, such as in the case in *Gooney Bird Greene* (Lowry, 2004) when the author uses this sentence: "'Hello,' Mrs. Pidgeon, the second grade teacher, said" (p. 1). From this appositive, a reader learns that Mrs. Pidgeon *is* the second-grade teacher. On other occasions, the appositional phrase defines a term of importance. Russell Freedman (1987) uses this structure in the following sentence to explain indentures: "Often they sold themselves as indentures for a period of twenty years, a form of voluntary slavery, just to eat and have a place to live" (p. 46). A reader who does not hold *indentures* in his oral vocabulary or who thinks that the word only applies to the use of paragraphs while writing now can use the appositional phrase to understand that *indentures* refer to voluntary slavery. Science, social studies, and math textbooks regularly rely on definitions with sentences such as: The *nucleus* is the center of the atom. Islands, bodies of land completely surrounded by water, can be found in the Pacific Ocean and other bodies of water.

■ *Example.* When an author provides an example, the reader must think (i.e., infer) what the example suggests about an unknown word's meaning. For example, in the first chapter of *The Midwife's Apprentice* (Cushman, 1995), the word *stench* appears in the following sentence: "Usually no one gets close enough to notice because of the stench" (p. 1). Prior to using this sentence, the author talks about animal droppings, garbage, and spoiled straw. A reader familiar with these things who then links this information with the sentence in which the unknown word, *stench,* appears could infer that a bad smell (the stench) kept people at bay. Examples can provide relatively straightforward assistance. Consider a reader who does not know the word *muffle* but who encounters this sentence from *The Slave Dancer* (Fox, 1973): "I lay motionless, my hands over my mouth to muffle my laughter" (p. 34). Visualizing what happens when people talk with their hands covering their face could support this reader's inference that the laughter would not be very loud. Other examples might demand more prior knowledge or background experiences. Any reader who uses examples must infer a meaning, and a teacher who explicitly presents and models how to use examples increases the chances for a reader's success with this strategy.

■ *Summary.* When an author uses a summary, a reader's understanding of an unknown word comes by integrating information provided across several sentences or longer paragraphs. Assuming that the word *championships* is unknown, the following summary offers assistance: The wrestlers had to win several matches to qualify for the final event. The final event had winners from each weight class. These *championships* were exciting to watch.

The following excerpt from *Walk Two Moons* (Creech, 1994) adds to our understanding of *pandemonium*:

> It was complete pandemonium at the Finneys'. May Lou had an older sister and three brothers. In addition, there were her parents and Ben. There were footballs and basketballs lying

all over the place, and boys sliding down the banister and leaping over tables and talking with their mouths full and interrupting everyone with endless questions. (pp. 46–47)

With summaries, as with other types of assistance, the reader must understand how to capitalize on this information. A reader can best understand this mental process from a teacher who makes this thinking public.

■ *Synonyms.* Consistent with its attributes, synonym help comes from an author's use of a word that holds a comparable meaning to the unknown word.

■ *Antonyms.* An author who offers a word or phrase that means the opposite of an unknown word takes advantage of antonyms. In the following sentences from *Because of Winn Dixie* (DiCamillo, 2000), the author provides this type of clue for *cooped up*: "My mama says you shouldn't be spending all your time cooped up in that pet shop and at that library, sitting around talking with old ladies. She says you should get out in the fresh air and play with kids your own age" (p. 89). Here, a reader must link the term *cooped up* with *get out* and infer the contrast in word meanings. As this example indicates, a reader often gets the best assistance by reading further. When appropriate, a knowledgeable teacher would encourage a reader to consider more than the single sentence in which the unknown word appears.

■ *Groupings.* In using groupings, a reader encounters a series of words that hold shared features. Assume that a reader does not know the meaning of *perch* as used in the following sentence: Troy caught a salmon, perch, and trout. If Troy knows that salmon and trout are fish, then he can infer that perch is, too. He still could not distinguish a perch from another fish, but he does correctly understand its general classification. This general information is often all a reader needs to understand a piece of text.

■ *Simile.* A simile links shared features between two words by using *like* or *as*. For a simile to help with inferring the meaning of an unknown word, a reader must have a solid sense of the concept the author uses for comparison. For example, to gain an understanding of *parliament* from "Parliament is like our House of Representatives," a reader must be informed about the House of Representatives.

Looking across these options and examples, two features about using context for inferring the meaning of an unknown word become clear: (1) readers benefit from broad and rich conceptual understandings and known vocabulary and (2) the inferential load for a reader varies across and within the types of clues a reader might encounter. Hence, an important task for teachers is joining a text's vocabulary demands with a reader's vocabulary strengths and needs to determine the appropriateness of expecting a reader to use context to understand unknown words. If readers hold gaps in their general understanding of the process of using context or specific gaps in this strategy's options, then explicit instruction assumes importance. As Isabel Beck, Margaret McKeown, and Linda Kucan (2002) remind us, "Because of the unreliability of natural contexts, instruction needs to be presented as a process of figuring out meaning within an individual context, rather than focusing on the product—a word's meaning" (p. 115). Figure 8.2 shows an example of an instructional plan that addresses using context for vocabulary learning.

FIGURE 8.2   An Example of a Vocabulary Lesson: Teaching a Contextual Cue for Word Learning

---

Declarative

"Today we are going to learn how to use groupings to figure out what an unknown word means."

Conditional

"The grouping strategy is helpful when there is a list of words and one word is unknown. Figuring out an unknown word helps you understand what you are reading."

Procedural: Information and Modeling

"First we need to understand what the grouping strategy is."

[Write the following sentence on the board: In Hawaii, you can buy pineapples, papayas, and coconuts.]

"I don't know what a papaya is, but I know that pineapples and coconuts are fruits. Therefore, I make an educated guess that a papaya is a fruit because it is in a list with other fruits."

Repeat with another example: I love the sound of a clarinet, saxophone, and oboe.

"I don't know what an oboe is, so I look at the rest of the words in the group, or list. I know that a clarinet and saxophone are instruments, so I can figure out that an oboe is probably an instrument also."

Guided Practice

Each student will receive a list with five sentences, each of which includes a group of items where one item is, most likely, unknown. Also have a copy of this list to use with a document camera or an overhead. Fill the sheet out as a group, having one student volunteer to discuss what he or she thinks the unknown word means and why. The questions after each sentence will be, "What do you think _____ means? What helped you figure out what that word means?"

> My dad is in the garage working on the *carburetor,* tires, brakes, and steering wheel today.
> My new sweater is gray, blue, and *chartreuse.*
> The woman said she owned a dalmatian, golden retriever, and *Pekingese.*
> We have daisies, *hydrangeas,* and roses in our backyard.
> The store had a special on chicken, *veal,* and pork.

Independent Practice

The students' future reading will promote practice by the use of grouping to derive meaning from unknown words that are grouped with known words.

Beyond teaching specific words and helping students learn words independently, James Baumann, Ed Kame'enui, and Gwynne Ash (2003) propose that a comprehensive vocabulary program should also "help students to develop an appreciation for words and to experience enjoyment and satisfaction in their use" (p. 778). A word-rich classroom that includes word play can foster this final goal. To accomplish it, Camille Blachowicz and Peter Fisher (2004) recommend activities such as a variety of vocabulary games, word puzzles, riddles, Hink Pink (e.g., an angry father—mad dad), drama, and art.

Connected Text

Armed with a large sight vocabulary, the known meanings of a multitude of words, and strategies to use when a bump in the road appears, a reader's effort to comprehend is not complete. Comprehension also depends on the mental tasks inherent in reading an array of connected texts. In this chapter, we focus on the general demands a reader encounters as well as those unique to narrative and informational texts: comprehension strategies.

General Demands. Much of what we know about the general demands of understanding connected text comes from close studies of what real readers do. Mary's recent reading of *The Three Questions* (Muth, 2002) serves as an example. Overall, because she was reading a story, she knew to expect its features: setting, character(s), plot, and theme. Initially, the title prompted her curiosity about the nature of the questions mentioned in the title, what they entailed, and why they mattered. She also wondered who asked them and how they got answered. These initial musings gave her reading a purpose. The author immediately introduced her to Nikolai and his three questions: When is the best time to do things? Who is the most important one? What is the right thing to do? These questions resonated with Mary and she considered them in light of her own life. In other words, she linked what she was reading with her personal experiences and background knowledge. As she read on, she met other characters (in this case, a series of animals) whom Mary considered self-serving in their responses to Nikolai. She compared her response with that of Nikolai, who, although not quite as critical of his friends, did realize that their answers were "not quite right." So, along with Nikolai, Mary moved beyond her initial questions to wonder if another animal (or person) would offer a wiser response. Nikolai next asked his three questions of a turtle. As the story progressed, Mary altered her questions, posited many guesses about what might happen next, and made numerous inferences to link the text's ideas. For example, this text demanded that she follow the use of quotation marks to understand dialogue, link pronouns to their referents, use sequence words such as *then* to keep the story's events in order, and understand cause-and-effect relationships. In addition, she needed to give herself over to the possibility that animals can speak with humans. As she read, she created many mental images suggested by this story's events and the author's wording. In the end, she understood the satisfaction Nikolai must feel with all he learned about himself and his life. Her involvement with the story did not end when she finished the last word on the last page. Mary continued to think about its ideas and shared them with several friends.

This brief account pinpoints the aspects of understanding connected text that many scholars identify as important *comprehension strategies* (e.g., Cunningham & Shagoury, 2005; Duffy, 2003; Duke & Pearson, 2002; Keene, 2002; Sweet & Snow, 2002). Readers pay attention to the *features of text*. They hold *purposes* for reading. Readers *self-question*. They make numerous *inferences* and continually use the author's words to spark pictures in their head (i.e., *visualize*). In addition, they *summarize* as they go and *monitor* their understanding. Finally, although Mary did not experience this need, good readers use *fix-up strategies* when comprehension failures occur.

This example stems from reading a story, narrative text. Readers also read exposition, informational texts, however. Shifting from narrative to exposition *text structure* introduces an additional challenge: an ability to shift between organizational frameworks rather than tapping a single expectation. Specifically, and as previously mentioned, stories have a predictable grammar: characters in a specific location do something that all comes together in the end and leaves a reader with a message to ponder. Stories may vary in sophistication, such as a reading of *Knuffle Bunny* (Willems, 2004) compared with *The Giver* (Lowry, 1993), but a reader still knows to expect a setting, characters, plot, and theme. This expectation disappears when a reader switches to exposition. Now, an author chooses from an array of options: (1) simple listing or description; (2) cause and effect; (3) problem–solution; (4) sequence, or time order; and (5) compare–contrast (Alvermann & Phelps, 2005). The author also often frequently shifts structures, sometimes within the same paragraph. On top of this complicating factor, nonfiction authors often use different fonts, insert headings and subheadings, link ideas to graphs and charts, and offer various text elements such as a table of contents, index, or glossary. Many students who read stories well stumble when reading expository texts. Starting early on, teachers must attend to narrative and informational reading. In Special Feature 8.1, Deanne McCredie describes several writing strategies she has found helpful when using informational texts with students.

SPECIAL FEATURE 8.1

Using Writing with Reading to Learn from Informational Texts

DEANNE MCCREDIE

Language serves a central role in content learning in the elementary classroom because students read, write, speak, and listen to construct meaning. A student is content literate when he or she possesses the ability to use literacy strategies to acquire new content in a given discipline: learning how to use language to learn (McKenna & Robinson, 2002).

When confronted with new information, good readers and listeners look for opportunities to connect the new information to their prior knowledge, or schema, in meaningful ways. Because no one brings the same prior knowledge to a text, no one finds meaning in the same way or in the same places. Many content literacy strategies effectively facilitate students' interaction with content, but a classroom that links reading and writing "invites students to explore ideas, clarify meaning, and construct knowledge . . . in ways not possible when

students read without writing or write without reading" (Vacca & Vacca, 2005, p. 353).

Writing in the content areas is sometimes discouraged, however, because teachers worry that the writing needs to be formally corrected or assessed. Writing need not always culminate in a polished, formal product. Simply recording rough thoughts on paper focuses students' thinking and prepares them to learn. The objective of the following before, during, and after learning activities is to use writing to maximize and motivate content learning, not to improve students' writing ability, although, as McKenna and Robinson (2002) point out, "this may follow as a by-product" (p. 12).

Before Reading

Quick-Write. The quick-write is a warm-up writing activity that helps students access their prior knowledge about a topic (Richardson & Morgan, 2000). In one or two minutes, students write what they know about the topic, considering, developing, and organizing ideas as they think through writing. Writing is thinking. Therefore, when students have a record of their thoughts, they can see their thinking and further ponder and elaborate their ideas.

Student-Generated Questions.   Another warm-up writing activity involves student-generated questions. In groups, students write questions that they would like answered about a topic (Richardson & Morgan, 2000). This activity not only helps students discover what they already know, but also piques their curiosity about the topic as they generate questions. Of equal importance, because this prereading activity links writing, listening, and speaking, students refine and deepen their understanding of ideas through speaking and compare their thinking with what they hear from their group members through listening.

Factstorming and Brain Writing.   During factstorming, in groups, or independently, students write down facts and associations about a topic (Richardson & Morgan, 2000). For example, during math class, students write anything they know about fractions.

Brown, Phillips, and Stephens (as cited in Richardson & Morgan, 2000) suggest a variation of factstorming called brain writing. During this activity, students first jot down their ideas, and then small groups of students switch their lists and add to each other's thinking. For instance, in social studies, students write what they think about when they hear the word freedom. Once the brain writing activity is complete, students have a record of both their thinking and their group members' thoughts to consider before they engage with a written text.

Not only do these prereading activities help students explore what they know about a topic, but they also help teachers to assess students' background knowledge and, if necessary, build that background knowledge for their students during subsequent instruction before or during reading.

During Reading

Write As You Read.   When students "write as they read," they make connections to what they already know instead of being intimidated by what they don't understand. They can record their thoughts on copies of the reading material, on Post-it Notes, on an overhead transparency, or in a journal. This strategy not only supports student learning, but also builds confidence. Everyone is an active participant. Jim Burke (2000) suggests "having students annotate or otherwise mark up texts is one of the most powerful ways of turning them into active readers" (p. 213).

Methods for this strategy might include:

- Underlining main ideas worth remembering
- Underlining ideas students might want to learn more about
- Underlining ideas students question and want to check
- Underlining parts students want to share with other learners
- Underlining ideas students agree with or disagree with
- Writing definitions or synonyms for difficult words
- Writing notes about personal connections and feelings
- Writing questions
- Summarizing a section of the text

When students are given the opportunity to choose a method or methods to mark up texts, their annotations reflect their unique thinking processes and schema and provide teachers important insights into their students' learning. By collecting the annotated texts, teachers have evidence of their students' learning. For instance, they can identify sections of a text or vocabulary that their students didn't understand and reteach the concepts during whole-group or small group instruction. They can also assess their students' overall comprehension of the text by analyzing the sections of texts they underlined and/or the questions and paraphrasing they wrote in the margins.

(continued)

Furthermore, following up with debriefing discussions encourages students to use their speaking and listening skills to spark new ideas about how to "write as you read" and how the strategy helped them interact with the text. These discussions give students opportunities to talk about their own reading processes and the thinking behind their annotations, and to learn from their peers' efforts. Through all these activities, students are actively engaged with a written text and constructing knowledge, "seeing how they think and how other kids' minds work" (Wilhelm, 1997, p. 142).

Crystal Ball.   Another during-reading strategy is called Crystal Ball (Billmeyer & Barton, 1998). At a pivotal point in the reading, teachers direct students to stop and write a prediction about what will happen next. Teachers then encourage students to support their predictions by using information from the reading to explain their thinking and to return to reflect on their predictions when they complete the reading.

Student VOC Strategy.   Learning vocabulary in the content areas is particularly challenging for students because it often means that they have no schema for the concepts. Rote memorization or use of a dictionary to look up definitions of words that are entirely new to them clearly does not help students build a meaningful understanding of the vocabulary. Students need time and practice learning how to relate vocabulary to experiences and ideas that are their own. Writing can assist them in this requisite but also provocative process.

The student VOC strategy (Billmeyer & Barton, 1998) uses writing to assist students in using context to analyze the meaning of words. After the teacher shares key vocabulary with students prior to reading, students identify the words that are new to them. They then use the VOC strategy while they read by

1. Writing the actual sentence in which the word appears

2. Writing a prediction about the word's meaning using the context of the sentence
3. Writing a definition of the word after consulting a friend, teacher, or other expert resource
4. Writing a sentence exhibiting their understanding of the word's meaning

Rachel Billmeyer and Mary Lee Barton go on to recommend that students link the word and its meaning to one of their senses by drawing a picture, miming an action, or relating the word to another familiar text such as a song or story. Students then write about the connection they made under the sentence they crafted. When students are asked finally to explain their understanding of the word and sensory association with the word to a partner, they use their speaking skills to further make clear their grasp of the word's meaning.

After Reading
First-Person Summary.   The National Reading Panel (2000) links students' successful summarization to improved comprehension. Despite its seeming simplicity, however, summarizing is a complex process that is often daunting for students. First-person summaries (Richardson & Morgan, 2000) allow students to work through the summarizing process by writing in their own words about a topic. Using the first person helps students become personally connected with the ideas so that they can distinguish between summarizing the important information and retelling all the information in the text, and so that they can better remember what they've learned.

First-person summaries need not be limited to writing from the perspective of characters in a narrative text. This writing activity also works well in a science, social studies, or math class. For example, when students study fractions, they could explain the process of reducing a fraction from the fraction's point of view. In science, when reading about ecosystems, students could write how the snail plays an important role in its ecosystem from the snail's point of view. The goal of first-person summaries, in any content area, is to help students decide on the information and the details, determine which examples are key, continually organize the information, and finally present the information in a concise form.

Cinquain. Writing a cinquain is an engaging language activity for students of all ages (Richardson & Morgan, 2000). Cinquains are patterned five-line poems:

> *Line 1:* a noun or the subject of the poem
> *Line 2:* two adjectives that describe the first line
> *Line 3:* three verbs or action words
> *Line 4:* four words that express a feeling
> *Line 5:* one word that refers back to line one, the subject of the poem

This activity requires focus and reflection as students exhibit their understanding of a concept through the careful composition of their poems.

"And the Winner Is . . ." According to Billmeyer and Barton (1998), the writing activity known as "And the winner is . . . " is particularly effective at the conclusion of a unit of study. Students begin by thinking about the following:

> The publisher of the textbook we use wants student input on the content of the chapter we are studying. Specifically, the publisher wants to know which individual or concept included in the chapter/unit has had the greatest impact on your life and why. (p. 157)

Students then write their argument in a letter to the publisher, explaining the effect the individual or concept has had on their lives. This authentic writing activity helps students reflect on their learning as they write to an actual audience. A real audience motivates students to do not only their best writing but also their best thinking and learning.

Final Thoughts

Thinking through writing in the content areas helps facilitate conversations students have with themselves and others that reveal and clarify their understandings before, during, and after learning, as they broaden and refine their new knowledge. And that new knowledge will be better understood and remembered because it is explored, cultivated, and organized through language that is meaningful and personal as students use their language to learn.

Go to the Assignments and Activities section of Chapter 8 in the MyEducationKit and complete the activity entitled "What Good Readers Do." As you watch the video and answer the accompanying questions, note what the children say good readers do when they read.

In summary, good readers use an array of comprehension strategies before, during, and after they read. They predict what they think might happen next. Whether novice readers or more expert in their achievement, good readers anticipate meaning and revise their predictions. As the cycle of reading continues, good readers question and monitor. Good readers imagine, combining prior knowledge with the descriptions and wording used by the author to envision the text's events or ideas. Good readers know when to use look-backs or fix-up strategies to rectify comprehension lapses. Good readers synthesize, summarize, and draw conclusions. When reading a narration, they grasp its theme. When reading exposition, they determine its main idea. Ultimately, good readers evaluate, making judgments or forming opinions stemming from a text's ideas. And, with a great deal of frequency, good readers understand what an author implies but does not directly state. The inferential load varies from text to text and reader to reader. Readers who make inferences understand how a character feels, where a story takes place, the ordering of a story's events, or a main idea that an author does not explicitly specify. Simply stated, making inferences is at the heart of understanding connected text. Figure 8.3 gives an example of a connected text instructional plan.

For purposes of convenience and clarity, we discussed these psychological components (word identification, vocabulary, and connected text demands) individually. For real readers, however, these components do not occur as separate entities. Instead, they represent intersecting spheres of components. When readers use them efficiently and in concert, they understand and enjoy a text.

Classroom Events

Armed with the information about reading as a process and the elements inherent in it, we turn to the practical task of designing a classroom program. This task requires attention to many complex features. Although options exist for each decision point, an overarching consideration applies: Do the various decisions place students' needs as readers at the heart of the classroom reading program? At this point, you might wonder whether this proposal for a child-centered pedagogy contradicts an attention to a standards-guided curriculum. We, however, consider that maintaining a combined focus on students and standards is the heart of the challenge rather than an either/or competition. So, how do teachers develop a reading program for the students in their classroom?

Determining a Schedule

Teachers must set aside ample time for reading and its instruction. Some literacy blocks are divided by the students leaving the room for library, physical education, or music. Other teachers enjoy an uninterrupted time frame. Although research does not establish a time-allotment preference, some time ago Charles Fisher and his colleagues (1978) found that teachers averaged a ninety-minute time frame. We consider a ninety-minute period necessary and reasonable for today's classrooms.

Once the time is set, teachers must use it wisely. Some teachers cleanly divide their time between teaching reading and writing without setting aside the mutual benefits that occur when readers write and writers read. David Pearson and Rob Tierney (1984) established these important relationships years ago, and teachers remain wise to act on them.

Selecting and Using Materials

Most teachers use trade books (i.e., narratives and exposition written by published authors) but also have basal materials (i.e., teacher manuals and student anthologies created by a publishing company) available to them. Some teachers, especially those in schools that receive federal funding, are often required to use published materials that this funding agency, the U.S. Department of Education, considers scientifically based. Other teachers combine their use of trade books and basal materials.

Research does not support basal readers or trade books over the other. In fact, the clear message from the first-grade studies (Bond & Dykstra, 1967) was that "children learn to read by a variety of materials and methods" (p. 67). No research today contradicts this conclusion. The choice of materials, however, does come with advantages and drawbacks.

FIGURE 8.3 An Example of a Connected Text Lesson: Determining Setting

Declarative

Today we're going to learn how to determine a story's setting.

Conditional

Every story has a setting, so you should determine it for every story you read. Knowing the setting helps you better understand any story's events and how to interpret them.

Procedural: Information and Modeling

First, let's define setting. It includes two things: where and when the story took place. *Where* includes the general location that applies to the entire piece. Certainly, characters can move from place to place, but when we determine the setting of the story we consider it as a whole. *When* refers to the time of the story: in the past, relatively modern times, or in the future. With many of the books you've read, the author directly states the setting. For example, *The Snowy Day* provides the setting in its title and in the first sentence when the author says "it was a winter morning." *Little Nino's Pizzeria* takes place in a city where a man owns a pizza restaurant. The title provides the first evidence of the importance of the restaurant and then the first events take place in one. Several events suggest that it is a city location: the crowdedness of the restaurant, the alley behind it, and the availability of someone to finance a larger restaurant. Because nothing in either story suggests that they took place a long time ago or in the future, I can infer that the author intended a reader to consider it modern. Without these settings, none of the events in either story could have happened.

Other books and stories require you to use text information to infer the setting. To understand where and when these stories take place, you need to put together clues that the author provides. These clues often appear in the beginning of the story, but they can appear throughout it. Let me give you an example. In *Wringer,* the author includes a newspaper article that says Waymer. So, even though he never mentions this town in the book, I can infer that this is the name of the town because the newspaper article talks about its events. Then, the events in the story—wide use of hunting, lack of mention of city landscapes—help me understand that it is a rural town. Because the author mentions the American Legion, I also know it is in the United States. So, *Wringer* takes place in a small rural town. Since none of the events in the story places it in a past or future time, I can infer that it is relatively modern.

Before we work together to determine a story's setting, let's review. What does setting include? What does a reader do to understand a book's setting?

Guided Practice

Today, I asked you to read *Thank You, Ma'am,* a short story by Langston Hughes. To determine its setting, what two things do we want to know? So, does this story take place in the country or in a city? How do you know? Now let's consider the clues about when it took place. Was this a modern-day story or one that took place in years past? What clues help you make this decision? Now let's combine this information to state its setting: a city in past times. Of course, the action is divided between the street and the woman's apartment, but setting needs to capture the whole story.

Independent Practice

Review the new information before reminding students to use it to determine the setting of stories they read in the future in their independent practice.

In some cases, published materials promote the use of a script rather than a responsiveness to readers' needs that we propose. Because teachers typically receive only grade-level basal readers, their students may find themselves expected to read books that are either too hard or too easy, mismatch their interests, or differ from their prior knowledge and experiences. On the other hand, teachers often find the sample lessons and curricular directions that these published materials offer helpful. Trade books allow a wider variety of choice and match "real reading." As real texts, they obviously demand the use of the psychological elements we previously explained. They easily lend themselves to instructional plans. Teachers must decide. Whatever their choice, a teacher must make certain that students read texts that allow them to grow and learn as readers and reading enthusiasts. In the end, we concur with Dolores Durkin (2004) that "every teacher must strive to become a knowledgeable decision maker, whether using basal materials or something else" (p. 333).

Considering Reading Options

Teachers have a variety of ways to read a text. First, they can *read to* students (a read-aloud). In this option, teachers take great care in selecting a text and consider the students' oral language, prior knowledge, and interests. As the name of this option implies, students listen as their teacher orally presents the text to them. This oral presentation by the teacher provides a common text for students to discuss, allows students to appreciate a text that they are perhaps unable to read by themselves, and offers them a model of their teacher's fluent oral reading.

Second, teachers can *read with* their students (a shared reading). In a shared reading, the teacher and students contribute to the oral presentation. A teacher who selects a text with the students' practice needs in mind can provide many important opportunities for students to hone their strategy use in the company of their peers and teacher.

Finally, teachers can assign *independent* reading. During independent reading, students silently read a text that matches their reading achievement and personal interests. At times, this independent reading becomes a whole-class activity (including the teacher). Called SSR (silent sustained reading), DEAR (drop everything and read), or HIP (high-intensity practice), the teacher sets aside a specific amount of time for *everyone* to read. With younger readers, this independent reading might last for five minutes. Teachers of older readers might set aside a twenty-minute period. This type of independent reading might occur daily or weekly, depending on the time available for it and the other options a teacher uses.

On other occasions, teachers link independent reading to guided reading groups (Fountas & Pinnell, 2001). In guided reading groups, teachers work with children who are at about the same level of reading development. Although students still read the text silently, they meet with the teacher in small groups before and after they read. During these small group meetings, teachers address the readers' comprehension needs for understanding this text and assess their understanding of text after the reading. Irene Fountas and Guy Su Pinnell (1996) outline these core components of a guided reading lesson:

- The teacher chooses a book that is relatively easy for this group of children to read, but one that poses a few problems for them to solve.
- The teacher briefly introduces the book.

- The students then read the text to themselves.
- The teacher invites children to share their personal responses to the story.
- The teacher selects one or two teaching points to present to the group following the reading.
- Students may read this book again during free-choice reading. Occasionally, the teacher engages children in extending the story through art, drama, writing, or additional reading.

Other teachers prefer book clubs (Raphael & McMahon, 1994). In book clubs, students read their text independently for a minimum of fifteen minutes, use writing to reflect on their reading, and then discuss their texts in peer-led discussion groups. Ralph Peterson and Maryann Eeds's (1990) classic book *Grand Conversations: Literature Groups in Action* contains wonderful examples of the deep discussions elementary students can have about good literature.

Regardless of the options a teacher uses, teachers must set aside regular chunks of time for students to read and hear texts. Students at all grade levels benefit from these options (read-alouds, shared reading, and independent reading). Time to read is insufficient without an instructionally supportive environment, however.

Providing Instruction

Previously, we outlined the word identification, vocabulary, and connected text strategies a teacher *might* teach. A student's reading of a specific text determines what strategy a teacher *should* teach, and when. In other words, teach what a student does not know and needs to know to comprehend a text successfully. Some students will need more support (often called scaffolding) than others.

Offering appropriate instruction depends on the formation of instructional groups. Sometimes an instructional group is composed of one student. On other occasions, the entire class or a small group of students benefit from a specific lesson. These options and varied needs lead teachers to consider *flexible grouping*. These groups are flexible in their composition (ranging from individual, small group, or whole-class membership), duration (lasting only as long as necessary for students to learn the unknown strategy), and topic (addressing what is unknown and necessary for the students to read a specific text). In addition to strategy instruction, teachers can also use flexible groups to accommodate students' mutual interests (reading everything available by a specific author or reading to understand a topic).

Once a teacher establishes the type of group and its membership, he or she plans the instruction. As each example in this chapter shows, and influenced by the combined work of Scott Paris and his colleagues (1984) and David Pearson and Linda Fielding (1994), we propose that instructional plans have three features. First, teachers tell the students *what* they plan to teach. Called a *declarative statement,* this step allows students to focus their attention on a topic and tap the information they might already hold about it. Second, teachers tell students *why* learning this information matters (a *conditional statement*). Students now understand what they will learn (the declarative statement) and why (the conditional statement). Finally, teachers develop a *procedural* component. In this section, teachers *provide information* about the topic and then model its use. Then, students engage in guided practice where the teacher and students work together to use a strategy to understand a text. The sequence ends with independent practice. At this time, students read alone and use their newly acquired strategy as the need naturally arises. This progression from the teacher to the student is called the gradual release of responsibility. The teacher initially takes the stage to provide information about a strategy and model its use, is followed by the students and teacher working together to apply the strategy, and ends with the student using the strategy during the student's independent reading time. In other words, the responsibility for using a strategy begins with the teacher, shifts to the teacher and student working together, and ends with the student working alone.

We propose the use of declarative, conditional, and procedural components for pre-planned instruction. Of course teachers also help students while they read. Mary Roe (2004) calls these opportunities *real reading interactions*. Such interactions occur while students read. As a teacher roams the room and kneels at a student's side, the teacher responds to the student's needs of the moment. These interactions might last a few seconds or a few moments. For them to matter, and like planned instruction, they must be intentional (i.e., linked to a student's need and the teacher's overall reading goals) and helpful (quickly targeted to the student's comprehension need). Teachers who respond quickly and helpfully select from a broad and quickly accessible knowledge base. A preservice teacher compared this knowledge to a Rolodex. Each card would hold information about the psychological elements that we explained in this chapter and then be able to "spin" to the one that holds the information that matters at this time and for this student.

As teachers identify the needs of a student or group of students, they must carefully balance their individual time with some students with their availability to others. To personalize their instruction, some teachers make sure that all students are meaningfully engaged with reading or a reading-related activity.

Assessing

Teachers use assessments to determine the psychological component a student needs to read better. These assessments can take several forms. Standardized and norm-referenced tests provide guidance about students' relative reading success. Performance on state tests (and all states now use them) can further identify the successful from less successful readers. (See Chapter 12 for a description of one state's English language arts test development.) To personalize instruction, however, a teacher needs specific direction. For that, teachers turn to informal and classroom-based tools. Informal reading inventories such as the Qualitative Reading Inventory-4 (Leslie & Caldwell, 2006) provide a way for teachers to establish students' reading levels. This important information allows a teacher to match this reading level to a specific guided reading group placement or basal text. For teachers who use basal readers, these published materials often provide their own informal reading inventory. If so, using the basal version makes sense. To maintain a close understanding of students' decoding, teachers regularly use running records, a recording of students' oral reading using check marks for correct words and a coding system for errors, or miscue analysis, a follow-up analysis

myeducationkit

Go to the Assignments and Activities section of Chapter 8 in the MyEducationKit and complete the activity entitled "Definition and Demonstration of a Running Record." As you watch the video and answer the accompanying questions, note how carefully the teacher records exactly what the student says as she reads.

that compares students' pronunciations with the words in the text. (Special Feature 12.3 provides instructions for administering running records.)

Attributes of a Successful Reading Teacher

The previous sections of this chapter suggest many attributes of the successful reading teacher. Successful reading teachers:

- Understand the reading process
- Articulate the psychological components that contribute to comprehension and understand the additional influences of attitude and motivation
- Create classroom environments that maximize the time available for reading and its instruction
- Tap a variety of reading options (read-alouds, shared readings, and independent reading)
- Select materials wisely and well
- Use assessments to guide instruction
- Have a familiarity with books appropriate for children in their classes to read

Now, consider the complex task of integrating these various features. In doing so, teachers must focus on the student. As Gerald Duffy (2003) reminds us, the overall goal is to "put students in control of their own efforts to make sense out of text" (p. 215). So, although teachers are "in charge," they should never remain center stage. They should strongly believe that all students can read better and openly share with their students the joy and wonder of reading.

Strategies for Teaching English Language Learners

LUISA ARAÚJO

Reading instruction beyond the earliest stages of reading, in particular, is an area where teaching accommodations or modifications are needed to enable ELL children to learn to read in English and to read in English to learn. Jeanne Chall (1996) documented the reading acquisition of first-language children and identified two distinct stages: in the first two years of schooling children learn to read and subsequently read to learn. ELL children, because they are learning a second language, go through the two phases concurrently. When ELL students have acquired literacy skills in a first language with an alphabetic system of writing, they already understand the alphabetic principle and can use this insight to decipher English words. However, they still need to develop their understanding of the phonology, morphology, syntax, and pragmatics of written English at the same time that they learn new vocabulary and new concepts (Herrell, 2000; Nagy, Berninger, & Abbott, 2006). This means that ELL students must learn to decipher groups of letters that make up words (word identification), learn about prefixes and suffixes that render specific meanings to words (word analysis), and develop syntactic knowledge, or the awareness of the grammatical use of a word and

(continued)

Strategies for Teaching English Language Learners   Continued

pragmatic awareness, or the understanding of how words are used to communicate (NICHD, 2007).

Literature-based reading instruction exemplifies how written language is used and can thus contribute to grammatical and pragmatic knowledge. Moreover, it introduces vocabulary in context and offers students opportunities to develop listening comprehension (Curtain & Pesola, 1994). Indeed, research indicates that ELLs benefit from the meaningful and motivating contexts created around literature-based instruction and that such contexts can help develop listening, speaking, reading and writing (Echevarria & Graves, 2003; Goldenberg, 2008). Teachers can create opportunities for listening and speaking by engaging in prereading or "book walks" and ask students to explore pictures and predict events. Similarly, teachers can ask students to draw semantic maps and Venn diagrams where they can write words and phrases related to the stories and explore their meaning with them.

Reading comprehension can be further explored by having students engage in journal writing, word theater (acting out the meaning of words), and drawing scenes from the book. In short, teachers should create learning environments that support the active engagement and participation of ELL learners. Adjusting speech interactions, choosing contextual clues and adjusting assignments to the language level of ELL learners will maximize their participation and support their learning. Tailoring reading instruction to their needs can also be done by implementing guided reading in the classroom. Studies of ELLs with learning disabilities (Ortiz & Graves, 2001; Ruiz, 1995a, 1995b) show that creating text for wordless books, shared reading with predictable text, literature conversations with read-alouds, and literature study with response journals are strategies that improve students' performance. According to Klingner and Vaughn (2004), for struggling ELL readers both phonics and phonemic awareness instruction should occur within the context of an integrated approach to developing students' comprehension and use of academic language and should focus on only one or two skills at a time.

Research indicates that good readers have strong oral vocabulary, strong print vocabulary, and good background knowledge (Kamil, 2003; Strickland & Alvermann, 2004). Listening to stories and engaging in recreational reading are two crucial activities that help children develop vocabulary knowledge. More specifically, good bilingual readers have been found to focus on increasing their vocabulary knowledge (Jiménez, García, & Pearson, 1996). Thus, they set up goals for themselves in order to master written information. Teachers should encourage such goal-oriented behavior and give ELLs direct instructional guidance, either strictly in English or using the students' primary language.

Such guidance can be provided by preteaching key vocabulary in expository texts, for example. This genre can be difficult for students because it is structured differently from a narrative (Moran et al., 2000). Moreover, expository texts use "non-specialized academic words that occur across content areas (e.g., examine, cause, formation) . . . and specialized content-area words that are unique to specific disciplines (ecosystem, foreshadowing, octagon)" (NICHD, 2007, p. 14). To facilitate this type of vocabulary knowledge, a teacher can say and write vocabulary words on the board, then ask students to repeat the words and to write them down, and finally show pictures, demonstrate or give relevant examples (Echevarria & Graves, 2003). In addition, there seem to be clear benefits in, whenever possible, using a biliterate approach (Cummins, 1999; Hornberger & Micheau, 1993). That is, in activating background knowledge in the students' first language and transferring it to the topic at hand. For example, key vocabulary about the American Revolution can be introduced in Spanish and the teacher can model his or her thoughts in both Spanish and English. Lastly, research suggests that when the meanings of academically useful words are taught to fifth-grade ELL students, together with strategies for using information from context, from morphology, from figuring out multiple meanings, and from cognates to infer word meaning, children improve their reading comprehension (Carlo et al., 2004).

Reading instruction, with these added ESL features and bilingual support, facilitates students' ability to comprehend text (Short & Fitzsimmons, 2007).

Strategies for Teaching English Language Learners   Continued

Pointing out high-interest/low-readability books and including culturally responsive literature in the classroom can also motivate students to read and foster ELL students' literacy development (Echevarria & Graves, 2003). As with first-language children, when teachers give students choice in recreational reading activities they are more motivated to read and this, in turn, affects their reading achievement (Guthrie & Humenick, 2004).

ELLs need learning environments that demonstrate and promote the interdependence of listening, speaking, reading, and writing. These learning environments, in turn, can best support reading develop-

ment by providing contexts for real communication, offering supplementary contextual information, preteaching key vocabulary, adapting content, and modifying testing situations. Importantly, as the report of the National Literacy Panel indicates, reading instruction is "insufficient to support equal academic success" without adequate support of ELLs' oral language proficiency (NELP, 2008, p. 32). Equally important is the realization that "Given that ELLs have more to learn—the regular curriculum that everyone must learn, plus English—it makes sense to consider ways to provide them with extra time for learning" (Goldenberg, 2008, p. 21).

Strategies for Children with Special Needs

KAREN BURSTEIN AND TANIS BRYAN

For many young children with or at risk for special needs, reading is an extremely difficult task. Many of these children benefit greatly from explicit instruction in the basic tools of reading (Chall, 1989; Slavin, 1989; Stahl & Miller, 1989) using a direct instruction model. Assessments of children's phonemic awareness (Torgesen, 1994) provide valuable information about the students' skills and deficits in basic manipulation of phonemes. Additionally, it is essential for teachers to match reading materials to the skills of students with special needs.

Once a student's instructional reading level has been identified and appropriate reading materials have been obtained, teachers can use the following strategies to help promote the reading development of the student with special needs:

- Use books without words to provide early readers with an overview of the sequence of story content.
- Teach students to use the context clues available in the text such as the title and pictures.

- Use cross-age tutors, pairing older children such as second-graders with kindergarteners, for drill and practice of sight words and newly learned words.
- Increase fluency by having students repeat readings often.
- Have students use a straightedge under a line of text to eliminate visual distractions and keep place and pace.
- Have students use their finger to point and keep place and pace.
- Tape text read by the teacher or other students. Have the student follow along and read aloud while listening to correct pronunciation, expression, phrasing, and punctuation.
- Echo-read with the students. Sit behind and to the side of the student out of his or her line of sight. Read the text with the student softly into his or her ear, providing a model of pacing, pronunciation, and corrective feedback.

Family Focus: Helping Children Read to Learn

Boring. Too many words. Hard to read.

Sadly, these are some of the words that parents often hear their children use to describe textbooks. By third grade children are introduced to expository (informational) texts. This type of text provides most of the curriculum content children will encounter for the remainder of their school career; in other words, children go from learning how to read to using reading as a tool for learning. Hence a child's ability to master schooling often depends on their success with the textbook.

So how can parents help young readers become expository experts?

1. *Read to children from informational children's books.* Children are very curious and they ask a lot of questions. Take advantage of this. Use encyclopedias, Web searches, and other nonfiction sources to find the information together.
2. *Use children's informational trade books to support and reinforce school textbook learning.* Trade books are found in libraries and sold in bookstores. They are often better written

and illustrated than textbooks. Young students are often more interested in reading these books and are better able to learn the content/information from trade books than from textbooks.

3. *Encourage children to read about topics of personal interest.* Whether a child is interested in dinosaurs or dolphins, s/he is reading expository style writing when she wants to learn more about his/her interest or hobby.
4. *Subscribe to a magazine for children.* Children's nature magazines often include excellent expository selections about topics of interest to children.
5. *Encourage children to read sections of the newspaper related to their interests.* Children can start a scrapbook on a sports team, country, famous person, and so on. When they find an article they may read it, cut it out, and mount it in their scrapbook for that topic.

It is never too early or too late for parents to engage children in expository text. Parents will be surprised at how much both they and their children learn together.

Summary

Readers benefit from teachers who are well versed in the reading process. They also benefit from teachers who design classroom environments that provide opportunities to engage in meaningful reading activities. Simply by reading, students can increase their fluency, add to their vocabulary, and practice many important reading strategies. However, students rarely acquire all the strategies they need to be proficient readers from just reading. In addition, readers benefit from teachers who wed the opportunity to read with personalized strategy instruction. Finally, readers benefit from teachers who explain what they do in light of students' needs and in consideration of district and state standards. We designed this chapter and the others in this book to help you be that teacher.

PEARSON
myeducationkit™

To check your comprehension on the content covered in this chapter, go to the MyEducationKit for your book and complete the Study Plan for Chapter 8. Here you will be able to take a chapter quiz and receive feedback on your answers.

- *What are the components of the reading process?*

The components of the reading process include several psychological pieces: (1) word identification, (2) vocabulary, and (3) connected text. For each component, a reader taps a number of strategies. For word identification, readers might use phonics, consider the context, or employ morphemic analysis. In addressing vocabulary, they might use strategies such as consulting a reference or using context. In addition, and when their strategy use is unsuccessful, readers might rely on their teacher's explicit instruction. For connected text, comprehension strategies include identifying a text's structure, understanding a purpose for reading, visualizing, posing questions, making inferences, and summarizing. Of importance, readers monitor their reading and use fix-up strategies when their understanding wanes.

■ *Beyond a reader's proficiency in the specific features of this process, what else contributes to reading achievement?*

Especially in a school setting, a number of classroom events contribute to reading achievement. Specifically, the amount of time designated for reading (i.e., scheduling), the choice of materials (i.e., finding the just-right book), the type of reading (i.e., independent, shared, or guided), and the quality of instruction add or detract from a student's reading success.

■ *What classroom events should occur during the time assigned for reading?*

Within a sufficiently long block of time (approximately ninety minutes), students should be seen reading an appropriate text, responding to that text, and receiving instruction from their teacher designed to help them read better.

■ *What attributes define a successful reading teacher?*

Good teachers have a deep understanding of the reading process. Based on this they select appropriate assessments and interpret the assessment results to offer appropriate instruction. They create an environment that maximizes the students' opportunities to read appropriate books. To support this responsibility, they possess a broad understanding of books that allows them to choose materials wisely and well.

LINKING KNOWLEDGE TO PRACTICE

1. Interview several elementary grade teachers and ask them about their views of the reading process. Compare their responses with what you learned about the process of reading and its psychological components.

2. Observe an elementary grade teacher during the teacher's reading time. Record what the students and teacher do. Overall, consider the question, How do the teacher and students spend their time?

9 A Comprehensive Elementary Reading Program: Teaching Meaning and Skills

When he was in sixth grade, Jim Christie recalls spending two hours every day engaged in round-robin oral reading of literary classics. He can still recall the "butterflies" that he got in his stomach as his turn to read approached. Every Friday, a lengthy multiple-choice test was given about the portion of the book that was read that week. He came to think of reading as unpleasant work, and it took years before he began reading books for pleasure again. Fortunately, fewer and fewer teachers are using this approach to literature.

Many adults remember reading experiences like Jim's. The teacher-assigned stories were followed by the teacher asking, actually reading, a set of very specific questions that typically had only one "right" answer. These "When did?" "Who did?" questions were designed to test the reader's comprehension of the story. Occasionally, the teacher varied this routine by requiring students to complete a fill-in-the-blanks test or to write a book report. Unfortunately, this approach to reading may have taught a number of lessons unintended by the teacher, as Nancy Atwell (1987, p. 152) describes:

- Reading is difficult, serious business.
- Literature is even more difficult and serious.
- There is one interpretation of a text: the teacher's.

Instead of a single "correct" interpretation of a piece of literature, the new approaches to the teaching of reading operate on the premise that individuals bring to the act of reading their unique prior experiences and beliefs that influence how they interpret the author's words. Likewise, a reader's interpretation may change and be influenced by ongoing life experiences (Rosenblatt, 1991). For instance, Billie Enz remembers reading Laura Ingalls Wilder's *On the Banks of Plum Creek* (Little House Heritage Trust, 1937) when she was nine years old. In Chapter 8, Laura described Pa's reactions after she and Mary disobeyed Pa's instructions and continued to tumble down the tall straw stack that Pa had carefully raked:

PA: Did you slide down the straw-stack?
LAURA: No, Pa.

PA: Laura!

LAURA: We did not slide, Pa. But we did roll down it.

Pa got up quickly and went to the door and stood looking out. His back quivered. Laura and Mary did not know what to think. (p. 60)

At nine, Billie Enz believed Pa to be so upset with Mary and Laura that he was phys-ically shaking with anger. Some twenty years later, however, when she was rereading this story to her class, her life experiences as a parent and teacher caused her to reevaluate her original view of Pa's reaction. Billie now believes that Pa was laughing at his children's silly antics! This example illustrates today's view of reading as being both transactive and inter-active; in other words, understanding is a combination of what the reader brings to the text and what the reader takes from the text (Cambourne, 2002; Eeds & Wells, 1991). Thus, the act of reading is social in nature; minimally, it consists of a conversation between one reader and an author. Optimally, reading may be enhanced when several readers discuss their personal interpretations and construct shared understandings (Peterson & Eeds, 1990; Rascon-Briones & Searfoss, 1995).

In this book, we encourage teachers to use a blended approach to the teaching of reading as a way to help students interact with high-quality literature. The approach offers students an opportunity to

- Read independently and study texts of their own choosing
- Read independently and discuss communally
- Work in temporary small groups to learn specific skills
- Work one-on-one with their teacher in individual conferences to learn specific skills
- Work in a whole-class group to learn those skills the teacher sees all students needing
- Lead and participate in discussions in which each member of the group has equal status
- Work in cooperative groups, governed by rules of respect, with everyone's ideas or interpretations respected and valued
- Practice working in self-governing groups
- Talk, share ideas, build new understandings with peers, and consider and value others' divergent perspectives

In this chapter, we will describe how teachers use the ideas presented in Chapter 8 to help their students learn to construct a personal understanding of text. In addition, we dis-cuss how they can teach specific decoding and comprehension skills within a blended approach to teaching reading. We begin with a rich description of three first-grade teachers. In Special Feature 9.1, our colleague, Sara McCraw, provides this careful description of these three teachers' daily reading instruction. These teachers integrate a writing workshop (see Chapters 6 and 10) into their literacy time block. Therefore, the description also pro-vides information about the teaching of writing in two first grades.

Teachers of older students also teach reading and help their students use their reading and writing skills to learn. Therefore, we invited a colleague, Deanne McCredie, to describe how she supported her third-grade students' use of their reading and writing skills within the context of the study of immigration in the United States (see Special Feature 9.2), and we provide a description of Mr. Sousa, a sixth-grade teacher, reading and writing program. From Delaware to Washington to Arizona, teachers across the country are using these strategies to support their students' development as readers (and writers).

Before Reading This Chapter, Think About . . .

- The type of reading instruction you experienced when you were in grade school. Were you in a reading group? Did you participate in round-robin reading (sometimes called popcorn reading), when one child read, and then another, and then another, until finally it was your turn?
- A favorite story that you read with your teacher and peers. Did you have a favorite book of poetry that you read again and again?
- How your teachers assessed your comprehension of the stories and books you read. Did you complete workbook pages? Were there weekly tests? Did you write book reports? Did you share your views with peers?

Focus Questions

- What organizational strategies do teachers use to implement a blended reading program?
- What types of grouping strategies are used in a blended reading program?
- How do teachers provide skill instruction in a blended reading program?
- How do teachers help students construct meaning and expand their understanding of text?

BOX **9.1**

Definition of Terms

book club: a time when a small group of students read the same book and gather to talk about their reading, deepen their understanding and strategy use, and clarify any questions.

individual conference: a time for a teacher to meet individually with a student to learn about reading strengths, needs, and areas of interest, monitor book selection, and set goals.

running record: an ongoing assessment by which a teacher determines the word decoding accuracy and strategy use a student has with different leveled text.

schema: a reader's background knowledge about a specific topic or experience.

strategy-based guided reading: grouping students by reading strategy need so that teachers can provide appropriate instruction. Students are usually reading on a similar level but are not confined to reading with only students at their specific level. These groups remain fluid; as student needs change, the group membership changes.

Using Reading and Writing for Learning: Grade 1

In Special Feature 9.1, note how children learn through reading while learning to read. Witness Mrs. Meszaros's first-grade students' learning about how horses sleep (standing up) from their reading of a book on horses. In recent years, many teachers have intentionally planned ways for their students to use their reading and writing skills to support their learning of the social studies or science content. These teachers are heeding the advice of the National Council of Teachers of English (NCTE, 1993):

PEARSON
myeducationkit™

Go to the Assignments and Activities section of Chapter 9 in the MyEducationKit and complete the activity entitled "Before and During Reading Strategies." As you watch the video and answer the accompanying questions, note how the teacher activates the children's knowledge of the strategies good readers use to improve comprehension.

Rather than working on subjects in isolation from one another and studying reading apart from writing, math, science, social studies, and other curricular areas, children learn best when they are engaged in inquiries that involve using literacy to learn about a variety of subject area. (Borman, Hewes, Overman, & Brown, 2003)

When the language arts are woven into the very fabric of all subject matter areas, it is a classic win–win situation. Subject matter content and the language arts are both learned more effectively. As teacher Tarry Lindquist (1995) points out:

It is through the language arts that my students most often reveal their knowledge and apply their skills. Reading, writing, listening, and speaking are integral to all learning. Without language arts, the construction of meaning in specific topics is impossible. (p. 1)

SPECIAL FEATURE 9.1

Lessons from Three Experienced First-Grade Teachers

SARA B. McCRAW

Sheila Roche-Cooper, Janelle Layton, and Chrissy Meszaros each knew that teaching from the reading series was not enough for the students in their classrooms. It seemed to reach students who were just about on grade level, but first-graders who were below felt lost and left behind and those above felt bored. These teachers decided to meet weekly and plan together to see if they could make a difference. During these weekly meetings they invited other staff members to share what was working for them and to uncover good resources for learning different ways to meet the needs of all their students in an engaging and motivating way. They also used this time to brainstorm and problem solve. They were willing to change their instruction if it was not

benefiting the students. What these teachers learned was that through collaboration they not only created a dynamic learning environment in their own classroom where students were actually asking for more time to read, but also formed a partnership that continues to grow and reduces the anxieties of trying to teach. No longer must they teach in isolation.

Each teacher has a strong foundation in teaching and recognizes that students need both explicit and implicit instruction in decoding and comprehension strategies to become proficient readers. The teachers believe in a systematic yet responsive model of instruction based on collecting ongoing assessment information about each student and designing instruction in students' zone of proximal development (be it in a whole group, flexible small group, or individually during

(continued)

reading conferences). These teachers do follow district guidelines in terms of meeting trimester goals, using district-adopted reading materials, and conducting established assessments used in all first-grade classrooms.

Mrs. Layton and Mrs. Meszaros share a classroom in a TAM (Team Approach to Mastery) model of including students with special needs with general education students, while Mrs. Roche-Cooper has a general education class. They all work in an early childhood center located in a rural, mid-Atlantic state where the building services all kindergarten and first-grade students in the district and those who qualify for prekindergarten. The average class size is twenty-three students and these children come from a variety of backgrounds. Each student is viewed as an individual who is capable and ready to learn and who also needs patience and guidance as they explore learning about themselves as readers, writers, listeners, and speakers. Since the teachers plan together they have a similar daily schedule, which is described on the following pages as a way to illustrate this responsive approach to literacy instruction that incorporates a reading and writing workshop model and time for word study each day.

Beginning the Day (8:10–8:40)

Students trickle into the classrooms when they are dropped off by parents, arrive on the bus, or have finished eating breakfast in the school cafeteria. By the second week of school, students know the routine of turning in homework, making their lunch selection, returning the book brought home to read the night before, and settling in to one of their morning literacy stations. Here students spend time reading and discussing books on the same theme (typically the upcoming or current science or social studies theme), listening to books on tape, practicing their fluency by reading into a tape recorder, working on a computer program to enhance their reading skills, or pairing up with a partner to practice high-frequency words. Students transition by cleaning up their station and joining together in the meeting area. A few students share

what they learned from reading a book in the theme tub and others share excitement about improved reading fluency and other successes.

Thinking about Reading (8:40–9:10)

The teachers are constantly modeling how they think about what they read as they share their "think-alouds" during reading (this occurs throughout the day across content areas). One morning, students in Mrs. Roche-Cooper's class gathered in the meeting area to listen to two stories about costume parades (it was October 31!). For the past two weeks, the students had learned about text-to-self and text-to-text connections and how good readers get ready to read by activating their *schema*. At this point, students were comfortable using the language of schema and connections correctly. More importantly, students had learned what kinds of connections help a reader understand (e.g., "I know what it feels like to lose a best friend, that happened to me when I moved.") versus ones that do not (e.g., "I have red shoes, too!"). The students learned about making connections with their reading series materials and other texts. An excerpt from a comprehension lesson using picture books follows:

One boy sits up high on a chair facing the students yet watching the teacher; today is his special day to sit in the chair and help the teacher. She reads the story with the book facing her as the students listen and visualize what is happening. At the end of each page she shows the pictures and the children automatically discuss with each other what they see and think. An atmosphere of a conversation is evident versus the "teacher talks, children raise their hands and one responds, and teacher repeats what the student said" model. In this conversational approach all students have a chance to share their thinking and ask questions with their classmates as authentic audience members. Near the end of the story Mrs. Roche-Cooper stops and asks a prediction question, "Why did the boy Gilbert in this story wear a ballerina costume?" Immediately the students turn to each other to respond, giggling about the question and sharing their own predictions as to why. A few moments later the teacher counts backward from five to indicate it's time to stop talking and listen. She continues to the end of the story, when the students take over the reading as they chant the poem told over and over in the story.

At the end of the story, the teacher facilitates the students sitting in pairs, knee to knee and eye to eye, as they share their connections from the story. The students have close to two minutes to share. Mrs. Roche-Cooper follows up with compliments and specific language models: "Remember to use our phrase when sharing connections, 'When I heard the part about blank it reminded me of blank.'" Students are invited to share their connections. One student shares, "I remember when I sang the same song from the story last year in class." She acknowledges that some students may not have made a connection in the first story. Mrs. Roche-Cooper reads a second story and lets the students know it is okay if they did not make a connection the first time but perhaps they will in the second one or they may even make a connection between the two stories.

She begins reading the second story, book facing her as she reads then sharing the pictures at end of each page. She compliments the students, reading behavior, "Thank you, Tyke and Jasmine, for listening politely." Mrs. Roche-Cooper naturally defines unfamiliar words during the reading experience and engages her class to see if they are familiar with the words. One student picks up on this habit and calls out, "gloomy means dark," as the teacher reads the sentence with the word *gloomy*. Other students look at her and nod their head in agreement. Interjecting is an accepted behavior when the comment or question is on topic and done so respectfully. Two thirds of the way through the second story Mrs. Roche-Cooper prompts students to share their connections with their same partners from before. She immediately gets up and roams around the pairs listening, coaching, and reminding. She brings them back together with more compliments for students who used the language of connections.

Next, Mrs. Roche-Cooper asks students to determine which book they made more connections with and to stand in groups accordingly. She broke these groups into small groups of three to four children and sent each group off with chart paper and markers to a section in the room to record their connections. One group (three girls and a boy) talk about what they are supposed to do: "You have to put a big *T* and a big *S* with an arrow in between." They end up taking up the entire paper with their big *T* and big *S,* then one girl points and states what each letter stands for: "text-to-self connection." Two of the girls take charge while the boy stands up looking for the teacher and the third girl tries to write her own *T* and *S* smaller on the chart. About this time Mrs. Roche-Cooper walks over and compliments their teamwork and comments that the *T* and *S* are too large so she flips the paper over and is more explicit about how to record their connections. She leaves and floats around to the other five groups, passing out compliments and facilitating when needed. The group of three girls and one boy is still having problems deciding how to share the writing experience. They each want to take turns writing one letter in each word. Mrs. Roche-Cooper returns and suggests they pick one recorder. The students raise their hands and eagerly look at the teacher. She says she will not pick the recorder and puts the responsibility back to the group to determine. She walks away and one girl decides to be the recorder and starts writing. The other group members offer help with spelling, spacing, and other conventions of writing.

Each group is given the responsibility of determining how to organize the writing and sharing the writing event. Two groups share the pen and write one connection together while the other four groups find a way to each record their own connections. Not one student complains they cannot write or spell. They each have the confidence to record using their best spelling. After about eight minutes (during which she continued to rotate between groups, offering support and guidance when needed), Mrs. Roche-Cooper lets students know they will gather together soon: "Put the caps on

(continued)

your markers and bring your chart back to the meeting area. Be sure to sit with your group." The students are so excited to share their charts that each holds a corner of the chart paper. Lots of chatter is heard in the room as the groups try to determine who will do the talking. Mrs. Roche-Cooper patiently reminds the group to gather in the meeting room then she calls up one group to share. She points out how well the group organized their work. "What do you notice about how they organized their connections?" Mrs. Roche-Cooper asks the class. One student comments, "They drew lines so they each had a place to write their own comment." The process of sharing continues until each group has had a chance to share. The teacher gives subtle reminders to look at the people speaking and compliments students for speaking clearly and sharing connections that helped them understand the story better. During transitions between groups, she asks the class if they made a similar connection to the last group that shared.

Applying What They Learned (9:10–9:40)

In previous years, each teacher used a centers approach for creating independence so they could meet in small groups for guided reading. This approach worked well, but the teachers became frustrated that the time could be used better and they wanted their students to spend more time reading and less time practicing disconnected skills (a.k.a. busy work). As a result, the teachers began to study the reading workshop model (see Figure 9.1) and decided to use this approach in their classrooms instead. They knew it would take time to build stamina for reading, so they began the year with just five minutes of independent reading time. Each day they extended the time until the students could read "just-right books" for ten minutes. At this point (about one week into school) the teachers began meeting with students for *individual conferences*. Here they interviewed students to learn about their interests and how each child viewed him/herself as a reader. The second conference was more of an assessment in which the teacher took a running record,

checked for comprehension, and shared the results with the student including strengths and areas of growth. Together the teacher and student set a goal for the student's reading, a way to measure the goal, and a time to check progress. About five weeks into school the students in both classes were able to read books from their book basket (a collection of books at students' independent and instructional level that were originally selected by the teacher, but the students have since taken over once they recognized what a just-right book looks like) and the teachers could meet with three students individually for a conference. The conferences shifted from simple assessment to more instruction as teachers offered support when needed. During a Thursday after-school meeting, the teachers discussed what was happening during their reading workshop time, and one teacher commented, "It's amazing! I cannot believe how engaged the students are in reading. I would never have believed this could happen last year." The teachers realized they knew more about their students' reading ability six weeks into school than they did all year in years past. An excerpt from a reading workshop follows.

A transition is made to reading workshop time by reviewing expectations, "We all want to be reading during this time." Mrs. Roche-Cooper reviews a few key strategies they can use while reading to help figure out words and to help with understanding. Then she asks the students to close their eyes and think about what their personal goal is for reading. "Remember, using strategies helps us to remember the story, to understand the story, and to enjoy the story." Students go get their reading basket of personal books at their independent level as she hands each student a rubric they will use to score themselves at the end of reading workshop time. They all sing a song together as they move through this transition, "There is a child who likes to read and _____ is her/his name-o, R-E-A-D read, R-E-A-D read, R-E-A-D read, and _____ is her/his name-o!" Students eagerly go straight to their cubbies to get their book baskets; some even skip. Each student finds a special place in the room to read (sitting on the ledge of the coat cubby, in a rocking chair, at a desk, at the writing center, under the kidney table, on the floor with a carpet square, in the book closet with a pillow). Immediately, students pull out their books and begin reading; some read leveled books, others read from the reading series. One child has a hard time getting started. He roams around the room watching other students until he finds a place to sit; then he looks at his goal notebook to see what his latest goal is.

Mrs. Roche-Cooper watches as the students begin reading then chooses a student with whom she will hold a conference. She approaches Connor, listens to him read a few moments, and then asks if she can hold a conference with him. The rest of the class is reading (out loud as they are apt to do at this stage of development) and do not seem to notice each other. One child stops periodically in his reading and comments on what is happening in the story. "This walrus is a wimp, he doesn't want to get in the cold water," he giggles. At the end he says to no one in particular, "This book is too easy for me." He reads a second book from his basket, and at the end he makes a text-to-self connection between the character and his own sister. Meanwhile, Mrs. Roche-Cooper finishes one conference in about four minutes and approaches Wen Li and asks if she can have a conference. She begins by asking why she chose the book she did. Wen Li responds that it is the next story in the book (anthology) and that it is her goal to read all the stories in it. The teacher asks Wen Li to determine if the story is too hard, too easy, or just right. She is not sure so she starts reading to decide. The teacher listens and occasionally records comments in Wen Li's conference notebook. When she needs help Mrs. Roche-Cooper prompts her with, "What can you do to figure it out?"

Elsewhere in the room a boy is reading *The Wide-Mouth Frog,* while another boy lingers and listens from behind, following the text with his eyes as the reader reads. It is difficult to see the faces of the students in the room because they hold their book close to their eyes and concentrate on reading. Some are pointing to the words. Many squiggle and move their legs, feet, bodies, but the whole time their eyes are focused on the book and they are reading. One boy walks to his cubby to find a book that was missing from his basket. Students in this room are reading books from a level two (just a few words on a page with high picture support and a repeated pattern) to a level seventeen (beginning of second-grade level with many words per page, past tense verbs, dialogue, and multi-syllabic words). One student pulls out the word bank from his basket and goes through reading all of his high-frequency words, quickly making a pile of the ones he knows and the ones he does not know. Another student is reading a "phonic book" that she made for practicing short-*e* word families. Yet another child reads a class-generated book of a poem that he illustrated. Off in a corner, a little girl curls up and flips through all the books in her basket. She seems to crave the quiet, small space as she begins reading. From this point on, she does not seem to notice anyone or anything else in the room.

Mrs. Roche-Cooper moves on to the third conference with Thomas. He chooses a class-made book to read. She listens to his reading, supporting when needed but really trying to see what Thomas can do on his own. At the end, she points out that he did a good job of reading. "At the beginning you had a hard time reading the word *pumpkin,* but later in the story you read it with no problem." She finishes by saying, "Thanks for letting me visit and happy reading!" She moves on to another conference while quietly letting two students know that they have a zero on their rubric for reading workshop at this point. She transitions the class to finish reading workshop by reminding them to choose a book from their basket to take home to read to someone for homework tonight. She also reminds them to score their rubrics and that they should have a two unless she spoke to them directly. The students gather in the meeting area to share their books and strategies used.

Eight weeks into the school year all three teachers realize some of their students are no longer making steady progress in their reading (an average of two levels every three weeks), so

(continued)

they decide it is time to begin small group instruction. Realizing that "fair" does not always mean "equal" time for every student, Mrs. Layton and Mrs. Meszaros set up a weekly schedule for reading workshop that allows the teachers to meet with students who are struggling the most three times a week in strategy-based, guided reading groups and three times a week for individual instruction later in the day. Students who are reading near the end of the first-grade level will meet in book clubs twice a week, and students who are reading on a level typical of this time of year will continue meeting individually with one teacher each week for a conference and will also meet once a week in a *strategy-based guided reading* group. The teachers are able to plan their instruction for small groups based on the information collected during individual conferences.

Differentiating Instruction (9:10–9:40)

During the time that the teachers meet with their students individually for conferences they also meet with small, guided reading groups based on student needs. At this time of year, Mrs. Layton and Mrs. Meszaros find themselves working with several groups of varying needs. Four students are already reading on a level near the end of first grade and participate in a book club. They read the same book and meet twice a week with a teacher to discuss the book, share strategies used, and increase their understanding. Three students in this inclusion class are still learning letter sounds and need to increase their phoneme manipulation skills. They meet as a small group for shared reading, phonics work, and phonemic awareness lessons four times a week. Four students are just beginning to apply voice–print–match skills and meet three times a week for guided reading. The rest of the class is reading on grade level, but have different strengths and needs. A group of four students meets twice a week in a guided reading group to strengthen their context clue use in combination to their strong decoding skills. Another group of five students uses context clues well but needs help with decoding; they

also meet twice a week for guided reading. The other four students reading on grade level are balancing their use of context and decoding strategies and continue to meet with the teachers for individual conferences. A strategy-based guided reading lesson with the group of on-level readers who need help with using context clues follows:

Five children and Mrs. Meszaros gather in a circle on the floor, each on their own carpet square. Some kneel and others sit with their legs crossed. Each student has his or her book basket and is reading a self-selected book as a warm-up. Mrs. Meszaros listens to Zane read the new book from the last time they met and takes a *running record* to check his accuracy and strategy use. About three minutes into the meeting, Mrs. Meszaros asks the students to find a stopping place in their reading, and then shares the strategies Zane used in his reading. "I like the way he went back and read the sentence again after he paused to sound out a word. This shows that he was paying attention to what the story was about." Then she asks, "Does anyone want to share a strategy they used when they got stuck on a word?" Olivia shares, "I got stuck on a word so I looked at it and I saw the little word *go* inside. Then I figured out the word was *going*." "Great," says Mrs. Meszaros, then she asks, "What else do readers do when they get stuck on a word?" "Sound it out!" calls out Zane. "Look at the beginning sound and match it to the pictures," says Miles. Mrs. Meszaros continues by describing how sometimes good readers get stuck on a word and sounding out or looking for chunks does not work, so they reread the sentence from the beginning to recall what the text is talking about and predict what word would make sense that has the same beginning sound. The group tries this with a few practice sentences (*When will we b____ our new jobs? School is the best place to l_____.*). The students match their predictions to the spelling of the word.

After the strategy lesson, Mrs. Meszaros prepares the students for their new book, *Sleeping Animals*. She passes out a copy of the book to everyone and they immediately begin taking a picture walk, looking at each page and making predictions about what the book will be about. Miles says, "It looks like horses sleep standing up, I wonder if this is true?" Olivia shares, "Hey I knew bats sleep upside down. We learned that when we read the bat book last week." After the picture walk, Mrs. Meszaros reminds the students to use their strategies if they get stuck on a word and to check their predictions. She invites one member of the group at a time to begin reading to ensure they each read on their own and use their own strategies to prevent choral reading (because the goal of guided reading is for students to learn how to read text on their own and rely on their strategies if they get stuck). Mrs. Meszaros listens to the readers, occasionally jotting down notes about each student on her lesson plan. These notes, in combination with the conference notes, will help her plan for the next guided reading lesson. Cole says, "I need help." And Mrs. Meszaros replies, "What can you do to figure it out?" "I can chunk it," he says. "Okay, show me." Cole finds *ing* and *sleep* and says the word is *sleeping*. His teacher smiles and Cole continues reading.

Latisha finishes reading first, so Mrs. Meszaros prompts her to find a word in the book that she had trouble with and be prepared to share with the group what she did to figure it out. As the others finish, they begin to talk about how animals sleep and confirm their predictions. "I was right! Horses do sleep standing up!" Miles shares. "I don't see how they do that. Why don't their legs get tired from standing all the time?" Latisha asks. Cole shares, "It's probably because that's how they were made. Yeah. Horses were made to stand up all the time that's why." The students decide they would like to learn more about horses and how they sleep so they ask Mrs. Meszaros to find more information about horses for them. She says they can look into it the next time they meet. Then she asks Latisha to share a strategy she used while reading. "I got stuck on this word. It was so big I didn't know how to sound it out so I tried reading the sentence again. Then the word popped into my head, *alligator*!

That made sense and it matched the picture, but when I looked at the word again I knew it couldn't be *alligator* because the word starts with a *c*. So I looked at the word again, read the sentence again and knew the word must be *crocodile*." Two others share a strategy they used to help them figure out a word.

Next, Mrs. Meszaros invites them to read the book again with a partner. "Now that you have figured out all the words and learned some new facts, when you read the book this time, work on your fluency. You want your reading to sound smooth and your voice to go up and down some, like when Mrs. Layton reads aloud to us. Take turns reading with a partner. When it is your turn to listen, follow the words with your eyes and let your partner know if they were reading fluently. I am going to listen to Zane read and take a running record on his reading." The students begin reading and don't seem to notice those reading near them. Latisha sounds like her teachers when Olivia asked for help and Latisha said, "What can you do to figure it out?" The students are learning how to rely on their own strategies while reading. When all are finished reading and commenting on each other's fluency, Mrs. Meszaros asks, "Would you recommend this book to other readers? Do you feel comfortable keeping this book in your book basket?" They all agree that other boys and girls would enjoy reading the book. Most want to keep it in their basket, but Cole decides it is too hard so he will not keep it in his book basket.

Ready to Write (10:10–11:00)

At this point in the school year the students understand the components and expectations of the writing workshop. On the day described below, the students are in the middle of writing a letter all about themselves to their special teacher who is out on maternity leave. In preparation for writing the letter, the class spent many weeks reading samples of different letters in literature, morning messages, and letters from home. Next the class created a list of characteristics common to friendly letters and began writing letters in

(continued)

whole-group and small group situations. Now the students are ready to produce their own letter.

> Mrs. Layton reminds students who were publishing yesterday to return to the same computer and continue typing. She asks the class, "What can you do if you are finished with your letters or are waiting for a computer?" One student states that they can read a book or play on the computer. Mrs. Layton reminds him that it is not the time to play on the computer but that it would be a great time to begin a new piece of free-choice writing. "You can write about anything you want. Maybe you could write a letter to someone else or make up a silly story." Mrs. Meszaros asks students who have a note from her about their writing (the teachers had read through the student writing and wrote comments to those who need to add more to their letters) to join her at the table. In the small group setting, she is able to guide students' writing when they need help. Some of the students have special needs and some just need help. Mrs. Layton confers individually with students who are ready to publish their letters. Together they read through the letter, stopping periodically to check if the writing sounds right and makes sense. At the end of the letter, they check the planning web to make sure everything is included. The students who are not publishing on the computer or meeting with a teacher are working independently on their writing. Some are focused on writing a web for a new writing piece, while others are reading through and revising their writing after a conference. One girl has a hard time getting started on her own, so Mrs. Layton asks her to move close so she can help motivate and monitor her work.
>
> Both teachers are acutely aware of each student's stage in writing (since they just read through the writing the day before) and can constantly monitor their progress. Today is one of the first days that the students have a choice to start writing something new if they are done. During the first six weeks of school, they received a great deal of scaffolded support in writing together about a similar topic. The challenge of writing independently is too much for one little girl, who just sits and "thinks" (tapping a finger on the side of her head). When Mrs. Layton asks Kaitlyn what she is writing, her eyes tear up and she comments that she has nothing to write about. Before she gets upset, Mrs. Layton joins her and helps her look through her writing folder to see if she has any unfinished writing or ideas for topics to write about. Kaitlyn smiles and pulls out a letter she started before but has never finished.
>
> In another part of the room two boys sit side by side working on separate tasks yet motivating each other with their level of focus. Mrs. Meszaros continues working with the same group of students who had notes on their letters. "It says here that you need to add more details to this part of the letter. I think Mrs. Sistare would like to know more about your family when she reads your letter." Then she leans across the kidney-shaped table to help other students with ideas, revisions, and stretching out words. She sends Abbey over to the editing center and explains there is a checklist of things to do. Abbey joins Karl on the carpet near the editor's checklist and begins to look through the list the class is creating together (adding items to check as they learn more ways to edit).

Word Study Time (1:30–2:00)

Although there are targeted skills that will be tested on the district assessment, these teachers realize that a more constructivist approach to understanding why words are spelled the way they are, versus teaching students to just sound out words at the phoneme level and memorizing words for a spelling quiz, is more useful. A snapshot of a word study lesson in Mrs. Meszaros and Mrs. Layton's class follows. The class spent several weeks studying short vowels, recognizing that when a one-syllable word has only one vowel in the middle it will most likely have the short sound. They also studied different word families, recognizing that the consonant that follows the vowel can alter the sound (e.g., *car, cat, call* all have short *a*, but the sound of the /a/ is altered by the *r, t, l*).

The students get a dry erase board, marker, and eraser and gather together in the meeting area. Mrs. Layton explains they are going to do a couple of examples together then they will each get a chance to do some on their own. "I'm going to ask you to spell a word. What is the first thing you would do to get all the sounds on the paper? If it's a word you know how to spell you can just write it. If you don't know how to, what can you do?" "Sound it out," says Darnell. "Right, show me how you can sound out the word *man*." Together the class chorally segments the word /m/ /a/ /n/ as they count out the sounds on their fingertips. Mrs. Layton says, "Yes, there are three sounds" and she records three dashes on the chart paper. The class segments the sounds in *man* again; this time they stop and decide what letter(s) represent each sound and fill it in on the chart. The /m/ sound was easy but short /a/ was difficult, so they paid close attention to the sound in the word and determined it was the letter /a/ making the short a sound. To clarify, Mrs. Meszaros showed the children how they can feel the difference between short /i/ and short /a/ by placing their hand under their chin and feeling how far their chin drops for the short /a/ sound but not for the short /i/ sound. They finish filling in the word together on the chart and start with the next word.

"Go ahead and try to count out how many sounds are in the word *grab*." The room fills with chatter as students segment the word *grab* and try counting out the sounds on their hand. Together the class segments the word in to four sounds and Mrs. Layton puts four dashes on the chart to represent the sounds. Then she prompts the students to do the same on their dry erase boards and lets them try filling in the letters for the sounds. Both teachers move around to assist students as they segment the word *grab,* then Mrs. Layton fills in the dashes with the appropriate letter on the chart for the students to check. Mrs. Layton is very explicit in her modeling and guided instruction as she clearly articulates the sounds. "We just learned these *r*-blend sounds this week so I know they are tough" she tells one student who looks worried. Mrs. Meszaros circulates around, but

mainly sits with two students who are in the prealphabetic stage and are still having trouble segmenting sounds.

Mrs. Layton prompts the class by saying, "The next word is tricky so listen carefully. The word is *trip*. How many sounds do you think it has?" The students again try to segment it. Then Mrs. Meszaros asks students to hold up enough fingers to show how many sounds are in it. A variety of fingers go up and Mrs. Meszaros calls on one student to share what the first two letters are that make the sound /tr/. They decide there are four sounds so each student records four dashes on the dry erase board. Although the students were very excited about using the dry erase boards and markers, they had used them enough before not to be too distracted by them. One boy had trouble focusing so he is asked to stop using his marker for a short time. He is invited to try again when he is ready (and immediately shows that he is ready!). Again Mrs. Layton prompts students to try recording the letters that correspond to the sounds. "Look at my mouth and listen to the sounds. Many of you wrote *i* but some wrote *e*. The sounds are close together. Listen as I say the sounds. Put your hand under your chin and feel how your chin moves when you make the short /e/ sound but not with the short /i/ sound. You can try this when you are spelling and not sure what vowel it should be.

"Everything's in my lap and my ears are listening," Mrs. Layton states to prompt the students to get ready to listen to a new word. "Okay, listen to my word. The word is *prop*. If I put my feet up, I could prop them on the chair. *Prop*. Okay, sound it out and show me with your fingers how many sounds you hear. Okay, this time I'm going to let you do it all on your own now." Students begin working on their own to spell the word, while both teachers move around, assisting students as needed, but first waiting to see what students can do on their own. Mrs. Meszaros says, "Jason, how many sounds did you hear in *prop*? Four? Okay, everyone, let's try it together." They all segment it out together. Then they spell the word together. Mrs. Layton says, "I must tell you it

(continued)

looks very impressive up here," as she refers to the students sitting near her who have written the word. She asks Mrs. Meszaros, who confirms the same thing is happening in the back of the room.

"Here are the directions. Listen carefully. I'm going to say the word, and you are going to sound out the word, count the sounds in the word, write that many dashes on your board, and then fill in the letters. Remember that every word has to have at least one vowel. The letters *a, e, i, o,* or *u* are vowels [she records these on the chart while stating them]. The word is *grin*". The chatter begins as students stretch out the word, talking about how many sounds they hear, and writing. Jason shows his board to Mrs. Meszaros for confirmation. Dyson asks to hear the word again so he can make sure he hears the end of the word correctly. "Let's tap it out together then I will have everyone help me spell it because everyone did an awesome job writing this word," Mrs. Layton says. The students grin with pride as they spell out the word *grin* together. Students are dismissed individually to return their materials and get their books from their book baskets in anticipation of meeting with their book buddies.

Reading with a Friend Once a Week (2:00–2:30)

Once a week, Mrs. Roche-Cooper's class joins Mrs. Layton and Mrs. Meszaros' class for book buddy time. At the beginning of the year students chose a buddy from the other class and now they share the books they can now read with each other every week. The teachers designed this weekly meeting time to create an authentic purpose for students to practice reading familiar texts and to create positive relations across classrooms.

Mrs. Meszaros reminds her class, "After your buddies reads their book to you, ask a few questions to see if they understand what they are reading. I think they will be surprised you ask questions, and I bet they can tell you what they are thinking while they were reading."

Students move to their book baskets to pick out just the right book to share with their buddy. Shaya carefully looks through each title, pulls one out, and then picks another book instead to share; she then returns her basket to her cubby above the coat rack. As the students wait for their buddy from the other class, they whisper to a neighbor what their book is about.

Soon Mrs. Roche-Cooper's students eagerly enter the room, books held tightly to their bodies, looking around the room for their buddy. No more directions are needed as the students begin sharing. Some sit knee to knee and eye to eye, others sit side by side. They all find a spot to share their reading. The room is buzzing with first-grade voices reading. "What's this word?" Byron asks Chloe. "No way, I didn't know that," Zack tells D.J. "I like your reading," James tells Sara. "Where do you want to sit?" Jaymen asks Tywon. One boy leans over to get a closer look at the pictures in another boy's book. Two girls sit on the floor then decide to lie down and look up at the books. While Susan reads, Tanika listens and helps her check her words when she needs help. Giggles come out when Cole reads *The Wide-Mouth Frog* to Bobby who's never heard the story before. The students read and share books for ten minutes, then Mrs. Meszaros counts backward from ten, giving the partners a chance to finish talking and get ready to listen. Mrs. Meszaros shares compliments with the children. "I noticed Patrick and Dylon were sitting knee to knee and eye to eye and having a conversation about their book after reading." Mrs. Roche-Cooper shares a compliment about how one student put his arm around his buddy, showing how he was really paying attention. Mrs. Layton shares how two sets of buddies found two different ways to sit with their buddy and invites them to sit and model in a "fishbowl," as the rest of the boys and girls stand in a large circle to watch and learn. "Okay, Antonio, pick a page to read so we can all watch what happens. Look at how Kyron put his arm around Antonio, looked at the words on the page and was quiet. Kyron was really showing Antonio that he was interested." A second set of buddies moves to the middle ready to model. "Stand back and

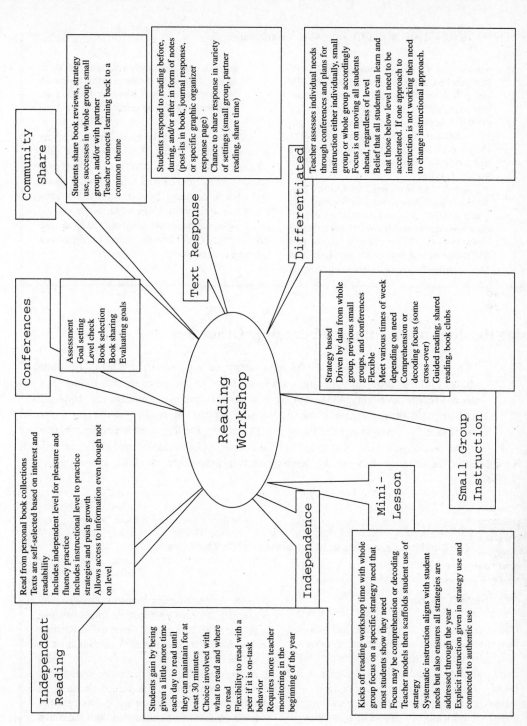

Community Share

Students share book reviews, strategy use, successes in whole group, small group, and/or with partner
Teacher connects learning back to a common theme

Conferences

Assessment
Goal setting
Level check
Book selection
Book sharing
Evaluating goals

Independent Reading

Read from personal book collections
Texts are self-selected based on interest and readability
Includes independent level for pleasure and fluency practice
Includes instructional level to practice strategies and push growth
Allows access to information even though not on level

Students gain by being given a little more time each day to read until they can maintain for at least 30 minutes
Choice involved with what to read and where to read
Flexibility to read with a peer if it is on-task behavior
Requires more teacher monitoring in the beginning of the year

Text Response

Students respond to reading before, during, and/or after in form of notes (post-its in book, journal response, or specific graphic organizer response page)
Chance to share response in variety of settings (small group, partner reading, share time)

Differentiated

Teacher assesses individual needs through conferences and plans for instruction either individually, small group or whole group accordingly
Focus is on moving all students ahead, regardless of level
Belief that all students can learn and that those below level need to be accelerated. If one approach to instruction is not working then need to change instructional approach.

Small Group Instruction

Strategy based
Driven by data from whole group, previous small groups, and conferences
Flexible
Meet various times of week depending on need
Comprehension or decoding focus (some cross-over)
Guided reading, shared reading, book clubs

Mini-Lesson

Kicks off reading workshop time with whole group focus on a specific strategy need that most students show they need
Focus may be comprehension or decoding
Teacher models then scaffolds student use of strategy
Systematic instruction aligns with student needs but also ensures all strategies are addressed through the year
Explicit instruction given in strategy use and connected to authentic use

Independence

Reading Workshop

FIGURE 9.1   A Balanced Approach to Teaching Reading

(continued)

SPECIAL FEATURE 9.1 Continued

admire what these two students are doing," Mrs. Roche-Cooper prompts the students. The two girls sit facing each other. Samantha reads one page, then turns the book to show her buddy, Manny, the pictures. Manny looks right at Samantha and listens until she gets to look at the picture. "Manny really showed Samantha that she was listening and paying attention to her good reading."

Mrs. Meszaros and Mrs. Layton's students put their books away, unprompted, and return to their desks as Mrs. Roche-Cooper's class lines up and walks out. "Bye, Darion," a buddy calls out. It is exciting to see the new friendships developing across the classrooms and the sense of community and mutual respect

expanding beyond their own classroom. These students also share the same recess time each day and have another chance to develop relationships across classrooms.

All three of these experienced teachers believe students need to learn how to be self-directed in their literacy activities by taking over choice in what text to read, what to write about, and what to discuss. These teachers also understand that children this age need to see models and receive support until they are ready to take over the responsibility for some of their own learning events.

Using Reading and Writing for Learning: Grade 3

In Special Feature 9.2, Deanne McCredie describes aspects of her third-grade students' study of immigration, highlighting how she used this social studies topic to support her students' literacy development. Most of her students have become proficient in decoding. Several are still struggling with the mechanical aspects of reading and receive special assistance. However, her general approach to teaching reading heavily emphasizes reading to learn as opposed to learning to read. Of course, as her students read and write to learn about immigration, they are also learning many advanced literacy skills at the same time.

SPECIAL FEATURE 9.2

The Immigrant Experience: An Integrated Unit in Third Grade

DEANNE MCCREDIE

Over the year, my third-graders had selected many topics for study. In this instance, however, topic selection was driven by my state's and district's standard curriculum-content mandates and by my interest in providing my students with meaningful multicultural experiences and learning events. Specifically, I wanted my students to

consider America's ethnic diversity. This diversity is possibly America's greatest national challenge as people of all backgrounds learn to live together and to appreciate one another's contributions to American life. One reason that the United States is so diverse is that it was settled by immigrants; everyone who lives in the United States is an immigrant or a descendent of an immigrant. I wanted my students to understand that their own family history is part of the story of America's immigration.

During the period of 1820 to 1920, the United States experienced the largest wave of immigrants in its history. I wanted my students to understand these immigrants' experiences, why the immigrants chose to leave their homelands, and to realize that immigrants continue to come to the United States in search of a new life for many of the same reasons immigrants came nearly a century ago.

What did my students already know about immigration? I began the unit with an introductory discussion to assess their existing knowledge about the topic. I learned quickly that my children knew very little about immigration. Therefore, defining what they wanted to learn was difficult. I decided to begin the unit by having the students engage in the behaviors of social scientists—historians—by examining primary sources of historical information and by recording and interpreting their findings. As the students acquired some knowledge about immigration, I asked them what else they wanted to learn, and I used their questions and discoveries to guide the direction of our investigations.

I wanted the students to understand that primary sources give us a firsthand look at the past and that studying primary sources helps us experience history. These students were eight- and nine-year-olds, though. How might we begin? I decided to start by examining primary sources that were significant to these children. I sent a letter to the children's parents requesting that they consider sending an item from their families' history to school for their child to share with the class. I suggested that the primary sources might include artifacts such as letters, journals, documents, photographs, and art.

The next day, the children arrived with many different pieces of their families' histories for sharing. A great deal of talk ensued. The artifact of greatest interest was an old glass bottle, probably dating from the Civil War. The students excitedly guessed whom the bottle might have belonged to and how it came to be buried in the

ground. I closed this sharing session by asking, "Has anyone read *Homeplace* by Crescent Dragonwagon, which was written in 1993? It's a story about a family who discovers several artifacts buried in the ground and imagines to whom the items might have belonged. You'll find a copy of it in the library corner."

In addition to *Homeplace,* the children found many other books in the library corner dealing with the topic of immigration. During the class's reading workshop, the children read books they chose from among the ones in that corner. As always, I conferred with the children, discussing their selections, learning what they had learned, and listening to them read selections they chose. The children also gathered in literature circles to discuss their books with other students. In addition, they raised questions, copied quotes they particularly liked, wrote drafts of letters to authors, and wrote drafts of letters to peers recommending their book (regular reading-response activities) in their reading-response journals.

In addition to their independent reading, my read-aloud sessions played a significant role in building the children's knowledge. I believed that the inclusion of children's literature would be crucial to the students' understanding of the immigrants' experiences. I selected books for specific purposes, all about children who had immigrated to the United States. Each time we read a story, we wrote the child's name on his or her homeland's flag, attached it to the child's homeland on a large map, marked the map indicating where the child landed in the United States, and connected the two locations with a string.

For example, I read and we discussed *Gooseberries to Oranges* (Cohen, 1982). First, however, we brainstormed a list of reasons why immigrants might choose to leave their homeland. What I thought would take five minutes took twenty minutes. The children had many thoughtful ideas on why people might leave their homeland. On another day, I read *Klara's New World* (Winter, 1992). The children commented on the similarities and differences between these two

(continued)

stories. To visualize the commonalities and differences, we created interconnecting circles, much like a Venn diagram.

I planned to have the children use learning logs to record their findings during our study. To illustrate how historians record their findings, I showed a slide of immigrants arriving on Ellis Island (photos, still and video, are important primary sources) and modeled how historians record their findings. I looked carefully at the slide. "What did this picture tell me about these immigrants?" I asked. I voiced some of my findings. I provided justification for each finding. I asked for the children's help. Together, we constructed a list of findings from this one slide, and I recorded our findings on the board. Then it was their turn. Over the remainder of our study, as we carefully considered the information in slides, in print, and in oral forms, we recorded our findings in our logs. Always, as the students wrote in their logs, I circulated about the classroom, speaking with them about their findings and learning much about their developing understandings of immigration.

By chance, there was a piece on the evening news about people immigrating from Mexico into the United States. Our focus to this point had been immigrants of the past; this news clip connected our study to the present day. As homework, the children were directed to skim newspapers and to watch the evening news broadcasts for information on immigration. (I brought copies of newspapers for those children who did not have access to them at home; none of my students lacked access to television.) Copies of the newspaper articles and notes taken while observing the news broadcasts were mounted on a classroom bulletin board. These became the topic of our morning current-events discussions. These articles and broadcasts verified that the items on our brainstormed list of reasons people immigrated to the United States in the past were equally relevant today. We decided that this discovery was important to record in our learning logs.

One child observed that it seemed as though when people immigrate, they do not bring much with them. "What would you choose to bring with you?" I asked. I brought a trunk to school the size of the trunks used by nineteenth-century immigrants. "If you could only bring what would fit in a trunk this size, what would you bring and why?" I asked. In groups, the children considered the possibilities. All groups concluded that money was important—even if it was not the currency of the new country—because any currency could be exchanged for appropriate currency. Perhaps stimulated by some of the family artifacts they had seen, the groups thought it would be important to bring things to remind them of their homeland and family (e.g., photographs, special gifts, favorite toys—small ones, of course). Also, they thought they would need food. One group thought that carrots would be a good idea; the thinking was that because no one likes them very much, they would not have to worry about their being stolen.

As the number of pieces of strings on our classroom map grew, the children's conversations around the map naturally turned to "My Pop-Pop immigrated [they liked to use that word, *immigrated*] from Sweden, just like Klara." Children made mental and written notes to check on their families' heritages. The children suggested making flags with their names on them and attaching the flags to the map to denote their own families' original homelands. Soon, conversations around the map indicated that the children were noting the many different original homelands represented by the children in the class: Puerto Rico, someplace in Africa, Poland, Croatia, Ireland, England, and many more.

I had wanted to introduce the children to the conditions that early African immigrants (i.e., unwilling immigrants) faced when they were brutally forced to come to this country. The children's interest in their families' countries of origin provided a reason for this discussion. I read excerpts from *Days of Slavery* (Kallen, 1990); *The Story of the Henrietta Marie* (Sullivan, 1994), showing the photographs of the actual shackles from the sunken slave ship; and Alex Haley's *Roots* (1974), the section describing the conditions of the slave ship that brought Kunta to America. Many of the students' recordings in their learning logs indicated their genuine concern regarding the conditions on the slave ships.

A colleague's middle-school students had been studying the slave experience. The day following our examination of the evidence of the conditions of the slave ships, three of her students came to our class to make brief speeches summarizing their research on life in the United States for the African Americans who were sold into slavery and how people such as Harriet Beecher Stowe helped some slaves escape to freedom. We ended this session with the reading of *Nettie's Trip South* (Turner, 1987), an excellent story told from the point of view of a ten-year-old girl, and the singing of "Follow the Drinking Gourd" (Winter, 1988), an African American freedom trail song. (The drinking gourd is the Big Dipper, which points the direction northward at night.) Again, the children's learning logs indicated their concern with the plight of the early African immigrants. Throughout the unit, I continually reinforced the connection between the immigrant experience and the slave experience so the children would understand that both groups contributed to the hopes and dreams that have built the United States.

One reason that people have immigrated to this country has been to worship their god or gods as they pleased. (We had noted this reason on our early brainstorming list, an indication that the children recalled our Thanksgiving-time discussion of why the Pilgrims came to America.) I decided to reread *Molly's Pilgrim* (Cohen, 1983), a book the children had enjoyed in November. Before reading the story, I wrote the Yiddish words used in the story on the board: *malkeleh, shaynkeit, paskudnyaks*. As I pronounced them, Zoe proudly told the class what they meant. As I read the book, we stopped often to discuss such points as why Molly's English was not perfect, why the other children teased Molly and how that must have made Molly feel, who the Cossacks

were, why Molly's family left Russia, what her class learned from Molly's doll, and Molly's definition of *Pilgrim*. I ended the presentation by indicating that we were going to make our own immigrant dolls to symbolize all the different people who came to live in the United States. Each student would select a different country and a specific person to research to understand how people in that country dressed when this immigrant came to the United States. They would use this information to dress their immigrant dolls. They would complete an immigration identification card for their dolls, with details such as the name of the immigrant, how old the immigrant was, the country of origin, the year of arrival, the reason(s) for immigrating, the conditions during their immigration journey, and the challenges faced when living in the United States. Finally, the students would use their research to write a piece that would tell their peers about their immigrant's journey. I closed the session with, "Think about the country of your choice overnight."

The next day, I posted a sign-up sheet for the students to note their selected countries. I provided sheets of poster board with the outline of a child traced on each board; various kinds of materials gathered from every neighbor of mine who sewed or knitted, to use for clothing and hair; informational books; an encyclopedia on CD-ROM; passes for trips to the library; and the children were off. Of course, I conferred, guided, formed discussion groups to resolve common problems or to consider clothing-customs discoveries made by children working on immigrants from similar parts of the world, negotiated material selections, conferred with writers, listened in on peer writing conferences, did minilessons addressing the needs I observed in the children's writing and researching, and so forth. The draft of one child's piece is presented in Figure 9.2.

Our culminating experience for the unit was to take a bus trip to Ellis Island. Although everything we had studied and learned was in preparation for this trip, I wanted to review the use of photographs as primary historical sources.

(continued)

SPECIAL FEATURE 9.2 Continued

I marked three photographs in each of several different books (*Ellis Island: New Hope in a New Land* by W. J. Jacobs [1990], *Ellis Island: Echoes from a Nation's Past* edited by S. Jonas [1989], *Ellis Island: A Pictorial History* by B. Benton [1985], *Keepers of the Gate: A History of Ellis Island* by T. M. Pitkin [1925]), divided the children into eight groups, and gave each group three overhead transparencies. The children were to work cooperatively as historians, examining the photographs and recording their findings about the immigrants pictured on the overhead transparencies. The transparencies would be used to present their discoveries to the class the next day.

①
X "Pack up!" "Where going to America
X Julia your only aloud to bring one
X doll. "Oh no!" said Julia "Which one
X do I bring?" "Bring Stacey," said nana
X Mana why are we going to America?
X "Because we are in the middle of a
X war sweety and we don't want to get
X hurt." "Oh. It was 1930 in
X the middle of world war 2. Very
X dangerous. "Paul" A bullet just broke
X the window. Julia started crying.

②
X Its o.k. sweety. It's just the war. Julia
X is only 4. "Oh!" "let's go!" Run!
X oh! oh! oh! oh! oh! oh! Then we're
X on the boat. It was very crowded on
X the boat, but I held my moms hand
X as tight as possible. I got sick on
X the 3rd day but I got better before
X anyone noticed. It wasn't very fun
X on the boat, but I had my doll on
X the boat. Stacey my doll was very
X scared also. My mom was with

③
X me. We only ate a little. The food
X that the people gave us was stale.
X I threw up because of it. After we
X ate we went to see the water on the
X top of the boat. The water was on
X rough it looked like a snake shaking
X like crazy. I thought it was real
X neat. Finally they got to Ellis
X Island safe and sound. We were
X in a big line for something. When
X It was my turn and my moms

④
X said "Go ahead. Then we went
to an intelligent test they
X said we were brilliant so we went on
suddenly we heard someone say Julia
X It was my dad!! He told us everything
X that happend to him on his
X way to America too
X When we got home. I was very
X shocked! It was a beautiful
X wooden house much better than
X our house. It was 12:00 A.M.
X My dad said to get to sleep

⑤
X because. I had school tomorrow.
X I loved my house in America!
x Home Sweet Home I said.

The End

FIGURE 9.2   The Story of Julia's Coming to America

As groups finished their observations and writing, they practiced their presentations. The children worked one day longer than I thought they would, carefully considering the information they gathered from the photographs, writing their sentences, and practicing their presentations.

One day later, the groups made their presentations. Photographs were shown; observations were read and justified. After each group's presentation, the class participated in an oral evaluation of their presentation, answering questions such as "What did this group do well?" and "What might they do better next time?" Generally, the presentations were marvelous. (Figure 9.3 shows the information one group presented on its overhead transparencies.)

Because we would be seeing the Statue of Liberty, we needed to learn something about it before we boarded the buses. I began by asking the children what they already knew about the Statue of Liberty. I listed the few known points on the board. I read *The Story of the Statue of Liberty* by Betsey and Guilio Maestro (1986). "Would the Statue of Liberty fit in this classroom?" I asked. Showing the students a meter stick, I asked the students to estimate the height of the Statue of Liberty in meters. I recorded their estimates on the board. Then I told them that the statue is one hundred meters tall. "How tall is that?" I asked. Although guesses were offered, the students seemed very unsure. We would measure the Statue of Liberty to exact scale on the grass outside the school building. I divided the class into four groups and made each group responsible for laying out a section of the statue (e.g., one group would mark the distance from the statue's chin to the top of the flame, another the distance from the statue's waist to its chin). I gave each group a container of Popsicle sticks. They were to place their meter stick on a beginning line and insert the Popsicle stick into the ground at the end of the meter stick. Then they would butt the meter stick to the Popsicle stick and place a second Popsicle stick at the end of the meter stick. The process would be repeated until they had reached the top of their section. Then the

group cut a piece of twine exactly as long as from their beginning line to their last Popsicle stick. When all groups had completed their tasks, we carefully laid the four pieces of twine end to end. The students exclaimed, "Wow! That's how big the Statue of Liberty is!" and "It looks as big as two eighteen-wheelers!!"

Fortunately, I had enlisted the assistance of several middle school students to help with our measuring. This hands-on measurement activity was meaningful to the children, but they definitely needed helpers. The next day, I used the middle school students' participation to teach the students about the social convention of writing a thank-you note when someone does something that pleases you. We talked about what might be included in a thank-you note. Interested students wrote thank-you notes.

Before leaving the unit, I wanted to pull the discussion back to our classroom and the twenty-four people who lived in it. During a read-aloud session, I read *Make a Wish, Molly* (Cohen, 1995). We live in a pluralistic culture in our society and in our classroom. We talked about what that meant. We also talked about several metaphors that describe our pluralistic culture: salad bowl, melting pot, and patchwork quilt. We decided that our classroom was a patchwork quilt. Our class was composed of different students with different backgrounds. We decided to make a patchwork quilt to symbolize our cohesiveness. Alone, each square would be lovely, together, all the squares would be a wonderful illustration of how we work together, just like how the immigrants had to work together to make our country.

The children decorated their squares with symbols telling about themselves and their heritage. Once the squares were sewn together, we proudly displayed the quilt in our classroom.

At the end of May, we boarded the buses for the long ride to Ellis Island and the Statue of Liberty. Throughout this unit of study, my students read, wrote, listened, talked, and observed. The materials in the classroom and in the school's

(continued)

SPECIAL FEATURE 9.2 Continued

library supported their investigations. Although the classroom schedule suggested reading workshop, writing workshop, social studies, and so forth, from the children's perspective, the day was seamless. Our investigation of immigration flowed across and was embedded within the various curriculum content areas. Although I had outlined goals and objectives for this interdisciplinary unit, the students' questions and observations guided our study as we learned together about the dreams and hopes that have built the United States.

1st picture.   ELLIS ILAND

1. The first thing we noticed was that you can not fit another person on the ship

2. Next we saw that most women are wearing scarfs on their heads.

3. Most of the men are wearing top hats or some sort of hat on his head, because of his religion.

4. We also noticed that the ship was huge! (As you can see.)

5. You know, if I were on that ship I would be so confused!!. (Just think how they feel.)

2nd picture.

1. The thing we really noticed most about this picture was that there is a huge American Flag on top of the front wall.

2. The Immigrants are waiting on benches or standing in long lines inside the railings

3. We also noticed that the ceiling is large and round, like a dome.

4. These are lots of huge windows.

FIGURE 9.3 Using Photographs to Gather Information about the Past

Using Reading and Writing for Learning: Grade 6

In this section, readers will observe how Mr. Sousa organizes and conducts his reading program with his sixth-grade students. We again encourage readers to make text-to-text connections between this description of the teaching of reading to upper elementary students with the previous descriptions of the teaching of reading to first-grade and third-grade students. How does student age affect the teacher's teaching? How does the upper-grade experience reflect the blended practices presented in Figure 9.1?

Mr. Sousa is part of a sixth-grade team that organizes the students' day into two major parts: the humanities class, which teaches the Arizona State social studies, and language arts standards, which are taught through careful curriculum integration (Figure 9.4) and the math–science inquiry lab. During the two-hour humanities block, Mr. Sousa teaches reading, writing, and oral communication skills by using social studies as the vehicle for this content. He has found this approach to be highly effective and efficient because it makes the best use of the limited time he has available to teach the course objectives for all these subjects.

He teaches this content to two sets of students: one class of thirty students in the morning and one class in the afternoon. On Monday and Tuesdays, he uses his time for text study and independent related reading. On Wednesdays and Thursdays, he uses his time for writers' workshop and research writing, and on Fridays, he uses his time for multiple assessment and group project work. He shares the students with Ms. Selina, who teaches the math and science content also using two 2-hour daily time blocks. The students come from predominately lower-socioeconomic homes, and, for many, English is their second language. The students' reading levels range from a third-grade to a ninth-grade level. The students are heterogeneously grouped overall, but both teachers often group homogeneously to teach specific skills.

Typical Monday and Tuesday Schedule

8:15–8:30.   Attendance, lunch count, settling in.

PEARSON
myeducationkit™

Go to the Assignments and Activities section of Chapter 9 in the MyEducationKit and complete the activity entitled "Reading for Information." As you watch the video and answer the accompanying questions, note how the teacher uses specific strategies to help students use reading to learn new information.

8:30–8:45.   During the last two weeks, the students read the sixth-grade social studies text, which provided a basic foundation for the study of early civilizations. Mr. Sousa begins each day with a focused minilesson or a minilesson review. Today, during this time, he reviews the use of a graphic organizer to help the students structure and summarize the information presented in the text (Figure 9.5). He also shows them how the graphic organizer helps them compare and contrast the different components of information.

8:45–9:00.   Independent reading. Because of the students' different reading levels and competency in speaking and reading English, Mr. Sousa found that they focus better on the social studies text when he organized their independent reading time into fifteen-minute segments. During this fifteen-minute segment, he asks the students to use their Post-it Notes to identify unknown vocabulary words.

9:00–9:15.   After a few minutes of finalizing their Post-it Notes, Mr. Sousa asks the students to share their vocabulary words. He writes their words on large word cards and asks all students to provide definitions. In most cases, someone in the class will offer an appropriate definition. Mr. Sousa gives the student who offers the correct definition the word card; that student gets to put the definition on the card and then sign his or her name. (To encourage the students to identify unknown vocabulary, Mr. Sousa gives the students extra credit points for each word card.) If the class cannot offer a definition, then Mr. Sousa

FIGURE 9.4   Sixth-Grade Language Arts–Social Studies Curriculum Map: First Quarter

Student Skills	Teacher Methodology	Social Studies Content
Reading *Decode new words in print* Decoding multisyllable words (Prefix, suffix, root word, dividing in syllables, and context clues) *Use comprehension skills* Vocabulary development Self-monitoring strategies Individual comprehension strategies ■ Visualizing ■ Summarizing ■ Predicting ■ Questioning to check for understanding ■ Questioning to clarify ■ Identifying big ideas and themes ■ Making text-to-text connections ■ Making text-to-self connections ■ Making text-to-world connections ■ Identify the main idea ■ Cause and effect ■ Description ■ Compare and contrast ■ Use of charts, graphs, sidebars, and structure (mainly with expository text) ■ Mapping (graphic organizers)	■ Reciprocal teaching ■ Independent reading ■ Guided reading (teacher directed) ■ Shared reading (partners) ■ Paired reading ■ Read-alouds ■ Rereading ■ Literature circles (substantive discussion) ■ Whole group (substantive discussion) ■ Guess the covered word ■ Graphic organizers ■ Response journals ■ Active reading activity (Post-it Notes)	**Social Studies** *Comparing early civilizations* ■ Aztec ■ Egyptian ■ Roman ■ Greek ■ Inca ■ Chinese ■ Informational texts How did early civilizations develop: ■ Architecture ■ Agriculture ■ Domesticate animals ■ Transportation What innovations and inventions did these civilizations develop? What religion did these civilizations practice? What supported these civilizations' economic systems? ■ Money ■ Trade Did these civilizations have a form of writing?

FIGURE 9.4   Continued

Student Skills	Teacher Methodology	Social Studies Content
Writing *Grammar* <ul><li>Adverbs (develop)</li><li>Conjunctions (developing)</li><li>Prepositions (developing)</li><li>Pronoun agreement (developing)</li><li>Quotations (developing)</li></ul> <ul><li>Generate, draft, revise, edit, publish different forms of written expression<ul><li>Fiction</li><li>Research papers/ reports</li><li>Comparative/contrast</li><li>Paragraph writing (topic sentence, supporting details & concluding sentence)</li><li>Short stories (Project Read Story form)/ Narrative</li><li>Book reviews</li></ul></li></ul> *Oral Presentation*<ul><li>Organize, sequence, practice, and deliver an oral presentation on the social studies project incorporating the skills of voice, projection, inflection, fluency and appropriate nonverbal language.</li><li>Use courtesy and consideration in communication situations.</li></ul>	*Grammar*<ul><li>Language book</li><li>Teacher created activities</li><li>District grammar book</li></ul> *Writing*<ul><li>Writer's Workshop (writer's process)<ul><li>Brainstorm</li><li>Graphic organizer</li><li>First draft</li><li>Conference (teacher & peer)</li><li>Revise</li><li>Second draft</li><li>Edit)</li></ul></li><li>Journal writing</li><li>Modeling</li><li>Minilessons</li></ul>	*Writing*<ul><li>Social studies project and research paper</li></ul> *Spelling* Content vocabulary will be added to spelling lists <ul><li>Social Studies presentations</li></ul>

uses the dictionary to find the definition. He reads the various definitions, and the students select the most appropriate response. Mr. Sousa believes that this extra effort to build vocabulary has had a positive effect on the students' oral language and reading comprehension. He also uses these words to build the unit spelling list.

9:15–9:30.   Mr. Sousa asks the students to work in pairs to complete the components of the graphic organizer (see Figure 9.5). While they do so, he circulates among the students, occasionally redirecting student behavior. For the most part, however, he offers vocabulary and language support to various students. Mr. Sousa has discovered that when the students know that they will be discussing their reading, they pay more attention to the text. For the students who are less confident in reading and English, the opportunity to talk helps them comprehend the text.

9:30–9:45.   Once again, Mr. Sousa redirects his students to the text. Once again, they use their Post-it Notes, but this time he has directed them to focus on the question, What innovations and inventions did the Egyptian culture develop? Mr. Sousa believes that by guiding their reading through the use of focus questions, he helps them learn to take notes, which also provides a basis for small group discussion. As the students read, Mr. Sousa monitors their behavior and offers decoding help where needed.

9:45–10:00.   Mr. Sousa asks the students to complete their graphic organizer for the Egyptian section. He encourages the students to work in pairs and to compare their answers. As the students work, he circulates to make sure that they are staying focused on the task at hand. After a few minutes, he draws the class's attention to the large graphic organizer chart he has placed on the wall. The class shares their responses as Mr. Sousa writes the information in the appropriate squares.

10:00–10:30.   Related independent reading time. The students have already determined which civilization they wish to study. They have already gone to the library and/or downloaded information from the Web to study their civilization further. Some students are reading

FIGURE 9.5   Graphic Organizer

Civilization	Where Located	Time Frame of Civilization	Type of Government	Innovations and Inventions	Religious Beliefs and Practices
Aztec					
Roman					
Greek					
Inca					
Chinese					
Egyptian					

historical fiction, others are reviewing expository texts. Each group of five or six students meets together to briefly review what they are reading and to read further. The students use an independent reading guide (Figure 9.6) to help them document and guide their reading.

During this time, Mr. Sousa monitors the groups briefly to make sure that the students are focused on their task. After the students begin reading, Mr. Sousa calls one or two students back to conduct a running record. His goal is to conduct a running record on each student every month. Although it is a daunting task, Mr. Sousa believes that it helps him guide his students to select appropriate difficulty-level texts and also helps him determine the content of the focus lessons he may conduct.

By 10:30, the students need to pack up their materials and go to other classes. The independent reading text and the reading guide go into their backpacks. Their reading guides are reviewed by Mr. Sousa and their peers each Friday. Independent reading at home is expected.

Typical Wednesday and Thursday Schedule

8:15–8:30. Attendance, lunch count, settling in.

8:30–9:00. The civilization groups begin to meet to review their research projects. Each person in the group is responsible for one of the following topics:

1. What innovations and inventions did this civilization develop?
2. What religion did this civilization practice?
3. What supported this civilization's economic system?
4. Did this civilization have a form of schooling, writing, numbers?
5. What was life like for a commoner in this civilization?

FIGURE 9.6   Independent Reading Guide

Name_____ **Date**_____

I'm reading

Text Title	Author	Publication Date
What pages have you read? Identifying big ideas and themes.		
What text-to-text connections can you make?		
What text-to-self connections can you make?		
What text-to-world connections can you make?		
What vocabulary do you need help with?		

The students have been collecting information about these subjects. They have gone to the school library, have conducted searches in the school's computer lab, and have visited the public library, where they checked out materials (including some DVDs and videos) about the topic. During this half hour, Mr. Sousa has given them the task of sharing the materials and information they have collected. The student groups buzz (somewhat loudly) as they share the information they have collected. Across the room, Mr. Sousa hears "I read that, too!" or "I found something that you could use." One group approaches Mr. Sousa to see if they can't schedule a DVD player to review a program together.

9:00–9:30.   Mr. Sousa reviews the parts of a research paper (Figure 9.7). To help the students learn about the parts of the paper, he has given them a copy of an excellent research paper that was written last year. He reviews the components of the paper step by step. The students are somewhat overwhelmed by the total research paper, but he reminds them to "take one step at a time."

9:30–10:00.   After reviewing the parts, Mr. Sousa returns to paragraph writing. He puts a good example of a paragraph on the overhead projector. He highlights the parts of the paragraph (topic sentence, supporting details, and concluding sentence) in different colors. Next, he gives the students a worksheet that has three different paragraphs. He asks them to identify the topic sentences in each paragraph. As the group moves to identifying supporting detail sentences, they realize that the second paragraph is very weak. Mr. Sousa asks the students to work in pairs to write supporting details. Within a few minutes, the students offer examples of supporting detail sentences. Finally, Mr. Sousa talks about the importance of a concluding sentence. The students once again find that one of the examples is very weak, and he asks them to rewrite the sentence and share with a partner.

10:00–10:30.   Mr. Sousa asks the students to begin to draft the first part of their reports, using their outlines that they developed last week. He reminds the students that they are in the first draft mode. He encourages them to get their ideas on paper and reminds them that tomorrow they will have time to work with a peer editor.

FIGURE 9.7   Parts of a Research Paper

- Title page
- List of figures
- Abstract
- Outline
- Body of the report
  - An introduction
  - Background information
  - Body of the paper
  - A conclusion
- Appendices
- Works cited

Typical Friday Schedule

8:15–8:30.   Attendance, lunch count, settling in.

8:30–9:00.   Spelling assessment and vocabulary matching. The words were selected by the students (see Monday–Tuesday schedule). Students complete the test, grade each other's work, and turn the papers in to Mr. Sousa.

9:00–10:30.   On Fridays, Mr. Sousa conducts writing conferences and running records as needed. The students sign up for ten-minute blocks of time. The remainder of the time the students work to complete the first drafts of each segment of their research report.

At the beginning of the semester, Mr. Sousa had difficulty managing student behavior during Friday work sessions, yet he continued to persist in his work expectations. Likewise, he also assigned lunch detention for students who misbehaved during this time. Within a month, nearly all the behavior challenges had faded.

Family Focus: Newsletters

In Chapter 4's Family Focus, we discussed the importance of communicating with parents. Though teachers are the primary source of classroom information for younger children, older students can begin to use their newly developed writing skills to communicate with their families. Trade Secret 9.1 shares third-grade teacher Mrs. Foley's approach to having each member of her class send home a weekly update about their learning.

TRADE SECRET 9.1
Student Notes

BY DAWN FOLEY

As a third-grade teacher, I have found another way that children can communicate about what they are learning in school with their parents: a personal weekly summary letter called a "note." For example, in Figure 9.8, Abby describes her view of things that she has learned during the week, ranging from the concept of probability in math to the literature she is reading. The letter is written in a form that leaves space for the teacher to make comments also. In this case, I commented on the fact that Abby won first place in our Academic Fair Project.

(continued)

TRADE SECRET 9.1 Continued

Fantastic Week!!

Dear Mom & Dad,

This week in March we did probability. We took a couple of time tests too. Also we learned about counting change. It was fun.

In reading we red Mrs. Piggie Wiggie. We read a few. They were called Mrs. Piggie Wiggie and the radish cure, Mrs. Piggie Wiggie and the selfishness cure, Mrs. Piggie Wiggie and the tiny bitetaker. They were really good books.

I can't wait till we get to make T-shirts . This was so fun!!! Do you think we'll do that in fourth grade? I hope so.

It was fun wearing P.J.'s to school.

We have a mistery and we've trying to find out who is the mistery guest is? We have a few clues. I don't remember what the clues are but I think it might be Mrs. Gayhart. But I'm not quite sure. I have a mother day gift for you but I'm not telling what it is.

Love,
Abby

> I am so proud of you and your Academic Fair Project!! WOW, WAY TO GO Abby 1st Place!!! Yeah!!!

FIGURE 9.8   Abby's Note to Her Parents

Strategies for Teaching English Language Learners

Developing Academic Reading for English Language Learners

LUISA ARAÚJO

As discussed in Chapter 4, ELL children need time to develop academic language (cognitive academic language proficiency, or CALP), even if they seem to make rapid progress in mastering conversational

English (basic interpersonal communicative skills, or BICS). This presents a challenge for regular classroom teachers who teach mainstream classes in the middle grades where there is more emphasis on learning academic concepts in the content areas.

We have seen how, in the beginning stages of learning to read, young ELLs can make rapid progress because the language requirements are very basic. As Claude Goldenberg (2008) states, "when the focus is on sounds, letters, and how they combine to form words that can be read, English learners can make progress in English that is comparable to that of English speakers, provided the instructions are clear, focused, and systematic" (p. 22). As children progress through the elementary grades, however, the complexity of language arts and of academic concepts increases and children need to develop domain knowledge in specific subjects.

To facilitate subject-matter learning, ESL teachers integrate the teaching of academic content with language instruction (Echevarria & Graves, 2003). In some school settings with a large ELL population, *sheltered content instruction* classes composed of ELL children may be used to "teach academic subject matter to English-language learners using comprehensible language and context, enabling information to be understood by the learner" (Echevarria & Graves, 2003, p. 8). Certified subject area teachers, with ESL training, are the best equipped to deliver instruction according to the sheltered instruction model. Their goal is to teach the core grade-level curriculum in a way that students can understand. For example, subject area learning can be facilitated by helping ELL students

to understand by modifying texts so that simpler and shorter sentences are used. Echevarria and Graves (2003) give an account of this practice: "The original directions said, 'once you have read the passage below, determine what the author is trying to express. Mark the keys words and the most important points.' The directions can be rewritten to say 'Read this paragraph. Underline one main idea. Circle three key words'" (p. 136); and "the number of science terms on a study sheet can be reduced or the assignment's due date can be extended" (p. 142). Using concise and simply worded study sheets, with repeated information and the same format for all units, will also help students master the information presented. These modifications maximize ELLs' comprehension of text that would otherwise be too difficult for them to understand.

The inability to understand what one reads precludes any real learning occurring in the classroom. However, it can also be the case that ELL students comprehend what they read, but have difficulties demonstrating their knowledge. According to Echevarria and Graves (2003), "Written expression is a common method used to assess subject matter knowledge. However, written expression is often problematic for students who are ELLs" (p. 81). Thus, they recommend the use of alternative ways of allowing students to demonstrate knowledge. For example, teachers can "let them speak into a tape recorder, to a peer, or to the teacher. Students can work in pairs to complete written assignments or can express their ideas in graphic or pictorial form rather than in words alone" (p. 81).

Strategies for Children with Special Needs

A specific learning disability is defined as "a severe learning problem due to a disorder in one or more of the basic psychological processes involved in acquiring, organizing, or expressing information that manifests itself in school as an impaired ability to listen, reason, speak, read, write, spell, or do mathematical calculations, despite appropriate instruction in the general education curriculum" (PI 11.36(6), Wis.

Admin. Code). In a special report published by the Center for the Improvement of Early Reading Achievement, Joanne Carlisle (2001) points out that about 5 percent of children in the elementary grades are identified as having a specific learning disability, and that most of these children have pronounced reading and spelling difficulties. Because of the trend toward mainstreaming, it is likely that general education

(continued)

Strategies for Children with Special Needs   Continued

teachers will have at least one child with a learning disability in their class. It is important that regular classroom teachers are able to foster these children's reading development.

Carlisle (2001, p. 5) presents a number of strategies that elementary grade teachers can use to promote the reading development of children with learning disabilities:

For word reading [decoding] instruction:

- Break down tasks
- Match the difficulty of the materials to students' skills

- Sequence short activities
- Focus children's attention on important aspects of the task

For reading comprehension instruction:

- Direct questioning
- Explain concepts and procedures fully
- Control difficulty of task demands
- Model steps and processes
- Provide cues to prompt children to use appropriate strategies
- Have children work in small groups

PEARSON
myeducationkit™

To check your comprehension on the content covered in this chapter, go to the MyEducationKit for your book and complete the Study Plan for Chapter 9. Here you will be able to take a chapter quiz and receive feedback on your answers.

Summary

Implementing a high-quality reading instructional program requires thoughtful planning, management, and organization as well as an ongoing and ever-changing understanding of student strengths, interests, and needs. For a blended approach to reading instruction like those described in this chapter to be successful, the teacher must purposefully structure a classroom environment that supports complex literacy and language communities and addresses each student's instructional needs. High-quality blended reading programs include all the features identified in Figure 9.1, carefully organized so that the teacher looks more like an orchestra conductor.

- *What organizational strategies do teachers use to implement a blended reading program?*

Teachers thoughtfully organize large blocks of time to begin to organize their teaching of reading. Teachers need to develop weekly schedules that consistently structure time for independent reading; whole-group, small group, and individual instruction; and community sharing. Teachers must also offer a number of procedural lessons that help students learn to be contributing members of the classroom learning community.

- *What types of grouping strategies are used in a blended reading program?*

Teachers who use the blended approach to reading instruction usually use both homogeneous (students with similar needs and abilities) and heterogeneous (students with different skills and abilities) grouping strategies. Teachers may also use whole-group or small group instruction, or provide individual instruction, depending on the needs of the students and the content that needs to be taught.

■ *How do teachers provide skill instruction in a blended reading program?*

Teachers usually deliver skill instruction through lessons. These lessons evolve from readers' immediate needs and concerns, or they may be based on teacher choice or district goals and objectives. There are two broad categories of lessons, including procedures for managing the instructional time, and how to choose interesting books, and how to select just-right books, or skill lessons, such as what students can do when they meet an unknown word or how to determine the main idea.

■ *How do teachers help students construct meaning and expand their understanding of text?*

High-quality reading instruction provides limitless possibilities for observant teachers to extend children's understanding of text. It can be accomplished during all components of a blended reading program: one-on-one teacher conferences, small group instruction, and whole-group instruction.

LINKING KNOWLEDGE TO PRACTICE

1. Interview a teacher about grouping practices for reading instruction. How does this teacher determine his or her students' reading abilities? Does this teacher use a running record to evaluate a student's independent and instructional reading levels? How often does the teacher assess student progress? How does the teacher use these data to create groups?

2. Visit a classroom during the time designated for reading instruction. Take field notes like those gathered by Sara McCraw. Compare your notes with those taken by Sara. Did the students engage in independent reading? Did the teacher hold individual conferences with the students? Were small groups of students pulled together for instruction based on their skill needs? In what ways did the teacher differentiate instruction? What conclusions can be reached about the observed teacher's teaching of reading? Are these students being offered a blended reading program?

3. Observe a classroom during the teaching of social studies or science. What reading, writing, and speaking skills has the teacher integrated into the social studies or science lesson?

CHAPTER
10 Creating Writers: Teaching Children to Write Well

Writing and writers are important in Deirdra Aikens's classroom. Ms. Aikens invites her students to join her on the rug for a writing lesson. She begins by saying, "I know you've been waiting for this! I'm going to reveal the next great beginning. Ta-dah!!" She uncovers the next statement on the Great Beginnings chart and reads: "It was a deep, dark, snowy Christmas Eve and presents were under the tree."

Referring to the example, she asks, "Where do you see it happening?" The students respond. "What could come after that?" Again, the students respond. She continues: "I've pulled together some beginnings from three of our favorite books. I really like how these authors started their pieces by setting the mood and creating an image of the setting. I'll read each beginning. You tell me where you see the story happening and how it feels."

Next, she reads the opening sentence of Tar Beach *by Faith Ringgold. "What did you see when you heard this sentence?" she asks. The students offer responses about the image the sentence created in their minds. Ms. Aikens accepts their answers and then shows the illustration that accompanies the sentence. "Was the picture in your head like the image created by the illustrator?" She moves on and repeats the process with the two other stories. "This is a different kind of beginning, isn't it? It's different from the other beginnings on our list. When you go back to your writing folders today, take a look at an old piece. Could using this kind of beginning make one of your old pieces better? If you start a new piece, think about using this kind of a beginning. Will this beginning work in all pieces?" The students answer "No!" in unison. "Of course not!" Ms. Aikens says. "You've got to think like a writer and make decisions about which kind of beginning to use. Team leaders, please get the writing folders out. Green folder writers, let's do a quick status of the class." Ms. Aikens calls on each green folder writer, gets a response ("start a new piece," "edit my piece"), and sends the writers off to write. The writing lesson is over.*

Writers return to their desks, where their writing folders have been placed. Some sit down, others move to be near a friend. One student selects the sharing chair as her writing place. In less than two minutes, all writers are writing. Students talk with each other while they write. Ms. Aikens begins a conference with a red folder writer; Monday is red folder writers' teacher–student conference day. Too quickly, the writing time ends and the students return their bulging folders by color group to the hanging file, all except the blue folder writers.

Blue folder writers share today. A blue folder writer sits in the sharing chair. His team leader stands beside him. The writer reads his piece. The team leader calls on a student to summarize. A student responds, and then several students and Ms. Aikens offer their comments. The team leader calls on another student to praise the author. The student responds, and then several students offer specific examples of what they like about the piece. The team leader calls on another student to question the author. The student responds, and then other students and Ms. Aikens state their questions. The team leader calls on a student to offer a suggestion. This student responds, and then another student offers a suggestion. Writing workshop is over.

This is how the teaching of writing happens in Ms. Aikens's classroom every day for forty-five minutes. Like many other teachers, Ms. Aikens calls this time "writing workshop." During writing workshop, the students use the writing process, the same process used by young and old writers. Some are prewriting. Some are looking off into space to discover what they know enough about to write about. Some immediately begin writing; they seem not to know what they have to say until they see the words appear on the paper. Some look at the list of topics they made for days like this one, days when they need an idea on what to write about. Others are making a graphic organizer or a list. Other students are writing their "sloppy copy" or first draft. While they write, they pause to read and reread what they wrote. Still other students cross out words; they draw arrows to shift the position of sentences. These students are revising. They change the spelling of a word. These students are editing. Finally, other students are recopying their revised and edited piece; they are publishing or doing their final draft. These students are using the writing process to write their ideas. This teacher has provided a structure within which she can create writers. These students know what it means to be a writer.

Before Reading This Chapter, Think About . . .

- Yourself as a writer. How do you prewrite? Do you make an outline or a graphic organizer, mull your thoughts over in your mind for several days, or just begin writing? Do you have a favorite writing tool, such as a special pen or the computer? Do you make lots of revisions while you write? Do you edit while you write?
- Writing instruction in your elementary school years. Did you write about topics of your choice? Did you share your writing with your peers? Did your teacher confer with you about your writing? Did you publish your writing?
- The kinds of writing you did in your elementary school years. Did you write stories? Did you write research reports? Did you write persuasive essays?
- How your writing was graded. Did your teacher write congratulatory words like "Good job!" or use a rubric to give you specific feedback about how effectively you used various writing traits? Did your teacher put a grade on your paper? Did your teacher encourage you to self-assess your writing?

Focus Questions

- What are the key structural features of a classroom where writing is taught and children write?
- What are the components of writing workshop?

BOX **10.1**

Definition of Terms

conference: conversation between a teacher and a student, or between or among peers, about a piece of writing.

editing: correcting mechanical errors in writing, such as spelling, punctuation, and grammar.

focus lesson: whole-class lessons on writing that typically occur at the beginning of writing workshop.

revising: making changes (adding, moving, deleting) in the content of a writing piece.

traits: qualities of writing (ideas, organization, voice).

writing process: recursive behaviors that all writers, regardless of age, engage in (prewriting, writing or drafting, revising, editing, final draft or publishing).

writing workshop: time in the schedule when all students meet to study the art and craft of writing.

- How do teachers explicitly teach writing and what kinds of lessons might they teach?
- What is the structure of a writing conference?
- How might teachers connect home and school in their teaching of writing?

The Essentials of Teaching Writing

Recently, Graves (2004) reviewed the fundamentals of the teaching of writing and identified the constants that two decades of research have confirmed are central to the teaching of writing. In the following section, we describe these essential features of a quality writing program.

Children Need Time to Write

Children need a block of time to write, from forty-five to sixty minutes daily. Regular, frequent times for writing are required to help children develop as writers. When children know to expect time to write, they come to school with ideas for topics and text construction. As Katie Wood Ray (2001) explains:

> It takes lots and lots of time over the course of years for writers to get the experience they need to become good writers. Along the way, writers need time to just write and write—a lot of it won't be very good, but all of it gives writers experience When it comes to TIME, quantity is what matters. (pp. 9–10)

Children Need Regular Response to Their Writing from the Teacher, Their Peers, and Others

Writing is a social act. Through interactions with others, writers come to understand the needs of their audiences. Because writers write about things they know, they make decisions about what information to include from their knowledgeable perspective. In sharing their writing with an audience, writers sometimes come to understand what information is needed to make their topic clear to an audience, or they watch the glazed look in their listeners' eyes and realize that too much detail has been provided, or they recognize the need to rearrange the information. Children want to share their writing with peers, know what their peers are writing, and ask for assistance with the construction of their text. Furthermore, having children share their writing with each other has a positive impact on the quality of their writing (Graham & Perin, 2008). Knowing this, teachers cluster children at tables or at desks that have been moved together. Most writing and *conferring* (talking with peers about writing) occur among the children in these clusters. This talk is not just any kind of talk; it is talk about the writers' texts. Writers need listeners who stop their writing, listen intently, and say, "Oh, your description of your dog is really good" or "Your characters' talk, your dialogue? Well, it sounds just like what teenagers would say" or "Hmmm. I don't get it. I'm confused here."

Children also want, and need, to talk with their teachers about their writing. They need to talk with a teacher who listens carefully to them, who makes considered honest responses to the writer's questions and statements, who asks genuine questions, and who supports the writer to become a better writer.

Children Need to Publish Their Writings

A key element of a quality writing program—that children need to publish their writings—is closely related to the previous fundamental element. Writing is meant for others to read. Yes, we write for ourselves, but few of us would sustain our effort if no one ever read our writings, if no one ever said, "Hey, I really enjoyed reading that piece!" Publishing need not be a complicated procedure. Children can publish by mounting their writings on a specially labeled bulletin board, by printing the final draft in a format that would allow the pages to be folded into a book, by joining with other writers to create a newsletter or newspaper, by stapling pages between two sheets of construction paper, and so forth.

By writing for real audiences, children come to think of themselves as authors. Further, writing for an unknown audience, one that is not present to ask clarifying questions, results in children developing an understanding for others' point of view.

Children Need to Choose Most of the Topics They Write About

Writers write about things they know. For those just beginning to be writers, the personal narrative (or memoir, telling their own stories) is the easiest kind of writing. Children need teachers who help them see that they can write about the everyday things that happen to them. Graves (1993) suggests that teachers need to help children discover those topics for which they "have a passion for the truth" (p. 2). In Trade Secret 10.1, Christine Evans describes how she helps young writers find a topic about which they have knowledge and maybe passion.

Yet there is more to writing than writing personal narratives. Children need teachers who help them build their background knowledge about topics of their choosing and then use what they know to write fiction, informative texts, poetry, persuasive essays, op-ed pieces, and more by selecting a corner of the topic to write about. In Graves's words, children need teachers who help them "penetrate a subject . . . enabling them to understand what it means to know in an unusual way (writing *as* Joan of Arc instead of *about* Joan of Arc, for example)" (2004, p. 90).

TRADE SECRET 10.1
Getting Started: Topics That Matter

CHRISTINE EVANS

Eight-year-old Peter stands by the writing center, new writing notebook and sharpened pencil in hand, listening to some of his friends as they talk about topics for their writing. It's Friday of the first week of third grade, and Peter, not unlike many others in the class, has difficulty finding topics for his writing. Peter's other teachers assigned topics, so he didn't need to have good ideas for his writing. And, like others in the class, Peter didn't like to write.

I wanted my third-graders to be motivated about writing, but so many didn't know where to begin to find ideas for good topics. I wanted them to be eager to develop personal topics and be passionate about their writing. I wanted them to share themselves through their writing. I wanted them to talk to each other about writing. So many "wants," but where should I start? How would I teach my students to find good topics? It dawned on me that I was asking my students to do something that I didn't do: write about myself. I wrote memos to the third-grade team, letters to my son's teacher, notes to my friends at Christmastime, but I never wrote a piece on a topic that was important to me. So I decided it was time for me to "walk the talk." That year I began to keep a writer's notebook.

Each year, writing workshop in my class begins with me sharing my notebook. I show my students the wonderings, reflections, quotes, and lists that fill its pages. I explain to my students that my notebook is the place where I write down, sometimes quickly, funny things that happen, curious things that I wonder about, and even favorite words or sentences from books I am reading.

Students notice that my notebook is always close at hand whenever I read aloud, and they watch as I enter the colorful words or images that authors use. I explain to my students that they are the ones who decide what goes in their notebooks. I tell them that the writing bits that fill their notebook pages will later become "seed ideas" for their pieces. These notebooks will hold the beginnings of longer pieces of writing; writing that matters.

Afterward, I invite my students to eavesdrop on my thinking as I page through my notebook and evaluate different ideas for my first writing piece. I mention three possibilities. Each one I consider individually, and then I decide on one. I let students "see" how I make the decision to write about my cat, Lotus. Then I share with students an entry from my notebook. I say, "Last night, when I got home from work, Lotus ran to the hallway closet and meowed and meowed. She wouldn't stop! So, I opened the closet door and remembered that was where I kept her favorite toy. I took it out and played a game with her. Well, I couldn't believe that a cat would 'talk' and play like that, so I decided to write about it in my notebook." *Sitting in my favorite chair, I waved the bird toy in circles over Lotus's head. Lotus leaped and somersaulted trying to get the bird in her mouth. One time she landed on her back and went skidding across the rug. It made me belly laugh to see her flipping and rolling while trying to catch the bird.*

My students learn how this entry becomes the seed for my first writing of the year. Together, the students and I write, revise, and edit my Lotus piece as I teach them both the process and the crafts of writing.

TRADE SECRET 10.1 Continued

Like Peter, some of my students experience writer's block and need help gathering ideas. To help them get started, I might read a particularly thought-provoking picture book (*The Memory String* by Eve Bunting, *Charlie Anderson* by Barbara Abercrombie, *Faithful Elephants* by Yukio Tsuchiya, or *The Other Side* by Jacqueline Woodson) or a poem and have students do a "quick-write" (students write quickly and freely for about two minutes everything that the text brings to mind) in their notebooks. Because quick-writes capture what is important or interesting, students often recover from their writer's block and develop these entries into polished pieces.

By the end of the year, my third-graders have filled their notebooks with facts, descriptions, stories, poems, and responses to literature. They have learned the power of the notebook—learning to write by writing. Many of the entries will never be used for topics of their published pieces but, more importantly, students have developed the writing habit. They have learned not only to write about their world but to observe it closely.

Children Need to Hear Their Teachers Talk Through What They Are Doing as They Write

What do writers think about as they create text? How writing happens is invisible; the work happens in the writer's head. Teachers can demonstrate or model how expert writers write. As they write, they say aloud what they are thinking. With the students watching, they engage in the writing process. They select a topic that they know something about and have some passion for writing about. They talk about how they might begin their piece (e.g., "I want to begin in a way that makes readers want to read my piece. I think I'll try beginning with a question and see if that works."). They talk about making changes, *revising* their text, and why they think a different word or sentence or sentence order would be better. They fix their spelling of a word (e.g., "Oops! That doesn't look right. Let me try it again.") and check their punctuation. Teachers model writing to show how experienced writers write and solve problems as they write. In this way, writers see (and hear) what is behind the print they read on the page. They catch a glimpse of the behind-the-scenes thinking. High levels of such modeling are positively related to improvements in children's writing (Taylor, Pearson, Peterson, & Rodriguez, 2003).

PEARSON
myeducationkit™

Go to the Assignments and Activities section of Chapter 10 in the MyEducationKit and complete the activity entitled "Portfolios as Assessment Tools." As you watch the video and answer the accompanying questions, note the similarities and differences between the two teachers' use of writing portfolios in their classrooms and how each involves her students in using the portfolio as a reflection tool.

Children Need to Maintain Collections of Their Work to Create a Portrait of Their Writing History

The only way to understand children's development as writers is to study the writings they produce over a period of time. By placing the writings in chronological order and looking closely at how the writer controls the *traits* or crafts of writing (e.g., organization, development, voice, conventions), the teacher and the writer can understand the writer's development over time. Often children's writing pieces are stored in a portfolio.

By studying the pieces in each child's portfolio, pieces written for a variety of purposes and audiences, teachers can get a comprehensive picture of the child's writing ability.

To Graves's list of the fundamentals of teaching writing, we add one more.

Children Need Teachers Who Explicitly Teach Writing, Not Just Make Writing Assignments

> Teaching kids how to write is hard because writing is not so much one skill as a *bundle* of skills that includes sequencing, spelling, rereading, and supporting big ideas with examples. These skills, however, are teachable. (Fletcher & Portalupi, 2001, p. 1)

Sometimes teachers say, "Oh, my students write every day." Yes, writing every day is important, but it is not enough. Teachers need to *teach* writing every day. As Sharan Gibson (2008, p. 324) said, "[W]riters need instruction." Teaching happens in several different ways. Teachers pull the whole class together to teach. Teachers group together several children who need the same information and teach them in a small group. Teachers confer with their students and teach them one-on-one. Students confer with each other, working in small groups. The class comes together to respond to each other's writings and teach through their responses. If teachers follow Steve Graham and Dolores Perin's (2007) advice, they will teach their students:

- Strategies for planning, revising, and editing their writing pieces
- Strategies and procedures for summarizing reading material
- Purposes of their writing product (e.g., to persuade) and the characteristics (or primary traits) of this kind of writing
- How to write increasingly complex sentences
- How to gather and organize their ideas before they begin writing their piece

In the following sections, we detail what teachers do to prepare the classroom environment, how teachers use the writing workshop structure to support their students' development as writers, and how to provide explicit instruction in the characteristics or traits and process of writing. We end this chapter with suggestions on how to assess children's development as writers and ideas for connecting home and school in the teaching of writing.

Preparing the Classroom Environment

Like younger writers, students in elementary school need materials to support their writing efforts. Return to page 186 in Chapter 6 to review the list of materials needed to support our youngest writers' writing efforts. In addition to these items, elementary-aged students need the following:

- Tools for revising their writing (e.g., scissors, tape, staples, staplers, glue sticks, paper clips, gum-backed paper, Post-it Notes, highlighters)
- Writer's notebooks for recording special language heard or read that they may want to use in their writing or ideas thought of when they are not writing

- Materials for bookmaking (e.g., construction paper, wallpaper, or poster board for making book covers; colored paper in various sizes; a long-arm stapler for binding; clear plastic covers with colored plastic spines)
- Reference materials (e.g., dictionaries, thesauri, spelling books and electronic spell-checkers, style handbooks)
- Teacher-made charts to guide their writing efforts (Figure 10.1 shows several charts that hang in Deirdra Aikens's classroom writing center)

Determining how to make effective use of the classroom's computers is an even greater challenge for teachers of older students than it is for teachers of younger children. Older children's writing pieces are longer; consequently, it takes longer to compose a first draft, revise, edit, and create a final draft. Note that the children are using the computer for the *entire* writing process (drafting, revising, editing, final draft), not just as a typewriter for the final draft. Older children tend to make more changes in their writing and need computer time to make these revisions. Some teachers assign a group of students to the computers. When this group completes their writing, another group begins to use the computers. While some students write with paper and pencils, others write with the computer. Many teachers respond to their students' cries for more time at the word processor by permitting them access before school, during class meetings, during recess, and whenever else time permits. The effect is that writing begins to pervade the school day. Very fortunate teachers and writers have word processors for every student or every two students.

Return to page 188 to look again at Figure 6.2. Like their colleagues who teach younger children, some teachers of elementary-aged children also place the classroom's shared writing materials in a writing center (or area). One difference is that elementary school teachers tend not to put a table and chairs in their writing centers. Instead, they ask their students to collect the materials they need from the writing center and to use them at a table or desk. Because students are known to forget to return borrowed items to their appropriate storage places, we strongly recommend that teachers create an inventory of the shared writing materials, post the inventory in the writing center, and assign a student to the task of checking the materials in the area against the inventory following each writing workshop. Other teachers of elementary-aged students make a "tool chest" (a plastic container) of regularly needed writing supplies (pencils, pens, scissors, tape, stapler and staples, paper clips) for each grouping of desks or each table. A student at each table or cluster of desks is responsible for ensuring that the shared supplies are returned to the tool chest and returned to the writing center at the end of writing workshop.

The Structure of the Teaching of Writing:
The Components of Writing Workshop

Nancie Atwell (1987) credits Graves (1983) with helping her discover a structure that was successful with her students. Teachers across the nation (world, really) have adopted and adapted this structure. Each *writing workshop* has three components. In most classrooms, they happen in the order described here.

Be Different!

Give a

R = Restate the question

A = Answer it!

R = Reasons! Reasons!

E = Examples! Examples!

The Best Endings

1. Surprise Ending
2. Emotional Ending
3. Circular Ending
4. Express your Feelings

and the rest are covered. Ms. Aikens hasn't taught them yet

Editing #1

⬭ misspelled word

My (frend) is here.

Editing #2

add a space

#
Mycat is smart.

Editing #3

∧ add this

new
Ihave a ∧ bike.

Editing #4

∦ no capital

My scⱮool is cool.

Editing #5

≡ needs a capital

Ms. aikens is here.
     ≡

Great Beginnings!

1. Question
       "Have you ever seen a cat?"
2. Arresting Sentence
       "She stole my mom's present!"
3. Astonishing Fact
       The Sun is 93 million miles from earth.
4. Spoken Words
       "Daddy is coming home today, Ben."
5. Setting the Mood (Setting)
       It was a deep, dark, snowy Christmas.

FIGURE 10.1   Examples of Charts in Deirdra Aikens's Writing Center

Go to the Assignments
and Activities section of
Chapter 10 in the MyEducationKit and complete the
activity entitled "Writing
Workshop Focus Lesson in
2nd Grade." As you watch the
video and answer the accompanying questions, note how
the teacher uses an example
of her own writing to teach
about writing pieces with
more than one paragraph.

Focus Lesson

When teachers first began to use writing workshop, each session always began with a focus lesson (a five- to ten-minute teacher presentation). Today, writing workshop experts are less concerned with the time factor and more attentive to the content and delivery of the lesson, so they, like Ray (2001), have shifted to calling the writing lesson a *focus lesson*. In the following section, our attention is on the focus lessons that teach students how writing workshop might be structured. These focus lessons are taught at the beginning of the year. These early lessons help the students learn about the teacher's expectations for their behavior and about what they can expect from the teacher. Procedural lesson topics include discussions about such items as conferences, editing, and publishing.

How to Confer with Peers.   "Collaborative activities have a strong impact on the quality of what students write" (Graham & Perin, 2007, p. 466). Students will not automatically know how to confer with their peers. While the teacher models conferring in the teacher–student conference, modeling likely will be insufficient to help students develop the necessary skills to offer constructive criticism. M. Colleen Cruz (2004) approached the teaching of conferring skills in the following ways. First, she generated a list of "some things writers talk to each other about" (p. 100), which included such things as asking advice, giving advice, identifying things that are going well and not so well, plot ideas, character traits, confusing parts, and word choice. Then, she sent her students off to talk as she walked around the room, eavesdropping on her students' conversations. Later, Ms. Cruz realized that her students needed to hear what thoughtful criticism might sound like. The model she provided her students included four points:

1. Start with a sincere compliment.
2. Be honest, but be kind.
3. Make suggestions that the writer can try right away.
4. Use examples from other authors' work. (p. 102)

Then, using a piece of her own writing (yes, the best teachers of writing are writers themselves), Ms. Cruz invited the students to use the model to critique her draft. When using this model, she noticed significant positive changes in her students' peer conferences.

Charles MacArthur (in Harris, Graham, Masson, & Friedlander, 2008) provides a set of six lessons that he uses to teach students a five-step peer conferring strategy, which he calls a revising strategy:

1. Define revision
2. Describe the roles of the two students (writer and listener) using the strategy
3. Describe how the students are to listen, read, recommend changes, discuss each paper, and make revisions
4. Describe how each writer is to use a checklist to proofread his writing
5. Describe how after the writer has made all of the revisions and proofread the paper, the listener will use the proofreading checklist to check for additional errors (pp. 324–325)

The first day's lesson introduces the students to the five-step strategy. During the remaining days' lessons, Mr. MacArthur provides students with opportunities for supervised practice of each of the revising steps. Like Ms. Cruz, Mr. MacArthur found this strategy effective in teaching students how to provide valuable response to each other. This kind of specific instruction in how to engage in peer conferring is required to ensure that students know how to provide feedback to their peers.

How Teacher–Student Conferences Will Occur. An important component of the teaching of writing is the teacher–student conference about the students' writing. These conferences occur while the students are writing. It is important that students understand two elements of teacher–student conferences. First, the focus lesson should describe how writers will be selected for a conference. Teachers report that it works well for them to go to the writer rather than have the writer come to them. By going to the student, teachers can control the length of the conference, and while moving from one side of the classroom to the other, the teacher will be able to monitor all the students' behavior.

Second, the lesson should tell the students about the teacher's and the students' roles during the conference. The students should know that the teacher will be an attentive listener, an audience genuinely interested in learning about the topics they have chosen; that they will be asked to read their piece to the teacher; that the teacher will be asking questions to learn more about their topic and proposing suggestions for their consideration; and that the conferences will be short (two to three minutes) so that they can get back to their writing. In addition, students understand the procedures better when the teacher models a teacher–student conference during the lesson.

PEARSON
myeducationkit™

Go to the Assignments and Activities section of Chapter 10 in the MyEducationKit and complete the activity entitled "Peer Editing." As you watch the video and answer the accompanying questions, note the peer editing procedures that this teacher has put in place to assist her students in making mechanical error corrections in their pieces.

Classroom Editing and Proofreading Procedures. Pieces that are to be published must be proofread and edited prior to publication. Writers edit by searching for the mechanical errors in their pieces and attempting to correct them. Directions on how to edit pieces and what will occur during the teacher–student editing conference should be presented in a focus lesson. Teaching students such procedures has been found to have significant effects on their writing (Graham, 2005).

How Publishing Will Be Done in the Classroom. Publishing includes preparation of the pieces for others to read. It is an important component of the writing process because most writing is meant to be read by an audience. There are many ways to publish students' writings. One teacher asked each student to bring a clear, plastic eight-by-eleven-inch picture frame to school. (She purchased frames for those children whose parents could not provide frames.) Her students published their work by mounting their selected pieces in their frames. The frames hung on the "Wall of Fame" on the back wall of the classroom. A teacher of older students purchased plastic covers with colored spines. Her students published by inserting their pieces in these covers. Anne Davis and Ewa McGrail (2009) describe how fifth-grade students published on their independent blogs and teacher podcasts. Davis and McGrail are convinced that podcasting is a particularly powerful tool for helping students "rethink and revise their writing to make it not only clear and precise but also engaging for readers" (p. 523).

Specific kinds of writing dictate publication in culturally defined ways (e.g., business letters, personal letters, invitations, thank-you notes). Each new way to publish means that the teacher must provide a lesson describing and illustrating the procedure for the children.

Writing Time

PEARSON
myeducationkit

Go to the Assignments and Activities section of Chapter 10 in the MyEducationKit and complete the activity entitled "Teacher-Student Conference." As you watch the video and answer the accompanying questions, note the similarities and differences between this teacher-student conference and the chapter's suggestions on how writing conferences might proceed.

The teacher who looks around the classroom during this component of the writing workshop will observe writers engaged in various aspects of the *writing process*. Some students will be selecting new topics, so they will be thinking, talking, writing, or observing. Others will be writing, with pauses to reread what they have written, reconsider their topic, or confer with the teacher or a colleague about the topic or the text. Others will be editing pieces in preparation for publication. Yet others will be publishing. In each writing workshop, writers will be engaged in the writing behaviors of all writers. The only differences will be the physical size and the experience of these writers.

During writing time, students write while the teacher moves about the room conferring with the writers. Students might also confer with other students. While the teacher confers with students at the students' writing place, peer conferences might occur with those around the writer or two or more writers might move to a special section of the room.

From Carl Anderson's (2000) perspective, *conferences* are conversations because they share the characteristics of a conversation:

- Conferences and conversations have a point to them; the point of the conference is to help students become better writers.
- Conferences and conversations have a predictable structure; the structure of a conference is to talk about the work a student is doing as a writer and how the student can become a better writer.
- In conferences and conversations, listeners pursue the talkers' (or readers') line of thinking; the line of thinking in a conference is driven by the student's concerns and the text.
- In conferences and conversations, speakers engage in a pattern of exchange: one talks and then the other talks, one leads and then the other leads; in conferences, the student sets the conference's agenda by describing what he or she is working on and then the teacher takes the lead to help the student write better.
- In conferences and in conversations, listeners show they care about each other; in conferences, teachers show students that they care by nodding, smiling, and celebrating what they did well.

Teacher–student conferences give teachers a chance to differentiate their instruction. In the next section, we outline how writing conferences might proceed.

Writer's Intent. The teacher might begin the conference with an opening such as, "Tell me about how your writing is going. What are you trying to do?" The teacher's goal is to discover the student's intentions. As the student speaks, the teacher listens intently. For example, is the writer working to tell this story in the clever way, to keep the reader's attention? Is the writer working to create a really engaging lead? Is the writer working to put spaces between the words? Is the writer trying out the strategy taught during the focus lesson? In this "research" or "understand the writer" part of the conference, the teacher searches for the way to match the teaching during the conference with the writer's goal for this piece of writing (Ray, 2001).

Writer's Need.   Knowing the writer's goal helps the teacher ask the right questions and focus the conversation in ways that will help the student become a better writer. In Ray's terms (2001), the teacher is making a "what-does-this-student-need-to-know" decision (p. 163). So the second part of the conference is assessing the writer's need and deciding what to teach. Remember that the goal of a writing conference is to help the student become a better writer, not just to make this piece of writing better. The challenge for the teacher is to figure out on the spot just one thing that will help this student as a writer, right now. All the writer's needs cannot be "fixed" in a single conference.

Teach the Writer.   Once the teacher has decided what would help the student be a better writer, the teacher teaches. Beware, however, conferences are not minilectures. The teacher might grab a book to illustrate a quality of writing that this writer needs ("Hmmm. I wonder if this lead will really grab your reader's attention. What leads have you tried? Can you think of any stories we have read recently that had a really great lead? Let's take a look at these three or four books."). The teacher might let the writer know that something is missing ("I got confused right here. As you were reading me this section, I couldn't figure out what you made out front when you write, 'Then I made one in the front.'"). Or, the teacher might label what the writer is trying to do ("Ah, so you are trying to write this piece from the perspective of your cat and you're having trouble always seeing things from your cat's perspective? Let's think about a story we have read recently where the author did just what you are trying to do.") Exactly what the teacher says will depend on the writer's intent. What is this writer trying to do? What can the teacher teach this writer now that will help the writer achieve his or her intent? What can the teacher teach now, what strategies or techniques, that the student can use not only in this piece but also in subsequent pieces?

Writer's Plan.   What did the writer understand the teacher to say? What will the writer do now? How will the writer use the conversation to make the writing better? Ray (2001) ends her conferences with, "Say back to me what I just talked to you about" (p. 168). Teacher Deanne McCredie ends her conferences by asking, "What will you do now? How will you use what we talked about?" Teacher Deirdra Aikens ends her conferences by saying, "So, what we talked about was . . ." and the student fills in the blank. Ms. Aikens then records a few key words from the student's summary on a piece of paper and staples it to the inside of the student's writing folder. She and the student now have a record of the content of the conference. Making a note about the content of the conferences helps remind Ms. Aikens and the student what was taught during the conference. Ms. Aikens departs from each conference by saying, "I'll check back with you in a few minutes to see how you are doing." In this way, her students know that they are to "have a go" at whatever strategy or technique she taught during the conference.

Like Ms. Aikens, most teachers record what they taught during each conference with each student. Not every teacher staples the note to the student's writing folder. Terry Analore, for example, records her notes on three-by-five-inch index cards. Following one conference she wrote "10/26— By reading the end of her piece, Constance saw that the last sentence didn't fit. She crossed it out and thought of a new ending." Here Ms. Analore taught the strategy of reading a piece aloud to hear how it sounds, which can help writers determine what needs revision. Other teachers record their notes on computer address label. They write each child's name on a label. As they confer with their students, they record their notes on each student's label. At a glance, they can tell whom they have conferred with and who might need support. As a student's label is filled with the teacher's notes, the label is removed from the sheet and attached to a sheet of paper in the student's portfolio.

Anderson (2005) suggests that teachers use an individual learning planning form to record their observations about each student. In the first column, he suggests that teachers describe what they learn about each student writer in response to the question, *What am I learning about this student as a writer?* In the second column, he suggests that teachers describe what they need to teach their students in response to the question, *What do I need to teach this student?*

Conferring with student writers, with any writer actually, is not easy. Students sometimes resist the teacher's suggestions. Teachers need time to develop the skills needed to teach writers a new strategy or technique in a way that keeps ownership of the piece with the writer. Following each conference, it is important that teachers step back and reflect on what they did and why they did it, and what the writer did and how the writer felt. Ray

The role of a teacher in a teacher–student writing conference is to listen carefully to the writer, to respond honestly to the writer's questions, and to offer suggestions that will help the student become a better writer.

Go to the Assignments and Activities section of Chapter 10 in the MyEducationKit and complete the activity entitled "Author's Chair." As you watch the video and answer the accompanying questions, note how the teacher encourages the class to provide specific comments that would help the child be a better writer and how she reinforces these comments so that all the children learn through their peers' sharing of their writing.

(2001) offers these words of advice: "Conferring is very challenging, and you will probably struggle with it for quite some time before you begin to feel at ease. But most things in teaching—as in all of life—are like that, aren't they?" (p. 171).

Sharing

Each writing workshop ends with a *group share session*. These sessions are a bit like the teacher–student and peer conferences from the writing portion of the writing workshop. An important difference is that during the group share session, two or three students sit, one at a time, in the author's chair and share their pieces with the other writers in the class. With young writers, the other writers typically gather at the sharing writer's feet. Older writers tend to remain at their desk or table. Regardless of the seating arrangement, the other writers listen attentively while the writer reads the piece, or a portion of the piece, preparing to ask meaningful questions. Trade Secret 10.2 describes group sharing in Jackie Shockley's classroom.

TRADE SECRET 10.2
Group Sharing

JACKIE SHOCKLEY

I glanced at the classroom clock—2:50.

"Boys and girls, writing time is over for today. Please put your folders away unless it is your turn to share, and meet us on the rug." Share time begins in Room 206.

The first author reads his piece in its entirety. He concludes; his audience applauds. Several hands shoot up. The author calls on a student: "I really like how you said you felt like biting him back. I liked hearing how you felt." The author smiles, replies with a thank you, and calls on another student. "I heard a lot of *ands* in your piece. Maybe you should go through and see if you need all of those *ands*." Sitting in the back of the group, I record that comment on a small piece of notepaper. The author again declines comment but calls on another student: "I liked your story a lot." I interrupt the student and ask, "What exactly did you like about it? Be specific so you can help the

author." The student responds that she liked how he wrote about his gerbil because she has one, too.

I tell the audience that I really like how they are helping each other when they make comments that are specific and refer to our focus lessons. I request another round of applause for our author and hand him the notes I wrote, asking, "Here are the suggestions that were made, but who's the boss of this piece?"

Two more authors read their pieces; each reading was followed by more comments and applause. Precious learning moments have occurred and have been reinforced during the ten-minute period. So ends a typical share time in my room. There is concrete evidence that helpful comments during share time have a positive impact on the students' writing. During a small group share, a writer (Kip) was reading a piece about a camping trip. In his attempts to be explicit, he included the time each activity began and ended. After one reading, a member of the audience

---

TRADE SECRET 10.2 Continued

commented, "Wow, you told the time on everything." He responded, "I know. I didn't like how it sounded. I think I'll take it out." I was thinking, "Hooray!" only to hear another member of the group saying, "I like it. I think you should leave it

in." The discussion continued. Kip wavered but prior to publishing decided to include only a few of the times. His final decision is not really the issue here. What is important is that these writers were thinking critically about the piece.

Teachers might organize several different kinds of group share sessions in their classrooms, a number of which originated some time ago with Calkins (1983). The typical group share session is like the sessions described in this chapter. In this kind of ten- to fifteen-minute share session, called a *share meeting,* as many writers as possible share their drafts and receive their peers' and teacher's questions. Some teachers select students who volunteer to be the presenters. Other teachers select those whom they have identified as having made a significant discovery to be the presenters. For example, teacher Margaret Hull asked student Charlie to share his piece about his fishing trip because he discovered how to use parentheses to explain words possibly unknown to his readers. Still other teachers ask writers who tried the strategy or technique taught in the focus lesson to share their revised draft and talk about how they used that strategy or technique. Deirdra Aikens invites all the students with a particular color folder to share on the same day. Many use a combination of these means of selecting writers for group share presentations.

A second kind of group share session is *writers' circle.* In this kind of share session, the teacher divides the class into several small groups of five or so students. Writers then simultaneously share pieces with their peers. Obviously, many experiences with share meetings are needed before young students can be expected to independently and effectively run writers' circles. Some educators insist that each participant in this kind of share session bring a piece of writing to the writers' circle.

A third share session is a *quiet share,* which requires the listeners to have access to paper, a writing tool, and a desk, table, or clipboard. When each of the two or three writers has finished reading a piece, the listeners write their questions or comments. They may or may not sign them. The comments are then given to the writers for their consideration.

In *focused shares,* the teacher asks the writers to read a specific aspect of their pieces. For example, the teacher might ask the students to gather to read their leads, titles, or sentence or sentences that describe the setting of their piece, or to show how they focused their topic. Sometimes, teachers link focused shares with the day's focus lessons, as Maryanne Lamont did. On the day when the topic of her focus lesson was the writing of focused pieces, Ms. Lamont decided that the group share session would be a focused share, during which time some of her young writers would read their old pieces and their revised pieces to illustrate how they had revised to focus on one aspect of their topic.

Occasionally, teachers will use the group share session for a *process share.* During these kinds of group share sessions, the students may be asked to bring illustrations of revisions they made in their texts and to be prepared to tell about why they made the changes. The students may also be asked to share their notes (like brainstorming webs), created to help them discover what they know about a topic, or their handling of problems they have solved in their pieces (such as Charlie's use of parentheses).

Giving or *celebration shares* are unlike all other group share sessions. During these share sessions, writers share the pieces they have published. Because the writers have completed their writing of these pieces, only comments are offered by the listeners. These authors' works then join those by other published authors (writers such as Maurice Sendak, Chris Van Allsberg, Tomie dePaola, and Eric Carle) in the classroom library corner. Like all other books in that corner, these works are available to be checked out and read by an appreciative audience. Like the other books in a library, these books need to have a library checkout card and a pocket in which to keep the card.

Using Technology in the Teaching of Writing

Teacher–student and peer–peer conferences, as described above, are 'live" ways to provide response to student writers. Today, technology can be used as an additional means for teachers and peers to respond to other writers and for collaboration among writers in the creation of texts. In Special Feature 10.1, Patricia Scott describes several ways to use technology to foster a collaborative, interactive environment that nurtures the writing process.

SPECIAL FEATURE 10.1

Integrating Technology into Writing

PATRICIA G. SCOTT

Research suggests that the effective use of technology fosters a collaborative, interactive environment that nurtures the writing process and supports the social perspective on learning (Hewett, 2000; Kamil, Intrator, & Kim, 2000; Karchmer, 2001; Leu, 2000; Selfe, 1999). Networked computers open the possibility to encourage a true sense of audience by cultivating an online community in which writers and readers are communicating and collaborating with each other. In an online community, students see a genuine purpose for the writing, beyond the assignment (Hawisher, LeBlanc, Moran, & Selfe, 1996; Spitzer, 1990).

Below I describe a few technology ideas to foster the social process of writing.

Software Programs

Educators often search for the perfect fix to help students write. Most educators seem not to know that there is a program already installed, for free, on most school computers that facilitates the writing process. When a student completes a writing piece on the computer, the writer often prints the document for the teacher and peers to read and respond, a step that is no longer necessary. Microsoft Word, a Microsoft Office product, comes installed with two revising tools: Comments and Track Changes. Teachers should ask their students to electronically send them or their peers their writing piece (via e-mail, shared network drive, jump drive, CD). Once received, the teacher and/or peers open the document and open Track Changes (Figure 10.2). (Track Changes is located under Tools on Mac computers and Review on PC computers on the top tool bar. By clicking on Track Changes, both that feature and Comments will be engaged.) To insert a comment, the teacher or peers click on the yellow folder.

With insert comment engaged, the teacher or peer is able to write detailed comments to

SPECIAL FEATURE 10.1 Continued

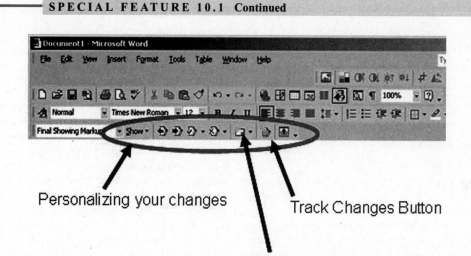

Personalizing your changes

Track Changes Button

Insert Comment

FIGURE 10.2

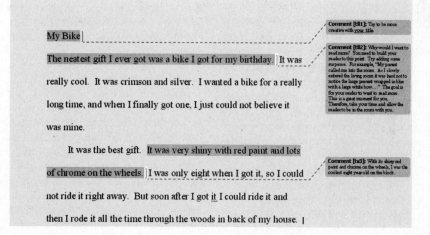

FIGURE 10.3

guide the writer through the revision process by moving the cursor and clicking at the spots in the document where he or she wishes to make a comment and typing the comment. Figure 10.3 gives an example of how the insert comments works. With Track Changes engaged (the background of the Track Changes icon is orange), teachers and peers can make suggested revisions directly in the writer's piece. Figure 10.4 shows how Track Changes allows readers to make suggested changes directly in the writer's piece.

(continued)

SPECIAL FEATURE 10.1 Continued

My Bike

_____The neatest best gift I ever got was a bike I got for my

birthday. It was really cool. It was croimsoncrimson and kind of

silver, but mostly red.

_____I wanted a bike for a really long time, and when I finally got

one, I just could not believe it was mine. It was the best gift I ever

got for a birthday presentmy birthday.

FIGURE 10.4

When the teacher or peers have responded, they will return the document via e-mail or jump drive to the writer. As soon as the writer opens the document, the feedback is obvious and easy to read.

Wikis and Blogs

Wikis and blogs are two examples of online applications to encourage writers to collaborate on the Internet. Wiki, the Hawaiian name for quick, is defined by Wikipedia (http://en.wikipedia.org/wiki/Wiki) as a Web application that allows users, anyone with a browser, to freely add and edit content on the Web. The idea behind wiki use in the classroom is for students to write collectively simply by clicking on the link "Edit This Page." Go to the Wikipedia site, an online wiki encyclopedia, for an example of how wikis enhance the community of learners. With the ease of creating, editing, and publishing pages immediately, wikis provide a simple way for asynchronous collaboration.

Another collaborative opportunity on the Internet are Web logs, or blogs, often referred to as online journals. This description, however, often ignores the interactive potential. A blog allows a writer to publish and permits readers to post comments in response to the original entry, idea, or question. Kennedy (2003, para. 2) identifies how a blog can enhance the social process of writing:

> Web publication gives students a real audience to write to and, when optimized, a collaborative environment where they can give and receive feedback, mirroring the way professional writers

use a workshop environment to hone their craft. Creating online communities where student writing takes center stage means inviting audiences to read and reflect on published work.

In a blog, the audience and the writers are able to connect to each other more readily in time and space, fostering and supporting an interactive community of writers. Blogs in the classroom provide opportunities for students to write in a personal space and also in a collaborative space where ideas are shared, questions are asked and answered, and social cohesion is developed (Huffaker, 2004).

The ways in which we write and learn with technologies need to shift from thinking about the hardware to thinking about the designs, set of activities, and the environments of technology that engage students to be active, constructive, authentic, and collaborative (Jonassen, Peck, & Wilson, 1998). The effective use of blogs and wikis is an example of how to think about technology as an environment to engage students in meaning-making processes. Writing with multimedia is another way.

Digital Storytelling

Teaching and learning with multimedia have a rich history in education. Instructional technology such as film, video, slides, and tapes has been used in the classroom for many years. The introduction of multimedia software in schools during the late 1980s, however, gave teachers the ability to capture, synthesize, and manipulate audio, video, and special effects with traditional media of text and images. Jonassen and colleagues (1998) define multimedia as "the integration to more than one medium (audio, video, graphics, text, and animation) into some form of communication" (p. 88). Digital storytelling is a way to write using a variety of multimedia practices. For the student, digital storytelling is an opportunity to share personal stories about the events, people, and places in their lives. For teachers, digital storytelling provides an engaging way for students to find their voices, communicate their stories, and connect with peers in a very special way.

What are the materials used and how do they create a story package? Although there are many software packages to purchase to create digital stories, often a program is already installed on the computer. Movie Maker 2, a program installed on computers with Microsoft Office XP, or iMovie, for Macintosh computers, is more than enough for students to create digital stories. Additional hardware might include a microphone, speakers, and a scanner. Before using the technology, there are excellent resources that provide teachers with student samples, adult samples, and lesson plans to learn more about digital storytelling. Listed below are a few "must" resources to investigate:

A Must List of Resources

- Digital Storytelling in Scott County: www .scott.k12.ky.us/technology/digitalstory telling/ds.html
- Center for Digital Storytelling: www .storycenter.org/

- Digital Storytelling Cookbook: www. story center.org/memvoice/pages/cookbook.html
- Digital Stories by Students and Teachers: www.digitalstories.org/

The focus of digital storytelling is the storytelling. Technology provides the environment and tools to create a story rich in voice and message.

Regardless of the technology—software programs, blogs, wikis, e-mail, instant messaging, or digital storytelling—online and multimedia writing challenges the way we interact, communicate, and think with writing. If technology matters to the social process of writing, then a central issue in the classroom use of computer technologies for literacy (specifically writing) and learning is how classroom teachers can integrate technology into the content and social context of the writing classroom as a means to support the writing process.

In Trade Secret 10.3 Noreen Moore describes another online program that many teachers of students in grades 4–12 use to support their students' development as writers. Unlike the use of technology described in Special Feature 10.1, this online program is a supplement to the teacher's and peers' feedback, providing direct feedback to students on their writing.

This chapter's Special Feature and Trade Secret descriptions suggest how educators can or have responded to the emergence of digital technologies. It is clear from these descriptions that the use of digital technologies changes how teachers facilitate their students' learning and how students interact with each other (Van Leeuwen & Gabriel, 2007). Teachers become facilitators, guides, and participants in the classroom's learning community. Students become more positive about and more engaged in the task of writing. Given the choice, they want to write with a word processor. Even students lacking proficiency in keyboarding prefer hunting for letters on the keyboard to writing by hand with paper and pencils (which is tiring). Making revisions to texts is so much easier with a word processor. But does technology make a difference in students' writing? Graham and Perin's (2008) meta-analysis of the writing research literature assures teachers and administrators that word processing "has a positive impact on the quality of [students'] writing" (p. 467). In short, digital technologies are helpful tools that positively impact children's writing—their enthusiasm for writing and the quality of their texts.

NOREEN MILLER

Mr. Jim's fifth-grade students file into the computer lab anxious to begin working on the first writing topic of the year. Mr. Jim asked them to write a personal narrative about a special day they had during their summer vacation. They have already brainstormed ideas in class and have created a plan for their narrative using a graphic organizer. Now, the students are prepared to begin drafting on the computer. All of the students go on to the Internet and type in the URL for the *MY Access!* writing program, www.myaccess.com. The brightly colored homepage appears, and the students enter in their log-in information. Now the students are ready to begin typing their personal narratives! As students are working on *MY Access!*, they can find tools and tips to help them plan, generate ideas, improve the organization of their narrative, and determine the best words to describe their day. Students are motivated by the interactive nature of the program and by the immediate feedback they know they will receive once they submit their drafts for online evaluation. Mr. Jim is free to circulate the room to conference with individual students as they are drafting and submitting their writing for feedback. The lab is buzzing with the clickety-clack of young writers' fingers typing away on the keyboard.

An online writing program designed for students in grades 4–12, *MY Access!* supports students throughout the writing process from idea generation to publication. Teachers can select and assign students a writing topic from a long list of already created topics and writing purposes; alternatively, teachers can create their own writing topics and purposes based on the specific interests of their students. *MY Access!* provides concept mapping tools and graphic organizers to support students as they brainstorm and plan. As students draft their pieces in *MY Access!*, writing tips and feedback are made available to support and motivate them. When students need more formal feedback on their writing, they are able to submit their writing to the program for immediate assessment and feedback. The system provides students with individualized feedback in six trait areas: focus and meaning, content and development, organization, language use and style, and grammar and mechanics. All feedback is genre specific, can be presented on two different reading levels (grades 4–6 or 7+), and can be given in English, Spanish, or Chinese. Students find the immediate feedback motivating as they work to craft their best writing. *MY Access!* provides teachers with a record of each student's submissions, performance, and feedback. Teachers can use this information to plan whole-class minilessons or individual student conferences.

Back in the computer lab several days have passed and the fifth-grade students in Mr. Jim's class feel confident that they have written wonderful narratives about a special day they spent that summer. In the computer lab, several students can be heard giggling and offering congratulations as they cluster around their neighbor's computer to read her narrative displayed in *MY Access!* After several revisions guided by the feedback provided by *MY Access!*, a conference with Mr. Jim, and feedback from their peers, the students feel ready to publish. *MY Access!* offers several creative layouts and templates on which students can publish their writing. Students enjoy playing with the colors, fonts, and layouts in order to get their narratives looking just right. Once their narratives are printed, students share during author's chair and Mr. Jim posts the final pieces on a bulletin board outside his classroom for the whole school to read.

MY Access! automatically creates a portfolio to organize and store students' writing. Mr. Jim's fifth-grade students will be able to view their special day narratives at the end of the school year and reflect on how they have grown as writers. In addition, Mr. Jim can use this information for assessment and instructional planning.

TRADE SECRET 10.3   Continued

The program is meant to enhance and complement quality instruction and assessment rather than to replace it. Students are motivated and intrigued by the technology and the immediate feedback on their writing and this motivation

encourages them to spend more time revising and reflecting on their writing. Soon, students come to understand and believe that revising is synonymous with being a writer.

The Explicit Teaching of Writing

As described earlier, procedural focus lessons happen at the beginning of the year. During the remainder of the year, the majority of the focus lessons should provide explicit instruction that teach students something about writing. These lessons can be grouped into three broad categories: characteristics or traits of good writing, writing process, and mechanics of writing.

Characteristics or Traits of Good Writing Lessons

Lessons about the characteristics or traits of good writing should make up the majority of the lessons presented during the year. These lessons are about the content of the children's pieces and what makes writing good.

Teachers of writing—such as William Zinsser, Donald Murray, Ralph Fletcher, and Stephen King—are a source for ideas for these lessons. From Zinsser (1998), teachers have gathered many ideas: use leads to suck readers into the piece and make them want to read on, select a *corner* (a small and interesting aspect) of the subject and focus on it, give the last sentence a special twist and make it a surprise, use action verbs, eliminate clutter, and watch the use of adjectives, to name a few. From Murray (1990), they have learned about choosing vivid, precise descriptive words; describing the sights, sounds, and smells so that readers will be put into the scene; using dialogue to enliven the piece; and writing in the present tense. From Fletcher (1993), teachers have learned about the art of writing with specificity, creating a character, writing with voice, creating dramatic leads, using various kinds of endings, creating tension in pieces, designing the setting, focusing, and choosing the best language. From King (2000), teachers can learn about what qualities writers need in their "toolbox" and tips such as: do not use long words just because you are a little ashamed of your short words; begin with the situations and then develop the characters; if you want to be a writer, then read a lot; and do not be afraid to imitate your favorite authors.

How should teachers teach their students about the qualities of good writing? Fortunately, teachers have a growing number of resources to access for support. For example, Steve Graham and his colleagues wrote numerous lessons to teach students to enhance their word choice and how to write a good story, an opinion essay, a persuasive essay, and a report (Harris et al., 2008). Key features of all lessons, according to Graham and Perin (2007), include: (1) clearly identifying the purpose of the writing (to persuade, to inform, to tell a story); (2) teaching the characteristics or primary traits of the kind of writing (e.g., in persuasive pieces, writers must address both sides of the argument); and (3) providing good models of each type of writing that is the focus of the instruction, having the students analyze the examples, and encouraging them to imitate the critical elements evidenced in each model. Lucy Calkins wrote *Units of Study* (2003). This resource provides lessons to guide teachers in the teaching of the traits of personal narrative, nonfiction, and poetry. Nell Duke and V. Susan Bennett-Armistead (2003) provide a step-by-step description of Pam Richardson's approach to teaching informational writing in her first-grade classroom. The Northwest Regional Education Laboratory provides lesson plans, sorted by early elementary and later elementary, on idea development, organization, voice, word choice, and sentence fluency (www.nwrel.org/assessment/lessonplans.php?odelay=1&d=1). Vicki Spandel (2009) offers a new series of books, one book for each grade level (grades 2–8), each of which provides 30 six-trait lessons per grade level. In short, a growing number of resources are available to help teachers explicitly teach their students about writing. We encourage teachers (and future teachers) to add these resources to their professional library and to use them to help them create writing trait lessons.

Writing Process Lessons

PEARSON
myeducationkit

Go to the Assignments and Activities section of Chapter 10 in the MyEducationKit and complete the activity entitled "Revising." As you watch the video and answer the accompanying questions, note how the teacher guides the student in the revision of his piece.

Writers engage in several behaviors as they write. When asked to describe their writing process, writers speak about where they get their ideas, how they draft their pieces (e.g., how many drafts they actually write; whether they use typewriter, longhand, or computer; where they write), how they revise, how they edit, and how their pieces are published. The writing process, then, includes prewriting, writing, revising, editing, and publishing. Writers make it clear that the process of writing is *not* a linear process. In lessons on the writing process, teachers want to show their writers the *behaviors* of writers, and make visible a process that is mostly invisible.

Some teachers find it helpful to children to share writers' descriptions of their writing process. Teachers and students can access interviews through the writers' or the writers' publishers' Web sites. For example, Scholastic (www2.scholastic.com/browse/video.jsp) advertises that teachers and students can meet their favorite authors and discover new ones through video interviews, classroom activities, and author profiles. Other teachers invite local authors into the classroom to write with the students; this has the advantage of making an author come alive for the students.

In addition to descriptions of writers' writing behaviors, children need to be shown how to plan and how to make revisions to their texts. Teaching children planning and revising strategies has been found to result in better writing (Chai, 2006; Graham & Perin, 2007). There are many different planning strategies. For example, a teacher can teach students to brainstorm ideas related to the selected topic, to organize those ideas into a draft, and to modify their plan as they write. Graphic organizers, talking with a partner for a few minutes, and asking the who, what, when, where, and why questions are planning strategies recommended by Patricia and Jim Cunningham (2010). Sharpening upper elementary students' skills of inquiry is suggested by Graham and Perin (2007):

> Effective inquiry activities in writing are characterized by a clearly specified goal (e.g., describe the actions of people), analysis of concrete and immediate data (e.g., observe one

or more peers during specific activities), use of specific strategies to conduct the analysis (e.g., retrospectively ask the person being observed the reason for their action), and application of what was learned (e.g., write a story where the insights from the inquiry are incorporated into the composition. (p. 467)

To revise a text means to change the meaning, content, structure, or style; to edit is to make surface changes to the text, to fix the spelling, punctuation, capitalization, or grammar. Revision does not just occur when the writer thinks the piece is finished; rather, it happens throughout the writing process. Teaching writers about the need to revise can be tricky. None of us likes to hear that the piece that we thought was "done" needs additional work. As Georgia Heard (2002) points out, when someone says, "I think you should add more," we translate it to mean, "My writing is not good enough." In her 2002 book *The Revision Toolbox: Teaching Techniques That Work,* Heard provides teachers with numerous strategies for helping children revise. A few of her strategies are summarized in Table 10.1, and we encourage readers to obtain a copy of her book, which illustrates these strategies using students' writings, for additional ideas.

TABLE 10.1   Selected Revision Strategies

Revision Tools	Purpose	Strategies
Cracking open words	To help students eliminate the use of words such as *fun, nice, pretty, wonderful,* and *scary* and replace them with words that bring a particular picture to the readers' mind	Ask students to create a list of tired, worn, and overused words and sentences from their writing. Then ask them to close their eyes and see or feel what *fun* or *nice* really looked or felt like and to write what they saw.
Collecting words	To help students expand the collection of words that they know so that they can access these words when they write	Ask students to begin a collection of "treasure" words in a notebook.
Give a yard sale for extra words	To help students obtain concise writing by cutting out extra unnecessary words in their writing, which will also help them understand which details of a story are essential	Have students practice cutting out extra words from a book excerpt, explaining to leave only the details that are really essential for the piece of writing. Then ask them to choose a piece of their own writing, cut out what they can, and share with the class.
Specificity of words	To help students learn how to write with detail, allowing them to express their specific thoughts in their writing correctly	Ask students to select a piece of their own writing and underline or highlight the verbs. Ask them to brainstorm or look in the thesaurus to replace those highlighted verbs with more detailed ones. Then ask students to repeat this exercise and underline nouns instead of verbs.

(continued)

TABLE 10.1   Continued

Revision Tools	Purpose	Strategies
Reseeing: Two-column writing	To help students observe and "resee" different objects or events with specificity and help them learn how to write with this kind of observational eye	Ask students to make a T-chart, labeling one side "ordinary" and the other side "poetic." Then ask them to observe a natural object and put the first words that come to mind under the "ordinary" column. Under "poetic," ask them to transform the "ordinary" descriptions into poetry by using metaphors and similes describing exact details. Then have them try writing the poetic side of the T-chart as a poem.
Asking questions, adding details	To help students discover what details they might need to add to their writing	Ask a student to choose a piece of writing in need of revision. Then, ask him or her to read the writing aloud while the rest of the class listens and jots down any questions they might want to ask the author. The class can then ask questions about the writing to the author, getting the author to think about what he or she might want to add to the story.

More recently, the Cunninghams (2010) suggested that teachers teach their students four general revising strategies:

1. *The Adding (Pushing In) Revising Strategy* This is the easiest revision strategy to learn so it should be the first strategy teachers teach. When writers use this strategy, they make their draft longer by adding a word or a phrase. Teachers can model using this strategy with a piece of their writing. They can show how they wrote on every other line, thus leaving a space for a revision, then adding a caret (^), inserting the new words, and rereading the text as revised.

   Instead of adding a word or a phrase, teachers might model adding dialogue to their text. Rereading that section of the text will show their students how much more interesting a piece can be with the addition of dialogue. For example, a teacher might say, "Oops! The writer forgot a very important piece of information right in the middle of the text!"

2. *Replacing (Trading) Revising Strategy* Writers aim to select just the right words for their text. Teaching students how to replace words or phrases with words or phrases that more clearly show the action or describe the object or event enlivens the text. This kind of focus lesson is illustrated in the vignette at the beginning of this chapter. In that lesson, Ms. Aikens showed her children one more Great Beginnings strategy and invited them to look at their writing to see if the great beginning she shared in the

lesson worked in their piece. Of course, it's possible to do the same kind of focus lesson about Great Endings.

3. *Reordering (Cutting and Sorting) Revising Strategy* The Cunninghams (2010) suggest that this lesson should be taught to each child individually. See the sections on teacher–student conferences and Teach the Writer earlier in this chapter for examples of how this lesson might be taught to a child.

4. *Revising While You Write Strategy* Sure, all published writers revise after they write. However, writers also revise *as* they write. Through thinking aloud, teachers can model how they make decisions to change the words they have just written.

Mechanical Skills Lessons

Finally, there are the lessons about the conventions of language: punctuation, grammar, usage, handwriting, capitalization, and spelling. Teachers can discover which mechanical skill lessons need to be presented through various sources. As with all lessons, the best source is the students' writing. What conventions do students need to use that they are not using correctly? They use dialogue, but is it incorrectly punctuated and capitalized, without quotation marks? If so, the topic of at least one lesson is clear.

Often, school districts have identified specific mechanical competencies that are to be covered at each grade level. Teaching these skills in lessons and then incorporating them into the editing stage of the writing process provides students with many practice opportunities. In districts in which a language arts textbook is issued, teachers often examine the textbook to discover the mechanical skills they are responsible for ensuring their students encounter. These skills are then taught through the lessons and reinforced as a part of the editing process in much the same way as the district-specified competencies were taught. Even when district competencies or a textbook are used as sources for mechanical-skill topic suggestions, teachers teach the skill *when their students' writing indicates a need for that skill* rather than following the order in which the skills are presented in the textbook or on the competency list. When students have a reason to learn particular skills and when the skills are taught in a meaningful context, students learn the skills much more quickly. Having said that, handwriting and spelling also must be explicitly taught, pulled out of writing workshop and taught in isolation. We provide evidence-based suggestions for how these mechanical skills of writing should be taught in Chapter 11.

As with other kinds of lessons, the content of mechanical skills lessons may need to be repeated. One mechanical skills lesson, how to write using your best guess of how to spell each word, for example, may need to be repeated often, particularly with kindergarten and first-grade students. Teachers of older students will want to present a similar lesson to their students, although their reason will be different. These teachers want their writers to use the words in their oral vocabulary in their writings. Hence, they need to convince their students that spelling every word correctly is *not* important in their rough drafts and to show them how to spell the words the best they can so that they can read them later.

Teaching the writer whose primary language is not English can sometimes be challenging. Teachers need to be aware of the textual organizational structures and cultural norms that might affect their students' writing. In Strategies for Teaching English Language Learners, Barbara Lutz offers some cautionary notes to teachers whose classrooms include students whose primary language is not English.

Strategies for Teaching English Language Learners

How Can We Help?

BARBARA GAAL LUTZ

Teachers sometimes view the pieces written by English as a second language (ESL) learners as being written in another language. Sometimes these students seem to make random word choices. Grammatical errors pepper their papers; in particular teachers see verb tense errors, article omissions, and the incorrect use of prepositions. Teachers often question, "What is the purpose of this paper?" because the paper seems to digress in several directions. Red pen in hand and with the intent of being helpful, teachers attack ESL learners' papers, editing heavily. Yet is this strategy the best? Teachers should know the why behind ESL writers' decisions.

Writing Personal Opinions

The assignment asked the students to write about their personal opinion on a topic under discussion in the classroom. U.S. students enjoy expressing their opinions, even when they are not well versed on the topic. Our educational system nurtures self-expression and individualism. For some ESL students, however, expressing personal opinions poses difficulties. In some cultures, students conform to the group, "subordinating the self for the 'we'" (Harris, 1994, p. 102); they are encouraged to voice those opinions that are commonly shared by the culture rather than express their personal views. Thus, an assignment that requires a personal opinion becomes an agonizing task for these students. Rather than take a stand, some students will persist in writing generalities, thereby avoiding personal comments or experiences to support specific points. Of course, other ESL students may be quite happy to write from a personal opinion, but they may not understand the need to defend their position by providing supporting evidence. In such cases,

merely expressing their opinions would be enough to satisfy their assignments in their own classroom cultures.

Taking these cultural differences into account when preparing assignments will greatly alleviate difficulties for both the ESL student and the teacher. For example, rather than one prompt for a writing assignment, teachers might consider several prompts, with each requiring a different kind response. In this way, both native speakers and ESL students could select the prompt that works best for them. In addition, directions that request the types of support the teacher expects to see in the development of the piece (e.g., examples from the textbook, examples from two outside sources, examples from real life) can be given.

Focus

English composition convention dictates that most pieces begin with a thesis in the first paragraph, clearly announcing the author's purpose. This pronouncement of purpose, which is continued in the piece with topic sentences, is a prominent feature of American discourse. For many ESL students, however, this convention does not exist. In fact, just the opposite rhetorical style may be employed. Long before the piece's main point is divulged, the writer may provide extensive background information to establish context and subtle suggestions that hint at the topic to be discussed. Only after such steady buildup does the writer arrive at the key point of the essay. Clearly, such a contrast in rhetorical styles can result in misreading and misunderstandings.

One way to overcome such differences in a piece's construction is to read the piece completely, resisting the urge to stop and search for the thesis. In doing so, the essay will unfold gradually, eventually revealing the writer's point. Once the main idea is clear, the teacher can then show the student how to work the main point closer to start of the piece. Another method is to ask the student how arguments and essays are constructed in the student's native language (Minett, 2004). Then, the teacher could explain the structure used in American writing. By comparing and contrasting ways in which texts are constructed, the student will come to see that by merely reorganizing an essay the meaning will be made clear for the American audience.

Coherence and Organization

When digression within the paper's paragraphs interferes with the American expectation for getting to the point, a handy exercise, called topical structural analysis, may help. Working through one paragraph at a time, the teacher and the student underline the subject of each sentence. These underlined "topics" are then placed in an outline diagram to determine the overall focus of the paragraph. This way, students can see the coherence and sequence of ideas in each paragraph and will be better able to make changes so that the paragraphs are developed for specific topics (Connor & Farmer, 1990).

Grammar and Form

A good way to view ESL grammatical errors is to view ESL writing as "a kind of foreign accent, only in writing instead of speech" (Leki, 1992, p. 129). As with accents in pronunciation, we can only expect modest improvement over time and, in many cases, no improvement at all. Thus it is with grammar. Correcting surface grammatical errors, even when the student wishes for such correction and when the teacher feels compelled to do so, will, according to research findings, produce "insignificant improvement in subsequent writing tasks" (Leki, 1992, p. 128). What is a teacher to do? The most beneficial help would be to focus on a few aspects of form in each paper. For example, if the overwhelming difficulty for the reader of the ESL piece comes from verb tense shifts, then let this one area be the focus of subsequent revision expectations.

Finally, it is important to note that some types of errors are usage rather than rule based and thus will not be something that a student will understand or learn simply by correcting in a single piece. On the other hand, rule-based errors will be the ones that practice and correction will eliminate to some degree over time. Overall, teachers cannot expect ESL students to write perfect papers. Teachers can, however, encourage them by valuing their ideas and assisting them in learning the conventions of American English writing.

Writing Instruction: Strategies for Children with Special Needs

The writing instruction program described in this chapter works with children with special needs as well as with "regular-education" students. Just ask Danling Fu and Nancy Shelton (2007); six of Shelton's nine special needs students met the state's writing assessment at the end of the year. Teacher Nancy Shelton and professor Danling Fu studied nine fourth-grade students with special needs (emotionally handicapped or with specific learning disabilities), studying the special needs children's progress as writers in an inclusive writing program.

Writing instruction in Ms. Shelton's classroom was for fifty minutes daily. Writing workshop began with a focus lesson, followed by a writing time, followed by two or three students sharing their work. Ms. Shelton conferred with small groups of writers and with individuals during writing time. Topics for the focus lessons initially were procedural lessons; later the lessons addressed skills that all or most of the students needed. Ms. Shelton evaluated her students regularly and worked with her students to set goals.

(continued)

Writing Instruction: Strategies for Children with Special Needs   Continued

The special needs children in this classroom made significant progress as writers. Fu and Shelton (2007) detail the why behind this progress. Shelton

- Met regularly with each student in her class and used this time to point out anything positive about the student's writing
- Allowed students time and space to work with each other
- Challenged each student appropriately

- Built a classroom in which each student was a member of the learning community
- Encouraged all students to take risks and to ask for help when they needed it

"The philosophy of the writing workshop model helped all students' learning regardless of their various abilities" (p. 327). All students can indeed be good writers.

Family Focus: Connecting Home and School

One of the points we have made in this chapter is the importance of students writing for authentic purposes and audiences. Families write for real purpose and real audiences regularly. Parents write notes or send e-mail or text messages to their children, reminding them that they'll be home a little later than usual. They make lists of items to be collected at the food store. Timothy Rasinski and Nancy Padak (2009) suggest that teachers help parents discover how to use everyday events like these as opportunities for their children to learn about the power of the pen (or keyboard). No ideas about the kind of writing parents might encourage their children to do? Rasinski and Padak provide a list for teachers. We summarize their suggestions in Table 10.2.

Families also can be an audience for completed texts. Teachers might send home completed texts for shared reading with family members or share the completed texts with families during an open house or parent–teacher conferences. Teachers also might involve parents in writing for their children. During an open house, Lisa Lang (Evers, Lang, & Smith, 2009), for example, asked parents to write an acrostic associating positive traits with the letters in their child's name. Jim, for example, might be *J* for joyful, *i* for inquisitive, and *m* for muscular. Her students beamed with pride as they shared their acrostic with their classmates. She reports, "Children love to read what their parents have written" (p. 468).

TABLE 10.2   Types of Family Writing

Types of Family Writing	Parents can ask children to:
List writing	Make a list of their activities for a day, birthday wishes, chores, or top-ten favorite foods
Notes, e-mail, or text messages	Write a note to remind themselves that their homework needs a parent signature or to another family member to stay out of their room
Journals/diaries	Write a summary of the significant events of their day
Dialogue journal	Communicate with each other in writing by asking questions, providing answers, offering encouragement, making apologies, and so on

TABLE 10.2   Continued

Types of Family Writing	Parents can ask children to:
Letters or e-mails	Write a letter or send an e-mail message to someone who doesn't live in the home telling about their day
Birthday and special event books	Share a kind thought or special memory for inclusion in a sibling's or relative's birthday or anniversary book

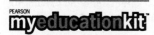

Summary

To become a competent teacher of writing will require considerable effort. Readers are encouraged to begin collecting models of good writing in all genres and to add copies of the many new books on the teaching of writing to their personal professional library. Entire books have been written on conferring, focus lessons, evaluating, and teaching writing within a writing workshop structure.

■ *What are the structural features of a classroom where writing is taught and children write?*

Before beginning the teaching of writing, teachers need to make preparations. They need to consider their daily schedule. Where will forty-five to sixty minutes of writing workshop each day fit into the schedule? They need to arrange the classroom environment for talk among peers and for quiet writing. They need to create an area where all the writers can gather to share their drafts and finished pieces. They need to gather the needed materials and determine how to arrange these materials for the writers' easy access. They need to make plans to teach their students how to write.

■ *What are the components of writing workshop?*

Many classrooms use writing workshop as the structure within which writing can be taught. The components of writing workshop happen in the following order each day: a focus lesson in which the teacher teaches the students something about writing or writing workshop procedures; writing time during which the students write, confer with the teacher, and confer with each other; and group sharing time during which two or three students share their writing with the group and receive responses.

■ *How do teachers explicitly teach writing and what kinds of lessons might they teach?*

Teachers explicitly teach about the qualities of good writing; the recursive nature of the writing process (prewriting, drafting, revising, editing, publishing) and how to use this process themselves; and the mechanical skills of writing (e.g., capitalization, punctuation, grammar, and spelling). Teachers can teach these same lessons, one-on-one, during teacher–student conferences. They can reinforce these lessons through the group share at the end of the writing time.

■ *What is the structure of a writing conference?*

Conferences have a predictable structure. The teacher begins by attempting to discover the student's intentions. Here, the teacher is searching for the way to match the teaching during the conference with the writer's goal for this piece of writing. Knowing the writer's goal helps the teacher decide what the writer needs to achieve the goal. The second part of the conference is assessing the writer's needs so as to decide what to teach. The third step is to teach the writer a needed strategy or skill. The teacher teaches something the student needs at the time but also something that will be useful in subsequent pieces of writing. The fourth step is to create a plan with the writer. What did the writer understand the teacher to say and what will the writer do now? The teacher then records the student's plan.

■ *How might teachers connect home and school in their teaching of writing?*

Families provide opportunities for students to be involved in writing for real purposes and audiences. At home, students can write lists, send notes or e-mail messages, write descriptions of special events in a journal or a diary, and more. Students can bring completed texts home to share with their parents. The students' parents can engage in writing pieces for the children. Such activities build students' enthusiasm for engaging in the writing process.

LINKING KNOWLEDGE TO PRACTICE

1. Visit a classroom to observe the teaching of writing. Make field notes of your observations of the classroom environment (the materials, the furniture arrangement, the writing area), the procedures used, the topic and content of the focus lesson, the models provided for the writers, how the teacher confers with the students, how peer conferring occurs, the availability of rubrics for the students' use, and how group sharing happened. Compare your observation data with your colleagues' data and against the description of the teaching of writing presented in this chapter.

2. Begin a writing support group with a group of colleagues. Challenge each other to write pieces in various genres. Gather models in each genre to "teach" you about the genre. Aim to publish your pieces.

3. Use Microsoft Word's two revising tools, Comments and Track Changes, to revise a piece of your own writing or to respond to a colleague's or a student's writing.

4. With a colleague, create a set of focus lessons to teach students about the traits of development, organization, voice, word choice, or sentence fluency in a persuasive essay or an informative piece, or create a set of focus lessons on components of the process of writing.

CHAPTER
11

Teaching the Mechanical Skills of Writing

Anton is ready to publish his story about his trip to Virginia Beach. He knows the classroom editing procedures. He collects the classroom's editing checklist (see Figure 11.1) from the writing center. With a blue pen, he circles any words he thinks might be misspelled. Then he searches his story to be certain he has put a punctuation mark at the end of each sentence, capitalized the first word in each sentence, indented the first word of each paragraph, capitalized the important words in the title, and capitalized the names of people and places. When he finishes with his search, he staples the editing checklist to his story and places both in "The Editing Box" in the writing center. Anton knows that before the next writing workshop his teacher will examine his edited piece and maybe will write him some notes, notes like "I see two more words that are misspelled. Can you find them?" or "I see three sentences in your second paragraph. Can you find them?" His teacher will also add the mechanical skills he used correctly to the list of skills he knows how to use on the inside cover of his writing folder. The next day during writing workshop, Anton will take a green pen and search the piece again to see if he can make the corrections the teacher's notes suggested. He can ask a friend to help him if he wishes. Following this search, he will sign up for an editing conference with his teacher. When he confers with his teacher, his teacher will celebrate the mechanical skills that he used correctly and teach him one or two additional skills. Then, he will publish his story by rewriting it on special theme paper using a felt-tip pen. He'll make a cover page with the title and his name. Then he'll insert the final draft and cover into a plastic sleeve and select a colored spine to hold it in place. Anton's story will be placed in the library center, alongside the work of other published authors.

Yes, it is important to engage all children in the kinds of activity described above, one that asks them to apply their knowledge about each of the mechanical skills of writing to edit their texts. Children should use editing checklists to hunt for errors in the pieces they are ready to publish. Teachers and their writers should meet together in editing conferences. However, we know that more is needed. "What contemporary research reveals is that although these aspects of literacy are not ends in themselves, they are nonetheless foundational. Serious deficits in [these skills] can undercut success in writing and reading" (Schlagal, 2007, p. 180). As described in Chapter 10, some focus lessons will be on topics in these areas. But focus lessons alone are insufficient; students will not learn these skills by hearing their teachers talk about or seeing their teachers demonstrate their use. Therefore, in the sections that follow, we provide evidence-based suggestions on the teaching of the mechanical skills of writing—spelling, grammar, capitalization, punctuation, and handwriting.

Before Reading This Chapter, Think About . . .

- How you learned to spell words. Did you learn to spell words by studying lists of words—the same list your peers studied—for Friday spelling tests? Do you think of yourself as a "good speller"?
- How you learned the rules of capitalization, punctuation, and grammar. Did you complete practice exercises?
- How you learned to form the letters of the alphabet. Did you practice by writing a page of *a*'s just like a model and then a page of *b*'s just like a model?

Focus Questions

- How will students learn about the mechanics of writing—spelling, grammar, capitalization, punctuation, and handwriting?
- How can teachers help children become better spellers?
- Which writing skills require not only teaching within the context of writing workshop but also more explicit teaching?
- How should teachers teach students to form the alphabet letters correctly?
- Given a choice, which handwriting style and form should teachers use? How should teachers teach students to form the alphabet letters?
- Is writing workshop and teaching the mechanical skills of writing within writing workshop appropriate for nonnative speakers of English?

BOX **11.1**

Definition of Terms

cursive-style writing: flowing form of writing in which the strokes of the letters in each word are joined.

early phonemic spelling: children represent one or two phonemes in words with letters.

editing conference: time when the teacher discusses the mechanical rules a student used correctly and teaches one or two rules he or she still needs to learn.

letter-name spelling: children break words into phonemes and choose letters to represent the phonemes based on similarity between the

sound of the letter names and the respective phoneme

manuscript-style writing: vertical form of writing with letters made with circles and straight lines.

prephonemic spelling: children form letters correctly, but they have not yet discovered that letters represent the sounds or phonemes in words.

transitional spelling: children write words that look like English words, though the words are not all spelled correctly.

Spelling

According to Bob Schlagal (2007, p. 180), spelling is one of the "least glamorous topics in today's language arts." But mastering spelling is important to both writing and reading. Steve Graham and his colleagues (2008) detail some of the reasons why teaching spelling is so important:

- Spelling errors make texts difficult to read.
- When writers need to focus on how to spell a word while writing, they might forget what they were planning to write.

| Editing Checklist |

Title _____

Name _____

Date _____

Are you ready to publish?

Check ✔ your piece for the following:

____ 1. Have you circled all the words you think might be misspelled?

____ 2. Have you punctuated the end of each sentence? (? ! .)

____ 3. Does each sentence begin with a capital letter?

____ 4. Have you capitalized the names of people and places?

____ 5. Did you indent the first word of each paragraph?

____ 6. Is your title capitalized?

____ 7. Have you read your piece aloud to check for errors?

| Editing Marks |

◯   Circle misspelled words

∧   Add word(s) or punctuation

≡   Capitalize a letter

¶   Begin a new paragraph

FIGURE 11.1   Editing Checklist

- When writers cannot spell a word, they often substitute a word they know how to spell.
- When writers focus heavily on how to spell words, they often put little attention on the text's organization or their audience's needs.
- When children have great difficulty with spelling, they often develop a mind-set that they cannot write, and their writing development is hampered.

How Children Learn to Spell

Children's emergent writing starts as pictures or scribbles and gradually becomes similar to conventional writing. Two decades ago Elizabeth Sulzby (1990) identified seven broad categories of emergent writing: drawing as writing, scribble writing, letterlike units, nonphonetic letter strings, copying from environmental print, invented spelling, and conventional spelling. A number of studies have focused solely on invented spelling, providing very detailed information about this stage of spelling development. These studies have provided important information to assist teachers in determining how to help children develop their ability to spell words conventionally. The following section briefly summarizes this research.

PEARSON
myeducationkit™

Go to the Assignments and Activities section of Chapter 11 in the MyEducationKit and complete the activity entitled "My Best Friend (K-2)." As you look at the artifact and answer the accompanying questions, note which stage of spelling this story represents.

Children who have had many experiences with print learn about how written language works through a process of discovery and experimentation. Children construct their own knowledge of written language as they interact with print and with people in everyday situations. Among the factors that contribute to children's discoveries about writing are being read to regularly, seeing adults who are important to them writing, and having access to writing tools. According to J. Richard Gentry and Jean Gillet (1993, pp. 22–24), three of children's first discoveries are that "print stays the same," that "writing is arranged horizontally" and moves from left to right across a page, and that "print is made up of certain kinds of marks."

At an early age, most children are able to detect the phonetic characteristics of words. They break words into their individual sounds and find a letter to represent each phoneme. These "finds," as Charles Read (1971) discovered, are not random. English-speaking children spell words by

- Using letter names (e.g., *C* for see, *LADE* for *lady*)
- Using only consonant sounds (e.g., *GRL* for *girl*)
- Omitting nasals within words (e.g., *ED* for *end)*
- Using phonetically based spelling patterns to represent artifacts ((e.g., *chr* for *tr* as in *CHRIBLES* for *troubles*)
- Substituting *d* for *t* (e.g., *prede* for *pretty*)

Children also employ several different strategies to spell words with short vowels, based on the place of articulation in the mouth. Short *i,* for example, is represented with an *e* (e.g., *FES* for *fish*), and short *o* is represented with an *i* (e.g., *CLIK* for *clock*). According to Schlagal (2007), this growing ability to map sounds to letters is very important to children's development; they are a "kind of glue that helps hold words in memory" (p. 181).

Children's invented spelling changes as they become aware of the many rules and patterns that govern the English language. Most children pass through the different stages of spelling in the same order. The five stages (using Temple, Nathan, Temple, & Burris's 1993 categories and labels) are as follows:

1. *Prephonemic stage*—Children can form letters correctly, but they have not yet discovered that letters represent the sounds or phonemes in words. Letters are strung together randomly. This stage is typical of three- to five-year-olds (for example, "RAVRDJRV" may be used for "ocean road").
2. *Early phonemic stage*—Children attempt to represent phonemes in words with letters, but they usually represent only one or two letters in words, generally the initial and the final sound. This stage is typical of five- and six-year-olds (for example, "MNMDF" may be used for "me and my dad fishing").
3. *Letter-name stage*—Children break words into phonemes and choose letters to represent the phonemes based on the similarity between the sound of the letter names and the respective phonemes. This stage is typical of six-year-olds (for example, "I WAT TO MAI FRNDZ BRATHDAY WE MAD AOI ON SUNDAY" for "I went to my friend's birthday. We made our own sundae.").
4. *Transitional stage*—Children write words that look like English words, though the words are not all spelled correctly. Typically, each syllable has a vowel. Unlike children in the earlier stages, transitional spellers no longer rely mostly on sounds to present written words; transitional spellers use a morphological and visual strategy also (e.g., *eightee* instead of *ate* for *eighty*). The child has a visual memory of spelling patterns. This stage is typical of seven- and eight-year-olds (for example, "Out back thar is a pass. it is hils. and thar is a huj hil. and I krassd on my bike." may be used for, "Out back, there is a pass. It is [between] hills. And there is a huge hill. And I crashed on my bike.").
5. *Correct spelling stage*—Children spell nearly all words correctly, though like all of us, assistance may be needed with occasional troublesome words. Children typically reach this stage by age eight or nine years. (For example, "I am nice, talented and aspeily smart BECAUSE I moved up to second grade. The week was very easy in first grade and just right in second grade. I really like second grade. In lunch a fly landed on Allen's nose today and it went buzzzzzzz!")

So learning to spell begins in the early years of children's literacy development. Children's early years, when they play with the forms and functions of print, are important because they lay the groundwork for children's later exploration of the alphabetic layer of spelling. By the early phonemic stage, children have some knowledge of the names of the alphabet letters and some awareness of sounds within spoken words. Now they can invent their spellings as they write. Notice how children are using consonants almost exclusively in the early phonemic stage. In English, according to Shane Templeton and Darrell Morris (1999), consonants emerge first in children's invented spellings because they are more salient acoustically and the children can feel their articulation. Vowels emerge later, in the letter-name stage.

By the time children move into the transitional stage of spelling, they have begun to understand how groups or patterns of letters work together to represent sound. A key indicator that children have progressed to this point is their use of silent letters in their invented spellings to represent long-vowel sounds. For example, for *tied* they might write *tide.* From letter patterns within single syllables, children will progress to understanding syllable patterns. Now, they grasp the understanding of "consonant-doubling/e-drop principles as it applies to simple base words and suffixes" (Templeton & Morris, 1999, p. 106). Understanding how syllables and suffixes work in spellings leads students to attend to the role of meaning in spelling. Now they correct words by relating words to the base. For example, they might write *oppisition,* look at it, see the word *oppose,* and understand how to correct their error.

By closely examining students' writings, teachers can understand the strategies children are using to construct written words. Each word can be categorized into one of the five spelling stages, and the percentage of words spelled using prephonemic, early phonemic, letter-name, transitional, and correct spelling strategies can be calculated. For example, if the word looks a lot like conventional English spelling, with a vowel in each syllable (e.g., "EGLE" for "eagle"), then the teacher knows the child used the sounds in the word and a visual pattern (*gle*) in constructing the word—strategies characteristic of a transitional speller. By engaging in this kind of analysis and calculating the percentage of words written at each stage, the teacher can identify the student as *primarily* exhibiting the strategies of a particular stage of spelling. (Children typically do not use strategies of one stage only.) Comparing two or more of a student's writing samples, written at different times during the year, helps the teacher understand the child's growth in spelling knowledge. With this information, the teacher can answer the question, is the child becoming a better speller?

Helping Children Become Better Spellers

Will children learn to spell words correctly by discovery on their own? Today's spelling experts (e.g., Gentry & Gillet, 1993; Graham et al., 2008; Schlagal, 2007; Temple et al., 1993; Templeton & Morris, 1999) suggest that independent discovery is not enough; children need instruction to become expert spellers.

While the theoretical and descriptive research has been "quite rich in describing what is happening cognitively as children learn to spell," what adults should *do* to assist children's development only recently has begun to be clarified.

Prephonemic and early phonemic spellers need help learning more about how alphabet writing works. Appropriate goals for these young spellers include learning letter names and sounds, developing a stable concept of what constitutes a word, and discovering both how to break words into their constituent parts—to phonemically segment words—and how to represent the parts with letters. Bernadette Watson's focus lesson on invented spelling is an example of an appropriate activity (see Trade Secret 6.4). As Bernadette wrote her piece on traveling to New York, she helped her young students break words into sound segments and select the best letter to represent these parts. She left spaces between the words and told the children why. As her children worked at writing their own pieces, Bernadette provided one-on-one instruction in these important skills as she conferred with each child.

These same kinds of activities are appropriate for letter-name spellers. As children move into this stage and have had many experiences with segmenting words and selecting the best letter to represent the spoken parts of each word, their accuracy will increase. More sounds are heard, including vowels. Occasionally, teachers might do as Elizabeth Sulzby has recommended. When a child says *went* is spelled *YNT,* the teacher might suggest that *YNT* is the way many children spell *went,* but soon they will learn that adults spell it a little differently—WENT.

Lawrence Sipe (2001) suggests another strategy, using an organizer such as Elkonin boxes to help students stretch out the phonemes or individual sounds in words. As they stretch out the sounds and identify the corresponding letters, they fill in the individual sound boxes to complete the word. For example, to write the word *trap,* the teacher might present the child with three boxes.

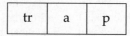

The use of such a strategy gives students a visual representation of how phonemes are combined to make words. It also emphasizes the number of letters that are used to make each word.

As letter-name spellers begin to move into the transitional stage, it is appropriate to begin asking students to study a short list of not more than ten words per week (Temple et al., 1993). Recall that, for the typical speller, this will occur sometime during the second half of first grade. Other children do not reach the transitional stage until later in the primary grades.

Recall our earlier statement that today teachers help students learn to spell by helping them understand how words work—the conventions that govern the structure of words and how these structures signal sound and meaning. Donald Bear, Marcia Invernizzi, Shane Templeton, and Francine Johnston (2003) provided teachers with specific helpful suggestions for, first, determining their children's developmental spelling level, and then, providing developmentally appropriate instruction that addresses each level, aimed at helping the children understand the patterns and structure of the English language. Such instruction is important not only because it helps children become better spellers but also because it improves their skills as readers. In Trade Secret 11.1, Gaysha Beard describes how she found her way to providing developmentally appropriate spelling instruction in her classroom using their ideas. We echo Ms. Beard's suggestions: readers should obtain copies of the *Words Their Way* materials for use in their classrooms.

Explicit Instruction in Spelling

Schlagal (2007) argues that a single grade-level spelling book does not meet the needs of every child in a class. The challenge for teachers, then, is to teach spelling without the use of a spelling book or to adapt spelling books to meet every child's needs. A key is that spelling instruction must be responsive to children's individual needs. In addition to needs-based explicit instruction, J. Richard Gentry and Jean Gillet (1993) suggest that formal instruction in spelling should possess five other characteristics: self-selection, student ownership, self-monitoring, collaboration, and feedback.

In the past, the words to be studied were selected by textbook writers. Today, the recommendation is for teachers and students to select the words to be learned. Which words should be chosen? Two teams of researchers (i.e., Gentry & Gillet, 1993; Temple et al., 1993)

TRADE SECRET 11.1
Using *Words Their Way* to Find My Way to Improved Spelling Instruction

GAYSHA BEARD

I wanted my classroom instruction to be based on students' individual needs. As a developing educator, I knew the importance of instructing at my students' developmental level. Naturally, in reading, I grouped my students based on their specific skill needs. For some reason, it took me some months before I made this link to spelling instruction. I like to think of *Words Their Way* (Bear et al., 2003) as the book that gave me that "aha" moment.

Words Their Way is a resource that every classroom teacher should own. This book was created on the principle that literacy development occurs in stages. Bear and his colleagues (2003) suggest that children develop knowledge of word features on a continuum. As students explore the English spelling system and make qualitative shifts from stage to stage, they use distinct spelling patterns and make distinct spelling errors. On average, K–3 teachers will find students working within the emergent, letter-name alphabetic, and within word pattern stages. At the beginning of the emergent stage, spellers' writing takes on the form of drawing and scribbling, and by the end students are spelling words representing the most salient sounds. Letter-name alphabetic spellers begin this stage accurately representing initial and final sounds, but eliminating vowels. As students approach the end of this stage their writing accurately represents short vowel patterns, digraphs, and blends. Students' writing during the within word pattern stage shows some confusion with long vowel patterns, and by the end of this stage students are accurately using complex vowel teams, and learning two- or three-letter complex consonant patterns. As children progress to the syllables and affixes stage, their writing suggests that they understand such concepts as silent *e,* other long vowels, and complex consonant patterns. However, they appear to be confused about the adding of suffixes and spelling multisyllabic words. The assessment tool provided

in *Words Their Way* makes it relatively easy for classroom teachers to assess and place each child in an appropriate instructional group.

I began, as recommended, by administering the *Words Their Way* Spelling Inventory to my entire class. The book provided user-friendly guidelines to administer and score the assessment. I said something like the following:

> *Today, boys and girls, all of you have a chance to help me become a better teacher. I want each of you to show me how well you can spell. Even if you cannot spell every word correctly, what you write on your papers are clues for me. These clues will teach me how to help you become an even better speller. Is everyone willing to help me become a better teacher?*

The assessment took no longer than fifteen to twenty minutes. It took me about one hour to score my classroom set.

I scored the papers using the Feature or Error Guide. The data chart revealed my students' developmental spelling stage. I grouped children with similar needs into small groups for instructional purposes. For example, children who made errors with short vowels were grouped together, and students who understood the silent *e* pattern but confused the other long vowel patterns were grouped in the "other long vowel patterns" spelling group.

After these groups were formed, my spelling instruction could begin. Because I could differentiate my instruction based on need, my students were not required to take the same twenty-word spelling test on Friday. I learned, for example, which children were not developmentally ready to spell multisyllabic words. Teaching spelling in this way begins with what children know and moves forward to advance their knowledge of how words work. Other than the assessment tool, the second best component of the *Words Their Way* book is the resources for teachers. Now teachers might feel a little overwhelmed if they discovered that they needed to create four different lesson

> ## TRADE SECRET 11.1 Continued
>
> plans for their various spelling groups. Not a problem! *Words Their Way* is divided into the literacy stages and provides examples of activities, word sorts, word lists, and reproducibles that teachers can easily adapt to their individual classroom needs. That's what I did. I provide a few examples of these authors' suggestions in the table at the end of this article. (See Table 11.1 for a list of sample activities that can be used for emergent to syllables and affixes spellers based on children's developmental needs.) The table is organized by developmental spelling stages, which I have learned are very important to keep in mind when designing any lesson. Each activity is designed for small-group instruction. In addition to the activities suggested in *Words Their Way*, Francine Johnston, Donald Bear, and Marcia Invernizzi recently published a set of additional teacher-friendly books with many activities for use with children at each stage.
>
> Now that I have been using this approach to guide my spelling instruction, I see a difference in my students' spelling abilities. They have discovered spelling patterns and are knowledgeable about how words work. As a class, we have moved from memorization to understanding!
>
> **TABLE 11.1 Sample Word Study Activities Based on Students' Developmental Needs**
>
> | Developmental Stage | Developmental Stage | Developmental Stage | Developmental Stage |
> |---|---|---|---|
> | Emergent
Late | Letter-Name
Alphabetic
Early
Middle
Late | Within Word Pattern
Early
Middle
Late | Syllables and Affixes
Early
Middle
Late |
> | **Areas of Need** | **Areas of Need** | **Areas of Need** | **Areas of Need** |
> | Initial Sounds | Final Sounds
Short Vowels
Consonant Digraphs
Consonant Blends | Consonant Blends
Long Vowel Patterns
Other Long Vowel
Patterns | Other Long Vowel
Patterns
Multisyllabic Patterns
Easy Prefixes &
Suffixes |
> | **Activities** | **Activities** | **Activities** | **Activities** |
> | **SORTS**
■ pictures or objects focusing on the beginning sounds; give students columns and ask them to sort the pictures | **SORTS**
■ begin with pictures and then introduce word sorts (focusing on final sounds, short vowels, digraphs, and blends); give students columns | **SORTS**
■ word sorts beginning with what the child knows and adding a new skill (focusing on silent -*e*, *r*-controlled vowels, diphthongs, & vowel teams); | **SORTS**
■ word sorts beginning with what the child knows and adding a new skill (focusing on adding -*ing*, doubling consonants, |

(continued)

TRADE SECRET 11.1 Continued

TABLE 11.1 Continued

Activities	Activities	Activities	Activities
SORTS ■ students complete concept sorts (e.g., sorting buttons) to develop their ability to compare and contrast **RHYME & ALLITERATION** ■ Games (bingo, Concentration; reading poetry; name game) **LITERATURE** ■ share children's literature that reinforces alliteration and rhyme	**SORTS** and ask them to sort the pictures and words ■ sort should include what the child knows and the new skill that they will learn **ACTIVITIES** ■ board games (focusing on key concepts at this stage); word hunts looking for words that follow the patterns; word hunts looking at word families (add new words to personal dictionaries); Concentration **LITERATURE** ■ share children's literature that reinforces learned skills	**SORTS** allow students to discover the pattern by creating their own columns for the sort; semantic sorts (compare and contrast word meanings, and content-specific words) **ACTIVITIES** ■ board games (focusing on key concepts at this stage); word hunts looking for words that follow the patterns; word hunts looking at word families (add words to personal dictionaries); playing Concentration using homophones; Jeopardy **LITERATURE** ■ share children's literature that reinforces learned skills	**SORTS** comparing open & closed syllables, comparing words that end in -er and -ure; allow students to discover the pattern by creating their own columns for the sort; semantic sorts (compare and contrast word meanings, and contentspecific words) **ACTIVITIES** ■ board games (focusing on key concepts at this stage); word hunts looking for words that follow the patterns; create a word study notebook); playing Concentration using homophones; Jeopardy including vocabulary and key features at this stage **LITERATURE** ■ share children's literature that reinforces learned skills

Go to the Assignments and Activities section of Chapter 11 in the MyEducationKit and complete the activity entitled "Introducing Sight Words through Spelling." As you watch the video and answer the accompanying questions, note how the teacher uses spelling to help children learn to recognize the word *she,* which they will encounter in a story they are about to read.

provide comparable advice: Some words should come from each student's reading and writing. To this advice, Shane Templeton and Darryl Morris (1999) add that, at the primary level, the words should be known as sight words in reading. As indicated above, words should be selected that the student will use frequently, which show a particular spelling pattern (e.g., [long vowel]-[consonant]-*e: name, hide, cute*), or which follow a consistent spelling generalization with no more than two different spelling patterns being evident in a student's weekly list. Good sources for these words include the books the student is reading, the student's personal dictionary, and the student's personal writings. A key is that the words should reflect features that the student uses but confuses in his or her own writing. Using these personalized words as the base, the teacher should add two or three words that share the same spelling pattern (e.g., *cat* and *fat* with *sat*), meaning pattern (e.g., synonyms and antonyms), or visual pattern (e.g., *ough* in *rough, cough,* and *enough*). Because the teacher and the student selected the initial words to be studied from the student's reading and writing, self-selection and student ownership is inherent in the word-selection process. How many words should be selected for study each week? Templeton and Morris recommend ten to twelve words as appropriate for second- and third-grade students and about twenty words for fourth-graders and beyond.

Collaboration occurs when students study their selected words with peers. Working with others helps students discover patterns in the spelling of words. Peers might study their words in pairs or they might administer tests of their words to each other. Working with other students reduces the tedium of studying for all students, both those with learning disabilities and those without disabilities. Some teachers suggest pairing students in the class (Burks, 2004), while others recommend at least occasional pairings with older "buddies" because the older student can serve as a positive model and provide significant support and scaffolding (Buschman, 2003). J. Richard Gentry and Jean Gillet (1993) and Charles Temple and his colleagues (1993) recommend using the following five-day schedule:

■ *Monday*—Each student's words should be called out, and each student should attempt to write the correct spellings. Obviously, because each student's list of words is different, the teacher cannot possibly call out each student's list. Students can work in pairs, taking turns calling out each other's list. Then each list should be returned to its owner so that the owner can compare the correct spellings against his or her spellings. Words spelled incorrectly should be crossed out, and the correct spelling should be written. Bob Schlagal (2007) suggests the children should copy the correct spelling twice because this focuses the children's attention on the words they need to attend to and to the features of the words they need to learn. The processes of collaboration, feedback, and self-monitoring are evident.

■ *Tuesday, Wednesday, and Thursday*—The students can work to learn those words they misspelled on the Monday pretest. Lynnette Bradley and Peter Bryant (1985) and Cassandra

Go to the Assignments and
Activities section of Chapter
11 in the MyEducationKit
and complete the activity
entitled "Spelling Practice."
As you watch the video and
answer the accompanying
questions, note how the strategy has children self-check
their spelling of the words
being studied.

Keller (2002) suggest that students be taught to study their words using a
multisensory study technique such as the one outlined in the following
eight steps (a technique that provides image feedback and a lot of self-
monitoring):

1. **Look** at the word, and **say** it aloud.
2. **Read** each letter in the word.
3. **Close** your eyes, try to **picture** the word, and **spell** it to yourself.
4. **Look** at the word. Did you spell it correctly?
5. **Say** each letter of the word as you **copy** it.
6. **Cover** the word, and **write** it again.
7. **Look** at the word. Did you write it correctly?
8. If you made any mistakes, **repeat** these steps.

On these days, the teacher might also bring together the students who are working on
words with a common pattern for some group work. Games and exercises that play on the
spelling patterns of the group's words can be profitable and fun. (Visit http://readwritethink
.org/lessons/index.asp for games and exercises.) Thursday might also be a practice-test day.
This instruction is clearly direct and based on needs. It is also fun.

Schlagal has different suggestions for Tuesday and Wednesday activities. On Tuesday, he suggests that teachers provide children with enlarged copies of their week's words.
These should be cut up so that the children can sort them by the patterns being emphasized
in the week's words. The children might play Concentration with their words, matching
words with similar patterns. On Wednesday, the children might do word hunts, looking for
words that evidence the same patterns as their week's words.

■ *Friday*—Students are tested on the words they selected (with the teacher's assistance)
for studying that week. Tests are administered and corrected, as they were on Monday. The
new words each student has learned to spell are celebrated. The students can record the
words they learned to spell correctly in a personal record-keeping book. Words that the student misspelled might be returned to the list for additional study next week or retired to be
reviewed at a later appropriate time. Self-monitoring, immediate positive feedback, and
student ownership evident.

This test–study–test method works equally as successfully with good and poor spellers,
although the efficacy of this procedure has not been specifically examined with students who
have learning disabilities. Of course, the presumption is that the students can spell some of the
words on the pretest. Otherwise, imagine the resentment against taking such tests. Further, the
procedures suggested for studying the spelling words are equally effective with students who
have and do not have learning disabilities. However, some data suggest that testing the students daily is an effective means of supporting daily practice (Graham, 1999).

This kind of spelling program—one that focuses on each student's word needs,
that provides direct instruction based on the student's spelling stage and demonstrated
knowledge, that celebrates each student without comparing his or her growth against that of
other class members, and that supports invented spellings as developmentally appropriate

for writers and not as errors—provides support for growing writers and spellers, helping them to tackle the challenges of writing and learning to spell with confidence and enthusiasm.

Back to Anton, the child in the vignette at the beginning of this chapter. Yes, editing his writing pieces with an editing checklist and participating in an editing conference with a peer and his teacher is important. However, it is not sufficient. In addition, his teachers need to engage him in activities like those described in this chapter to develop his spelling skills. As Stephen Graham and his associates (2008, p. 800) point out, spelling will not be "acquired as naturally and easily as speaking, by immersing children in literacy-rich environments where they have plenty of opportunities to read and write for real purposes. . . . It is necessary to directly and systematically teach children how to spell."

Grammar

Children come to school knowing a lot about how language works. By the age of six years, they know the basic grammar of the language used in their home. They have internalized the rules for creating language. Their grammatical knowledge is *implicit*—that is, children cannot tell their teachers the rules they are using, but they can intuitively use the rules to construct their oral texts. As Neil Daniel and Christina Murphy (1995, p. 226) point out, "All normal humans have full control of the grammar they use every day."

For some children, the grammar that works well at home is different from the grammar they meet at school. School's grammar is "a set of conventions, collectively known as usage, that govern written [and oral] discourse" (Daniel & Murphy, 1995, p. 226). School's grammar is an arbitrary system of rules, rules to be learned and demonstrated by students.

In the past, teachers tried to teach their students the rules of grammar or usage through drill. Readers may recall filling in tedious workbook exercises such as, "The children _____ (was or were) playing." Years of researching the effectiveness of this approach to teaching grammar led diverse scholars to the same conclusion: Students make almost no connection between this traditional grammar instruction and the production of their own texts (Hillocks, 1986). Even those students who successfully completed the exercises and scored well on the Friday tests rarely used what they had learned in their own writing and speaking. The main predictable outcome was that most students developed an aversion to studying grammar. A new method of teaching grammar was clearly needed. Note that the question was not, to teach grammar or not to teach grammar. As Constance Weaver, Carol McNally, and Sharon Moerman (2001) suggest, "That is *not* the question." As with spelling, educators cannot afford to assume that students will acquire an accurate understanding of formal language structures through reading, writing, and speaking. Grammar must be explicitly taught.

The constructivist perspective suggests that grammar should be taught as children engage in meaningful uses of language. More than anything else, humans need to be engaged with significant tasks (Csikszentmihalyi, 1990). Within these meaningful tasks, grammar instruction

PEARSON **myeducationkit**

Go to the Assignments and Activities section of Chapter 11 in the MyEducationKit and complete the activity entitled "Grammar and Punctuation." As you watch the video and answer the accompanying questions, note how the teacher gives students feedback on one or two skills at a time and sets the stage for peer editing.

can help children understand that there are many ways of saying the same thing. As George
Hillocks Jr. (1986) suggests, teachers should show writers how to use a variety of syntactic
structures (word orderings) and how to select the most effective structure for the current situation. For example, the grammatical structures used in writing a letter for publication in a
newspaper are different from those used to write a letter to a grandmother.

Constance Weaver (2008) updates Hillocks' suggestions with 12 principles to guide
teachers' teaching of grammar:

1. Teaching grammar divorced from writing doesn't strengthen writing and therefore
   wastes time.
2. Few grammatical terms are actually needed to discuss writing.
3. Sophisticated grammar is fostered in literacy-rich and language-rich environments.
4. Grammar instruction for writing should build on students' developmental readiness.
5. Grammar options are best expanded through reading and in conjunction with writing.
6. Grammar conventions taught in isolation seldom transfer to writing.
7. Marking corrections on students papers does little good.
8. Grammar conventions are applied most readily when taught in conjunction with editing.
9. Instruction in conventional editing is important for all students but must honor their
   home language or dialect.
10. Progress may involve new kinds of errors as students try to apply new writing skills.
11. Grammar instruction should be included during various phrases of writing.
12. More research is needed on effective ways to teaching grammar to strengthen writing.

The teaching of grammar, then, does not mean requiring students to memorize a collection of dos and don'ts! It does mean helping students learn how to manipulate language.
For example, students can be assisted in selecting words to modify nouns, or they can learn
to combine sentences by discovering the processes of embedding, deletion, substitution,
and rearrangement of elements (Brosnahan & Neuleib, 1995). Yes, teachers should expose
their students to grammar's vocabulary: *noun, verb, adjective, adverb,* and *clause,* yet students need very little of this to learn the conventions of written English. The difference today
is that grammar's vocabulary and the structure of the language is studied within the context
of a meaningful task.

The writing workshop provides a meaningful context within which to facilitate students' study of grammar. Within the writing workshop, writers produce products that are
published in various forms for others to read. As Wendy Bishop (1995, p. 187) points out,
"There is nothing like [publishing] to make us try to make ourselves and our writing pre-
sentable!" The opportunity to publish supplies considerable motivation for students to follow the conventional rules of grammar.

The components of the writing workshop—focus lessons, writing and conferring (content and editing conferences), and group sharing—provide for grammar teaching and learning opportunities. For example, during a focus lesson, Deanne McCredie shared with her
students a piece that she had written about her dogs. She finished by saying, "You remember I was working on this last week? Well, I thought it got kind of boring. It was funny when
it happened, but my story didn't sound funny. I remembered the story of the wolf's view of
his adventures with the three little pigs, and I thought, 'Why don't I try this piece from my

dogs' perspective!' Here's what it sounds like now." Her students agreed that the story from the dogs' perspective made it "funnier"—though they professed to like the story from her perspective also. The lesson continued with a brief comparison of the two perspectives. Ms. McCredie ended by saying, "When you work on your pieces today, you might think about writing about your topic from one of the characters' perspective." So, as Weaver and her colleagues (2001) suggest and Deanne McCredie demonstrates, the important question to ask is, "What aspects of grammar can we teach to enhance and improve students' writing, and when and how can we best teach them?" (p. 19). Dawn Downes (see Trade Secret 11.2) would respond, "in the context of writing in writing workshop." The goal is to see students incorporating the grammatical constructions teachers teach into their writing, to see them using the grammatical constructions in their writing.

Focus lessons on grammatical constructions can take many forms. For example, teachers might model and ask students to generate sentences with particular kinds of grammatical constructions like those found in literature, or they might show students how to use the five senses in their writing to sharpen the details in their descriptions of objects and experiences in their writing. Carol McNally (Weaver et al., 2001) used Lois Lowry's *The Giver* (1993) in one of her focus lessons. She selected a paragraph from chapter 9 and, "through a regression process," turned it into a piece of writing that sounded just like what her students wrote (p. 24). When her students read the passage, they thought it was "too choppy." So they combined sentences, rewrote the altered passage, and revised the paragraph to make it sound like what they thought Lowry would have written. Then they compared what they had written with what Lois Lowry wrote. Ms. McNally encouraged her students to think about how they might incorporate what they had learned about how to combine sentences in their own writings. What she discovered was increased use of participial phrases, appositives, and subordinate clauses in her students' writing—all without telling them they were studying grammar. So, grammatical constructions can be topics of focus lessons.

TRADE SECRET 11.2
Building Language: A Constructivist Approach to Grammar

DAWN DOWNES

The first year that I initiated a writing workshop in my classroom, my students brainstormed ideas, drafted writing, conferred with me and each other, made revisions, and published their writing in a class anthology. I gave focus lessons on topics, leads, revision strategies, organizing ideas, and a host of other skills and strategies related to writing, the writing process, and living and working in a

writers workshop. I felt good about what was happening in my classroom. The kids were writing, and I felt like I was making a difference in the literate lives of my students. Several weeks into the workshop, however, one of my students came up to me and very innocently asked, "When are we going to do English?"

After I recovered from the surprise of her question, I stammered that we *were* doing English. Writing is, after all, the summation of all of those

(continued)

TRADE SECRET 11.2 Continued

grammar skills. Right? Besides, marching students through the chapters of a grammar book did not make them better writers. Satisfied with my less than polished answer, Sarah walked away to join her writing circle, but she left me with a nagging question in the back of my head that wouldn't go away: What was I doing about grammar in the writing workshop?

I knew that many teachers teach formalized grammar lessons because they believe that it improves the quality of their students' writing. They also think that learning grammar makes the writing more concrete, improves test scores, facilitates foreign language learning, improves social status, and makes our students better users of language (Weaver, 1996).

In reality, more than fifty years of research suggest that teaching the grammar book in a traditional manner does not improve the quality of students' writing. In fact, "if schools insist upon teaching concepts of traditional school grammar (as many still do), they cannot defend it as a means of improving the quality of writing" (Hillocks, 1986, p. 138). Moreover, "the conclusion can be stated in strong and unqualified terms: the teaching of formal grammar has a negligible or, because it usually displaces some of the instruction and practice in actual composition, even a harmful effect on the improvement of writing" (Braddock, Lloyd-Jones, & Schoer, as quoted in Calkins, 1986, p. 195). Such strong words confirm what I had learned through classroom experience and intuition: teaching the grammar book is a waste of instructional time.

To teach grammar in the context of student writing means that we follow a constructivist approach to teaching that builds on students' knowledge of the English language. In traditional grammar curricula, the language (or whole) is broken down into a system of rules (parts) that describe and prescribe how we use language. English teachers hope that their students will somehow manage to apply these "rules" and transfer them to their writing and speech. Usually the anticipated and miraculous transfer of grammatical skill never happens.

Students enter school with the knowledge of some version of English (a grammar). Students learn best when their teachers help them to apply what they already know about the language in their writing and then instruct them on those aspects of language they don't know, but need to know in order to complete the writing task and craft meaning. This contrasts sharply with a traditional grammar classroom where students are overwhelmed with rules and structures that are not directly applied to their writing and cannot be internalized. The rules and patterns may be momentarily memorized for a test or quiz, but in the end they are lost. In a constructivist classroom, students build their knowledge by learning in the context of authentic tasks. Students have the opportunity to write, and as the teacher sees a need for grammatical coaching, a lesson is taught. The simultaneous integration of the grammatical rule with its application to an authentic task, adds value to the new knowledge. Instead of learning the grammatical skills in isolation, the grammar will be attached to meaningful texts in a powerful way (Brooks & Brooks, 1993).

There are four different kinds of grammar lessons that can be embedded in writing workshop. All of these lessons start with student work; the teacher assesses the work, determines the grammatical needs of the writing, and plans lessons (coaching sessions) around those needs:

1. *Incidental lessons* are lessons that are not taught through direct instruction. They take place during a student conference or casually as the teacher moves about the room, coaching students on their writing. The emphasis is on exposing students to the rules of grammar at the moment of greatest impact: right when they find that they don't know how to do or say what they mean. The application is immediate and meaningful (Weaver, 1996).

2. *Inductive lessons* are some of the most powerful lessons that students can learn. This is when students are presented with a collection of data (like student work) and they draw conclusions and formulate a rule

---

TRADE SECRET 11.2 Continued

based on the work (Weaver, 1996). As suggested by Brooks and Brooks (1993), inductive lessons require students to construct knowledge and come to their own conclusions based on their own observations. Because the lesson came out of students' needs, the application of the rule derived inductively is immediate.

3. *Focus lessons* are short, five- to ten-minute lessons. Several lessons in a sequence may be used to teach larger concepts. In general, the students are not required to practice the skill immediately, outside of the context of their writing, and the skills that are presented are not tested in isolation from the student writing. However, students are expected to apply these grammatical concepts as they are needed in the writing.

4. *Extended focus lessons* should take place when a concept is complex and the students would benefit from some practice. The teacher teaches a regular focus lesson and then the students are asked to apply the concept in a short activity. The focus of the practice is to clarify the concept, not necessarily to master it. Again, the students will not be tested in isolation on this topic. Instead, the teacher should assess whether the students grasp the ideas based on their writing and their application of the grammatical rule or structure.

Altogether, grammar lessons that are taught through these four types of instruction will fit into a curriculum in which the application of grammatical patterns is contextualized in response to student work. As I reflect upon my conversation with Sarah about "doing English" in the writing workshop, I realize that I was misguided in my thinking about how grammar and writing workshop fit together. I thought that writing was the cumulative activity that grows from the application of other discrete skills. I was approaching the workshop from a parts to whole pedagogy. I ignored explicit grammar instruction because the students were "doing English" by using their grammar in writing.

Now I approach English and grammar from a different perspective. Students must use their prior knowledge of grammar to create a new piece of writing. Then, as a coach, I study their writing and create a grammar game plan that teaches them the grammar they need to know in the context of when and why they need to know it. Together we construct their knowledge of language so that their use of grammar contributes to effective and purposeful writing. I no longer ignore grammar, but my students will never "do English" the way that Sarah from my first writing workshop wanted. Instead, my students will learn grammar as they craft their writing around meaningful experiences, playing with language inside and outside the rules of grammar, searching for a clear voice to express their thoughts and ideas.

During teacher–student conferences, teachers can discuss the decisions their students make about their sentences or the perspective they decide to take on their topic, or many of the other grammatical and stylistic decisions writers must make to construct text. During *editing conferences,* teachers can help their writers consider the conventions of grammar needed to meet the demands of a specific text's situation. Is it going to the writer's grandmother or to the newspaper? As different grammatical constructions are taught in focus lessons, they can be added to the editing checklist. Joan Berger (2001) did this. As well as providing instruction during focus lessons, Ms. Berger's peer editor's checklist gave specific directions on what peers should look for as they edited each other's papers. For example, items on this checklist included, "Commas are used correctly after adverb phrases or with compound sentences. Place a check mark in the margin where commas are not used or used incorrectly." Through focus lessons, her students had the "verbal equipment" to recognize "adverb phrases" and "compound sentences" (p. 47).

This kind of grammar teaching provides support for growing writers and users of the language. It helps them to tackle the challenges of writing and to begin "to share in what every writer knows is grammar's 'infinite power'" (Hunter, 1995, p. 246).

Now, it is possible that some readers are feeling moderately unsure that the grammar instruction *they* received helped *them* recognize adverbial phrases and compound sentences. For assistance with personal grammar questions, readers might wish to visit the Guide to Grammar and Writing site maintained in memory of Charles Darling (http://grammar.ccc .commnet.edu/grammar/). Readers who find themselves overwhelmed with all the information on this site might turn to the Big Dog's Grammar site, a bare bones guide to English (http:// aliscot.com/bigdog/).

Capitalization and Punctuation

Students who learned capitalization and punctuation rules as needed in the context of their own writing perform equally as well on a standardized test as students who are taught using the more traditional skill-and-drill method (e.g., Calkins, 1980; Cordeiro, Giacobbe, & Cazden, 1983). Lucy Calkins (1980) also discovered that the students who learned the rules as needed within the context of their writing used more kinds of punctuation correctly within their pieces and explained the reasons why punctuation is used more clearly than did students taught using the traditional approach. Further, Pat Cordeiro, Mary Ellen Giacobbe, and Courtney Cazden (1983) discovered that teaching the rules in the context of the students' writing actually seems to provide students with *more* opportunities to practice using the rules than does the language-arts book and workbook they might have used.

Once a rule is introduced in Deirdra Aikens' classroom, it becomes an item on the classroom's editing checklist. As with all items on this checklist, writers search the pieces they have selected for publication for words that should be capitalized that are not or words that are capitalized that should not be, as well as for punctuation that is missing or is used incorrectly. The practice of searching for errors and correcting them in one's own work provides instruction. Additional instruction occurs during the editing conference. The teacher can reinforce the rule supporting each self-correction made by the student and can call the student's attention to one or two words incorrectly capitalized or one or two punctuation marks used incorrectly. As in handwriting instruction, during the editing conference, the teacher has the opportunity to provide direct instruction on those rules of capitalization and punctuation the student needs.

Unfortunately, however, a student's piece typically has many capitalization and punctuation errors. The teacher cannot teach all rules simultaneously! Which rule should the teacher focus on first? Teacher Judy Patton used her school district's language-arts textbook to guide her decision making. Ms. Patton decided to teach those punctuation and capitalization rules that her students' writings indicated they needed and that her district (by its selection of the language-arts textbook) identified as important. Teachers who have no textbook to guide their decisions have the advantage of focusing solely on their students' needs, selecting those most in need of attention, as determined by frequency of use in the students' pieces. Teachers may wish to use resources like *The Elements of Style* (Strunk & White, 2005), *Writers Express* (Kemper, Nathan, & Sebranek, 1994) or *The Write Track* (Kemper, Nathan, & Sebranek, 1995) to guide their recall of capitalization and punctuation rules.

Handwriting

What is the best way to teach children how to form letters? In the past, the idea of teaching letter formation was pushed away. Today, the data clearly indicate that teaching handwriting improves students' writing. Further, teachers, test readers, potential employers, and others form impressions of the student as a writer based on the quality of the handwriting. On scored writing pieces, students with the poorer handwriting typically score considerably lower than students with better handwriting (Graham, Harris, & Fink, 2000). Because handwriting instruction facilitates learning to write, more and more educators believe teachers should provide their students with handwriting instruction. But, as Schlagal (2007) asks:

> Should children be introduced to writing through a traditional manuscript alphabet and later bridged into cursive, as was common throughout most of the 20th century? Should students begin with cursive to prevent the difficulties of learning a new way to write in later grades? Or should they be taught a slanted or italic version of print that is designed to connect with cursive and so ease the difficulty of transition? (p. 193)

So many questions. So few evidence-based answers.

Manuscript or Cursive Style?

Prior to the 1920s, U.S. children of all ages were taught only the *cursive style* (Hackney, n.d.). Marjorie Wise's 1921 arrival in the United States from England marked the commencement of U.S. children being taught the manuscript style. Wise's introduction of the *manuscript style*, a vertical form of letters made with circles and straight lines, was quickly embraced by teachers as the writing style most appropriate for young children. Several reasons have been put forth to support the teaching of the manuscript style to young children (Barbe & Milone, 1980; Duvall, 1985; Farris, 1982; Graham, 1993–1994, 1999; Hackney, n.d.; Schlagal, 2007). These include the following:

- Manuscript letters are very similar to the print forms used in books. Only two lower-case letters, *a* and *g,* are different in type than in handwriting.
- The print in children's world outside the classroom (e.g., "STOP," "SCHOOL BUS") is mostly in manuscript style.
- The manuscript style is easier to produce than is the cursive style.
- The basic strokes (mostly circles and lines) used in the manuscript style parallel young children's perceptual and motor development; the basic shapes are in their drawings.

The typical pattern has been to introduce students to the manuscript style first and then to the teach them cursive style in second or third grade.

Vertical or Slanted Form?

Which manuscript form: vertical or slanted? The title of Steve Graham's (1993–1994) article "Are Slanted Manuscript Alphabets Superior to the Traditional Manuscript Alphabet?"

summarizes the debate. Beginning in the 1960s, some educators began to question children's introduction to the vertical manuscript alphabet—a form like that used by the Zaner-Bloser Company in their handwriting program, *Hand-writing: A Way to Self-Expression* (1993; see www.zaner-bloser.com/Zaner-Bloser-Handwriting.html). Two concerns have been raised most frequently: (1) Young children often reverse some of the very similar lowercase letters (e.g., *b* and *d*), and (2) young children are being required to learn two distinctly different handwriting forms in the span of only two or three years. Concerns such as these resulted in the introduction of slanted manuscript alphabets, a manuscript form purportedly more similar than the vertical form to cursive writing. Today, for example, Donald Thurber's (1999) D'Nealian slanted manuscript alphabet is used in the Scott Foresman handwriting program *D'Nealian Handwriting* (see www.dnealian.com/).

Do the slanted alphabets really ease children's transition from the manuscript to the cursive style? Does the use of a slanted alphabet truly help children become better cursive writers? Several researchers (e.g., Duvall, 1985; Farris, 1982; Graham, 1992, 1993–1994, 1999; Ourada, 1993) contend that there is insufficient evidence to support the claims made by the supporters of slanted alphabets of the benefits of this form to writers. Instead, their findings indicate the following:

- The use of slanted alphabets does not help children to learn cursive more easily or quickly.
- The slanted alphabets' manuscript and cursive letter forms are, like the vertical manuscript and cursive forms, dissimilar.
- There is no evidence that using the slanted alphabets' continuous strokes to form manuscript letters resulted in children having a better writing rhythm, a faster writing speed, or a smaller number of reversed letters than when using single strokes.
- Slanted alphabets require young children to engage in fine-motor motions that are beyond their physical developmental level.

Hence, the present evidence seems to suggest that, if given a choice, teachers should choose to introduce their students to the vertical manuscript style like that from the students' environment outside the school. Learning the vertical manuscript style is also recommended for students with learning disabilities, even though there is no research examining the effectiveness of different scripts with these special needs students (Graham, 1999). Steve Graham adds a word of caution, however. Regardless of which script teachers teach their students, children will develop their own style. Teachers ought not to insist on a strict adherence to any particular model.

Handwriting Instruction

Careful teaching and practice of handwriting can facilitate fluency in writing and may prevent writing disabilities (Graham et al., 2000). Bob Schlagal's recent review (2007) of the suggestions for teaching handwriting identified several key features of handwriting instruction including:

- Explicit instruction in short daily sessions
- Sufficient opportunities to practice correct letter formation

- Teacher modeling of correct letter formation, both visual and verbal, for students in the primary grades but not for students in the upper grades
- Copying a letter from a correct model, with numbered arrows and a simple visual memory technique

An increasing number of school districts are purchasing handwriting programs to teach their elementary students correct letter formation. A program with growing popularity is the *Handwriting Without Tears* program (visit www.hwtears.com/). Other school districts are turning to technology to teach letter formation. Programs like WriteOn! (www.incrediblekid.com) have received positive response from teachers and children.

Left-Handed Writers

Given that 10 to 15 percent (a percentage that is growing) of the population is left-handed, most teachers will have at least some left-handed students in their classrooms. Instruction for left-handed students is only slightly different from the instruction provided for right-handed students. First, it is important for teachers to determine each student's hand preference. Most children develop a preference for their left or right hand sometime during the first four years of life (Bloodsworth, 1993). When unsure of a student's choice, the teacher can ask the student to throw a ball, to cut with scissors, to paint, to string beads, or to hold a pencil or crayon. These will provide clues regarding the student's hand preference. Sometimes these observations will provide conflicting information. Carol Vukelich, one of the authors of this book, writes with her left hand, holds a tennis racket in her right hand, paints walls with her right hand, throws a ball with her right hand, manipulates puzzle pieces with her right hand, pours water with her left hand, and pours sand with her right hand. Fortunately, her first-grade teacher, Ms. Peggar, permitted her to choose which hand she preferred to use to write.

Three instructional adjustments are recommended for left-handed writers (Hackney, n.d.; Howell, 1978):

1. Left-handed writers might wish to hold their writing tools an inch or more farther back from the tip than right-handed writers. This change permits them more easily to see what they have just written.
2. Left-handed writers should tilt the paper to slope downward slightly to the right about 30 to 40 percent, with the lower-right corner pointed toward their midsection. (Right-handed writers tilt the paper slightly upward and to the left.) Too severe a tilt results in a backward slant to the letters.
3. Teachers should permit left-handed writers to slant their handwriting slightly backward.

Of the three suggestions, the paper tilting is the most critical (see Figure 11.2). If the left-handed child fails to position the paper correctly, the child may end up writing with a hooked wrist, a problem that affects legibility and fluency and can cause erasure or smudging of what has been written. Carol Vukelich knows about these problems from personal experience. She has received many smudged notes from her left-handed father, whose teacher, Ms. Peggar, would not let him tilt his paper to the right. Fortunately, a generation later, when Ms. Peggar was Carol's first-grade teacher, she had changed her approach to teaching handwriting and allowed Carol to tilt her paper in the proper direction.

FIGURE 11.2   Correct Paper Slant for Right- and Left-Handed Writers

The kind of support needed by developing writers comes from handwriting instruction that focuses on each student's letter-formation needs, provides direct instruction in how to form the selected letters, and adapts to student's hand preferences.

Strategies for Teaching English Language Learners

According to David Francis and colleagues' research-based recommendations, while ELLs are learning conversational English, they must also quickly begin to develop academic language if they are to be successful in school. "Mastery of academic language is arguably the single most important determinant of academic success for individual students" (Francis et al., 2006, p. 7). Academic discourse is a specialized language, one that is distinctly different from conversational discourse. Understanding complex sentence structures and the corresponding syntax of English is only one aspect of academic language and is not the key aspect, vocabulary (specifically understanding the multiple meanings of English words) is.

How is academic language learned? ELLs will learn many structural sentence patterns unconsciously through hearing them used by good models, their teachers and their peers. But just hearing good models is not enough; teachers need to use strategies in addition to those described above that are effective for all students.

- ELLs' grammar will improve over time if they are provided with many opportunities to engage in structured, academic talk; practice stringing words into complex sentences; and receive tactful feedback for their speaking efforts. As language is used, conceptual understanding and ability develops. ELL students need ample opportunities to use language in context.
- Talk is one context for learning grammar. Writing provides an excellent comparable opportunity for teachers to provide models, explicit grammar focus lessons, practice, explanations, and feedback. ELLs, as any other students, want to write about topics that they truly care about. Writing letters, keeping diaries, or dialogue writing are learning tasks that give

students the opportunity to write about something that motivates them to do more and better writing.
- Teacher modeling is a beneficial tool for ELLs to see how the writing process is used.
- Specific feedback on writing furthers the student's comprehension of academic language. As a student writes a journal entry or a letter, a teacher can provide feedback on the student's paper's content and language. Written as well as oral feedback affords ELLs specific information to improve their academic language.
- Activities that combine reading, writing, listening, and speaking enable students to practice academic language on a daily basis.

Experiences and interactions in the classroom provide a foundation for ELLs to master academic language, allowing them to be successful. In Special Feature 11.1, Luisa Araújo presents a number of strategies for promoting the writing development of ELL students.

SPECIAL FEATURE 11.1
The Writing Development of English Language Learners

LUISA ARAÚJO

Writing can be seen as the "flip side" of reading. Indeed, researchers agree that "many of the skills that are involved in writing, such as spelling and grammar, are reinforced by reading skills" (NICHD, 2007, p. 32). Writing requires good instruction so that students can increase their ability to communicate and to learn. Good writers are goal-oriented; employ strategies to help them plan, organize, and revise their work; and have a good sense of audience (Wollman-Bonilla, 2001). These aspects are stressed in a process-oriented approach to writing and the methodology for teaching ESL writing has embraced this approach. It can be defined as "a process of discovery in which

ideas are generated and not just transcribed as writers think through and organize their ideas before writing and revising their drafts" (Lee, 2006, p. 308). However, can you imagine how hard it will be for students to utilize a language they barely know to write a coherent narrative or a persuasive letter? Much like in the beginning stages of reading development, in the beginning stages of writing development, young ELLs' development is similar to that of first-language children. For older elementary children, the complexity of writing requirements can make writing to learn and to communicate daunting tasks.

It is well documented that young children adopt a letter-name strategy to spell words. As Pollo, Kessler, and Treiman's (2005) research indicates,

(continued)

SPECIAL FEATURE 11.1 Continued

English-speaking children tend to make more mistakes in representing vowels and "they are more likely to include a vowel in their spelling when the vowel is a letter name than when it is not" (p. 4). In Portuguese, young children have also been observed to include more phonetically accurate letters in their writing when the letter's name occurred in the word (Silva & Martins, 2002). Young ELLs, armed with knowledge of the English alphabet, can be expected to make the same mistakes and have greater ease in producing letters that say their names. Similarly, when given opportunities for controlled spelling practice and for free production activities, they can move from invented spellings to conventional forms of writing, regardless of their oral language proficiency level (Araújo, 2002a). However, the writings of ELL children may indicate that their knowledge of English syntax is still limited (Silva, 1993). For example, during writer's workshop, an ESL child wrote a story with the ending "and they falled in the love" (Araújo, 2002b). The sentence is marked ungrammaticality because the child used the wrong verb inflection and the word *the* incorrectly. Nonetheless, this ending is akin to the happy endings of fairy tales (e.g., lived happily ever after) and the child began the story with the canonical narrative beginning "Once upon a time").

In order to support this type of writing development, teachers need to teach reading and writing in an integrated way. Reading good-quality literature in the classroom and giving children opportunities to write in response journals about readings will allow children to interiorize language patterns. In addition, as children progress in school, it is necessary for teachers to teach them strategies for accomplishing specific types of writing tasks, such as writing a story a persuasive essay or taking notes (De La Paz & Graham, 2002; Graham, 2005). Whether for regular students or for ELLs, research shows that explicitly teaching process-writing strategies for planning, revising, and/or editing has a strong impact on the quality of their writing (Graham & Perrin, 2007; NICHD, 2007). In fact, it seems that, for ELLs, process approaches that do not focus on explicit instruction in particu-

lar writing skills and subskills are not sufficient to promote writing development (Genese, Lindholm-Leary, Saunders, & Christian, 2006).

Even mainstream students with average reading abilities may find writing particularly difficult. This is because "[w]hile readers form a mental representation of thoughts written by someone else, writers formulate their own thoughts, organize them, and create a written record of them using the conventions of spelling and grammar" (Graham & Perrin, 2007, p. 8). Thus, to improve ELL students' writing teachers must ensure they have plenty of opportunities to practice the mechanics of writing and to express their thoughts in English. The ability to spell accurately and to express thoughts using correct grammar will enable ELL children to communicate effectively in writing. Again, as with mainstream children, "It will be harder for students to utilize strategies to write a coherent summary or persuasive essay if they are not fluent in the lower-level skills. At the same time, students who have difficulty with either lower-level writing skills or higher-level writing strategies will find it difficult to write to learn" (Graham & Perrin, 2007, p. 24).

Teaching learning strategies such as a specific way to take notes can help students write to learn. One strategy worth teaching comprises writing notes, writing key words, remembering, and studying. Echevarria and Graves (2003) explain how a teacher implemented this specific learning strategy:

> The students were taught to divide each notebook page into two columns by drawing a vertical line down the paper about 2 inches from the left margin. The left column was to remain blank until the students wrote notes on the right column. During the next class, the notes in the right column were used to recall key points and the key points were written in the left column adjacent to the notes. After the key words were written, the students covered the right column with a piece of paper and looked only at the key words to trigger their memories. (p. 141)

Strategy instruction may involve teaching other processes: for example, brainstorming, how to construct graphic, semantic organizers and word maps, and how to interact with peers for collaborative writing and peer revising (NICHD, 2007).

Importantly, writing should be regarded as an avenue for personal learning, as a collaborative endeavor, and as a tool for real communication. When students collaborate to write a persuasive letter to their school principal to convince him or her to address a school problem, they use writing to solve a real problem. This will teach them both literacy and social skills and, as recent research suggests, students' quality of writing may depend on their level of social awareness. It appears that social competence and academic skill are interconnected in writing, both for monolingual and bilingual children (Dray, Selman, & Schultz, 2009). Children with high levels of social awareness may have a better sense of audience and be more persuasive in their writing.

A classroom environment for ELLs should promote writing as both a collaborative and a personal activity that aids learning and serves real communicative needs. Thus, students should have experiences with the following four activities:

1. Interactive journals, in which the teacher responds to students' daily entries in writing each day to provide modeling of written dialogue
2. Writer's workshop based on writing-as-a-process, in which students go through planning, drafting, editing, revising, final drafting, and publishing a written product
3. Patterned writing, in which students use patterned language from books as a basis to create a new story (e.g., Brown bear, brown bear what do you see)
4. Literature study with response journals

The roles of learning to write and of writing to learn are interdependent and develop more efficiently in ELL children with explicit teaching of skills and strategies. Listening, speaking, reading, and writing also develop interdependently. Thus, without adequate oral language development ELL students will be unable to discuss ideas, to understand arguments, and to state points of view and opinions. Giving children choice in writing assignments can also support their motivation to write. Motivated writers show high levels of task engagement, self-determination, and self-regulation (NICHD, 2007). In Chapter 8 we discussed how teachers can use literature that explores ELLs' native language and culture to motivate them to read. Culturally and linguistic responsive teaching (Graves, 1995) should also include opportunities for students to write about their language and culture and their personal experiences. More skills-based initiatives may be implemented and include, for example, a spelling bee in Spanish—a clear message that teachers value ELLs' language (Cummins, 2009).

Strategies for Children with Special Needs: Spelling Instruction

To understand what strategies primary teachers use to help children experiencing difficulty spelling, Graham and his colleagues (2008) surveyed teachers of grades 1–3 across the United States. Their data analysis revealed that 70 percent or more of the survey respondents used the following practices (there is experimental evidence to support the use of each of these practices with struggling spellers):

- Teaching phonological awareness
- Phonics for spelling
- Spelling rules

(continued)

Strategies for Children with Special Needs: Spelling Instruction   Continued

- Strategies for spelling unknown words
- Feedback on words the children misspelled and praised the children for correctly spelling words
- Using games at least weekly
- Peer learning activities
- Encouraging children to use invented spellings
- Encouraging children to use spell-checkers
- Encouraging children to proofread

The surveyed teachers used these strategies with all of their students. Unfortunately, few of the surveyed teachers reported that they adapted their instruction for their weaker spellers. Those who did make adaptations made two evidence-based adaptations: fewer words to learn each week by weaker spellers and reteaching spelling skills and strategies more often to weaker spellers. Bottom line: It is important that teachers make adaptations for weaker spellers.

Family Focus: Helping Children With Spelling

Most parents remember taking spelling tests. We easily remember writing the words three times and using each word in a sentence. Everyone in class had the same words and all of us hoped we would pass the practice test on Thursday so we could flaunt our free time on Fridays.

Some of us were wonderful spellers and a few of us made the finals for the annual spelling bee. But many more of us dreaded the Friday spelling test. So how come spelling is so difficult?

Spelling English words is not easy. English is often said to be a difficult language to learn to read and write because of the irregularities and inconsistencies, for example:

- English has 1,100 different ways to spell its forty-four separate sounds (phonemes) by combining the twenty-six letters of the alphabet.
- English contains hundreds of words borrowed from other languages with different phonetic combinations.
- English contains words that sound the same (homophones), but have different meanings and spellings (*to, too, two*; *principal* or *principle*).
- English has many different spellings rules (twenty-eight) but the only foolproof rule is that all spelling rules in English have exceptions.
- Some words, called sight words, don't rely on strategies or rules to spell, they require children to simply recognize them on sight and then to memorize in order to spell them.

So how can parents help their child learn to spell? We believe that it is best to combine practice with fun!

- To start studying, children should:
  1. **Look** at the word, and **say** it aloud.
  2. **Read** each letter in the word.
  3. **Close** their eyes, try to **picture** the word, and **spell** it out loud.
  4. **Look** at the word again. Did they spell it correctly?
  5. **Say** each letter of the word as you **copy** it.
  6. **Cover** the word, and **write** it again.
  7. **Look** at the word. Did they write it correctly?
  8. If they made any mistakes, **repeat** these steps. (Bradley & Bryant [1985]; Keller [2002])
- Play "spot the mistake." Have children give you the spelling test. Deliberately misspell a couple of the words. See if children can spot the error and correct it.
- Use speed spelling. Have children write/type their words as quickly as possible, which provides plenty of practice.
- Play "travel bee." Ask children to practice spelling words as you travel from place to place in the car/bus/subway.
- Always write down a spelling when children ask. A verbal response is harder to remember because it lacks a visual prop.

- Provide a selection of dictionaries and thesauri.
- After children have studied, spell the words to them, in random order, and have them name the word you spelled.

- Finally, admitting to children that you need to look up words occasionally provides good role modeling, so don't be afraid of using a dictionary or spell-checker yourself.

Summary

In this chapter, we have focused on the mechanical skills of writing—spelling, grammar, capitalization, punctuation, and handwriting. Some of these skills are best taught, explicitly and through practice, within the context of a strong writing program, like the program described in Chapter 10. Other skills, while used by writers, need more attention and must be explicitly taught in ways beyond writing program focus lessons.

- *How will students learn about the mechanics of writing—spelling, grammar, capitalization, punctuation, and handwriting?*

PEARSON
myeducationkit™

To check your comprehension on the content covered in this chapter, go to the MyEducationKit for your book and complete the Study Plan for Chapter 11. Here you will be able to take a chapter quiz and receive feedback on your answers.

Instruction in the mechanics of writing occurs within two contexts: some are embedded in the writing workshop through focus lessons and editing checklists and some are explicitly taught in isolation (like letter formation and spelling). Students are provided instruction on the mechanics of writing during the focus lessons that begin each writing workshop. The students' needs determine which mechanical skills are taught. For example, the observant teacher notices when many of the students are not capitalizing the names of the months in their pieces and teaches a lesson on the importance of capitalizing proper names. Or the teacher might notice that the students write in short, choppy sentences and decide to teach a lesson on sentence combining. Then, when the writers have decided that the content of their pieces is just right, and they wish to publish their pieces, they turn their attention toward the mechanical details. They search their piece, attempting to discover their errors. They circle the words they think are misspelled. They look for words that should be capitalized that are not or words that are capitalized that should not be. They look carefully at how their letters are formed, circling those they think look odd. They search for places that need punctuation marks. They look carefully at the grammatical structures they have used. They might search with a friend after they have searched alone for their errors. Then, the students and the teacher edit the pieces to be published, and the teacher provides one-on-one direct instruction on one or two rules the students need in order to correct mistakes in their pieces because the pieces will be read by a particular audience.

- *How can teachers help children become better spellers?*

Children need instruction to become better spellers. Spelling instruction varies by the stage of the speller. Prephonemic and early phonemic spellers, for example, have different spelling needs than children in the transitional stage. Spelling instruction must be responsive to children's individual needs. When teachers can select the words children will learn to spell, they should select words that reflect the spelling features that students use but confuse when they write, various spelling patterns, and sight words (at the lower levels). Instruction should focus on helping the students understand how words work. Teachers should use a test–study–test method because it is equally as successfully with good and poor spellers. The spelling program should focus on each student's word needs, provide direct instruction based on the student's spelling stage and demonstrated knowledge, celebrate each student's growth without comparison to other class members, and support invented spellings as developmentally appropriate for writers and not treat them as errors.

- *Which writing skills require not only teaching within the context of writing workshop but also more explicit teaching?*

Spelling and handwriting need to be explicitly taught. When children begin to write, it is important that they be encouraged to use what they know about words and their sounds. Becoming a competent speller is a developmental journey, with all children progressing through five stages. At each stage, children need to be provided with spelling instruction; formal spelling instruction—being assigned particular words to study each week—will begin when the child reaches the fourth stage. Some of the words the students will study will be selected from their writing and reading. The teacher will add some words that share the same spelling pattern (e.g., if a particular student needs to learn to spell *cough,* then *rough* and *tough* might also be added to the week's spelling list). There will be spelling tests on Friday for students who receive formal spelling instruction. There is some evidence that spelling instruction embedded in writing workshop and taught directly yields greater gains in spelling performance than either one alone. This is true for students who have learning disabilities and those who do not. This is also true for nonnative English-language speakers.

- *How should teachers teach students to form the alphabet letters correctly?*

Students do need instruction in how to form letters. Some teachers will provide this instruction during the editing stage of the writing process. They will select one or two letters that the student seems to be having difficulty forming correctly. They will give verbal directions for how to form each of the two letters, model how to construct the letters, and observe the student as the student repeats the steps in making the letters while saying the directions softly. They will provide the student with corrective feedback and observe while the student correctly forms the letters three or four times. They will ask the student to select the best-formed letter. They will not ask students with learning disabilities to verbalize the steps for forming a letter while learning it. Instead, they will have them examine a model of the letter marked with numbered arrows and then reproduce the letter from memory. Other teachers will find that their school district has purchased a handwriting program or technology tools as a guide for teaching its students to form letters correctly.

- *Given a choice, which handwriting style and form should teachers use? Manuscript or cursive style? Vertical or slant form?*

The answers are manuscript and vertical for students who have learning disabilities and those who do not.

- *Are writing workshop and teaching the mechanical skills of writing within writing workshop appropriate for nonnative speakers of English?*

Absolutely! Nonnative speakers of English have the same needs as native speakers of English. The focus of the writing workshop is to address the needs of each student. Hence, within the writing workshop, teachers can meet the needs of many different kinds of learners. Through writing workshop, second-language learners can and do engage in writing for multiple purposes and audiences, at first in their native language and then later in English. In the process, they learn about written language and about how to use it effectively.

LINKING KNOWLEDGE TO PRACTICE

1. Work with a colleague to develop a focus lesson plan on capitalization, punctuation, or grammar for a group of students.

2. Visit a classroom to observe the teaching of spelling. What activities were the students doing? Were all students doing the same activity or were the students engaged in different activities, presumably based on their developmental needs? If possible, ask the teacher to describe the schedule used to help the children learn the words and whether or not the test–study–test method is used. Compare your findings with your colleagues' data and against the description of the teaching of spelling presented in this chapter.

3. View the video on WriteOn! Handwriting Program (www.incrediblekid.com/videosample/index.php) and the free download Handwriting Without Tears material (www.hwtears.com/learninglounge). Which do you like better and why?

CHAPTER

12 Assessment: Determining What Older Students Know and Can Do

In Chapters 8–11, we presented strategies for implicit and explicit instruction in literacy for primary- and elementary-aged students. While these instructional activities form the core of an effective reading, writing, and speaking program, they cannot stand alone. To ensure that instructional strategies meet the needs of every student in the class, teachers need to assess whether these activities achieve their intended aims.

We began the discussion of assessment in Chapter 7 with a focus on determining what young children know and can do. In this chapter, our focus is on determining what older students (primary- and elementary-aged students) know and can do. As we did in Chapter 7, we begin this chapter by returning first to the topic of goals or standards. What is it that primary and upper-elementary students should know and be able to do? Because it is common practice for states to mandate that students take a standards-based standardized test, typically in the spring of the academic year, following the discussion of states' expectations for primary- and elementary-aged students, we turn our attention to what teachers should know about this on-demand test. We end this chapter with suggestions on how teachers can assess students' reading and writing skills and the role that parents might play in the classroom's assessment program and the school's testing program.

Before Reading This Chapter, Think About . . .

- How your teachers assessed your literacy progress. Did you take a spelling test on Fridays? Did you read stories and answer comprehension questions?
- The on-demand tests you have taken. Did you take reading and writing tests throughout elementary, middle, and high school? Were you required to take a test, like the Scholastic Aptitude Test or the Graduate Record Examination, and score above a minimum level to gain admission to your undergraduate or graduate program? What are your memories of these tests?

Focus Questions

- What should teachers know about students' literacy development?
- How might teachers prepare their students for standardized tests?

BOX 12.1

Definition of Terms

achievement test: a standardized test designed to measure how much a student has learned and to compare this student's learning with a standard or norm.

analytic scoring: a type of rubric scoring that separates the whole into categories of criteria that are examined one at a time. For example, a rater might judge a piece of writing in the categories of organization, development, sentence sense, word choice/style, and mechanics, one score per category.

assessment: the process of observing, describing, collecting, recording, scoring, interpreting, and sharing with appropriate others (like parents) information about a student's learning.

benchmark: examples of actual student performance that illustrate each point on a scale and then are used as exemplars against which other students' performance can be measured.

criterion-referenced test: a test used to compare a student's progress toward mastery of specified content, typically content the student had been taught. The performance criterion is referenced to some criterion level such as a cutoff score (e.g., a score of 60 is required for mastery).

evaluation: use of information from assessments to make a decision about continued instruction for a student.

holistic scoring: assigning a single score based on the overall assessment of the student's performance.

norm-referenced test: a test designed to compare one child against a group of children.

on-demand assessment: a type of assessment that occurs during a special time set aside for testing. In most cases, teaching and learning come to a complete stop while the teacher conducts the assessment. *See also* standardized test

ongoing assessment: a form of assessment that relies on the regular collection of student work to illustrate students' knowledge and learning. The students' products are created as they engage in daily classroom activities; thus, students are learning while they are being assessed

performance task: an activity that allows students to demonstrate what they know and can do.

rubric: a scoring guide that describes the characteristics of performance at each point on a scale.

running record: systematically observing and recording children's oral reading behavior.

standardized test: a test in which the teacher reads verbatim the scripted procedures to the students. The conditions and directions are the same whenever the test is administered. Standardized tests are one form of on-demand test.

- How might teachers assess their students' writing development?
- How might teachers assess their students' reading growth?
- How might teachers involve students in self-assessment?

What Should Teachers Know About Children's Literacy Development?

Nearly all states have defined *content standards*—what their young citizens (grades pre-K–12) should know and be able to do at specific *benchmark* years (e.g., grades 3, 5, 8, and 10). Figure 12.1 provides an example of one state's literacy standards, in this case developed by teachers, administrators, parents, and businesspeople for Delaware's grade 5 citizens.

FIGURE 12.1   Delaware's English Language Arts Content Standards and the Performance Indicators for the End of K–5

English Language Arts Content Standards

Standard One: Students will use written and oral English appropriate for various purposes and audiences.

Standard Two: Students will construct, examine, and extend the meaning of literary, informative, and technical texts through listening, reading, and viewing.

Standard Three: Students will access, organize, and evaluate information gained through listening, reading, and viewing.

Standard Four: Students will use literary knowledge gained through print and visual media to connect self to society and culture.

(Indicators of required performance for each standard at four grade clusters—K–3, 4–5, 6–8, and 9–10—are provided. One such set of indicators for K–5 students for one standard, Standard One, is detailed below.)

Performance Indicator for the End of K–Grade 5

Writers will produce texts that exhibit the following textual features, all of which are consistent with the genre and purpose of the writing:

Development: The topic, theme, stand/perspective, argument, or character is fully developed.

Organization: The text exhibits a discernible progression of ideas.

Style: The writer demonstrates a quality of imagination, individuality, and a distinctive voice.

Word Choice: The words are precise, vivid, and economical.

Sentence Formation: Sentences are completed and varied in length and structure.

Conventions: Appropriate grammar, mechanics, spelling, and usage enhance the meaning and readability of the text.

Writers will produce examples that illustrate the following discourse classifications:

1. **Expressive** (author-oriented) texts, both personal and literary, that
   a. reveal self-discovery and reflection;
   b. demonstrate experimentation with techniques, which could include dialogue;
   c. demonstrate experimentation with appropriate modes, which include narration and description;
   d. demonstrate experimentation with rhetorical form.
2. **Informative** (subject-oriented) texts that
   a. begin to address audience;
   b. exhibit appropriate modes, which could include description, narration, classification, simple process analysis, simple definitions;
   c. conform to the appropriate formats, which include letters, summaries, messages, and reports;

FIGURE 12.1   Continued

      d. contain information from primary and secondary sources, avoiding plagiarism.
  3. **Argumentative and persuasive** (audience-oriented) texts that
      a. address the needs of the audience;
      b. communicate a clear-cut position on an issue;
      c. support the position with relevant information, which could include personal and expert opinions and examples;
      d. exhibit evidence of reasoning.

Speakers demonstrate oral-language proficiency in formal and informal speech situations, such as conversations, interviews, collaborative group work, oral presentations, public speaking, and debate. Speakers are able to

  1. **Formulate** a message, including all essential information.
  2. **Organize** a message appropriately for the speech situation.
  3. **Deliver** a message,
      a. beginning to control volume, tone, speed, and enunciation appropriately for the situational context;
      b. using facial expression to reinforce the message;
      c. maintaining focus;
      d. creating the impression of being secure and comfortable, and in command of the situation;
      e. incorporating audiovisual aids when appropriate.
  4. **Respond** to feedback, adjusting volume and speed, and answering questions.

PEARSON
myeducationkit™

Go to the Assignments and Activities section of Chapter 12 in the MyEducationKit and complete the activity entitled "Using Standards to Focus Students' Performance: Designing a Plan." As you watch the video and answer the accompanying questions, note how state standards guide the teachers' planning.

Further, states have brought teachers together to define what students at each grade level should know and be able to do. These grade level expectations (GLEs) aim to help teachers measure their students' progress toward the state's benchmark year expectations (e.g., grades 3, 5, 8, and 10). (For an example of one state's English Language Arts Grade Level Expectations, visit www.doe.k12.de.us/infosuites/staff/ci/content_areas/ela.shtml).

High-Stakes Assessment

States aim to ensure that the standards impact teachers' teaching by administering annual standardized *achievement tests* linked to each state's standards. As described in Chapter 1, each school must meet adequate yearly progress goals, with 100 percent of the school's students "meeting the standards" in reading and mathematics by the 2013–14 school year. Each state will make the determination of whether every student in each school has met the state's reading and mathematics standards by examining each school's students' performance on the statewide standardized achievement test. Preservice teacher education candidate readers of this book

PEARSON
myeducationkit

Go to the Assignments and
Activities section of Chapter
12 in the MyEducationKit
and complete the activity
entitled "The Test." As you
watch the video and answer
the accompanying questions,
note why Florida's FCAT test
is truly a "high-stakes"
assessment.

likely participated in their state's high-stakes assessment program as elementary, middle, and high school students. These tests are used to make judgments about students and schools. As Kay Fukuda (2007, p. 431) notes, "they are used to compare schools, to determine the future of a school, to measure the degree to which children are learning and teachers are teaching, and to determine whether a student will be promoted to the next grade or receive a high school diploma." No wonder they are known as "high-stakes assessments." The increased importance of the use of on-demand assessments has not gone without educators raising concerns. We identify four of these areas of concern below:

1. Current standardized assessments tend to focus on a narrow sampling of all-purpose skills and strategies. Literacy is more than a set of skills and strategies. Therefore, current assessments undersample the full range of literate behaviors. For example, the current literacy assessments fail to assess such literate dispositions as reciprocity or the "willingness to engage in joint learning tasks, to express uncertainties and ask questions, to take a variety of roles in joint learning enterprises, and to take others' purposes and perspectives into account" (Carr & Claxton, 2002, p. 16). Current literacy assessments also fail to assess resilience or the willingness to "focus on learning when the going gets tough, to quickly recover from setbacks, and to adapt" (Johnston & Costello, 2005, p. 257).

2. Literacy assessment practices affect teachers' instructional practices. When the *standardized test* focuses on a narrow set of skills and strategies, and teachers' salaries, student retention, student graduation, and more are affected by the students' performance on the test, teachers may eliminate the more complex instructional practices from their repertoire (Rex & Nelson, 2004). Educators fear that only those skills assessed on the test will be taught. Further, they fear that these skills will be taught solely in the format of the test. Test practice becomes the reading curriculum (Santman, 2002).

3. Current assessment policies are too focused on accountability; assessment should be used as a tool for teachers to diagnose children's learning needs so that instruction can be adjusted to meet the children's needs (Olson, 2005).

4. Teachers are unsure about "whether to teach *to* the content of the test, teach students *about* the genre of tests and test-taking, teach . . . students to take a stance *against* the test, or all of the above" (Short et al., 2002, p. 199).

In Special Feature 12.1, Bonnie Albertson begins by acknowledging that many educators have written about the shortcomings of high-stakes assessment.

Lucy Calkins, Kate Montgomery, and Donna Santman (1998) suggest that teachers hired to teach in a new district ask questions like the following to help them understand the district's testing policies:

- Is the district's test *norm-referenced* or *criterion-referenced* and standards-based?
- How are the students' scores reported to the public? Raw scores? Percentile scores? Cut-score percentages (below standard, meets standard, above standard)?

SPECIAL FEATURE 12.1
The Evolution of One State's High-Stakes Assessment

BONNIE ALBERTSON

Much has been written about the shortcomings of high-stakes assessment, accountability based on one-shot tests, and the negative impact that these tests have on students, teachers, and classroom practice in general. Researchers agree that when assessments have high stakes and high visibility, for both individual and program accountability, they influence teacher practice and often determine what will be taught (e.g., Hillocks, 2002; Mabry, 1999; Madaus, 1988; National Commission on Testing and Public Policy, 1990). However, "teaching to the test" may not necessarily be all bad; in fact, many assessment and literacy scholars (e.g., Black & Wiliam, 1998; Huot, 2002; Weigle, 2002) note that the future of such assessments lies in their potential to inform instruction. Similarly, many scholars argue for more local control of assessment systems and getting teachers involved in all aspects of assessment design (e.g., Huot, 2002; Winograd & Arrington, 1999). Calls for local control are based on a situated, contextual view of learning and assessment. Increased local control allows for open-ended dialogue among educators and helps to balance power relationships. These are the kinds of collaboration supported by the teacher-change literature (e.g., Anders & Richardson, 1992; Winograd & Arrington, 1999).

If we know that high-stakes assessments can lead to "teaching to the test," it stands to reason that at the very least, stakeholders should make sure that they are aware of what teaching to the test actually looks like (see Guthrie, 2002, for information about the effects test-taking strategies and familiarity with test format have on test performance). To this end, having teachers involved in every stage of the assessment process increases teachers' knowledge about what content is being tested, what the test looks like, and how it is scored. Surely this is important knowledge if we want to give students every opportunity to truly show what

they "know and can do" in reading and writing. The development of literacy assessment in one state, Delaware, did indeed evolve into a system that influenced instruction in many of the ways promoted by scholars (e.g., Black & Wiliam, 1998; Huot, 2002).

Delaware's current assessment system is not 100 percent "local"; it is, in fact, a hybrid. It calls for a partnership between the "client" (Delaware) and the test "vendor" (PearsonPerson, Inc.). What does such a system look like and what are the positive elements of assessment systems such as Delaware's DSTP (Delaware Student Testing Program)?

Nuts and Bolts

Such a partnership is time-consuming; indeed, shared ownership is both a burden and a privilege. Exactly what roles do teachers play in Delaware's assessment system? In fact, teachers are involved in virtually every phase from passage selection to scoring resolution and publication of released items and anchor papers.

Teacher Selection

Teachers are nominated to serve on test development "steering committees." These teacher committees represent all three of Delaware's counties. In addition, every attempt is made to have committees reflect the makeup of Delaware's school population (gender, ethnic, racial) and represent a cross-section of students.

Test Development

Delaware teachers write the writing prompts; they locate, select, and screen reading passages; they write all the comprehension items (multiple choice, short answer, and extended responses). Committee members also conduct local passage and item "classroom trials" and student–teacher interviews to assess informally passage and item appropriateness. Throughout the development phase, Pearson staff provide constant feedback.

(continued)

SPECIAL FEATURE 12.1 Continued

Field Test and Scoring Protocols

Following the item development phase, the process moves to field testing and scoring. PearsonPerson selects a range of papers from reading and writing field tests. From these they arrange a preliminary set of "proposed anchors" for every written reading and writing test response. They make notes regarding the initial assessment of these pieces. These sets are brought to Delaware on designated days (for English language arts [ELA], usually three full days are allotted). Teachers are released from their schools to participate, although benchmarking often also runs into Saturdays. For each grade level, there are two representatives from Pearson and several teachers, including steering committee members. Participants take turns recording careful notes about scoring discussions.

The first task is to read through the proposed set of anchors and come to consensus on them. This can take four to five hours of "lively" debate but always results in a "Delaware-sanctioned" anchor set. Then teachers turn their attention to additional "training sets" and "decision sets," to be used to train scorers once the Pearson trainers are back in Texas.

At the end of these grueling sessions, the two trainers for each grade level leave with the anchor/training/decisions sets and two sets of notes. But Delaware's teachers leave with even more: they return to their respective districts declaring that participation in these sessions constitutes "the best staff development opportunity they've ever had," at least for the test. Individual scoring biases are exposed, overall student strength and weaknesses become evident, teachers learn about curriculum initiatives across the state, and they learn about what other teachers value in terms of content knowledge.

Live Scoring

Following the "live" assessment in March, Delaware Department of Education (DOE) staff and steering committee members travel to Texas to oversee the "training of scoring leaders." Districts are also invited to send representatives (often department chairs, curriculum leaders), and many do take advantage of this opportunity. These educators observe the scoring training and the actual scoring process. The Pearson staff assigned to "the Delaware project" explain thoroughly the scoring process, covering everything from read-behind protocols to computer features that allow scorers to reverse-image for easier visibility—all information that reassures Delaware educators: "Yes, we all do have college degrees," and "No, lightning will not strike if a student writes his/her answer a bit outside the boxed lines."

Even after Delawareans have returned home, Pearson stays in touch with DOE. They send odd papers, seeking Delaware's decision about papers that do not "fit" the anchors. The following account illustrates the process:

One particularly difficult reading passage was selected by the tenth-grade steering committee to develop for the reading assessment. In keeping with Delaware's stated desire to have "authentic" texts whenever possible and the ELA standard's stated goal of including some informative/technical text, the committee chose to develop a brochure about the Cape May (New Jersey)–Lewes (Delaware) Ferry. One of the questions required students to propose an itinerary for a hypothetical trip to the area, using information about both towns in the proposal. The ferry runs across the Delaware Bay, at the mouth of the inlet leading to the Atlantic Ocean. The two towns—Cape May and Lewes—are in New Jersey and Delaware, across the river from one another. Both are resort towns. There was no apparent problem with the question during the initial anchor-setting activities. However, when it came time for "live" scoring, the Pearson folks noticed a scoring anomaly. Scorers became confused by a few responses that used the terms "beach" and "shore" when referring to Delaware and New Jersey respectively. Since neither of those terms is used in the brochure, and because the ferry runs across a river, the scorers were puzzled by words that referred to a sandy beach/seashore. Delaware teachers, however, were not the least bit puzzled. It's common knowledge—among Delawareans and Jerseyites that is—that when one says she is going to "the beach," she is going to one of Delaware's coastal resorts; when one says he is going to "the shore," he is undoubtedly headed for New Jersey. Once we explained the regionalism, a "scoring note" took care of the apparent dilemma. However, without a mutually respectful relationship between "client" and "vendor," many students would have received lower scores due to the inclusion of what a non-Delawarean would consider "irrelevant" information.

Other Teacher Resources

Teachers have access to a wealth of information on the DOE/DSTP Web site. Information about the reading and writing test configuration, item specifications used by item writers to compose the test, and sample items with benchmarked answers are all available to teachers and parents. The writing prompts and anchor papers for prompts dating back to 1998 are also released and available for teachers to download and use instructionally. In fact, teachers can access their own students' writing samples.

Conclusions

Testing is still testing, and the purpose of this section is not to paint an unrealistically rosy picture. However, we agree with Winograd and Arrington who note that "no particular assessment is a best practice in and of itself; rather, the quality of assessments lies largely in how wisely they are used" (1999, p. 214). Furthermore, the purpose of this section is not to argue for or against high-stakes assessments. Rather, this section explores the ways in which teacher

participation influences one state's large-scale assessment system.

Finally, DSTP has changed the discourse of teachers. Across the state, teachers use the same terms to describe student performance, set achievement goals, and write curriculum. At the very least, consistency and clear expectations are positive outcomes of the DSTP. In addition, teachers have the power to define what is valued. Remember that it is Delaware teachers who "sanction" anchor sets; therefore, teachers make the decisions so teachers do not need to "guess" about the features that make up top-scoring responses. They don't have to guess whether the five-paragraph is privileged or penalized (neither is true); whether students must restate the question in the answer (no) or cite specific information from the test (yes) to earn top scores on the reading test. And finally, although it may be too early to make any predictions about the long-term performance of Delaware's schoolchildren, Delaware's National Assessment of Education Progress scores have steadily increased over the last ten years.

Postscript

In 2009, Delaware entered into negotiations with other testing vendors for the next generation of test. At this writing, the blueprint for the new testing system has not been finalized; thus, the future of teacher–vendor partnerships such as the one enjoyed for more than a decade with Pearson, Inc., is in question. Teachers, however, have expressed their continued commitment to improving the quality of their own classroom formative and summative assessments based on what they learned from the DSTP era.

■ Is a school's score compared with that of other schools and used to rank the school? Are all students' (special education, English language learners) scores counted in the school's ranking?

Preparing Students for On-Demand Assessments

Each state's department of education expects its mandated standardized achievement test to impact the classroom teaching practices of the state's teachers. Of course, when a test is directly linked to a state's content standards, both classroom curriculum/instruction and the test are driven by the standards. In theory, if teachers are teaching to the standards (providing learning opportunities that help students develop the knowledge specified in the content standards), their students should do well on the test. Even so, teachers, like Donna Santman (2002), pause from their rich units of study to teach their students the test genre. Note that Ms. Santman does *not* spend the year teaching to the test. Rather, her reading and writing curriculum builds the knowledge her students require to perform well on the test.

So the pause is to teach her students the particular challenges of reading associated with the test—to approach the test as a kind of genre and to teach her students how to negotiate the unique qualities of the test genre. Ms. Santman recommends teachers use the following test genre teaching strategies:

- Begin by having students work in groups to create lists of what they already know about this genre. From previous years' experiences, what do they remember about the test? This provides teachers with information on what their students' already know about the tests.
- Immerse students in materials *exactly like* the format of the test they will take. Many test publishers sell practice books. Some states (e.g., www.doe.k12.de.us/infosuites/ Students_family/reading/files/reading_readsamp_1999.pdf) provide item samplers for teachers' use with their students.
- Invite students to explore the materials (e.g., read through the test passages to consider how they are organized and the types of questions asked).
- Time students as they work through a number of passages, if the test is a timed test. If not, invite them to read and respond to a number of passages. Then, talk about the strategies they used to read and respond to the questions.
- Role-play the strategies you use when taking a test. Do you, for example, avoid looking ahead so that you are not overwhelmed by all that is left to do? Do you stop between sections to give yourself a short break in order to feel refreshed and ready to proceed? Do you change pencils to help you feel refreshed? Tell them what works for you and invite them to share their successful strategies.
- Focus on the test questions. Ask students to work in groups to identify "tricky phrases." Translate the generated list into words the students know and have been using all year.
- Focus on the test answers. Show students how to avoid overanalyzing and to check passages for answers to the questions.
- Invite students to "act as if they are test writers" (p. 210). Being a test writer themselves will help them look at the questions and answers from a new perspective.

Reconsidering Teaching Practices

It is unacceptable if a teacher is still teaching the same way she/he was teaching twenty years ago. We, as a profession, have learned incredible amounts about how students learn best. . . . If [we] teach well, maintain best practices, make instructional decisions based on [our] students' needs, and make decisions that are reflective of [the principles of learning we hold], [our] students will learn. They will learn well, and they will pass the test. (Buckner, 2002, p. 215)

The authors of this book acknowledge that no single test score should be used alone to judge students' progress in reading and writing. However, *if* most of the students in a school do not perform as expected on a standardized test, then teachers must be prepared to reconsider their methods of teaching reading and writing. Teachers need to ask themselves, What could I have done better or differently? Others certainly will raise this question. Is it the reading curriculum? A district administrator might recommend that a new basal anthology be purchased. Someone, maybe even a state legislator, might mandate that phonics be taught to all kindergartners through third-graders for thirty minutes a day. Teachers must be able to respond by defending their teaching practices and by learning what legitimately needs revising to support students' development as readers and writers. Teachers at each grade level and within each school need to study the reported testing data to understand what their students could do well and what was challenging for their students. These data can guide teachers' examination of their teaching practices.

Assessing Students' Writing Performance

Central to teachers' implementation of a high-quality writing program is their ability to answer the following kinds of questions: What do these writers need? Do they need information on how to pull their readers into their pieces, on good leads? Do they, perhaps, need information on how to make their writing come alive, using dialogue? When children use dialogue, do they know how to punctuate their texts? Do they need information on the traits of an opinion essay? To answer these questions, teachers need to use formative assessment:

> Effective teachers of writing are engaged in an ongoing process of assessing student needs and teaching to meet those needs. In this . . . approach to assessing student learning, teachers engage in what we often call *formative assessment* or assessment for learning. (Glasswell & Parr, 2009, p. 353)

By examining the pieces in the students' writing folders or writing notebooks, rereading the anecdotal notes made during teacher–student conferences and the vignettes of significant breakthroughs demonstrated by their writers, and reading and evaluating their students' writing pieces, teachers acquire the information they need to make instructional decisions. This information will also help teachers judge their writers' development and accomplishments.

Anderson (2005, p. 2) encourages teachers to "take an assessment stance" and assess student writers every day. He is *not* suggesting that teachers *test* student writers every day by having them write to a prompt. Rather, Anderson suggests that good teachers gather information about their student writers by observing them, talking with them, and studying their writing pieces. By observing, teachers can gather information about the students' initiative, what the students know about writing well, and about the students' writing process. By conferring, teachers can learn what the students are thinking about as they write, as well as what they know about writing and their writing process. By studying the writing pieces (not just the finished pieces but all the drafts), teachers can learn what the students do well, what revising strategies they use, and what their editing shows that they know about the mechanics of writing. Using these strategies, good writing teachers learn about their students' writing strengths and weaknesses, how to tailor their conversations with their students during conferences to meet each student's needs, and how to design focus lessons and units of study that best meet the collective needs of the class of writers.

Using Writing Rubrics

Rubrics are an important tool teachers use to evaluate their students' finished pieces. Rubrics help teachers answer the questions: How good is this piece of writing? What qualities of good writing did this writer use effectively in crafting this piece? (The answer to this question helps teachers know what to celebrate in their students' writing, and celebrating what is good is as important as uncovering each writer's instructional needs.) What qualities of good writing did this writer not use as effectively in crafting this piece? (The answer to this question helps teachers know what lessons to teach this student.) Rubrics, then, help teachers understand their students' development. Rubrics enable teachers (and students) to assign a score or rating (beginning, developing, proficient) to a piece of writing.

Classic writing rubrics typically describe student writing in several areas (writing traits), such as organization, development or ideas, sentence variety, word choice, voice, and conventions. Descriptors outline the expectations or criteria for each of the possible point values or performance levels, usually on a three- to six-point scale, for each area. The clearer the criteria, the more likely the student writers will know what is expected of them in each writing trait. Vicki Spandel (2001, p. 21), for example, describes the level of detail needed to describe the *organization* writing trait. She suggests that the criteria describing proficient organization might be: "(1) inviting, purposeful lead; (2) effective sequencing; (3) smooth, helpful transitions; (4) good pacing; and (5) effective conclusion that makes the reader think." The criteria describing developing performance might be: "(1) introduction and conclusion present, (2) sequencing sometimes works, (3) transitions attempted, and (4) pacing sometimes too rapid or too slow." Finally, the criteria for beginning organization might be: "(1) no real lead or conclusion yet, (2) sequencing creates confusion, and (3) pacing slows reader down—or pushes the reader too hard." Notice how these criteria are clearly written, identify significant aspects of an important writing trait, give clear distinctions among the three performance levels, and describe what the writer should do. The students could use these criteria to guide the development of their writing, and they and their teachers could use this rubric to judge the quality of this writing trait (organization) in the students' writing pieces.

Three kinds of scoring rubrics for teachers and students are in use today: primary trait, holistic, and analytical.

PEARSON
myeducationkit™

Go to the Assignments and Activities section of Chapter 12 in the MyEducationKit and complete the activity entitled "Writing a Personal Narrative: Rubric." As you watch the video and answer the accompanying questions, note how the students have help to construct the rubric that is used to evaluate their writing.

Primary Trait Scoring Rubrics. These rubrics vary with the writing's purpose and audience. If the writers are to write to persuade a person in authority, for example, then the traits that are central to putting forth an argument might be to articulate a position and to prepare a well-written discussion of the reasons for the position, taking into account the knowledge of the audience about the topic. Because the audience is a person in authority, an additional trait might be to offer a counterargument for at least one of the audience's possible positions on the topic. An example

FIGURE 12.2   Primary Trait Scoring Rubric for Persuasive Writing

---

6   Extensively elaborated. In these pieces, students articulate a position for or against the topic, or they suggest a compromise, and they present an extended, well-written discussion on the reasons for their position. These responses may be similar to "5" responses, but they provide an extended discussion of the reasons for their position.

5   Elaborated. In these responses, students articulate a position for or against the topic, or they suggest a compromise, and they provide an extended discussion of the reasons for their position.

4   Developed. In these responses, students take a position for or against the topic, or they suggest a compromise, and they discuss the reasons for their position. Although the reasons may be more clearly stated than in papers that receive lower scores, the discussions may be unevenly developed.

3   Minimally developed. In these responses, students state or imply a position for or against the topic. Rather than support their position with reasons, however, these papers tend to offer specific suggestions or to elaborate on the students' opinions.

2   Undeveloped. In these responses, students state or imply a position for or against the topic, but they offer no reasons to support their point of view.

1   Off-topic or no response. In these responses, students do not take a position or write nothing.

---

of a primary trait scoring rubric is presented in Figure 12.2. Using this rubric, how would you score the persuasive letter in Figure 12.3?

Holistic Scoring Rubrics.   These rubrics require raters to consider how a writer used all the writing traits (organization, ideas or development, voice, word choice, sentence variety, mechanics) in harmony in a piece to achieve an overall effect. In essence, the scorer reads the piece and gets a general impression of how well the writer has used the writing traits in the crafting of the piece. To help scorers, exemplars (or anchor papers) are selected to illustrate typical performance at each score point. The scorers, then, can compare the piece they are reading against the anchor papers to help them arrive at a single score. Unlike primary trait scoring rubrics, the same holistic scoring rubric can be used to score writing in all discourse categories (persuasive, expressive, informative, narrative). An example of a holistic scoring rubric developed by a group of teachers is shown in Figure 12.4. Consistent with suggestions regarding how a rubric should be created, these teachers researched the characteristics of expressive texts and read published pieces when preparing a list of the important characteristics exhibited by these kinds of tests. They incorporated these characteristics into the highest category, labeled "advanced," on their rubric. Using this rubric, how would you score the writing in Figure 12.5?

Analytical Scoring Rubrics.   The final type of rubric "acknowledges the underlying premise that, in writing, the whole is more than the sum of its parts, but it adds that, if we are to teach students to write, we must take writing apart—temporarily—in order to focus on one skill at a time" (Spandel, 2001, p. 26). An analytical scoring rubric, then, takes each significant writing trait and, using specific language and criteria, describes what each trait looks like at various levels of proficiency. For example, Ruth Culham (2003) describes a 6 + 1 analytic scoring rubric used by many teachers to describe students' writing. The traits on this rubric

Jason
I think you
Shouldn't give us
homework becusase
I think we should
have a free Spring
break. becusase I think
you Should Let us
have a break becusase
it's Our time
off. and plus I'm
going to west Vrginia with
my dad

FIGURE 12.3   Jason's Persuasive Letter

FIGURE 12.4   Teacher-Designed Expressive Rubric

Three Rubrics: Basic, Proficient, Advanced

Pieces rated as basic *should exhibit the following characteristics:*
- The piece has a good topic sentence.
- Piece focuses on one topic.
- The sequence of the events is appropriate.
- The description of the setting (where the event occurred) might be stated or implied.
- The piece has a beginning, a middle, and an end. The beginning and middle probably are more developed than the end.
- The transition between sentences and paragraphs is typically clear.
- The piece has a title that is consistent with its main idea.

Pieces rated as proficient *should exhibit the preceding characteristics, with some elaboration, and the following characteristics:*
- The setting is stated and developed, probably through the use of an adjective or two.
- The piece has a beginning, a middle, and an end that exhibits more development (particularly of the middle) than pieces rated as basic. One event may be detailed, or there may be brief details for multiple events.
- The vocabulary is selected to create a picture of the event or events, the character, the setting, and so on. Fresh adverbs and adjectives are often used.

Pieces rated as advanced *should exhibit the following characteristics:*
- The lead is catchy, grabbing the reader's attention and making him or her want to read on.
- The setting is explicitly described, using imagery.
- The beginning catches the reader's attention, arousing his or her interest and helping him or her to anticipate the middle. It provides the information necessary to understand the rest of the narrative. The middle sustains interest by depicting events with details. The piece ends with an effective "bang" that reveals the outcome.
- The dialogue provides insights into the character's (or characters') thoughts and feelings, in addition to advancing the plot/storyline.
- The writer uses appropriate words to signal transitions.
- There is cohesion within the paragraphs (each idea is developed in a paragraph) and coherence across paragraphs. One event moves smoothly to another.
- Multiple events are described. Events, details, and dialogue are carefully chosen with the purpose of telling the story.
- The writer selects and sustains
   - a language natural to the narrative,
   - a point of view appropriate to the narrative, and
   - a tense (or tenses) consistent with the flow of the narrative.

---

include *ideas* (the content), *organization* (the internal structure, the logical pattern of the ideas), *voice* (the writer's style, what makes the writer's feelings and convictions come out through the words), *word choice* (the rich, colorful, precise language that moves the piece), *sentence fluency* (the flow of the language), and *conventions* (the level of correctness), plus *presentation* (the form and layout of the writing). Culham then defines the qualities of each

There once was a very tiny family. The largest one was six inches tall. They all had tals they lived in the walls of the Bigg family. Nobody ever noticed them. One Halloween the 2 yongest ones Were thinking of something to Scare there family with. The oldest was listening to the radio. The little boy told his plan to scare his family with to his Sister They wen to the microphone on the radio If this tiny family was discoverd they would be destroyed The little boy turned on the microphone and said "There has been discoverd a Small family living inside the walls If you think you have them call this number 738-9828 we will Send you a destroer for them. The whole family went wild they Started packing there things The yongest 2 told them it was just a joke They unpacked there things and settled down.

True story

T.HI.

The day I went to the Carnival in wildwood

Oneday I went to wildwood and we stayed in a motel in wildwood for 20 days in the Summer I went in the Spooky house and It was Fun My brother My cousin they went Into It was Fun we went pass Dracule My cousin thought that It was a staten so he said Boo! that Dracula said Boo! back to him and we jumped We almost jumped and the water. It was all over a man at the door was beating the door and I never went in a Spook house again And we had fun. That all I can Say now By The End

FIGURE 12.5   Two Third-Graders' Stories

trait at five levels of performance. For guidance in how to focus on each trait to score students' writing, see Culham's book and complete the exercises on scoring samples of students' papers. An additional resource is the Northwest Regional Educational Laboratory's 6+1 analytic scoring rubric: available at www.nwrel.org/assessment/pdfRubrics/6plus1traits.PDF.

The analytical scoring rubric is the most useful rubric for teachers. By scoring students' writing along each significant writing trait, teachers can determine the writing needs of individual students and an entire class. With that information, teachers know what the topics of the classroom's focus lessons should be and what to teach. An example of an analytical scoring rubric is shown in Figure 12.6. Using this rubric, how would you score the writing in Figure 12.7?

FIGURE 12.6   Analytical Scoring Rubric

The following characteristics determine the success of the response in meeting the needs of the audience and fulfilling the writing purpose.

Score of 5		Score of 4	Score of 3	Score of 2	Score of 1
Score point 5 meets all the criteria listed in score point 4. In addition, a paper receiving this score shows an exceptional awareness of readers' concerns and needs. *The student may have shown an exceptional use of:* *Development strategies specific to the purpose for writing* *Distinctive style, voice, tone* *Literary devices* *Compositional risks*	*Organization*	Unified with smooth transitions, a clear and logical progression of ideas, and an effective introduction and closing.	Generally unified with some transitions, a clear progression of ideas, and an introduction and closing.	Minimally unified and may lack transitions or an introduction or closing.	Lacks unity.
	Development	Sufficient, specific, and relevant details that are fully elaborated.	Specific details but may be insufficient, irrelevant, or not fully elaborated.	Some specific details but may be insufficient, irrelevant, and/or not elaborated.	No or few specific details that are minimally elaborated.
	Sentence Formation	Consistently complete sentences with appropriate variety in length and structure.	Generally complete sentences with sufficient variety in length and structure.	Some sentence formation errors and a lack of sentence variety.	Frequent and severe sentence formation errors and/or a lack of sentence variety.
	Style/Word Choice	A consistent style with precise and vivid word choice.	Some style and generally precise word choice.	Sometimes general and repetitive word choice.	Often general, repetitive, and/or confusing word choice.
	Lang. Conventions	Few, if any, errors in standard written English that do not interfere with understanding.	Some errors in standard written English that rarely interfere with understanding.	Several kinds of errors in standard written English that interfere with understanding.	Frequent and severe errors in standard written English that interfere with understanding.

Source: Delaware Department of Education.

Large-Scale Writing Assessment

In the above sections, we described classroom-based assessment tools. Teachers could use any one of the rubrics to assess their students' writing using *ongoing assessment* (e.g., teachers assess a student's or all of their students' writing pieces using one of the above rubrics) or *on-demand assessment* (e.g., teachers require all students to respond to a writing prompt). States, gathering writing samples from all students in select grade levels in the state, and

Do you know how to play soccer? Well, Matt and I do. This is how you start. First, you sign up. Then you get your coach. After that, the coach gets the whole team together and you have your first practice. Then you practice all the kicks and moves. Now we are going to tell you how to do them.

(1)

First we will tell you the way you should use your feet. You use the inside of your feet to dribble, pass and score. Also, you use the inside of your feet to block the ball.

Now we will tell you about kicks. One kick is the dribble and kick. It is when you dribble and then you kick the ball.

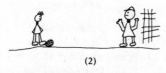

(2)

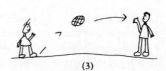

(3)

Since we have been talking about dribbling, we will tell you how to dribble. You use the inside of your feet. Then you kick it with the inside of your feet. If you kick it with your toes, sometimes it will hurt. Also if you kick it with the outside of your foot, the person can steal the ball. Also you might twist your ankle. But if you want to kick the ball like that you should be a professional or if you had a lot of experience. If you want to, you can try it; but we're just telling you that you shouldn't try it.

Now we will tell you more kicks. This play is called the "give and go." First, you dribble the ball. Then you pass it to your teammate. Then their teammate kicks the ball and makes a score.

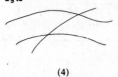

(4)

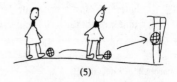

(5)

Now we will tell you about the banana kick. The banana kick is when the defender is charging. You should strike the ball with the outside of your foot. It will curve around him to your teammate. The banana kick is a very famous kick because it is made by famous Peli.

(6)

Now we will tell you how to act on the field. First, you be kind to your teammates. If you yell at the ref, you will get a yellow card. If you yell at the ref again, you will get another yellow card. That means you got a red card and you will get kicked out of the other next game.

(7)

FIGURE 12.7   How to Play Soccer by Matt and Scott

Now we will tell you about the tournaments. Later on in the season, there will be tournaments. Your coach will sign your team up and you will go on the day that it is done. You also will play lots of teams. There will be an ice cream truck at the side walk. There will also be a concession stand and it will have hot dogs and candy bars and lots of other candy. Then there will be more tournaments later on. Just so you know, a tournament is a scrimmage too.

Soccer is one of the best games in our state. If you like football, you should like soccer too. That's how soccer is.

by Scott Myers and Matt Hearn

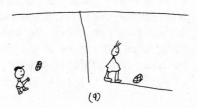

(8)   (9)

FIGURE 12.7   Continued

the National Education of Educational Progress (NAEP), gathering data from a representative sample of select students in states agreeing to participate, are examples of large-scale writing assessments.

On a specific day, typically in the spring, all students at specified grade levels are required to produce a piece of writing. The procedures for gathering this sample of students' performance are standardized. Typically, teachers across the state, at each of the grade levels, present their students with the same prompt. For example, the students might be directed to write to the following prompt (from the Delaware Department of Education): The editor of your newspaper is putting together a student section of the newspaper. Students have been asked to write about their favorite holiday or tradition for this section. Write an article about your favorite holiday or tradition to send to the newspaper. Once the allotted time has passed, the teachers box the students' writing samples and deliver them to the school's office. The office staff then forwards the test to the district office or the state for scoring by trained scorers. (For additional prompt suggestions, see Spandel, 2001, pp. 32–33, and www.doe.k12.de.us/aab/English_language_Arts/Writing_Standalone.shtml. The Web site has prompts and examples of students' writing at grades 3, 5, 8, and 10. The students' writing has been critiqued for strengths and weaknesses.)

This kind of writing for large-scale assessments is different from what typically occurs in writing workshops. In writing workshops, students write about topics in which they have vested interests. Real audiences read their writing. Students have time to prewrite, write, revise, edit, and write a final copy. Students use the resources (e.g., dictionary, thesaurus, spell-checker) they need. Perhaps it is not surprising that, given such differences, all teachers are not enthusiastically supportive of large-scale assessments. Some teachers find these assessments threatening and intimidating, especially when their students' performance is used to judge their teaching or their school's or district's performance. David Coker and William Lewis (2008) agree and encourage researchers to design writing tests or alternate forms of *evaluation* that are more authentic. They suggest that new writing assessments need to be more consistent with the varied writing practices students experience, including such possibilities as eliminating the imposed time limits, evaluating more than one piece of the students' writing, allowing students to select the topic, and permitting students to work collaboratively on the writing.

NAEP's large-scale writing assessment uses a procedure similar to that described above. NAEP assesses students in grades 4, 8, and 12 and reports data at the state and national levels in writing, usually at grades 4 and 8, and not in writing every year. Following the administration and scoring of the students' writing, NAEP releases the Nation's Report Card, informing the public about the writers' performance and comparing performance among states, urban districts, public and private schools, and student demographic groups. Readers can find a copy of the most recent report card for writing at http://nationsreportcard.gov/writing_2007/.

Assessing Students' Reading Performance

Consider these scenarios:

A teacher pulls each of her students aside, one at a time, to have them read the same book, a book unknown to all of them. While each child reads, the teacher records the child's reading errors. When the child finishes reading, the teacher asks the child to retell the story. Later, the teacher might use a miscue analysis system to analyze the children's reading errors and a story structure form to analyze the children's retellings. The teacher analyzes every child's reading and retelling exactly the same way.

A group of children finish reading Charlotte's Web *by E. B. White (1952, HarperCollins). The teacher has participated occasionally in the group's book discussions so the teacher has a sense of the group's understanding of the story. However, the teacher wants to know more about each child's understanding of the text. The teacher develops a set of four open-ended questions to which all children will respond in writing and identifies the criteria to be used to score the children's work. All children in the group take the test on the same day, writing for as much time as they need, and are given the same directions: to use details from the story to support their answers. To score the test, the teacher compares what the children wrote and the degree to which they supported their ideas (rarely to thoroughly and sufficiently) against the previously defined criteria.*

On two days in March, all third-, fifth-, eighth-, and tenth-graders in the state read several passages and demonstrate their understanding of the passages by bubbling-in answers to multiple-choice questions and writing answers to open-ended questions. The multiple-choice questions are scored by machine; the open-ended questions are scored by trained raters using a rubric written by and anchor papers selected by teachers. (Because the items on the test have been linked to the state's content standards, this on-demand assessment would be called a "standards-based state-mandated" assessment because it is linked to the state's standards and mandated by the state's legislators.)

Notice the shared features of these on-demand assessments. A central feature is that during on-demand assessments the teacher stops instruction and the children stop their learning to demonstrate what they know and are able to do. The children are, as the name implies, required to show what they know "on-demand." (Recall that, in ongoing assessment, assessment and instruction were interwoven.)

Standardized Tests

Many on-demand assessments, such as those in the third example above, are administered, scored, and interpreted in the same way for all test takers. Each student taking the test reads the same passages, answers the same questions, and hears the same directions or writes to the same prompt in the same amount of time. When all variables are held constant, the assessment would be known as a "standardized" on-demand test. Table 12.1 provides a number of reading assessments for older children. Evaluating older students' reading development requires a broader look at literacy, decoding, vocabulary, listening comprehension, silent reading comprehension, and fluency. The standardized tests listed in Table 12.1 are widely used across the United States and have strong psychometric measures for reliability and validity. These types of assessments can provide teachers with valuable information about a student's literacy

TABLE 12.1 Standardized Reading Tests for Older Students

Name of Test and Publisher	Type of Test	Skills Assessed	Administration Age Range	Time to Administer
Diagnostic Assessment of Reading (DAR) ■ Riverside	Diagnostic	Decoding Vocabulary	Individual Ages 5–adult	10–30 min.
Dynamic Indicators of Basic Early Literacy Skills (DIBELS)	Diagnostic Progress monitoring	Phonological awareness Letter naming Phoneme segmentation Nonsense word fluency Oral reading fluency Retelling fluency Word usage fluency	Ages 5–8	Timed tests; usually 1 minute per subtest
Gates MacGinitie Reading Test, 4th ed. (GMRT) ■ Riverside	Diagnostic	Vocabulary Comprehension	Group Pre-K–Grade 6	70 minutes for both subtests (35 each)
Gray Oral Reading Test (GORT-IV) ■ Pro-Ed	Diagnostic	Oral reading fluency Comprehension	Individual Ages 6–18	10–15 minutes
Group Reading Assessment and Diagnostic Evaluation (GRADE) ■ American Guidance Service	Diagnostic, Progress monitoring	Word reading Vocabulary Comprehension Listening	Group or individual Ages 4–18	45–60 minutes
Qualitative Reading Inventory III (QRI-III) ■ Allyn & Bacon Longman	Diagnostic	Decoding Fluency Vocabulary Comprehension	Individual Ages 5–13	30 minutes

strengths and areas of need. This type of assessment, especially group administered testing, can quickly provide teachers with needed information that guides instruction at the beginning of the school year. Special Feature 12.2 provides an overview of how one of these tests, Dynamic Indicators of Basic Early Literacy Skills (DIBELS), is used in primary-grade classrooms.

SPECIAL FEATURE 12.2
Dynamic Indicators of Basic Early Literacy Skills (DIBELS)

CHRISTINE EVANS

It's the end of September and all the students in Matthew's kindergarten class are taking the DIBELS Initial Sound Fluency test. The Initial Sound Fluency (ISF) test measures phonological awareness with beginning sound identification tasks. Matthew's teacher shows him four pictures: a mouse, flowers, a pillow, and letters. She points to each picture while saying its name: *This is mouse, flowers, pillow, letters.* Then she says: *Mouse begins with the sound /m/* (points to the mouse). *Listen: /m/, mouse. Which picture begins with the sounds /fl/?* Matthew says *flowers* and points to the picture of the flowers. Alternate forms of the ISF test used for progress monitoring will ask Matthew to produce the initial sound for the picture instead of identifying the picture for the sound. These brief one-minute screening tests will identify a subset of students who are in danger of reading failure, those that need early intervention as quickly as possible.

In September the median performance of all students in Matthew's class on the ISF test is 10 correct initial sounds per minute. Matthew scores a 10, and therefore is on an average level with his peers and not in need of further assessment or intervention. In December, the teacher repeats the assessment using an alternate form of ISF. The median score for the class increases to 15 initial sounds per minute. Matthew's score remains at 10 initial sounds per minute. Thus, Matthew's December test score is below the class median and is an indicator of a trend toward lower reading performance than that of his peers. At this time, Matthew's teacher further assesses his

phonological awareness and provides him with intervention in January.

Effective, comprehensive reading programs include assessments that screen, diagnose, monitor, and evaluate (Fuchs, Fuchs, & Vaughn, 2008). Currently, schools seek early identification of struggling students like Matthew and provide these students with interventions that will increase the likelihood that they will be successful. Dynamic Indicators of Basic Early Literacy Skills (DIBELS) are a set of problem-solving procedures and measures for assessing students' early literacy and reading skills from kindergarten to third grade (more recently to sixth grade). Each DIBELS measure contains two cut scores that divide the students into categories: "low risk" for reading failure, "some risk" for reading failure, and "at risk" for reading failure. Those students categorized as "at risk" are below the lowest cut score and in need of intense intervention. DIBELS measures provide different cut scores depending on whether screening takes place in the beginning, middle, or end of the year (Fuchs et al., 2008, pp. 28–29). There are seven subtests in all and kindergarten typically uses three of these measures:

1. *Initial Sound Fluency (ISF).* This subtest measures phonological awareness with beginning sound identification tasks (see previous description), and is administered late pre-school through winter of kindergarten.
2. *Letter Naming Fluency (LNF).* This measures letter knowledge and rapid naming ability. The teacher presents the student with a printed page containing upper- and

lowercase, randomly arranged letters and asks the student to name as many letters as he can in one minute. It is administered fall of kindergarten through fall of first grade.

3. *Phoneme Segmentation Fluency (PSF).* This subtest measures a student's ability to break short words into individual phonemes, or sounds. It is administered winter of kindergarten through spring of first grade (Good & Kaminski, 2002).

When students approach or have reached ceiling on a particular measure, the teacher changes the measurement material to a more challenging task (Good & Kaminski, 1996). By February, Matthew's kindergarten class had reached ceiling on the ISF, so the teacher administered Phoneme Segmentation Fluency (PSF). In this measure, the teacher says the words for one minute. After each word, the student segments the word into specific phonemes. For example, the teacher says to the student: *I am going to say a word. After I say it, you tell me all the sounds in the word. So, if I say, "cat," you would say /k/ /a/ /t/. Let's try one. Tell me the sounds in "top."* The student responds: /t/ /o/ /p/. Matthew's score on PSF was consistent with his peers in February. The teacher monitored Matthew's progress with alternate forms of DIBELS PSF measures during March and April. She discovered that he was not responding adequately to the core instructional program in the general education classroom. Thus, she implemented a second intervention for Matthew. By the end of May, Matthew's phonological awareness skills had increased to forty-seven segments per minute. Thirty-five to forty-five segments per minute is predictive of reading success (Good & Kaminski, 1996, p. 334). Because of DIBELS screening and progress monitoring, Matthew was considered no longer at risk of reading failure in first grade in the area of phonological awareness.

In first grade DIBELS recommends continuing letter naming fluency and phoneme segmentation fluency screening with the addition of a fourth measure:

4. *Nonsense Word Fluency (NWF).* This subtest measures alphabetic principle including letter–sound correspondence skills as well as decoding skills. This measure can be administered for *most* students from the winter of kindergarten through fall of second grade. Older students benefit from NWF progress monitoring if they are at risk in alphabetic principle. The benchmark for NWF is fifty correct letter sounds per minute by mid-first grade (Good & Kaminski, 1998). With Nonsense Word Fluency, the teacher presents the student with a page of randomly ordered "pseudo" words and asks the student to "read" the words (Fuchs et al., 2008). The student has one minute to produce as many letter sounds as he can correctly. Students who blend the sounds and read the nonsense word score higher than those students who just pronounce the letter sounds in isolation.

DIBELS suggests two other subtests intended for students from the middle of first grade to the end of third grade:

5. *Oral Reading Fluency (ORF).* This subtest measures accuracy and fluency with short passages. The teacher directs the student to read a passage for one minute. Similar to a running record, the teacher notes words omitted, substituted, or incorrect as errors. The benchmark goals for students are 40 correct words per minute (wpm) in the spring of first grade, 90 correct wpm in the spring of second grade, and 110 correct wpm in the spring of third grade (Good & Kaminski, 2002). Good, Kaminski, and Dill (2002) note that the ORF assessment provides one of the most reliable measurements of reading proficiency for students in grades one through three.

(continued)

SPECIAL FEATURE 12.2   Continued

6. *Retelling Fluency (RTF).* This subtest measures the comprehension of the passage read for the ORF assessment. The teacher asks the student to tell as much as he can about what he just read.

The last subtest in the DIBELS assessment is:

7. *Word Usage Fluency (WUF).* This subtest is intended to measure vocabulary and oral language of students from the fall of kindergarten through the end of third grade. The teacher uses a word in a sentence, for example, "The word is *bird*. The bird is building a nest. " Then the teacher gives the student a word and asks him to use it in a sentence. Due to the need for additional research, DIBELS does not provide benchmark goals for WUF and schools often choose not administer this subtest.

Through biweekly progress monitoring using DIBELS alternate forms, Matthew's kindergarten teacher was able to "catch" Matthew's

reading deficiencies early in his school career. She provided appropriate interventions for Matthew two times during his kindergarten year, and Matthew entered first grade on an average instructional level consistent with his peers. According to Good and Kaminski (1996, p. 335), the skills measured by DIBELS are not the only skills teachers need to instruct and assess. The measures are indicators of *key* skills but there are other important skills young students need in order to be successful readers. Therefore, it is important that teachers use a variety of reading assessments to

- Evaluate the effectiveness of reading programs
- Identify students who are at risk for reading difficulty
- Determine if students are making adequate progress
- Inform instructional decisions

Dynamic Indicators of Early Literacy Skills are measures that will tighten the link between instruction and assessment and, therefore, ensure the reading success of all students.

PEARSON
myeducationkit

Go to the Assignments and Activities section of Chapter 12 in the MyEducationKit and complete the activity entitled "Running Record." As you watch the video and answer the accompanying questions, note how a running record is conducted and think about how a teacher might interpret the results of this assessment.

Running Records

Another form of on-demand testing is the *running record*. Running records are used to document students' reading behaviors. As Peter Johnston (1992, p. 69) suggests, "learning to record oral reading errors and figure out what they [mean]" takes practice. The recording and interpretation of oral reading errors are very important skills for teachers to develop. Once teachers have learned the procedures, they can record their students' oral reading behaviors at any time, from any book, without any preparation such as photocopying of the story's pages or having extra copies of the book available. Running records also provide information about how difficult a passage or book is for a particular student: Is the text at the student's independent level (can read on his/her own), instructional level (can read with help from the teacher), or frustration level (too difficult, even with help)? To monitor more than decoding, teachers typically combine a word-error analysis with a retelling (a request for the readers to use their own words to retell a story or capture an informational text's central messages). Some districts provide specific texts and times for collecting these running record and

Running Records

The running record is a means of systematically observing and recording a student's reading behavior (Clay, 1985). This procedure is very popular with classroom teachers because of its ease of use and the valuable information it provides. In a one-on-one setting, the student reads a brief passage from a book while the teacher uses a special symbol system to make a written record of what occurs: ticks (check marks) are used to record each correct response and other symbols are used to note the errors and other behaviors that occur (see Figure 12.8). No special transcript of the passage

✓	correctly read word	
ride / run	incorrectly read/substitution (error each time misread – proper name counted as error 1st time only)	error
/ r/run / ri- / ride	record all trials	1 error
/ ride/run / ran / run / SC	*self-correct–child corrects error	no error
walk	omission	error
to	insertion	error
T TOLD / ride / up and / R /	child given word *repetition	1 error no error
/ (slash)	*hesitation (errors of pronunciation not counted as reading error)	no error
ACCURACY	$\dfrac{\text{Running Words} - \text{Countable Errors}}{\text{Running Words}}$	

*Not counted as an error

FIGURE 12.8 Conventions for Recording a Running Record

(continued)

is needed. The marks are made on a blank piece of paper. After the reading is finished, comprehension can be checked by asking the student to retell the story in his or her own words.

After a running record has been taken, the written record can be analyzed to determine the accuracy of the student's reading. The first step is to subtract the number of countable errors (words supplied by the teacher and non-self-corrected substitutions, omissions, and insertions) from the number of words in the passage. The next step is to divide this number by the number of words. The resulting percentage indicates the proportion of words that the student recognizes accurately and is an indication of the relative difficulty of the passage for that particular student:

95 to 100 percent accuracy: independent-level material, suitable for pleasure reading
90 to 95 percent accuracy: instructional-level material, suitable for instruction

Less than 90 percent accuracy: frustration-level material, too difficult

This calculation gives the teacher an idea of the difficulty level of material that the student is capable of reading for different purposes. In the example running record in Figure 12.9, the student's accuracy is 90 percent, indicating that the passage is on the boundary between the frustration and the instructional level for this particular student. The only time that students should read material that is this difficult is when passage information is of particularly high interest or utility (e.g., needed for a class project).

Additional information about students' reading strategies can be obtained by using miscue analysis to analyze the errors contained on a running record (Goodman, Watson, & Burke, 1987). Miscue analysis involves examining errors in terms of cue systems and self-monitoring behavior. Errors are compared with their text counterparts and the

TEXT

Jimmy was a little boy. He was walking home from school when he saw an old house on the corner. Jimmy and his dog Spot walked up to the old house. Jimmy knocked on the door, but no one answered. Jimmy was brave. He went inside.

Jimmy looked around the house, and he saw a door to his right. He opened the door and went inside. The room was very dark. Jimmy tried to find a light and he fell down. He sat on the floor and began to cry. Spot heard Jimmy crying and ran into the room, Spot found Jimmy and led him out of the dark room.

RUNNING RECORD

$$\text{ACCURACY} = \frac{110 \text{ (running words)} - 11 \text{ (countable errors)}}{110 \text{ (running words)}} = 90 \text{ percent}$$

FIGURE 12.9   Example Running Record

surrounding context to determine whether students are attending to the following:

- Graphophonic cues: substituted words look like the text words
- Syntactic cues: substituted words are the same part of speech, and other errors maintain grammatical acceptability
- Semantic cues: errors make sense in the context in which they occur

In the example in Figure 12.9, most of the reader's substitutions look like the text words, but many do not make sense in terms of the preceding or subsequent context. Notice that several are also different parts of speech than their text counterparts. This analysis indicates that the reader is relying heavily on graphophonic cues (letter–sound relationships) but is not paying adequate attention to context cues. Only one of the serious, meaning-disrupting errors was self-corrected, hinting that the reader may not be self-monitoring her reading to make sure that what is read makes sense. Detailed instructions for conducting and interpreting miscue analysis can be found in the manual by Yetta Goodman, Dorothy Watson, and Carolyn Burke (1987).

retelling assessments. Teachers, however, can use them with any text at any time. Special Feature 12.3 gives directions on how to take a running record of a child's reading behavior.

On-Going Assessment

Beyond on-demand assessments, teachers benefit from viewing ordinary classroom events as assessment opportunities. For example, Peter Johnston (1997) reminds teachers of all the things they can learn from listening to students as they respond in the classroom and engage in personal conversations with their friends about books and reading. For example, Drop Everything and Read (DEAR) time can become a time when teachers have an opportunity to systematically observe students engaging with text (Pikulski & Chard, 2005). Adding an additional five to ten minutes for students to share what they have just read with a partner allows the teacher to listen and document these interesting conversations as described in Chapter 7.

Another way to collect ongoing assessment information is through reader response logs. Again, after DEAR, allow an additional 5 to 10 minutes for students to write in their logs. The logs do not have to be written in each day, but they must reflect the students' thinking about literature as they read. Log entries should include the date, the book title and author, and the student's response to the text read. Early in the year, model log entries and provide an outline of the format as well as some prompting questions as a handout or poster in the classroom. To help students begin sometimes it is helpful to have literature log prompts such as:

- I began to think . . .
- I love the way . . .
- I felt sad when . . .
- If I were (name of character) . . .
- I was surprised . . .
- I wonder . . .
- I predict that . . .

In addition, Beverly DeVries (2004) notes classroom products that also serve as assessment tools; for example, completion of a graphic organizer provides evidence of students' comprehension. Remember that one of this book's main tenets is that assessment is the lynchpin between assessing and planning. For this goal to be practical and doable, teachers must remember that helpful assessment occurs systematically, develops over time, and taps an array of assessment tools. In combination, these assessments provide teachers with rich data about students' development as readers and supply information that can be used to direct instruction.

Student Self-Assessment

As students mature it is also important for teachers to begin to share the responsibilities for monitoring achievement and progress with the learner. As students progress through the grades, the shift from learning to read to reading to learn becomes more evident in the types of learning activities children participate in. As students mature they learn to interpret and apply new information, providing their teachers with multiple ways to determine what was clear to students and what needs to be retaught or refined. Special Feature 12.4 shows how Mr. Chavez, a fifth-grade teacher, uses a number of student contracts, rubrics, and self-assessments in his teaching.

SPECIAL FEATURE 12.4

Working Together

Mr. Chavez usually develops four-week units. He enjoys using direct instruction to provide most of the foundational information, then later allows the students multiple ways to deepen their knowledge through laboratory experiments, Internet exploration, case studies, and video observations. Since Mr. Chavez uses PowerPoint to highlight the main concepts from the science text, he is able to give students notes that are generated by the PowerPoint program. Mr. Chavez also believes it is important to have frequent assessments. He often gives true-false, multiple-choice, matching, or short-answer quizzes to hold students accountable for listening and taking notes during his presentations. These criterion-referenced tests provide him with a great deal of information that continues to help

him refine his instruction and work with individuals who need more support.

Mr. Chavez also uses a learning contract that gives students options in the ways they wish to demonstrate their growing understanding of science concepts. Further, he believes learning contracts help students to develop personal responsibility for their learning. Figure 12.10 presents the learning contract and the choices his students could make. The following pages offer examples of the different performance rubrics Mr. Chavez uses to guide student projects.

The learning contract is used on a daily basis as both students and Mr. Chavez record student scores. If a student appears to be falling below his/her learning contract obligation, Mr. Chavez

SPECIAL FEATURE 12.4 Continued

I, _____, a student in Mr. Chavez's fifth-grade class at Green Valley School, do hereby contract to complete the following learning goals during my investigation of the ocean. I agree to complete these tasks by *November 1*. I understand that the point values listed below are the maximum number that can be earned for each task and that fewer points may be awarded.

❖ I also understand that certain assignments are required.

❖ I have identified my other choices with an "X."

❖ Items marked with a * have rubrics that will help me develop the project.

Points Needed to Earn Specific Grades

90–100 = A	80–89 = B	70–79 = C	60–69 = D	59 or less = F

Required Assignment	Points Possible	Points Earned
Chapter 3 Exercises (page 90)	5	
Matching Quiz	5	
True-False Quiz	5	
Multiple-Choice Quiz	5	
Short-Answer Quiz	5	
Observations Forms—Critical Periods	5	
Ocean Booklet *	25	
Student and Teacher Assessment of Effort *	5	

Choice Assignments (choose 2)		
Assignment	*Points Possible*	*Points Earned*
_____ 3-D Model/Diagram of Ocean Zones *	20	
_____ Presentation of an Ocean Zone *	20	
_____ Literature Review—Research Summary *	20	
_____ Special Student-Designed, Teacher-Approved Project	20	
Total	**100**	

Student Signature	Date
Teacher Signature	Parent Signature

FIGURE 12.10   Sample Unit Learning Contract

(continued)

meets with the student individually and they determine their next course of action. Mr. Chavez also uses the Weekly Behavioral Assessment Checklist, which details the students' classroom behavior (see Figure 12.11). The student and teacher then determine a plan of action to improve the students' performance that is cosigned by the parents.

Mr. Chavez also uses a number of literacy rubrics that focus on specific aspects of the student projects. For example, Figure 12.12 is Mr. Chavez's Literature Review and Research Summary Rubric. Mr. Chavez offers minilessons to describe how each

aspect (research summary, Internet, and book or article citation) of the assignments are completed.

Figure 12.13 is Mr. Chavez's presentation rubric. This type of guidance helps students know how to prepare for a presentation and clearly understand what is expected of them.

Mr. Chavez acknowledges that this approach initially takes a great deal of preparation. However, he also finds that the students do a much better job of learning when they have options and clear expectations.

Name	Date		
Behavior	**Outstanding**	**Satisfactory**	**Needs Improvement**
Homework turned in on time			
Class work completed			
Exhibits acceptable classroom behavior			
Participates orally in class discussions			
Participates in classroom activities			
Assumes responsibility for own actions			
Comes to class prepared with supplies			
Is ready to work when class begins			
Performs well on quizzes and tests			
Shows good listening skills			
Is attentive and focused during class			
Shows good organizational skills			
Respects the property of others			

Identify areas of strength:

Identify areas of improvement:

_____	_____	_____
Student Signature	Teacher Signature	Parent Signature

FIGURE 12.11   Weekly Behavioral Assessment Checklist

SPECIAL FEATURE 12.4 Continued

Name _____   Teacher _____

Subject _____   Period _____   Date _____

This is a record of research skills demonstrated by the student. The student initials, verifying completion, and the teacher's score indicates the degree to which the skill was successfully demonstrated. It is the student's task to bring this form and the documentation to the teacher for review.

Student Initial	Teacher Score	Research Skill
	/5	Located a book on Ocean Zones. List book.
	/5	Used Internet to find three research articles on Ocean Zones.
	/5	Summarized (1 page) each research article. Sites are included.
	/5	Wrote summary (2 paragraphs) interpreting graph, chart, or diagram. Graph, chart, or diagram is attached.
Total	**/20**	Comments:

FIGURE 12.12   Literature Review and Research Summary Rubric

Name	Date	
Presentation Requirements	**Criteria**	**Points**
Introduction	Provided an engaging introduction with accurate information about the topic. Comments:	/5
Content	Adequately covered the presentation topic in an organized manner with accurate information, referencing specific areas of information. Comments:	/5
Summary	Summarized findings and provided a meaningful closure. Comments:	/5
Presentation Skills	Consistently engaged audience, spoke with a loud and clear voice, completed presentation in allotted time. Comments:	/5
Total		**/20**

FIGURE 12.13   Presentation Rubric

Assess-Plan-Teach-Assess

The assessment procedure of greater value to classroom teachers is ongoing assessment. Therefore, doing ongoing assessment well is critically important. As Dylan Williams is quoted as saying, "A focus on 'assessment for learning' can yield 'radical effects'" (quoted in Olson, 2005, p. 7).

So how does a project or school "get it right"? In any effective assessment system, teachers use multiple measures or tools as described in this book (e.g., anecdotal notes, vignettes, checklists, work samples), sometimes along with on-demand assessment, to guide their instruction. Simply directing teachers to use the tools is not sufficient. Teachers must be shown how to make sense of the data and to use the data to drive their classroom instruction. Teachers need to reflect on and understand student data by asking questions like the following:

- Where do the children score the highest/lowest?
- Do you see any patterns?
- What factors contribute to this pattern?
- In what categories do you see the biggest growth?
- What did you do in the classroom to contribute to this growth? (Heidemann, Chang, & Menninga, 2005, p. 90)

Armed with this information, teachers can begin to form goals, lesson plans, and learning experiences that meet students' needs. Teachers can use the wide range of instructional strategies and ideas suggested in Chapters 8–11 of this book to create these plans. With strong support, teachers can learn how to engage in data-driven planning. In the end, the teachers' effective use of assessment can translate into literacy success for all students.

Family Focus: Helping Parents Understand Report Cards

1, 2, 3, S, P, N? What does it all mean? Helping parents understand how their children are progressing is a significant part of a teacher's job. It is therefore important for teachers to explain the district grading procedures and codes to parents prior to report card time. The purpose of a report card is to clearly, fairly, and objectively communicate how a child is doing in school. In most districts teachers are responsible for summarizing a student's achievement and efforts into one single grade or comment code. To help parents make sense of all this information many teachers create a "conversion chart" that helps

to explain what each symbol means. For example, in some districts there are multiple aspects of a child's grade (see Figure 12.14). For instance, children could be assessed on their effort, achievement, and performance level—with each category using different symbols!

At the beginning of the school year it is essential that parents receive a document demystifying this information (Enz, Kortman, & Honaker, 2008). Likewise, it is essential that teachers use this grading system to assess formative work that students complete. Smiley faces, while wonderful to receive, do

Effort		Achievement		Performance Level	
Outstanding	O	A	1	Excellent	Above level	+
Satisfactory	S	B	2	Above Average	At level	✓
Inconsistent	I	C	3	Average	Below level	--
Needs Improvement	N	D	4	Below Average		
Unsatisfactory	U	F	5	Failing		

FIGURE 12.14   Examples of Grade Symbol Systems

not easily translate into grades, so teachers need to be consistent.

Report cards highlight information that school districts expect teachers to assess. Many teachers will give a copy of the district report card to parents at open house. Through the grading term (typically six or nine weeks), teachers will collect and document information about each student's oral reading fluency, comprehension, and vocabulary. Likewise teachers will need to determine each child's independent reading level and determine a way to assess each child's effort. Teachers should share this information during curriculum night or send home newsletters explaining their grading procedures. Currently, report cards appear in many forms but the most prevalent types are the Category Report Card and the Standards-Based Report Card.

Figure 12.15 presents an example of a category report card. Category report cards broadly define different aspects of reading but do not, for example, explain what specific skills the students were learning.

In the past decade, we have seen the emergence of a new report card—one that reflects the standards-based educational reform of the past decade. Standards-based report cards (SBRCs) provide more explicit information regarding the skills that are being taught. These report cards give more information about what children know and can do and where more help is needed (see Figure 12.16). SBRCs may use the same symbols as traditional report cards or the marks might show whether the student is exceeding (E), meeting (M), or below (B) for each standard. Most SBRCs still provide separate marks for effort and work habits.

READING	1st Period	2nd Period	3rd Period	4th Period
EFFORT:				
ACHIEVEMENT:				
GRADE LEVEL WORK:				
Oral Reading Fluency				
Comprehension				
Vocabulary				
Independent Reading Level				

FIGURE 12.15   The Reading Section of a Category Report Card

(continued)

Family Focus: Helping Parents Understand Report Cards   Continued

Grade Level 4—Standards for Fourth-Grade Reading (Performance Objective—PO).			
Child's Name_____ Grading Period: First 9 weeks			
Performance Area—Vocabulary	E	M	B
1. Use knowledge of root words and affixes to determine the meaning of unknown words			
2. Use context to determine the relevant meaning of a word			
3. Determine the difference between figurative language and literal language			
4. Identify figurative language, including similes, personification, and idioms			
5. Uses a variety of reference aids, e.g., dictionaries, thesaurus, glossaries, etc			
6. Identify antonyms, synonyms, and homonyms for given words within text			
Comments:			
Performance Area—Comprehension	E	M	B
1. Explain the problem or conflict in a story and how it is resolved			
2. Analyze similarities and differences between the actions, motives, and appearance of a character in a narrative text and self or people in own life			
Comments:			

FIGURE 12.16   A Standards-Based Report Card

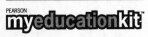

To check your comprehension on the content covered in this chapter, go to the MyEducationKit for your book and complete the Study Plan for Chapter 12. Here you will be able to take a chapter quiz and receive feedback on your answers.

Summary

In Chapters 8–11, we presented the instructional strategies that create the framework for an effective language and literacy program for primary- and upper-elementary-aged students. However, these strategies by themselves are not sufficient to construct a program that ensures optimal language and literacy learning for all students. In this chapter, we presented information on a key ingredient—assessment.

■ *What should teachers know about children's literacy development?*

Teachers need a thorough knowledge of the language and literacy accomplishments or goals or objectives that have been judged by the professional community and the public as important. For primary- and upper-elementary-aged students, this information may be obtained from several sources, including state and local school district guidelines.

■ *How might teachers prepare their students for standardized tests?*

Immerse the students in materials *exactly like* the format of the test they will take. Many test publishers sell practice books. Give students practice working under testing conditions, for example, listening to directions only once, or taking the practice tests under timed conditions. Discuss test strategies that help students feel more "in control."

■ *How might teachers assess their students' writing development?*

Rubrics are an important tool teachers use to evaluate their students' finished writing. Rubrics help teachers teach aspects of good writing and help students analyze their work. Rubrics, then, help teachers understand their students' development. Rubrics enable teachers (and students) to assign a score or rating (beginning, developing, proficient).

■ *How might teachers assess their students' reading growth?*

Teachers have a wide range of standardized tests to evaluate students' reading development. Running records and ongoing assessments provide valuable information about what children know and can do relating to reading. Once again this information should guide teacher's planning of instruction and adjustments to teaching.

■ *How might teachers involve students in self-assessment?*

Teachers may use learning contracts, rubrics, and self-reflection guides to help students learn how to evaluate their products, efforts, and achievement. This approach takes a great deal of initial preparation but ultimately teaches students a great deal about their own learning.

LINKING KNOWLEDGE TO PRACTICE

1. One way teachers determine what they want and need to know about students' literacy development is by reviewing national, state, and local standards. Search your state's Web site or contact the state or a school district to obtain a copy of the state or local standards for language arts. Given what you have learned about students' literacy development in this textbook, do these standards appear reasonable goals for language arts instruction at the grade level of your choice? Why or why not?

2. Interview an elementary or middle school teacher about the information-gathering tools that he or she typically uses to collect information about his or her student's writing and reading development. How does the teacher use this information to plan and adjust instruction?

3. Review a report card. What type of report card is this district using? How are the symbols explained to parents?

REFERENCES

Adams, M. (1990). *Beginning to read: Thinking and learning about print.* Cambridge, MA: MIT Press.

Adams, M., Foorman, B., Lundberg, I., & Beeler, T. (1998). The elusive phoneme: Why phonemic awareness is so important and how to help children develop it. *American Educator, 21*(1 & 2), 18–29.

Allen, R. (1976). *Language experiences in communication.* Boston: Houghton Mifflin.

Altwerger, B., Diehl-Faxon, J., & Dockstader-Anderson, K. (1985). Read-aloud events as meaning construction. *Language Arts, 62,* 476–484.

Alvermann, D. E., & Phelps, S. F. (2005). *Content reading and literacy* (4th ed.). Boston: Allyn & Bacon.

Anders, P., & Richardson, V. (1992). Teacher as game-show host, bookkeeper, or judge? Challenges, contradictions, and consequences of accountability. *Teachers College Record, 94,* 382–396.

Anderson, C. (2000). *How's it going?* Portsmouth, NH: Heinemann.

Anderson, C. (2005). *Assessing writers.* Portsmouth, NH: Heinemann.

Anderson, G., & Markle, A. (1985). Cheerios, McDonald's and Snickers: Bringing EP into the classroom. *Reading Education in Texas, 1,* 30–35.

Anderson, R. C., Pichert, J. W., & Shirey, L. L. (1983). Effects of reader's schema at different points in time. *Journal of Educational Psychology, 75,* 271–279.

Araújo, L. (2002a). The literacy development of English-language learners. *Journal of Research in Childhood Education, 16* (2), 232–247.

Araújo, L. (2002b). An ESL child´s emergent literacy development. *Academic Exchange, 6,* 167–171.

Ashton-Warner, S. (1963). *Teacher.* New York: Simon & Schuster.

Atwell, N. (1987). *In the middle.* Portsmouth, NH: Heinemann.

Au, K. (2006). *Multicultural issues and literacy achievement.* Mahwah, NJ: Erlbaum.

August, D., & Hakuta, K. (Eds.) (1997). *Improving schooling for language-minority children: A research agenda.* National Research Council and Institute of Medicine, Washington, DC: National Academy Press.

Baghban, M. (1984). *Our daughter learns to read and write.* Newark, DE: International Reading Association.

Barbe, W., & Milone, M., Jr. (1980). *Why manuscript writing should come before cursive writing* (Zaner-Bloser Professional Pamphlet No. 11). Columbus, OH: Zaner-Bloser.

Barbour, A. (1998–1999). Home literacy bags: Promote family involvement. *Childhood Education, 75*(2), 71–75.

Barrentine, S. (1996). Engaging with reading through interactive read-alouds. *The Reading Teacher, 50,* 36–43.

Bateson, G. (1979). *Mind and nature.* London: Wildwood House.

Bauer, E., & Manyak, P. (2008, October). Creating language-rich instruction for English-language learners. *The Reading Teacher, 62,* 176–178.

Baumann, J. F., Kame'enui, E. J., & Ash, G. E. (2003). Research on vocabulary instruction: Voltaire redux. In J. Flood, D. Lapp, J. R. Squire, J. M. Jensen (Eds.), *Handbook of research on teaching the English language arts* (2nd ed., pp. 752–785*).* Mahwah, NJ: Erlbaum.

Bear, D., Helman, L., Templeton, S., Invernizzi, M., & Johnston, F. (2007). *Words their way for English learners.* Upper Saddle River, NJ: Prentice Hall.

Beck, I., & McKeown, M. (2007). Increasing young low-income children's oral vocabulary reper-toires through rich and focused instruction. *The Elementary School Journal, 107,* 251–271.

Beck, I., McKeown, M., & Kucan, L. (2002). *Bringing words to life: Robust vocabulary instruction. Solving problems in the teaching of literacy.* New York: Guilford.

Becker, H., & Epstein, J. (1982). Parent involvement: A study of teacher practices. *Elementary School Journal, 83,* 85–102.

Benton, B. (1985). *Ellis Island: A pictorial history.* New York: Facts on File.

Berger, J. (2001). A systematic approach to grammar instruction. *Voice from the Middle, 8,* 43–49.

Bhavnagri, N., & Gonzalez-Mena, J. (1997). The cultural context of infant caregiving. *Childhood Education, 74,* 2–8.

Bialystok, E. (Ed.) (1991). *Language processing in bilingual children.* Cambridge: Cambridge University Press.

Biemiller, A. (2004). Teaching vocabulary in the primary grades: Vocabulary instruction needed. In J. F. Baumann & E. J. Kame'enui (Eds.), *Vocabulary instruction: Research to practice* (pp. 28–40). New York: Guilford.

Biemiller, A., and Slonim, N. (2001). Estimating root word vocabulary growth in normative and advantaged populations: Evidence for a common sequence of vocabulary acquisition. *Journal of Educational Psychology, 93,* 498–520.

Biggar, H. (2005). NAEYC recommendations on screening and assessment of young English-language learners. *Young Children, 60*(6), 44–46.

Billmeyer, R., & Barton, M. L. (1998). *Teaching reading in the content areas: If not me, then who?* (2nd ed.). Aurora, CO: McRel.

Bishop, W. (1995). Teaching grammar for writers in a process workshop classroom. In S. Hunter & R. Wallace (Eds.), *The place of grammar in writing instruction: Past, present, future* (pp. 176–187). Portsmouth, NH: Boynton/Cook.

Bissex, G. (1980). GNYS AT WRK: A child learns to read and write. Cambridge, MA: Harvard University Press.

Blachowicz, C. L. Z., & Fisher, P. (2004). Keep the "fun" in fundamental: Encouraging word awareness and incidental word learning in the classroom through word play. In J. F. Baumann & E. J. Kame'enui (Eds.), *Vocabulary instruction: Research to practice* (pp. 218–237). New York: Guilford.

Black, J., Puckett, M., & Bell, M. (1992). *The young child: Development from prebirth through age eight.* New York: Merrill.

Black, P., & Wiliam, D. (1998). Assessment and classroom learning. *Phi Delta Kappan, 80*(2), 139–148.

Bloodsworth, J. (1993). *The left-handed writer.* Arlington, VA: ERIC Document Reproduction Service, ED356494.

Bodrova, E., & Leong, D. J. (2003). Building language and literacy through play. *Early Childhood Today, 18,* 34–43.

Bond, G. L., & Dykstra, R. (1967). The cooperative research program in first-grade reading instruc-tion. *Reading Research Quarterly, 2,* 5–141.

Borman, G., Hewes, G., Overman, L., & Brown, S. (2003). Comprehensive school reform and achievement: A meta-analysis. *Review of Educational Research, 73,* 125–230.

Boroski, L. (1998). The what, how, and why of interactive writing. In S. Collom (Ed.), *Sharing the pen: Interactive writing with young children.* Fresno, CA: San Joaquin Valley Writing Project.

Bowman, M., & Treiman, R. (2004). Stepping stones to reading. *Theory into Practice, 43,* 4, 295–303.

Brabham, E. G., & Lynch-Brown, C. (2002). Effects of teachers' reading-aloud styles on vocabulary acquisition and comprehension of students in the early elementary grades. *Journal of Education Psychology, 94,* 3, 465–472.

Bradley, P., & Bryant, L. (1985). *Children's reading problems.* New York: Oxford University Press.

Bransford, J. D., Barclay, J. R., & Franks, J. J. (1972). Sentence memory: A constructive versus interpretive approach. *Cognitive Psychology, 3,* 193–209.

Bredekamp, S. (1989). *Developmentally appropriate practice.* Washington, DC: National Association for the Education.

Brock, D., & Dodd, E. (1994). A family lending library: Promoting early literacy development. *Young Children, 49*(3), 16–21.

Brooks, J., & Brooks, M. (1993). *In search of understanding: The case for constructivist classrooms.* Alexandria, VA: Association for Supervision and Curriculum Development.

Brosnahan, I., & Neuleib, J. (1995). Teaching grammar affectively: Learning to like grammar. In S. Hunter & R. Wallace (Eds.), *The place of grammar in writing instruction: Past, present, future.* Portsmouth, NH: Boynton/Cook.

Brown, J. (1994). Parent workshops: Closing the gap between parents and teachers. *Focus on Early Childhood Newsletter, 7*(1), 1.

Bruner, J. (1980). *Under five in Britain.* Ypsilanti, MI: High/Scope.

Bruner, J. (1983). Play, thought, and language. *Peabody Journal of Education, 60*(3), 60–69.

Buckner, A. (2002). Teaching in a world focused on testing. *Language Arts, 79,* 212–215.

Burke, J. (2000). *Reading reminders: Tools, tips and techniques.* Portsmouth, NH: Heinemann.

Burks, M. (2004). Effects of classwide peer tutoring on the numbers of words spelled correctly by students with LD. *Intervention in School and Clinic, 39,* 301–304.

Burns, M. S., Griffin, P., & Snow, C. E. (Eds.). (1999). *Starting out right: A. guide to promoting children's reading success.* Washington, DC: National Academy Press.

Bus, A., van IJzendoorn, M., & Pellegrini, A. (1995). Joint book reading makes for success in learning to read: A meta-analysis on intergenerational transmission of literacy. *Review of Educational Research, 65,* 1–21.

Buschman, L. (2003). Buddies aren't just for reading, they're for spelling too! *The Reading Teacher, 56,* 747–752.

Butler, A., & Turbill, J. (1984). *Towards a reading-writing classroom.* Portsmouth, NH: Heinemann.

Cabell, S. Q., Justice, L. M., Vukelich, C., Buell, M. J., & Han, M. (2008). Strategic and intentional shared storybook reading. In. L. M. Justice & C. Vukelich (Eds.), *Achieving excellence in preschool literacy instruction* (pp. 198–220). New York: Guilford.

Calkins, L. (2003). *Units of study: K–2.* Logan, IA: Perfection Learning.

Calkins, L. (1980, February). Punctuate! Punctuate! Punctuate! *Learning Magazine,* 86–89.

Calkins, L. (1983). *Lessons from a child: On the teaching and learning of writing.* Portsmouth, NH: Heinemann.

Calkins, L. (1986). *The art of teaching writing.* Portsmouth, NH: Heinemann.

Calkins, L. (1994). *The art of teaching writing.* Portsmouth, NH: Heinemann.

Calkins, L., Montgomery, K., & Santman, D., with Falk, B. (1998). *A teacher's guide to standardized reading tests.* Portsmouth, NH: Heinemann.

Cambourne, B. (1988). *The whole story: Natural learning and the acquisition of literacy in the classroom.* Auckland, New Zealand: Ashton Scholastic.

Canizares, S. (1997). Sharing stories. *Scholastic Early Childhood Today, 12*(3), 49–52.

Carey, S. (1979). The child as word learner. In M. Halle, J. Bresnan, & G. Miller (Eds.), *Linguistic theory and psychological reality* (pp. 264–293). Cambridge, MA: MIT Press.

Carlisle, J. (2001). *How can I help children with learning disabilities?* Ann Arbor, MI: Center for the Improvement of Early Reading Achievement.

Carlo, M. S., August, D., Mclaughlin, B. Snow, C. E., Dressler, C., Lippman, D. N., Lively, T. J., & White, C. E. (2004). Closing the gap: Addressing the vocabulary needs of English-language learners in bilingual and mainstream classrooms. *Reading Research Quarterly, 39*(2): 188–215.

Carnine, D., Silbert, J., & Kame'enui E. (2004). *Direct instruction reading.* NJ: Prentice Hall.

Carr, M., & Claxton, G. (2002). Tracking the development of learning dispositions. *Assessment in Education, 9*(1), 9–37.

Casbergue, R., McGee, L., & Bedford, A. (2008). Characteristics of classroom environments associated with accelerated literacy development. In L. Justice & C. Vukelich (Eds.), *Achieving excellence in preschool literacy instruction* (pp. 167–180). New York: Guilford.

Cazden, C. (1976). Play with language and meta-linguistic awareness: One dimension of language experience. In J. Bruner, A. Jolly, & K. Sylva (Eds.), *Play: Its role in development and evolution* (pp. 603–608). New York: Basic Books.

Cazden, C. (1988). *Classroom discourse.* Portsmouth, NH: Heinemann.

Chai, C. (2006). Writing plan quality: Relevance to writing scores. *Assessing Writing, 11*(3), 198–223.

Chall, J. (1989). Learning to read: The great debate 20 years later—A response to "Debunking the great phonics myth." *Phi Delta Kappan, 70,* 521–538.

Chall, J. S. (1996). *Stages of reading development.* New York: McGraw-Hill.

Chomsky, C. (1969). *The acquisition of syntax in children from 5 to 10.* Cambridge, MA: MIT Press.

Chomsky, N. (1965). *Aspects of the theory of syntax.* Cambridge, MA: MIT Press.

Christian, K., Morrison, F., & Bryant, F. (1998). Predicting kindergarten academic skills: Interaction among child-care, maternal education, and family literacy environments. *Early Childhood Research Quarterly, 13,* 501–521.

Christie, J. (2008). The SBRR approach to early literacy instruction. In L. Justice & C. Vukelich (Eds.), *Achieving excellence in preschool literacy instruction* (pp. 25–40). New York: Guilford.

Christie, J., Johnsen, E. P., & Peckover, R. (1988). The effects of play period duration on children's play patterns. *Journal of Research in Childhood Education, 3,* 123–131.

Christie, J., & Stone, S. (1999). Collaborative literacy activity in print-enriched play centers: Exploring the "zone" in same-age and multi-age groupings. *Journal of Literacy Research, 31,* 109–131.

Christie, J. F., Roskos, K., & Vukelich, C. (2002). *Literacy in Play. Doors to Discovery: An Early Literacy Program.* Bothell, WA: McGraw-Hill/The Wright Group.

Chukovsky, K. (1976). The sense of nonsense verse. In J. Bruner, A. Jolly, & K. Sylva (Eds.), *Play: Its role in development and evolution* (pp. 596–608). New York: Basic Books.

Clark, E. (1983). Meanings and concepts. In J. Flavell & E. Markman (Eds.), *Handbook of child psychology: Vol. 3. Cognitive development* (4th ed., pp. 787–840). New York: Wiley.

Clarke, A., & Kurtz-Costes, B. (1997). Television viewing, educational quality of the home environment, and school readiness. *Journal of Educational Research, 90,* 279–285.

Clarke, L. (1988). Invented spelling versus traditional spelling in first graders' writing: Effects on learning to spell and read. *Research in the Teaching of English, 22,* 281–309.

Clay, M. (1975). *What did I write?* Auckland, New Zealand: Heinemann.

Clay, M. (1985). *The early detection of reading difficulties* (3rd ed.). Portsmouth, NH: Heinemann.

Clay, M. (1991). *Becoming literate.* Portsmouth, NH: Heinemann.

Clements, D. H., & Sarama, J. (2003). Young children and technology: What *does* the research say? *Young Children, 58,* 34–41.

Cobb, C. (2003). Effective instruction begins with purposeful assessment. *The Reading Teacher, 57*(4), 386–388.

Cochran-Smith, M. (1984). *The making of a reader.* Norwood, NJ: Ablex.

Cochran-Smith, M., Kahn, J., & Paris, C. (1986, March). *Play with it; I'll help you with it; Figure it out; Here's what it can do for you.* Paper presented at the Literacy Research Center Speaker Series, Graduate School of Education, University of Pennsylvania.

Cohen, B. (1982). *Gooseberries to oranges.* New York: Lothrop, Lee & Shepard.

Cohen, B. (1983). *Molly's pilgrim.* New York: Lothrop, Lee & Shepard.

Cohen, B. K. (1995). *Make a wish, Molly.* New York: Bantam Doubleday Dell.

Coker, D., & Lewis, W. E. (2008). Beyond writing next: A discussion of writing research and instructional uncertainty. *Harvard Educational Review, 78*(1), 231–251.

Coleman, M. R., Buysse, V., & Neitzel, J. (2006). *Recognition and response: An early intervening system for young children at risk for learning disabilities. Full report.* Chapel Hill: University of North Carolina at Chapel Hill, FPG Child Development Institute.

Collier, V. P. (1987). The effect of age on acquisition of a second language for school. Washington, DC: National Clearinghouse for Bilingual Education. http://www.ncela.gwu.edu/pubs/classics/focus/φ2aage.html

Collin, B. (1992). *Read to me: Raising kids who love to read.* New York: Scholastic.

Collins, M. (1997). Sounds like fun. In B. Farber (Ed.), *The parents' and teachers' guide to helping young children learn* (pp. 213–218). Cutchoque, NY: Preschool Publications.

Collins, M. (2005). ESL preschoolers' English vocabulary acquisition from storybook reading. *Reading Research Quarterly, 40,* 406–408.

Connor, U., & Farmer, M. (1990). The teaching of topical structural analysis as a revision strategy for ESL writers. In B. Kroll (Ed.), *Second language writers: Insights for the classroom.* New York: Cambridge University Press.

Copeland, J., & Gleason, J. (1993). *Causes of speech disorders and language delays.* Tucson: University of Arizona Speech and Language Clinic.

Corballis, M. C. (1991). *The lopsided ape: Evolution of the generative mind.* New York: Oxford University Press.

Cordeiro, P., Giacobbe, M., & Cazden, C. (1983). Apostrophes, quotation marks, and periods: Learning punctuation in the first grade. *Language Arts, 60,* 323–332.

Cowley, F. (1997, Spring/Summer). The language explosion. *Newsweek: Your Child* (special edition).

Creech, S. (1994). *Walk two moons.* New York: HarperCollins.

Cruz, M. C. (2004). *Independent writing: One teacher—thirty-two needs, topics, and plans.* Portsmouth, NH: Heinemann.

Crystal, D. (1995). *Cambridge encyclopedia of the English language.* New York: Cambridge.

Csikszentmihalyi, M. (1990). *Flow, the psychology of optimal experience.* New York: Harper.

Culham, R. (2003) *6 + 1 traits of writing: The complete guide grades 3 and up.* New York: Scholastic.

Cummins, J. (1994). Primary language instruction and the education of language minority students. In California State Department of Education (Ed.), *Schooling and language minority students: A theoretical framework* (2nd ed., pp. 3–46). Los Angeles: Evaluation, Dissemination, and Assessment Center, California State University, Los Angeles.

Cummins, J. (1999, Autumn). The ethics of double-think: Language rights and the bilingual education debate. *TESOL,* 13–17.

Cunningham, P. M., & Cunningham, J. W. (2010). *What really matters in writing: Research-based practices across the elementary classrooms.* Boston: Allyn & Bacon.

Cunningham, A., & Shagoury, R. (2005). *Starting with comprehension: Reading strategies for the youngest learners.* Portland, ME: Stenhouse.

Curtain, H., & Pesola, C. (1994*). Languages and children: Making the match.* NY: Longman.

Cushman, K. (1995) *The midwife's apprentice.* New York: HarperCollins.

Cuyler, M. (1991). *That's good! That's bad!* New York: Henry Holt.

Daniel, N., & Murphy, C. (1995). Correctness or clarity? Finding answers in the classroom and the professional world. In S. Hunter & Ray Wallace (Eds.), *The place of grammar in writing instruction: Past, present, future* (pp. 225–240). Portsmouth, NH: Boynton/Cook.

Danst, C., Lowe, L., & Bartholomew, P. (1990). Contingent social responsiveness, family ecology, and infant communicative competence. *National Student Speech-Language-Hearing Association Journal, 17*(1), 39–49.

Davis, C., & McGrail, E. (2009). "Proof-revising" with podcasting: Keeping readers in mind as students listen to and rethink their writing. *The Reading Teacher, 62,* 522–529.

De La Paz, S., & Graham, S. (2002). Explicitly teaching strategies, skills, and knowledge: Writing instruction in middle school classrooms. *Journal of Educational Psychology, 94,* 687–698.

Delpit, L. (1997). Ebonics and cultural responsive instruction. *Rethinking School Journal, 12*(1) 6–7.

Demo, D. (2000). *Dialects in education* (ERIC/CLL Resources Guide online). Washington, DC: ERIC: Clearinghouse on Language and Linguistics.

dePaola, T. (1975). *Strega Nona.* New York: Prentice Hall.

dePaola, T. (1978). *Pancakes for breakfast.* New York: Harcourt Brace Jovanovich.

DeVries, B. A. (2004). *Literacy assessment and intervention for the elementary classroom.* Scotts- dale, AZ: Holcomb Hathaway.

Dewey, J. (1938). *Experience and education.* New York: Collier.

DiCamillo, K. (2000). *Because of Winn Dixie.* Cambridge, MA: Candlewick.

Dickinson, D. K., McCabe, A., Anastaspoulos, L., Peisner-Feinberg, E. S., & Poe, M. D. (2003). The comprehensive language approach to early literacy: The interrelationships among vocabulary, phonological sensitivity, and print knowledge among preschool-aged children. *Journal of Edu- cational Psychology, 95*(3), 465–481.

Dickinson, D. K., McCabe, A., Clark-Chiarelli, N., & Wolf, A. (2004). Cross-languge transfer of phonological awareness in low-income Spanish and English bilingual preschool children. *Applied Psycholinguistics, 25,* 323–347.

Dickinson, D., & Tabors, P. (Eds.) (2001). *Beginning literacy with language: Young children learning at home and school.* Baltimore, MD: Paul H. Brookes Publishing.

Dodge, D., & Colker, L. (1992). *The creative curriculum for early childhood education.* Washington, DC: Teaching Strategies.

Dodge, D., Heroman, C., Charles, J., & Maiorca, J. (2004). Beyond outcomes, how ongoing assessment supports children's learning and leads to meaningful curriculum. *Young Children, 59(1),* 20–28.

Dragonwagon, C. (1993). *Homeplace.* New York: Alladin Books.

Dray, A., Selman, R. L., & Schultz, L. (2009). Communicating with intent: A study of social aware- ness and children's writing. *Journal of Applied Developmental Psychology, 30,* 116–128.

Dudley-Marling, C., & Lucas, K. (2009). Pathologizing the language and culture of poor children. *Language Arts, 86,* 362–370.

Duffy, G. G. (2003). *Explaining reading: A resource for teaching concepts, skills, and strategies.* New York: Guilford.

Duke, N. K., & Bennett-Armistead, V. S. (2003). *Reading & writing informational text in the primary grades: Research-based practices.* New York: Scholastic.

Duke, N., & Pearson, P. D. (2002). Effective practices for developing reading comprehension. In A. E. Farstrup & S. J. Samuels (Eds.), *What research has to say about reading instruction* (pp. 205–242). Newark, DE: International Reading Association.

Dunn, L., & Dunn, L. (1997). *Peabody Picture Vocabulary Test III.* Circle Pines, MN: American Guidance Service.

Durkin, D. (1966). *Children who read early.* New York: Teachers College Press.

Durkin, D. (2004). *Teaching them to read* (6th ed.). Boston: Pearson.

Duvall, B. (1985). Evaluating the difficulty of four handwriting styles used for instruction. *ERS Spec- trum, 3,* 13–20.

Dyson, A., & Genishi, C. (1983). Children's language for learning. *Language Arts, 60,* 751–757.

Early Childhood Research Institute on Measuring Growth and Development. (2000). *Individual Growth and Development Indicator* (IGDI). Minneapolis, MN: University of Minnesota.

Echevarria, J., & Graves, A. (2003). *Sheltered content instruction: Teaching English-language learn- ers with diverse abilities* (2nd ed.). New York: Allyn & Bacon.

Edelman, G. (1995, June). Cited in J. Swerdlow, Quiet miracles of the brain, *National Geographic, 187*(6).

Eeds, M., & Wells, D. (1991). Talking and thinking and cooperative learning: Lessons learned from listening to children talk about books. *Social Education, 55*(2), 134–137.

Ehri, L. (1997). Phonemic awareness and learning to read. *Literacy Development in Young Children, 4*(2), 2–3.

Ehri, L., Nunes, S., Willows, D., Schuster, B., Yaghoub-Zadeh, Z., & Shanahan, T. (2001). Phonemic awareness instruction helps children learn to read: Evidence from the National Reading Panel's meta-analysis. *Reading Research Quarterly, 36,* 250–287.

Ehri, L., & Roberts, T. (2006). The roots of learning to read: Acquisition of letters and phonemic awareness. In S. Neuman & D. Dickinson (Eds.), *Handbook of early literacy research* (2nd. ed., pp. 113–131). New York: Guilford.

Elbow, P. (1973). *Writing without teachers.* New York: Oxford University Press.

Enz, B. (1992). *Love, laps, and learning to read.* Paper presented at the International Reading Association Southwest Regional Conference, Tucson, AZ.

Enz, B., & Christie, J. (1997). Teacher play interaction styles: Effects on play behavior and relationships with teacher training and experience. *International Journal of Early Childhood Education, 2,* 55–69.

Enz, B., & Cook, S. (1993). *Gateway to teaching: From pre-service to in-service.* Dubuque, IA: Kendall-Hunt.

Enz, B., & Searfoss, L. (1995). Let the circle be unbroken: Teens as literacy teachers and learners. In L. Morrow (Ed.), *Family literacy: Multiple perspectives* (pp. 115–128). Reston, VA: International Reading Association.

Enz, B. J., & Foley, D. (2009). Sharing a language and literacy legacy—A middle-class family's experience. In. Li (Ed.), *Multicultural families, home literacies, and mainstream schooling* (pp. 153–174). Charlotte, NC: Information Age Publishing.

Enz, B. J., Kortman, S., & Honaker, C. (2008). *Managing the primary and elementary classroom.* Dubuque, IA: Kendall-Hunt.

Enz, B. J., Prior, J., Gerard, M., & Han, M. (2008). Exploring intentional instructional uses of environmental print in preschool and primary grades. In *Here's How, Here's Why: Developing Early Literacy Skills* (pp. 53–66). Ypsilanti, MI: High/Scope Press.

Ericson, L., & Juliebö, M. (1998). *The phonological awareness handbook for kindergarten and primary teachers.* Newark, DE: International Reading Association.

Evers, A. J., Lang, L. F., & Smith, S. V. (2009). An ABC literacy journey: Anchoring in texts, bridging language and creating stories. *The Reading Teacher, 62,* 461–470.

Faltis, C. (2001). *Joinfostering: Teaching and learning in multilingual classrooms* (3rd ed.). Upper Saddle River, NJ: Prentice Hall.

Farris, P. (1982). *A comparison of handwriting strategies for primary grade students.* Arlington, VA: ERIC Document Reproduction Service.

Feitelson, D., & Goldstein, Z. (1986). Patterns of book ownership and reading to young children in Israeli school-oriented and nonschool-oriented families. *The Reading Teacher, 39,* 924–930.

Feldgus, E. G., & Cardonick, I. (1999). *Kid writing: A systematic approach to phonics, journals, and writing workshop.* Bothell, WA: McGraw-Hill/The Wright Group.

Fernandez-Fein, S., & Baker, L. (1997). Rhyme and alliteration sensitivity and relevant experiences among preschoolers from diverse backgrounds. *Journal of Literacy Research, 29,* 433–459.

Fessler, R. (1998). Room for talk: Peer support for getting into English in an ESL kindergarten. *Early Childhood Research Quarterly, 13,* 379–410.

Field, T. M., Woodson, R., Greenburg, R., & Cohen, D. (1982). Discrimination and imitation of facial expression by neonates. *Science, 218,* 179–181.

Fisher, B. (1995). Things take off: Note taking in the first grade. In P. Cordeiro (Ed.), *Endless possibilities: Generating curriculum in social studies and literacy.* Portsmouth, NH: Heinemann.

Fisher, C. W., Filby, N. N., Marliave, R., Cahen, L. S., Dishaw, M. M., Moore, J. E., & Berliner, D. C. (1978). *Teaching behaviors, academic learning time, and student achievement.* (Technical Report V–1). San Francisco: Northwest Regional Lab.

Fisher, D., Flood, J., Lapp, D., & Frey, N. (2004). Interactive read-alouds: Is there a common set of implementation practices? *The Reading Teacher, 58,* 8–17.

Fletcher, R. (1993). *What a writer needs.* Portsmouth, NH: Heinemann.

Fletcher, R., & Portalupi, J. (2001). *Writing workshop: The essential guide.* Portsmouth, NH: Heinemann.

Fountas, I., & Pinnell, G. (1996). *Guided reading: Good first teaching for all children.* Portsmouth, NH: Heinemann.

Fox, P. (1973). *The slave dancer.* New York: Random House.

Fractor, J., Woodruff, M., Martinez, M., & Teale, W. (1993). Let's not miss opportunities to promote voluntary reading: Classroom libraries in the elementary school. *The Reading Teacher, 46,* 476–484.

Francis, D. J., Rivera, M., Lesaux, N., Kieffer, M., & Rivera, H. (2006). *Practical guidelines for the education of English language learners: Research based recommendations for instruction and academic interventions.* Portsmouth, NH: RMC Research Corporation, Center on Instruction. Available online at www.centeroninstruction.org/files/ELL1-Interventions.pdf

Freedman, R. (1987) *Lincoln: A photobiography.* New York: Clarion.

Freeman, Y., & Freeman, D. (1994). Whole language learning and teaching for second language learners. In C. Weaver, *Reading process and practice: From sociopsycholinguistics to whole language.* Portsmouth, NH: Heinemann.

Fu, D., & Shelton, N. R. (2007). Including students with special needs in a writing workshop. *Language Arts, 84,* 325–336.

Fuchs, D., Fuchs, L. S., & Vaughn, S. (Eds.). (2008). *Response to intervention.* Newark, DE: International Reading Association.

Fukuda, K. (2007). Test development, test taking, and the right to learn. *Language Arts, 84,* 431–440.

Galda, L., Cullinan, B., & Strickland, D. (1993). *Language, literacy, and the child.* Fort Worth, TX: Harcourt Brace Jovanovich.

Gallas, K. (1992). When the children take the chair: A study of sharing in a primary classroom. *Language Arts, 69,* 172–182.

Gambrell, L., & Mazzoni, S. (1999). Principles of best practice: Finding the common ground. In L. Gambrell, L. Morrow, S. Neuman, & M. Pressley (Eds.), *Best practices in literacy instruction* (pp. 11–21). New York: Guilford.

Gamse, B. C., Jacob, R. T., Horst, M., Boulay, B., and Unlu, F. (2008). *Reading First Impact Study Final Report (NCEE 2009-4038).* Washington, DC: National Center for Education Evaluation and Regional Assistance, Institute of Education Sciences, U.S. Department of Education.

Garvey, C. (1977). *Play.* Cambridge, MA: Harvard University Press.

Gelfer, J. (1991). Teacher-parent partnerships: Enhancing communications. *Childhood Education, 67,* 164–167.

Geller, L. (1982). Linguistic consciousness-raising: Child's play. *Language Arts, 59,* 120–125.

Genese, F., Lindholm-Leary, K., Saunders, W., & Christian, D. (2006). *Educating English language learners.* New York: Cambridge University Press.

Genishi, C. (1987). Acquiring oral language and communicative competence. In C. Seefeldt (Ed.). *The early childhood curriculum: A review of current research.* New York: Teachers College Press.

Gentry, J., & Gillet, J. (1993). *Teaching kids to spell.* Portsmouth, NH: Heinemann.

Gersten, R., Baker, S. K., Shanahan, T., Linan-Thompson, S., Collins, P., & Scarcella, R. (2007). *Effective literacy and English language instruction for English learners in the elementary grades: A practice guide* (NCEE 2007-4011). Washington, DC: National Center for Education Evaluation and Regional Assistance, Institute of Education Sciences, U.S. Department of Education. Retrieved from http://ies.ed.gov/ncee/wwc/publications/practiceguides

Glasswell, K., & Parr, J. M. (2009). Teachable moments: Linking assessment. *Language Arts, 86*(5), 352–362.

Gleason, J. (1967). Do children imitate? In C. Cazden (Ed.), *Language in early childhood education.* Washington, DC: National Association for the Education of Young Children.

Goals 2000: Educate America Act. (1994). H.R.1804. www.ed.gov/legislangion/GOALS2000/TheAct/Index.html

Good Start, Grow Smart: The Bush administration's early childhood initiative. (2002, April). Washington, DC: The White House.

Goldenberg, C. (2008, Summer). Teaching English-language learners: What the research does—and does not—say. *American Educator,* 8–24.

Golinkoff, R. (1983). The preverbal negotiation of failed messages: Insights into the transition period. In R. Golinkoff (Ed.), *The transition from prelinguistic to linguistic communication* (pp. 57–78). Hillsdale, NJ: Erlbaum.

Gonzalez-Mena, J. (1997). *Multicultural issues in childcare* (2nd ed.). Mountain View, CA: Mayfield.

Good, R. H., & Kaminski, R. A. (1996). Assessment for instructional decisions: Toward a proactive/prevention model of decision-making for early literacy skills. *School Psychology Quarterly, 11*(4), 326–336.

Good, R. H., & Kaminski, R. A. (1998). Assessing early literacy skills in a problem-solving model: Dynamic indicators of basic early literacy skills. In M. R. Shinn (Ed.), *Advanced applications of curriculum-based measurement.* New York: Guilford.

Good, R. H., & Kaminiski, R. A. (Eds.). (2002). *Dynamic indicators of basic early literacy skills* (6th ed.). Eugene, OR: Institute for the Development of Educational Achievement.

Goodman, Y. M., Watson, D. J., & Burke, C. L. (1987). *Reading miscue inventory: Alternative procedures.* New York: Richard C. Owen.

Graham, S. (1992). Issues in handwriting instruction. *Focus on Exceptional Children, 25,* 1–4.

Graham, S. (1993–1994). Are slanted manuscript alphabets superior to the traditional manuscript alphabet? *Childhood Education, 70,* 91–95.

Graham, S. (1999). Handwriting and spelling instruction for students with learning disabilities: A review. *Learning Disability Quarterly, 22,* 78–98.

Graham, S. (2005). Strategy instruction and the teaching of writing: A meta-analysis. In C. MacArthur, S. Graham, and J. Fitzpatrick (Eds.), *Handbook of writing research* (pp. 187–207). New York: Guilford.

Graham, S., Harris, K., & Fink, B. (2000). Is handwriting causally related to learning to write? Treatment of handwriting problems in beginning writers. *Journal of Educational Psychology, 92,* 620–633.

Graham, S., Morphy, P., Harris, K. R., Fink-Chorzempa. B., Saddler, B., Moran, S., & Mason, L. (2008). Teaching spelling in the primary grades: A national survey of instructional practices and adaptations. *American Educational Research Journal, 45,* 796– 825.

Graham, S., & Perin, D. (2007). *Writing next: Effective strategies to improve writing of adolescents in middle and high schools* (Carnegie Corporation Report). Washington, DC: Alliance for Excellent Education.

Graves, D. (1983). *Writing: Teachers and children at work.* Portsmouth, NH: Heinemann.

Graves, D. (1993). Children can write authentically if we help them. *Primary Voices K–6, 1,* 2–6.

Greenewald, M. J., & Kulig, R. (1995). Effects of repeated readings of alphabet books on kindergartners' letter recognition. In K. Hinchman, D. Leu, & C. Kinzer (Eds.), *Perspectives on literacy research and practice: Forty-fourth yearbook of the National Reading Conference* (pp. 231–234). Chicago: National Reading Conference.

Grosjean, F. (1982). *Life with two languages.* Cambridge, MA: Harvard University Press.

Guthrie, J. T. (2002). Preparing students for high-stakes testing in reading. In *What research has to say about reading instruction.* Newark, DE: International Reading Association.

Guthrie, J., & Humenick, N. (2004). Motivating students to read: Evidence from classroom practices that increase reading motivation and achievement. In P. McCardle & V. Chhabra (Eds.), *The voice of evidence in reading research.* Baltimore, MD: Brookes.

Hackney, C. (n.d.) *Standard manuscript or modified italic?* Columbus, OH: Zaner-Bloser.

Haley, A. (1974). *Roots: The saga of an American family.* New York: Doubleday.

Hall, N. (1991). Play and the emergence of literacy. In J. Christie (Ed.), *Play and early literacy development* (pp. 3–25). Albany: State University of New York Press.

Hall, N. (1999). Real literacy in a school setting: Five-year-olds take on the world. *The Reading Teacher, 52,* 8–17.

Hall, N., & Robinson, A. (1995). *Exploring writing and play in the early years.* London: David Fulton.

Hansen, C. (1998). *Getting the picture: Talk about story in a kindergarten classroom.* Unpublished doctoral dissertation, Arizona State University.

Hargrave, A. C., & Senechal, M. (2000). A book reading intervention with preschool children who have limited vocabularies: The benefits of regular reading and dialogic reading. *Early Childhood Research Quarterly, 18,* 1, 75–90.

Harris, K. R., Graham, S., Manson, L. H., & Friedlander, B. (2008). *Powerful writing strategies for all students.* Baltimore, MD: Brookes.

Harris, M. (1994). Individualized writing instruction in writing centers: Attending to cross-cultural differences. In J. A. Mullin & R. Wallace (Eds.). *Intersections: Theory-practice in the writing center.* Urbana, IL: NCTE.

Hart, B., & Risley, T. (1995). *Meaningful differences in the everyday experience of young American children.* Baltimore, MD: Brookes.

Hart, B., & Risley, T. (2003). The early catastrophe. *American Educator, 27*(4), 6–9.

Hawisher, G. E., LeBlanc, P. L., Moran, C., & Selfe, C. L. (1996). *Computers and the teaching of writing in American higher education, 1979–1994: A history.* Norwood, NJ: Ablex.

Hazen, K. (October, 2001). *Teaching about dialects.* Educational Resources Information Center, ERIC: Clearinghouse on Language and Linguistics. EDO-FL-01-01.

Healy, J. (1994). *Your child's growing mind: A practical guide to brain development and learning from birth to adolescence.* New York: Doubleday.

Healy, J. (1997, August–September). Current brain research. *Scholastic Early Childhood Today, 12*(1), 42–44.

Heard, G. (2002). *The revision toolbox: Teaching techniques that work.* Portsmouth, NH: Heinemann.

Heath, S. (1982). What no bedtime story means: Narrative skills at home and school. *Language in Society, 11,* 49–76.

Heath, S. (1983). *Ways with words.* Cambridge: Cambridge University Press.

Heidemann, S., Chang, C., & Menninga, B. (2005). Teaching teachers about assessment. *Young Children, 60*(3), 86–92.

Herrell, A. L. (2000). *Fifty strategies for teaching English language learners.* Upper Saddle River, NJ: Prentice Hall.

Hewett, B. L. (2000). Characteristics of interactive oral and computer-mediated peer group talk and its influence on revision. *Computers and Composition, 17,* 265–288.

Hillocks, G., Jr. (1986). *Research on written composition: New directions for teaching.* Urbana, IL: National Conference on Research in English.

Hillocks, G., Jr. (2002). *The testing trap: How state writing assessments control learning.* Berkeley, CA: National Writing Project.

Hirsch, E. D. (2003). Reading comprehension requires knowledge of words and the world. *American Educator, 27*(1), 10–14.

Hirschler, J. A. (1994). Preschool children's help to second language learners. *Journal of Educational Issues of Language Minority Students, 14,* 227–240.

Holdaway, D. (1979). *The foundations of literacy.* Sydney: Ashton Scholastic.

Hornberger, N., & Michaeu, C. (1993). Getting far enough to like it: Biliteracy in the middle school. *Peabody Journal of Education, 69*(1), 30–53.

Howard, S., Shaughnessy, A., Sanger, D., & Hux, K. (1998). Lets talk! Facilitating language in early elementary classrooms. *Young Children, 53*(3), 34–39.

Howell, H. (1978). Write on, you sinistrals! *Language Arts, 55,* 852–856.

Huey, E. (1908). *The psychology and pedagogy of reading.* New York: Macmillan.

Huffaker, D. (2004, June). The educated blogger: Using weblogs to promote literacy in the classroom. *First Monday, 9*(6). Retrieved September 5, 2005, from http://firstmonday.org/issues/issue9_6/huffaker/index.html

Hunter, S. (1995). Afterword. In S. Hunter & R. Wallace (Eds.), *The place of grammar in writing instruction: Past, present, future* (pp. 243–246). Portsmouth, NH: Boynton/Cook.

Huot, B. (2002). *(Re)articulating writing assessment.* Cedar City: Southern Utah University Press.

Huttenlocher, J. (1991). Early vocabulary growth: Relations to language input and gender. *Developmental Psychology, 27,* 236–248.

Invernizzi, M., Meier, J., Swank, L., & Juel, C. (1999). *Phonological Awareness Literacy Screening Teacher's Manual* (2nd ed.). Charlottesville, VA: University Printing Services.

IRA/NCTE. (1994). *Standards for the assessment of reading and writing.* Newark, DE, & Urbana, IL: International Reading Association & National Council of Teachers of English.

IRA/NAEYC. (1998). Learning to read and write: Developmentally appropriate practices for young children. *Young Children, 53*(4), 30–46.

Isenberg, J. P., & Jalongo, M. R. 1993. *Creative expression and play in the early childhood curriculum.*

Jackman, H. (1997). *Early education curriculum: A child's connection to the world.* Albany, NY: Delmar.

Jacobs, W. (1990). *Ellis Island: New hope in a new land.* New York: Scribner.

Jalongo, M. (1995). Promoting active listening in the classroom. *Childhood Education, 72*(1), 13–18.

Jiménez, R. T., García, G. E. Pearson, E. P. (1996). The reading strategies of bilingual Latina/o students who are successful English readers: Opportunities and obstacles. *Reading Research Quarterly, 31,* 90–112.

Johnson, J., Christie, J., & Yawkey, T. (1999) *Play and early childhood development* (2nd ed.). New York: Allyn & Bacon/Longman.

Johnston, P. (1997). *Knowing literacy: Constructive literacy assessment.* York, ME: Stenhouse Publishers.

Johnston, P., & Costello, P. (2005). Principles for literacy assessment. *Reading Research Quarterly, 40*(2), 256–267.

Jonas, S. (Ed.). (1989). *Ellis Island: Echoes from a nation's past.* Montclair, NJ: Aperture.

Jonassen, D. H., Peck, K. L., & Wilson, B. G. (1998). *Teaching with technology: A constructivist perspective.* Upper Saddle River, NJ: Merrill.

Jones, E., & Reynolds, G. (1992). *The play's the thing: Teachers' roles in children's play.* New York: Teachers College Press.

Joyce, B. (1999). Reading about reading: Notes from a consumer to the scholars of literacy. *The Reading Teacher, 52,* 662–671.

Justice, L., Bowles, R., & Skibbe, L. (2006). Measuring preschool attainment of print concepts: A study of typical and at-risk 3- to 5-year-old children. *Language, Speech, and Hearing Services in Schools, 37,* 1–12.

Justice, L., & Ezell, H. (2002). Use of storybook reading to increase print awareness in at-risk children. *American Journal of Speech-Language Pathology, 11,* 17–29.

Justice, L., Kaderavek, J., Fan, X., Sofka, A., & Hunt, A. (2009). Accelerating preschoolers' early literacy development through classroom-based teacher-child storybook reading and explicit print referencing. *Language, Speech, and Hearing Services in Schools, 40,* 67–85.

Kadohata, C. (2004). *Kira-kira.* New York: Atheneum.

Kalb, C., & Namuth, T. (1997, Spring/Summer). When a child's silence isn't golden. *Newsweek: Your Child (*special edition).

Kallen, S. (1990). *Days of slavery: A history of black people in America.* Edina, MN: Abdo & Daughters.

Kamil, M. (2003). Adolescents and literacy: Reading for the 21st century. Washington, DC: Alliance for Excellent Education.

Kamil, M. L., Intrator, S. M., & Kim, H. S. (2000). The effects of other technologies on literacy and literacy learning. In M. Kamil, P. Mosenthal, P. D. Pearson, & R. Barr (Eds.), *Handbook of reading research, Volume III* (pp. 195–206). Mahwah, NJ: Erlbaum.

Keene, E. O. (2002). From good to memorable: Characteristics of highly effective comprehension teaching. In C. C. Block, L. B. Gambrell, & M. Pressley (Eds.), *Improving comprehension instruction: Rethinking research, theory, and classroom practice.* San Francisco: Jossey-Bass Publishers.

Keller, C. (2002). A new twist on spelling instruction for elementary school teachers. *Intervention in School and Clinic, 38,* 3–7.

Kemper, D., Nathan, R., & Sebranek, P. (1994). *Writers express.* Burlington, WI: The Write Source.

Kemper, D., Nathan, R., & Sebranek, P. (1995). *The write track.* Burlington, WI: The Write Source.

Kennedy, K. (February 15, 2003). Writing with web logs. *Techlearning.* Available online at www .techlearning.com/db_area/archives/TL/2003/02/blogs.html

Kim, K. H., Relkin, N. R., Lee, K. M., & Hirsch, J. (1997). Distinct cortical areas associated with native and second languages. *Nature, 388,* 171–174.

Kiefer, B., Hepler, S., & Hickman, J. (2007). *Charlotte Huck's children's literature* (9th ed.). New York: McGraw-Hill.

Klingner, J. K., & Vaughn, S. (2004). *Strategies for struggling second-language readers.* In T. L. Jetton & J. A. Dole (Eds.), *Adolescent literacy research and practice* (pp. 183–209). New York: Guilford.

Kotulak, R. (1997*). Inside the brain: Revolutionary discoveries of how the mind works.* Kansas City, MO: Andrews McMeel.

Krashen, S. (1987). Encouraging free reading. In M. Douglass (Ed.), *51st Claremont Reading Conference Yearbook.* Claremont, CA: Center for Developmental Studies.

Krashen, S. D. (1981). Bilingual education and second language acquisition theory. In California State Department of Education (Ed.), *Schooling and language minority students: A theoretical framework* (pp. 51–79). Los Angeles: Evaluation, Dissemination, and Assessment Center, California State University, Los Angeles.

Kuhl, P. (1993). *Life language.* Seattle: University of Washington.

Kuhl, P. (2004). Early language acquisition: Cracking the speech code. *Nature Reviews, 5,* 831–843.

Kuhl, P. K. (2008). Linking infant speech perception to language acquisition: Phonetic learning predicts language growth. In P. McCardle, J. Colombo, & L. Freund (Eds.), *Infant pathways to language: Methods, models, and research directions* (pp. 213–243). New York: Erlbaum.

Lass, B. (1982). Portrait of my son as an early reader. *The Reading Teacher, 36,* 20–28.

Lazar, A. M. (2004). *Learning to be literacy teachers in urban schools*. Newark, DE: International Reading Association.

Leal, D. (1994). Storybooks, information books, and informational storybooks: An explication of the ambiguous gray genre. *The New Advocate, 6,* 61–70.

Lee, Y. (2006). The process-oriented ESL writing assessment: Promises and challenges. *Journal of Second Language Writing, 15,* 307–330.

Leki, I. (1992). *Understanding ESL writers: A guide for teachers*. Portsmouth, NH: Boynton/Cook.

Leslie, L., & Caldwell, J. (2006). *Qualitative Reading Inventory—4*. Boston: Allyn & Bacon.

Lessow-Hurley, J. (2000). *The foundations of dual language instruction*. New York: Longman.

Leu, D. J. (2000). Literacy and technology: Deictic consequences for literacy education in an Information Age. In M. Kamil, P. Mosenthal, P. D. Pearson, & R. Barr (Eds.), *Handbook of reading research, Volume III* (pp. 195–206). Mahwah, NJ: Erlbaum.

Levin, D., & Carlsson-Paige, N. (1994). Developmentally appropriate television: Putting children first. *Young Children, 49,* 38–44.

Lewis, R., & Doorlag, D. (1999). *Teaching special students in general education classrooms*. Columbus, OH: Prentice Hall.

Lindfors, J. (1987). *Children's language and learning* (2nd ed.). Englewood Cliffs, NJ: Prentice Hall.

Lindquist, T. (1995). *Seeing the whole through social studies*. Portsmouth, NH: Heinemann.

Lipson, M. Y., & Wixson, M. Y. (2003). *Assessment and instruction of reading and writing difficulty*. New York: Allyn & Bacon.

Lowry, L. (1993). *The giver*. New York: Houghton Mifflin.

Lowry, L. (2004). *Gooney bird greene*. New York: Dell Yearling.

Luke, A., & Kale, J. (1997). Learning through difference: Cultural practices in early childhood language socialization. In E. Gregory (Ed.), *One child, many worlds: Early learning in multicultural communities* (pp. 11–29). New York: Teachers College Press.

Mabry, L. (1999). Writing to the rubric. *Phi Delta Kappan, 80,* 673–679.

MacArthur, C. (2008). Peer revising. In K. Harris, S. Graham, L. Mason, & B. Friedlander (Eds.), *Powerful writing strategies for all students* (pp. 323–338). Baltimore, MD: Brookes.

MacLean, P. (1978). A mind of three minds: Educating the triune brain. In J. Chall & A. Mirsky (Eds.), *Education and the brain, 77th yearbook of the National Society for the Study of Education*. Chicago: University of Chicago Press.

Madaus, G. F. (1988). The influence of testing on curriculum. In L. N. Tanner (Ed.), *Critical issues in curriculum: Eighty-seventh yearbook of the National Society for the Study of Education* (pp. 83–121). Chicago: University of Chicago Press.

Maestro, B., & Maestro, G. (1986). *The story of the Statue of Liberty*. New York: Lothrop, Lee & Shepard.

Manning-Kratcoski, A., & Bobkoff-Katz, K. (1998). Conversing with young language learners in the classroom. *Young Children, 53*(3), 30–33.

Martinez, M., & Roser, N. (1985). Read it again: The value of repeated readings during storytime. *The Reading Teacher, 38,* 782–786.

Martinez, M., & Teale, W. (1987). The ins and outs of a kindergarten writing program. *The Reading Teacher, 40,* 444–451.

Martinez, M., & Teale, W. (1988). Reading in a kindergarten classroom library. *The Reading Teacher, 41,* 568–572.

Mathews, M. (1966). *Teaching to read: Historically considered*. Chicago: University of Chicago Press.

Mayberry, R. I., & Nicoladis, E. (2000). Gesture reflects language development: Evidence from bilingual children. *Current Directions in Psychological Science, 9,* 192–196.

McCardle, P., & Chhabra, V. (2004). *The voice of evidence in reading research*. Baltimore, MD: Brookes.

McGee, L., & Richgels, D. (1989). "K is Kristen's": Learning the alphabet from a child's perspective. *The Reading Teacher, 43,* 216–225.

McKenna, M. C., & Robinson, R. D. (2002). *Teaching through text: Reading and writing in the content areas* (3rd ed.). Boston: Allyn & Bacon.

Menyuk, P. (1988). *Language development: Knowledge and use.* Glenview, IL: Scott Foresman.

Miller, S. (1997). Family television viewing: How to gain control. *Childhood Education, 74*(1), 38–40.

Minett, A. J. (2004). Earth aches by midnight: Helping ESL writers clarify their intended meaning. In S. Bruce & B. Rafoth (Eds.), *ESL writers: A guide for writing center tutors.* Portsmouth, NH: Boynton/Cook.

Moats, L. (1999). *Teaching reading is rocket science.* Washington, DC: American Federation of Teachers.

Moran, C., Stobbe, J., Baron, W., Miller, J., & Moir, E. (2000). *Keys to the classroom.* Thousand Oaks, CA: Corwin Press.

Moffett, J., & Wagner, B. (1983). *Student-centered language arts and reading, K–13: A handbook for teachers* (3rd ed.). Boston: Houghton Mifflin.

Moir, A., & Jessel, D. (1991). *Brain sex: The real differences between men and women.* New York: Carol.

Morisset, C. (1995). Language development: Sex differences within social risk. *Developmental Psychology, 31,* 851–865.

Morrow, L. (1983). Home and school correlates of early interest in literature. *Journal of Educational Research, 76,* 221–230.

Morrow, L. (1985). Reading and retelling stories: Strategies for emergent readers. *The Reading Teacher, 38,* 870–875.

Morrow, L. (1988). Young children's responses to one-to-one story readings in school settings. *Reading Research Quarterly, 23,* 89–107.

Morrow, L. (2005). *Literacy development in the early years* (5th ed.). New York: Pearson.

Morrow, L. (2001). *Literacy development in the early years: Helping children read and write* (4th ed.). Boston: Allyn & Bacon.

Morrow, L., & Tracey, D. (1997). Strategies used for phonics instruction in early childhood classrooms. *The Reading Teacher, 50,* 644–651.

Morrow, L., & Weinstein, C. (1982). Increasing children's use of literature through program and physical changes. *Elementary School Journal, 83,* 131–137.

Murray, D. (1990). *Write to learn.* New York: Holt, Rinehart, and Winston.

Muth, J. J. (2002). *The three questions.* New York: Scholastic.

Nagy, W., Berninger, V., & Abbott, R. (2006). Contributions of morphology beyond phonological literacy outcomes of upper elementary and middle-school students. *Journal of Educational Psychology, 98,* 134–147.

Nagy, W. E., & Scott, J. A. (2000). Vocabulary processes. In M. L. Kamil, P. B. Mosenthal, P. D. Pearson, & R. Barr (Eds.), *Handbook of Reading Research Volume III* (pp. 269–284).

National Commission on Excellence in Education. (1983). *A Nation at Risk: The Imperative for Educational Reform. A Report to the Nation and the Secretary of Education United States Department of Education.* Washington, DC: Author. Retrieved January 3, 2006, from www.ed.gov/pubs/NatAtRisk/index.html

National Commission on Testing and Public Policy. (1990). *From gatekeepers to gateway: Transforming testing in America.* Chestnut Hill, MA: Boston College.

National Early Literacy Panel. (2008). *Developing early literacy: Report of the National Early Literacy Panel: A scientific synthesis of early literacy development and implications for intervention.*

Washington, DC: National Center for Family Literacy, National Early Literacy Panel, National Institute for Literacy.

National Education Goals Panel. (1997). *Special early childhood report.* Washington, DC: Department of Education.

National Institute for Literacy. (2007). *What content-area teachers should know about adolescent literacy.* Washington, DC: National Institute for Literacy, National Institute for Child Health and Human Development (NICHD).

National Reading Panel. (2000). *Report of the National Reading Panel: Teaching children to read.* Bethesda, MD: National Institute for Child Health and Human Development. Available at www .nichd.nih.gov/publications/nrp/smallbook.htm

National Research Council. (1999). *Starting out right: A guide to promoting children's reading success.* Washington, DC: National Academy Press.

National Council of Teachers of English. (1993). *Elementary school practices: Current research on language learning.* Urbana, IL: Author.

Neuman, S. (1995). *Linking literacy and play.* Newark, DE: International Reading Association.

Neuman, S. (1998). How can we enable all children to achieve? In S. Neuman & K. Roskos (Eds.), *Children achieving: Best practices in early literacy* (pp. 5–19). Newark, DE: International Reading Association.

Neuman, S. (1999). Books make a difference: A study of access to literacy. *Reading Research Quarterly, 34*(3), 286–311.

Neuman, S., & Dwyer, J. (2009). Missing in action: Vocabulary instruction in pre-K. *The Reading Teacher, 62,* 384–392.

Neuman, S., & Roskos, K. (1992). Literacy objects as cultural tools: Effects on children's literacy behaviors during play. *Reading Research Quarterly, 27,* 203–223.

Neuman, S., & Roskos, K. (1993). *Language and literacy learning in the early years: An integrated approach.* Fort Worth, TX: Harcourt Brace Jovanovich.

Neuman, S., & Roskos, K. (1997). Literacy knowledge in practice: Contexts of participation for young writers and readers. *Reading Research Quarterly, 32,* 10–32.

Neuman, S., & Roskos, K. (2005). What ever happened to developmentally appropriate practice in early literacy? *Young Children, 60*(4), 22–26.

Neuman, S., & Roskos, K. (2007). *Nurturing knowledge: Building a foundation for school success by linking early literacy to math, science, art, and social studies.* New York: Scholastic.

Norris, A., & Hoffman, P. (1990). Language intervention with naturalistic environments. *Language, Speech, and Hearing Services in the Schools, 21,* 72–84.

Oken-Wright, P. (1998). Transition to writing: Drawing as a scaffold for emergent writers. *Young Children, 53*(2), 76–81.

Olson, L. (2005, October 19). Purpose of testing needs to shift, experts say. *Education Week.*

Orellana, M., & Hernández, A. (1999). Taking the walk: Children reading urban environmental print. *The Reading Teacher, 52,* 612–619.

Oritz, A., & Graves, A.W. (2001). English-language learners with literacy related learning disabilities. *International Dyslexia Association Commemorative Booklet Series, 52,* 31–36.

Ourada, E. (1993). Legibility of third-grade handwriting: D'Nealian versus traditional Zaner-Bloser. In G. Coon & G. Palmer (Eds.), *Handwriting research and information: An administrators handbook* (pp. 72–87). Glenview, IL: Scott Foresman.

Owocki, G. (2005). *Time for literacy centers.* Portsmouth, NH: Heinemann.

Paley, V. (1990). *The boy who would be a helicopter.* Cambridge, MA: Harvard University Press.

Paris, S. G., Cross, D. R., & Lipson, M. Y. (1984). Informed strategies for learning: A program to improve children's reading awareness and comprehension. *Journal of Educational Psychology, 76,* 1239–1252.

Pearson, P. D., & Fielding, L. (1994). Reading comprehension: What works? *Educational Leadership, 51*(5), 62–67.

Pearson, P. D., & Tierney, R. J. (1984). On becoming a thoughtful reader: Learning to read like a writer. In A. Purves & O. Niles (Eds.), *Becoming readers in a complex society.* Chicago: National Society for the Study of Education.

Peterson, R., & Eeds, M. (1990). *Grand conversations: Literature groups in action.* New York: Scholastic.

Pikulski, J. J., & Chard, D. J. (2005). Fluency: Bridge between decoding and comprehension. *The Reading Teacher, 58*(6), 510–519.

Pinker, S. (1995). *The language instinct.* UK: Perennial (HarperCollins).

Piper, T. (1993). *Language for all our children.* New York: Macmillan.

Pitkin, T. (1975). *Keepers of the gate: A history of Ellis Island.* New York: New York University Press.

Pollo, T. C., Kessler, B., & Treiman, R. (2005). Vowels, syllables, and letter names: Differences between young children's spelling in English and Portuguese. *Journal of Experimental Child Psychology, 92,* 161–181.

Power, B. (1998). Author! Author! *Early Childhood Today, 12,* 30–34.

Price, L., van Kleeck, A., & Huberty, C. (2009). Talk during book sharing between parents and preschool children: A comparison between storybook and expository book conditions. *Reading Research Quarterly, 44,* 171–194.

Prior, J., & Gerard, M. (2004). *Environmental print in the classroom: Meaningful connections for learning to read.* Newark, DE: International Reading Association.

Raines, S., & Isbell, R. (1994). *Stories: Children's literature in early education.* Albany, NY: Delmar.

Rascon-Briones, M., & Searfoss L. (1995, December). *Literature study groups in a preservice teacher education class.* Paper presented at the meeting of the National Reading Conference, New Orleans.

Rasinski, T., & Padak, N. (2009). Write soon! *The Reading Teacher, 62,* 618–620.

Ray, K. (2001). *The writing workshop: Working through the hard parts (and they're all hard parts).* Urbana, IL: National Council of Teachers of English.

Read, C. (1971). Pre-school children's knowledge of English phonology. *Harvard Educational Review, 41,* 1–34.

Reese, E., & Cox, A. (1999). Quality of adult book reading affects children's emergent literacy. *Developmental Psychology, 35,* 20–28.

Rex, L. A., & Nelson, M. C. (2004). How teachers' professional identities position high-stakes test preparation in their classrooms. *Teachers College Record, 106,* 1288–1331.

Rice, M., Huston, A., Truglio, R., & Wright, J. (1990) Words from Sesame Street: Learning vocabulary while viewing. *Development Psychology, 26,* 421–428.

Richardson, J. S., & Morgan, R. F. (2000). *Reading to learn in the content areas* (4th ed.). Belmont, CA: Wadsworth/Thomson Learning.

Richgels, D., & Wold, L. (1998). Literacy on the road: Backpacking partnerships between school and home. *The Reading Teacher, 52,* 18–29.

Ringgold, F. (1991). *Tar beach.* New York: Crown.

Roberts, T. (2008). Home storybook reading in primary or second language with preschool children: Evidence of equal effectiveness for second-language vocabulary acquisition. *Reading Research Quaterly, 43,* 103–130.

Roe, M. F. (2004). Real reading interactions: Identifying and meeting the challenges of middle level unsuccessful readers. *Childhood Education, 81*(1), 9–15.

Rosenblatt, L. (1991). Literacy theory. In J. Flood, M. Jensen, D. Lapp, & J. Squire (Eds.), *Handbook of research on teaching the English language arts* (pp. 57–62). New York: Macmillan.

Roskos, K., & Christie, J. (Eds.). (2000). *Play and literacy in early childhood: Research from multiple perspectives.* Mahwah, NJ: Erlbaum.

Roskos, K., & Christie, J. (2004). Examining the play-literacy interface: A critical review and future directions. In E. Zigler, D. Singer, & S. Bishop-Josef (Eds.), *Children's play: The roots of reading* (pp. 95–123). Washington, DC: Zero to Three Press.

Roskos, K., & Christie, J. (Eds.). (2007). *Play and literacy in early childhood: Research from multiple perspectives* (2nd ed.). Mahwah, NJ: Erlbaum.

Roskos, K., & Neuman, S. (1993). Descriptive observations of adults' facilitation of literacy in play. *Early Childhood Research Quarterly, 8,* 77–97.

Roskos, K., Tabor, P., & Lenhart, L. (2009). *Oral language and early literacy in preschool* (2nd ed.). Newark, DE: International Reading Association.

Rowe, D. (1994). *Preschoolers as authors: Literacy learning in the social world.* Cresskill, NJ: Hampton.

Ruetzel, R. (2009, February). *Teaching the letters of the alphabet: Something old is new again.* Paper presented at the International Reading Association Annual Conference, Phoenix.

Ruiz, N. T. (1995a). The social construction of ability and disability I: Profile types of Latino children identified as language learning disabled. *Journal of Learning Disabilities, 28,* 476–490.

Ruiz, N. T. (1995b). The social construction of ability and disability II: Optimal and at-risk lessons in a bilingual special education classroom. *Journal of Learning Disabilities, 28,* 491–502.

Sakai, K. (2005). Language acquisition and brain development. *Science, 310*(4), 815–819.

Santman, D. (2002). Teaching to the test? Test preparation in the reading workshop. *Language Arts, 79*(3), 203–211.

Santos, R. M. (2004). Ensuring culturally and linguistically appropriate assessment of young children. *Young Children, 59*(1), 48–50.

Saville-Troike, M. (1988). Private speech: Evidence for second language learning strategies in the "silent period." *Journal of Child Language, 15,* 567–90.

Schickedanz, J., & Casbergue, R. (2004). *Writing in the preschool: Learning to orchestrate meaning and marks.* Newark, DE: International Reading Association.

Schickedanz, J. A. (1998). What is developmentally appropriate practice in early literacy? Consider the alphabet. In S. Neuman & K. Roskos (Eds.), *Children achieving: Best practices in early literacy (*pp. 20–37). Newark, DE: International Reading Association.

Schlagal, B. (2007). Best practices in spelling and handwriting. In S. Graham, C.A. MacArthur, & J. Fitzgerald (Eds.), *Solving problems in the teaching of literacy.* New York: Guilford.

Schnabel, J. (2009). The black box. *Nature, 459,* 765–768.

Schon, D. (1983). *The reflective practitioner: How professionals think in action.* New York: Basic Books.

Segal, M., & Adcock, D. (1986). *Your child at play: Three to five years.* New York: Newmarket.

Selfe, C. (1999). Technology and literacy: A story about the perils of not paying attention. *College Composition and Communication, 50*(3), 411–436.

Sénéchal, M. (1995). Individual differences in 4-year-old children's acquisition of vocabulary during storybook reading. *Journal of Educational Psychology, 87,* 218–229.

Sénéchal, M., Ouellette, G., & Rodney, D. (2006). The misunderstood giant: On the predictive role of early vocabulary to future reading. In D. Dickinson & S. Neuman (Eds.), *Handbook of early literacy research* (vol. 2, pp. 173–184). New York: Guilford.

Serna, I., & Hudelson, S. (1993). Emergent literacy in a whole language bilingual program. In R. Donmoyer and R. Kos (Eds.), *At-risk students: Portraits, policies and programs.* Albany, NY: SUNY Albany Press.

Shannon, P. W. (1988). *Broken promises: Reading instruction in twentieth-century America.* Glenview, IL: Greenwood.

Shepard, L., Kagan, S., & Wurtz, E. (1998). Goal 1 early childhood assessments resource group recommends. *Young Children, 53,* 52–54.

Shore, R. (1997). *Rethinking the brain: New insights into early development.* New York: Families and Work Institute.

Short, D., & Fitzsimmons, S. (2007). *Double the work: Challenges and solutions to acquiring language and academic literacy for adolescent English language learners—A report to Carnegie Corporation of New York.* Washington, DC: Alliance for Excellent Education.

Short, K. G., Schroeder, J., Kauffman, G., & Kaser, S. (2002). Thoughts from the editors. *Language Arts, 79*(3), 199.

Silva, C., & Alves-Martins, M. (2002). Phonological skills and writing of presyllabic children. *Reading Research Quarterly, 37,* 466–483.

Silva, T. (1993). Toward an understanding of the distinct nature of L2 writing: The ESL research and its implications. *TESOL Quarterly, 27,* 657–677.

Sipe, L. (2001). Invention, convention, and intervention: Invented spelling and the teacher's role. *The Reading Teacher, 55,* 264–273.

Skinner, B. (1957). *Verbal behavior.* East Norwalk, CT: Appleton-Century-Crofts.

Slavin, R. (1989). Students at risk of school failure: The problem and its dimensions. In R. Slavin, N. Karweit, & N. Madden (Eds.), *Effective programs for students at risk.* Boston: Allyn & Bacon.

Smith, F. (1998). *Understanding reading* (4th ed.). Hillsdale, NJ: Erlbaum.

Smith, M., Brady, J., & Anastasopoulos, L. (2008). *Early Language and Literacy Classroom Observation, Pre-K Tool.* Baltimore, MD: Brookes.

Smith, M., & Dickinson, D. (1994). Describing oral language opportunities and environments in Head Start and other preschool classrooms. *Early Childhood Research Quarterly, 9,* 345–366.

Smith, M. W., & Dickinson, D. K. (2002). *Early language and literacy classroom observation toolkit.* Baltimore, MD: Brookes.

Snow, C. (2002). Second language learners and understanding the brain. In A. Galaburda, S. Kosslyn, & C. Yves (Eds.), *The languages of the brain* (pp. 151–165). Cambridge, MA: Harvard University Press.

Snow, C., Burns, M. S., & Griffin, P. (1998). *Preventing reading difficulties in young children.* Washington, DC: National Academy Press.

Snow, C., & Ninio, A. (1986). The contracts of literacy: What children learn from learning to read books. In W. Teale & E. Sulzby (Eds.), *Emergent literacy: Writing and reading* (pp. 116–137). Norwood, NJ: Ablex.

Sochurek, H. (1987, January). Medicine's new vision. *National Geographic, 171*(1), 2–41.

Spandel, V. (2001). *Creating writers through 6-trait writing assessment and instruction.* New York: Addison Wesley Longman.

Spandel, V. (2009). *Creating 6-trait revisers and editors for grade 2: 30 revision and editing lessons.* New York: Longman.

Spitzer, M. (1990). Local and global networking: Implications for the future. In D. Holdstein & C. Selfe (Eds.), *Computers and writing: Theory, research, and practice* (pp. 58–70). New York: Modern Language Association of America.

Sprenger, M. (1999). *Learning and memory: The brain in action.* Alexandria, VA: Association for Supervision and Curriculum Development.

Stahl, S. (1992). Saying the "p" word: Nine guidelines for exemplary phonics instruction. *The Reading Teacher, 45,* 618–625.

Stahl, S. (2003). How words are learned incrementally over multiple exposures. *American Educator, 27*(1), 18–19, 44.

Stahl, S., Duffy-Hester, A., & Stahl, K. (1998). Everything you wanted to know about phonics (but were afraid to ask). *Reading Research Quarterly, 33,* 338–355.

Stahl, S., & Miller, P. (1989). Whole language and language experience approaches for beginning reading: A quantitative research synthesis. *Review of Educational Research, 59,* 87–116.

Stainback, S., & Stainback, W. (1992). *Curriculum considerations in inclusive classrooms.* Baltimore, MD: Brookes.

Stanovich, K. (1986). Matthew effects in reading: Some consequences of individual differences in the acquisition of literacy. *Reading Research Quarterly, 21,* 360–407.

Stern, D. (2000). The interpersonal world of the infant: A view from psychoanalysis and developmental psychology. New York: Basic Books.

Strickland, D. S., & Alvermann, D. E. (2004). Learning and teaching literacy in grades 4–12: Issues and challenges. In D. S. Strickland and D. E. Alvermann (Eds.), *Bridging the literacy gap, grades 4–12* (p. 1–13). NY: Teachers College Press.

Strickland, D. S., & Schickedanz, J. A. (2004). *Learning about print in preschool: Working with letters, words, and beginning links with phonemic awareness.* Newark, DE: International Reading Association.

Strunk, W., & White, E. B. (2005). *The elements of style.* New York: Penguin.

Sullivan, G. (1994). *Slave ship: The story of the Henrietta Marie.* New York: Dutton.

Sulzby, E. (1985a). Children's emergent reading of favorite storybooks: A developmental study. *Reading Research Quarterly, 20,* 458–481.

Sulzby, E. (1985b). Kindergartners as writers and readers. In M. Farr (Ed.), *Advances in writing research, Vol. 1: Children's early writing development* (pp. 127–200). Norwood, NJ: Ablex.

Sulzby, E. (1990). Assessment of emergent writing and children's language while writing. In L. Morrow & J. Smith (Eds.), *Assessment for instruction in early literacy* (pp. 83–109). Englewood Cliffs, NJ: Prentice Hall.

Sulzby, E., & Barnhart, J. (1990). The developing kindergartner: All of our children emerge as writers and readers. In J. McKee (Ed.), *The developing kindergarten: Programs, children, and teachers.* Ann Arbor: Michigan Association for the Education of Young Children.

Sulzby, E., Barnhart, J., Hieshima, J. (1989). Forms of writing and rereading from writing: A preliminary report. In J. Mason (Ed.), *Reading and writing connections* (pp. 31–63). Boston: Allyn & Bacon.

Sulzby, E., & Teale, W. (1991). Emergent literacy. In R. Barr, M. Kamil, P. Mosenthal, & P. D. Pearson (Eds.), *Handbook of reading research* (vol. 2, pp. 727–757). New York: Longman.

Sylvester, R. (1995). *A celebration of neurons: An educator's guide to the human brain.* Alexandria, VA: Association for Supervision and Curriculum Development.

Tabors, P. (1998). What early childhood educators need to know: Developing effective programs for linguistically and culturally diverse children and families. *Young Children, 53*(6), 20–26.

Tabors, P., Paez, M., & Lopez, L. (2003). Dual language abilities of bilingual four-year-olds: Initial findings from the Early Childhood Study of Language and Literacy Development of Spanish-speaking Children. *NABE Journal of Research and Practice, 1,* 70–91.

Tabors, P., & Snow, C. (1994). English as a second language in preschool programs. In F. Genesee (Ed.), *Educating second language children: The whole child, the whole curriculum, the whole community* (pp. 103–126). New York: Cambridge University Press.

Tabors, P., Snow, C., & Dickinson, D. (2001). Homes and schools together: Supporting language and literacy development. In D. Dickinson & P. Tabors (Eds.). *Beginning literacy with language: Young children learning at home and school* (pp. 313–334). Baltimore, MD: Brookes.

Taylor, D. (1986). Creating family story: "Matthew! We're going to have a ride." In W. Teale & E. Sulzby (Eds.), *Emergent literacy: Writing and reading* (pp. 139–155). Norwood, NJ: Ablex.

Taylor, B. M., Pearson, P. D., Peterson, D. S., & Rodriguez, M. C. (2003). Reading growth in high poverty classrooms: The influence of teacher practices that encourage cognitive engagement in literacy learning. *Elementary School Journal, 104,* 3–28.

Teale, W. (1986). Home background and young children's literacy development. In W. Teale & E. Sulzby (Eds.), *Emergent literacy: Writing and reading* (pp. 173–205). Norwood, NJ: Ablex.

Temple, C., Nathan, R., Temple, F., & Burris, N. A. (1993). *The beginnings of writing*. Boston: Allyn & Bacon.

Templeton, S., & Morris, D. (1999). Questions teachers ask about spelling. *Reading Research Quarterly, 34,* 102–112.

Thomas, W., & Collier, V. (1997). Two languages are better than one. *Educational Leadership, 55*(4), 23–26.

Thousand, J., & Villa, R. (1990). Sharing expertise and responsibilities through teacher teams. In W. Stainback & S. Stainback (Eds.), *Support networks for inclusive schooling: Interdependent integrated education* (pp. 151–166). Baltimore, MD: Brookes.

Thurber, D. (1993). *D'Nealian handwriting*. Glenview, IL: Scott Foresman.

Torgesen, J. (1994). *Torgesen test of phonemic awareness*. Shoal Creek, TX: Pro-Ed.

Treiman, R., & Kessler, B. (2003). The role of letter names in the acquisition of literacy. In R. Kail (Ed.), *Advances in Child Development and Behavior, 31,* 105–135.

Trelease, J. (1989). *The new read-aloud handbook*. New York: Penguin.

Trelease, J. (2006). *The read-aloud handbook* (6th ed.). New York: Penguin.

Turner, A. (1987). *Nettie's trip south*. New York: Macmillan.

U.S. Citizenship and Immigration Services (formerly the Immigration and Naturalization Service), Census Bureau. (2001). *Immigrants, Fiscal Year 2001*. Washington, DC: Author.

Vacca, R. T., & Vacca, J. L. (2005). *Content area reading: Literacy and learning across the curriculum* (8th ed.). Boston: Pearson Education.

Van Leeuwen, C. A., & Gabriel, M. A. (2007). Beginning to write with word processing: Integrating writing process and technology in a primary classroom. *Reading Teacher, 60,* 420–428.

van Manen, M. (1995). On the epistemology of reflective practice: Teachers and teaching. *Theory and Practice, 1,* 33–50.

Veatch, J., Sawicki, F., Elliot, G., Flake, E., & Blakey, J. (1979). *Key words to reading: The language experience approach begins*. Columbus, OH: Merrill.

Vukelich, C. (1993). Play: A context for exploring the functions, features, and meaning of writing with peers. *Language Arts, 70,* 386–392.

Vukelich, C. (1994). Effects of play interventions on young children's reading of environmental print. *Early Childhood Research Quarterly, 9,* 153–170.

Vukelich, C., Evans, C., & Albertson, B. (2003). Organizing expository tests: A look at possibilities. In D. M. Barone & L. M. Morrow (Eds.), *Literacy and young children: Research-based practices. Solving problems in the teaching of literacy* (pp. 261–290). New York: Guilford.

Vygotsky, L. (1962). *Thought and language*. Cambridge, MA: MIT Press.

Vygotsky, L. (1978). *Mind in society: The development of psychological processes*. Cambridge, MA: Harvard University Press.

Walker, D., Greenwood, C., Hart, B., & Carta, J. (1994). Prediction of school outcomes based on early language production and socio-economic factors. *Child Development, 65,* 606–621.

Weaver, C. (1996). *Teaching grammar in context*. Portsmouth, NH: Boynton/Cook.

Weaver, C. (2008). *Grammar to enrich and enhance writing*. Portsmouth, NH: Heineman.

Weaver, C., McNally, C., & Moerman, S. (2001). To grammar or not to grammar: That is *not* the question. *Voices from the Middle, 8,* 17–33.

Wells, G. (1986). *The meaning makers: Children learning language and using language to learn*. Portsmouth, NH: Heinemann.

Weir, R. (1962). *Language in the crib*. The Hague: Mouton.

Weiss, C., Lillywhite, H., & Gordon, M. (1980). *Clinical management of articulation disorders*. St. Louis: Mosby.

Weizman, Z. O., & Snow, C. E. (2001). Lexical input as related to children's vocabulary acquisition: Effects of sophisticated exposure and support for meaning. *Developmental Psychology, 37*(2), 265–279.

White, B. (1985). *The first three years of life.* Englewood Cliffs, NJ: Prentice Hall.

Whitehurst, G., & Lonigan, C. (2001). Emergent literacy: Development from prereaders to readers. In S. Neuman & D. Dickinson (Eds.), *Handbook of early literacy research* (pp. 11–29). New York: Guilford.

Wilhelm, J. D. (1997). *"You gotta BE the book."* New York: Teachers College Press.

Willems, M. (2004). *Knuffle bunny.* New York: Hyperion.

Winograd, P., & Arrington, H. (1999). Best practices in literacy assessment. In L. Gambrell, L. Morrow, S. Neuman, & M Pressley (Eds.), *Best practices in literacy instruction* (pp. 210–241). New York: Guilford.

Winter, J. (1998). *Follow the drinking gourd.* New York: Knopf.

Winter, J. (1998). *Klara's new world.* New York: Knopf.

Wollman-Bonilla, J. (2001). Can first-grade writers demonstrate audience awareness? *Reading Research Quarterly, 36,* 184–201.

Wong-Fillmore, L. (1991a). Second-language learning in children: A model of language learning in social context. In Bialystok (Ed.), *Language processing in bilingual children* (pp. 49–69). New York: Cambridge University Press.

Wong-Fillmore, L. (1991b). When learning a second language means losing the first. *Early Childhood Research Quarterly, 6,* 232–346.

Wong-Fillmore, L., & Snow, C. (April, 2000). *What teachers need to know about language.* Educational Resources Information Center, ERIC Clearinghouse on Language and Linguistics. ED-99-CO-0008.

Woodard, C. (1984). Guidelines for facilitating sociodramatic play. *Childhood Education, 60,* 172–177.

Wright Group/McGraw-Hill. (2002). *Doors to Discovery: A new pre-kindergarten program.* Bothell, WA: Author.

Yaden, D., Smolkin, L., & Conlon, A. (1989). Preschoolers' questions about pictures, print conventions, and story text during reading aloud at home. *Reading Research Quarterly, 24,* 188–214.

Yaden, D., Smolkin, L., & MacGillivray, L. (1993). A psychogenetic perspective on children's understanding about letter associations during alphabet book readings. *Journal of Reading Behavior, 25,* 43–68.

Yarosz, D. J., & Barnett, W. S. (2001). Who reads to young children? Identifying predictors of family reading activities. *Reading Psychology, 22,* 67–81.

Yopp, H. (1992). Developing phonemic awareness in young children. *The Reading Teacher, 45,* 696–703.

Yopp, H., & Stapleton, L. (2008). Conciencia fonémica en Español (Phonemic awareness in Spanish). *The Reading Teacher, 61,* 374–382.

Yopp, H., & Yopp, R. (2000). Supporting phonemic awareness in the classroom. *The Reading Teacher, 54,* 130–143.

Zaner-Bloser. (1993). *Handwriting: A way to self-expression.* Columbus, OH: Author.

Zinsser, W. (1998). *Worlds of childhood: The art and craft of writing for children.* Boston: Houghton Mifflin.

AUTHOR INDEX

Abbott, 253
Adams, M., 136, 168, 169, 170, 174, 175, 178
Adcock, D., 115
Albert, L., 148
Albertson, B., 138, 354, 355, 356, 357
Allen, R. V., 153
Altwerger, B., 79
Alvermann, D., 244, 254
Anastasopoulos, L., 139, 168, 189
Anders, P., 355
Anderson, C., 301, 303
Anderson, R. C., 131, 231, 359
Araujo, L., 60, 122, 253, 285, 343, 344
Arrington, H., 355, 357
Ash, G., 242
Ashton-Warner, S., 184
Atwell, N., 258, 297
Au, K., 231
August, D., 60

Baghban, M., 176
Baker, L., 170, 194
Barbe, W., 339
Barbour, A., 143
Barclay, J., 231
Barnhart, J., 28, 85
Barnett, W., 137
Barrentine, S., 73
Bartholomew, P., 69
Barton, M., 246, 247
Bateson, G., 31
Bauer, E., 194
Baumann, J., 242
Bear, D., 194, 327, 328
Beard, G., 328
Beck, I., 116, 136, 241
Becker, H., 143
Bedford, A., 98
Beeler, T., 170, 175
Bell, M., 32, 47
Bennett-Armistead, V., 137, 312

Berger, J., 337
Berninger, V., 253
Bhavnagri, N., 57
Bialystok, E., 60
Biemiller, A., 115
Biggar, H., 223
Billmeyer, R., 246, 247
Bishop, W., 334
Bissex, G., 78
Blachowicz, C., 242
Black, J., 32, 47, 355
Blakey, J., 153
Blamey, K., 148
Bloodsworth, J., 341
Bobkoff-Katz, K., 69, 104
Bodrova, E., 153
Bond, G. L., 248
Borman, G., 261
Boroski, W., 157
Bowles, R., 183
Bowman, M., 177, 202
Boulay, B., 9
Brabham, E., 136, 141
Bradley, L., 332, 346
Brady, J., 189
Brady, S., 139
Bransford, J., 231
Bredekamp, S., 145
Brice Heath, S., 31, 57, 83
Brock, D., 143
Brooks, J., 336, 337
Brooks, M., 336, 337
Brosnahan, I., 334
Brown, J., 79, 261
Bruner, J., 106, 110
Bryan, T., 160, 196, 212, 255
Bryant, F., 32, 77
Bryant, P., 332, 346
Buckner, A., 224, 358
Buell, M., 25
Burns, M. S., 17
Burns, S., 104, 106, 178
Burke, C., 374
Burke, J., 245

Burks, M., 331
Burris, N., 325
Burstein, K., 160, 196, 215, 255
Bus, A., 78
Buschman, L., 331
Butler. A., 147
Buysse, 30

Cabell, S., 25, 144, 183
Caldwell, J., 252
Calkins, L., 175, 305, 312, 336, 338, 354
Cambourne, B., 259
Canizares, S., 71, 112
Cardonick, I., 189
Carey, S., 50
Carlisle, J., 286
Carlsson-Paige, N., 76
Carnine, D., 168
Carr, M., 354
Carta, J., 56
Casbergue, R., 98, 186
Cazden, C., 99, 113, 114, 338
Chall, J., 175, 253, 255
Chai, C., 312
Chang, C., 202
Chard, D., 375
Charles, J., 203
Chhabra, V., 115
Chomsky, N., 40
Christian, K., 32, 77, 344
Christie, J., 17, 26, 53, 110, 111, 150, 151, 153
Chukovsky, K., 113
Clarke, A., 50, 75, 76, 182
Clark-Chiarelli, E., 195,
Clay, M., 25, 28, 112, 235, 373
Claxton, G., 354
Clements, D., 187
Cobb, C., 202
Cochran-Smith, M., 141, 187
Cohen, L., 32, 48, 273
Coker, D., 367
Coleman, M. R., 30

405

SUBJECT INDEX